CONTENTS

Chapters 2, 12-13, and 3 form a sequence and are best read in that order.

ABBREVIATIONS

Libraries and archives are identified with the *sigla*-system of the *Répertoire international des sources musicales* (RISM).

AC 1966	Ursula KIRKENDALE, *Antonio Caldara: Sein Leben und seine venezianisch-römischen Oratorien*, Graz/Cologne, Hermann Böhlaus Nachf, 1966.
AC 2007	Ursula KIRKENDALE, *Antonio Caldara: Life and Venetian-Roman Oratorios*, revised and translated by Warren Kirkendale, Florence, Leo S. Olschki, 2007.
AfMw	«Archiv für Musikwissenschaft».
AMl	«Acta Musicologica».
AmZ	«Allgemeine musikalische Zeitung» (Leipzig, unless specified as Vienna).
CMM	«Corpus Mensurabilis Musicae».
DTÖ	«Denkmäler der Tonkunst in Österreich».
GR	*Graduale Romanum.*
HR	Ursula KIRKENDALE, *Handel with Ruspoli: New Documents from the Archivio Segreto Vaticano, December 1706 to December 1708*, SM XXXII, 2003, pp. 301-348 and XXXIII, 2004, pp. 249-250.
JAMS	«Journal of the American Musicological Society».
LU	*Liber Usualis.*
MGG[1-2]	*Die Musik in Geschichte und Gegenwart*, editions of 1949-86 and 1994–.
MD	«Musica Disciplina».
NG[1-2]	*The New Grove Dictionary of Music and Musicians*, editions of 1980 and 2001.
PäM	«Publikationen älterer praktischer und theoretischer Musikwerke».
P.G.	*Patrologiae ... Series Graeca*, Paris, Migne, 1857-1912.
P.L.	*Patrologiae ... Series Latina*, Paris, Migne, 1844-64.
PS	Postscriptum: revisions in square brackets to the original versions of ch. 9 (= *RD*, often with reference to *HR*) and ch. 11 (= *HR*).
RIdM	«Rivista italiana di musicologia»
RD	Ursula KIRKENDALE, *The Ruspoli Documents on Handel*, JAMS XX, 1967, pp. 222-273 and 517f.

SL	Claudio SARTORI, *I libretti italiani a stampa dalle origini al 1800*, Cuneo, Bertola & Locatelli, 1990-94.
SM	«Studi musicali».
s.n.	*Sine nomine* (publisher's name not mentioned).
UP	University Press.
VjMw	«Vierteljahrsschrift für Musikwissenschaft».
ZfMw	«Zeitschrift für Musikwissenschaft».

PLATES

VII.3   Louis XIV as Apollo. Engraving by Alexis Étienne Rousselet [or Jacques Rousselet] after a lost drawing by Charles Lebrun (1619-90).

VII.4   Anne d'Autriche with Louis (recto) and Val-de-Grâce (verso). Medal by Jean Warin commemorating the beginning of the church, 1645.

VIII.1   Ferdinando Carlo Gonzaga, Duke of Mantua. Anon. oil on canvas, 260 × 146 cm., 1671, Mantua, private collection. Cf. also the portrait in *AC* 2007, Plate 2.

IX.1   Libretto of *La resurrezione*, title page, with the arms of Ruspoli-Marescotti.

IX.2   Libretto of *La resurrezione*, page 3.

IX.3   Doc. 24: Bill of Antonio Giuseppe Angelini for copies of 11 cantatas of Handel, receipted 9 Aug. 1708. Archivio Segreto Vaticano, Archivio Ruspoli Marescotti, *Giustificazioni di Roma*, A 45, after fasc. 133, 10 July - 19 Sept. 1708.

IX.4   Doc. 27: Bill of Antonio Giuseppe Angelini for copy of the parts for Handel's cantata *Il Tebro* ("O come chiare e belle" HWV 143), receipted 10 Sept. 1708. *Ibid.*

IX.5   Doc. 29: Bill for payment of instrumentalists who performed an unidentified cantata of Handel and *Il Tebro* HWB 143, issued 2 Sept., receipted 25 Sept. 1708. *Ibid.* A 46, after fasc. 165, 24 Sept. - 9 Nov. 1708.

IX.6   Doc. 35: Bill of Francesco Lanciani for copies of 21 cantatas of Handel, receipted 31 Aug. 1709. *Ibid.* A 47, after fasc. 113, Aug. 1709.

X.1   Organ of Luca Blasi and Giovanni Battista Montani, 1599, in San Giovanni in Laterano. Photo courtesy of the Fondazione Pro Musica e Arte Sacra, Rome.

XI.1   Francesco Maria Ruspoli, Prince of Cerveteri. Antonio David, oil on canvas, 115 × 89 cm., 1709, Rome, Palazzo Ruspoli in Via del Corso.

XI.2   Palazzo Bonelli. Engraving by Alessandro Specchi (1668-1729) from *Il quarto libro del nuovo teatro delli palazzi in prospettiva di Roma moderna*, Rome, Domenico de' Rossi, 1699, f. 39.

XI.3   *Nuova pianta di Roma*, Giovanni Battista Nolli, Rome, 1748. Detail showing the locations of Palazzo Bonelli (no. 273), Palazzo Ruspoli al Campidoglio (no. 985), Santa Maria in Aracoeli (no. 917), Palazzo Colonna (no. 281), SS. Apostoli (no. 283), Palazzo Capizucchi (no. 987), S. Maria in Campitelli (no. 989), S. Maria di Loreto (no. 274).

XI.4   Margarita Durastante. Caricature by Anton Maria Zanetti, drawing in brown ink, 90 × 56 cm., ca. 1721 (when Zanetti moved his lodgings from the house of John Christopher Smith sr. to that of Durastante), Venice, Fondazione Cini, f. 14.

XI.5   Piazza d'Aracoeli, with Palazzo Ruspoli al Campidoglio (now Palazzo Pecci Blunt) to the right of Giacomo Della Porta's fountain, behind the horses. Engraving by Giovanni Battista Falda (1643-78) from his *Fontane di Roma ... libro primo*, Rome, Giovanni Giacomo de' Rossi, n. d. and 1691, f. 18.

XI.6   Brigantine. Anonymous, oil on canvas, 86 × 114.5 cm. One of several paintings with the brigantine in Cerveteri, Castello Ruspoli.

XI.7   Receipts of *camerieri* for clothing allowance, 5 Jan. 1707. Line 7: sample of Domenico Castrucci's handwriting. Archivio Segreto Vaticano, Archivio Ruspoli Marescotti, *Giustificazioni di Roma*, A 44, after list 20.

I.

CIRCULATIO-TRADITION, *MARIA LACTANS*, AND JOSQUIN AS MUSICAL ORATOR

Bernhard Meier in memoriam

The phenomenon of the circle has not only fascinated mathematicians, astronomers, and philosophers since earliest times; it has also impressed itself on music in various ways: one need think only of the music of the spheres, the 'rounded' forms of the medieval rondeau and the classical rondo, the (perfect) circle as a notational symbol for *tempus perfectum*, the circle of fifths, and the circle canon (Latin *'rota'*, English 'round'), which can be written also in the shape of a circle.[1] And then there is that circle which constitutes one of the most interesting, but still little known figures of musical rhetoric: the *circulus* or *circulatio*, the subject of this study.

In art music, as in elevated speech, a figure is a conscious, clearly defined *deviation* from the simplest mode of writing, intended to embellish the expression and to represent a particular meaning or affect contained in the text.[2] Such figures were already employed in large numbers during the Renaissance, when the humanist respect for the word made music more and more into an expressive language. Franco-Flemish and Italian composers surely identified them in oral instruction with the Greek and Latin terminology of rhetoric. But it remained for the German music theorists of the seventeenth and eigh-

---

[1] E.g. cf. John BERGSAGEL, *Cordier's Circular Canon*, «Musical Times», CXIII, 1972, pp. 175f, and Virginia NEWES, *Turning Fortune's Wheel: Musical and Textual Design in Machaut's Canonic Lais*, MD, XLV, 1991, pp. 115f.

[2] QUINTILIAN, *Institutio oratoria*, IX.i.3: "de recta et simplici ratione cum aliqua dicendi virtute deflectitur" ["is deflected to some rhetorical advantage from the straightforward and simple mode of speaking"]. He goes on to distinguish between tropes and figures. Cf. also IX.iii.3: "a simplici rectoque loquendi genere deflexa" ["deflected from the simple and straightforward manner of speaking"] and Joachim BURMEISTER, *Musica poetica*, Rostock, Myliander, 1606, p. 55: "qui a simplici compositionis ratione discedit" ["which deviates from the simple manner of composition"].

teenth centuries to expound the so-called 'Figurenlehre' in print, not always escaping the danger of fabricating crutches for lame muses. Only with the romantic era, which showed little interest in the rational aspects of musical composition, was this repertoire of figures more or less lost, along with the motive-traditions of iconology and the *topoi* of literature. Thus musicologists, in the first half of our century, had to rediscover the relationships between rhetoric and music. Arnold Schering and his pupils dug up the figures from the writings of music theorists.[3] Others have shown how figures were applied by single composers – to mention only the small, but important book by Arnold Schmitz on J. S. Bach's musical imagery or *Bildlichkeit*.[4]

But Schmitz also warned against false speculations: "only a thorough analysis of the entire musical complex" will help; one should not deal with figures "like fruit picked out of a cake".[5] We must agree with him, yet raise the question whether a composer like Bach really stands in such splendid isolation, or whether his figures – nay, more modestly – one single figure should not be seen in a larger context, that of a longer tradition. Only before such a background can the details of a particular work be fully measured. We must ask, then: Does the *circulatio* come down to us as a carrier of meaning? And, if it does, where does it begin? I shall therefore have to interpret the *circulatio*, and I beg the readers' indulgence if for some arguments better ones might be substituted.

The *circulatio* is mentioned and defined for the first time in theoretical literature by Athanasius Kircher in 1650:[6]

---

[3] Arnold SCHERING, *Die Lehre von den musikalischen Figuren*, «Kirchenmusikalisches Jahrbuch», XXI, 1908, pp. 106-114; *id., Geschichtliches zur 'ars inveniendi' in der Musik*, «Jahrbuch der Musikbibliothek Peters», XXXII, 1925, pp. 25-34; Heinz BRANDES, *Studien zur musikalischen Figurenlehre im 16. Jahrhundert* (diss. Berlin), Würzburg, Triltsch & Huther, 1935; Hans Heinrich UNGER, *Die Beziehungen zwischen Musik und Rhetorik im 16.-18. Jahrhundert* (diss. Berlin), Würzburg, Triltsch, 1941. A summary of figures is provided in the article *Rhetoric* in NG[1], reprinted in NG[2]. Cf. also the compilation by Dietrich BARTEL, *Handbuch der musikalischen Figurenlehre*, Laaber, Laaber-Verlag, 1985; revised English ed. London, Lincoln, 1997.

[4] *Die Bildlichkeit der wortgebundenen Musik Johann Sebastian Bachs*, Mainz, Schott, 1950.

[5] *Die oratorische Kunst J. S. Bachs – Grundfragen und Grundlagen*, in Gesellschaft für Musikforschung, *Kongress-Bericht Lüneburg 1950*, Kassel, Bärenreiter, n.d., p. 44.

[6] *Musurgia*, Rome, Corbelletti, 1650, II, 145, taken over literally by Thomas Balthasar JANOWKA, *Clavis ad thesaurum magnae artis musicae*, Prague, Labaun, 1701, p. 56. ARISTIDES QUINTILIANUS already designated as περιφερής, "turning", one of his three melodic types, e.g. ascending stepwise through the tetrachord and then descending in disjunct motion – *De musica* [ca. 3rd c.], Leipzig, Teubner, 1963, pp. 16ff; hence Manuel BRYENNIUS, *Harmonica* [ca. 1320], Groningen, Wolters-Noordhoff, 1970, pp. 360-363. The term *circulus* was used much earlier in music theory, but with a somewhat different meaning and hardly as a musical-rhetorical figure: HUCBALD understands by "circulus" a short group of notes which ends on the note with which it began, such as might be notated by the torculus neume – *De harmonica institutione*, in Martin GERBERT, *Scriptores ecclesiastici*

Κύκλωσις sive *circulatio* est periodus harmonica, qua voces in circulum agi videntur, servitque verbis actiones circulares exprimentibus, uti Philippi de Monte, 'Surgam et circumibo civitatem'.

[*Kyklosis* or *circulatio* is a musical passage in which the voices seem to move in a circle; it serves for words expressing circular actions, as Philippe de Monte 'Surgam et circumibo civitatem' [*Canticum canticorum*, 3:2].

Thus Kircher describes the *circulatio* as the expression of an action. He gives no musical examples. These we find only 1677 in Printz,[7] 1719 in Vogt,[8] and 1732 in the music lexicon of J. S. Bach's cousin Johann Walther[9] (Exx. 1-3). These authors depict the musical circle clearly as a sine curve. Since music unfolds not in space, but in time, and the notes of a melody are normally written from left to right, the upper and lower halves of the circle in a single voice can

---

de musica sacra [St. Blasius, Typis San-Blasianis, 1784], I, 104. This anticpates the rhetorical κύκλος or *circulus* as defined by HERMOGENES TARSENSIS in his *De inventione*, IV.8: "cum a quo quis nomine vel verbo incipit, in idipsum rursus desinet" ["when someone begins with that noun or verb, he ends with the same"] – *De arte rhetorica praecepta*, Venice, Sessae, 1539, f. 59. A longer *circulatio* is called *complexio* by Johannes NUCIUS, *Musices poeticae*, Neisse, Scharffenberg, 1613, sig. G3: "Cum harmoniae initium in fine repetitur, ad imitationem poetarum, qui saepe uno eodemque vocabulo versum incipiunt et claudunt" ["When the beginning of the music is repeated at the end, in imitation of the poets who often begin and end a verse with one and the same word"]. In poetry, the *circulus/complexio* most often involved the repetition of the entire opening line at the end – cf. the definition of the *circulus* as a "poematis genus" ["kind of poem"] in Piero VALERIANO BOLZANI, *Hieroglyphica*, Basel, s.n., 1556, f. 287*v*: "poema illud circulus appellant, cuius finis idem est cum principio" ["they call that poem a *circulus* whose end is the same as its beginning"]. This device was revived by the English metaphysical school in poems of several strophes, with the last line of one strophe being repeated as the first line of the next, and the last line of the last strophe identical with the first line of the first, e.g. George HERBERT, "Sinnes Round", in *The Temple*, Cambridge, Buck, 1633, p. 114; or John DONNE, "La Corona" and "A Valediction", in *Poems*, London, Marriot, 1633, pp. 28-32, 193f – cf. John FRECCERO, *Donne's "Valediction: Forbidding Mourning"*, «E[nglish] L[iterary] H[istory]», XXX, 1963, pp. 335-376, and Margaret MAURER, *The Circular Argument of Donne's "La Corona"*, «Studies in English Literature», XXII, 1982, pp. 51-68. The rhetorical *circulus* (or even Hucbald's and Nucius's) is much less perfect than Kircher's musical *circulatio*, for it merely returns to its point of departure, without describing a circular motion.

7 Wolfgang Caspar PRINTZ, *Phrynis mytilenaeus ... Ander Theil des Satyrischen Componistens*, Sagan, Okel, 1677, f. [35]: "*Circulo* ist, wenn zween *circuli mezi* also zusammen gesetzt werden" ["A *circulus* is when two *semicirculi* are thus set together"]; repeated literally in his *Compendium musicae*, Dresden, Mieth, 1689, p. 52, and 1714, unpaginated.

8 Moritz Johann VOGT, *Conclave thesauri artis musicae*, Prague, Labaun, 1719, pp. 148f.

9 Johann Gottfried WALTHER, *Musicalisches Lexicon*, Leipzig, Deer, 1732, p. 166: "wenn zweene *Circoli mezzi* also zusammen- und an einander gehänget werden, daß, so [= wenn] sie über einander gesetzt werden solten, sie einen vollkommenen Circul darstellen würden" ["when two *semicirculi* are hung together so that, when they should be superimposed, they form a perfect circle"] and tab. VIII, fig. 9. Meinrad SPIESS, *Tractatus compositorio-practicus*, Augsburg, Lotter, 1746, p. 156, still describes the "*Circolo*, ein Circul- oder Creiß-Figur, bestehend aus 8 geschwinden Noten; wird also genennet, weil sie gleichsam einen Circul formiert" ["*Circolo*, a circle-figure, consisting of eight fast notes, so named, because it forms, as it were, a circle"]. But his musical example, p. 159, is not a true *circulus*.

be placed only beside each other. Much less frequently, composers will align the two halves of the circle vertically in two simultaneous voices (Ex. 8).[10]

Ex. 1. Printz: Circulo.

Ex. 2. Vogt: Circulus.

Ex. 3. Walther: Circul.

The *circulatio* belongs to those musical figures which have no direct analogies in language. It is closer to the visual arts and can be classified among the larger category of *hypotyposis* figures. Such a figure, says Burmeister in 1606, depicts the meaning of the text so that it seems to come alive,[11] or, in Vogt's words, "painted from life".[12]

The *circulatio* has been mentioned only briefly in musicological literature.[13] Not all of the examples given have been happily chosen: when they

---

[10] Thus for the words of Jacopone da Todi, "Amor, tu se' cerchio rotondo" ["Love, you are a round circle"] in Luigi DALLAPICCOLA's *Concerto per la notte di Natale*, 1956, Milan, Suvini Zerboni, 1958, p. 33ff. Here the melody does not move by step, but by leaps.

[11] P. 62: "Hypotyposis est illud ornamentum, quo textus significatio ita deumbratur, ut ea, quae textui subsunt & animam vitamque non habent, vita esse praedita, videantur" ["A *hypotyposis* is that ornament with which the meaning of the text is so reflected that those things which are contained in the text and do not have soul and body seem to be endowed with life"]. Cf. QUINTILIAN, IX.ii.40: "ὑποτύοσις dicitur proposito quaedam forma rerum ita expressa verbis, ut cerni potius videatur quam audiri" ["*hypotyposis* is called a certain form of things expressed with words so that it seems to be seen rather than heard"], and the authors quoted by Martin Ruhnke in *Das Erbe deutscher Musik*, XLII, Lippstadt, Kistner & Siegel, 1958, p. VII.

[12] "depinxit ad vivum", p. 157. It is not surprising that quasi-visual figures were favored especially in the baroque era, an age which delighted in picture-rhymes, e.g. written in the shape of a heart or a cross and expressing amorous or religious ideas, respectively. If Leibniz, in 1717, can list a long series of words which begin with "W" and which, as he imagines, are derived from the wave-shape of this letter – like "Wogen", "Wellen", "Wirbel", "Walze", "winden", "wenden", etc. – then we may all the more easily understand how notes which actually move in a circle were understood as depicting a circular object or motion; Gottfried Wilhelm LEIBNIZ, *Collectanea etymologica*, Hanover, Foerster, 1717, II, 282f, also I, 307f. Unger, from whom I take these remarks, quoted the passage (p. 95) from a secondary source and misattributed it to Martin Opitz.

[13] CMM, 14: Cipriani RORE, *Opera Omnia*, III, 1961, p. V; Bernhard MEIER, *Wortausdeutung*

— 4 —

contain leaps or do not return to their point of departure and thus do not form a complete circle. In some of them the 'circular' motion is so free as to be probably unintended, in others, the melody has no circular form at all.[14] The following pages will give a small, but representative selection of genuine *circulationes* with their respective texts, in order to determine the history and the conceptual nature of this figure.[15] It extends from the sixteenth into the nineteenth century, thus illustrating the continuity of figurative language in European music. In place of the rigid, abstract formulas of the theorists, we shall see the manifold shapes from actual compositions, animated by rhythmic and melodic variants and always tied to some kind of circular concept.

Ex. 4. Haydn: circle (orch.).[16]

Ex. 5. Rore: laurel wreath.[17]

un lau - ro ver - de

---

und Tonalität bei Orlando di Lasso, «Kirchenmusikalisches Jahrbuch», XLVII, 1963, pp. 83f. The posthumously published article of Arnold SCHERING, *Einige Grundsymbole der Tonsprache Beethovens*, in *Ludwig van Beethoven*, ed. Ludwig Finscher, Darmstadt, Wissenschaftliche Buchgesellschaft, 1983, contains, on pp. 10-17, a discussion of *circulus* figures which is questionable only in its 'identification' of Beethoven's literary 'models'.

[14] E.g. the very disjunct melodies set to "aeternum" by LASSO, *Sämmtliche Werke*, Leipzig, Breitkopf & Härtel, n.d., XV, 158f. and XVII, 148f. Lasso's settings of the words "aurum" ["gold"] and "ch'intorno gira" ["which turns around"], on the other hand, are exemplary *circulationes* (see below, Exx. 8, 15). The method of this study was misunderstood and misapplied to a composer (and a period) where it is no longer justified, with misleading results. Peter TENHAEF, *Magische Kreise in Franz Schuberts Melodram 'Die Zauberharfe'*, in *Festschrift Klaus Hortschansky zum 60. Geburtstag*, Tutzing, Schneider, 1995, pp. 367-384, believes to illustrate *circulationes* with musical examples which have neither a circular form nor a direct connection with words conveying a circular concept.

[15] I thank Juliane Riepe for references to the examples by Schütz, Mazzocchi, Cazzati, and Bononcini, added to this version of the article.

[16] "In frohen *Kreisen* schwebt, sich wiegend in der Luft, der munteren Vögel Schar" ["In joyous *circles* the lively flock of birds hovers rocking in the air"] in *Die Schöpfung* (1798), no. 18, Zürich, Eulenburg [ca. 1925], p. 166. Due to limitations of space, the musical examples in this article quote *circuli* out of their context. In order to gain a true impression of the role of this figure, one must consult the full scores with their (usually conspicuous) repetitions and/or imitations.

[17] "Signor mio", from *Il primo libro de madrigali a quatro voci*, Ferrara, Buglhat & Hucher, 1550; *Opera*, IV, 1969, p. 15.

Ex. 6. Rore: sun.[18]

Ex. 7. Caldara: sun.[19]

Ex. 8. Lasso: gold [ring or coin].[20]

These concepts extend from simple physical objects (Exx. 4-8)[21] and similes (Ex. 9) to complex tropes, often metaphors. Bernhard Meier has noted a most graphic passage where Lasso draws, in the two upper voices, not only the sine curves in imitation, but also a real two-dimensional circle, with its upper and lower halves superimposed (Ex. 8). He interprets these measures as the image of a round coin or a ring of gold, from the treasury of the Magi.[22] With a little practice in musical rhetoric, one can often conclude from a text what kind of music will be used for it and vice versa. The theorist Vogt, in 1719, included "waves" in a long list of words which composers should depict with a *hypotyposis*,[23] so we are not surprised to see

---

[18] "Quand'io son", from *I madrigali a cinque voci*, Venice, Scotto, 1542; *Opera*, II, 1963, p. 17. The same word "sole" ["sun"] is set to a huge *circulus* in Domenico MAZZOCCHI, "A travestirsi di passibil velo", *Musiche sacre e morali*, Rome, Grignani, 1640, p. 3.

[19] *Oratorio per S. Francesca Romana* (1710), quoted in *AC* 1966 pp. 270f = *AC* 2007 pp. 339, 341; for further, more sophisticated examples cf. *AC* 1966 pp. 285, 308, also 177f, 264f = *AC* 2007 pp. 358, 385f, also 227, 332.

[20] "Videntes stellam", *secunda pars*, "Et apertis thesauris suis", from *Sacrae cantiones quinque vocum*, Nuremberg, Montanus & Neuber, 1562; *Werke*, V, p. 25.

[21] Also "Stern" ["star"] in Heinrich SCHÜTZ, *Historia der Geburt Jesu Christi* [1623], in *Neue Ausgabe sämtlicher Werke*, I, Kassel, Bärenreiter, 1955, pp. 28f; "occhi" ["eyes"] and "ruota" ["wheel"], in MAZZOCCHI, "Homai le luci eranti" and "Cinta intorno d'insidie", *op. cit.*, pp. 9, 35.

[22] MEIER, *Wortausdeutung*, p. 83.

[23] P. 157.

how Benedetto Marcello sets his "onda" ["wave"]: as an undulating *circulus* (Ex. 9).[24] As often in the Baroque, the composer takes as his point of departure a figure of speech which the poet provided in the first sentence of his text. Hence the 'simile-' or 'metaphor-arias'. In a cantata of J. S. Bach (Ex. 10), the basso continuo presents a long chain of *circulus*-motives while the vocal recitative declaims the text "Wenn er mich auch gleich wirft ins Meer, So lebt der Herr auf großen Wassern noch, ... Drum werden sie mich nicht ersäufen, Wenn mich die Wellen schon ergreifen ..." ["Although he casts me into the ocean, the Lord still lives on great waters; ... thus they will not drown me when the waves already seize me"]. In another of Bach's cantatas (Ex. 11), an entire aria is permeated by wave-motion generated by the words "rauschend Wasser" ["roaring water"]; in the St. Matthew Passion (Ex. 12) a persistent *semicirculus* is set in motion by the words "Wiewohl mein Herz in Tränen schwimmt" ["although my heart is floating in tears"]; in the St. John Passion a *circulus* depicts the "Regenbogen" ["rainbow"] after the flood.[25] The figure may represent even a preposition, as seen by Monteverdi's and Handel's conspicuous *circulationes* for the word "around" (Ex. 13f).

Ex. 9. Marcello: wave.[26]

Co - me l'on - da fu - ri - bon - da

Ex. 10. Bach: ocean, waters, wave (b.c.).[27]

---

[24] Likewise Alessandro Scarlatti for the words "Inter *udas* fluctuantes" in his motet "Iam sole clarior", from his *Motetti sacri*, Naples, Mutij, 1697; modern edition in preparation by Luca Della Libera, A-R Editions.

[25] *Ibid.*, Ser. II, Bd. IV, 1973, p. 74, mm. 26f. Manfred Karl HOPFENMÜLLER, *Elemente der barocken Figurenlehre in der Johannespassion von Johann Sebastian Bach*, ms. M. A. thesis, Universität Regensburg, 1984, p. 47, note 161.

[26] The cantata "Senza gran pena" (*Stravaganze d'amore*), US-NYp Mus. Res. * MP (Italian); no. A 321 in Eleonor SELFRIDGE-FIELD, *The Music of Benedetto and Alessandro Marcello: A Thematic Catalogue*, Oxford, Clarendon, 1990, p. 175. The aria is edited in Carl PARRISH, *A Treasury of Early Music*, New York, Norton, 1958, p. 308.

[27] From the cantata "Ich habe in Gottes Herz und Sinn", BWV 92, in Johann Sebastian BACH, *Neue Ausgabe Sämtlicher Werke*, Ser. I, Bd. VII, Kassel, Bärenreiter, 1956, p. 57.

Ex. 11. Bach: rushing water (voice and orch.).[28]

Ex. 12. Bach: swimming, floating (orch.).[29]

Ex. 13. Monteverdi: around.[30]

Ex. 14. Handel: around (orch.).[31]

Kircher's "actiones circulares" refer only to verbs, such as "circumibo" ["I shall go around"]. To his example could be added "intorno gira" ["turns around", Ex. 15], "revertere" ["to turn"],[32] "circuit" ["goes around", Ex. 16, in all voices], "circumdatum" ["surrounded"],[33] or "circumdabit" ["will surround", Ex. 17]. In Ex. 17 Christ says to His disciples on Maundy Thursday, "nunc videbitis turbam, quae circumdabit me" ["You will see the crowd which will surround me"]. In this exemplary *circulatio* the word "me" is in the center of the circle, literally "surrounded"

[28] From the cantata "Ach, wie flüchtig" BWV 26, *ibid.*, Bd. XXVII, 1968, pp. 42-49.

[29] *Ibid.*, Ser. II, Bd. V, 1972, p. 53. Of the various connotations of the musical *circulus*, it was the obvious 'aquatic' one which still persisted in romantic music, watered down to mere tone-painting – cf. Franz DUBITZKY, *Das Wasser in der Musik*, Langensalza, Musikalisches Magazin, 1913.

[30] Claudio MONTEVERDI, "Dolcemente dormiva", from *Il secondo libro de madrigali a cinque voci*, Venice, Raverii, 1607; *Opera omnia*, III, Cremona, Fondazione Monteverdi, 1979, p. 150.

[31] *Theodora* (1751), *Georg Friedrich Händel's Werke*, VIII, Leipzig, Breitkopf & Härtel, 1860, pp. 109ff: "your thickest veil *around* me throw". See below, note 35, for another setting of the same word.

[32] Costanzo FESTA, "Florentia", I-Rvall S. Borromeo E.I.55-66 [ca. 1530/31] and *Novum et insigne opus musicum*, Nuremberg, Grapheus, 1537; *Opera omnia*, CMM, XXV, vol. V, 1979, p. 88, tenor I, mm. 45ff.

[33] Claudin SERMISY, "Quous-que non reverteris pax", *Liber undecimus 26 musicales ...*, Paris, Attaignant, 1534; *A Gift of Madrigals and Motets ...*, ed. H. Colin Slim, Chicago UP, 1972, II, 8, altus, mm. 99ff.

by the adjacent notes. Another perfect *circulatio* on "circumdedit" ["surrounded"], in a plainsong Tractus for Holy Saturday (Ex. 18), has been identified by Bernhard Meier – interestingly but not surprisingly – as an addition to the plainchant melody by the humanistically oriented editors of the *Editio Medicea*![34] Purcell's drunken poet asks for assistance, "Turn me round" (Ex. 19). We recall that to this day the word "turn" designates an ornament in the form of a *circulus*, abbreviated with a small sine curve (∾). Passages like Ex. 19 and 21 led Daniel Webb, in his *Observations on the Correspondences between Poetry and Music*, 1769, to conclude that "Purcell ... accompanies every idea of roundness with an endless rotation of notes".[35] This author, however, regards the *circulatio* as mere tone-painting; notwithstanding the title of his book, he no longer knows about musical-rhetorical figures.

Ex. 15. Lasso: the heavens turning around.[36]

il ciel, ch'in - tor - no gi - ra

Ex. 16. Lasso: go around.[37]

cir - - - cu - it

Ex. 17. Lasso: surround.[38]

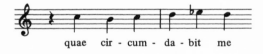

quae cir - cum - da - bit me

---

[34] *Modale Korrektur und Wortausdeutung im Choral der Editio Medicea*, «Kirchenmusikalisches Jahrbuch», LIII, 1969, p. 125.

[35] London, Dodsley, 1769, p. 143. Cf. also Purcell's setting of "like olive branches *around* thy table" in the anthem "Blessed are they that fear the Lord" (1687/8) or "Thou tun'st this *world* below the *spheres* above, Who in the heavenly *round* to their own music move" from the *Ode on St. Cecilia's Day* (1692), *Works*, XXVIII, 1959, p. 50, and VIII, 1897, pp. 42-47.

[36] "Signor, le colpe mie", from *Madrigali*, Nuremberg, Gerlach, 1587; *Werke*, VI, p. 96.

[37] "Fratres: sobrii", from *Liber secundus sacrarum cantionum quatuor vocum*, Leuven, Phalèse, 1569; *Werke*, I, 130.

[38] "Tristis est anima mea", from *Modulorum Orlandi de Lassus ... secundum volumen*, Paris, Le Roy & Ballard, 1565; *Werke*, V, 48.

Ex. 18. *Editio Medicea*: surround.[39]

cir - cum - - - de - dit

Ex. 19. Purcell: turn around.[40]

turn me round

With such texts, and more profound ones, composers produced a musical equivalent to the circle symbolism of hieroglyphics and astronomy. Renaissance humanists were, of course, fascinated by hieroglyphics, and though they did not yet understand properly their principles, they drew upon them for their own sign language, especially for emblems.[41] Today, art historians are using these symbols to discover the meaning of paintings. And indeed, the preoccupation of eminent humanists with hieroglyphics could not have escaped the attention of educated musicians in the sixteenth century.[42] Horapollo, who transmitted very imperfectly the meaning of ancient Egyptian symbols to the first centuries of the Christian era and hence to the Renaissance, explains the hieroglyph of the ουροβόροσ, a snake in the form of a circle, as a symbol for "saeculum" ["eternity" etc.] or "terra" ["earth", "world"].[43] Adriano Banchieri, in 1613, draws a huge circle in notes for the word "terra" (Ex. 20), whereas Purcell places his *circulus* on the modifier "round" (Ex. 21). The same hieroglyph of the serpent appears in emblem books especially as a symbol of eternity and immortality (see Plate I.1 and below pp. 13-16),[44] also of the year.[45] Thus Handel's chorus of Babylo-

[39] Tractus "Vinea facta est", *Graduale de tempore*, Rome, Typogr. Medicea, 1614, f. 153*v*.

[40] *The Fairy Queen* (1692), *The Works of Henry Purcell*, XII, London, Novello, 1903, pp. 21f. Likewise "girando" ["turning"], in Maurizio CAZZATI, "Mortali, che fate", *Cantate morali e spirituali a voce sola*, Bologna, Benacci, 1659, p. 184.

[41] Karl GIEHLOW, *Die Hieroglyphenkunde des Humanismus in der Allegorie der Renaissance*, «Jahrbuch der kunsthistorischen Sammlungen des allerhöchsten Kaiserhauses», XXXII/1, 1915, pp. 1-232.

[42] As MEIER, *Wortausdeutung*, pp. 84f, suggested.

[43] HORAPOLLO ALEXANDRINUS [4th c.], *Hieroglyphica*, Bologna, apud H. Platonidem, 1517, f. 1*r-v*.

[44] Andrea ALCIATI, *Emblemata*, Paris, Wechel, 1536, p. 45, and the commentary in the edition of Lyons, Rovillius, 1557 = 1566, p. 153. Otho VAENIUS, *Amorum emblemata*, Antwerp, the author, 1536, p. 1; Barptolomaeus ANULUS, *Picta poesis ut pictura poesis erit*, Lyons, Bonhomme, 1552, p. 9; Hadrianus JUNIUS, *Emblemata*, Antwerp, Plantin, 1575, no. 3. Reproductions in Arhur HENKEL and Albrecht SCHÖNE, *Emblemata*, Stuttgart, Metz, 1967, col. 654ff.

[45] Juan DE BORIA, *Empresas morales*, Prague, Nigrin, 1581, p. 30; HENKEL/SCHÖNE, col. 653.

nians in *Belshazzar* includes both the sun and the cycle of the year: "Twenty times the *sun round* the great year his *course* shall run", with a circulus for "course" (Ex. 22). Valeriano's *Hieroglyphica* of 1556, the most important handbook of symbolic images in the Renaissance, gives a substantial list of interrelated objects and concepts which are symbolized by the circle. I find them to be precisely those words which composers set to a *circulus*: the heavenly spheres, world, universe, all, perfection, eternity, God; also the cycle of the year or life, wheel of Fortune, etc.[46] Valeriano's list includes, for example, "cuncta" ["tutto", "all"], a concept set by Rore as a *circulus* (Ex. 23) and associated by Marino with roundness: "The large wheel of all in a little circle".[47] It may be no accident that Kircher, who dealt with the circle at length in three large works on hieroglyphics,[48] was also the first music theorist to describe the *circulatio*.

Ex. 20. Banchieri: world.[49]

et ter - - - - - - ram

Ex. 21. Purcell: round world.[50]

the round_____ world

---

[46] F. 286v-290. Cf. also Ludwig VOLKMANN, *Bilderschriften der Renaissance*, Leipzig, Hiersemann, 1923, pp. 7, 10, 17, 19; Otto BRENDEL, *Symbolik der Kugel*, «Mitteilungen des deutschen archaeologischen Instituts, Römische Abt.», LI, 1936, pp. 1-95.

[47] "La gran rota del tutto in picciol tondo" – Giambattista MARINO, *L'Adone*, X.174, Paris, Di Varano, 1623, p. 225.

[48] *Obeliscus pamphilius, hoc est, interpretatio nova & hucusque intentata obelisci hieroglyphica*, Rome, Grigani, 1650, pp. 379-384; *Oedipus aegyptiacus*, Rome, Mascardi, 1652-54, II/2, pp. 85-96; *Obelisci aegyptiaci nuper inter isaei romani rudera effossi interpretatio hieroglyphica*, Rome, Varese, 1666, pp. 27, 37, 52. Kircher's immense labor proved to be more or less in vain, since it was still based on false premises – cf. VOLKMANN, pp. 112ff. True understanding of the Egyptian hieroglyphics was achieved only in 1822 by Jean François Champollion, who recognized the phonetic (alphabetic and syllabic) as well as ideographic function. On Kircher cf. also Sergio DONADONI, *I geroglifici di Athanasius Kircher*, in *Athanasius Kircher: il museo del mondo*, ed. Eugenio Lo Sardo, Rome, De Luca, 2001, pp. 101-110.

[49] "In voluntate tua", from *Terzo libro di nuovi pensieri ecclesiastici*, Venice, Amadino, 1613; published in W. KIRKENDALE, *L'Aria di Fiorenza, id est Il Ballo del Gran Duca*, Florence, Olschki, 1972, p. 99. See also above, note 35, "world".

[50] "The Lord is King" (1688), *Works*, XXXII, 1962, p. 30.

Ex. 22. Handel: sun round ... his course.[51]

course___

Ex. 23. Rore: all.[52]

cun - cta sunt po - si - ta

Though it is unlikely that many composers, even in the sixteenth century, were consciously aware of the similarities between the principles of hiero-glyphics and those of musical-rhetorical figures, these similarities are so close as to be worth pointing out. We see that the same figure may be used for dif-ferent parts of speech – nouns ["Kreise" = "circles"], verbs ["circuit" = "goes around"], adjectives ["round"], prepositions ["intorno" = "around"], etc. – in various languages and that it may represent both direct, concrete meanings ["onda" = "wave"] and indirect, abstract ones (see below, "God"). The same holds true for hieroglyphics. The sole of a shoe or sandal, for example, has both literal and metaphorically transferred meaning, in the latter sense as a verb, "to subjugate", as a past participle, "subjugated", or as a noun, "sub-ject". The image of the hawk stood not only for that bird, but also for all swift things, hence "swiftness". No better explanation of the function of musical figures for both composer and listener could be given than an art historian's characterization of hieroglyphics: "A succession of Renaissance hieroglyphic signs expresses a series of ideas without grammatical relation, and ... the bur-den of deciding what parts of speech to assign to each hieroglyph falls on the translator, whose job is to transform an ideographic sequence into a fully dis-cursive one".[53] We need only substitute 'figures' for 'hieroglyphs'.

The philosophical, theological, and cosmological literature on the circle is, of course, more extensive and likewise very old.[54] Here too, a few examples

[51] "Dominus Deus" from *Il terzo libro di motetti a cinque voci*, Venice, Gardano, 1549; *Opera*, I, 1959, p. 133.

[52] *Belshazzar* (1746), *Werke*, XIX, 1864, p. 21.

[53] Charles DEMPSEY, *Renaissance Hieroglyphic Studies and Gentile Bellini's 'St. Mark Preaching in Alexandria'*, in *Hermeticism and the Renaissance: Intellectual History and the Occult in Early Mod-ern Europe*, ed. I. Merkel and A. G. Debus, Washington, Folger, 1988, p. 355.

[54] Manfred LURKER, *Der Kreis als Symbol im Denken, Glauben und künstlerischen Gestalten der Menschheit*, Tübingen, Wunderlich, 1981, writes from the standpoint of an anthropologist, rather than that of a historian of ideas. More useful is Dietrich MAHNKE, *Unendliche Sphäre und Allmittel-*

must suffice. Philosophers such as Plato[55] and Aristotle[56] regarded the circle as the most noble type of motion, as perfect and eternal, since it had no beginning or end.[57] These qualities had already made the circle a symbol for 'god' in Babylonia, Egypt, or in Orphic poetry.[58] And so Eusebius can remark in his *Praeparatio evangelica*: "the sphere and everything round are attributed to God, the world ..., sun, and moon".[59] The medieval tradition of geometrical religious symbolism was continued above all by Nicolaus Cusanus.[60] Kircher quotes a very influential formulation which can be traced back through the theological literature from Cusanus[61] via Berchorius,[62] Master Eckhart,[63] and Alanus de Insulis[64] (always without mention of the source) to the pseudo-hermetic *Liber XXIV philosophorum* ca. 1200:[65] "God is a circle or intelligible sphere, whose center is everywhere and circumference nowhere".[66] This neoplatonic concept was taken up with enthusiasm by Renais-

---

punkt, Halle, Niemeyer, 1937; also Georges POULET, *Le symbole du cercle infini dans la littérature et la philosophie*, «Revue de métaphysique et de morale», LXIV, 1959, pp. 257-275, and *id.*, *Les metamorphoses du cercle*, Paris, Plon, 1961. With the discovery of the circulation of the blood, medical writers were quick to allude to the philosophical and theological concepts of the circle, and were delighted to have a further analogy between the microcosm and the macrocosm, confirming the complementary relationship between anatomy and astronomy – cf. Walter PAGEL, *The Circular Motion of the Blood and Giordano Bruno's Philosophy of the Circle*, «Bulletin of the History of Medicine», XXIV, 1950, pp. 398f, and Frank L. HUNTLEY, *Sir Thomas Browne, M. D., William Harvey, and the Metaphor of the Circle, ibid.*, XXV, 1951, pp. 236-247.

[55] *Timaeus*, 33B: "most perfect" form for the universe; 34A: "belongs especially to reason and intelligence".

[56] *Physica*, VIII.viii, 264B: "perpetual", "self-completing", "continuous"; *De coelo*, 1.2, 269A-B: "primary", "continuous", "eternal". Cf. also PLINIUS SECUNDUS, *Historia naturalis*, II.ii: "ad motum ... aptissima" ["most suitable for motion"].

[57] Cf. Friedrich SOLMSEN, *Aristotle's System of the Physical World*, Ithaca, Cornell UP, 1960, pp. 36f, 225, 237, 289.

[58] MAHNKE, *passim*; DOREN (quoted below, note 111), p. 81 and note 31.

[59] "Pila et rotunda omnia Deo, mundo ..., soli, lunae attribuuntur" – P.G. XXI. The passage is quoted by KIRCHER, *Obeliscus*, p. 383, and *Obelisci ... interpretatio*, p. 52.

[60] MAHNKE, pp. 78, 81.

[61] *Id.*, pp. 78, 146.

[62] Petrus BERCHORIUS [Pierre Bersuire, ca. 1290-1362], *Repertorium morale perutile predicatoribus*, Nuremberg, Bindonus, 1489, f. clxxv.

[63] Heinrich DENIFLE, *Meister Eckeharts lateinische Schriften*, «Archiv für Litteratur- und Kirchengeschichte des Mittelalters», II, 1886, p. 571; MAHNKE, pp. 146ff *et passim*.

[64] *Regulae de sacra theologia*, regula VII, in P.L. CCX, 627.

[65] Published in DENIFLE, p. 428, and Clemens BAEUMKER, *Das pseudo-hermetische 'Buch der vierundzwanzig Meister'*, «Beiträge zur Geschichte der Philosophie des Mittelalters», XXV/1-2, 1927, p. 208.

[66] "Deus circulus est, seu sphaera intelligibilis, cuius centrum est ubique, circumferentia nusquam", quoted here from KIRCHER, *Obeliscus*, p. 380 (also in *Oedipus aegyptiacus*, II/2, pp. 84, 86). The oldest ms. of the *Liber XXIV philosophorum* reads: "Deus est sphaera infinita" – MAHNKE, p. 173. Cf. also HIPPOLYTUS, *Refutatio omnium haeresium* [third century A.D.], I.i.1: "Divinum autem

sance architects such as Alberti,[67] Filarete,[68] Francesco di Giorgio,[69] and Palladio,[70] who, in their treatises, sing the praises of the circle's perfection and, in their churches, replace the rectangular basilica with the domed circular plan symbolic of God.[71] The architectural symbolism was by then already documented for famous circular temples of antiquity. According to the *Legenda aurea*, the Pantheon's roundness demonstrated the eternity of the gods,[72] and Palladio himself explains the circular form of the Roman temple of Vesta, goddess of the earth, as reflecting the shape of the terrestial globe.[73] This imagery was, of course, cultivated also by poets. A modern historian of literature even finds that "No metaphor was more loved by Renaissance poets than that

---

id esse quod neque principium habeat neque finem" ["Divine, moreover, is that which has neither beginning nor end"]; MECHTHILD VON MAGDEBURG, *Das fließende Licht der Gottheit* [13th c.], VI.31: "Wie Gott einer Kugel gleicht" ["How God resembles a sphere"]; BERCHORIUS, f. clxxv: "circulus ... potest ... significare ... Dei perfectionem" ["a circle can signify the perfection of God"]; VALERIANO, f. 287: "Sarraceni quoque, & pleraeque aliae nationes Deum circulum appellabant" ["Also the Saracens and very many other nations call God a circle"]; KIRCHER, *Oedipus*, II/2, p. 95: "Circulus demonstrat, quomodo in Deo omnia identificentur" ["The circle demostrates how everything is identified with God"]; *id.*, *Obelisci ... interpretatio*, p. 52: "nil nisi divinum" ["nothing unless the divine"]; MAHNKE, pp. 146-150, 169-215. According to Karsten HARRIES, *The Infinite Sphere: Comments on the History of a Metaphor*, «Journal of the History of Philosophy», XIII, 1975, pp. 5-15, it was Cusanus who transferred the metaphor "Deus est sphaera" from God to the universe.

67 Leon Battista ALBERTI, *De re aedificatoria* [ca. 1450], Florence, Alamani, 1485, f. [114*v*], passage beginning "Rotundis naturam in primis delectari ...".

68 Antonio AVERLINO, detto il FILARETE, *Trattato di architettura* [1464], Milan, Polifilo, 1972, I, 230f.

69 Francesco di Giorgio MARTINI [d. 1501], *Trattati di architettura, ingegneria e arte militare*, Milan, Polifilo, 1967, II, 372: "Tre sono le principali spezie di templi. ... La prima e più perfetta delle altre è la figura rotunda" ["There are three kinds of temples. ... The first, more perfect than the others, is the round plan"].

70 Andrea PALLADIO, *I quattro libri dell'architettura*, Venice, De' Franceschi, 1570, IV, 6: the circular form is "la più perfetta, & eccellente", "attissima a dimostrare la unita, la infinita essenza, la uniformita, & la giustitia di DIO"; "faremo i tempij ritondi" ["the most perfect and excellent", "most apt to demonstrate the unity, the infinite essence, the uniformity, and the justice of GOD"; "let us make temples round"].

71 Louis HAUTCŒUR, *Mystique et architecture: Symbolisme du cercle et de la coupole*, Paris, Picard, 1954, and especially Rudolf WITTKOWER, *Architectural Principles in the Age of Humanism* («Studies of the Warburg Institute», XIX), London, Warburg Institute, 1949, Part One, "The Centrally Planned Church and the Renaissance", pp. 1-28. Already in the Middle Ages, centrally planned churches and dome-like baldachins were associated with the cult of the Virgin – cf. Antje MIDDELDORF/KOSEGARTEN, *Zur Bedeutung der Sieneser Domkuppel*, «Münchener Jahrbuch der bildenden Kunst», 3. Folge, XXI, 1970, pp. 84-88.

72 JACOBUS DE VORAGINE [ca. 1230-98], *Legenda aurea*, Bratislava, Koebner, 1890, p. 719: "ut ex ipsa forma Deorum aeternitas demonstretur" ["so that the eternity of the gods is demonstrated from the same form"]. On the circular plan for temples and for the ideal cosmic *civitas* of antiquity, with the ruler or god in the center, cf. Tommaso CAMPANELLA, *La città del sole* [1602], Modena, Rossi, 1904, p. 3, and H. P. L'ORANGE, *Studies on the Iconography of Cosmic Kingship in the Ancient World*, Oslo, Aschehoug, 1953, pp. 9-27.

73 PALLADIO, IV, 6.

of the circle".[74] To these I would add the English metaphysical poets of the seventeenth century. John Donne exclaimed, "O Eternall, and most gracious God, who ... art a circle",[75] and Henry Vaughan "saw Eternity the other night, / Like a great ring of pure and endlesse light".[76]

Considering the immense currency of the circle's symbolism in the philosophy, theology, literature, and visual arts[77] of the Renaissance, it is not surprising to find this symbol also in the music of the period. We can now understand why Lasso employs the *circulatio* for the mystical words of God from the burning bush (Ex. 24): Moses asks what he should tell the Israelites when

Ex. 24. Lasso: [God].[78]

they ask him the name of this god, and God replies, "Ego sum, qui sum" ["I am that which I am"]. That God and the sun should share the same hieroglyphical and musical symbol is only natural when we recall how closely the two have always been linked.[79] As giver of life, the sun was the principle god of primitive peoples. They celebrated the birth of the sun at the time of the winter solstice. Hence the early Christians, having no record of the date for Christ's birth, assigned it to that period, just as they assigned the Lord's day to Sun-day. Matthew says Christ's face "shone like the sun";[80] the altar in Christian churches often faces the rising sun; and baroque monstrances

---

[74] Majorie Hope NICHOLSON, *The Breaking of the Circle: Studies in the Effect of the "New Science" upon Seventeenth Century Poetry*, Evanston, Northwestern UP, 1950, p. 34.

[75] *Devotions upon Emergent Occasions*, London, Jones, 1624, p. 16.

[76] "The World", from *Silex scintillans*, London, Blunden, 1650, p. 91.

[77] Cf. also Milard MEISS, *Masaccio and the Early Renaissance: The Circular Plan*, in *Studies in Western Art: Acts of the 10th International Congress of the History of Art*, Princeton UP, 1963, II, 135: "Though the circular plan began to appear in Trecento painting, its great diffusion came with the Early Renaissance". Horst de LA CROIX, *Military Architecture and the Radial City Plan in Sixteenth Century Italy*, «Art Bulletin», XLII, 1960, p. 263: the circular plan became "the perfect vehicle for the expression of Renaissance urban ideals" (for military architects, admittedly, it came to have only functional, not philosophical or theological meaning). Irving LAVIN, *The Story of O from Giotto to Einstein* will be published in *The A. W. Mellon Lectures in the Fine Arts*, Princeton UP.

[78] "Ego sum, qui sum" [*Exodus*, 3:14], from *Selectiorum aliquot cantionum sacrarum ... fasciculus*, Munich, Berg, 1570; *Werke*, XIII, 4.

[79] Cf. Gosbert SCHÜSSLER, *Das göttliche Sonnenauge über den Sündern: Zur Bedeutung der 'Mesa de los pecados mortales' des Hieronymus Bosch*, «Münchener Jahrbuch der bildenden Kunst», 3. Folge, XLIV, 1993, pp. 121f.

[80] MATTHEW, 17:2.

show the rays of the sun emanating from the Host, the body of Christ.[81] For theologians, such as Albertus Magnus and Bonaventure[82] the circular crown signified life everlasting. And because the circle represented perfection and eternity, the crown became the attribute of a king; the nimbus or halo, that of divine or saintly persons who enjoy eternal life, as even Kircher observed.[83] Thus Filippo Picinelli referred to the circle as "symbol ... of eternity", or "of beatitude".[84] Both concepts were known to musicians. When the Nuremberg composer Sigmund Theophil Staden designed ca. 1655 a visual allegory of heavenly and earthly music, he explained in his commentary that the cherubim singing the praises of the Lord form a circle to symbolize the eternity of the Holy Trinity, represented by the triangle.[85] And Willaert crowned the martyr St. Stephen with the halo of beatitude (Ex. 25), just as Rore

Ex. 25. Willaert: crowned.[86]

co - ro - na - - - - tus

(Ex. 26), Schmeltzer (Ex. 27), or Biber (Ex. 28) painted the gloria-nimbus, extended in Ex. 29 to baroque excess (many measures continue in this man-

---

81 Oskar MONTELIUS, *Das Sonnenrad und das christliche* [griechische] *Kreuz*, «Mannus», I, 1909, pp. 177-185. Montelius refutes the common view that Christian churches were built to face Jerusalem by pointing out that also Asiatic churches north of Jerusalem face the east.

82 ALBERTUS MAGNUS (1193?-1280): "... vitam interminabilem, quae significatur in corona, quae est circularis et circulus non habet principium nec finem" ["... everlasting life, which is represented by a crown, which is circular, and the circle does not have a beginning or end"]. BONAVENTURE (1221-74): *De VII donis Spiritus Sancti*, ch. II: "Rotunditas coronae significat illius regni aeternitatem" ["the roundness of a crown signifies the eternity of that reign"]. Both quoted by Filippo PICINELLI, *Mondo simbolico*, Milan, Vigone, 1669, p. 754.

83 *Obeliscus*, pp. 382f. On 'eternity' cf. also above, HORAPOLLO; VALERIANO, ff. 286v, 288; KIRCHER, *Oedipus aegyptiacus*, II/2, 86, *Obelisci ... interpretatio*, p. 52. On the halo, cf. Henri MENDELSOHN, *Der Heiligenschein in der italienischen Malerei seit Giotto*, Berlin, Cassirer, 1903 – mere description of a "Stimmungselement" [!], doesn't deal with concepts; Karl KÜNSTLE, *Ikonographie der christlichen Kunst*, Freiburg, Herder, 1928, I, 25-28; the relevant lexica: *Dictionnaire d'archéologie chrétienne et de liturgie*, *Enciclopedia cattolica*, *Lexikon für Theologie und Kirche*, etc. and the literature quoted there.

84 "simbolo ... dell'eternità" or "della beatitudine", p. 754. On the circle as a symbol of life after death, cf. also above, p. 10; HENKEL/SCHÖNE, col. 5f: emblem from Theodorus BEZA, *Icones* [Genua, Laonius, 1580]; and *Apoc.* 2:10: "dabo tibi coronam vitae" ["I shall give you the crown of life"].

85 "... dero Ewigkeit durch den Zirkel um den Triangel angezeiget wird" ["... whose eternity is indicated through the circle around the triangle"] – Hans H. EGGEBRECHT, *Zwei Nürnberger Orgel-Allegorien des 17. Jahrhunderts*, «Musik und Kirche», XXVII, 1957, pp. 180f.

86 "Patefactae sunt", from *Musica quatuor vocum liber primus*, Venice, Scotto, 1539; CMM, III: *Adriani Willaert Opera omnia*, I, Rome, American Institute of Musicology, 1950, p. 111.

Ex. 26. Rore: gloria.[87]

Ex. 27. Schmeltzer: gloria.[88]

Ex. 28. Biber: gloria.[89]

Ex. 29. [Biber?]: gloria.[90]

ner). We are reminded of Shakespeare's words, "Glory is like a circle in the water, / Which never ceaseth to enlarge itself".[91] Such is the arrangement of the souls in Dante's *Paradiso* (XXIV.13ff), as drawn by Botticelli, with Christ again represented as the sun (Plate I.2).[92] In the visual arts, the circle was the traditional pose for the souls in paradise, as exemplified by Tintoretto's painting for the Sala del maggior consiglio of the doges' palace in Venice (Plate I.3).[93]

---

[87] "O qui populos suscipis", from D-Mbs Mus. ms. B; *Opera*, VI (1975), p. 72.

[88] *Missa nuptialis, Sanctus*, DTÖ, XLIX, Vienna, 1918, p. 66.

[89] *Missa Sancti Henrici* (1701), *Gloria, ibid.*, p. 12.

[90] *Festmesse, Gloria, ibid.* XX (1903), p. 32. This Mass was composed probably not by Orazio Benevoli, but by Heinrich Biber in 1682 – cf. Ernst HINTERMAIER, *'Missa salisburgensis': Neue Erkenntnisse über Entstehung, Autor und Zweckbestimmung*, «Musicologica Austriaca», I, 1977, pp. 154-196.

[91] 1 *Henry VI*, I.ii.133f.

[92] Dante ALIGHIERI, *La Divina commedia illustrata da Sandro Botticelli*, Rome, Canesi [1965], pp. 267, 269, 271. When Dante saw the Virgin in her heavenly court, he heard a song of the "amore angelico": "Così la circolata melodia / si sigillava, e tutti li altri lumi / facean sonare il nome di Maria" ["Thus the circular melody was sealed, and all the other lights sounded the name of Mary"] – *Par.* XXIII.108ff.

[93] Many gloria circles from the interior of domes are reproduced in Karl MÖSENEDER, *Die Inversion der Glorie: Johann Evangelist Holzers Deckengemälde in Partenkirchen und verwandte Fresken*, «Münchener Jahrbuch der bildenden Kunst», 3. Folge, XXXIX, 1988, pp. 133-174.

Dante, of course, conceives not only the souls in nine concentric circles in the eighth heaven, but also the heavens themselves as a series of nine concentric circles, according to the Ptolemaic system of astronomy (*Paradiso*, XXVIII.34; Plate I.4).[94] Centuries later, Mozart writes conspicuous *circulus*-figures where the text speaks not of the heavens, but of the flames of hell (Ex. 30). Earlier

Ex. 30. Mozart: flames of hell.[95]

composers have used the same recipe, since hell too consisted of nine circles, for instance in Botticelli's drawing of Dante's *Inferno* (XXIII.21, Plate I.5; cf. Virgil, *Aen.*, VI.439). Petrus Berchorius, whose voluminous *Repertorium morale* provided rich material for preachers, wrote in the fourteenth century of the "circle, infernal closure and orbit".[96] And still Gottfried Taubert, in his *Rechtschaffener Tanzmeister* of 1717, quotes the church father Cyprianus:[97]

'Chorea est circulus, cuius centrum est diabolus, qui in medio tripudiantium ignem concupiscentiae inflammabat'; Der Tanz ist ein Kreiß, allwo sich der Teufel in der Mitten befindet, und unter den Tanzenden ein Feuer geiler Brunst und verbotener Lust anzündet.

'The dance is a circle, whose center is the devil, who inflamed among the dancers a fire of lasciviousness' ...

Bach paints a ghastly picture of hell with a *circulatio* on the words "wie ein Tod den andern fraß".[98] "One cadaver swallows up the other" at the rate of four per measure in a very close canon. Finally, I may cite an example from the instrumental repertoire. Here too, figures have their meaning, if we approach them with caution. Once texts have provided clues for our under-

---

[94] Cf. also the circle as a symbol of heaven in BEZA, no. 1 (HENKEL/SCHÖNE, col. 6), etc.; and *Dante historiato da Federico Zuccaro*, Rome, Salerno, 2004, containing, like Botticelli's series, many circles.

[95] *Requiem* (1791), *Dies Irae*, "Confutatis maledictis, flammis acribus addictis" – Wolfgang Amadeus MOZART, *Neue Ausgabe sämtlicher Werke*, Ser. I, Werkgruppe 1, Abt. 2, Teilband 1, Kassel, Bärenreiter, 1965, pp. 41-43.

[96] "circulus, clausura et ambitus infernalis", f. clxxv.

[97] Leipzig, Lanckischen, 1717, p. 63.

[98] Cantata "Christ lag in Todesbanden" BWV 4, in Johann Sebastian BACH, *Neue Ausgabe sämtlicher Werke*, Ser. I, vol. IX, Kassel, Bärenreiter, 1985, p. 29; cf. also the edition of Gerhard Herz, New York, Norton, 1967, pp. 103f.

standing of musical formulations in the vocal repertoire, the same formulations can easily be recognized when they occur in instrumental music, with the same or similar meaning (e.g. below, pp. 437f, Exx. 6, 5). In the slow movement of his string quartet Op. 59, no. 2, Beethoven draws a splendid series of *circuli* (Ex. 31). But why did he do it here? According to his pupil Czerny, Beethoven conceived this movement "once when he observed the starry sky and thought of the music of the spheres".[99]

Ex. 31. Beethoven: [music of the spheres].[100]

I am convinced that, at least from the late Renaissance until the Enlightenment, educated listeners saw such clearly formulated, conspicuous *circuli* with their ears. This is confirmed by contemporary witnesses for single composers such as Lasso, perhaps the greatest composer of the sixteenth century, whom Burmeister singles out as the best model for figures.[101] When Samuel Quickelberg designates motets of Lasso as "musica reservata", he turns to a visual analogy: "accommodating the subject matter and the words, expressing the force of the single affects, and placing the content almost as acted before [our] eyes".[102] Like Kircher's "actio circularis", this reminds us that in classical rhetoric "actio" designated the delivery of the oration with voice and gesture.[103] Also Quickelberg's words "res et verba" reveal the source of his formulation in ancient rhetoric, and what he describes here is simply the *evidentia*, the "palpability" of rhetoric, which Quintilian says displays the facts "to the eyes of the mind".[104] The

---

[99] "als er einst den gestirnten Himmel betrachtete und an die Harmonie der Sphären dachte" – Alexander Wheelock THAYER, *Ludwig van Beethovens Leben*, II, Leipzig, Breitkopf & Härtel, 1922, p. 532. Beethoven possessed a copy of Johann Elert BODE, *Anleitung zur Kenntnis des gestirnten Himmels mit Kupfern*, Berlin, Himburg, 1801[7] – Albert LEITZMANN, *Ludwig van Beethoven*, Leipzig, Insel, 1921, II, 383.

[100] Werke, Abt. VI, Bd. 4, Munich, Henle, 1968, p. 49, mm. 37-39 (V. 1), 40-42 (Vc.).

[101] Pp. 57-65.

[102] "res et verba accommodando, singulorum affectum vim exprimendo rem quasi actam ante oculos ponendo" – quoted by Adolf SANDBERGER, *Beiträge zur Geschichte der bayerischen Hofkapelle unter Orlando di Lasso*, I, Leipzig, Breitkopf & Härtel, 1894, p. 56, note 2.

[103] Cf. QUINTILIAN, XI.ii.51.

[104] Cf. *ibid.*, IV.ii.64, VIII.iii.62.

Nuremberg printer Johann Ott had already made similar observations on motets of Josquin in 1538: "what painter could express so graphically the face of Christ?", "adorns sacred things so elegantly", "almost paints the gesture".[105]

Now Josquin has long been recognized as the first great master of text interpretation.[106] In theoretical writings of his time, 'rhetoric' in the narrow sense is, of course, less in evidence than in the late sixteenth or seventeenth century. But since we are proceeding empirically, we are justified in looking for circle figures here too. We searched extensively for them in the works of the earlier fifteenth-century composers.[107] But only in two of Josquin's pieces did we find them for the first time in the classical formulation and unambiguously associated with appropriate texts.[108] Both compositions, like almost everything he wrote, are undated. Petrucci printed them in 1501 and 1504, respectively.[109] Edward Lowinsky has argued that Josquin, in his canzona "Fortuna d'un gran tempo", depicted the turning of Fortune's wheel by means of modulation in a circle of fifths.[110] In art and literature, this fickle goddess is nearly always shown with the attribute of the wheel, which no sooner has raised people to power and success than it plunges them back down into misfortune (Plate I.6).[111] But Josquin formulated also his melody it-

---

[105] "quis pictor eam Christi faciem ... exprimere tam graphice potuit?", "sacras res sic eleganter ornat" and "gestum quasi ping[e]t", Preface to *Secundus tomus novi operis musici*, Nuremberg, Grapheus, 1538; RISM 1538³.

[106] Helmuth OSTHOFF, *Der Durchbruch zum musikalischen Humanismus*, International Musicological Society, *Report of the Eighth Congress New York 1961*, Kassel, Bärenreiter, 1962, II, 31-39; Ludwig FINSCHER, *Zum Verhältnis von Imitationstechnik und Textbehandlung im Zeitalter Josquins*, in *Renaissance-Studien: Helmuth Osthoff zum 80. Geburtstag*, Tutzing, Schneider, 1979, p. 69, attributes to Josquin's motet "Ave Maria ... Virgo serena" [ca. 1476?] "the historically decisive step from text presentation to text interpretation", without furnishing any demonstration.

[107] A huge *semicirculus* is appended to the 'wheel' of St. Catherine – *Antiphonale Sarisburiense*, London, Plainsong and Mediaeval Music Society, 1901-24, IX, plate Y. And a two-dimensional *circulus* occurs in a two-part conductus with the words "novus annus *circulari* ductu renovatus" ["the new year renewed with *circular* shape"] – Robert FALCK, *The Notre Dame Conductus*, Henryville, Institute of Medieval Music, 1981, p. 76; this circle is more evident when the higher voice is written above the lower. With such texts, it is tempting to interpret these passages as rhetorical *circuli*. However, I prefer not to draw conclusions from only two examples, but to reserve judgment until a systematic search for such phenomena in medieval music has been made.

[108] The ostinato figure in Johannes Martini's *Fortuna desperata* is not an "early example of this *circulatio* figure", but an *anabasis* – contrary to Dietrich KÄMPER, *"Fortuna rota volvitur": Das Symbol des Schicksalsrades in der spätmittelalterlichen Musik*, «Miscellanea mediaevalia», VIII, 1971, pp. 363ff; nor does Isaac's "Corri Fortuna", quoted on p. 366, contain a *circulus*. This figure does depict the wheel of Fortune in Giovanni Maria BONONCINI, *Zenobia prigioniera* and *Fortuna arruota Cortelli*, in *Cantate per camera a voce sola, libro primo ... opera decima*, Bologna, Monti, 1677, pp. 19, 44ff.

[109] *Odhecaton* and *Motetti C*.

[110] *The Goddess Fortuna in Music: With a Special Study of Josquin's Fortuna dun gran tempo*, «Musical Quarterly», XXIX, 1943, pp. 45-77.

[111] Cf. Wilhelm WACKERNAGL, *Das Glücksrad und die Kugel des Glücks*, «Haupt-Zeitschrift für

Ex literarum studiis immortali-
tatem acquiri.

Neptuni tubicen,cuius pars vltima cetum,
  Aequoreum facies indicat effe Deum:
Serpentis medio Triton comprehenditur orbe,
  Qui caudam inferto modicus ore tenet.
Fama viros animo infignes,præclaráque gefta
  Profequitur:toto mandat & orbe legi.

  Triton Neptuni tubicen, exauditam eloquentiam, profun-
damque rerum fcientiam defignat. Anguis in fefe reuolutus,
æternitatem:Concha perfonans,famã,quibus vnà conuenien-
tibus,æterna fcientiæ & eloquentiæ fama fignificatur.

K 5

I.1. Serpent circle, symbol of immortality and eternity. Andrea Alciati, *Emblemata*, Lyon, Rovillius, 1557, p. 153. Cf. p. 10.

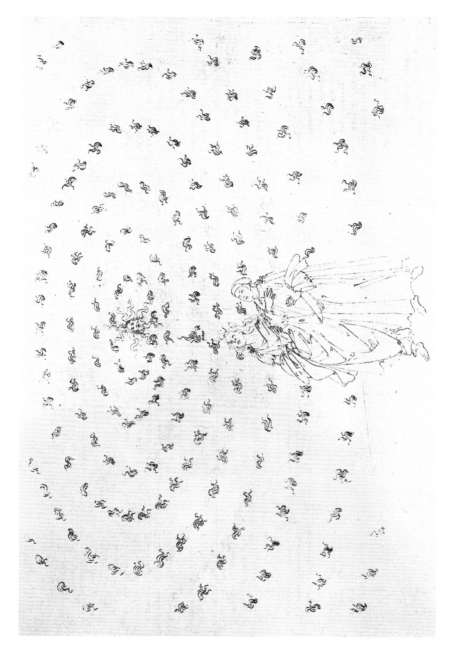

I.2. Blessed souls in paradise. Sandro Botticelli, illustration for Dante's *Divina commedia*, ca. 1492-97. Cf. p. 17.

I.7. *Maria lactans*. Jean Fouquet, Melun diptych, ca. 1450, Musée d'Anversa. Cf. p. 23.

self as a huge *circulus*, encompassing the entire octave (Ex. 32). The notes of very unequal duration depict the erratic motion of Fortune's wheel.[112] (I shall be returning to this rhythm later). One might perhaps object that Josquin, like many other composers, merely took over the melody of the popular Fortuna song. However, a comparison with the other arrangements of this song[113] shows that only the first descent is taken from the traditional melody. Thus the idea of drawing the wheel of Fortune with a powerful circle probably remains Josquin's ingenious innovation.

Ex. 32. Josquin: [wheel of Fortune].[114]

The other example is the last one in this article. But it displays such consummate art that I should like to comment on the few measures in detail. They are from Josquin's motet "Ave Maria ... benedicta tu". The first half of the well known *Ave Maria* text is found as early as the sixth century, in the Marian liturgy since the tenth, but common only since the twelfth, especially in Josquin's homeland, Hainault.[115] It combines the 'angelic greeting' with the salutation of Elizabeth.[116] These make up two thirds of the motet's text. But what interests us here is what follows. At the time of Josquin there was no unified type. Not until after his death was the text extended in Catho-

---

deutsches Altertum», VI, 1846, pp. 134-149; Gustav HEIDER, *Das Glücksrad und dessen Anwendung in der christlichen Kunst*, «Mittheilungen der k. k. Central-Commission zur Erforschung und Erhaltung der Baudenkmale», IV, 1859, pp. 113-124; A. MEDIN, *Ballata della Fortuna*, «Propugnatore», n. s. II/1, 1889, pp. 101-144; A. DOREN, *Fortuna im Mittelalter und in der Renaissance*, «Vorträge der Bibliothek Warburg», II/1, 1922/23, pp. 71-144; Joseph SAUER, *Symbolik des Kirchengebäudes und seiner Ausstattung des Mittelalters*, Freiburg, Herder, 1924, pp. 272-276; Howard R. PATCH, *The Goddess Fortuna in Medieval Literature*, Cambridge MA, Harvard UP, 1927.

[112] Fortune's wheel turns "not uniformly, for her motions ocur erraticly and unpredicatably" – DOREN, p. 84.

[113] Cf. the seven melodies superimposed by Jaap VAN BENTHEM, *Fortuna in Focus: Concerning 'conflicting' Progressions in Josquin's Fortuna dun gran tempo*, «Tijdschrift van de Vereniging voor Nederlandse Muziekgeschiedenis», XXX, 1980, p. 49.

[114] *Werken van Josquin Des Prez*, Supplement, Amsterdam, Vereniging voor nederlandse Muziekgeschiedenis, 1969, pp. 62-65.

[115] On the history of the *Ave Maria*, cf. Stephan BEISSEL, *Geschichte der Verehrung Marias*, Freiburg, Herder, 1909-10, I, 228-250, II, 5-16; Fernand CABROL and Henri LECLERCQ, *Dictionnaire d'archéologie chrétienne et de liturgie*, Paris, Letouzey, 1924-53, X/2, col. 2055-60; *Lexikon für Theologie und Kirche*, Freiburg, Herder, 1957-67, I, 1141; *Lexikon der Marienkunde*, Regensburg, Pustet, 1957ff, col. 477-501.

[116] LUKE, 1:28 ("Ave, gratia plena, Dominus tecum, benedicta tu in mulieribus") and 1:42 ("Benedicta tu inter mulieres, et benedictus fructus ventris tui"), combined since the turn of the eighth century.

3

lic regions with the familiar formulation "Sancta Maria, Mater Dei, ora pro nobis" (admitted to the *Breviarium Romanum* in 1568; *LU* 1861). Josquin's continuation, however, reads, "Et benedicta sint beata ubera tua, quae lacta-verunt regem regum" ["And blessed be thy breasts, which nursed the King of Kings"].[117] This text, used as early as 1100 by Anselm of Canterbury,[118] be-longs to the seventh Gregorian Responsory for Matins of the Christmas week (*LU* 390). My readers may by now suspect where Josquin uses the *circulus* (Ex. 33). He depicts the "ubera", the "breasts" of the Mother of God with

Ex. 33. Josquin: breasts.[119]

---

[117] On the various other settings of the *Ave Maria* by Josquin cf. Daniel E. FREEMAN, *On the Origins of the Pater Noster – Ave Maria of Josquin Desprez*, MD, XLV, 1991, pp. 169-213.

[118] *Oratio* LVIII, in P.L. CLVIII, 963.

[119] In this connection I would not mention that, according to ancient legend, the *circulus lacteus* or Milky Way originated from milk (Greek γάλα, hence "galaxy") spilled from the breast of Juno,

a genuine, classical *circulus* in the form of a sine curve. (We recall, moreover, that the Latin word "sinus" means "bosom").[120] The nourishing breasts of the Virgin are sung in numerous hymns since the fourth century in the entire Christian world, east and west.[121] But nowhere except in Josquin's motet have I seen this particular text combined with the *Ave Maria*. Whether the text was compiled by Josquin himself or by someone else is uncertain. More important is that Josquin here sets to music what he must have long known from paintings: the iconographical type of the nursing Madonna, the *Maria lactans*.

The earliest depictions of the Virgin already show her as a nursing mother.[122] They were intended above all as proof of motherhood, in support of the title θεοτόκος, against the scepsis of the first centuries. With the Council of Ephesus in 431 A. D. the virginal maternity of God became dogma, thus establishing the Marian cult.[123] From this point on, the iconographical type became widely diffused, first in Coptic art of the fifth and sixth centuries, influenced by depictions of the nursing Isis.[124] But it was cultivated especially in the fourteenth and fifteenth centuries in Italy and Flanders,[125] and then declined after the Council of Trent censured nudity in religious art. A *Maria lactans* by Jean Fouquet (Plate I.7), for example, from the period and homeland of Josquin, illustrates very clearly the *circulus* figure.[126] (The overly explicit in-

---

were not this legend subsequently christianized by replacing Juno with Mary and the infant Hercules with St. Bernhard – cf. Wilhelm GUNDEL, *Sterne und Sternbilder*, Bonn/Leipzig, Schroeder, 1922, p. 52, and Tintoretto's painting, reproduced in DE VECCHI, tav. IL.

[120] Many are quoted by Lazare MIRKOVIĆ, *Die nährende Gottesmutter (Galaktotrophusa)*, «Studi bizantini e neoellenici», VI, 1940, pp. 297-304.

[121] *Werken, Motetten*, I, 1922, pp. 12f.

[122] Cf. Natalia BALDORIA, *La Madonna lattante nell'arte del medio evo*, in R. Istituto di scienze, lettere e arti, «Atti», ser. VI, vol.VI, 1887/88, pp. 777-798, and especially Paul EICH, *Die Maria lactans: Eine Studie ihrer Entwicklung bis ins 13. Jahrhundert und ein Versuch ihrer Deutung aus der mittelalterlichen Frömmigkeit*, ms. diss. Frankfurt, 1953, containing references to many literary sources. Brief indications in *Handbuch der Marienkunde*, ed. Wolfgang Beinert and Heinrich Petri, Regensburg, Pustet, 1984, pp. 563, 571.

[123] Cf. F. A. VON LEHNER, *Die Marienverehrung in den ersten Jahrhunderten*, Stuttgart, Cotta, 1886, pp. 37-85, and EICH, pp. 14-21; *Handbuch* cit., pp. 112ff.

[124] Gabriel MILLET, *Recherches sur l'iconographie de l'évangile aux XIVᵉ, XVᵉ et XVIᵉ siècles*, Paris, Fontemoing, 1916, p. 627; EICH, pp. 9, 11, 22f; Louis RÉAU, *Iconographie de l'art chrétien*, Paris, Presses universitaires, 1955-59, II/2, 96f; H. W. MÖLLER, *Die stillende Gottesmutter in Agypten*, Hamburg, Nordmark, 1963; *Lexikon der christlichen Ikonographie*, Freiburg, Herder, 1968-76, III, 158.

[125] *Lexikon der christlichen Ikongraphie*, III, 186, 190. Cf. also Georgiana GODDARD KING, *The Virgin of Humility*, «Art Bulletin», XVII, 1935, pp. 474-491; Millard MEISS, *The Madonna of Humility*, *ibid.*, XVIII, 1936, pp. 435-464; Dorothy C. SHORR, *The Christ Child in Devotional Images in Italy during the XIV Century*, New York, Wittenborn, 1954, pp. 58-82.

[126] Likewise the *Mariae lactantes* of Joos van Cleve (active in Antwerp, ca. 1511-40) in Max J. FRIEDLÄNDER, *Die altniederländische Malerei*, Berlin, Cassierer, 1924-37, IX, Tafel xxxii, xxxv, xxxix, and in the Art Institute, Chicago.

terpretation may be connected with the fact that this 'Virgin' has the facial features of Agnes Sorel, mistress of the French king). More typical of Josquin's time are kind, motherly, very human girls, in a domestic setting.[127] Bernet Kempers characterized Josquin's Virgin not inappropriately as a dear relative who has come for a visit;[128] but he did not connect her with this iconographical tradition, found especially in private house altars. Josquin himself had a Marian altar in his house.[129] (I might add that Italian painters of the Renaissance frequently placed the Virgin and child in a *tondo*, accentuating their divinity with the circular frame).[130]

Breasts belong, of course, to the oldest and most long-lived symbols of mankind – as symbol of fertility and of nature in primitive art, in the multibreasted Artemis πολυμαστή of Ephesus to Faust's "infinite Nature, you breasts"[131] or Schiller's "at the breasts of Nature" in Beethoven's Ninth Symphony.[132] But especially in Christendom, breasts and their milk – likewise an ancient and many-faceted folk symbol[133] – were associated not only with physical, but also with spiritual nourishment.[134] Thus Paul says to the Corinthians, "I give you milk to drink".[135] Clement of Alexandria writes at great length about the miracle of the virginal milk and interprets this as a symbol of the *logos*, the doctrine of the gospels, which nourishes the Christians.[136] (The opposite, Heresy, was

---

[127] E.g. the famous Madonna by the Master of Flémalle in the National Gallery, London, reproduced in Erwin PANOFSKY, *Early Netherlandish Painting*, Cambridge MA, Harvard UP, 1964, II, pl. 90.

[128] K. Ph. BERNET KEMPERS, *Jacobus Clemens non Papa und seine Motetten*, Augsburg, Filser, 1928, p. 76.

[129] Herbert KELLMAN, *Josquin Desprez and Notre-Dame at Condé-sur-Escaut*, paper presented at the congress of the International Musicological Society, Strasbourg 1982 (not published in the congress report).

[130] For paintings of *Maria lactans* in *tondi* from the school of Botticelli cf. Ronald LIGHTBROWN, *Sandro Botticelli*, Berkeley, California UP, 1978, II, 132, 137.

[131] "unendliche Natur, Euch Brüste", I – GOETHE, *Faust*, 455f.

[132] "an den Brüsten der Natur". Cesare RIPA, *Iconologia*, Rome, Gigliotti, 1593, p. 175, describes nature as a "donna ignuda, colle mammelle cariche di latte" ["a nude woman, with breasts full of milk"].

[133] J. B. FRIEDRICH, *Die Symbolik und Mythologie der Natur*, Würzburg, Stahel, 1859, pp. 673-676; Robert EISLER, *Orphisch-Dionysische Mysteriengedanken in der christlichen Antike*, «Vorträge der Bibliothek Warburg», II/2, 1922/23, ch. 41; Louis CHARBONNEAU-LASSAY, *Bestiaire du Christ*, Paris, Desclée, 1940, pp. 197-201.

[134] Cf. BERCHORIUS, f. ccxxxviv: "Sunt duo genera uberum: s[cilicet] divina et humana" ["There are two kinds of breasts: namely divine and human"].

[135] I *Cor.* 3:2.

[136] *Paidagogus*, I.6, in P.G. VIII, 291-311. HONORIUS AUGUSTODUNENSIS (d. ca. 1125), *Expositio in Cantica Cantic.*, equates the two breasts with the "doctrina de duobus Testamentis" ["doctrine of the two Testaments"] – P.L. CLXXII, 361; cf. BERCHORIUS, f. ccxxxvi: "Deus enim habet duo ubera sacrae scripturae s. vetus et novum testamentum" ["For God has two breasts of the sacred scripture, namely the Old and New Testament"].

symbolized as a woman with dry, withered breasts, for example by Cesare Ripa in his *Iconologia*.[137] Incidentally, a most notorious traffic in relics was that of the Virgin's milk, satirized by Erasmus;[138] this consisted, at best, of a mixture of water and chalk from a cave in Bethlehem).[139] The nursing Madonna is identified further with the *ecclesia lactans*, the mother Church,[140] and with the *sedes sapientiae*, Solomon's throne of wisdom.[141] St. Bernard thus refers to Mary as "dispenser of wisdom".[142] These ideas are connected with the age-old notion that mother's milk formed also the character and intellect – as the nurse says to Shakespeare's Juliet, "Were not I thy only nurse, / I would say thou hadst suck'd wisdom from thy teat",[143] or "the breasts of wisdom" in Goethe's *Faust*.[144] (A satirical drawing by a Lutheran,[145] 1599, shows Calvin at the breast of Philosophy, regarded with suspicion by Luther). But with *Maria lactans* the situation is much more complex, because Mary, in the words of Balai, "nursed the universal nourisher";[146] or St. Jerome, "he sucked your breasts, which he himself filled".[147] With the 'nourishment of the nourisher' I am caught in a vicious circle which I must leave to the theologians.[148]

---

[137] Padua, Tozzi, 1625, p. 289.

[138] "Peregrinatio religionis ergo", in his *Colloquia*, Basel, Froben, 1526, pp. 425-462.

[139] BEISSEL, I, 298; EICH, pp. 148-161.

[140] CLEMENT OF ALEXANDRIA, in P.G. VIII, 299; EICH, pp. 4ff, 118-126; J. A. SCHMOLL, *Sion – Apokolyptische Weib – Ecclesia lactans*, in *Miscellanea pro arte* [Festschrift Hermann Schnitzler], Düsseldorf, Schwann, 1965, pp. 91-110; Max SEIDEL, *Ubera matris: Die vielschichtige Bedeutung eines Symbols in der mittelalterlichen Kunst*, «Städel-Jahrbuch», N. F., VI, 1977, pp. 41-98.

[141] I *Kings* 10:18-20; Wilhelm MOLSDORF, *Christliche Symbolik der mittelalterlichen Kunst*, Leipzig, Hiersemann, 1926, pp. 138ff. The twelfth-century commentaries on the *Cantica Canticorum* (Alanus de Insulis, Bernard of Clairvaux, Honorius Augustodunensis) identify Mary with Solomon's bride (i.e. God's Church), her breasts with those of the Church. Cf. also *Handbuch* cit., p. 595.

[142] "dispensatrix sapientiae", *Ad laudem gloriosae V. Matris*, subtitle, quoted from William S. HECKSCHER, *Bernini's Elephant and Obelisk*, «Art Bulletin», XXIX, 1947, p. 180 (not in P.L. CLXXXII).

[143] *Romeo and Juliet*, I.iii.67f. Cf. RIPA's description of Educazione, Padua 1625, p. 193: "Donna di età matura ... mammelle piene di latte" ["A lady of mature age ... breasts full of milk"], and William S. HECKSCHER's review in «The University of Toronto Quarterly», XVI, 1947, pp. 212f. Especially the earliest phase of education, *grammatica*, was symbolized by a nursing woman – SEIDEL, pp. 50-56.

[144] "der Weisheit Brüste" – 1, 1892.

[145] Lieselotte MÖLLER, *Bildgeschichtliche Studien zu Stammbuchbildern*, «Jahrbuch der Hamburger Kunstsammlungen», I, 1948, Abb. 21. On the derivation of the *Philosophia lactans* from the *Maria lactans* cf. also her *Nährmutter Weisheit: Eine Untersuchung über einen spätmittelalterlichen Bildtypus*, «Deutsche Vierteljahrsschrift für Literaturwissenschaft und Geistesgeschichte», XXIV, 1950, pp. 347-359.

[146] *Ausgewählte Schriften der syrischen Dichter Cyrillonas, Baläus, Isaak von Antiochien und Jakob von Sarug*, Kempten/Munich, Kosel, 1912, p. 94. Cf. similar formulations in the *Coptic Apocryphal Gospels*, Cambridge UP, 1896, pp. 39, 46, 53, 61, 77, 101.

[147] "sugeret tua ubera, quae ipse implevit" – *Epistola* X, in P.L. XXX, 149. Likewise Pseudo-AUGUSTINUS, *Sermo* 188,2, P.L. XXXVIII, 1004: "crearetur ex matre quam creavit, ... sugeret ubera

The question arises whether Josquin's music goes beyond the visual effect of the *circulus* and expresses something of this theological symbolism. Now in works of great masters musical-rhetorical figures seldom stand alone. Even more than language, music can express several ideas simultaneously, and such counterpoint of affects is carried to almost unbelievable intensity in the works of J. S. Bach.[149] Josquin presents his *circulus* simultaneously as the figure of the *fuga*, i.e. a fragmentary canon. Tenor and soprano form a small canon at the upper octave, alto and bass the same at the lower octave. Such figural canons often signify "one thing issuing from another, ... a forceful connection", as Schmitz says of Bach.[150] In Masses by Dufay, Ockeghem, Josquin, and up to the b-minor Mass of Bach, the union of Godfather and -son is symbolized again and again by canonic passages for words like "ex Patre natum" ["born of the Father"].[151] For the equation of the mother and son of God, Josquin uses similar canonic duos in his Antiphon "Alma Redemptoris Mater"[152] and here in the *Ave Maria*. Also the interval of the octave for canonic imitation in our example is probably not chosen by chance, for imitation at the octave is the most literal, equivalent to the rhetorical *mimesis*, the imitation of someone else's manner of speaking .[153] Like the circle, also the octave was regarded as perfect. Josquin's compatriot Johannes Legrense calls it ca. 1460 "the most perfect of the consonances", which begets all other intervals "as a pious mother fosters and nourishes in her bosom".[154] These

---

quae implevit" ["He was created from the mother which He created, ... He sucked the breasts which He filled"]. The Council of Ephesus had made this paradox into a dogma.

[148] Cf. Anton L. MAYER, *Mater et filia: Ein Versuch zur stilgeschichtlichen Entwicklung eines Gebetsausdrucks*, «Jahrbuch für Liturgiewissenschaft», 1927, pp. 60-81. Of his many examples I quote only the words of a poet well known to music historians, ALFONSO EL SABIO, *Cantigas de Santa Maria*, Madrid, Aguado, 1889, I, 574: "da filla fez madr" ["from the daughter He made the mother"]. Cf. also KING, p. 485.

[149] Cf. SCHMITZ, *Bildlichkeit*, and Reinhold HAMMERSTEIN, *Der Gesang der geharnischten Männer: Eine Studie zu Mozarts Bachbild*, AfMw, XIII, 1956, pp. 11f.

[150] *Bildlichkeit*, p. 41.

[151] Fritz FELDMANN, *Untersuchungen zum Wort-Ton-Verhältnis in den Gloria-Credo-Sätzen von Dufay bis Josquin*, MD, VIII, 1954, pp. 167f; Willem ELDERS, *Studien zur Symbolik in der Musik der alten Niederländer*, Bilthoven, Creyghton, 1968, pp. 86-91; id., *Das Symbol in der Musik von Josquin des Prez*, AMl, XLI, 1969, p. 171ff; Arnold SCHERING, *Bach und das Symbol: Insbesondere die Symbolik seines Kanons*, «Bach-Jahrbuch», XXII, 1925, pp. 44, 46; SCHMITZ, *Bildlichkeit*, pp. 48f.

[152] *Werken, Motetten*, IV (1922), pp. 107f, with the words "genuisti ... tuum sanctum genitorem" ["you gave birth to your holy parent"], text by Hermannus Contractus, A.D. 1013-54.

[153] QUINTILIAN, IX.ii.58, and below, pp. 65ff, 439.

[154] "perfectissima consonantiarum", "ut pia mater in sinu suo foveat ac enutriat" – *Joannis Gallici dicti Carthusiensis seu de Mantua Ritus canendi vetustissimus et novus*, in E. DE COUSSEMAKER, *Scriptorum de musica medii aevi nova series*, Paris, Durand, 1864-76, IV, 302. Similarly Pietro AARON, *De institutione harmonica*, Bologna, Di Ettore, 1516, f. 14v: "tamquam foecunda parens" ["as much as a fertile parent"].

words, of course, fit my argument very well, as does Zarlino's designation of the octave a century later as "parent, mother, source, origin".[155] Just as in religious painting of the fifteenth century, especially in the Netherlands, almost every detail of everyday life points to a higher sphere – that's the "spiritual things in a corporal metaphor" of Thomas Aquinas[156] – thus these physical *ubera* give more, namely divine nourishment. The continuation of the motet text, "quae lactaverunt", is then set to the musical-rhetorical figure of the *katabasis*, a descending line, which soon became a standard device for fluids,[157] in this case milk.

But in addition to melody and counterpoint, we must consider also the rhythm, for in this music all means are at the service of text expression. Josquin sets the entire *Maria lactans* episode as a tripla interpolation, i.e. a temporary shift to triple time or *tempus perfectum*. Winfried Kirsch observed that such sections are normally homophonic; when they are not, we have "a personal ... stylistic attitude, which is really incompatible with the normal function of such sections in triple time".[158] We therefore have all the more reason to regard Josquin's conscious use of canonic figures as text interpretation. As in other tripla passages, here too the change of measure serves to accentuate significant words and to set them off from their context.

It is not difficult to see why Josquin presents his *circuli* in trochaic triple rhythm: that combination results in the style of the cradle song. Since the fourteenth century, European lullabies for the Christmas season were composed in this rhythm. Some of them, such as "In dulci jubilo", are found in Catholic songbooks to this day. Mattheson still associates this rhythm with "cradle or slumber songs" and says it has "something quite innocent about it".[159] Already in Josquin's day, physicians recommended that infants, after nursing, be rocked to gentle music.[160] A sixteenth-century painting of the hall of the

---

[155] "genitrice, madre, fonte, origine" – Gioseffo ZARLINO, *Istitutioni harmoniche*, Venice, s.n., 1558, p. 158.

[156] "spiritualia sub metaphoris corporalium" – *Summa theologiae*, 119. PANOFSKY, I, pp. 131-148, has made us aware of the importance of this concept.

[157] Cf. the words "rio fluente" ["flowing stream"], in Claudio MONTEVERDI, *L'Incoronazione di Poppea* (1642), *Tutte le opere*, Asolo, Malipiero, 1926-43, XIII, 134, and the tears of the saint in Caldara's *Oratorio per Santa Francesca romana*, AC 1966 p. 274 = AC 2007 p. 344.

[158] *Zur Funktion der tripeltaktigen Abschnitte in den Motetten des Josquin-Zeitalters*, in *Renaissance-Studien: Helmuth Osthoff zum 80. Geburtstag*, Tutzing, Schneider, 1979, p. 146. Josquin concludes the *tertia pars* of the motet "Vultum tuum" (*Werken, Motetten*, VII, 1924, p. 122) with a different elaboration of the same tripla material, but without employing a *circulatio*, since the text contains no 'circular' concept.

[159] "Wiegen- oder Schlaf-Liedern","ziemlich-unschuldiges an sich" – Johann MATTHESON, *Der vollkommene Capellmeister*, Hamburg, Herold, 1739, p. 166.

[160] E.g. Paulus BAGELLARDUS, *Libellus de aegritudinibus infantium*, Padua, Valdezoccho & De

wet-nurses in the hospital of Santo Spirito in Rome[161] shows a single flute player providing this music. Another indication is given by a Christmas motet of Costanzo Festa which sets the words "natus in presepio" as a *semicirculus* in triple time (Ex. 34). The musicians at the Nativity were, of course, the shep-

Ex. 34. Festa: [pastoral cradle song].[162]

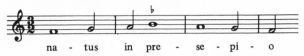

na - tus in pre - se - pi - o o

herds; their instruments, the bagpipes and the shawm.[163] At Christmas time, to this day, real shepherds come in pairs from the mountains of Abruzzo to Rome and play the ancient cradle song in the streets and before Marian altars or crèches, for instance as Louis Spohr described them in 1816: "Usually there are two of them, of which one plays the bagpipe, the other the shawm".[164] Their smooth, gently rocking melody in triple time does not differ very much from Josquin's cradle song. This ancient pastoral style belongs to the *topos* of Christmas music in Italy. Also Handel, surely influenced *inter al.* by Corelli's 'Christmas' concerto Op. 6, no. 8 (Amsterdam, Roger, 1714), used it in *Messiah* to introduce the shepherds at Bethlehem.[165]

Aboribus, 1472, f. [4]. For paintings showing the *Maria lactans* with the sleepig child, cf. Hans KÖRNER, *Hans Baldings 'Muttergottes mit der Weintraube'*, «Pantheon», XLVI, 1988, pp. 50-55.

[161] Reproduced in Werner Friedrich KÜMMEL, *Musik und Medizin*, Munich, Salber, 1977, Abb. 16.

[162] "Angelus ad pastores ait", from *Motetti novi libro secundo*, Venice, Antico, 1520; *The Medici Codex*, «Monuments of Renaissance Music», IV, Chicago UP, 1968, p. 79.

[163] Cf. Master of Flémalle, Dijon *Nativity* (ca. 1420-25), reproduced in PANOFSKY, II, pl. 88, and Christoph Hellmut MAHLING, *Der Dudelsack in westeuropäischer Plastik und Malerei*, in *Studia instrumentorum musicae popularis*, IV, Stockholm, Musikmuseet, 1976, pp. 64f.

[164] "Gewöhnlich sind sie zu zweien, wovon der eine den Dudelsack und der andere die Schalmei spielt", *Selbstbiographie*, Kassel/Göttingen, Vigant, 1860-61, I, 318. Hans GELLER, *I pifferari: Musizierende Hirten in Rom*, Leipzig, Seemann, 1954, reproduces 19th-century German drawings of Italian bagpipers and gives a transcription of their music, "Quando nascette Ninno a Bettelemme" (p. 62f). The melody still most played by the *pifferari* today is "Tu scendi dalle stelle" (18th c.). On such pastoral music, cf. Rudolf BERLINER, *Die Weihnachtskrippe*, Munich, Prestel, 1955, pp. 192f; Hermann JUNG, *Die Pastorale*, Bern, Franke, 1980; Helmut LOOS, *Weihnachten in der Musik*, Bonn, Schröder, 1991; Joachim STEINHAUER, *"Fare la ninnananna": Das Wiegenlied als volkstümlicher Topos in der italienischen Kunstmusik des 17. Jahrhunderts*, «Recercare», IX, 1997, pp. 49-93; Friedrich LIPPMANN, *Berlioz, Gounod, Spohr, Nicolai, Landsberg, Liszt und die Pifferari*, «Analecta Musicologica», XXXVI, 2005, pp. 489-558.

[165] *Messiah* (1741), "Pifa", «Hallische Händel-Ausgabe», XVII, Kassel, Bärenreiter, 1965, pp. 66f.

If an ancient rhetorician were to classify this mild, tranquil style, he would surely associate it with *aequalitas*, the 'evenness' which Quintilian recommends for a good movement of the voice. This, he says, includes variety and thus maintains the middle between the two extremes, of inequality and monotony.[166] These extremes are rhetorical *vitia*, unless they are necessitated by the subject matter; then they become virtues. By this criterion we may now interpret both Josquin's erratic rhythm for the wheel of Fortune and Mozart's monotonous tremolo – each an extreme – as a virtue.

But rhetoricians from Cicero to Gottsched, when dealing with the *pronuntiatio*, considered the motion not only of the voice, but also of the body, the rhetorical gestures, and emphasized that they must be synchronized with the content of the speech.[167] Of the ancient authors, only Quintilian writes about them at length. And he mentions "seven" gestures as indispensable for the orator. What interests us here is the seventh, "which returns to itself, a circle".[168] In the Middle Ages, Quintilian was, of course, read now and then, but only in fragments. Only after 1416, when Poggio Bracciolini discovered a complete manuscript, did he become a favorite author of the humanists. But it was not until 1468 that his work appeared in print. From then on, a flood of editions appeared. They must be regarded as a prime cause for the new rhetorical concept of music in the Renaissance.[169] Josquin found the *concept* of circle symbolism already ripe in the world of ideas; but he may have derived his compositional *technique* from the ancient Roman's teachings on gesture. We recall that in 1538 Johann Ott spoke of him "painting" the gestures. As long as we have no proof that Josquin knew Quintilian from a manuscript – and it is very unlikely that such proof will ever be found – we may suggest that our two examples may have been composed after the first edition of Quintilian. In them, "words, ... gesture, and motion"[170] coincide. Here he shows himself, at one of the most marked turning points in the history of Western music, as a perfect orator in the sense of the ancient rhetoricians.

* * *

---

[166] QUINTILIAN, XI.iii.43f.

[167] *Id.*, XI.iii.65ff, 88ff. Johann Christian GOTTSCHED, *Vorübung der Beredsamkeit*, Leipzig, Breitkopf, 1754, pp. 236f.

[168] "qui in se redit, orbis" – QUINTILIAN, XI.iii.105. Quintilian's seven categories of motion are derived from PLATO, *Timaeus*, 34A, 43B.

[169] For the most consistent application of Quintilian's teachings to music, cf. below, ch. 12. On the subsequent application of this research, see below, p. 118, note 137.

[170] "verba, ... gestus, motusque", QUINTILIAN, XI.iii.9.

The end, if any, of the circle is its beginning, and this study too has been little more than a beginning. So much remains to be done. To anticipate misunderstandings, I conclude with some remarks on method. With my musical examples I immediately plunged into deep water, because I believe that talk about method makes sense only when one demonstrates concretely on actual compositions what one is attempting to do. No one would deny that the task of scholarship is to recognize problems and to develop the methods to solve them. Yet it is not so widely recognized today that a central problem in the history of the arts is the *content* of the work. Iconology[171] and research on literary *topoi* – publications by Warburg, Panofsky, Curtius, to name only a few – have yielded brilliant contributions to our understanding of works of art, precisely because they were directed no longer merely at form, but also at content. But musicology has hitherto participated little in this kind of research – understandably perhaps, for the content of a musical composition is less easily accessible than that of a literary or visual work of art. The first attempts at musical hermeneutics did not help, because they did not go beyond a subjective, layman's aesthetic, for example when Hermann Kretzschmar in his concert guide designated Schubert's C-major Symphony as a "magnificent spring landscape", complete with mountains, sunbeams, and birdsongs.[172] Confidence in the interpretation of musical content was further weakened by Schering's late fantasies on the alleged literary models for Beethoven's instrumental works. But we must not, because of this, throw out the baby with the bath water and renounce all musical exegetics, for both the theory and the practice of music from the Renaissance until the early nineteenth century no longer leave any doubt that music was conceived as a language, i.e. as a vehicle for ideas and affects. Exaggerating intentionally, one might say: what we still need – and this was recognized already by Rousseau and Forkel – is a conceptual dictionary for this language of notes which would explain the meaning of its vocabulary, etymologically and historically.[173] But

---

[171] I.e. the explanation of the meaning of visual art by identifying its (usually ancient) literary sources and by tracing motif-traditions – not to be confused with iconography, the mere collecting and cataloguing of visual data. I attempted to apply the iconological method to music itself also below, ch. 15. Cf. p. 592, note 25.

[172] *Führer durch den Concertsaal*, 1. Abt., Leipzig, Breitkopf & Härtel, 1887, pp. 120f.

[173] Jean-Jacques ROUSSEAU, *Essai sur l'origine des langues*, in his *Traités sur la musique*, Geneva, s.n., 1782, p. 296: "c'est une langue dont il faut avoir le dictionnaire" ["it is a language for which it is necessary to have the dictionary"]. Hence Johann Nikolaus FORKEL, *Allgemeine Geschichte der Musik*, Leipzig, Schwickert, 1788-1801, I, 41: "da die Musik eine solche Sprache ist, zu welcher nur sehr wenige Zuhörer ein vollständiges Wörterbuch besitzen" ["since music is such a language, for which only very few listeners possess a complete dictionary"]. The difficulty of such an undertaking lies, of course, in the unspecific nature of most musical formualtions.

this could be undertaken only with the help of the neighbouring disciplines. For even though music is – fortunately – not an "art without concepts", as Kant imagined,[174] we still need literary and visual sources in order to unlock the meaning of its concepts. The first key is, of course, the text which is set to music. In the Renaissance and the Baroque, this is most often taken literally, or at least in content, from the Scripture or from classical mythology. Those are precisely the sources upon which painters based their pictures. A composer can thus take his concepts either directly from this literature, or from one of the numerous commentaries on it, or indirectly from the visual arts. Men of the Renaissance and Baroque still possessed a common educational ground, their interests were not limited to their own professions. Music did not exist in a vacuum, as an abstract pattern of sounds, but was bound by manifold ties to the intellectual and social life of its time – much to its advantage. To uncover these connections is perhaps the most interesting task of musicology. But this must be done with all methodical rigor, for there is nothing more annoying than vague and superficial analogies between the different arts. In our comparisons we must insist upon objective criteria and historical documentation, if we are to achieve credibility. The point of departure should, of course, be a careful musical analysis. But that is only the first step, what might be called 'pre-historic' method. The parallel phenomena from the neighbouring disciplines must be examined in the same way, at first independently of music.[175] The next task is to make plausible that the composer was aware of the extramusical ideas. One can never have too much documentation for this, which, in turn, is dependent upon the state of bio-bibliographical research. Also very old ideas, like circle symbolism, are not to be excluded, when one knows that they were still current at the time of the composer (cf. above, Beethoven). In some cases we cannot assume a conscious intention. Mozart, for example, may not have been aware that he applied a musical-rhetorical figure. But every composer, whether he wishes or not, subordinates himself to the principles of musical rhetoric, just as every verbal expression is subject to the rules of grammar and to the universal system of literary rhetoric, already perfected in antiquity. The choice of a certain musical formulation for a certain content is always influenced by the associations in the historical repertoire known to the composer. Since the humanities are not exact sciences, we shall not be able, in many cases, to prove one hundred percent

---

[174] "begriffslose Kunst" – *Kritik der Urtheilskraft* (1790), § 53, in *Kant's gesammelte Schriften*, V, Berlin, Reimer, 1913, p. 328.

[175] Edward E. LOWINSKY, *The Concept of Physical and Musical Space in the Renaissance*, «Papers of the American Musicological Society», 1941, p. 64.

the intentions of the composer, especially when he does not formulate his ideas clearly, as often with lesser talents. We must therefore avoid overstraining our interpretations, if we do not wish to arrive at conclusions which would surprise the composer, make him amused, or even angry. But when we find that many masters, even over a period of centuries, have associated a certain figure with the same or related content, then we begin to understand their language.

II.

CICERONIANS VERSUS ARISTOTELIANS
ON THE RICERCAR AS EXORDIUM, FROM BEMBO TO BACH

Erich Schenk in memoriam

Of the various facets of ancient culture – art, literature, philosophy, law, medicine, and so on – which inspired the scholars and artists of the Renaissance, none received more attention than the art of rhetoric, inherited from antiquity as a fully developed system and still the climax of every schoolboy's curriculum, coming after the more elementary subjects of grammar and dialectic. Though with the decline of democracy it was no longer the key to political power, it did form the essential preparation for the preacher and the lawyer, and hence for a large segment of the educated; it was cultivated in the academies; and it dominated the humanist theories of literature and art.[1] In this context, music was undergoing perhaps the most profound change in its history, loosening its medieval bond with the mathematical disciplines of the quadrivium and becoming an expressive language. In other words, it became more and more aligned with the trivium.[2] The aim of

---

[1] On the latter see John R. SPENCER, *Ut rhetorica pictura: A Study in Quattrocento Theory of Painting*, «Journal of the Warburg and Courtauld Institutes», XX, 1957, pp. 26-44; Michael BAXANDALL, *Giotto and the Orators*, Oxford, Clarendon, 1971. Götz POCHAT, *Rhetorik und bildende Kunst in der Renaisssance*, in *Renaissance-Rhetorik*, ed. Heinrich Plett, Berlin, De Gruyter, 1993, pp. 266-284, and Patricia RUBIN, *Raphael and the Rhetoric of Art*, in *Renaissance Rhetoric*, ed. Peter Mack, New York, St. Martin's Press, 1994, pp. 165-182, demonstrate how humanist writers such as Bembo and Vasari used rhetorical categories (*imitatio, inventio, dispositio, argumentatio, persuasio, demonstratio, varietas, ethos, pathos, concetto, muovere, maniera,* the *genera,* etc.) to describe rhetorical elements in paintings such as those of Raphael's *stanze* for Leo X. Paul Oskar KRISTELLER, *Renaissance Thought and its Sources*, New York, Columbia UP, 1979, pp. 213-259, provides a survey of the role of rhetoric since antiquity.

[2] In his review of Helmut Osthoff's *Josquin Desprez*, «Renaissance News», XVI, 1963, pp. 256f, Edward LOWINSKY observed that in a fresco of the seven Liberal Arts attributed to Jean Perréal (ca. 1500) Musica is actually grouped with the language arts of the trivium rather than, as heretofore, with the quadrivial disciplines – perhaps, I may add, because QUINTILIAN, in book I of his *Institutio oratoria*, dealt with music immediately after grammar, before rhetoric. In the fresco she is represented by Tubal-Cain with the features of Josquin, the composer whose work did much to accom-

movere-delectare-docere [to move, to delight, and to teach] was transmitted to music from the common knowledge of rhetoric rather than from the much less accessible ancient writings on music theory or from the specific legend of Orpheus. Not until about 1600 did a music theorist, Joachim Burmeister, apply the system of rhetorical figures to music, thus establishing a basis for German baroque theory (*Figurenlehre*). But in the sixteenth century and in Italy, the implications of rhetoric for music are to be traced not so much through treatises on music, as through those on rhetoric itself. Though these have hitherto received almost no attention in musicological literature, they represent, directly and indirectly, the most pervasive and enduring influence of classical antiquity on music. And, as will be seen, they provide the greatest quantity of contemporary statements on one of the most important types of Renaissance music: the ricercar. The neighboring discipline of rhetoric can thus add a third dimension to the investigations by Eggebrecht and Slim of the ricercar's terminology and repertoire, respectively.[3]

Most instrumental music of the sixteenth century belongs to one of three categories: 'abstract' pieces, dances, and instrumental adaptations of vocal music (intabulations). The so-called abstract pieces[4] largely fulfilled a preludial function, and went by a variety of originally more or less interchangeable names, such as ricercar and fantasia. As secular music, especially for lute, they were followed by songs, madrigals, instrumental intabulations, or dances; as liturgical organ music they served as preludes to Mass sections, motets, or psalms. On the basis of the more familiar organ repertoire, the ricercar has long been described as an instrumental counterpart of the motet, with its style of continuous imitation making it the forerunner of the baroque fugue.[5] It is also recognized, however, that a totally different type of ricercar existed prior to and

---

plish this shift. Cf. also Klaus Wolfgang NIEMÖLLER, *Zum Paradigmenwechsel in der Musik der Renaissance: vom numerus sonorus zur musica poetica*, Akademie der Wissenschaften in Göttingen, phil.-hist. Klasse, «Abhandlungen», dritte Folge, no. 208, 1995, pp. 187-215; and Manfred Hermann SCHMID, *Musica theorica, practica und poetica: zu Horaz-Vertonungen des deutschen Humanismus*, in *Zeitgenosse Horaz: Der Dichter und seine Leser seit zwei Jahrtausenden*, ed. Helmut Krosser and Ernst A. Schmidt, Tübingen, Narr, 1996, pp. 52-67.

[3] Hans Heinrich EGGEBRECHT, *Der Terminus 'Ricercar'*, AfMw, IX, 1952, pp. 137-147; *id.*, *Studien zur musikalischen Terminologie*, Akademie der Wissenschaften und der Literatur in Mainz, geistes- und sozialwiss. Klasse, «Abhandlungen», 1955, no. 10; H. Colin SLIM, *The Keyboard Ricercar and Fantasia in Italy, c. 1500-1550*, ms. diss., Harvard University, 1960.

[4] The results of this article suggest that 'abstract' may be a 20th-century misnomer for these pieces, which, in function at least, must be regarded as 'concrete'.

[5] The customary analogy between the motet and the imitative ricercar is valid as long as it is not carried too far. The differences between the two have been pointed out by Gordon SUTHERLAND, *The Ricercari of Jacques Buus*, «Musical Quarterly», XXXI, 1945, pp. 448-463, and Willi APEL, *The Early Development of the Organ Ricercar*, MD III, 1949, pp. 141f.

concurrently with this one. It was not in the strict, contrapuntal style, but rather like a freely improvised prelude; sometimes, as when included in instruction books, it fulfilled a function comparable to that of the étude in the nineteenth century.[6] The existence of a single nomenclature for two so divergent types of music – the free and the imitative ricercar – has been one of the more baffling problems in the history of music. I shall show that the explanation can be found in a passage from Aristotle's *Ars rhetorica*, Cicero's reaction to it, and the persistence of their respective ideas throughout the sixteenth century and later.

Aristotle's *Rhetoric* (ca. 336 B.C.) was known in the Middle Ages especially through the widely diffused Latin translation by Guillelmus de Moerbeke (ca. 1270). The original Greek text was first published by Aldus in his *Rhetores Graeci* (Venice, 1508-09), and many new translations, paraphrases, and commentaries, mostly in Latin, followed during the course of the sixteenth century.[7] Of the three Aristotelian *genera causarum* – the epideictic or demonstrative, for praise and censure, the deliberative, for persuasion and dissuasion, and the judicial or forensic, for prosecution and defense – only the first flourished during the absolutistic sixteenth century: in church sermons, public festivities, wedding celebrations, funerals, academies, and court entertainments, playing a role similar to that of music.[8]

In speaking of the introduction or proem (Greek *procemion*, Latin *exordium*)[9] of a speech in the epideictic genus, Aristotle compares it to the prelude of the flute player (Greek *proaulion*):[10]

Τὸ μὲυ ὀυν προοίμιόν ἐστιν ἀρχὴ λόγου, ὅπερ ἐν ποιήσει πρόλογος καὶ ἐν αὐλήσει	The proem is the beginning of a speech, like a prologue in poetry and a prelude in

---

[6] See Imogene HORSLEY, *The Solo Ricercar in Diminution Manuals*, AMl, XXXIII, 1961, pp. 29-40.

[7] See Moïse SCHWAB, *Bibliographie d'Aristote*, Paris, Welter, 1896, pp. 285-298, and *National Union Catalog: Pre-1956 Imprints*, XXI, London, Mansell, 1969, pp. 11-20, for a fairly complete listing. Keith V. ERICKSON, *Aristotle's Rhetoric*, Metuchen, Scarecrow, 1975, pp. 1-18, gives a brief survey of the manuscript tradition and publication. R. G. BOLGAR, *The Classical Heritage and its Beneficiaries*, Cambridge UP, 1954, pp. 465-468, lists 15th-century mss. in and from Italy. Cf. also the listings of mss. of the various Latin translations in George LACOMBE, *Aristoteles Latinus*, Cambridge, Typis Academiae, 1939-1955.

[8] See Paul Oskar KRISTELLER, *Music and Learning in the Early Italian Renaissance*, «Journal of Renaissance and Baroque Music», I, 1946, p. 273. In the 17th century a sermon could be compared to an operatic entertainment: "quasi ad una musica di comedia si va alla predica, per osservare la rettorica, la bella grazia, le inventioni, la voce, il gesto del predicatore" ["almost as to an opera one goes to the sermon, to observe the rhetoric, the beautiful grace, the invention, the voice, the gesture of the preacher"] – Domenico DE GUBERNATIS, *Quaresimale*, Milan, Malatesta, 1672, p. 272.

[9] Classical rhetoric divides the speech into four to six parts: *exordium, narratio, partitio* (Cicero), *argumentatio* (subdivided by Cicero and Quintilian into *probatio* and *refutatio*), and *peroratio*. See ARISTOTLE, *Ars rhetorica*, III.1414b; CICERO, *De inventione*, I.xiv.19; QUINTILIAN, *Institutio oratoria*, III.ix.1; and below, Appendix I.

[10] III.1414b. All translations in this article are my own and aim at literal rendition.

προαύλιον· πάντα γὰρ ἀρχαὶ ταῦτ᾽ εἰσί, καὶ οἷον ὁδοποίησις τῷ ἐπιόντι. τὸ μὲν οὖν προαύλιον ὅμοιον τῷ τῶν ἐπιδεικτικῶν προοιμίῳ· καὶ γὰρ οἱ αὐληταί, ὅ τι ἂν εὖ ἔχωσιν αὐλῆσαι, τοῦτο προαυλήσαντες συνῆψαν τῷ ἐνδοσίμῳ, καὶ ἐν τοῖς ἐπιδεικτικοῖς λόγοις δεῖ οὕτω γράφειν ὅ τι γὰρ ἂν βούληται εὐθὺ εἰπόντα ἐνδοῦναι καὶ συνάψαι.

flute playing; for all these are beginnings, and pave the way, as it were, for what follows. Indeed, the prelude is like the proem of epideictic [speeches]; for as the flute players begin by playing whatever they can execute skillfully and connect it with the keynote, so also should be, in epideictic speeches, the composition [of the proem]; [one should] say at once whatever one likes, give the keynote,[11] and continue.

The Latin translations and paraphrases of this passage are by no means always literal (like, e.g., Latin *tibia* or *fistula* for Greek *aulos*), as can be seen from the occasional substitution of the stringed instruments lyre and cithara for the aulos, surely influenced by the Renaissance practice of playing preludes on lutes and viols. Thus we find the words "ἐν αὐλήσει προαύλων" ["prelude in flute playing"] rendered also as "in lyrae pulsatione praeludium",[12] "in pulsu lyrae praecentio",[13] and "citharoedorum praeludia".[14] And the αὐληταί ["flute players"] occur in phrases implying singing as well as playing: "qui fistula canunt",[15] "cytharoedi canunt, antequam certamen legitimum incohent",[16] "quae ante legitimum sonum a tibicine canuntur",[17] "tibicines quodcunque commode canere possunt".[18]

Aristotle's prelude, consisting of "whatever [the player] can execute skillfully" would seem to come close to the free, improvisatory type of ricercar. And indeed, we find that in the Italian translations and paraphrases of this passage the word *proaulion* is rendered as "ricercata", "ricerca", or "sonata", corresponding to the Latin *praeludium*. The very same usage is followed by Italian rhetoricians in their own treatises, with or without approval or ac-

---

[11] QUINTILIAN, stressing the importance of the study of music to the rhetorician (I.x.22-33), mentions a famous Roman orator who set the pitch of his voice with the help of a musician standing behind him and sounding a *tonarion* (pitchpipe).

[12] Georgius TRAPEZUNTIUS (1395-1484), *Aristotelis ... rhetorica* (first ed. Paris, ca. 1475), Venice, 1550, f. 26v.

[13] Ermolao BARBARO (1454-93), *Rhetoricorum Aristotelis libri*, Venice, Tridino, 1544, f. 183.

[14] Martin BORRHAUS, *In tres Aristotelis de arte dicendi libros commentaria*, Basle, Operinus, 1551, p. 401. The earliest Latin translation (anonymous, 13th c.) already rendered αὐληταί as "citharizantes", whereas MOERBEKE, only slighty later, wrote "fistulatores" – *Aristoteles Latinus*, XXXI,1-2, Leiden, Brill, 1978, pp. 149, 308.

[15] TRAPEZUNTIUS, f. 26v.

[16] BARBARO, f. 183v.

[17] Pietro VETTORI, *Commentarii* (first ed. Basle, 1547), Florence, Giunta, 1548, p. 584.

[18] Carlo SIGONIO, *Aristotelis ... Rhetorica* (first ed. Cracow, 1557), Bologna, Benatius, 1565, p. 180.

knowledgment. It will suffice to quote here the earliest Italian translation; a dozen more examples are given in Appendix II of this article.[19]

Lo proemio si è lo principio de l'oratione ... come ... nel sonar de la lira quel primo toccar de le corde. ... Et spetialmente li proemi de le orationi dimostrative sono somiglianti a le ricercate de li sonatori prima che comincino il suono. Percioché essi quando debbono sonare alcuna buona danza, allhora primamente corrono per li ponti de le corde, lequali sono principali ne la danza, laquale intendono di sonare, et continuando appresso cominciano a sonare distintamente tutto ciò, che haveano trascorso. Et così avviene ne le orationi dimostrative, perché primamente in brevità di parole si dà ad intendere a li auditori il tema de l'oratione intorno al quale intende di laudare o di biasmare.

The proem is the beginning of the oration ... like that first touching of the strings in lyre playing. ... And especially the proems of epideictic orations are similar to the ricercars of the instrumentalists before they begin to play, since they, when they must play some good dance, first run over the frets of the strings which prevail in the dance they intend to play, then continuing they begin to play distinctly everything which they have run through. And thus it happens in epideictic orations, because first one lets the listeners hear briefly the theme of the oration, about which one intends to praise or censure.

Authors writing in the sixteenth century obviously would not have rendered Aristotle's word *proaulion* as 'ricercar' if his description did not correspond closely to the kind of music which was called 'ricercar' in their own time. And indeed, the Greek passage contains three essential elements, all of which fit precisely the sixteenth-century phenomenon: 1) the *proaulion*-ricercar is an instrumental piece with a preludial function, therefore comparable to the proem in rhetoric; 2) it is very free ("maxime liberum"),[20] quasi-improvisatory, not related to the piece it introduces; 3) it attaches itself to the following piece by sounding the "keynote" (I use this modern term with all due reservations). For the ricercar, these three elements can be further demonstrated from musical and from other literary sources.[21] I shall begin with the second, since the first and third must be considered together.

---

[19] [Felice FIGLIUCCI, 1518-95], *Tradottione antica de la rettorica d'Aristotile, nuovamente trovata*, Padua, Fabriano, 1548, f. 167*r-v*. Figliucci's statement in the dedication to the effect that this earliest Italian translation was made "già più secoli" ["already several centuries ago"] has little credibility; it is quite possible that he was the translator. I have yet seen no source prior to the 16th century which uses the word 'ricercata' in the musical sense.

[20] BARBARO, f. 183*v*; Marc'Antonio MAJORAGIO, *In tres Aristotelis libros* (*editio princeps* Venice, 1547), Venice, Conti, 1571, p. 422. Lodovico CARBONE, *De disposizione oratoria*, Venice, Ciotti, 1590, p. 78.

[21] My arguments will be supported by citations from the relevant sources, though some of these have already been quoted in the literature on the ricercar (with the help of Nicolò TOMMASEO and Bernardo BELLINI, *Dizionario della lingua italiana*, Turin, UTET, 1916, VI, 187, article 'ricerca').

4

The style of the earliest notated ricercars, those in the lute tablatures of Spinacino, Dalza, and Bossinensis published by Petrucci between 1507 and 1511,[22] might be described as that of written improvisation. These little pieces lack formal organization, thematic unity, and even thematic material, but consist rather of a free alternation of short runs and chordal passages, such as a lutenist would improvise while warming up. Their very modest length speaks against their use for anything but a preludial function. The improvisatory character is underlined during a discussion in Sperone Speroni's *Dialogo dell'historia* on whether historiography can be considered an art; here Paolo Manuzio, son of Aldus, is made to compare histories with ricercars: "... licentious pieces, made at the whim of the instrumentalist, without any art which would regulate their beginning or end".[23] The ricercar remained associated with improvisational practice well into the eighteenth century. Mersenne's definition is derived, directly or indirectly, from Aristotle: "And when the musician takes the liberty to apply there everything which comes into his head, without expressing there the passion of any word, this composition is called *fantaisie* or *recherche*".[24] Brossard's statement, on the other hand, "It is a kind of prelude or fantasy, ... normally improvised, without preparation",[25] taken over literally by Walther and Rousseau,[26] is indebted to Quintilian (see below, note 221). Mattheson characterizes ricercars, particularly those for viola da gamba, as "things governed by nothing but the imagination", "improvised, not written".[27]

---

[22] To these may be added the two earliest lute mss., dating from the first and second decades of the 16th century: see G. THIBAULT, *Un manuscrit italien pour luth des premieres années du XVI⁰ siè-cle*, in *Le luth et sa musique*, ed. J. Jacquot, Paris, CNRS, 1958, pp. 43-76, and *Compositione di Messer Vincenzo Capirola*, ed. Otto Gombosi, Neuilly-sur-Seine, Soc. musique d'autrefois, 1955.

[23] "Ricercari comunemente sono appellati sì fatti suoni licentiosi, fatti ad arbitrio del sonatore, senza arte alcuna che dia lor legge di cominciare, né di finire" – *Dialoghi*, Venice, Aldi filii, 1550, p. 365. Francesco PANIGAROLA, *Modo di comporre una predica*, Venice, Vincenti, 1603, f. 42*v*: "& come le ricercate ponno essere di diece mila foggie, così questi prologhini non havendo che far altro, che destar gli animi, vengono ad essere così senza legge, e così senza regola" ["And as the ricercars can be in ten thousand different manners, thus these little prologues, having no other function than to arouse the spirits, thus come to be without law and thus without rule"].

[24] "Et lors que le musicien prend la liberté d'y employer tout ce qui luy vient dans l'esprit sans y exprimer la passion d'aucune parole, cette composition est appellée Fantaisie ou Recherche" – Marin MERSENNE, *Harmonie universelle*, Paris, Cramoisy, 1636, II, 164; used almost verbatim by Sebastian DE BROSSARD, *Dictionnaire de musique*, Paris, Ballard, 1702, s.v. 'motetto', but with the Italian words "fantasia & ricercata".

[25] "C'est un espèce de prélude ou de fantaisie. ... Cela se fait ordinairement sur le champs & sans préparation", s.v. 'ricercata'.

[26] Johann Gottfried WALTHER, *Musicalisches Lexicon*, Leipzig, Deer, 1732, p. 526; Jean Jacques ROUSSEAU, *Dictionnaire de musique*, Paris, Duchesne, 1768, p. 398.

[27] "Sachen, die ... sich nach nichts als der Fantesey richten", "a mente, non a penna" – Johann MATTHESON, *Das neueröffnete Orchestre*, Hamburg, Verfasser, 1713, pp. 175f, and *Der vollkommene Capellmeister*, Hamburg, Herold, 1739, p. 87.

The relationship of the proem to the ricercar was established in two stages: first Aristotle's simile compared the proem with the prelude; then Renaissance authors replaced 'prelude' with 'ricercar', substituting a modern term for an ancient one. Aristotle's analogy is perfectly natural in view of the unity of poetry and music in classical antiquity, for in ancient poetry the proem was often a musical one. This is reflected in the very etymology of the word *procemion*, for, as Quintilian and Aristotle's commentators take care to point out,[28] the literal meaning is: that which comes "before the song" (πρό + οἴμη), "quasi ante cantum".[29] Already in Homeric times, professional singers played a proem on the cithara before singing a section of an epic, and it was this prelude which gave them the opportunity to display their art,[30] "whatever they can execute skillfully". (There is no doubt that musicians of the Renaissance regarded their instrumental preludes and solo songs to the accompaniment of a stringed instrument as a revival of ancient practice;[31] the Florentine humanist Marsilio Ficino, for example, appeared in the company of Lorenzo il Magnifico as a new Orpheus singing to the accompaniment of his lyre).[32] One composer, at least, employed the word *procemium* as the title for musical compositions: Hans Kotter in his organ tablature of 1513 onwards.[33] It is surely no accident that the Greek terms *procemion* and *anabole* are employed here (f. 58*v*) in a manuscript written for a humanist, Bonifacius Amerbach in Basle, who prefaced the collection with Greek quotations. Vincenzo Galilei uses the word *proemio* in the table of contents of his *Fronimo* (Venice, Scotto, 1584) to refer to the "Fuga [i.e. canon] a cinque voci" at the beginning of the volume.

---

[28] QUINTILIAN, IV.i.1f: "οἴμη 'cantus' est et citharoedi pauca illa, quae, antequam legitimum certamen inchoent, emerendi favoris gratia canunt, procemium cognominaverunt" ["*oime*, 'song', is those little things which the cithara players sing to acquire favor before beginning the contest proper; they were called *procemium*"]; BORRHAUS, p. 401; Antonio RICCOBONI, *Paraphrasis*, Frankfurt, Wechel, 1588, p. 331; CARBONE, p. 33; likewise various commentaries on the *Rhetorica ad Herennium*, I.iv.6.

[29] SLIM, pp. 411, 414ff, quotes numerous 16th-century lexicographers, including Thomas Eliot (1538, 1548), Thomas Cooper (1565), and Ambrogio Calepino (1572), who define a prelude as a proem.

[30] Jacques HANDSCHIN, *Musikgeschichte*, Lucerne, Rüber, 1948, pp. 55ff.

[31] Dietrich KÄMPER, *Studien zur instrumentalen Ensemblemusik des 16. Jahrhunderts in Italien*, Cologne/Vienna, Böhlau, 1970, pp. 22ff.

[32] Arnaldo DELLA TORRE, *Storia dell'Accademia Platonica di Firenze*, Florence, Carnesecchi, 1902, pp. 788-791, 793; Lorenzo de' MEDICI, *Opere*, Florence, Molini, 1825, II, 165: "Pensai che Orfeo al mondo ritornasse, ... Sì dolce lira mi parea sonasse" ["I thought that Orpheus returned to the world, ... so sweetly did he seem to play the lyre"].

[33] CH-Bu Mus. F.IX.22, ff. 48*v*-49*v*, 59*v*-60*v*. Cf. Wilhelm MERIAN, *Drei Handschriften aus der Frühzeit des Klavierspiels*, AfMw, II, 1919/20, pp. 22-47. These pieces are published in MERIAN, *Der Tanz in den deutschen Tabulaturbüchern*, Leipzig, Breitkopf & Härtel, 1927, pp. 60, 63f, and «Schweizerische Musikdenkmäler», VI, Kassel, Bärenreiter, 1967, pp. 44, 52f.

The first equation cited above, between the prelude and the ricercar, has already been well documented in musicological literature. Particularly Egge-brecht and Slim have demonstrated that in the sixteenth century a large num-ber of names were used more or less interchangeably for instrumental pre-ludes: fantasia, intonatio, praeambulum, preludio, ricercar, tastar, tiento (in Spain), toccata, etc.[34] During most of the century these different names did not imply different musical styles. A contemporary table of contents may list a composition under a name different from the one in its caption, or the same piece may be found under another name in a different source. The use of *praeludium* and its derivatives as an alternate title indicates that all of these pieces had a preludial function.[35] In the case of the ricercar, we have substan-tial literary evidence from Tommaseo/Bellini[36] for its use as a prelude to sing-ing, especially in the epic. In Tasso's *Gerusalemme liberata*, completed in 1574, a musician prepares the listeners for his song with low-pitched ricercars: "That courteous musician, before loudly loosing his clear tongue for the song, prepares the minds of others for the harmony with sweet ricercars in low modes".[37] Paolo Del Rosso and Vincenzo Galilei tell us that Emperor Nero "first made with his fingers a beautiful ricercar on it [the lyre], and then be-gan to sing".[38] A lutenist in Bartolomeo Corsini's *Torracchione desolato* ad-heres to the same practice: "He took his lute to his chest and, playing ricercars masterly on the faithful strings, thus he released the voice to the agreeable sound".[39] In another mock epic, *Ricciardetto*, Niccolo Forteguerri introduces an incorrigible clerical musician who "takes the lyre, and after hundreds of ricercars he sang" in order to seduce the young nuns in a monastery.[40] With

---

[34] See also Richard MURPHY, *Fantaisie et recercare dans les premieres tabatures de luth du XVIe siècle*, in *Le luth et sa musique* cit., pp. 135f.

[35] See Filippo VENUTI, *Dittionario generale volgare & latino*, Venice, Valvassori, 1568, col. 684: "ricercata nel sonare hoc [est] praeludium" ["ricercar in instrumental music, i.e. prelude"]. A. Soler writes on 27 June 1765: "Ricercate, o siano preludi" ["ricercars or preludes"] – Santiago KASTNER, *Algunas cartas del P. Antonio Soler dirigidas al P. Giambattista Martini*, «Anuario musical», XII, 1957, p. 237. Honoré Francois Marie LANGLÉ, *Traité de la fugue*, Paris, 1805, l'auteur, p. 54, defines the "ricercato" as "une espèce de caprice ou prélude fugué" ["a sort of capriccio or fugal prelude"].

[36] *Op. cit.*, VI, 17f.

[37] "Qual musico gentil, prima che chiara / Altamente la lingua al canto snodi, / A l'armonia gli animi altrui prepara / Con dolci ricercate in bassi modi" – XVI.43.

[38] "fece prima in essa una bella ricercata con le dita, & dipoi cominciò a cantare" – GALILEI, *Dialogo della musica antica, et della moderna*, Florence, Marescotti, 1581, p. 39, taken over from DEL ROSSO, *Le vite dei dodici Cesari*, Venice, Costantini, 1554, I, 30. See also below, note 135.

[39] "Ad un liuto suo diede di piglio, / Adattosselo al petto, e ricercando / Di quel, con maestria, le fide corde, / Così sciolse la voce al suon concorde" – VII.21; written ca. 1660; first ed. London, Prault, 1768, I, 171.

[40] "prende la lira / E dopo cento ricercate e cento / Cantò" – XX.6, Paris, Pitteri, 1738, II, 108.

Italian translations of the *Odyssey* (I.155) we come the full circle, back to Homer: "now, playing ricercars on the strings, he began a beautiful song"[41] and "while he played ricercars on the strings with masterful fingers ...".[42]

Also the pairing of ricercars and instrumental arrangements of vocal pieces in the musical sources illustrates the preludial function. In the lute manuscript of Mme. Thibault, a "Recerchar de benedictus" is followed by an intabulation of a Benedictus by Heinrich Isaac,[43] and in Spinacino's tablature[44] of 1507_1 two ricercars are designated by their titles as preludes to two other pieces in the same book, intabulated from Petrucci's *Odhecaton* and *Canti C*: "Recercare De tous biens" and "Recercare a Juli amours". The two lute books of Bossinensis (1509_1 and 1511_1) conclude with a total of 46 ricercars, assigned by letters as preludes to the 126 frottolas. And in the Capirola lute book some pieces are associated with specific ricercars by headings such as "Oublier veuil nel ton del primo ricercar", "Sit nomen Domini benedictum nel ton del recercar terzo", and "Padoana francexe nel ton del recercar terzo".[45] This musical evidence that ricercars were followed by an intabulated motet, madrigal, song, or by a dance corroborates the rhetorical literature cited on pages 37 and 83ff: Figliucci, Cavalcanti, Caro, Piccolomini, De Nores, and Panigarola.[46]

An essential function of preludial pieces, running consistently through their history until the disintegration of tonality, is to establish the pitch, mode, or key for the piece which follows. Caro's translation of Aristotle (below, p. 83) accurately describes sixteenth-century practice: with the ricercar the instrumentalists "enter into the key of the motet or madrigal which they intend to play".[47] If our lute ricercars were to fulfil this function, they

---

[41] "or questi ricercando / Le corde, incominciava un vago canto" – [Anton Maria SALVINI], *Odissea d'Omero*, Florence, Tartini & Franchi, 1723, p. 7.

[42] "Mentr'ei le corde / Ne ricercava con maestre dita ..." – Ippolito PINDEMONTE, *Odissea di Omero*, Verona, Soc. Tip. Editrice, 1822, I, 9.

[43] THIBAULT, pp. 47, 52.

[44] Dates with subscript numbers refer to listings in Howard BROWN, *Instrumental Music Printed before 1600*, Cambridge MA, Harvard UP, 1967.

[45] Daniel HEARTZ, *Preludes, Chansons, and Dances for Lute ...*, Neuilly-sur-Seine, Soc. musique d'autrefois, 1964, p. x.

[46] A closely related but clearly exceptional practice is the employment of a ricercar as a postlude to a dance or intabulated motet – Dalza 1508_2, f. 48*v*: "Calata spagnola" + "recercar detto coda"; lute book of Jörg Fugger, DTÖ, XXXVII, Vienna, 1910, p. 108: "Recercar ad imitationem del motetto primo".

[47] That the pitch link between two successive sections of a musical complex had been an important consideration since very early times is illustrated by the system of *differentiae* for the psalm tones in plainsong.

would obviously have to be played on a well-tuned instrument. Since the lute is notoriously difficult to tune (it has been said that a lutenist spends half his time tuning, the other half playing out of tune), it is not surprising to find the word 'ricercar', particularly in its verbal forms, used frequently in the sense of 'testing' the tuning of the instrument. Dalza, 1508[2], couples a "tastar de corde" with a "recercar dietro".[48] Judenkünig, 1523[2], says he composed a preamble to be used to test the tuning of the lute.[49] Ganassi, in his treatise on viol playing, 1543[2], prefixes a madrigal with two such ricercars:[50]

Io voglio che questi duoi recercari ti sia abastanza per quanto lo ricercar l'istromento per il servitio in parte di giustar li tasti & acordar le corde ma che tu seguiterai che ti serà mostrato uno madregal da sonare e cantare con ditta viola.	I want these two ricercars to suffice for you to try out (*ricercar*) the instrument for use, partly in adjusting the frets and tuning the strings, but you will continue and be shown a madrigal to play and sing with the said viol.

Two authors make the musician's trial ricercar the subject of their own proems. Francesco Panigarola's example of a "prologhino" for a sermon begins with a description of a prelude for "viuola o cetra" before a motet or madrigal:[51]

Trascorre tutte il sonator le voci, tutti que' tasti tocca, tutte quelle minuge va tentando, tutte (se così si può dire) sollecita le corde, ne prima viene all'opra, che egli o gruppo, o fantasia, o qualche ricercata habbia premessa.	The player runs through the whole range, touches all the frets, goes on trying all those strings, urging them on (if one may say so), not arriving at his work until he has introduced it with either a group, or fantasia, or some ricercar.

Also the major Italian prose writer of the Seicento, the Jesuit Daniello Bartoli, who depicts the world as an immense repertoire of religious symbols, bears witness to this musical practice, after comparing the world to a well tuned harp:[52]

---

[48] See SLIM, pp. 242f, on the use of the word 'tastar' to refer to the tuning of strings (Francesco da Milano, De Barberiis, Brossard).

[49] Quoted by SLIM, p. 413.

[50] *Lettione seconda*, cap. XVI, sig. F1.

[51] *Il predicatore*, Venice, Giunti & Ciotti, 1609, p. 288.

[52] *La ricreatione del savio*, Rome, De' Lazzeri, 1659, p. 77 (lib. I, cap. V: "L'harmonia del mondo").

Così Iddio il [= il mondo] compose, così l'accordò, e il tiene in mano, e continuò il ricerca, e ne fa udire la musica.

... un valentissimo sonator d'arpa, che dopo una brieve ricercata, ch'è l'esame dell'accordatura, dia nelle più vaghe e artificiose sonate, ch'egli sappia d'ogni tuono e d'ogni modo le proprie, e Dorico grave, e Lidio guerriero, e Frigio mesto ...

Thus God composed the world, tuned it, and holds it in his hand, continually tries it out (ricerca), and lets the music be heard from it.

... a most capable harpist, who, after a brief ricercar (which is the examination of the tuning), leads into the sweetest and most elaborate pieces he knows, proper to each key and mode: the grave Dorian, warlike Lydian, and sad Phrygian ...

And then:[53]

Col fin hora discorso, io non voglio haver fatto altro, di quel che sogliono i sonatori di liuto, un proemio, come dicevano i Greci, o come noi, una ricercata, sonando un qualche bel gruppo di fantasia; e vale non tanto ad esaminar lo strumento per tutte le sue corde, a saper se si accordano; quanto a raccogliere l'attentione de gli uditori, e affissar loro l'anima ne gli orecchi per la sonata da vero che le vien dietro.

With what has been said thus far I do not want to have made other than that which is the custom of the lutenists, a proem, as the Greeks said, or, as we say, a ricercar, playing some beautiful group of improvisation; and this is useful not so much to examine the instrument in all its strings, to see if they are in tune, but to attract the listeners' attention and attach their soul to their ears for the real piece which follows.

This meaning of 'ricercar' is still given by Walther: "to play ricercars on an instrument ... to determine if it is tuned".[54]

The problem of tuning having been solved, the ricercar will establish, with its final cadence (quasi *endosimon*), the tonality of the ensuing composition. This function of *intonatio*, which the ricercar shares with all preludial pieces, is evident from three further considerations. First, such pieces are frequently given a tonal designation, beginning with the earliest sources – for instance "Preludium in fa", "Preambulum super d", "Recercada per b quadro del primo tono", "Toccata del quarto tono", and so on. (A special group is constituted by those which go through a series of cadences in many keys and which could be terminated whenever the desired one had been reached: for example

---

[53] *Dell'ultimo e beato fine dell'huomo, ibid.*, 1670, pp. 5f, indebted to Caro's translation of Aristotle, quoted below, p. 83.

[54] "'Ricercar' uno stromento ... ein Instrument ... versuchen, obs gestimmt sey" – p. 526. Likewise the Italian translations of Homer, quoted above ("ricercando le corde").

Spinacino's "Recercar de tutti li toni", 1507[1]; the "Prelude sur chacun ton" published by Attaignant, 1531[6]; and Gerle's "gut Preambel auff allerley Claves", 1533[1], with the instruction "you may abbreviate it where you wish").[55] Second, they are very often arranged in groups according to mode or key, usually in ascending order, to facilitate selection to match the tonality of the pieces they were to introduce.[56] Such groupings are a tradition extending from the medieval tonaries at least to Chopin's twenty-four Preludes Op. 28[57] and including the *Inventions* and the *Well Tempered Clavier* of J. S. Bach. Significantly, the *Inventions* were originally entitled "Praeambula"; the latter collection preserves also the connotation of a 'well tuned' instrument. Third, contemporary theorists confirm the intonation function of the musical proem: "Thus in music, whose relationship with poetry is great, we express the key in the exordium itself"[58] and "in ricercars ... one searches the mode".[59] It should by now be clear that an answer to the question posed by the *Bezeichnungsfragment* 'ricercar', "What is being sought (ricercato)?" It is, as Eggebrecht has stated,[60] the tuning of the instrument, the tonality of the piece to follow. Brossard's suggestion, retained by Walther, is not far off the mark: "it appears that the composer *searches* the features of the harmony which he wishes to employ in the regular pieces which he must subsequently play".[61] But I shall return to this question later.

Non-Italian writers have unnecessarily dissected the word 'ricercar' into 'ri-cercare', 'wieder-suchen',[62] without realizing that in Italian 'ricercar' does

---

[55] "Das magstu kürtzen, wo du wilt". For two additional examples, from the 17th century, see EGGEBRECHT, *Studien*, p. 94. We may add that this type of piece survived well into the 18th century, under the name of 'harmonic labyrinth' (one such is dubiously attributed to J. S. Bach, BWV 591), though not necessarily intended to be abbreviated ad libitum.

[56] The rare exceptions of mismatched modes (Bossinensis 1509[1], 1511[1] and De Barberiis 1546[2], title page; see SLIM, pp. 247f, 281) merely suggest that a few composers regarded also more-or-less related modes as a satisfactory preparation, just as *differentiae* did not always end on the same note with which the antiphons began.

[57] According to a communication from Nicholas Temperley, these were intended as actual preludes to be played before longer compositions.

[58] "Ita nos in musica cujus cum poesi magna est cognatio tonum in ipso exordio exprimamus" – Gallus DRESSLER (see below, note 140), p. 244, referring to the beginning of a vocal composition.

[59] "nelli ricercari si ... ricerca il modo" – Pietro PONZIO, *Dialogo*, Parma, Viothi, 1595, p. 48.

[60] *Studien*, p. 98.

[61] "semble que le compositeur *recherche* les traits d'harmonie qu'il veut employer dans les pieces reglées qu'il doit joüer dans la suite", s.v. 'Ricercata'. Cf. WALTHER, p. 526: "es scheine, ob suche der Componist die harmonischen Gänge oder Entwürffe, so er hernach in den einzurichtenden Pieces anwenden wolle" ["it would seem as if the composer searches for the harmonic passages or design, which he subsequently will apply to the pieces to be prepared"].

[62] EGGEBRECHT does this in his studies of 1952 (p. 137) and 1955 (p. 97), but abandons the error in his article 'Ricercar', in *Riemann Musik-Lexikon*, Mainz, Schott, 1967. Nevertheless, Chris-

not normally imply a repeated action any more than the related English words 'research' or 'require' do. The prefix 'ri', like the Latin 're-', has two separate meanings: repetition *or* intensification of an action. In many verbs the first meaning is subordinate or lacking entirely. Musicologists have often regarded 'ricercar' as an exclusively musical term, ignoring the fact that it is a very ordinary word in Italian, one which musically untrained natives today would not associate with music. Theorists use it also in this ordinary sense – which itself is no reason for quoting them in musicological literature: Zarlino entitles a chapter "That which one searches for in every composition".[63] He is perfectly consistent in following 'ricercar' with its logical result 'ritrovare'.[64] No competent translator would render these words as 'search again' and 'find again'. Gombosi's speculation that "the writer of a ricercar wants to 'look up again' something he had before"[65] can only be regarded as unnecessary.

Concluding our discussion of the 'Aristotelian' ricercar, or, to be less anachronistic, our sixteenth-century commentary on a simile in Aristotle's description of the epideictic proem, we should reflect on this connection established across the centuries. Since, in the sixteenth century, a humanistic education was a prerequisite for success in music as in any other profession, many composers would have known of Aristotle's figure of speech, either directly or indirectly. This probably even helped to confirm the style of the free ricercars. But Aristotle was himself thinking of musical practice. Thus rhetorical theory and musical practice cannot be clearly distinguished as cause and effect, for each influenced the other. There was, of course, no question of sixteenth-century composers imitating Greek music, unknown to them, or of reviving an ancient practice through exercise of the intellect and of historical-philological interests, which was the nature of much humanistic activity. Rather, the striking congruence between Aristotle's description and sixteenth-century practice

---

toph WOLFF's article in the *Handwörterbuch der musikalischen Terminologie*, Wiesbaden, Steiner, 1973, indebted to Eggebrecht, begins: "von ri-cercare, wieder-suchen, von neuem suchen" ("from ri-cercare, to search again"). Likewise SLIM, p. 417, "to search for again", although the footnote quotes an Italian-English dictionary of 1567: "Ricercare, to search or seeke out".

[63] "Quel che si ricerca in ogni compositione", *Istitutioni harmoniche*, Venice, Dei Franceschini, 1573, p. 199; see also p. 200: words should be set "secondo che ricerca la materia contenuta in esse" ["according to what the subject matter contained in them requires"].

[64] ZARLINO, pp. 199f. "Tromba ... inventori" on p. 75 is indexed as "Tromba ritrovata", i.e. "invented", not "re-invented". Cf. also Giovanmaria MEMO, *L'oratore*, Venice, De' Fari, 1545, f. 71*v*: "Però havendosi in ogni causa due cose a ricercare, l'una ritrovar ciò che si ha da dire, & l'altra come si ha da dire il ritrovato" ["Having, however, in every case two things to search for: one is that which one has to say, and the other how one must say that which has been found"].

[65] Capirola Lute-Book, p. XXXII. Likewise MURPHY's argument, pp. 136f, based on Dalza's singular usage of "Tastar de corde" + "Recercar dietro" (see note 46 above): the "toccata" searches for the tonality and the ricercar "re-searches" it.

is to be seen primarily as resulting from the continuation, perhaps uninterrupted, of a natural manner of musical expression. This suggestion, particularly the word 'uninterrupted', may seem overly bold to anyone conditioned by northern historiography, which tends to see the Renaissance as the rebirth of cultural phenomena lost during the 'Dark Ages'. But this view, though it may have some validity for events north of the Alps, does not do justice to Italy. Here alone, the land and to a certain degree even the language which produced ancient and sixteenth-century culture remained the same. Though even in this more favorable situation ancient learning was lost and had to be retrieved by intellectual effort, such an interruption did not occur in the many simpler customs which did not need to be sustained by learning. The more one becomes familiar with modern Italian attitudes and customs, the more one discovers that many have persisted from antiquity with a tenacity astonishing only to a non-Italian. To begin a musical performance or poetic declamation with a freely improvised prelude not related to what follows but joined to it in pitch is such a natural, almost obvious procedure that it could have been preserved by the Mediterranean mentality not only from Periclean, but even from Homeric times.[66] Aristotle's description is sufficiently general to accommodate the inevitable changes in musical style, yet specific enough for sixteenth-century Italian writers to recognize immediately its validity for a type of music from their own time. Because the earliest lute tablatures, at the very beginning of the continuous repertoire of notated Italian instrumental music, already contain large numbers of ricercars, we can safely assume

---

[66] We can still trace it in Mozart's letter of 22 Jan. 1783, to his father: "ich habe die Eingänge in Rondeau noch nicht verändert, denn wenn ich dieses Concert spiele, so mache ich allzeit was mir einfällt" ["I haven't changed the entries [of the solo instrument in a concerto, in the style of a free improvisation] in the rondo [K. 382], because whenever I play this concerto, I always do whatever occurs to me"] – *Briefe und Aufzeichnungen*, Kassel, Bärenreiter, 1962-75, III, 251. Such entries are found occasionally in later concertos, such as Beethoven's piano concerto Op. 73 and Brahms's double concerto Op. 102, and also in Beethoven's Choral Phantasy Op. 80. That it is not far-fetched to regard works this late as exemplars of the Aristotelian tradition is proven by a statement of Friedrich KALKBRENNER in the preface to his *Traité d'harmonie ... pour apprendre à préluder et à improviser*, Paris, l'auteur, 1849: "Les notions les plus intéressantes sur cet art depuis Aristote jusqu'a nos jours y sont passées en revue" ["The most interesting notions on this art from Aristote to our time are reviewed"] in 18th-19th-century music-theoretical writings. The formulations of the ancient rhetoricians (not only of Artistotle, but also of Cicero – see below) on the exordium still remained current throughout the late 18th and 19th centuries with reference to preludial pieces, and they continued to influence the musical style, as can be deduced from the music cited in Maria Grazia SITÀ, *Preludi, fantasie, capricci: modi dell'improvvisazione nella musica per tastiera italiana tra Settecento e Ottocento*, ms. thesis, Conservatorio di Milano, 1991/92, and *Il concetto di fantasia nella trattatistica musicale italiana tra Settecento e Ottocento*, ms. thesis, Università di Venezia, 1993/94. Edward BULWER-LYTTON was aware of the ancient practice when he twice had a song introduced by a "short [instrumental] prelude" in *The Last Days of Pompeii*, 1834, III,ii and IV,iii]. Aristotle's concept is still alive in the German expression "präludieren" for "improvise" – cf. below, pp. 522f.

that they merely fix in writing a kind of music already widely practised in the fifteenth century, as improvisation or from memory – a conclusion supported also by iconographical evidence. In view of what has been said above, we suggest that even the musical style of the instrumental preludes changed only very slowly over the centuries preceding the earliest notation.

* * *

But towards the middle of the sixteenth century a quite different style begins to emerge. Just as ricercars were contained in the earliest sources of Italian lute music (1507 onwards), we find them also in the earliest Italian edition of music originally composed for keyboard: Marc'Antonio Cavazzoni's *Recerchari, mottetti, canzoni* (Venice, Vercelli, 1523_1). Each of the two ricercars is followed by a motet in the same mode, "Salve virgo" and "O stella maris". (The motets, like the four canzonas, were surely based on vocal models). A comparison immediately reveals some striking differences between these two preludes and the typical lute ricercars. Not only are they of much greater length – 127 and 150 breves, respectively – but they are less improvisatory, more unified, based on only two or three continually recurring elements. They also exhibit close stylistic congruence with the following piece. Both the first ricercar and the first motet, for example, are pervaded by scalar motion in quarter notes and a rhythmically uniform 'turn' on the leading note in cadential progressions; also the eighth-note 'trills' in the motet are anticipated in the ricercar. Since these elements are by no means unique to these pieces,[67] but commonplaces of early sixteenth-century keyboard music, Jeppesen was rightly skeptical of Benvenuti's assumption of conscious thematic unification of ricercar and motet.[68] Nevertheless, compared to the lute pieces, the much greater stylistic coherence, both within the ricercar and between members of a pair, is inescapable.

At the time Cavazzoni's edition appeared, instrumental preludes were still exhibiting almost no trace of that fundamental change in the compositional process – one of the most significant in the history of music – which had been taking place in sacred vocal music during the preceding decades: the establishment of the imitative principle, the new equivalence of voices sharing in succession the same melodic material. Imitative writing entered the instrumental media through the extraction of instrumental duos and trios from

---

[67] They occur also in Cavazzoni's other pieces. Especially the turn-formula is standard practice in keyboard music of this period – cf. Kotter's tablature, the Castell'Arquato mss., etc.

[68] Giacomo BENVENUTI (ed.), *Marco Antonio Cavazzoni: Ricercari, motetti, canzoni*, «I classici musicali italiani», I, Milan, Bravi, 1941, pp. 91f; Knud JEPPESON, *Die italienische Orgelmusik am Anfang des Cinquecento*, Copenhagen, Hansen, 1960, I, 89f; likewise SLIM, p. 76. Even the similar openings c′-c′-e′-f′♯-g′ in the second pair could be coincidental.

two- and three-part Mass sections,[69] through the playing of motets from the original vocal parts,[70] and through their arrangement for a single instrument, retaining imitative passages. However, instrumental music not based on vocal shows only a very slight increase in contrapuntal texture and use of imitation during the third and fourth decades of the century.[71] Jacopo Fogliano's keyboard ricercars in the Castell'Arquato manuscripts[72] have been characterized, not without some justification, as "well on the way to the motetic ricercar".[73] However, their 'motetization' rarely goes beyond two brief entries per motive. And though Hans Neusidler promises "vil schöner fugen" in a "Preambel oder Fantasey" (1536_7, sig. Aa1*v*), the long piece contains little in the way of imitative writing. Real points of imitation, with exposition of motives by all four voices, are applied consistently to instrumental music for the first time in the *Musica nova accommodata per cantar et sonar sopra organi et altri strumenti* (Venice, Andrea Arrivabene, 1540_3), a collection of part-book ricercars composed mostly by Julio da Modena (Giulio Segni), with some by Adrian Willaert and a few by other masters such as Girolamo Parabosco and Hieronimo da Bologna (Girolamo Cavazzoni).[74] From the Franco-Flemish polyphonic idiom, which is here applied to instrumental media, Slim singles out the motets of Gombert, appearing in Italian editions from 1539, as possibly the most direct influence.[75] That this style found immediate acceptance in the instrumental repertoire is suggested by a gross understatement in the dedication of the next major landmark in the history of the ricercar: Girolamo Cavazzoni, Marc'Antonio's son, characterized the contents of his *Intavolatura cioè recercari, canzoni, himni, magnificati ... libro primo* (Venice, s.n., 1543_1) as "com-

---

[69] See «Monuments of Renaissance Music», VI, Chicago UP, 1975, p. 44.

[70] KÄMPER, pp. 115, 117. This practice is sometimes reflected on the title pages themselves, e.g. of Gombert's motet collection, *Musica quatuor vocum lyris maioribus, ac tibijs imparibus accomodata* ["accomodated for larger lyres and flutes of different ranges"], Venice, Scotto, 1539.

[71] SLIM, pp. 286-300. The consistently imitative writing in the lute fantasia of Marco Dall'Aquila, 1536_9, f. 7, is quite exceptional for this period, though some imitative ricercars appear later in the publications of Valentin Bakfark and in the *Tablature de luth italienne dit Siena Manuscript (ca. 1560-1570)*, facs. ed. Geneva, Minkoff, 1988.

[72] Published in BENVENUTI and JEPPESEN.

[73] GOMBOSI, p. xxxv.

[74] New ed. by Colin SLIM in «Monuments of Renaissance Music», I, Chicago UP, 1964. The title of this collection and of Willaert's publication of 1559 (see below, p. 52) — notwithstanding the historical importance of the music — may have been taken somewhat too seriously by scholars who have attempted to explain it through stylistic innovations. In Italian literature of the period, the title "Opera nova" was very common for chapbooks of popular poetry, even if they had already been printed in several editions under different titles; cf. the six 'Opere nuove' quoted below, pp. 131, 137, 195, notes 13, 40, 285.

[75] SLIM, diss., p. 339.

mon, ordinary ... music".[76] With this collection – the next printed Italian keyboard score extant after his father's – Girolamo already brought the imitative organ ricercar to an astonishingly high level.[77] Such ricercars obviously exhibit a still greater degree of stylistic coherence with their following motets or Mass sections than did those of Marc'Antonio.

With Girolamo Cavazzoni, observes Jeppesen, (and, we may add, with *Musica nova*), "the ricercar changes its appearance completely and makes such sharp turn as is very seldom seen in the history of musical forms";[78] or, as Apel asked, "Are we to assume that the word 'ricercar' meant so little to musicians of that time as to admit a change of meaning into its very opposite?"[79] Yet the two types retained some common features: the preludial function, the grouping by modes, and the association with practical and theoretical pedagogy.[80] Even improvising was not abandoned: one of the tests given candidates for the position of organist at St. Mark's in Venice consisted of improvising a ricercar on a plainsong melody chosen at random.[81] Following our investigation of the free ricercar we must question whether the fundamental change in style is to be explained, as hitherto, solely in musical terms (adoption of motet style), or whether the rhetorical theory of the proem may throw further light on the history of the ricercar. In other words, does the rhetorical literature provide a second analogy, describe an alternate type of proem which might be related to the imitative ricercar? Later in this article I shall demonstrate that a precise analogy can indeed be found: in Cicero. But in order to determine whether his writings may have exerted an influence on the ricercar I shall first fill in the historical background by considering some biographical facts and the phenomenon of Ciceronianism.

* * *

The *arbiter litterarum* during the period under discussion, the champion of purity of style represented by Cicero for Latin and Petrarch for Italian, was,

---

[76] "musica ... comune e dozinale". The dates which KÄMPER, p. 117, suggests for the ricercars of Segni, Willaert, and G. Cavazzoni are too early – cf. SLIM, *Musica Nova*, note 46. The younger Cavazzoni's ricercars must have been composed shortly before their publication.

[77] Though we are justified in associating primarily the free ricercar with the 'secular' lute and the imitative ricercar with the church organ, we should not overlook that the latter type eventually occurs also in the lute repertoire (s. above, note 71), sometimes as arrangements (e.g. Segni in 1548₄), and that free preludes and occasional free "ricercars" are found in keyboard music for several centuries.

[78] I, 92.

[79] P. 140.

[80] On this, see HORSLEY, and especially KÄMPER, pp. 118-127.

[81] Francesco CAFFI, *Storia della musica sacra nella già cappella ducale di S. Marco in Venezia*, Venice, Bollettino bibliogr. mus., 1854-55, I, 28.

of course, Pietro Bembo (1470-1547, Plate II.1). Precisely because Bembo wrote such elegant, 'Ciceronian' Latin, the humanist Pope Leo X made him his secretary. Upon Leo's death in 1521, Bembo carried the Roman curia's cult of Latin and Cicero with him to Padua and Venice. It was again his reputation as a stylist – certainly not as a historian – which led to his appointment as official historiographer of the Venetian Republic in 1529.[82] Yet Bembo's immense authority was due to the fact that he did not confine his efforts to Latin, but applied them also to Italian. His *Prose della volgar lingua*,[83] a dialogue supposedly taking place in Venice in 1502 but published only in 1525, became the most important document of vernacular humanism, used as a guide by Ariosto and Castiglione – to name only the most eminent. Highly refined critical ability rather than poetic genius made Bembo the strongest single influence on the development of Italian language and literature during the Renaissance, as witness his relations with most of the leading contemporary men of letters. His many friends included also rhetoricians such as Bernardino Tomitano and Francesco Sansovino, authors of the first two monographs on rhetoric written in Italian.[84] Sansovino, who was later to edit Bembo's *Prose*, *Rime*, and *Lettere*, illustrates his handbook with quotations from Petrarch and Bembo, and mentions incidentally a symbol of Venice's pride in her achievements in the sister arts of music and oratory: the statues of Apollo and Mercury (1540-45) by his father Jacopo Sansovino on the bell tower of St. Mark's Square, "designating music and eloquence, two things in which the Venetian gentlemen excel superbly, the first represented by Apollo, the second by Mercury".[85] Other rhetoricians, quoted above and in my Appendix II, who contributed to this tradition in Venice include Ermolao Barbaro and his grandnephew Daniel, B. Cavalcanti, and G. De Nores. The Venetian schools, particularly the Scuola di Rialto, were known for their teaching of rhetoric, but they could not confer higher degrees. Venetian citizens who wished to continue their studies were obliged by law to do so at the University

---

[82] The publication of breves written for Leo X, *Epistolae ... Latinae puritatis studiosis ad imitandum utilissimae*, 1535 etc., and of the *Historiae Venetae libri XII*, Venice, apud Aldi filios, 1551, was planned by Bembo partly with the intention of furnishing models for Ciceronian prose style.

[83] Dedicated not to Leo X, as Bernard WEINBERG, *A History of Literary Criticism in the Italian Renaissance*, Chicago UP, 1961, II, 1116, states, but to Clement VII.

[84] *Ragionamenti della lingua toscana: la rhetorica secondo l'artificio d'Aristotile & Cicerone*, Venice, De' Farri, 1546, and *L'arte oratoria secondo i modi della lingua volgare*, Venice, Del Griffo, 1546, respectively.

[85] "il segno della musica e dell'eloquenza, nelle quai due cose i Signori Venitiani sommamente sono eccellenti, che della prima ne è dimostratore Apollo della seconda Mercurio" – *L'arte oratoria*, f. 52v.

of Padua, the nearby city under Venetian rule. Venice/Padua thus can be regarded as a single bastion of rhetoric. At the university in the fourteenth century the philosophers propagated Aristotle, and Giovanni di Conversino expounded Cicero, as did Secco Polentone in the early fifteenth century.[86] Many of the authors cited in this article studied in Padua: D. Barbaro, Bembo, Daniello, De Nores, Dolet, Musso, Ricci, and B. Segni. Even more taught there: E. and D. Barbaro, Beni, De Nores, Longueil, Muret, Piccolomini, Riccoboni, Sigonio, Speroni, and Tomitano. The close contact between these persons is illustrated also by their membership in the Paduan Accademia degli Infiammati during the 1540s,[87] and, especially vividly, by their appearance as interlocutors in each other's treatises in the classical dialogue form: E. Barbaro in Bembo's,[88] Speroni in Tomitano's, Figliucci and Sansovino in Francesco Patrizi's,[89] D. Barbaro as editor of Speroni's,[90] and others to be mentioned later. The vast majority of sixteenth-century Italian books, including the Latin and vernacular texts on rhetoric, were, of course, published in Venice.

Bembo emerges also as the strongest link between the rhetoricians and the composers. It has not yet been observed that all of the first masters of the imitative ricercar were associated with him. For Marc'Antonio Cavazzoni "da Bologna, detto d'Urbino" and for Giovanni Maria Crema, as for Bembo, the court of Urbino had been a stepping-stone to Rome.[91] All three could thus come to know each other in the Castiglionian situation before they entered the service of Leo X. At the court of this pope, whose passion for Cicero was surpassed only by that for music,[92] they certainly encountered Leo's or-

---

[86] Georg Voigt, *Die Wiederbelebung des classischen Alterthums*, Berlin, Reimer, 1893, II, 432, 434f.

[87] D. Barbaro, Piccolomini, Sansovino, Speroni, Tomitano. See Michele Maylender, *Storia delle accademie d'Italia*, Bologna, Cappelli, 1926-30, III, 266-270.

[88] *De Virgilii culice et Terentii fabulis*, Venice, Sabius, 1530.

[89] *Della retorica*, Venice, Sanese, 1562.

[90] *Dialoghi*, Venice, Aldus, 1544. Also Speroni's funeral oration for Bembo and Caro's edition of Bembo's *Rime* (Rome, Dorico, 1548) illustrate these relationships.

[91] Both Bembo and Marc'Antonio left Urbino for Rome in 1512. Only after further travels does the composer appear on the papal payrolls, from Feb. 1520 to May 1521 – cf. Jeppesen, I, 78ff, and Herman-Walther Frey, *Regesten zur päpstlichen Kapelle unter Leo X. und zu seiner Privatkapelle*, «Die Musikforschung», IX, 1956, p. 140. In the dedication of his organ tablature of 1523 to Francesco Cornaro, he states that he was in the service of this Venetian patrician before and after his sojourn in Rome. Cornaro was the nephew of the ex-queen of Cyprus, whose court in Asolo had provided the setting for Bembo's Ciceronian dialogue *Gli Asolani* (Venice, Aldus, 1505). Crema is documented at Urbino in 1510 and was on the payroll of Leo X from 1515 until the latter's death in 1521. He renamed himself "Giovanni Medici" after that pontiff, and arranged imitative ricercars of G. Segni for lute – see his *Intavolatura di liuto libro primo*, 1546₁₀, Florence, Maurri, 1955, pp. VII-VIII; Frey, VIII, 430f, IX, 155f; and Slim, *Musica Nova*, pp. XXXVI, 40ff.

[92] Cf. Pietro Aaron, *Thoscanello de la musica*, Venice, De' Vitali, 1523, sig. a²; André Pirro,

ganist G. Segni, who was later to become the principal composer of the *Musica nova*.[93] Bembo may have been reunited with Marc'Antonio Cavazzoni in Padua during the 1520s[94] and probably had something to do with Segni's appearance as first organist at St. Mark's in Venice from 1530 to 1533.[95] Willaert had become chapel master there in 1527; two years later Bembo was appointed librarian of the Nicena (Marciana). It is hardly conceivable that the chapel master and the librarian of St. Mark's did not know each other. In fact Willaert's *Musica nova* – a collection of motets and madrigals published in 1559 but composed possibly much earlier, not to be confused with the ricercar collection of 1540 with the same title – can be understood only in this connection. Taking all but one of its madrigal texts from Petrarch's *Canzoniere*, it represents the massive and decisive entry of Bembo's Petrarchism into music, establishing for a generation the favorite source of madrigal texts.[96] Marc'Antonio Cavazzoni, Willaert's close friend and the executor of his estate, had already been identified with Bembo's literary taste by receiving the dedication of a Petrarch edition published by his pupil Giovanni Lanzo Gabbiano in 1523, where it is said that he provided the source for the edition and "da Papa Leone è stato sommamente venerato et amato". Girolamo Cavazzoni's dedication of his epoch-making *Recercari ... libro primo* to his own godfather, Pietro Bembo, reflects a close relationship for two generations.[97] Girolamo may

---

Léon X et la musique, in *Mélanges ... offerts a Henri Hauvette*, Paris, Presses françaises, 1934, pp. 221-232; JEPPESON, I, 76.

[93] The publisher of this collection, Andrea Arrivabene in Venice, brought out an edition of Bembo's *Prose* in 1557.

[94] See below, note 97.

[95] On Segni's activities in Rome and Venice, see Luigi Francesco VALDRIGHI, *Di Bellerofonte Castaldi*, «Atti e memorie della r. deputazione di storia patria per le provincie dell'Emilia», n.s. V/1, 1880, p. 91, and Giacomo BENVENUTI, *Andrea e Giovanni Gabrieli e la musica strumentale in San Marco*, Milan, Ricordi, 1931, I, xi.

[96] Armen CARAPETYAN, *The Musica Nova of Adriano Willaert*, «Journal of Renaissance and Baroque Music», I, 1946/47, pp. 200-221.

[97] Girolamo's statements in the dedication of 25 Nov. 1542 that he was born as the son of Bembo's "old friend and devoted servant" Marc'Antonio, and that these compositions are the "first fruits of his youth", when he was "anchor quasi fanciullo" ["still almost a boy"], have been used by JEPPESEN, I, 81, to deduce that Marc'Antonio must have been "in the service" of Bembo around 1524-26. But here the word 'servidore' does not mean 'employee'; nor does it exclude reference to Marc'Antonio's contacts with Bembo before (Urbino) or after the date of Girolamo's birth. Bembo, of course, did not have his own court or even a large retinue. He had no occasion to employ musicians. Later, as cardinal, he didn't even engage a clavichord teacher for his daughter, since he regarded playing an instrument to be beneath her social status, "cosa da donna vana e leggiera" ["attribute of a vain and frivolous woman"], and preferred her to pursue literary studies – see his letters of 31 Oct. 1540, and 10 Dec. 1541, *Opere*, Venice, Hertzhauffer, 1729, IV, 300, 342. SLIM, in summarizing Jeppesen's arguments (*Musica nova*, pp. XXIXf), takes not only "servidore" but also "fanciullo" somewhat too literally (Girolamo said "*quasi* fanciullo"). Just as the former was an ubiquitous

have been a pupil of Willaert.[98] With all these arguments we may amplify the conclusion reached by a modern scholar of Bembo: not only "in the literary life of the period", but also in the development of the ricercar, "one sees that all roads lead to Bembo".[99]

Having established the close biographical links between the composers of ricercars and the foremost advocate of Ciceronianism, I shall examine briefly this movement itself.[100] During an era which looked to classical antiquity for its models, the imitation of Cicero was regarded as "the most perfect single instrument of education".[101] His works made up the lion's share of sixteenth- and seventeenth-century curricula, both south and north of the Alps.[102] No concept was more central to Renaissance artistic production than that of imitation. In order to understand it, we must free it from the derogatory connotations which it acquired only with the advent of romantic 'confessional' art and the modern trend to originality at the price of intelligibility. It did not mean mere copying or aping (condemned in any age),[103] but was rather an honest acknowledgment of the sources of inspiration for a new production, and it embraced the possibility that the models, even Cicero, could be sur-

---

compliment in a letter written to anyone, the understatement of one's own works as *juvenilia* was a common *topos* of dedications, certainly no indication that the composer was "at most, fifteen to sixteen" at this time. However, Jeppesen's arguments (cf. also JAMS, VIII, 1955, p. 84) are closer to the truth than those of Mischiati, who seems to have confused the composer with another organist Girolamo documented in Mantua in 1525. Our Girolamo was surely born about 1520, probably in Padua or Venice, since Bembo was his godfather.

[98] Contrary to my statment in this article of 1979, the composer Andrea Gabrieli was *not* the nephew Andrea († 1571, age 68) of the Venetian philosopher Trifone Gabrieli, as I discovered in 1980 from this Andrea's testament (I-Vas Arch. Notarile, Testamenti, b. 156, no. 52, and b. 1263/IV, ff. 46v-48) after drafting an article on Trifone. Thus I abandoned my hypothesis and draft after I had comunicated them privately to Edward Lowinsky, but I was unable to persuade him to do the same. He added Trifone and Andrea to a lecture he had presented at Duke University, *Humanism in the Music of the Renaissance*, when he pubished it in *Medieval and Renaissance Studies*, Durham NC, Duke UP, 1982, p. 220, note 161. Soon afterwards it was revealed that the composer was no more than thirteen years of age when Bernardino DANIELLO's *Della Poetica* was published in 1536 (Venice, Nicolini) and, contrary to Lowinsky, would not been Trifone's nephew who participated in it as an interlocutor (cf. Martin MORELL in «Early Music History», III, 1983, pp. 111ff).

[99] W. Theodor ELWERT, *Pietro Bembo e la vita letteraria del suo tempo*, in his *Studi di letteratura veneziana*, Florence, Sansoni, 1958, p. 137.

[100] Cf. Remigio SABBADINI, *Storia del Ciceronianismo*, Turin, Loescher, 1885; Th. ZIELINSKI, *Cicero im Wandel der Jahrhunderte*, Leipzig, Teubner, 1908²; Izora SCOTT, *Controversies over the Imitation of Cicero*, New York, Teachers' College, 1910; Morris W. CROLL, *Style, Rhetoric, and Rhythm*, Princeton UP, 1966; Marc FUMAROLI, *L'âge de l'éloquence*, Geneva, Droz, 1980, ch. 2; *Historisches Wörterbuch der Rhetorik*, II, Darmstadt, Wissenschaftliche Buchgesellschaft, 1994, col. 225-247.

[101] CROLL, p. 120.

[102] Two sample curricula are communicated by SCOTT, pp. 120-123.

[103] See (pseudo-) DEMETRIUS PHALEREUS, *De elocutione*, II.112f, and QUINTILIAN, X.ii, who emphasizes the importance of *inventio* as well as *imitatio*.

passed.[104] Renaissance music provides with the parody Mass and the instrumental elaborations of vocal music a perfect embodiment of this attitude. Until well into the eighteenth century, critics intended to be complimentary when they said that an author was highly successful in imitating a certain great master. Thus Lodovico Beccadelli (1501-72) said of his friend Bembo: "Among the admirable qualities of Messer Pietro was the virtue of imitation, in which he was always most felicitous".[105] Poets were proud to be continuers (i.e. not merely copiers) of a great tradition. For this reason, most ancient and Renaissance literary criticism was preoccupied with the discovery of the best models.[106]

Both Plato and Aristotle, of course, had defined art as 'imitation', of nature and of human actions, respectively[107] (the latter followed by Sir Philip Sidney in his *Defense of Poesie*, 1579-81: "Poesie therefore, is an art of imitation: for so Aristotle termeth it μίμησις").[108] But by the time of Cicero a large corpus of literature worthy of emulation had accumulated, and 'imitation' came to mean first and foremost the imitation of literary style.[109] This rhetorical concept of imitation naturally prevailed in the sixteenth century, when "rhetoric was the central doctrine about which the edifice of ... learning was constructed".[110] The controversy on the imitation of Cicero never se-

---

[104] BEMBO, *Opere*, IV, 339. Though successful artistic and scholarly production goes beyond that which can be taught, most of the necessary learning is acquired even today by imitation, conscious or unconscious.

[105] "Cosa mirabile era fra l'altro in Messer Pietro la virtù della imitatione, nella quale fu felicissimo sempre" – *Monumenti di varia letteratura*, Bologna, Ist. delle scienze, 1797-1804, I/2, p. 236.

[106] The concepts of imitation are traced in, e.g., Berhard SCHWEITZER, *Der bildende Künstler und der Begriff des Künstlerischen in der Antike: ΜΙΜΗΣΙΣ und ΦΑΝΤΑΣΙΑ*, «Neue Heidelberger Jahrbücher», 1925, pp. 28-132; Hermann GMELIN, *Das Prinzip der Imitatio in den romanischen Literaturen der Renaissance*, «Romanische Forschungen», XLVI, 1932, pp. 83-360 (pp. 173-229 deal with Bembo, pp. 358ff = bibliography); Giorgio SANTANGELO, *Il Bembo critico e il principio d'imitazione*, Florence, Sansoni, 1950; BOLGAR, ch. 7; T. ELWERT, *Il Bembo teorico dell'imitatio'*, in his *Studi* cit., pp. 11-24; BAXANDALL, *passim*; Götz POCHAT, *Imitatio und Superatio: Das Problem der Nachahmung aus humanistischer und kunsthistorischer Sicht*, in *Klassizismus: Epoche und Probleme: Festschrift für Erich Forseman zum 70. Geburtstag*, Hildesheim, Olms, 1987, pp. 317-335; Martin L. MCLAUGHLIN, *Literary Imitation in the Italian Renaisance: The Theory and Practice of Literary Imitation in Italy from Dante to Bembo*, Oxford, Clarendon, 1995; *Historisches Wörterbuch der Rhetorik* cit., IV, 1998, col. 235-285; and articles in the following journals: «Philologus» (1933-34), «Modern Philology» (1936), «Wiener Studien» (1949), «Quarterly Journal of Speech» (1951), «Commentari» (1956), and «Classical Philology» (1958). See also WEINBERG, II, 1170. My application of these concepts to music was continued by Howard M. Brown – see below, p. 90.

[107] PLATO, *Laws*, 889B-D, *Republic*, book X; ARISTOTLE, *Poetica*, 1447a-48b. The treatise of DIONYSIUS OF HALICARNASSUS, *De imitatione*, is preserved only in fragments.

[108] *The Prose Works*, III, Cambridge UP, 1962, p. 9.

[109] CICERO, *De oratore*, II.xxii, asserts that rhetoric is learned from models, especially Greek ones; I.xxxiv was a starting point for the renaissance theory of imitation.

[110] R. EVANS in CROLL, p. 104.

riously questioned the validity of imitation; the issue was whether one should imitate only Cicero or other models as well. Most of the Cicero enthusiasts before Bembo – they include Quintilian in the first century, the church fathers Ambrose, Augustine, and Jerome in the fourth, and Petrarch in the fourteenth – did not go so far as to suggest that all Latin prose should imitate Cicero.[111] It was only in the fifteenth and sixteenth centuries, when Poggio Bracciolini, Paolo Cortese, and Bembo set up Cicero as the exclusive model, that controversy was provoked, with Lorenzo Valla, Angelo Poliziano, and Giovanni Francesco Pico, respectively. Bembo's epistle *De imitatione*, the manifesto of Ciceronianism, was written in January 1513, in reply to Pico, and published in Rome the following year.[112] Erasmus joined the battle with his *Ciceronianus* of 1528, a witty satire directed not against Cicero or Bembo, but against the blind and narrow-minded aping of the Roman orator by lesser talents, particularly Christophe Longueil. (Bembo, it will be remembered, championed also a vernacular prose based on fourteenth-century models). The debate was continued by the authors of Cicero-lexica and their opponents,[113] often assuming a personal, nationalistic, or confessional bias. Not until the last quarter of the century did the anti-Cicero reaction, with the *genus humile* and Attic style of the essay, begin to prevail, albeit through the efforts of non-Italians (Muret, Lipsius, Montaigne, Bacon). In the land where to this day rhetorical speech is a natural mode of expression, Cicero remained the supreme authority. (The Venetians, who called their ambassadors 'orators', conferred 'Ciceronianus' as a title of literary distinction and forbade the reading of Erasmus).[114] Also in Germany the Ciceronian tradition remained strong until the time of Gottsched and J. S. Bach, especially in Leipzig, which like Padua/Venice combined the resources of university and book-publishing center. In quoting any post-classical handbook on rhetoric for its author's ideas, great caution is in order, since almost identical formulations are found in earlier treatises and often can be traced to Cicero.

* * *

---

[111] QUINTILIAN, X.ii.24ff. Cicero himself, II.xxii.91f, implies that one should imitate a single model, the best one.

[112] Both authors' treatises are included in BEMBO's *Opere*, IV, 329-341, and, together with a subsequent reply of Pico, in G. SANTANGELO (ed.), *Le epistole 'De imitatione'*, Florence, Olschki, 1954.

[113] Also by Étienne DOLET, *Dialogus de imitatione Ciceroniana*, Lyon, Gryphius, 1535; Giulio Camillo DELMINIO, *Trattato della imitazione*, Venice, De' Farri, 1544; Johannes SAMBUCUS, *De imitatione Ciceroniana*, Paris, Gorbinus, 1561; and Johannes STURM, *De imitatione oratoria*, Strasbourg, Jobinus, 1574.

[114] CROLL, p. 127.

When Aristotle compared the proem in oratory to the prologue in poetry and to the prelude in flute-playing, he immediately specified that the second of these similes, the one which gave rise to so many references to the ricercar in the sixteenth century, applied only to the epideictic proem. Eventually he revealed that his first simile referred to another genus of rhetoric, that of the law courts: "As for the proems of the forensic speech, ... they produce the same effect as dramatic prologues and epic proems (for those of dithyrambs resemble epideictic proems), ... [and] provide a sample of the subject in order that the hearers may know beforehand what it is about".[115] The forensic proem is, then, like a prologue which indicates the 'argument' of the play.[116] But opponents of Aristotle usually overlooked that he admitted this type of proem also for epideictic oratory: "either foreign or closely connected with the speech".[117] Their criticism is directed primarily against his description of the 'separate' or free proem,[118] with its musical overtones.

Of the ancient treatises containing descriptions of the proem, those of Cicero and pseudo-Cicero were studied much more than Aristotle's, for the fragmentary *De inventione* and the spurious *Rhetorica ad Herennium*,[119] very widely diffused in manuscripts during the Middle Ages, had become the basis of instruction in rhetoric. First printed in 1470, they had already gone through at least nine and twenty-four editions, respectively, by the end of the fifteenth century. Cicero's *De oratore*, rediscovered in 1422, had a dozen editions during this period and was one of the first books ever printed in Italy (Subiaco, Sweynheym & Pannartz, 1465). Cicero is, in fact, one of the most frequently published authors of all time and particularly during the Renaissance.[120]

---

115 III, 1415a. Johann MATTHESON, *Plus ultra*, Hamburg, Martini, 1754, p. 148, alludes to this type of proem: "Und aus dieser nothwendigen Musik- oder Melodieregel haben die Redner ihre Eingänge, mehr oder minder, so zu bestimmen getrachtet, daß man die Absicht derselben schon überhaupt zum Voraus merken kann" ["and from this necessary rule of music or melody orators have more or less endevoured to arrange their exordia, so that one can generally perceive their intention already in advance"].

116 See [Thomas HOBBES], *A Briefe of the* [Aristotle's] *Art of Rhetorique*, London, Cotes, 1635, p. 180.

117 III, 1415a.

118 Examples of such separate proems are ISOCRATES, *Helena* (see below, note 234), and SALLUST, *De conjuratione catilinae* and *Bellum iugurthinum*.

119 This earliest complete rhetorical handbook in Latin was written ca. 86-82 B.C., not long after *De inventione*, and misattributed to Cicero throughout the Middle Ages. The close similarities in the treatment of the exordium and elsewhere suggest that the two works used a common oral source. Rolf DAMMANN, *Der Musikbegriff im deutschen Barock*, Cologne, Volk, 1967, ch. 2 *passim*, mistakes Herennius, the dedicatee of the work, for its author.

120 See the editions of his rhetorical works in the *National Union Catalog*, CIX, 1970, pp. 509-525.

In his youthful *De inventione* (ca. 90 B.C.), the first section of an unfinished handbook of rhetoric, Cicero writes about the exordium as follows: [121]

Igitur exordium in duas partes dividitur: principium et insinuationem. Principium est oratio perspicue et protinus perficiens auditorem benevolum aut docilem aut attentum. Insinuatio est oratio quadam dissimilatione et circumitione obscure subiens auditoris animum. ...

Si non omnino infesti auditores erunt, principio benevolentiam comparare licebit. ...
Insinuatione igitur utendum est cum admirabile genus causae est, hoc est, ... cum animus auditoris infestus est. ... Oportet ... dissimulare te id defensurum quod existimeris. ...
Exordium sententiarum et gravitatis plurimum debet habere et omnino omnia quae pertinent ad dignitatem in se continere, propterea quod id optime faciendum est quod oratorem auditori maxime commendat; splendoris et festivitatis et concinnitudinis minimum, propterea quod ex his suspicio quaedam apparationis atque artificiosae diligentiae nascitur, quae maxime orationi fidem, oratori adimit auctoritatem.

Vitia vero haec sunt certissima exordiorum quae summopere vitare oportebit: vulgare, commune, commutabile, longum, separatum, translatum, contra praecepta. ... Separatum, quod non ex ipsa causa ductum est nec sicut aliquod membrum annexum orationi.

The exordium, then, is divided into two species: *principium* and *insinuatio*. The *principium* is a speech which immediately and in plain language makes the listener benevolent, receptive, or attentive. The *insinuatio* is a speech which by a certain dissimilation and indirection unobtrusively steals into the mind of the listener. ...
If the listeners are not completely hostile, it will be permissible to win their benevolence by a *principium*. ...
The *insinuatio*, then, must be used when the case is difficult, that is, ... when the mind of the listener is hostile. ... You must ... conceal your intention of defending what you are expected to defend. ...
The exordium must have a high degree of sententiousness and gravity, and generally contain in itself everything which pertains to dignity, because the best thing to do is that which most commends the speaker to the listener; very little brilliance, ornamentation, or elegance, because these give rise to a suspicion of a certain preparation and excessive ingenuity, which greatly detracts from the conviction of the oration and the authority of the speaker.
The following are indeed the most certain faults of exordia, which one will by all means have to avoid: the general, common, interchangeable, verbose, separate, out of place, or contrary to fundamental principles. ... The separate is one which is not derived from the case itself or connected with the speech, like some limb [to a body].

[121] I.xv-xviii. In referring to Cicero and his followers, I shall use the Latin 'exordium' rather than the Greek 'proem(ion)'.

In *De oratore*, Cicero's masterwork on rhetoric, written at the height of his career (55 B.C.), the discussion of the exordium is renewed: [122]

Principia autem dicendi semper cum accurata et acuta et instructa sententiis, apta verbis, tum vero causarum propria esse debent. ... Haec autem in dicendo non extrinsecus alicunde quaerenda sed ex ipsis visceribus causae sumenda sunt; idcirco tota causa pertemptata atque perspecta, locis omnibus inventis atque in structis considerandum est quo principio sit utendum. ...

Omne autem principium aut rei totius quae agetur significationem habere debebit aut aditum ad causam et communitionem aut quoddam ornamentum et dignitatem; sed oportet, ut aedibus ac templis vestibula et aditus, sic causis principia pro portione rerum praeponere. ...

But the opening remarks, though they should always be careful, pointed, provided with significance, and suitably expressed, must at the same time be appropriate to the cases; ... But in speaking these must not be taken from some outside source but from the very heart of the case; consequently, when the whole case has been examined and surveyed, and all our topics thought out and arranged, it must be considered what opening to employ. ...

Every beginning will have to have either an indication of the whole matter that is to be put forward, or an approach and introduction to the case, or some ornament and dignity; but one should put at the beginning of the cases opening passages proportioned to the facts, as fore-courts and entrances to mansions and temples.[123] ...

---

[122] II.lxxviii-lxxx. Bembo added annotations to his own (15th-c.?) ms. copy of this work, GB-Lbl Add. 10965. He possessed also a copy of Artistotle's *Ars Rhetorica* in the edition of Venice, Tridino Montis, 1534, with the extensive commentary by Hermolao Barbaro. – Massimo DANZI, *La biblioteca del cardinale Pietro Bembo*, Geneva, Droz, 2005, pp. 324, 168.

[123] If an art historian were to explore the (doubtless demonstrable – cf. above, note 1) impact of Ciceronianism on the visual arts, he too might take an exordium simile as his point of departure, namely Cicero's comparison with the "forecourts and entrances to mansions and temples". Venetian pupils of Bembo's friend Trifone Gabrieli were sufficiently convinced by this figure of speech to use it in their own rhetorical works: SANSOVINO, f. 5: "Il proemio nell'oratione non è altro che una bella e ricca entrata d'un magnifico e ben inteso palazzo" ["The proem in the oration is nothing else but a beautiful and rich entrance to a magnificent and well conceived palace"]; Giasone DE NORES, *Della rhetorica*, Venice, Megietto, 1584, f. 86: "sì come le entrate de i tempij, et delle case ... così devono ancho essere i proemij" ["just like the entrances of the temples and houses ... so should be also the proems"]. Sansovino's father, the friend and colleague of Bembo, designed such an "entrata" for the Biblioteca Marciana, his architectural masterwork. Another member of Bembo's circle, Titian, may well have been inspired by Cicero when he created with the peristyle of a temple a visual exordium for his Pesaro Madonna in S. Maria dei Frari (1519-26) – a motive hardly employed earlier. Staale SINDING-LARSEN, *Titian's Madonna di Ca' Pesaro and its Historical Significance*, «Acta ad archaeologiam et artium historiam pertinentia», I, 1962, pp. 140-147, demonstrated that the columns were not part of the original composition. More recent X-rays have revealed, however, that the addition was made not posthumously, but by Titian himself. Titian's portrait of Bembo is reproduced in Plate II.1.

Connexum autem ita sit principium con-
seguenti orationi ut non tamquam citharoedi prooemium affictum aliquid sed
cohaerens cum omni corpore membrum
esse videatur. Nam non nulli, cum illud
meditati ediderunt, sic ad reliqua tran-
seunt ut audientiam fieri sibi non velle videantur. Atque eiusmodi illa prolusio debet esse, non ut Samnitium, qui vibrant
hastas ante pugnam quibus in pugnando
nihil utuntur, sed ut ipsis sententiis quibus proluserint vel pugnare possint.

But the opening passage should be so
connected with the following speech that
it does not seem to be like some appended proem of a cithara player, but a
limb coherent with the whole body. For
some, when they have produced that after
due practice, pass on to the remainder as
though they seem not to want to be listened to. Also, that opening must not be
like that of the Samnites, who before a
fight brandish spears which they are not
going to use at all in the [actual] combat,
but it must be so that they can fight with
the same ideas used in the opening.

In revealing his knowledge of Aristotle, Cicero tactfully takes issue with
him, without mentioning him by name. While he is a clever enough lawyer
to warn against the appearance of excessive preparation, he makes it clear that
the exordium must be carefully thought out in advance, coherent with the
body of the oration, not like the nonchalant prelude of Aristotle's musician,
whom he mentions with little respect.[124] In direct reaction to Aristotle, Cicero
classifies the 'separate' exordium as a rhetorical *vitium*, as does his loyal disciple Quintilian.[125] In the sixteenth century the two views again come into
conflict, Cicero's eventually prevailing. While some authors follow Aristotle,[126] others echo Cicero,[127] and even some commentators of Aristotle repeat
Cicero's reprimand of the flute player (Vettori, p. 584; Borrhaus, p. 401).

---

[124] This desideratum is applied to the operatic overture by Francesco ALGAROTTI, *Saggio sopra
l'opera in musica*, Venice, Pasquali, 1755, p. 14: "La sinfonia dovrebbe essere parte integrante del
dramma, come appunto l'esordio dell'orazione" ["The overture should be an integral part of the drama, just like the exordium of an oration"], or, in the later revision (Livorno, Coltellini, 1763), p. 26:
"Suo principal fine è di annunziare in certo modo l'azione, di preparare l'uditore a ricevere quelle impressioni di affetto che risultano dal totale del dramma. E però da esso ha da prendere atteggiamento e
viso, come appunto dalla orazione l'esordio" ["Its principle aim is to announce the plot in a certain
manner, to prepare the listener to receive those affective impressions which result from the drama
as a whole. And from it, however, he must assume the posture and countenance, just as the exordium
does from the oration"]. There follows, p. 27, a negative criticism of the "sinfonia distaccata". Composers such as Verdi were to compile overtures as potpourris of themes from the operas.

[125] IV.i.53.

[126] Most of those quoted in Appendix II of this article.

[127] E.g. Antonio LULLO, *De oratione*, Basle, Operini, 1558, p. 197: "neque qui mos est tibicinis,
ante cantilenam fiat alterius rei praeludium" ["nor let there be made, before the song, a prelude
based on other matter, which is the custom of the flute players"]; Alessandro CARRIERO, *Breve et
ingenioso discorso contra l'opera di Dante*, Padua, Meietto, 1582, p. 46. PANIGAROLA, in a passage
quoted below, p. 44, accepts the Aristotelian *procemium separatum*, but adds to it the Ciceronian
element of "preparation" ["the musician ... must take great care"].

The coherence and preparation emphasized by Cicero find their musical equivalents in the new, stylistically coherent ricercars of the Cavazzonis, especially Girolamo, and in the later admonitions of theorists to examine first the subject for its possible use in stretto, inversion, and so on[128] – the contrapuntal artifices which became more and more characteristic of the imitative ricercars from Andrea Gabrieli onwards. Also these can be considered things which were *sought* in the ricercar. More than any other kind of music, the sometimes unjustly maligned *alla breve* subjects of the organ ricercars fulfill perfectly Cicero's requirements of sententiousness, gravity, dignity, lack of superficial brilliance – quite unlike the free ricercar which displayed the instrumentalists' technique ("whatever they can execute skillfully").

A reader conditioned by later thematic processes may be interested in whether the ricercar takes its melodic material from the following motet or Mass section, in this way meeting fully Cicero's requirement of coherence. This question cannot be answered satisfactorily, because the imitative ricercars are collected separately in editions of instrumental music and we do not know what vocal composition followed a particular ricercar. (Paul Oskar Kristeller informed me that collections of exordia, from Demosthenes' to modern after-dinner speakers', were sometimes published separately).[129] Outside the mainstream of the genre, which was in the Emilia, Veneto, and Ferrara, the monothematic ricercars of Giuliano Tiburtino (1549₇) in Rome may have been derived thematically from vocal pieces by Josquin.[130] Improvised ricercars – obviously not available for examination – may have used melodic material of the following vocal piece, just as versets and chorale preludes do. And toccatas originated not as free rhapsodies – the view long held – but as cantus firmus compositions based on a psalm tone, the same one then used for singing the following psalm, either as chant or as falsobordone.[131] On the other hand, perceptible thematic relationships between successive pieces seem to be rather limited in sixteenth-century instrumental sources, i.e. to pairs of dances in proportional sequence. The lack of such obvious relation-

[128] Beginning with Michael PRAETORIUS, *Syntagma Musicum*, III, Wolfenbüttel, Holwein, 1619, pp. 21f, and continuing through the textbooks on fugue.

[129] Cf. also his *Iter Italicum*, London, Warburg Institute, 1963-92, indices, s.v. 'exordia', and especially I, 430 and IV, 200 for examples of ms. collections of exordia to be used for various occasions (13th-15th c.).

[130] This derivation of Tiburtino's rather non-committal solmisation subjects is argued by James HAAR, *The Fantasie et Recerchari of Giuliano Tiburtino*, «Musical Quarterly», LIX, 1973, pp. 223-238; see also BENVENUTI, *Gabrieli*, I, lxxxviii.

[131] Murray C. BRADSHAW, *The Origin of the Toccata*, Dallas, American Institute of Musicology, 1972; he believes psalm tones were ideally present even in some early lute toccatas (pp. 60f). See above, p. 15, on ricercars improvised on subjects from plainsong.

ships in ricercars may be a reason why rhetoricians normally use the musical comparison only when speaking of the separate, Aristotelian proem.[132] But composers may well have regarded the shared imitative style of ricercar and motet as providing sufficient coherence in the Ciceronian sense. Johannes Nucius, one of the first to apply the rhetorical figures to music theory, doubtless remembered the Roman orator when he said that the ricercar is the test of the composer's ability "to connect imitations duly with good coherence".[133] The internal coherence of this style, which overlaps thematic entries and eschews the subdivision into sections by the clear cadences characteristic of secular music, is analogous to the rhetorician's description of the exordium: "Divisions and subdivisions are absent from exordia".[134]

Of even greater musical implications than Cicero's characterization of the exordium in general is his distinction between two types: the *principium*, in plain and direct language, identified by other authors with the Greek *procœmion*;[135] and the *insinuatio* or 'subtle approach', used to captivate a hostile audience by approaching the arguments unobtrusively and indirectly.[136] Gioseffo Maria Platina, taking issue with Aristotle's simile, argues that all exordia are *insinuationes*: "As performers of the ricercar insinuate themselves into the *sonata* ...".[137] The two types have their clearly distinguished counterparts in the preludial repertoire of the Renaissance and baroque (Andrea and Giovanni Gabrieli, Frescobaldi, etc.): the *principium* is realized musically, e.g. in the *intonazioni* and toccatas, those preludes which begin directly with plain, full chords and are of brief duration (Ex. 1); and the *insinuatio*, in the imitative ricercars, where the

---

[132] An exception is Figliucci's paraphase of Aristotle's description, quoted above; it arbitrarily introduces Ciceronian elements. See also below, Platina.

[133] "fugas ... bona *cohaerentia* rite jungere" – *Musices Poeticae*, Neisse, Scharffenberg, 1613, sig. G2 (my italics), quoted by PRAETORIUS, p. 22, and WALTHER, p. 526.

[134] "Absint in exordiis divisiones et subdivisions" – Justus Christoph BÖHMER, *Dissertatio academica ideam eloquentiae sacrae sistens*, Helmstadt, Hammius, 1713, p. 31.

[135] *Rhetorica ad Herennium*, I.iv.6. It is from the word 'principium' (SUETONIUS, *De vita Caesarum*, VI.xxi.2: "peracto principio") that Del Rosso and Galilei derived "fece ... una ... ricercata" (see above, note 38).

[136] At least one author had reservations about this method. Alessandro LIONARDI, *Dialogi della inventione poetica*, Venice, Pietrasanta, 1554, p. 52, says: "havete ritrovata una maniera di essordio, che chiamate insinuazione, ... mescolate la verità con la bugia, ... più tosto inganno che essordio" ["you have found a kind of exordium which you call insinuation, ... you mix the truth with lies, ... more deceit than exordium"]. E. W. BOWER, *ΕΦΟΔΟΣ and Insinuatio in Greek and Latin Rhetoric*, «Classical Quarterly», LII, 1958, pp. 224-230, concludes that, *pace Ad Herennium*, the doctrine of *insinuatio* was never really accepted by the Greeks, but propagated primarily by Cicero in his *De inventione* and revived in the fourth and fifth centuries by Roman rhetoricians influenced by him.

[137] "Siccome i suonatori della ricercata s'insinuano nella suonata ..." – *Arte oratoria*, Bologna, Benacci, 1716, p. 495.

Ex. 1. Andrea Gabrieli: *Intonazione del primo tono*,[138] mm. 1-5.

Ex. 2. Girolamo Cavazzoni: *Ricercar primo*, mm. 1-10.

---

[138] From *Intonationi d'organo ... primo libro*, Venice, Gardano, 1593₄.

voices creep in quietly one by one, gradually and almost imperceptibly increasing the number of parts from one to two, three, four, with unobtrusive subjects avoiding large leaps or faster rhythms (Exx. 2, 4). The first note of a new entry may have been heard already in a preceding part (in Ex. 2, the *e'* in mm. 2 and 3, the *a* in mm. 4 and 6, the *e* in mm. 7 and 9), thus avoiding the prominence of a clearly different register. Or it may be so close to the preceding note in an adjacent part that it sounds like the continuation of that part (Ex. 2, m. 9, *f + e*), rather than a new entry. A subject often will enter not as part of a new chord, but on a note belonging to a chord already in effect (Ex. 3, the two entries after the rests). Other means of disguising an entry are to present it in a inner voice (Exx. 3 and 4) or in a harmonic unison or octave with another part (Ex. 4 and *Musica nova*, Ricercar XVII, m. 2); to overlap entries (i.e. not separate them by the codettas often used in baroque fugues); or to introduce them in close stretto (Ex. 4 and *Musica nova*, Ricercars VI, XII, XIV, XVI; still more frequently after the initial exposition). Ricercars and fugues can be regarded as insinuations to the extent to which they exhibit these elegant stylistic features.[139] In general, late baroque fugues in

Ex. 3. Girolamo Cavazioni: *Ricercar primo*, mm. 16ff.

Ex. 4. *Musica nova*: *Ricercar XVIII* (Hieronimo Parabosco), mm. 1-4.

---

[139] The six-part ricercar in Bach's *Musical Offering* illustrates admirably the *insinuatio* style.

Germany, especially those with dance-like subjects and marked entries, have much less *insinuatio* character than the Italian ricercars. In the Italian churches of the sixteenth and seventeenth centuries the imitative ricercars flourished simultaneously with their rhetorical counterparts, the *insinuationes* in the sermons of Ciceronian preachers such as Cornelio Musso (disciple of Bembo), Francesco Panigarola, Paolo Aresi, Emanuele Orchi, and the Jesuits Daniello Bartoli and Paolo Segneri.

Evidence that musicians followed Cicero, directly or indirectly, is provided by northern music theorists who derive their precepts from the practice of Franco-Flemish and Italian composers. Most of them, as cantors, taught Cicero to schoolboys. They actually adopt the term 'exordium' (usually for the first section of a vocal composition, rather than for an independent instrumental prelude), and also make the twofold distinction. Thus Gallus Dressler's *Praecepta musicae poëticae*, based on lectures first given in Magdeburg in 1559/60,[140] include a "Caput XII: De fingendiis exordiis", where we read:

Est autem exordium cantilenarum duplex,[141] videlicet plenum et nudum. Plenum est, cum omnes voces uno tempore ictu incipiunt ut in 'Bewahr mich hehr'. ... In huiusmodi exordijs quaedam voces nonnumquam ex imperfectis constant consonantiis.	But the exordium of musical compositions is twofold, viz. full and bare [i.e. *principium* and *insinuatio*]. 'Full' (*plenum*) is when all voices begin at the same time, as in 'Bewahr mich, Herr'.[142] ... In such exordia certain voices sometimes consist of imperfect consonances.
Nudum appellamus exordium quando non (simul) omnes voces prorumpunt sed aliae post alias ordine procedunt. Hujusmodi exordia ex fugis plerumque constituuntur, ... ut 'Adesto dolori meo'.	We call an exordium 'bare' (*nudum*) when all voices don't break out at the same time, but proceed one after the other in series. Such exordia are generally formed from imitations, ... such as 'Adesto dolori meo'.[143]

Also Joachim Burmeister, in his *Musica poetica*,[144] admits that exordia are either imitative or homophonic, i.e. consist of either a "fuga" or a "noema" (homophonic passage):

---

[140] D-B Ms. Theor. 4.⁰ 84, dated 1564 and probably taken down hastily by a pupil from lectures, published in «Geschichts-Blätter für Stadt und Land Magdeburg», XLIX, 1914, pp. 213-250.

[141] This formulation parallels closely the Ciceronian handbooks of rhetoric, e.g. the anonymous *Praeceptiones rhetoricae*, Paris, 1717, p. 95: "Duplex igitur est Exordium, scilicet Principium, & Insinuatio" ["The exordium, then, is of two kinds, namely *principium* and *insinuatio*"].

[142] A contrafact of Lasso's chanson "Ton feu s'eteint" from the *Treiziesme livre de chansons*, Paris, Le Roy & Ballard, 1559, in *Sämtliche Werke*, Leipzig, Breitkopf & Härtel, 1894-1926, XII, p. 109.

[143] From *Liber sextus ecclesiasticarum cantionum*, Antwerp, Susato, 1553; CLEMENS NON PAPA, *Opera omnia*, American Institute of Musicology, 1966, XIII, p. 33.

[144] Rostock, Myliander, 1606, p. 72.

Exordium eo usque pertingit, quo fugae affectio prorsus desijt sub introductione clausulae verae, vel tractuli harmonici speciem clausulae habentis. Hoc fieri animadvertitur ilico, ac nova affectio a fugae affectione prorsus aliena introducta apparet. Quod autem omnes cantilenae a fugae ornamento initium faciant hoc exemplis non comprobatur. ... Noema locum quandoque in exordio obtinet.

The exordium extends to that point where the fugal subject ceases completely at the introduction of a true cadence or of a harmonic progression having a kind of cadence. This is perceived to happen there and a new subject completely different from the fugal subject appears introduced. However, that all pieces begin with the ornament of a fugue, this is not proven with examples. ... Sometimes the noema takes place in the exordium.

Johann Andreas Herbst, in a chapter *De exordio*, uses the same words as Dressler: "plenum" and "nudum".[145] From the 1540s on, the title 'ricercar' was applied predominantly, though not exclusively, to the imitative (*nudum*) prelude, whereas a variety of other names were eventually preferred for the homophonic preludes, such as 'intonatio', 'toccata', 'praeludium', etc. Thus the *intonatio* is defined by Mattheson as 'plenum': "The *intonatio* occurs with some few full chords, though also certain broken chords ... may serve well here".[146] Both Ciceronian types, the *principium plenum* and the *insinuatio nuda*, continue and dominate the non-dance keyboard repertoire of the baroque. Even later, the title 'ricercar' is still used occasionally for the *principium* type (Wagenseil).

A question which at first may appear far-fetched is whether the new imitative musical style has any conceptual relationship to the other kinds of *imitatio* in vogue at this time. Imitation of Cicero's style was only one of these, albeit the most important. *Imitatio* conditioned all aspects of Renaissance intellectual life (and nowhere more than in Bembo's circle, from which all of the following examples are taken). Contemporary historians such as Donato Giannotti taught that worthy institutions of antiquity should be imitated in modern times (Venice), and they regarded historiography itself as a kind of *mimesis*.[147] Poetry itself was defined as 'imitatio'.[148] Individuals prided them-

---

[145] *Musica poetica*, Nuremberg, Dümler, 1643, p. 81.

[146] "Die Intonatio geschiehet am besten mit einigen wenigen *vollen* Griffen; wiewol auch gewisse gebrochene Accorde ... Dienste hiebey thun können", *Capellmeister*, p. 477 (my italics).

[147] On the humanist historians' concept of their discipline as a branch of rhetoric see Felix GIL-BERT, *Machiavelli and Guicciardini*, Princeton UP, 1965, pp. 216, 272f; on their inclusion of orations in their histories see Donald J. WILCOX, *The Development of Florentine Humanist Historiography in the Fifteenth Century*, Cambridge MA., Harvard UP, 1969, pp. 123-126, 167-171, 200f.

[148] E.g. Giovanni Antonio VIPERANO, *De poetica*, Antwerp, Plantin, 1579, pp. 9ff.

selves on imitating famous ancients, as when Bernardino Daniello compared his relationship to Trifone Gabrieli with that of Plato to Socrates. Such parallels were invariably drawn with complimentary intentions. Trifone is repeatedly apostrophized by his contemporaries as the 'new Socrates' or said by Pietro Aretino to have imitated Christ. Bembo's friend Andrea Molino was "il Roscio della nostra età" ["the Roscius [comedian and friend of Cicero] of our time"], and Bembo himself, praised as "Cicero ... renatus",[149] imitated Petrarch's habits, just as he and the Roman curia imitated Cicero in all details of private life: in their villas, walks, number of guests, etc.[150]

Also the older Platonic and Aristotelian concepts of *mimesis* – i.e. of imitation of nature[151] and of human actions – were of course very much alive in Renaissance music and eventually provided a basis for the baroque *Affektenlehre*. For the word-oriented age of humanism, this was achieved especially by rendering the meaning of the text in music, as Giovanni Gabrieli says of his uncle Andrea: "one sees clearly how singular he was in imitation and in finding sounds expressing the energy of the words and concepts".[152] When Burmeister entitles the last chapter of his *Musica poetica* "De imitatione", he does so still in the sense of style-imitation[153] and proceeds to identify a dozen sixteenth-century composers to serve as models. However, by this time the word 'imitation' was already well established in musical terminology for the successive entries of a melody in different voices. Bartolomeo Ramos de Pareia's *Musica practica*, begun ten years before its publication in 1482, already uses the verbal form in this sense.[154] Johannes Frosch in 1532 and Johannes Stomius in 1537 designate canonic writing (fuga) as "mimesis",[155] i.e. the Greek equiva-

---

[149] Petrus NANNIUS, hexameters prefixed to *Commentarii rerum gestarum in India*, Louvain, Rescius, 1539.

[150] GMELIN, pp. 222, 176ff.

[151] This aspect of imitation is discussed in Armen CARAPETYAN, *The Concept of imitazione della natura in the Sixteenth Century*, «Journal of Renaissance and Baroque Music», I, 1946/47, pp. 47-67.

[152] "si vede apertamente quanto egli sia stato singulare nell'imitatione in ritrovar suoni esprimenti l'energia delle parole e de' concetti" – *Concerti ... libro primo et secondo*, Venice, Gardano, 1587.

[153] P. 74: "Imitatio est studium & conamen nostra musica ad artificium exempla, per analysin dextre considerata, effingendi & formandi" ["Imitation is the study and endevour of depicting and formulating our music according to examples of the masters, skilfully considered by analysis"]. Cf. Johannes FROSCH, *Rerum musicarum opusculum*, Strasbourg, Scheffer & Apiarius, 1532, index: "De imitatione authorum" ["On the imitation of authors"], on parody technique.

[154] Bologna, De Colonia and De Hiriberia, 1482, II.i.1: "Est tamen modus organizandi optimus, quando organum imitatur tenorem in ascensu aut descensu, non in eodem tempore, sed post unam notulam vel plures incipit" ["However, the best manner of composing is when the organal voice imitates the tenor in ascending and descending, not at the same time, but beginning after one or more notes"].

[155] FROSCH, cap. XIX: "non uno temporis ictu exorsa sed per mimesim, & imitationem, & ceu

lent to the Latin *imitatio*, familiar especially from chapters 1-3 of Aristotle's *Poetica*.[156] Zarlino, Willaert's pupil and indirect successor as chapel master at St. Mark's, lists the various expressions for the imitative procedure, such as *fuga, risposta, reditta, conseguenza*, and concludes by saying: "But some others have called it 'imitation', since he who follows the first [singer] tries to imitate him as much as he can, in the intervals and in the duration [of the notes] as well as in the motions, and takes pains to repeat everything which the first has said".[157] Like most theorists, he gives preference to this term, entitling his next chapter *"Delle imitationi"*.[158] It is significant that he is not abstract, but concrete, speaking not of one melody but of one singer imitating another; thus his statement relates to the above-mentioned imitation of individuals.

I do not consider it mere coincidence that the imitative ricercar originates in Bembo's circle and precisely at the time – the 1530s and 1540s – when the controversy on the imitation of Cicero reached its peak – a controversy characterized by one eminent scholar as "the most important event in the history of ideas during this period".[159] Composers, unlike architects and men of letters, could hardly imitate antiquity directly, for no ancient musical models were yet known. But they had discovered that a melody could imitate itself, and they were making this procedure the basis of polyphonic composition. This too had its analogies in literature, for the Ciceronian Petrarch, for example, was known for his self-imitations,[160] and rhetoricians such as Bembo's disciple Bartolomeo Ricci recommend also imitation "in contraria" etc.,[161] already familiar to com-

---

fugam iterata" ["not entering at the same time, but repeated by *mimesis* and imitation or fugue"]; index: "De mimesi, & ceu fuga imitanda". STOMIUS, *Prima ad musicen instructio*, Augsburg, Ulhard, 1537, sig. C2v: "Ingeniosa, quas mimeses seu fugas appellant: ubi eadem vox a pluribus, sed certis temporum spacijs intervenientibus, consequenter canitur" ["Those *mimeses* or fugues [= imitations] are said to be ingenious where the same voice is sung by several in succession, but with certain intervals of time intervening"], adding an example by Senfl.

[156] Aristotle's 'mimesis' was rendered invariably as 'imitatio' ever since the Latin translation by Giorgio Valla in 1498.

[157] "Ma alcuni altri l'hanno detto imitatione, percioché quello che segue il primo quanto puote cerca di imitarlo, sì ne gli intervalli et ne i tempi, come anco nelli movimenti; et si sforza di ridire tutto quello, che ha detto il primo" – *Istitutioni harmoniche*, 1573, p. 257. This definition is not yet included in the corresponding passage in the first edition of 1558, pp. 212f. Zarlino surely derived the title of his work from Quintilian's *Institutio oratoria*.

[158] ZARLINO, 1558, pp. 217-220; 1573, pp. 262-267.

[159] CROLL, p. 107.

[160] GMELIN, p. 167.

[161] *De imitatione*, Venice, Aldus (*editio princeps* 1541), 1545, p. 49: "Contrariorum igitur plura sunt genera: in omnibus autem aptissime cadit imitatio" ["There are, then, more kinds of *contraria*: but imitation belongs most suitably to all of them"]. See also below, notes 208, 211.

posers. Though 'imitation' had many shades of meaning, the basic concept was common to all usages: musical, literary, artistic, moral. I therefore venture to designate this most important and characteristic musical technique of the Renaissance as a component of the 'imitation mentality' of the time.

Both the musical and literary imitation of Cicero are combined in Girolamo Cavazzoni's landmark publication of 1543, if, as argued, the ricercars imitate the Ciceronian *insinuatio*, for the dedicatory letter, addressed to no other than Girolamo's godfather Bembo, is an unmistakable imitation of the Ciceronian epistle. (At the same time it serves, like all such dedications, as an exordium to the publication).[162] It is, in fact, one of the few dedications I have seen in Italian music which begins with the standard opening formula of classical Latin letters: the *salutatio* of the writer to the receiver, both of whom are immediately named. Girolamo translates this literally into Italian, with only one necessary concession to modern etiquette: the reversal of the position of writer and addressee (subject and indirect object). Thus instead of "Tullius s[alutem] p[lurimum] d[icit] Terrentiae",[163] he writes "All'Illustriss. et Reverendiss. Signore il Cardinal Bembo, devotissimo servidor Girolamo Cavazzoni da Bologna fa humil reverenza". In normal Italian letters of the time, the compliments and name of the writer came, of course, at the end, not at the beginning of the letter as here. Also the elaborately balanced phrases which follow in the dedication are pure Cicero, translated into Italian: "nato, non fatto" (*antithesis*), "compare e servidor ... antichissimo e devotissimo" (*synchrysis*, for "antichissimo compare e devotissimo servidor"), and so on.[164] (Bembo, as we know, was never happier than when he received a letter on which he could bestow his highest praise: 'Ciceronian').[165] Girolamo goes on to say that his work "trahe radici da scienza lodata e eseguita" ["has roots in worthy studies pursued"], and by now I hardly need to say what these "roots" and "studies" were.

There is every reason to believe that Bembo was knowledgeable about music.[166] His lover in 1500 was, according to his testimony, an incompar-

[162] Cf. Wolfgang LEINER, *Der Widmungsbrief in der französischen Literatur (1580-1715)*, Heidelberg, Winter, 1965, p. 91, for 17th-century Ciceronian comparisons of the exordial dedication with the 'exordial' architecture.

[163] Example from Cicero to his wife. Cf. also BEMBO, *De imitatione*: "Petrus Bembus Jo. Francisco Pico S. P. D." (*Opere*, IV, 333) and the dedication of Gioseffo ZARLINO, *Sopplimenti musicali*, Venice, De' Franceschi, 1588.

[164] The entire dedication is quoted in Claudio SARTORI, *Bibliografia della musica strumentale italiana stampata in Italia fino al 1700*, Florence, Olschki, 1952, pp. 9f, and in G. CAVAZZONI, *Orgelwerke*, Mainz, Schott, 1959-61, I, vi.

[165] GMELIN, p. 192.

[166] On the influence of his poetry and poetics on madrigal composers see Walter H. RUBSAMEN, *Literary Sources of Secular Music in Italy*, Berkeley and Los Angeles, California UP, 1943, pp. 27ff,

able musician.[167] In a letter of 15 June 1503 to his brother, he complained about the poor quality of some viol strings, and in one of 3 January 1546, to Trifone Gabrieli, the 75-year-old cardinal boasted that he not only celebrated, but also sang a Mass in the presence of Pope Julius III, the college of cardinals, and "molto popolo".[168] The usual assumption that a composer dedicates to a patron music which is to the latter's taste is a safe one in the case of G. Cavazzoni, if one recognizes that his ricercars imitate Cicero's *insinuatio*. In the *Prose* Bembo indeed exhibits a preference for the skillfully constructed exordium over the more straightforward tale.[169] We may also draw some indirect conclusions on Bembo's musical taste from the discussion of imitation in Castiglione's *Cortegiano*, II.xxix-xxxix, inspired by the *Prose*. Castiglione's manuscript, published by the Aldine press in 1528, had already been sent to Bembo for comment in 1518. Words assigned to Bembo were ultimately transferred to another interlocutor, his friend Federigo Fregoso, while Lodovico da Canossa serves as Castiglione's mouthpiece. Bembo's view is that there should be an elevated style of written vernacular prose, based on fourteenth-century models and distinct from spoken usage (cf. Cicero's statement that the exordium should be carefully thought out in advance); this suggests that in music he would favor the learned style of the imitative ricercar. Castiglione, on the other hand, would model literary style on the contemporary spoken language of the courts, and it is no accident that one word he uses to characterize this freer style, 'sprezzatura',[170] is taken up by Giulio Caccini to describe the new monody, closer to natural speech and diametrically opposed to the imitative ricercar.[171] The ricercars from Caccini's vicinity, composed by Vincenzo Galilei, are, like those of lutenists generally, much closer to the free, 'Aristotelian' type.[172] Since Galilei is critical of the rhetorical concept of music and prefers the

---

and especially Dean T. MACE, *Pietro Bembo and the Literary Origins of the Italian Madrigal*, «Musical Quarterly», LV, 1969, pp. 65-86.

[167] *Opere*, III, 350, 367: "Ella forse ora tra suoni e canti dimorando, de' quali nessuna viva di lei maggior maestra ..." ["She, perhaps now dwelling among instrumental music and singing, of which no one living [is] a greater master ..."].

[168] *Opere*, III, 99, 107.

[169] Venice, Tacuino, 1525, f. xxxiii, with reference to Boccaccio.

[170] Spontaneous grace, as opposed to premeditated affectation (*Cortegiano*, I.xxvii-xxviii). See Edward WILLIAMSON, *The Concept of Grace in the Work of Raphael and Castiglione*, «Italica», XXIV, 1947, pp. 316-324, and W. KIRKENDALE, *The Court Musicians in Florence during the Principate of the Medici*, Florence, Olschki, 1993, pp. 155-158.

[171] Dedication of *L'Euridice*, Florence, Marescotti, 1601, and preface to *Le nuove musiche*, *ibid.*, 1602.

[172] *Fronimo*, Venice, Scotto, 1568² and 1584⁵.

style of folksong,[173] it is not surprising that he speaks disparagingly of the imitative ricercar in his *Dialogo* (p. 87).

Another aspect of literary style explains the origin of a tempo designation, the one normally associated with the imitative ricercar. The quality which the Bembists praised most of all in Cicero and Petrarch is *gravità*.[174] Of the three traditional *genera dicendi* distinguished in rhetorical theory and poetics for different situations and social classes, i.e. the *genus humile* or *subtile*, the *genus mediocre*, and the *genus grande* or *sublime*,[175] it was the *genus grande* which was characterized by *gravitas* and sometimes referred to as *genus grave*.[176] Renaissance musicians regarded *gravità* as characteristic of ancient music and therefore worthy of imitation: "The ancient musicians ... performed grave and learned things, elegantly composed", "full of severity and gravity".[177] Giovanni Gabrieli's dedication of 1587, quoted above, praises Andrea Gabrieli "perché sia stato grave" ["because he was grave"]. By the middle of the seventeenth century, the *stilus gravis* was generally associated with the sixteenth century: Christoph Bernhard equates it with *stilus antiquus* or *ecclesiasticus*, i.e. with the style of the *a cappella* motet, which in the broader sense embraces also the imitative ricercar;[178] and in 1677 Fabrizio Fontana published in Rome "Ricercari d'organo in stile antico e grave". These authors were merely adapting a concept already current in Italian rhetorical theory: "The ancient style ... is characterized by gravity, and lowers rather than raises itself".[179] Titian painted his 'visual exordium' in the *stilus grandis*, with ancient columns (cf. note 123).

---

173 See DAMMANN, pp. 107-111. Claude V. PALISCA, *Vincenzo Galilei and some Links between 'Pseudo-Monody' and Monody*, «Musical Quarterly», XLVI, 1960, pp. 344-360.

174 See BEMBO's *Prose*; TOMITANO, p. 145: "gravità ... sopra tutte l'altre cose commendabili" ["gravity ... above all other commendable things"]; Bernardino DANIELLO's various publications, 1536-68; and MACE.

175 See CICERO, *Orator*, XXI.69; QUINTILIAN, XII.x.58.

176 E.g. by TOMITANO, pp. 169ff, who includes Cicero, Horace, Ovid, Virgil, Boccaccio, and Petrarch among its masters, and by Giovanni GIACCHETTI, *Rhetoricarum eruditionum epitomae*, Rome, Caballus, 1636, p. 133.

177 "Gli antichi musici ... recitavano cose gravi, dotte, et composte elegantemente", "piene di severità et di gravità" – ZARLINO, 1558, p. 65.

178 *Die Kompositionslehre Heinrich Schützens in der Fassung seines Schülers Christoph Bernhard*, ed. Joseph Müller-Blattau, Kassel, Bärenreiter, 1963, pp. 42, 63. See also Athanasius KIRCHER, *Musurgia*, Rome, Corbelletti, 1650, I, 585: "Motectus stylus, ... gravis, maiestate plenus" ["motet style, ... grave, full of majesty"]. None of the fundamental ancient literary and rhetorical concepts is mentioned in Christoph WOLFF's *Der Stile antico in der Musik Johann Sebastian Bachs*, Wiesbaden, Steiner, 1968.

179 "Lo stile antico ... ha ... del grave, e più tosto s'abbassa, che e' si alza" – Orazio LOMBARDELLI, *Gli aforismi scolastici*, Siena, Marchetti, 1603, p. 139.

An indirect but conclusive proof that the ricercar belonged to the *genus grave* is provided by Cicero and his followers, who teach that the exordium, more than any other part of the oration, should be 'grave', dignified: "The exordium must have a high degree of sententiousness and gravity, and generally contain in itself everything which pertains to dignity".[180] This leaves no doubt as to the derivation of Herbst's characterization of the musical exordium as "of dignity and worthiness",[181] or of Kircher's as "grave, sweet, full of sounds and with harmonious gravity".[182] Numerous musical sources of the seventeenth century confirm the slow tempo of the ricercar and other preludial pieces.[183] The slow introductions to the later overtures, church sonatas, symphonies, and even waltzes of Johann Strauss are likewise musical manifestations of the *exordium grave*.

It must be emphasized that what today is regarded merely as a tempo indication originally designated much more: an entire style, recognized as a mu-

---

[180] CICERO, *De inventione*, I.xviii.25, quoted more fully above. See also LULLO, p. 192, and CARBONE, p. 92 (quoting Cicero?): "Initio quidem oratio prodit tranquille, pedententim [*sic*], ac moderate" ["At the beginning the oration indeed unfolds calmly, gradually, and moderately"]. MEMO, f. 79: "I principi dever esser gravi, i fini veramente brevi & affrettati" ["The beginnings must be grave, the conclusions truly brief and hasty"]. SANSOVINO, f. 4*v*, 5: "il proemio, il quale è grave e maturo principio del ragionamento", "Il Diretto, ... dando principio con grave discorso all'oratione" ["the proem, which is the grave and mature beginning of the discourse", "The direct [i.e. Cicero's *principium*], ... beginning the oration with a grave discourse"]. Daniel BARBARO, *Della eloquenza*, Venice, Valgrifio, 1557, p. 52: "La maestà è usata per lo più ne i proemi" ["Majesty is used mostly in the proems"]. CAVALCANTI, p. 277: "un certo movimento grave, ... che habbia qualche degnità" ["a certain grave motion, ... which has some dignity"]. Orazio TOSCANELLA, *La retorica di M. Tullio Cicerone ... ridotta in alberi*, Venice, Degli Avanzi, 1561, f. 124*v*: "Nel principio ... se useremo intervalli lunghi: cioè se faremo pausa, et ci fermeremo a i punti de i commi, coli, et periodi ..." ["At the beginning ... if we shall use long intervals: i.e. if we shall make a pause at the commas, colons, and periods ..."]. Desiderius ERASMUS, *De recta Latini Graecique sermonis pronuntiatione*, Cologne, Soter, 1529, p. 88: "in exordiis, in quibus oportet sedatam esse dictionem, longiore mora pronuntiant syllabas, ... prior pars lentius sonatur quam posterior. – Fit idem a musicis" ["In exordia, in which the diction must be sedate, they pronounce syllables with a long delay. ... The first part is sounded more slowly than the following. – [Reply of the interlocutor:] The same is done by musicians"].

[181] "aus dignitet und würdigkeit" – p. 82.

[182] "grave, suave, sonorum & harmonica gravitate plenum" – II, 143.

[183] Adriano BANCHIERI, *Moderna armonia di canzoni alla francese*, Venice, Amadino, 1612, *avvertenze*: "la prima fiata devesi suonare adagio in guisa di ricercar" ["The first time it must be played adagio in the manner of a ricercar"]. Girolamo FRESCOBALDI, *Toccate e partite*, Rome, Borboni, 1615: "I principij delle toccate sian fatti adagio" ["The beginning of the toccaas are to be made adagio"]. *Id.*, *Il primo libro di capricci*, Rome, Soldi, 1624: "Si devono i principii cominciarli adagio" ["The beginnings must be adagio"]. *Id.*, *Il primo libro delle canzoni*, Rome, Robletti, 1628: "la presente opera ... in gravità e dottrina perfettissima; aggiunga anco i capricci & ricercari del medesimo se vuole gravità di stile" ["the present work ... most perfect in gravity and learning; add also the capriccios and ricercars of the same if you desire gravity of style"]. Giovanbattista FASOLO, *Annuale*, Venice, Vincenti, 1645: "Le ricercate delli otto toni cominciano gravi" ["The ricercars of the eight modes begin *grave*"]. Giovanni SCIPIONE, *Intavolatura di cembalo et organo*, Perugia, Bartoli & Laureni, 1650: "Gl'incominciamenti delle toccate si faranno adagio" ["The beginnings of the toccatas will be made adagio"].

sical counterpart to the *genus grande* in language.[184] Thus 'grave' implied not only slow tempo, but also 'low' dynamics, 'low' pitch (compare Tasso's "ricercate in bassi modi", quoted above), and *stilus antiquus* (Bernhard). Singers, choir directors, and organists will perform this music intelligently only if they realize that the skillful orator begins his speech not only slowly, but also quietly: "Beginning a case, care must be taken that the speech be soft";[185] "A gentle delivery is most often best suited to the exordium".[186] Composers understood this when they constructed their musical *insinuatio* as an unnotated crescendo, with a gradual increase in the number of parts, thus achieving a perfect musical correspondence to Giasone De Nores' description of exordia: "which always go from somewhat mild and moderate beginnings, then gradually rising and becoming animated, imitating the things produced by nature, which arrive at their due perfection not immediately, but *poco a poco crescendo*"[187] – words which could be found in a musical score. Shortly before the designation 'grave' came to be included in the musical notation of the ricercar, we have literary references to the 'grave' character of the improvised organ preludes or composed ricercars which introduce the Elevation of the Host during the Mass: in the *Caeremoniale episcoporum iussu Clementis VIII* (Rome, Typ. linguarum externarum, 1600)[188] and in Adriano Banchieri's *Organo suonarino* (Venice, Amadino, 1605).[189] (Banchieri was not only one of the first composers to apply tempo designations to music, but also one of the most articulate in writing about music as a rhetorical art).[190] Marco da Gagliano, in the preface to his *Dafne* (Florence, Marescotti, 1608), says that the prologue must be performed "con gravità", "pieno di maiestà" ["with gravity", "full of majesty"] – a style already employed by Jacopo Peri in the prologues to his *Dafne* and *Eu-*

---

184 Irmgard HERRMANN-BENGEN, *Tempobezeichnungen*, Tutzing, Schneider, 1959, did not recognize the relation of this or any other tempo designation to rhetoric.

185 "Exordienda causa servandum est ut lenis sit sermo" – *Ad Herennium*, I.vii.ii.

186 "Procœmio frequentissime lenis convenit pronuntiatio" – QUINTILIAN, XI.iii.161. Cf. TOSCANELLA, f. 124*v*: "Se cominceremo ... con bassa voce, ... la voce leggiera, molle, et bassa ha virtù di conciliarsi benevoglienza" ["If we shall begin ... with a low voice, ... the light, soft, and low voice has the advantage of winning benevolence"]; the orator should not become heated at the beginning.

187 "che sempre da alquanto lievi e mediocri comminciamenti vadino poi inalzandosi e pigliando spirito di grado in grado, imitando le cose prodotte dalla natura, le quali non così al primo tratto ma *poco a poco crescendo* pervengono alla loro debita perfezione" – *Breve trattato dell'oratore*, Padua, Galignani, 1574, f. 20*r-v* (my italics).

188 F. 52.

189 P. 38. Cf. FASOLO, *Annuale*: "La elevatione vuole essere gravissima". BANCHIERI's *Organo suonarono*, Venice, Vincenti, 1622³, contains a "Sonata grave ... alla Levatione".

190 See especially his *Cartella musicale*, Venice, Vincenti, 1614, pp. 165f.

ridice. Beethoven still showed awareness of this tradition when he wrote an orchestral "Praeludium" as Elevation music in his *Missa solemnis*, an imitation of the organ improvisation, complete with slow tempo, low dynamics, low pitch, and *stilus antiquus* or *contrapunctus gravis*.[191]

To the etymological question raised above, "What is being sought (*ricercato*) in the ricercar?", purely musical answers were suggested (pp. 41-44), based on musical references in literary sources: the tuning of the instrument, or the key of the following piece. The question may now be considered again, within the context I have reconstructed from rhetorical theory. While the function and style of the ricercar are identified with the first of the *partes orationis* (i.e. exordium), its etymology is closely related to the first of the five *partes artis*, i.e. the *inventio* (see Appendix I).[192] The orator begins his work by exploring his material, 'searching' for ideas, arguments, and refutations, and these he finds (*invenit*) in the rhetorical system of 'search-formulas' or 'places', the *loci* (Greek *topoi*). In their literal meanings of 'search' and 'find', the terms 'ricercar' and 'invention' are thus complementary,[193] a fact which has eluded lexicographers who attempted unsuccessfully to explain the latter in purely musical terms,[194] not realizing that it was taken over by Bach from the discipline of rhetoric, to replace his original designation "praeambulum". The search formulas for the exordium, as mentioned in almost every discussion of this section of the speech from Cicero to John Quincy Adams, aim at a threefold effect on the listener: "The exordium is a speech preparing the mind of the listener suitably for the rest of the oration; this will result if it renders him benevolent, attentive, and ready to understand".[195] This most tenaciously

---

[191] See pp. 521f. For the important role of *gravità* at the court of Louis XIV see below, pp. 225-234.

[192] The five phases of the orator's activity are *inventio, dispositio, elocutio, memoria*, and *pronuntiatio* (CICERO, *Orator*, xiv-xvii; QUINTILIAN, III.iii.1). CICERO's *De inventione* is the first section of an incomplete treatise on the *partes artis rhetoricae*.

[193] André MAUGARS, *Response faite à un curieux, sur le sentiment de la musique d'Italie, éscrite à Rome le premiere octobre 1639*, Paris, 1639, p. 13, praised Frescobaldi's toccatas "pleines de recherches & d'inventions admirables" ["full of admirable *recherches* and inventions"].

[194] E.g. Willi APEL, *Harvard Dictionary of Music*, Cambridge MA, Belknap, 1969, p. 422: "Bach's reason for choosing these terms [invention and sinfonia] is entirely obscure". Also the obscurity in the use of the term 'sinfonia' for the three-part inventions vanishes once we realize their preludial character, shared with the Italian sinfonia (overture). EGGEBRECHT, *Studien*, pp. 72-82, correctly emphasizes that 'inventio' always retained its elementary, general significance and never became a specific musical term. Cf. notes 8, "invenzioni", and 199, "inventione"; also DAMMANN, pp. 114-125.

[195] "Exordium est oratio animum auditoris idonee comparans ad reliquam dictionem; quod eveniet si eum benevolum, attentum, docilem confecerit" – CICERO, *De inventione*, I.xv.20. Cf. ARISTOTLE, III, 1415a; John Quincy ADAMS, *Lectures on Rhetoric and Oratory*, Cambridge MA, Hilliard & Metcalf, 1810, I, 402: the exordium is to "prepare the minds of the hearers ... or ... to engage their good will, their attention, and their docility". The rendering of the Greek ευμαθής as the English

repeated formulation in all rhetorical theory suggests, then, that the ricercar may be 'searching' for the listeners' goodwill, attention, and receptiveness. For the function of *docere* ('to make *docilem*', 'to teach'), the learned contrapuntal style was found appropriate. The idea of 'preparing the listener' is echoed in a Viennese document of the late fifteenth century mentioning a minstrel who makes "a preamble... [with] which he moves the people to be attentive to him",[196] in Tasso's words, quoted above, "He prepares the minds of others for the harmony with sweet ricercars", in Corsini's "He proceeded to play, and made ricercars which would render tame every Megaera [one of the three furies of the underworld]",[197] in my second quotation from Bartoli (see above, p. 43), and in theorists' almost literally Ciceronian descriptions of the musical exordium, from Burmeister and Kircher to Mattheson.[198]

Zarlino, in his chapter "That which is sought in every composition", suggests that many things may be "sought", but the first is the "subject".[199] This, as in poetry, may be either borrowed or freely invented.[200] To Zarlino's analogy to literature we might add one to the visual arts, for here we find the dis-

---

"docile" is inadequate, since the ancients intended by this: "prepared for intelligent listening by having been given the subject of the following speech". See Francis P. DONNELLY, *A Function of the Classical Exordium*, «Classical Weekly», V, 1911/12, pp. 204-207.

[196] "ain preambel ... das er die lewt im auf ze merkchen bewege" – quoted by SLIM, diss., p. 413, and others.

[197] "Seguì sonando, e fece ricercari / Da render mansueta ogni Megera" – CORSINI, I, 172.

[198] BURMEISTER, p. 72: "Exordium est prima carminis periodus, sive affectio, fuga ut plurimum exornata, qua auditoris aures & animus ad cantum attenta redduntur, illiusque benevolentia captatur" ["The exordium is the first section of the music or the affect – adorned as much as possible with imitation – with which the ears and spirits of the listener are rendered attentive to the song and his goodwill is won"]. KIRCHER, II, 143: "Exordium melodiae est modulatio auditoris animum idoneum ad reliqua reddens" ["The exordium of the melody is a passage rendering the mind of the listener suitable for the rest"]; cf. also I, 465: "organoedus ... praeambulis quibusdam auditorum animos praeparet" ["the organist ... prepares the minds of the listeners with certain preambles"]. MATTHESON, *Capellmeister*, p. 236: "Das Exordium ist der Eingang und Anfang einer Melodie, worin zugleich der Zweck und die gantze Absicht derselben angezeiget werden muss, damit die Zuhörer dazu vorbereitet, und zur Aufmercksamkeit ermuntert werden" ["The exordium is the entrance and beginning of a melody, in which at the same time the purpose and the whole intention of the same must be announced, so that the listeners are prepared for it and are stimulated to attentiveness"]. Cf. also below, p. 83, TOSCANELLA.

[199] "Quel che si ricerca in ogni compositione"; "si ricercano molte cose; ... la prima e il soggetto" – 1573, p. 199; p. 200 defines "soggetto" as "quella parte, sopra la quale il compositore cava la inventione di far le altre parti della cantilena" ["that part from which the composer derives the invention for making the other parts of the song" through imitation]. Thus 'inventione' is sometimes used for 'soggetto', e.g. in Pietro PONTIO, *Ragionamento di musica*, Parma, Viotto, 1588, pp. 159f: "Il modo per far un ricercar' è tale, che l'inventioni vogliono esser lunghe. ... Anco sia lecito seguire dal principio fin'al fine con un'istesso soggetto" ["The manner of making a ricercar is such that the inventions are to be long. ... It may also be permitted to procede from beginning to end with the same subject"] – anticpating the monothematic baroque fugue.

[200] ZARLINO, 1573, pp. 199f; see also HAAR, p. 236.

tinction between "imitatione icastica" of "a thing formed by nature", and "imitatione fantastica" in which the artist paints "a caprice/fantasy of his [own], never drawn by another".[201] Clearly related to this latter formulation are the musical terms 'capriccio' and 'fantasia' designating pieces which, like ricercars but unlike the early canzonas, did not normally make use of pre-existing subjects.[202] Indeed, words such as 'subject', 'invention', 'imitation', 'fantasia', 'capriccio', etc. are commonly used together in a much broader and more ancient context than writers on music suspect. Greek theory of visual art complemented *mimesis* (imitation) with the stoic concept of *phantasia*,[203] just as Quintilian later balanced *imitatio* with *inventio*.[204]

As demonstrated above, the verb 'ricercar' in ordinary sixteenth-century usage meant simply 'to search', and it has retained this meaning to the present day. However, beginning with the end of the century, its past participle acquired an additional significance, identical to the German equivalent 'gesucht', designating an elaborate style of language, characterized by artifice rather than sincerity. Orazio Lombardelli (1603) is one of the first authors to use the word 'ricercato' in this sense as a subdivision of style: "The diligent, the *recherché* ... show the art openly".[205] This usage of the past participle soon became the normal one, also in French.[206] 'Ricercato' thus implies the (over)-use of artifices, i.e. of the rhetorical figures.

---

[201] "cosa formata della natura"... "un suo capriccio non più disegnato da alcun altro" – Gregorio COMANINI, *Il Figino ovvero del fine della pittura*, Mantua, Osanna, 1591, pp. 29, 53. Paul Oskar Kristeller kindly informed me that this concept of icastic and phantastic imitation is derived from PLATO, *Sophist*, 266D. See also below, note 233. Agostino MICHELE, *Discorso in cui ... si dimostra come si possono scrivere ... le commedie e le tragedie in prosa*, Venice, Ciotti, 1592, ff. 40*v*-41, describes the distinction in literature, tracing it to Aristotle, who subdivided each into a 'narrative' and a 'dramatic' species..

[202] Cf. KIRCHER's description of the "phantasticus stylus", I, 585: "Phantasticus stylus aptus instrumentis, est liberrima, & solutissima componendi methodus, nullis, nec verbis, nec subiecto harmonico adstrictus ad ostentandum ingenium, & abditam harmoniae rationem, ingeniosumque harmonicarum clausularum fugarumque contextum docendum institutus, dividiturque in eas, quas *phantasias, ricercatas, toccatas, sonatas* vulgo vocant" ["*Phantasticus stylus*, suitable for instruments, is a very free and loose manner of composing, compelled by nothing, neither words nor musical subject, to display ingenuity and the hidden principle of harmony and the ingenious context of the harmonic cadences and imitations, established for teaching, it is divided into those [genres] which in the vernacular are called *fantasias, ricercatas, toccatas, sonatas*"].

[203] Cf. SCHWEITZER, and «Philologus», LXXXVIIIf, 1933f.

[204] See above, note 103.

[205] "L'accurato, e ricercato ... mostrano l'arte scopertamente" – pp. 134, 141.

[206] Sforza PALLAVICINO, *Istoria del Concilio di Trento*, Rome, Bernabò, 1656-57, I, 356: "questo discorso ... più ricercato e declamatorio che vero ed efficace" ["this discourse ... more *recherché* and declamatory than true and effective"]; the edition of Rome, 1664, I, 381, replaces "declamatorio" with "rettorico", illustrating the emergence of the modern negative usage of the word 'rhetoric', still unknown in the 16th century, and the continuing correlation between 'ricercar' and rhetoric. Vin-

It is interesting to observe also here the perfect analogy in music. We have seen (notes 177 and 183) that from Zarlino to Frescobaldi 'dottrina' was associated with 'gravità'. Beginning with Andrea Gabrieli, the imitative ricercar soon became the most elaborately contrived music of its time, a true counterpart of Ciceronian oratory, characterized by contrapuntal artifices such as augmentation, diminution, inversion, and syncopation of the themes. For this the Flemish motets did not provide the models.[207] Modern writers on music have remained unaware that all these devices originated, or at least had their counterparts, in rhetoric.[208] Prosecution lawyers augment the vices and diminish the virtues of the defendant; these arguments may be inverted by the defense in the *refutatio* if the prosecutor is not careful to avoid the *vitium* of the *commutabile* (cf. p. 57). Syncope, in rhetoric, is the omission of a syllable from the middle of a word, e.g. 'dixti' for 'dixisti', thus shifting the expected position of the following syllable(s). Augmentation and diminution were used especially in epideictic oratory, and Quintilian associates them with the exordium.[209] As in music, such devices were applied to the 'subject',[210]

---

cenzo GRAVINA, *Della ragion poetica*, Rome, Gonzaga, 1708, p. 63: "Quindi negli scrittori, e poeti di quei secoli si ravvisa maggior acume, che naturalezza, maggior dottrina, che senno, e maggior lusinga di ricercate parole, ed arguzie, che fedeltà e verità di sentimenti" ["Hence in the writers and poets of those centuries" after the death of Augustus "one saw more acumen than naturalness, more learning than judgement, and more allurement with *recherché* diction and subtleties than faithfulness and truth of sentiments"]. Anton Maria SALVINI, *Discorsi accademici*, II, Florence, Manni, 1712, p. 273: "orazioni ... affaticate, e con troppo squisito e ricercato ripulimento lavorate" ["labored orations, worked out with too exquisite and *recherché* polish"]. ANON., *Memorie per le belle arti*, I, 1785, p. xv: "Il secolo decimosettimo celebre per la caricata maniera di scrivere in prosa, ed in verso, pieno di metafore e di ricercati concetti" ["the 17th century, famous for the overloaded manner of writing in prose, full of metaphors and *recherché* conceits"].

207 APEL, *The Early Development* ..., p. 145.

208 On *augmentatio* (or *incrementum*) see ARISTOTLE, II, 1391b; QUINTILIAN, VIII.iv.3-8, 28. On *diminutio* (or *minutio*), QUINTILIAN, VII.iv.1, 28; CICERO, *De oratore*, III.liii.202; TOSCANELLA, *op. cit.*, f. 165*v*. On *inversio* (or *contrarium*) CICERO, III.liii.207; QUINTILIAN, IX.i.34, IX.iii.90; Pierre SAINCT-FLEUR, *Institutionum rhetoricarum libellus*, Paris, Brumennius, 1561, f. 13; TOSCANELLA, *loc. cit.*; *id.*, *Libro primo degli artifici osservati ... sopra l'orationi di Cicerone*, Venice, Sessa, 1568, f. 18; Bartolomeo ZUCCHI, *L'idea del segretario*, Venice, Comp. Minima, 1600, ch. VI: "L'imitatione nel contrario", and above, p. 67, "imitatio in contraria". On syncope, Peter SCHADE, *Tabulae de schematibus et tropis*, Paris, Vilhardus, 1535, p. 7. Even retrograde motion, though of little use in rhetoric, has its precedents and analogies in language, from the ancient Greek boustrophedon writing to a motet text of Josquin; on the latter, cf. Virginia CALLAHAN, '*Ut Phoebi radiis': The Riddle of the Text Resolved*, in *Josquin des Prez: Proceedings of the International Josquin Festival Conference*, ed. Edward E. Lowinsky, London, Oxford UP, 1977, pp. 560-563.

209 IV.i.15.

210 E.g. Gabriel François LE JAY, S. J. (1657-1734), *Ars rhetorica ad Tullianam rationem exacta*, Venice, Balleoniana, 1748, p. 250: "Quid sunt opposita, seu contraria? R[esponsum]: Sunt ea, quae in eodem subjecto vel esse non possunt, vel si in eodem fuerint, necessario inter se pugnant" ["What are opposites or *contraria*? R[eply]: They are those things which either cannot be in the same subject, or if they were there, necessarily conflict with each other"].

and were regarded as varieties of imitation.[211] Music theorists as late as Beethoven's teacher Johann Georg Albrechtsberger still knew of their debt to rhetoric and therefore designated the contrapuntal artifices as "figures": "Augmentation, diminution, abbreviation, syncopation, and stretto of the fugue subject are the main figures (adornments) and artifices in a fugue. Yet one can rarely employ all of them at once in a single fugue".[212] It has been demonstrated that Beethoven was challenged by this passage to write a *Große Fuge* which did employ all of the 'figures' and therefore was entitled "... tantôt recherchée".[213] He was undoubtedly aware that music theorists of the eighteenth century used the term 'ricercar' for a *Kunstfuge*, a fugue employing elaborate contrapuntal artifices.[214] And had not J. S. Bach devised an acrostic on the word 'ricercar' as a subheading in his *Musical Offering*, the most *recherché* composition of the baroque era, including a great variety of erudite canons and two "ricercars"?

With this work we come to a final problem in need of solution. It is well known that Bach left no clear indication of the sequence of components. Various modern reconstructions have issued from merely subjective, aesthetic criteria (David, Moser/Diener, Gerber, etc.). Christoph Wolff added greatly to their number,[215] then concluded by denying that Bach intended performance

---

[211] Cf. Bernardino PARTENIO, *Della imitatione poetica*, Venice, Ferrari, 1560, p. 17: "Havendosi dunque da imitare tutta una intera materia, mi pare che le si debba dare altro sesto et forma. Il che si farà col disponer, col dilatare, col ristringere, col mutare, con i contrarij" ["Having, then, to imitate an entire subject, it seems to me that one has to give it a different order and form. One will be able to do this by dilating [augmentation], restricting [diminution (or stretto)], mutating, [or] by *contraria* [contary motion or inversion]"].

[212] "die Vergrösserung (*augmentatio*), die Verkleinerung (*diminutio*), die Abkürzung (*abbreviatio*), die Zerschneidung (*syncope*), die Engführung (*restrictio*) des Fugenthema sind die Hauptfiguren (Zierlichkeiten) und Künste in einer Fuge. Doch kann man selten alle zugleich in einer einzigen Fuge anbringen", *Gründliche Anweisung zur Composition*, Leipzig, J. G. I. Breitkopf, 1790, p. 189. Only William JONES, *A Treatise on the Art of Music*, Colchester, the author, 1784, p. 43, explains augmentation, diminution, and imitation as "the figures of rhetoric ... transferred to music". Many other musical terms derived from rhetoric are listed below, p. 88, note 3. See above, p. 1, and note 2 for an explanation of the term 'figure'.

[213] W. KIRKENDALE, *Fugue and Fugato in Rococo and Classical Chamber Music*, Durham NC, Duke UP, 1979, pp. 262-265; also below, ch. 17. A review of a Mass by Beethoven's friend August Friedrich Kanne speaks of a "fuga ricercata", full of contrapuntal artifices – AmZ, XIII, 1811, col. 505f.

[214] See Marpurg and the other theorists quoted in *Fugue and Fugato, loc. cit.*

[215] *Der Terminus 'Ricercar' in Bachs Musikalischem Opfer*, «Bach-Jahrbuch», LIII, 1967, p. 72; *Ordnungsprinzipien in den Originaldrucken Bachscher Werke*, in *Bach-Interpretationen*, ed. Martin Geck, Göttingen, Vandenhoeck, 1969, pp. 157f; *New Research on Bach's Musical Offering*, «Musical Quarterly», LVII, 1971, p. 407; J. S. BACH, *Neue Ausgabe sämtlicher Werke*, Ser. VIII, Bd. I, Kassel, Bärenreiter, 1974; *ibid., Kritischer Bericht*, 1976, pp. 48f, 125 (nos. 1, 2, 4). Also the descriptions of the sources are contradictory – compare 1967, p. 72; 1969, p. 157; and 1976, pp. 48f.

as a cyclic composition.[216] He published in the new Bach edition a version beginning with the two ricercars in succession.[217] This is not a "sinnvolle Gliederung", but a sequence as meaningless as two exordia or two overtures in succession.

To understand Bach's two ricercars we must approach them through the archways of rhetoric, rather than through the narrow cellars of the 'pre-historic' diplomatic method, which reveals only one aspect. Spitta already observed that the three-part ricercar lacks the contrapuntal qualities of other fugues of Bach. Without being aware of the function of the sixteenth-century ricercars, he correctly characterized the piece as "präludienartig" and identified it with the fugue which Bach improvised on the *thema regium* during his audience with Frederick the Great in Potsdam.[218] After Eggebrecht clarified the distinctions between the improvisatory and imitative types of ricercar, Wolff (1967) applied this dichotomy to explain the very different character of Bach's two ricercars, designating the second as a later substitute for the second, six-part fugue which Bach had improvised at the king's request, now using the *thema regium* for the written composition.[219] The two ricercars thus correspond to the distinction made by Bach's friend Walther between the two types: "improvised and without preparation" and "composed artificially, through strong reflection".[220] But Walther's description of the first type is derived ultimately from Quintilian: "let the entire oration seem improvised, whose beginning displays nothing prepared".[221] And we now see that Bach's ricercars are carried by the much broader stream of Cicero's 'duplex' exordia: the direct *principium* and the carefully thought-out *insinuatio*. Also we find realized here, more perfectly than in any other music, the Ciceronian 'coherence', for the ricercars, sharing the *thema regium* with the other sections of the work, are like those exordia which draw their ideas from the body of the speech.

The key to the position of the two ricercars in Bach's work, hitherto overlooked, is the widespread practice of dual exordia. Quintilian taught that a

---

[216] 1969, p. 160; 1971, pp. 403f, 407f.

[217] Here he follows a contemporary newspaper advertisement – a mere summary of the components, not a table of contents – and disclaims any "Ordnungsgrundsätze" (1976, pp. 125f).

[218] Philipp SPITTA, *Johann Sebastian Bach*, Leipzig, Breitkopf & Härtel, 1873-80, II, 672f. Werner NEUMANN and Hans-Joachim SCHULZE, *Bach-Dokumente*, I, Kassel, Bärenreter, 1963, p. 241. Johann Nikolaus FORKEL, *Über J. S. Bachs Leben*, Leipzig, Hoffmeister & Kühnel, 1802, p. 10.

[219] In Potsdam Bach had not dared to use this for a six-part improvisation, but chose a theme himself – see FORKEL, *loc. cit.*

[220] "ex tempore und ohne praeparation" and "künstlich durch starckes Nachsinnen aufgesetzt" – p. 526.

[221] "videatur tota extemporalis oratio, cuius initium nihil praeparati habuisse manifestum est" – IV.i.54. See above, p. 38.

second exordium can be inserted before the *argumentatio*, parallel to the first one before the *narratio*.[222] In Ciceronian rhetoric the *principium*, as its name indicates, was used at the beginning; also an *insinuatio* could serve as a single initial exordium, but more characteristically it was the second of two, i.e. before the *argumentatio*. The speculations on Bach's "Ordnungsprinzipien" ignore the rhetorical basis of the composer's art in favor of an 'optical' approach. One arrangement favored by Wolff is 'symmetrical', with the trio sonata in the middle and the two ricercars framing the whole. But the works which he cites to support this view[223] are not symmetrical: the internal overtures in the *Goldberg Variations* and the suites of the *Klavierübung*, BWV 825-830, do not form a central axis, they open the second half of the group, just as the second ricercar does in the *Musical Offering*. In all these works it is not a question of symmetry, which would be inaudible anyway, but of a musical equivalent to, e.g., the second exordium in Virgil's *Aeneid*, at the beginning of the second half.[224] To place the second ricercar at the end would be like ending a speech with an exordium, or a concert with a prelude. As Ursula Kirkendale has proven in a sequel to this article (below, ch. 12, continued below, ch. 3), Bach modeled not only the sequence of movements, but also the total conception of the *Musical Offering*, in every stylistic detail, after Quintilian's *Institutio oratoria*; and the old Bach-Gesellschaft edition indeed presented the movements in the correct sequence. The components to follow the first ricercar correspond to the *narratio*, while those to come after the second are analogous to the *argumentatio* and *peroratio*.

The dual exordia of the *Musical Offering* are not without precedents in cyclical musical compositions. Bach knew not only Quintilian's treatise[225] but also Frescobaldi's *Fiori musicali* (Venice, Vincenti, 1635),[226] containing three organ Masses which all begin with a "toccata avanti la Messa" and insert a "ricercar dopo il Credo", that is, the same arrangement of *principium* and

---

[222] IV.iii.9. Chirius FORTUNATIANUS, *Artis rhetoricae libri III*, II.20, calls this second exordium "ananeosis": "Ananeosis quo differt a procemio? procemium in quacumque orationis parte potest poni, ananeosis autem non nisi post narrationem ante quaestiones" ["How does the *ananeosis* differ from the proem? The proem may be placed in any part of the oration, the *ananeosis*, however, nowhere except after the *narratio*, before the *argumentatio*"]. Also some later authors say that an exordium can be used wherever an important new topic is introduced: TOSCANELLA, *Libro primo*, f. 8v; DE NORES, f. 86v; PLATINA, pp. 538f.

[223] 1969, p. 154; 1971, p. 405.

[224] VII.37-45. Other examples of internal exordia may be seen in CICERO, *Pro lege Manilia*, VIII.20, *Philippica II*, XX.50, XXVIII.70; QUINTILIAN, IV-VIII, XII. Another 'internal exordium' by Bach is the 'French' chorale fughetta BWV 681, mentioned by Wolff, 1969, p. 154.

[225] NEUMANN/SCHULZE, II, 1969, pp. 331ff.

[226] See SPITTA, I, 418, on the copy in Bach's possession.

insinuatio as in the *Musical Offering*. These Masses can be understood only in the dual context of Roman liturgy[227] and rhetorical practice, not from a Protestant or abstract viewpoint. Their ricercars have been designated paradoxically as "postlude ricercars", "independent instrumental pieces" separated from the "Intonationsfunktion".[228] But a ricercar "after the Creed" is, of course, not a postlude to the Credo, but a prelude to what follows, for it marks the very basic division between the Liturgy of the Word ('Vormesse') and the Liturgy of the Eucharist ('Hauptmesse'). Toccata and ricercar thus correspond precisely to what a German ecclesiastical rhetorician called in 1713 the "general" and "special" exordia of the Mass, the first coming at the beginning, the second after the Lessons, before the real Mass: "After ... the Scripture has been read, follows the special exordium, with the function of preparing the spirits in the highest degree for the action at hand".[229] Frescobaldi invariably employs the *principium* (toccata) at the beginning of the Mass and the *insinuatio* (ricercar) after the Lessons and Credo, when, if I may use the words of an ancient rhetorician, "the mind of the listener has been fatigued by listening to those who spoke before"[230] and needs to be made attentive by subtle means. Though most collections of organ pieces, unlike the organ Masses, did not adhere to the liturgical sequence, organists doubtless selected from them the proper type of piece for the corresponding place in the Mass.

Iconologists and students of literary *topoi* have achieved impressive results by tracing the elements of artistic expression to specific passages of classical authors or the Scripture. Yet discussions of humanism in musicological writings have for the most part remained rather vague, rarely citing chapter and verse of ancient literature as is necessary if any influence of antiquity is to be argued convincingly. Having traced the repercussions of a few passages from Aristotle and especially Cicero on a vast musical repertoire from the sixteenth to the eighteenth century, I venture to say that classical literature – and not merely ancient music theory – holds the hidden keys which may explain many

---

[227] The interreaction of liturgy, rhetoric, and music in the Mass is an interesting problem worthy of further study. I have approached it in *L'Aria di Fiorenza*, Florence, Olschki, 1972, pp. 35-41 (a Mass by Banchieri) and below, ch. 15.

[228] WOLFF, in *Handwörterbuch*, s.v. 'Ricercar', p. 6.

[229] "Post ... praelectum textum, sequitur exordium speciale, cuius munus est, ad praesentem maxime tractionem animos praeparare", BÖHMER, p. 30.

[230] "animus auditoris ... defessus est eos audiendo qui ante dixerunt", *Ad Herennium*, I.v.9, on the *insinuatio*. Cf. CICERO, "when the case is difficult, ... when the mind of the listener is hostile" (quoted above), and QUINTILIAN, "si dicendum apud fatigatos est" ["if one must speak to tired persons" – IV.i.48].

musical phenomena of the Renaissance and Baroque, if we only look for them. Music too, though lacking ancient specimens, could not fail to be profoundly revitalized by the powerful 'Nachleben der Antike', particularly by the revival of ancient rhetoric, the "omnium artium domina" (Tacitus).

* * *

In an editorial published in 1949 Curt Sachs engaged himself in an imaginary conversation, where an "educated person" protests:[231]

I am not interested in the various structures of ballades or ricercari or the downward resolution of dissonances in the sixteenth century. I am, however, deeply interested in the destinies of music as an extreme expression of human individuals. ... Does none of your musicologists ever realize that music has more than technique, that it is part of the humanities?

And a general historian of culture admits:

I do not know what a ricercare is, nor am I particularly eager to grasp its details; but show me what a ricercare ... stands for in the history of the mind, and I will be earnestly interested.

The choice of the example was a better one than Sachs could have realized.

[*Continued in ch. 12*]

---

[231] JAMS, II, 4.

APPENDIX I

RHETORICAL CATEGORIES

GENERA CAUSARUM

Genus iudicale, forense (for accusation and defense in the courts of law)
Genus deliberativum (for persuasion and dissuasion, e.g. in legislative assemblies, council meetings)
Genus epideicticum, demonstrativum (for praise and censure, e.g. in public ceremonies)

GENERA DICENDI

Genus grande, grave, sublime
Genus medium
Genus subtile, humile

PARTES ARTIS

Inventio
Dispositio
Elocutio
Memoria
Actio, pronuntiatio

PARTES ORATIONIS

See below, p. 103, note 65

APPENDIX II

FURTHER REFERENCES TO THE RICERCAR AS EXORDIUM
(cf. above, p. 37)

Bernardo SEGNI (d. 1558), *Rettorica et poetica d'Aristotile tradotta di greco*, Florence, Tormentino, 1549, p. 215:

Il proemio ... è il medesimo ... che è nel suono la ricerca. ... La ricerca adunche ne' suoni è simile al principio dimostrativo.[232]	The proem ... is the same ... which the ricercar is in instrumental music. ... The ricercar, then, in instrumental music is similar to the epideictic *principium*.

---

[232] TOMMASEO, s.v. 'ricerca', refers to this passage, hence cited briefly in a footnote by EGGE-

Bartolomeo CAVALCANTI (1503-62), *La retorica*, Venice, De' Ferrari, 1559, p. 395:

I proemij in questo genere dimostrativo ... sono simili alle ricercate de i sonatori: percioché, sì come essi facendo quella ricercata, che vogliono innanzi alla canzone, la quale intendono di sonare, congiungono la canzone con la ricercata.	The proems in this epideictic *genus* ... are similar to the ricercars of the instrumentalists, because they, making that ricercar which they wish before the song they intend to play, join the song with the ricercar.

Oratio TOSCANELLA (ca. 1510-80), *La retorica di M. Tullio Cicerone ... ridotta in alberi*, Venice, Degli Avanzi, 1561, f. 2, reverses the analogy:

Ma propriamente proemio era quella ricercata.	But that ricercar was actually a proem.

Annibal CARO (1507-66), *La rettorica d'Aristotile fatta in lingua toscana*, Venice, Salamandra, 1570, p. 246:

Ma la ricercata è simile al proemio del genere dimostrativo. Che sì come i sonatori sonando prima qualche bel gruppo di fantasia, entrano successivamente nel tuono del mottetto, o del madrigale, che intendono di sonare.	But the ricercar is similar to the proem of the epideictic *genus*. As the instrumentalists, first playing some beautiful group of improvisations, subsequently enter into the key of the motet or madrigal which they intend to play.

Alessandro PICCOLOMINI, Bishop of Siena, *I tre libri della retorica d'Aristotele*, Venice, Varisco, 1571), p. 264:

Il proemio ... non è altro che ... appresso de i sonatori di tibie, o di flauti, quella prima sonata, che fanno di fantasia.	The proem ... is no other than ... the instrumental prelude improvised by the players of pipes or flutes.

Id., Piena et larga parafrase ... nel terzo libro della retorica d'Aristotele, Venice, Varisco, 1572, pp. 413ff:

Il proemio ... non è altro che ... appresso di quei musici, che suonano o flauti, o lire, o liuti, o cetere, o simile instrumento, vediamo havere a i mottetti, o alle canzoni, che sonar vogliono, elle prime sonate d'aria, & di fantasia,[233] che nel pigliar gli stromenti in mano, con un certo toccargli & trascorrergli	The proem ... is no other than those first instrumental pieces that we see among those musicians who play flutes, lyres, lutes, or citterns, or a similar instrument – pieces, either based on a standard progression or freely improvised, which they are accustomed to make for motets or canzonas they wish to play, [be-

---

BRECHT, *Der Terminus 'Ricercar'*, p. 143. SLIM, diss., pp. 425f, quotes an English translation of Aristotle's passage, and adds the Latin version of E. Barbaro, placing it more than half a century too late. No author pursues the rhetorical implications or mentions Cicero.

[233] Sonata d'aria = instrumental piece based on a standardized bass or harmonic progression ("Aria di Ruggiero", "Romanesca", etc.). Sonata di fantasia = freely composed or improvised piece which does not use a pre-existing cantus firmus or vocal model. On the former type of composition, cf. W. KIRKENDALE, *L'Aria di Fiorenza*, on the latter, Slim's dissertation and above, pp. 74f.

come a caso, soglion far prima, che vengano alla principal sonata. ... Il proemio [è simile] a quelle sonate di fantasia, che fanno i musici ricercando, & toccando vagamente i loro instromenti, prima che vengono alla sonata lor principale. ... Sì come coi proemij del gener giudicale tiene spetial somiglianza il prologo de i poemi ... così a proemij del gener demostrativo, la tengon quelle prime preparative sonate, che fanno i musici, la qual somiglianza, non solo consiste nella brevità (in cui la fa consister l'interprete greco), essendo così questi proemij demostrativi, come quelle prime sonate, principij brevi; ma molto più consiste nell'uso, & nel modo loro. Conciosiacosa che questi, ... prima che vengono a sonar la canzone, o'l mottetto che gli hanno in animo; se in qualche maniera di sonata si senton dotti, artificiosi & valenti, han per costume di prenderla come per un principio; & in esso vagando, & mostrando alquanto la loro eccellentia in quell'arte, finalmente con destro, & bel modo l'adattano & la congiungono (non ad una terza sonata di mezo ..., com'afferma un espositor latino [Pietro Vettori]) ma con la sonata principal stessa. Questo medesimo ha libertà di far l'oratore nelle cause demostrative; essendo egli libero in esse di potere per materia del suo proemio eleggere a modo suo quello, che più gli venga commodo, o che prima gli venga innanzi.

fore] arriving at the principal instrumental piece, taking the instruments in their hands, and touching and running over them in a certain manner, as if by chance. ... The proem [is similar] to those improvised fantasies which the musicians make, trying out (*ricercando*) and touching beautifully their instruments, before coming to their principal instrumental piece. ... Just as the prologue of poems has a special resemblance to the proems of the forensic genus, ... thus those first preparatory instrumental pieces made by musicians [are similar] to the proems of the epideictic genus. This similarity consists not only in their brevity (as defined by the Greek interpreter), these epideictic proems thus being, like those preludes, brief beginnings; but much more consists in their use and manner. Because these [musicians], ... before playing the song or motet which they have in mind, give with some kind of instrumental piece the impression of being learned, skilled, and clever, being accustomed to take it as a beginning. And rambling in it and showing somewhat their excellence in that art, finally in an adroit and beautiful manner they adapt it and join it (not to a third, intermediate instrumental piece ... as affirms a Latin commentator [Pietro Vettori]), but with the principal instrumental piece itself. The orator has the liberty to make the same in epideictic cases, being free there to select, in his own way, as subject matter for his proem that which he finds most comfortable or whatever first occurs to him.

Alessandro Car[r]iero (1548-1626), *Breve et ingenioso discorso contra l'opera di Dante*, Padua, Meietto, 1582, p. 46:

Aristotele ... dice il proemio degli oratori essere nelle loro orazioni il medesimo ch'è ... il ricercar dei musici nei loro suoni armonici.

Aristotle ... says that the proem of the orators in their speeches is the same as ... the ricercar of the musicians in their harmonies.

Giasone De Nores (1530-ca. 1590), *Della retorica*, Venice, Megietto, 1584, f. 86:

De i proemij, alcuni sono liberi, et sciolti, che solamente convengono al genere dimostrativo, i quali possiamo rassomigliare alle ricercate, che sogliono usar i musici a loro arbitrio,

Of the proems, some are free, which usually are suitable for the epideictic *genus*. We can compare them to the ricercars which the musicians are accustomed to use arbitrarily be-

II.1. Pietro Bembo. Titian [Tiziano Vecellio], oil on canvas, 94.5 × 76.5 cm., Washington, National Gallery. Cf. p. 50.

avanti che comincino a sonar o motteto, o madrigale, o canzone alcuna, sì come è quello di Isocrate ... in laude di Helena.[234]

fore they begin to play any motet, madrigal, or song, like that of Isocrates ... in praise of Helen.[234]

Lodovico CARBONE (d. 1597), *De dispositione oratoria*, Venice, Zenarus, 1590, p. 31:

Exordium in oratione, ut praeludium in cantu, et symphonia; ... atqui praeludium ... non est cantus, sive symphoniae pars.

The exordium in the oration, like the prelude in vocal and instrumental music; ... and the prelude ... is not part of this.

Francesco PANIGAROLA (1548-94, Bishop of Asti), *Modo di comporre una predica*, Venice, Vincenti, 1603, ff. 26*v*-27, 42*r-v*:

Quanto al prologhino diciamo, che questo non è parte di predica, sì come la ricercata non è del madrigale, ma è solamente un preludio, come concede anche Aristotele. ... Tuttavia deve il musico haver molt'avvertenza a far gentilmente quella ricercata, che egli vi promette prima, che se lo ponga a sonare. Perché ... da lei cavano subito i circonstanti quello che possono sperare della virtù del sonatore.

As for the little prologue, we say that this is not part of the sermon, just as the ricercar is not [part] of the madrigal, but is only a prelude, as also Aristotle concedes. ... However, the musician must take great care to make that ricercar pleasantly which he promises before he sets about playing. Because ... from it the [listeners] present perceive immediately what hopes they may have for the ability of the performer.

Id., Il predicatore, Venice, Giunti & Ciotti, 1609, p. 284:

Ma ad alcune altre cose gli [i.e. i prologhini] troviamo commodi; e fra l'altre ad operare quello, che oprano presso a musici le ricercate inanzi a madrigali. ... Apparecchia grandemente gli animi de gli ascoltanti il musico; ove prima, che entri a sonare il madrigale, alcuna ricercata, o fantasia, o gruppo vi prepone. ... Aristotile anche i veri proemi oratorij, nel genere dimostrativo permette, che siano sciolti dalla necessaria congiettura col rimanente dell'oratione a guisa di ricercate inanzi a musici componimenti.

But we find the little prologues useful for some other things, among others to fulfil that function which ricercars fulfil for musicians before madrigals. ... The musician greatly prepares the minds of the listeners, where before beginning to play the madrigal he prefixes some ricercar, fantasy, or group. ... Aristotle permits also true proems of orations in the epideictic genus, which are detached from the necessary connection with the rest of the speech in the manner of ricercars before musical compositions.

Gioseffo Maria PLATINA, *Arte oratoria*, Bologna, Benacci, 1716, p. 495:

Siccome i suonatori della ricercata s'insinuano nella suonata; così gli oratori dal proemio ... s'insinuano nell'assunto.

As the performers of the ricercar insinuate themselves into the instrumental piece, thus the orators insinuate themselves from the proem into the undertaking.

---

[234] I.e. the example given by Aristotle.

III.

ON THE RHETORICAL INTERPRETATION OF THE RICERCAR AND J. S. BACH'S *MUSICAL OFFERING*

When my wife and I published a pair of interrelated articles in 1979-80,[1] we hoped to have presented new conclusions, but did not claim to have introduced a novel method, for the basic principle of our approach was not new. Since historians of the arts aim at explaining works which were produced in remote times and places, the qualitatively greatest part of their work has consisted of overcoming chronological and geographical barriers. Their success in making the composers', poets', and artists' intentions understood – which should be considered the highest priority of their respective disciplines – has depended upon the degree to which they could reconstruct 'die verlorengegangenen Selbstverständlichkeiten', that complex network of roots which the work of art had in its own context. To arrive at this goal – for which there are no short cuts – the historian must attempt no less than to go through the same educational process, to subject himself to the same impressions and experiences which formed the thinking and thus the artistic productions of the author. He must also exclude systematically attitudes which originated only in his own time and place if he is to avoid doing violence to the work of art with anachronistic and irrelevant judgements. Especially American music historians working in the earlier periods of European music history in the 1950s, '60s and '70s often succeeded admirably in overcoming the above-mentioned barriers. They recognized that this could be accomplished only by voracious reading of the sources and literature from the composers' own time, sparing no effort (travel!) to gain access to such rare material in the old libraries and archives.

The vast area of musical rhetoric provides a particularly clear example of the necessity of restoring contemporary attitudes and eliminating modern

---

[1] Above, ch. 2, continued in ch. 12 (see pp. 601ff for various presentations and editions).

ones when studying works from the past. In our time, 'rhetoric' is generally understood as 'insincere speech', such as used by one's political opponents. And it no longer exists as a subject taught in schools and universities. Very few persons living in this context can imagine the supreme role of rhetoric in the educational system and thus in the artistic production of the Renaissance and Baroque. This *ars liberalis* was very highly regarded, not yet burdened with the negative connotations which became current only in the nineteenth century, with the ungrateful petty-bourgeois aesthetic of the 'original genius', with sentimental 'confessional' art, and the reaction against the rational aspects of artistic production. All human inventions, even worthwhile ones, can of course generate excess and abuse, and the modern negative view of rhetoric has focussed one-sidedly on its degeneration, ignoring that this discipline for centuries formed with good reasons the core and pinnacle of the curricula. Rhetoric embraced all aspects of literary style, including what today would be called literary criticism.[2] Investigations of artistic productions of the Renaissance and Baroque which ignore the supremely important *ars bene dicendi* do so at their own peril.

Writings on music, also by non-musicians, since the late sixteenth century refer continually to music as 'oratio', 'Klangrede', etc., and a large part of our musical terminology is derived from rhetoric.[3] The reasons for this are traceable back to the Renaissance with its immense respect for the culture of classical antiquity and the desire to imitate it. Here, composers were at a disadvantage because, unlike artists and men of letters, they had no ancient works which they could use as models. They discovered, however, with the help of the humanists' passion for ancient rhetoric, another, less direct way to benefit from antiquity. Thus they became increasingly aware that music has much in common with language, since it, like the spoken word, is perceived in time and through the ear. Like speech, it makes use of higher and lower pitch, volume, and styles, of slower and faster tempi, of a variety of repetitive formulas, of intended, effective *deviations* from the simplest for-

---

[2] Ernst Robert CURTIUS, *Europäische Literatur und lateinisches Mittelalter*, Tübingen/Basel, Franke, 1993[11], p. 435, is not alone in recognizing "that from Roman imperial times until the French Revolution all literary art was based on school rhetoric".

[3] Cf. p. 76 and the following: accidental, *Affekt*, ambitus, anticipation, auditor[ium], augmentation, breve, clausula, [isometric] color, compose, [*stile*] *concitato*, conjunct, consonance, contrary [motion], crescendo, decrescendo, *differentia*, diminution, disjunct, dolce, *dur*, exposition, extempore, figure, *genus*, grave, imitation, *interruptio*, invention (this term used as a title by Giovanni Battista Vitali 1689, Francesco Antonio Bonporti 1712, and J. S. Bach 1723 had long eluded explanation), inversion, *moll*, mutation, ornament, parody, partita, recapitulation, recital, [*recitativo*] *secco*, subject, suspension, syncopation, tempo, transition, trope, *Vortrag*.

mulations (i.e. of figures), of a more or less elaborate *dispositio*, and of expression of specific affects (including, in particular instances, praise; see below), etc. It was thus understood that the ancient rhetoricians, studied at every higher school and university, had much to offer to musicians.[4]

The rhetorical nature of music was still understood by Bach's first biographer Forkel and by Goethe,[5] only to be almost eclipsed until Arnold Schering and his pupils conducted the first modern musicological research on the subject.[6] In the meantime, a vast literature[7] – albeit of uneven quality – has appeared on musical rhetoric, and few music historians would deny the importance of the phenomenon. However, the predominantly German writers on the subject have unjustifiably narrowed their horizon by two limitations: 1) they focussed one-sidedly on the use of the figures, which belongs to *elocutio*, only one of the five *partes artis* (*inventio, dispositio, elocutio, memoria, actio;*[8]

---

[4] This is not understood by many musicians specializing in early music today. In an exaggerated reaction against the excesses of romanticism, many seem to believe that, in order to be historically 'authentic', music must be deprived of all expression and variety. The result is music which is no longer like eloquent language, as expected by audiences of the Renaissance and the Baroque, but is characterized by the rhetorical *vitium* of *monotonia*, as if performed by robots (cf., for example, the cold, arid rigidity of Glenn Gould or Robert Hill, etc. and, on the other hand, the eloquence of Emilia Fadini, who succeeds in making the harpsichord 'speak'). Here it is not realized that music, without coherent melody and without a judicious use of rubato, is dead (as I once learned especially from preparing the 'cello suites of J. S. Bach for public performances and for the master classes of Pablo Casals). Cf. the prophetic observation in Johann Joachim QUANTZ, *Versuch einer Anweisung die Flöte traversiere zu spielen*, Berlin, Voß, 1752, p. 113: "Man könnte eine musikalische Maschine durch Kunst zubereiten, daß sie gewisse Stücke mit so besonderer Geschwindigkeit und Richtigkeit spielte, welche kein Mensch ... nachzumachen fähig wäre. Dieses würde auch wohl Verwunderung erwecken, rühren würde es aber niemals" ["One could prepare a musical machine artificially, so that it played certain pieces with such particular velocity and correctness as no human being were capable of imitating. This would surely arouse amazement, but it would never move"]. Many German choirs now sing always with a brutal staccato, like barking dogs, destroying the melodic line; but an eloquent orator does not speak staccato. The tendency for string players to execute every note with a crescendo and diminuendo has a similar effect, comparable to a pedal harmonium gasping for breath. The mechanization of early music is not only analogous to, but also influenced by musicologists lacking comprehension of rhetoric – see the last paragraph of this article.

[5] Cf. Michael von ALBRECHT (professor of Latin, University of Heidelberg), *Musik und Rhetorik bei Goethe und Quintilian*, in *Musik in Antike und Neuzeit*, ed. *id.*, Frankfurt, Lang, 1987, pp. 31-50.

[6] It is easy for revisionist writers to find fault with Schering and Albert Schweitzer, who did not have the advantage of the musicological resources available today (and, in the case of Schweitzer, worked largely from intuition), but were undoubtedly on the right track and are certainly less harmful than the extreme reaction in the opposite, positivistic direction.

[7] The bibliography of George J. BUELOW, *Music, Rhetoric, and the Concept of the Affections*, «Notes», XXX, 1973/74, pp. 253-259, could be substantially expanded; my own file currently [1997] includes ca. 300 titles.

[8] *Actio* (*pronuntiatio*), especially as taught by Quintilian, is the subject of Don HARRÁN, *Toward a Rhetorical Code of Early Music Performance*, «Journal of Musicology», XV, 1997, pp. 19-41. The

see above, p. 82, for the terminology of rhetorical categories), and ignored the more elusive musical equivalent of *dispositio*, undeniably relevant for composers; 2) they documented their work almost exclusively with provincial north German music theorists of the Baroque and completely ignored not only the derivative postclassical rhetorical literature, but also – more important – the primary sources of all rhetorical teaching, i.e. the classical authors so widely read, especially in Italy in the fifteenth and sixteenth centuries, but also in other countries, foremost Germany, until the eighteenth, at least. With our pair of articles, we made a first attempt to remedy these deficiencies,[9] confronting the difficult problem of *dispositio* and drawing upon the real sources, those from classical antiquity.

In my article of 1979 (above, ch. 2) I applied to music something already well understood by literary historians: the *rhetorical* concept of *imitatio*,[10] which played such a predominant role in the artistic production of the Renaissance and Baroque. Chapters and entire treatises were often entitled *De imitatione* (Pietro Bembo 1513, Joachim Vidianus 1518, Étienne Dolet 1535, Bartolomeo Ricci 1541, Giulio Camillo Delminio 1544, Giovanni Pietro Capriano 1555, Bernardino Partenio 1560, Joh. Sambucus 1561, Roger Ascham 1570 [posth.], Joh. Sturm 1574, Giovanni Antonio Viperano 1579, Bartolomeo Zucchi 1600, Joachim Burmeister 1606, etc.). Like 'rhetoric', this term did not yet carry negative connotations; it did not imply 'copying' or 'aping', but choosing good models and adding something new to them, possibly even surpassing them. The relevance for music was quickly accepted by musicologists.[11] Howard M. Brown recognized the importance of the concept and took my article as a point of departure for his *Emulation, Competition, and Homage: Imitation and Theories of Imitation in the Renaissance*,[12] where he pursued further the musical implications. Considering the general lack of understanding of Latin rhetoric in the twentieth century,[13] it is not surprising

---

approach could be extended profitably to the work of QUANTZ, whose *XI. Hauptstück* begins: "Der musikalische Vortrag kann mit dem Vortrag eines Redners verglichen werden" ["The musical performance can be compared with the speach of an orator" – p. 46; examples follow].

[9] These characterize also the articles 'Rhetoric' in NG[1-2].

[10] Cf. above, pp. 54f, 65-68.

[11] E.g. J. Peter BURKHOLDER, *Johannes Martini and the Imitation Mass of the Late Fifteenth Century*, JAMS, XXXVIII, 1985, p. 503; letters to the editor by Leeman L. Perkins and Burkholder, *ibid.*, XL, 1987, pp. 133f, 137.

[12] JAMS, XXXV, 1982, pp. 1-48 (cf. p. 38, note 39).

[13] The connection has not yet been severed in Italy, closest to the source. I have heard President Oscar Luigi Scalfaro quote still relevant classical authors in the original language during public appearances, something one would not expect from Presidents Carter, Reagan, Clinton, or Bush jr., but certainly from President John Quincy Adams, author of a book on rhetoric (1810).

that such work would not be appreciated by writers who may not have enjoyed a classical/literary education and who prefer 'purely' musical analysis. They attempted to criticize our work, however, without acquiring familiarity with its basis, ancient rhetoric. The article of Honey Meconi of the University of Texas, *Does Imitation Exist?*,[14] though undertaking to deal with a key concept of rhetoric, does not cite classical or even postclassical rhetoricians, and its references to rhetoric are derived, with only one exception, from recent secondary literature in English. In her attempt to revise Brown and to answer negatively the question posed in the title of her article, she thus tends to ignore rhetorical considerations while assembling an impressive number of purely musical arguments against 'imitation', a concept which cannot be discussed without its rhetorical context.[15] Though some of these arguments may seem well reasoned, the article is flawed by a misunderstanding of the nature of rhetoric and of the analogies between language and music. The author seems unwilling to recognize that, just as imitation involves variation and original additions, analogies are not copies – otherwise they would cease to be analogies and become identities, in this case no longer music, but literature. Analogies between language and music have obvious limitations[16] and thus

---

[14] «Journal of Musicology», XII, 1994, pp. 152-178.

[15] For a useful corrective to Meconi's article, see the section "Imitatio" in Klaus Wolfgang NIE-MÖLLER, *Die musikalische Rhetorik und ihre Genese in Musik und Musikanschauung der Renaissance*, in *Renaissance-Rhetorik*, ed. Heinrich Plett, Berlin, De Gruyter, 1993, pp. 300-304. My own article (above, p. 67, note 157) is quoted by Meconi in a single footnote (p. 162, note 43) expressing surprise that I "even" implied that Gioseffo Zarlino imitated Quintilian's *Institutio oratoria* in formulating his title *Istitutioni harmoniche*. If one looks beyond music, one sees that he is, of course, only one of a number Renaissance authors who did this. I might add that Zarlino, like Girolamo Cavazzoni (cf. above, p. 68), imitated also the Ciceronian form of address in the dedication of his *Supplimenti musicali*, Venice, De' Franceschi, 1588. And in his *Dimostrazioni harmoniche, ibid.*, 1571, p. 210, he spoke of forming "a guisa dell'Oratore perfetto di Marco Tullio Cicerone un perfetto musico" ["a perfect musician in the manner of the perfect orator of Marcus Tullius Cicero"]. Some echoes of classical rhetoric in music-theoretical writings of the sixteenth century are mentioned also in Blake McDowell WILSON, *"Ut oratoria musica" in the Writings of Renaissance Music Theorists*, in *Festa Musicologica: Essays in Honor of George J. Buelow*, ed. Thomas J. Mathieson and Benito V. Rivera, Stuyvesant, Pendragon, 1995, pp. 341-361.

[16] As is well known from Joachim Burmeister's important, but not always successful attempts to apply the Greek names of rhetorical figures to music. Many of Burmeister's terms, however, are more useful than any other methods yet devised to describe music in words, because, as in literary studies, they recognize *topoi*, avoid lengthy circumlocutions, and emphasize the affinity with language (eloquence, expressive content, syntactical function). How much more concise and meaningful – to the initiated – is, for example, the term 'noema' than the description 'a brief homophonic interpolation in a polyphonic context', traditionally used to invoke, e.g., the name of a holy person and comparable to the use of larger type for such names in early printed texts (e.g. Bibles). Or 'hyperbole', defined by Burmeister as a voice rising above the upper limit of its ambitus, as frequently for words such as 'laus' ['praise'] and thus a component of epideictic musical rhetoric (for a very conspicuous example see below, pp. 441-444, Bach's canon referring to the fortune of the king).

cannot be expected to be complete in all aspects. Musical imitation will of course be different from literary imitation, will have aspects absent in literature, and will lack some of the characteristics of literary imitation, as Meconi took pains to demonstrate. But this by no means invalidates the analogy. Composers were free – or forced – to make a *selection* from the very large number of options and in many cases did this unconsciously. But they could not possibly escape a concept so firmly rooted in the thinking of their own era. I would *not* consider it a coincidence that the parody Mass was most widely cultivated precisely at the time when *imitatio* was most discussed in literature.[17] Johannes Frosch, in the index of his *Rerum musicarum opusculum* (Strasbourg, Schöffer & Apiarus, 1532), explicitly refers to his discussion of parody technique with the words "De imitatione authorum" [*sic*]. With an excess of postmodern scepticism, Meconi questions whether composers had any knowledge of rhetoric, presumably believing that this can be proven only by very specific documentation, such as references in composers' letters, or even records of their examinations in school, something which, however desirable, has not been found and probably will never come to light. But in the Renaissance and Baroque, the Seven Liberal Arts dominated the curriculum completely and did not have to compete with the multiplicity of modern subjects which threaten the very existence of the humanities today. And none of the seven received as much attention as rhetoric. The older European libraries are full of books on the subject. There must be good reasons for Cicero being one of the most published authors of all time and Quintilian going through ca. 130 [!] editions in the sixteenth century alone – to mention only the most famous. We are surely safe in assuming that *such books were very widely used* and that the subject was part of the awareness of all educated persons. For lawyers, preachers, statesmen, diplomats (called 'orators' in Venice!), teachers, men of letters, and, I would dare say, composers and artists – i.e. for most of the educated population of the time – it was an indispensable prerequisite for success.[18]

---

[17] Meconi objects that Masses based on models of the same composer [still exemplified by J. S. Bach's Mass in B minor] had no counterpart in literary *imitatio*. But the rhetorical literature recognizes the practice of self-imitation (cf. above, p. 67, the well known example of Petrarch).

[18] Also art historians have come to recognize its importance (cf. above, p. 33, note 1). In January 1996 an interesting congress was held by the Bibliotheca Hertziana (the splendid German institute for art history) and the Istituto Olandese in Rome, which began its title very appropriately with the most familiar of rhetorical concepts: *Docere – delectare – movere: Affetti, devozione e retorica nel linguaggio artistico del primo barocco romano*, illustrated by a concert of Gustav Leonhardt with music of Frescobaldi. For a few of the many rhetorical elements in Frescobaldi's music cf. Emilia FADINI, *L'aspetto retorico del linguaggio Frescobaldiano*, in *Girolamo Frescobaldi nel IV centenario della nascita*, Florence, Olschki, 1986, pp. 329-340; English translation in *Frescobaldi Studies*, ed. Alexander Silbiger, Durham, Duke UP, 1987, pp. 284-297.

Though biographical documents relevant to musical rhetoric may be rare, plenty of arguments for the rhetorical-musical method can be found in musical and theoretical sources. Modern writers who question the validity of this method betray a misunderstanding of rhetoric when they expect every observation of an analogy to be documented by a relevant source.[19] In the great majority of cases we have done this, but when we have not, the analogy does not become invalid. Rhetoric is a timeless, infinitely flexible and adaptable system, already perfected in antiquity, which was applied to almost all aspects of human thought. Just as even the simplest formulation in language is subjected to the rules of grammar, any expression going beyond this and assuming some degree of elegance, as associated with works of art in any time or place, immediately operates with rhetorical categories, whether the author is conscious of them or not.[20] It is therefore no more necessary to prove that a poet knew certain rhetorical treatises than it is to document his understanding of grammar. The same goes for musical rhetoric. Modern writers on music have, however, often taken music theorists too seriously, as infallible lawgivers. While theorists can be helpful in revealing contemporary attitudes (usually after the fact), they do not really constitute primary sources, and composers, especially in Italy where rhetoric is a natural mode of expression inherited from antiquity, did not need pedantic music theorists to make them aware of rhetoric.[21] They learned their art by *imitating* musical *exempla*, applying the principles of rhetoric learned in school.

* * *

Since the article of Paul Walker, *Rhetoric, the Ricercar, and J. S. Bach's «Musical Offering»*[22] bears directly on our work, I must discuss it in greater detail. Here the writer attempts to demonstrate that the imitative ricercar did

---

[19] I have emphasized elsewhere the necessity of insisting on documentation in biographical research, but also of daring to risk well-founded hypotheses when interpreting musical works within their historical context; cf. my *Court Musicians in Florence during the Principate of the Medici*, Florence, Olschki, 1993, p. 20, note 13. With my criticism of the excesses of one-sided positivism I do *not* wish to identify myself with Joseph Kerman's disparagement of well documented historical work and his interminable crusades to convert music historians into music critics.

[20] Cf. above, p. 31.

[21] As observed, with reference to Bach, also by E. Fred FLINDELL, *Bach's Tempos and Rhetorical Applications*, «Bach: Journal of the Riemenschneider Bach Institute», XXVIII, 1997, pp. 154-157. Thus we by no means imply that every rhetorical effect observable in music is attributable to the direct influence of a rhetorician. Though I once demonstrated that Beethoven took a theoretical work, one dealing *inter al.* with musical-rhetorical figures, as the point of departure (no more) for a musical composition, the *Grande Fugue ... tantôt recherchée*, Op. 133, this must be regarded as an exceptional case; cf. ch. 17.

[22] *Bach Studies*, II, ed. Daniel R. Melamed, Cambridge UP, 1995, pp. 175-191.

not have a preludial function[23] and that thus not only the rhetorical *dispositio*, but the entire conception argued by Ursula Kirkendale for the *Musical Offering* is unfounded. Like Meconi, Walker makes numerous purely musical points which might appear convincing if they did not ignore precisely the rhetorical context which he undertakes to criticize. Here too, notwithstanding the word "rhetoric" in the article's title, classical rhetorical texts are not cited. The new arguments are drawn almost exclusively from the German musical and theoretical sources with which he has familiarized himself through the work on his dissertation.[24] But we are dealing here with an *Italian* word, 'ricercare', and with a repertoire which was produced almost exclusively in Italy. If, as Walker concedes (p. 189), the numerous quotations from Italian authors in my article prove beyond all doubt that this word, with reference to the free ricercars of the lutenists, had primarily a rhetorical meaning, designating a musical equivalent to the orator's exordium, how, then, can we possibly conclude that this meaning was suddenly forgotten when the name was applied, still in Italy, to imitative ricercars?[25] Language, particularly sixteenth-century Italian, deserves more respect than this! Since the designation was retained, some concept must have linked the two quite different types of music, and since it cannot have been the *style*, it must have been the preludial *function*, especially in view of the two very different types of rhetorical exordia (free and strict, i.e. 'Aristotelian' and 'Ciceronian', or, to quote only Cicero, *principium* and *insinuatio*), so closely analogous to the two musical styles. Since the word 'ricercar' *meant* 'prelude' in Italy, it was no more necessary to specify this in musical practice than to say 'prelude means a musical introduction'.[26] That the bulk of the Italian literary testimonies relates to the free ricercar is not because their authors did not consider the imitative ricercars to be preludes; it

---

[23] This criticism was repeated in a paper of Markus GRASSL, *Überlegungen zur Vor- und Frühgeschichte des Ricercars*, presented in October 1996 at the annual meeting of the Gesellschaft für Musikforschung in Regensburg and kindly sent to me by him after completion of my article. Since he has already made his criticism of my research known publicly, I cannot pass over it in silence, though it was already refuted in my manuscript of this article. I informed him of this, and he may possibly modify his views, making some of my counterarguments irrelevant to him, but not necessarily to others who may write on the subject in a similar manner. – Leo SCHRADE, *Die ältesten Denkmäler der Orgelmusik als Beitrag zu einer Geschichte der Toccata* (diss., Leipzig, 1927), Münster, Helios, n.d., p. 9, seems to have been the first musicologist to recognize "the meaning of the proem" in the organ ricercar.

[24] *Fugue in German Theory from Dressler to Mattheson*, ms. diss., State University of New York at Buffalo, 1987.

[25] Cf. Jeppesen's observation and Apel's well motivated but unanswered question quoted above, p. 49.

[26] Grassl's construction "Präludien-Ricercar" can thus be regarded only as a pleonasm, not as a means of distinguishing the free ricercar from the imitative.

is simply because these writers are commenting, directly or indirectly, on a famous simile of Aristotle. Cicero's treatment of the exordium provided no new simile which would have inspired such 'musical' commentaries. The commentators were men of letters, preoccupied with the functions of language, not musicians who might have been interested in making technical distinctions for future musicologists.

As is well known, *both* types of ricercars, free and imitative, were arranged in collections (like the separate collections of orators' exordia) and identified like other preludial pieces (toccatas!) by modes or keys, *precisely in order to facilitate matching the music which followed*, i.e. for their function as *preludes*.[27] This arrangement is one of the most tenacious organizational principles in music, extending at least from the time of Aristotle to the medieval tonaries and the 24 preludes Op. 28 by Chopin.[28] And in this enormous repertoire, the choice of the first piece was left to the performers, not prescribed by the composers. Only in rare instances are we able to reconstruct a sequence of two pieces, even in the case of the obviously preludial free ricercars.[29] Thus it is by no means necessary, as Walker believes, to cite pairs of movements (pp. 182f: "ricercars ... explicitly linked ... to particular vocal pieces") in order to prove that the imitative ricercars fulfilled a preludial function.

Curiously, one very important and relevant instance of imitative ricercars functioning as preludes is used by Walker to argue the opposite: he believes that the ricercars "dopo il Credo" in Frescobaldi's organ Masses (1635) have a "non-preludial function", whereas they serve, like the internal exordia of rhetoric, to introduce the second main section, the 'Mass of the Faithful'

---

[27] Not only the ricercar, but almost all instrumental music of the sixteenth century, with exception of dances and intabulations of vocal music, had a preludial function, not to mention more or less interchangeable nomenclature (p. 40). Murray BRADSHAW, *The Origin of the Toccata*, American Institute of Musicology, n.p., 1972, has argued that the organ toccata derived from the *intonazione*. The modal designations were already common for the free ricercars, and there is no reason to assume that they did not indicate a preludial function also for the imitative ricercars, as for the toccatas. This nomenclature is most consistently applied in the complete cycles arranged in numerical sequence of modes by Andrea and Giovanni GABRIELI, *Intonationi d'organo ... libro primo*, Venice, Gardano, 1593 (one cycle by each composer), A. GABRIELI, *Ricercari ... libro secondo*, ibid., 1595 (one cycle), and Giovannbattista FASOLO, *Annuale*, Venice, Vincenti, 1645; see the tables of contents in Claudio SARTORI, *Bibliografia della musica strumentale italiana ...*, Florence, Olschki, 1952, pp. 81, 396f.

[28] Above, p. 44. Maria Grazia SITÀ, *Preludi, fantasie, capricci: modi dell'improvvisazione nella musica per tastiera italiana tra Settecento e Ottocento*, thesis, Conservatorio di Milano, 1991/92, p. 36, lists two dozen collections of preludes in all keys, ca. 1762-1828.

[29] These exceptions which prove the rule are mentioned above, p. 41. They do not include Tiburtino's ricercars; as WALKER rightly points out (p. 183), these were hardly intended as preludes to vocal pieces by Josquin.

('Mass of the Eucharist'), following the 'Mass of the Catechumens' ('Mass of the Word').[30] This position of the ricercar in the liturgy is confirmed also by Banchieri, Bottazzi, Croci, and Fasolo.[31] At St. Mark's in Venice, where most of the early composers of imitative ricercars were employed, the organ did not *replace*, but surely *introduced* a vocal Offertory following the Credo, because the *alternatim* practice, where the organ replaces alternate verses, was not used there for polyphonic Masses.[32] This would seem to apply generally, for musical sources do not combine substitute organ pieces designated by liturgical text-incipits (i.e. components of 'organ Masses') with vocal polyphony.[33] Since ricercars 'dopo il Credo', on the other hand, do not bear such designations, they did not serve as a substitute for (or, more correctly, an accompaniment to the spoken) Offertories even of plainsong Masses, but as preludes to them.[34] Thus the *Caeremoniale Episcoporum* – first published in 1600 and frequently reprinted – very clearly prescribes organ music immediately after the Credo only "ad offertorium".[35] This was the first musical item of the 'Hauptmesse', occurring at the point in the liturgy where, for centuries to come, music without specific liturgical designation was most widely used. Lutheran musicians would have little awareness of this usage, because their polyphonic *Missae breves* (Kyrie + Gloria) concluded already with the 'Wortmesse'. The Offertorium, that part of the Roman liturgy to which the Lutherans objected most strenuously, was eliminated, and the rest of the music consisted mostly of German chorales. The ricercars, having no stylistic relationship to this music, were replaced by the chorale preludes.

---

[30] Above, pp. 79f.

[31] Adriano BANCHIERI, *L'organo suonarino*, Venice, Amadino, 1605, p. 38; Bernardino BOTTAZZI, *Choro et organo*, Venice, Vincenti, 1614; Antonio CROCI, *Frutti musicali, ibid.*, 1642; FASOLO, *op. cit.*: "Se li Graduali Offertorij saranno troppo brevi, potranno sonare una Ricercata". Cf. SARTORI, pp. 195, 382, 396.

[32] James H. MOORE, *The Liturgical Use of the Organ in Seventeenth-Century Italy: New Documents, New Hypotheses*, in *Frescobaldi Studies* cit., p. 367.

[33] Andreas MIELKE, *Untersuchungen zur Alternatim-Orgelmesse*, Kassel, Bärenreiter, 1996, pp. 77f.

[34] MIELKE does not deal with them, not because they were not used in the Mass, but because his dissertation is limited to organ pieces played in alternation with plainsong and bearing liturgical titles derived from the chants they replaced. Frescobaldi's organ Masses are exceptional in including ricercars together with such pieces, but at the same time they serve as a valuable indication of their location in the liturgy. Normally the ricercars were either selected by the organists from the collections or improvised. On the improvisation of ricercars as a test for applicants for organists' positions, cf. Arnaldo MORELLI, *Concorsi organistici a San Marco e in area veneta nel Cinquecento*, in *La cappella musicale di S. Marco nell'età moderna*, Venice, Fondazione Levi, 1998, p. 261.

[35] *Caeremoniale Episcoporum iussu Clementis VIII*, Romae, ex typographia linguarum externarum, 1600, p. 135; repeated literally in editions of 1606, 1614, 1633, 1651, 1670, 1713, 1727, 1729, 1732 (Frankfurt), etc.

Most of both Catholic and Protestant organ repertoire, including improvisation, had a clearly preludial function right up to the twentieth century.
Thus Biagio Rossetti referred to organists who played "praeambula ... super
missarum partibus ex tempore".[36] Beethoven still spoke of "Preludien [plur-
al!] zu meiner Messe [Op. 86]" and "Preludieren des Kyrie von organisten".
In his time 'preludieren' still meant 'to improvise'.[37] And Bach's *principium*-
type ricercar *a 3*, of course, fulfilled the challenge to improvise on a given
theme, to exhibit the "ex tempore dicendi facultas", regarded by Quintilian
as "maximus vero studiorum fructus", indispensable for the forensic orator
(X.vi.1).

In attempting to dissociate the imitative ricercar from any function and
regarding it as part of a "purely musical tradition", as "contrapuntal writing
in its purest and most distinguished form" (pp. 178, 183, 191), Walker embraces a discredited, late nineteenth-century view of 'absolute' music (Hanslick's fatal "tönend bewegte Form" [music = "sounding form in motion"],
which unfortunately escalated in the twentieth century, with catastrophic results).[38] This notion, implying that any music which has a function is 'impure',
is anachronistic in pre-romantic music, which had very specific functions and
was not ashamed of them. This is especially true for music like the organ repertoire, which was part of the liturgy. In view of what has been said in chapter 2 and above (ch. 3) we must ask: to what extent does Walker's category of
"independent [i.e. liturgically irrelevant] pieces" for organ exist at all in the
middle of the eighteenth century? And if the ricercars did not have a preludial
function, what were they used for? Discussions of the ricercar which completely ignore both rhetoric and liturgy – the two highly important spheres in
which the genre was so firmly anchored – cannot begin to explain this music.

I do not doubt that at least the more provincial Protestant musicians in
Germany, the country from which Walker draws his arguments, no longer understood the rhetorical meaning of the foreign word 'ricercare'. Though the
revival of classical antiquity emanating from Italy in the Renaissance was so
immensely powerful as eventually to penetrate and dominate the thought
and art even of transalpine countries, its assimilation there required an addi-

---

[36] *Libellus de rudimentis musices*, Verona, Nicolini, 1529, sig. n ij*v*.

[37] Cf. below, pp. 522f, with notes 112, 114.

[38] The discreditation of this view, as applied to the *Musical Offering*, is mentioned by WOLFF,
New Reseach on Bach's «Musical Offering», «Musical Quarterly», LVII, 1971, p. 400, and Michael
MARRISSEN, *The Theological Character of J. S. Bach's «Musical Offering»*, in *Bach Studies* cit., II, 86.
The idolization of Bach in Germany and the U.S. resulted from an overrating of cerebral counter-
point (not to mention German chauvinism) and a disregard for southern elegance. Cf. Anselm GER-
HARD, *Händels Musik gegen Bachs Liebhaber verteidigt*, «Händel-Jahrbuch», L, 2004, pp. 285-306.

tional intellectual effort, compared to Italy, where people lived with the ancient culture and experienced it as second nature.[39] In the case of the ricercar, the general awareness of the rhetorical function was clearly weakened by the Protestant mutilation of the Latin liturgy (comparable to the *Bilderstürme* of the Reformation and the damage done to mankind's greatest musical heritage in our own time by the Second Vatican Council). As a result, many Protestant musicians, some possibly misled also by Praetorius (see below), were probably no longer aware of the use of imitative ricercars as preludes to one of the two major subdivisions of the Tridentine Mass, the second of which they no longer supplied with Latin polyphonic music. But Bach, though a devout Lutheran, was not a bigoted one. He wrote not only Lutheran *Missae breves*, but, unlike most Protestant composers, also a "große catholische Messe" in B minor (albeit a kind of auto-parody assembled over a longer period). He possessed copies of Frescobaldi's organ Masses, a Mass of Palestrina, and six of Giovanni Battista Bassani.[40] This indicates not only that he was well aware of the full structure of the Mass, but also that his knowledge of the Italian ricercar was transmitted to him especially via Frescobaldi.

According to Walker (p. 186), the title of Chapter X of Michael Praetorius' *Syntagma Musicum*, part II,[41] is "extremely damaging" to my arguments, for it classifies the ricercar among the "independent pieces which Praetorius calls *praeludiis* [*recte: praeludia*][42] *vor sich selbst*". But with this title Praetorius still explicitly designates the ricercars as preludes [!], though he no longer seems to have understood their specific function. The reason for this is very clear and simple. The Italian organ ricercars, as musical equivalents to the *insinuatio*-type exordia, were normally used not at the beginning, but as the *internal* preludes within the Mass, introducing the Mass of the Eucharist.[43]

---

[39] This is certainly a reason why it was possible for the Italian language to achieve an unsurpassed elegance already in the fourteenth century while German still remained crude and awkward in the eighteenth. It is also a reason why in Italy public latrines, first installed in Rome by Emperor Vespasian, could still be called 'Vespasiani' in modern times. I mention this not to entertain readers, but simply to illustrate the immense tenacity and general awareness of ancient traditions in Italy. Many more examples could easily be added.

[40] Kirsten BEIßWANGER, *Johann Sebastian Bachs Notenbibliothek*, Kassel, Bärenreiter, 1992, nos. I/F/2, I/P/2, I/B/48.

[41] Wolfenbüttel, the author, 1619, p. 21.

[42] Praetorius knew, of course, that the declination of Latin nouns must be respected, also when they are quoted in a German context ("Von den *praeludiis* vor sich selbst").

[43] The internal exordium of the Mass was known in Germany: cf. p. 80 with note 229 (Böhmer 1713); Paul GRAFF, *Geschichte der Auflösung der alten gottesdienstlichen Formen in der evangelischen Kirche Deutschlands*, Göttingen, Vandenhoeck & Ruprecht, 1937-39, I, 171; and D. William NAGEL, *Geschichte des christlichen Gottesdienstes*, Berlin, De Gruyter, 1970, pp. 174f: in the services of the Protestant church of St. Nicolai in Berlin, 1778, the 'Glaubenslied' was followed by an exordium.

When this 'Opfermesse'[44] was curtailed by the Lutherans, the imitative ricercars were left dangling "vor sich selbst" ["by themselves"]. In this way they came to be misunderstood as "independent pieces" by Protestant musicians and musicologists. Their 'Wortmesse', on the other hand, continued to be introduced by free, often chordal preludes, the counterparts of the *principium*-type exordia preferred at the beginning of an oration. Thus German musicians never had any difficulty in recognizing the preludial function of toccatas.

A fundamental error committed by Walker (and by his uncritically accepted German authority Praetorius) and misattributed by him also to me is his equation of 'ricercar' with 'fugue' (pp. 184; 189: "ricercar/fugue", "fugue/ricercar").[45] Since a preludial function has not often been documented for fugues,[46] Walker would exclude also the imitative ricercar from this function. But it is precisely to dissociate his ricercars from fugues which follow preludes in eighteenth-century Germany, familiar from *Das Wohltemperierte Klavier*, that Bach uses the designation 'ricercar', a genre which has no established tradition of following preludes. The rare instances of the pairing of a very brief free prelude and a much longer imitative ricercar,[47] which have been used as an argument against the preludial function of the ricercar,[48] actually confirm their composers' adherence to the letter of the rhetorical doctrine of the exordium, albeit in these cases mistranslated from the Latin. It very probably resulted from an easy misinterpretation of Cicero's famous definition of the exordium in his *De inventione*, the most widely used textbook of rhetoric in the schools: "Igitur exordium in duas partes dividitur: principium et insinuationem".[49] As only to be expected, some composers took this to mean "The exordium, then, is divided into two parts [i.e. sections]: the

---

[44] The relationship to «Musikalisches Opfer» could be more than coincidental – cf. below, p. 107, 'gloria'.

[45] Years ago, Ursula Kirkendale already corrected in correspondence with colleagues this imprecision committed herself, with reference to the three-part ricercar (*The Source*, 1980, p. 96, where, however, she had stressed the non-fugal elements of the piece). Though its episodes have long been recognized as free, improvisatory, Marissen curiously would regard them as "learned" (*op. cit.*, p. 92).

[46] It was done by Adriano Banchieri in 1605 and 1611, where 'fuga' is to be understood as a brief imitative piece, rather than as a 'fugue' in the later sense. Cf. Stephen BONTA, *The Uses of the Sonata da Chiesa*, JAMS, XXII, 1969, p. 72. An anonymous 18th-century *Messa in sesto tono* includes a "Fuga per l'Offertorio" – *Musiche pistoiesi per organo*, ed. Umberto Pineschi, Brescia, 1988², fasc. 1, p. 42.

[47] Five ricercars in ms. 244 from the library of Laurence Feininger in Trent, two in Frescobaldi's *Fiori musicali*, one by J. H. Buttstedt, and one in I-Bc ms. 360A.

[48] WALKER, p. 186.

[49] I.xv, quoted more fully on p. 57.

principium and the *insinuatio*", rather than "divided into two species or types", an error understandably committed also by Alfred Dürr in a letter of 12 September 1980 to Ursula Kirkendale. (Cicero himself, with his immediate continuation of this passage, left no doubt as to his meaning,[50] and the translations, paraphrases, and derivatives of his work rightly understand "partes" to mean not "sections", but "species"). Thus when Frescobaldi couples a toccata of only 13 or 14 semibreves with a ricercar of 56 or 69 breves in the same key, he surely intends this as two parts of a single prelude.[51] One genre very widely diffused in Bach's time, the French overture, also included a fugal movement as the second, major component of a single prelude, and I assume that no one would question the latter's preludial function.

In order to deny the ricercar such a function, Walker then, like Marissen (see below, p. 114), equates it with fugue, a genre which for music-historical laymen is synonymous with the *Well-Tempered Clavier*, part of a repertoire of preludes + fugues which is chronologically and geographically much more limited than that of the ricercar. But the Italian imitative ricercar, with its inconspicuous ('insinuated') entries and rhetorical *genus grave* or *stylus ecclesiasticus* (*stile antico*), i.e. permeated by the *gravitas* so widely documented for both musical *and* literary exordia,[52] is not equivalent to the north German fugue, which is characterized by clearly marked entries and often has lively, even dance-like subjects.[53] Nor were the *gravitas* and artifices already typical of the free, 'Aristotelian' ricercars for lute, but resulted only from the application

---

[50] *Loc. cit.*: "Principium est ..." and "Si non ..." on the one hand, and "Insinuatio est ..." and "utendum est ..." on the other. Cf. also p. 64, Dressler.

[51] The suspicion is justified that the pairs of preludes (toccatas, fantasias, etc.) and fugues in the late German Baroque – undoubtedly used in the church – might have some connection with this misreading of Cicero's text, though it must be emphasized that most of these fugues are not characterized by exordial-*insinuatio* style consistently used for ricercars (see next paragraph). That such errors may be fruitful and thus need not be judged negatively was pointed out by Erwin PANOFSKY in the penultimate public lecture delivered before his death: *The Value of Error in the History of Art*, Duke University, 4 Nov. 1967.

[52] Cf. pp. 70-73 This style was still intentionally adopted by Beethoven in the "Preludium" [*sic*] for the Elevation in his *Missa solemnis* – cf. p. 521.

[53] That also fugues were fraught with rhetorical elements has been convincingly demonstrated by Gregory G. BUTLER, *Fugue and Rhetoric*, «Journal of Music Theory», XXI, 1977, pp. 49-109. Daniel HARRISON, *Rhetoric and Fugue: An Analytical Application*, «Music Theory Spectrum», XII, 1990, pp. 1-42, though much indebted to this important and original article, practices unnecessary and offensive criticism of it (e.g. p. 1), not appreciating/understanding its legitimate historical method, but preferring "present-day [i.e. anachronistic, quasi-Schenkerian] analytical tools". Most of his valid observations merely confirm and supplement those of Butler, but they soon become bogged down in arid descriptive minutiae (esp. pp. 10-39) such as often render analytical articles unreadable; one cannot see the forest for the trees.

of essential features of the Ciceronian exordial style to music. Thus I never implied that the "supporting evidence for a rhetorical analogy to the exordium ... consist[ed] almost exclusively of an Italian translation of Aristotle" (Walker, pp. 190f).[54] As my article amply demonstrated, the analogies between the imitative ricercar and the Ciceronian *insinuatio*-type exordium are *more numerous, varied, and specific* than those between the free ricercars and Aristotle. Only when a fugue made extensive use of contrapuntal artifices was it designated, by those German theorists who still understood the terminology, as a "fuga ricercata", i.e. qualified by a past participle derived from a different genre.[55] And it is precisely such artifices – *imitatio* [! – see above, pp. 90ff] in augmentation, diminution, inversion etc., all having their counterparts in rhetoric and therefore called 'figures' by musicians[56] – which had made the ricercar the musical equivalent of the Ciceronian exordium at its most elaborate, as only to be expected from its origins in Bembo's circle.[57] When J. S. Bach employed the antiquated Italian term so prominently, with all its rhetorical associations, for two ricercars and an acrostic in his *Musical Offering* – and only there – he thus had a good reasons for doing so and surely knew what it meant.[58] This was not because King Frederick's musical taste was conservative, as stated by Walker (p. 190), for it is well known that it was quite the opposite. But it could have something to do with the fact that the king was an ardent Ciceronian, and it surely announced Bach's rhetorical intention with this work, demonstrated by so many other arguments as well (see below).

---

[54] Aristotle's concept was, however, still very much alive in the nineteenth century – cf. p. 46, note 66, the quotation from Kalkbrenner; M. von ALBRECHT, *Musik und Rhetorik*, pp. 36f (especially Goethe's words "seine Flöte *versuchen*" and "preludieren ... *ohne Gesetz*" ["to *try out* his flute" and "to play preludes ... *without rules*"]; cf. the Italian word 'ricercare' and, above, p. 38, note 23, the two quotations "senza ... legge"). SITÀ, pp. 15, 22, 32, 34, presents additional late echoes of Aristotle, without recognizing them as such: C. P. E. Bach 1762, F. Galeazzi 1791, C. Gervasoni 1800, P. Lichtenthal 1836, C. Czerny 1836.

[55] W. KIRKENDALE, *Fugue and Fugato*, p. 264.

[56] As first pointed out above, pp. 76f.

[57] Grassl rightly adds Ferrara to Venice as an early center of ricercar composition, while overlooking the role of Rome and Urbino (above, p. 51) and completely ignoring the powerful literary currents in which these composers were immersed in these cities (Ciceronianism; the presence of Bembo and the many other rhetoricians identified *op. cit.*). He attaches undue importance to the use of imitative writing for instruments before G. Cavazzoni, already identified p. 48, note 71, which cannot explain the sudden and massive influx of this style in ricercars. Particularly overstated is his case for the didactic repertoire, which as a mere means to an end (instruction) loses its significance once the end has been achieved; the elaborate organ ricercars for the Venetian liturgy are anything but 'secular', pedagogical exercises for students.

[58] Christoph WOLFF, *Der Terminus 'Ricercar' in Bachs Musikalischem Opfer*, «Bach-Jahrbuch», LIII, 1967, p. 80, could assume that Frederick understood the term 'ricercar' to signify the two different types of preludes, as defined by Johann Gottfried Walther in 1732.

We would not expect Bach to have written a chordal, homophonic prelude as his first exordium, for the *thema regium* was not suitable for such treatment, and he wished to demonstrate his characteristic contrapuntal mastery, even in an improvisation, at the court. But the improvisatory aspects of the three-part ricercar have caused authors since Spitta rightly to associate it with the impromptu performance at Potsdam, and eventually with the freer type of preludial ricercar, analogous to the *principium*-type exordium.[59]

Some of the objections advanced by Walker had come to mind while preparing my article, but I did not consider them serious enough to jeopardize the case which I was making. By now it should be clear why I did not insist on more explicit documentation for the preludial function of ricercars in Germany. This would be neither necessary nor reasonable, because not only was this country's production of ricercars almost negligible, compared to that of Italy; its literature contains hardly any references to specific functions also of other types of baroque instrumental church music, much of which had no prescribed place in the Lutheran service.[60] Even in Italy, the printed collections of such music contain very few specific instructions for the use in the liturgy. This indicates that traditions were well established and explanations were not considered necessary,[61] least of all for pieces with the caption 'ricercar', understood by natives to mean 'prelude'. Also, I quoted Dressler's description of the two different exordial styles (*plenum et nudum*) fully realizing that this theorist was referring not to instrumental preludes, but to the opening section of motets,[62] which, in turn, could be preceded by preludes. Though I may quote theorists for what they are worth, I certainly do not rely heavily upon them, as Walker suggests (p. 184; cf. above, p. 93), least of all on German writers such as Herr Schulz alias Praetorius, a preacher's son totally immersed in his Lutheran context, whom one cannot regard as an authority on the complexities of Italian liturgy.[63] In the case of Dressler, I

---

[59] P. 78.

[60] W. KIRKENDALE, *Fugue and Fugato*, p. 22. Protestant German songbooks and *Kirchenordnungen* of the sixteenth century almost never mention the organ (which does not mean that it was not used), regarded by Luther as "des römischen Abgottes Baal Feldzeichen" ["banner of the Roman idol Baal"]; cf. Georg RIETSCHEL's learned treatise, *Die Aufgabe der Orgel im Gottesdienst bis in das 18. Jahrhundert*, Leipzig, Dürr, 1893, pp. 23-25, 40. As is well known, the overzealous Calvinists destroyed many precious organs.

[61] As observed by BONTA, p. 54.

[62] Dressler's rudimentary *dispositio* has been discussed by Howard M. BROWN, *Clemens non Papa, the Virgin Mary, and Rhetoric*, in *Musicologia Humana: Studies in Honor of Warren and Ursula Kirkendale*, Florence, Olschki, 1994, pp. 139-156. See below, p. 118, note 137, and p. 423, note 29, on the *dispositio* in music of Dufay, Corelli, Bach, and Marcello.

[63] Praetorius himself regretted that he was never able to visit Venice, to study music at its

merely called attention to a close stylistic relationship between instrumental and vocal exordia (the rhetorical term used by Dressler) of both types and to this dichotomy in rhetoric (the *principium* and the *insinuatio*, respectively).

It is not surprising to see that the function of the imitative ricercar, for which Walker, unnecessarily excluding Praetorius (cf. above, p. 98: "praeludiis"), found little evidence in Protestant Germany, was still understood in Catholic countries long after Bach's death. What more indication of this is needed than the definition of the ricercar as a "prélude fugué" [!] by Honoré François Marie Langlé (1741-1807)?[64] In this connection, we may remember that the preferred language of the Prussian aristocracy and especially of the king himself was French. However, a more eloquent and accurate testimony than any music theorist could provide has been found in a unique German composition, the *Musical Offering*, with its exemplary adherence to the rhetorical theory and practice of the exordium (initial and internal) as well as of the other *partes orationis*.

* * *

Proceeding from the exordium/ricercar to the *dispositio* of the following *partes orationis* (*exordium/principium – narratio – exordium/insinuatio – argumentatio – peroratio*) as demonstrated for the *Musical Offering*,[65] I address a principal criticism by Wolff and Walker of Ursula Kirkendale's interpretation: that the ricercars and the trio sonata, i.e. the 'exordia' and 'peroratio', are 'too extended' to be balanced by the sometimes brief canons assigned to the other

---

source. The problem of the use of instrumental music in the Italian liturgy is made especially complex by the fact that the practice was not uniform and, in the case of the organ, that much of it was improvised. The extant 'organ Masses' represent only a small part of the music actually heard.

[64] Quoted above, p. 40, note 35, but ignored by Walker. The free ricercar was still defined as «une espèce de prélude ou de fantasie» by Pasquale RICCI, *Methode ou recueil*, 1786, p. 9 (SITÀ, pp. 40, 76). A modern connoisseur of rhetoric recognized: "To prelude, in the music of the 17th century, is less to find than to search ('rechercher') ... The geographic area of this voyage ... is the Roman, Italianized Europe" – Marc FUMAROLI, *L'école du silence*, Paris, Flammarion, 1994, p. 9.

[65] See below, pp. 475ff, Appendix II, which may be simplified as follows:

QUINTILIAN	BACH
Exordium I (Principium)	Ricercar a 3
Narratio brevis and/or:	Canon perpetuus super thema regium
Narratio ornata	[5] Canones diversi super thema regium
	("Thematis regii elaborationes canonicae")
Egressus	Fuga canonica
Exordium II (Insinuatio)	Ricercar a 6
Argumentatio (Quaestiones)	[2 enigmatic canons] ("Quaerendo invenietis")
Probatio	Canon a 2
Refutatio	Canon a 4
Peroratio in adfectibus or:	Sonata sopr'il soggetto reale (Fl., V., B.c.)
Peroratio in rebus	Canon perpetuus (Fl., V., B.c.)

partes orationis, the *narratio* and *argumentatio*. But none of the shorter canons was compared to an entire section of the oration. No less than five canons[66] are assigned to one section, the *narratio ornata*,[67] and the *argumentatio* has two longer ones. Not only were the shorter canons intended to be repeated; their musical content is much denser than that of the ricercars and the sonata. Actually, the number of measures assigned by Bach to 'Exordium I – Narratio – Exordium II – Argumentatio' does not vary greatly, being in the ratio of 135:111:103:112, respectively, *not* counting the 'perpetual' repetitions of canons.

The concern about 'disproportion' can be dispelled also by reading rhetorical literature. The classical rhetoricians provide a full description of the oration's structure only for the *genus judicale*, i.e. for the forensic oration. For the other two rhetorical genres, the epideictic (demonstrative) and deliberative, the scheme was freely modified at the orators' discretion, adapting the forensic form to accommodate, for example, also epideictic content. This is perhaps one reason why Bach supplied both the shorter and longer versions of the 'narratio' and 'peroratio', the shorter versions each consisting of a single canon. Quintilian himself already seems to have anticipated some overzealous scepticism in our time when he wrote: "Some, it is true, have thought that [the bases of the forensic oration] were peculiar merely to forensic themes, but their ignorance will stand revealed when I have treated all three kinds of oratory" (III.vi.1); and "all three bases [forensic, epideictic, deliberative] may fall into this work [epideictic oratory]" (III.vii.28).

Quintilian does not describe the forensic oration as a rigid scheme, but emphasizes that it should be modified to fit the particular circumstances. Thus, in some cases, the exordium may be omitted entirely, or an internal exordium can be introduced in any part of the oration (IV.i.72f), though its place was normally before the *argumentatio* (IV.iii.9). The same applies to the use of the organ in the Mass. Any organ piece preceding (rather than replacing or accompanying) an item in the liturgy can be regarded as a prelude. Already in 1431, priests were known, on occasion, to have abbreviated the Preface before the Sanctus to allow more time for the organist to play.[68]

---

66 Not "four", as stated by WALKER, p. 191.

67 Both the rhetorical *virtus* of clarity and the late-baroque 'unity of affect', so characteristic of Bach's single movements, precluded his presenting Quintilian's five forensic and five epideictic qualities in a single piece. Thus he utilized the *partitio* (five canons) recommended by the rhetorician for the *narratio ornata*, combining one forensic quality with one epideictic one in each canon; cf. pp. 431-448.

68 BONTA, p. 60, note 20.

Contrary to what some musicians might expect today from a prelude or postlude, the exordium and the peroration were not necessarily brief sections subordinated to those which they frame. Especially the *insinuatio*-type exordium is described as an elaborate construction full of sophisticated devices and delivered slowly. The length and elaboration of music for the liturgy is always a function of (i.e. proportionate to) the solemnity of the feast.[69] For *very* solemn religious festivities in Venice there is not only ample iconographical evidence but also literary testimony, such as Thomas Coryat's description of a marathon musical-liturgical function in 1608.[70] That the Venetians, "sommamente eccellenti" in music and oratory,[71] had a weakness for extended organ pieces is indicated also by the fines they imposed upon priests for interrupting the organ by beginning the chant too soon.[72] It is thus not surprising that Mozart could write to Padre Martini: "our church music is quite different from that of Italy, all the more because a Mass ... may not last longer than three quarters of an hour".[73]

Also the length of Bach's 'peroratio in adfectibus', i.e. the trio sonata, is to be explained by a rhetorical consideration. Here too, Bach modified the forensic *dispositio* for an epideictic purpose. As documented from Quintilian, this was the section of the oration where all the floodgates of eloquence were opened to give full expression to the affects.[74] Bach could implement this only by abandoning, for the only time in the *Musical Offering*, the strict contrapuntal genres of ricercar and canon, unsuitable for affective expression. As pointed out,[75] he finally turned to the 'empfindsamer Stil' of the Prussian court. Only here could he pay homage to the king by writing in Frederick's preferred musical style, and he did so generously.[76] So it need not surprise

---

[69] Thus imitative ricercars, if regarded as too long for a particular service, could be terminated at an internal cadence (Frescobaldi, preface to his *Fiori musicali*: "finire nelle sue cadenze"), continuing a practice already established by the free ricercars of the lutenists (above, p. 44) – a further indication of the common preludial function of the free and imitative ricercars. Similarly, an organist playing variations (with "alio modo", "terzo modo", etc.), was free to omit any of the variations, as documented also by partially concordant sources of different length. The same probably holds true for J. H. Buttstedt's 'stanzas', mentioned by WALKER, p. 182.

[70] Quoted in Stephen BONTA, *Liturgical Problems in Monteverdi's Marian Vespers*, JAMS, XX, 1967, pp. 97f.

[71] See p. 50, note 85, the quotation from Jacopo Sansovino, 1546.

[72] BONTA, *The Uses*, p. 55, note 2.

[73] "la nostra musica di chiesa è aßai differente di quella d'Italia, e sempre più, che una Meßa ... non ha da durare che al più longo 3 quarti d'ora" – letter of 4 Sept. 1776, *Briefe und Aufzeichnungen*, Kassel, Bärenreiter, 1962-75, I, 533.

[74] "Totos effundere adfectus" (IV.i.28), "totos eloquentiae aperire fontes" (VI.i.51).

[75] Below, pp. 455f.

[76] MARISSEN, *The Theological Character*, pp. 94ff, would like to minimize the generally recog-

us that the *peroratio in adfectibus* was particularly extended in this *Huldigungskomposition*. This is merely another modification of the forensic technique for an epideictic purpose, as authorized by Quintilian. With its affective content and fuller instrumentation, now involving the royal flautist also as a performer, the piece represents a climax and thus can come *only* at the end.[77] While this position for the *sonata* is dictated primarily by secular epideictic rhetoric (not to mention court protocol: the most important person appears last),[78] it is consistent also with the position of canzonas and their successors, the *sonate da chiesa*, at the end of the Mass, accompanying the extended liturgical action of the *Communio*. Contrary to the allegation of Wolff, Ursula Kirkendale did not interpret the sonata and the canon perpetuus as an "absurdity" of a "double peroration".[79] Because Quintilian's two types of peroration are not sequences, but *alternatives* ("aut in rebus aut in adfectibus",[80] i.e. *"either ... or"*, not understood by Wolff?), she *repeatedly* designated the two pieces as such (cf. pp. 455, 458, 464: "alternatives", "the other [!] conclusion of his work", "one ... might be omitted").[81]

The *narratio* and *argumentatio*, on the other hand, may be abbreviated or even omitted entirely in epideictic oratory (Wolff's reference, *loc. cit.*, to these sections as Quintilian's "centerpieces" thus misses the mark) because the task here is not to prove a case in court, but to praise an eminent personage. The rhetorical and musical *genus epideicticum* was as relevant to the Mass[82] as, in

---

nized gallant aspects of the sonata, even regarding the piece as "learned". But the term is relative: when Bach chooses to use this style, the result will obviously be less 'gallant' than that of his less conservative contemporaries.

[77] Contrary to what is stated by Christoph WOLFF, *Bach: Essays on his Life and Music*, Cambridge MA, Harvard UP, 1991, p. 422, Ursula Kirkendale did not designate the last canon perpetuus as "the most extraordinary movement" or the "crowning of the entire work". The word "coronat", below, p. 454, was applied to the presence of the king and thus to the fuller instrumentation in *both* the sonata and the canon, certainly not to the canon alone. And the characterization of the canon as an "extraordinary contrapuntal coup" may not be too enthusiastic when one recognizes that the artistry here consists precisely in *concealing* the "compositional sophistication" ("ars est celare artem"; cf. Quintilian, VIII.ii.2) in "a mirror canon, combining two different solutions ... without the slightest modification of the given melody", yet still appearing 'gallant'.

[78] Politicians take this for granted. Ronald Reagan admitted learning it in Hollywood: "We save the best things for the last act", referring to his own political comeback (*Die Zeit*, 27 Feb. 1987, p. 2). Or when Raissa Gorbachev provided a royal reception for Anne Burda in Moscow, the elderly fashion queen was the last person to mount the podium (*Mittelbayerische Zeitung*, 5 Mar. 1987). The examples could be multiplied *ad infinitum*.

[79] WOLFF, *loc. cit.*, with reference to the article cited below, note 120.

[80] Quintilian, VI.i.1, on the two types of peroratio: "Eius duplex ratio est posita aut in rebus aut in adfectibus".

[81] Any reader troubled by the presence of two *narrationes* may consult Heinrich LAUSBERG, *Handbuch der literarischen Rhetorik*, München, Huber, 1973², I, 176, on the double *narratio*.

[82] Cf. John O'MALLEY, *Praise and Blame in Renaissance Rome: Rhetoric, Doctrine, and Reform in the Sacred Orators of the Papal Court c. 1450-1521*, Durham, Duke UP, 1979.

turn, the organ Masses of Frescobaldi were to Bach's *Huldigungskomposition*; the latter, of course, both involve the concept 'gloria'. Bach's title immediately identifies the genus as epideictic, meaning that the composer was free to adapt the classical forensic *dispositio* to his epideictic purpose. And, as always when a composer adopts rhetorical elements for his music, he was even freer than the orators in deciding to what extent he would adhere to the textbook description and to what degree he would modify it. Here again, there is no need to demonstrate an absolutely complete analogy, provided enough evidence for a rhetorical conception is produced. We must only overcome the chronological-geographical obstacles (e.g. modern impatience with slower tempi and lengthy liturgies) and the misunderstanding of the rhetorical *genera causarum*.

Neither the article of Walker nor the one of Michael Marissen on the *Musical Offering*,[83] published together in a volume edited by a pupil of Christoph Wolff, dared to criticize the publications of Wolff or to cite Ursula Kirkendale's detailed review of his facsimile edition (below, ch. 13), where additional refutations of his opinions are presented. But with each new publication Wolff had changed his mind and proposed new 'solutions' to the sequence of movements – altogether ca. sixteen different ones! –,[84] only to end up by capitulating and denying that any sequence was ever intended. The long series of self-contradictions cannot be disguised by the categorical pronouncements ("an infallible sign", "it is indisputable that ...", "very clear that the idea of a sophisticated cyclical structure has to be rejected", etc., where none of this is true).[85] Wolff's own defense, after eleven years, was much weaker than Walker's article. It presented only the 'disproportion' objection (refuted above), confused well known baroque devices of musical rhetoric (for the depiction of the 'gods') with irrelevant romantic "program music",[86] resorted again to categorical pronouncements, saying in effect that 'the interpretation is wrong because I say it is wrong',[87] and for the rest relied on the most im-

---

[83] *The Theological Character of J. S. Bach's «Musical Offering»*, in *Bach Studies* cit., II, pp. 85-106.

[84] Below, p. 419, note 11. When WALKER, p. 177, refers to "the [!] order deduced by Christoph Wolff from the original print and manuscript copies", we must ask which one is intended and how is it justified.

[85] *NBA* VIII/1, *Kritischer Bericht*, Kassel, Bärenreiter, 1976, pp. 122, 124; *New Research*, pp. 403f. Cf. below, p. 423, note 27 *et passim*, and pp. 483f. The "irrefutable" symmetry was soon rejected by Wolff himself.

[86] Cf. the distinctions made by Manfred BUKOFZER, *Allegory in Baroque Music*, «Journal of the Warburg and Courtauld Institutes», III, 1939/40, pp. 18-21.

[87] *Bach*, p. 422: "The irregular makeup of the original print ... can under no circumstances [!]

perceptive of witnesses, who writes in a similar vein.[88] Another *ex cathedra* judgement, i.e. without arguments, was made by Wolff's collaborator in the *Neue Bach-Ausgabe* who undertook to defend the vested interest.[89] But the *NBA* has always been limited to the printing notes and critical reports, not explaining musical content.[90] Owen Jander, in his interesting and methodically sound article *Beethoven's "Orpheus in Hades": The Andante con moto of the Fourth Piano Concerto*, unlocking musical meaning with the help of a classical author (Ovid), likewise misapplied the term "program music", but corrected this in his sequel to that article.[91] As he rightly points out, the term should be restricted to works, especially of the nineteenth century, for which the composers themselves provided the often specific but unsophisticated literary indications. I would add: provided for the benefit of lay audiences which were no longer capable of understanding the subtleties of the musical rhetoric ubiquitous in the Baroque repertoire. Thus when Wolff asserts that such subtleties are "fundamentally different from what is known about this relationship in the seventeenth and eighteenth centuries",[92] he reveals only that they are unknown to himself. The authorities quoted below, pp. 437f, are not Berlioz and Liszt, but Monteverdi and Kuhnau (Bach's predecessor in Leipzig!), and their number could easily be expanded. Jupiter's thunderbolts were still known to and depicted by Mozart,[93] and also Mars and Neptune were of course omnipresent at court festivities throughout Europe (for Prussia, see below, p. 439, note 71). These three principal gods frequently formed a triad in panegyric literature, where sovereigns were invariably compared to classical deities and heroes. A *Huldigungskantate* by Karl Ditters von

---

be explained by means of rhetorical methods". Except for the revocation of some of the 'solutions' to the sequence of movements discredited by U. Kirkendale, the articles dealing with the *Musical Offering* reprinted in this volume contain only minor revisions and retain many of the errors already pointed out. The chapter "Apropos the Musical Offering: The Thema Regium and the Term Ricercar", not surprisingly, ignores my article relevant to "the term ricercar" (ch. 2), first published in 1979.

[88] I.e. the article cited below, note 120.

[89] Alfred DÜRR, in «Notes», XLIX, 1992/93, p. 510.

[90] WOLFF's *Kritischer Bericht*, NBA VIII/1, represents an immense amount of painstaking labor of the most arid nature, fulfilling the prophecy of Friedrich Blume, quoted below, p. 112. It contributes almost nothing to our understanding of Bach's composition, but much to its misunderstanding.

[91] «Nineteenth Century Music», VIII, 1984/85, p. 196; *ibid.*, XIX, 1995/96, p. 31.

[92] *Bach*, p. 422.

[93] Cf. *Thamos, König in Ägypten*, in *Neue Mozart-Ausgabe*, II,6/1, Kassel, Bärenreiter, 1956, pp. 228f; also Purcell's *katabasis* for "thunder" in *Dido and Aeneas*, in *The Works of Henry Purcell*, III, London, Novello, 1889, p. 57.

Dittersdorf for the birthday of Frederick the Great in 1773 is thus entitled *Il tribunale di Giove* (ms. in GB-Lcm).

The extreme positivistic approach, based on printing technology, such as practised by Wolff, has now been continued by Michael Marissen.[94] Some of the observations would appear valid, e.g. that the five numbered canons were traced from Bach's autograph or that the parts for the sonata were divided among two different engravers, whose undistinguished names are now known.[95] But this does not have the slightest bearing on the order of the pieces. Johann Christoph Oley's manuscript copy of the work, cited as an authority, is based on the print and thus has no value as a source; its solution to one of the canons is wrong (see below, p. 442). I must also reject Marissen's interpretation of the heading, *Canon a 2 Quaerendo invenietis*.[96] In order for this cardinal number '2' to have originally designated the position of the canon rather than the number of its parts, it would have to have come before the word "Canon", not after the Italian word "*a*" (cf. the headings of the five numbered canons). Marissen argues that the number '2', here written with the angular form resembling the letter 'Z', was originally '7' and that the original edition shows faint traces (which "cannot be seen in the reproduction") of the bottom line having been added later. Rather than accept this on faith, I examined the original print with a magnifying glass and found no such "traces". Actually, the Z-form of the number '2' is very common in older sources. To mention only one example: in an anonymous seventeenth-century painting of the *Seduta del Concilio nella chiesa di Santa Maria Maggiore* in the Castello del Buon Consiglio, Trent, which identifies the various persons by numbers, the digit '2' in the number '12', more than the one in Bach's print, looks like a '7' with a (shorter) bottom line 'added later'.[97] Marissen himself observes that Schübler's writing of this number is inconsistent: not only in the print of the *Musical Offering*, but also in that of the six 'Schübler' chorales BWV 645-650, where the engraver again wrote predominately '2', but also, "curiously", '1Z' for '12'. But even if he did change the number for the canon – which he did

---

[94] *More Source-Critical Research on Bach's «Musical Offering»*, in «Bach: Quarterly Journal of the Riemenschneider Bach Institute», XXV, 1994, pp. 11-27; also Gregory BUTLER, *The Printing History of J. S. Bach's 'Musical Offering': New Interpretations*, «Journal of Musicology», XIX, 2002, pp. 306-331.

[95] Also the single editions of Handel's opera I-III were executed by two different engravers; cf. Donald BURROWS, *Walsh's Editions of Handel's Opera 1-5*, in *Music in Eighteenth-Century England: Essays in Memory of Charles Cudworth*, Cambridge UP, 1983, pp. 80f, 83.

[96] Pp. 16f and note 21.

[97] The Z-form is consistently used, for example, also for the foliation of the *Medici Codex*; cf. the facsimile, *Monuments of Renaissance Music*, V, Chicago UP, 1968.

not – he would have been correcting an error. The thrust of Marissen's arguments (on his ulterior, "theological" motive, see below) is to sustain the 'systematic' sequence (ricercars – sonata – canons) suggested by the newspaper advertisement (Leipzig, 1747), G. B. Pauli's letter to Padre Martini (1750), and the obituary listing, subsequently adopted by the *Neue Bach-Ausgabe* (which we regard as one big typographical error).[98] However, these listings are mere summaries, intended to indicate as simply and briefly as possible the contents of the whole. In no case did their writers want to enumerate thirteen pieces separately in sequence, especially when the sequence was not too clear from the unbound source. The statement by Marissen (p. 14, note 9, repeated p. 15) to the effect that "the ordering of Martini's materials corresponds to the ... newspaper announcement" is blatantly false, since the pieces in a single printer's unit cannot possibly be separated from each other. This statement (intentionally?) obscures the fact that canons were contained also in units with the ricercars and the sonata, and implies that the unit with the "canons" contains all of them, when it actually consists only of the five numbered *canones diversi*, plus the *Fuga* canonica (see below, p. 418, Table 1). The shelf numbers assigned in Bologna have no significance whatsoever for Bach's intentions.

We believe that the print – except for an autograph of the six-part ricercar the only extant source for the work – must be taken seriously and be given a *much* higher priority than any simplified systematic listing. It is, of course, unlikely that Bach presented his manuscript to the engraver in a layout corresponding exactly to the print; the pieces may well have been written on separate folios (e.g. the *Fuga canonica* separate from the five numbered canons). But the sequence which we consider correct is not "a nineteenth-century ordering",[99] nor was it "accept[ed] from the old collected edition".[100] On the contrary, it is one of the very few possibilities presented in 1747 and was arrived at through an independent investigation of the source and the musical-rhetorical content. The only question was the sequence of the four units B-E.[101] Contrary to what has generally been assumed, this never constituted a great mystery. Almost anyone knowledgeable about music who examined these units [not too] thoughtfully would arrive at the same conclusion as Spitta and the editor of the old Bach edition, even without knowing the detailed

---

[98] I state this explicitly, since Alfred Dürr requested us to point out typographical errors.

[99] MARISSEN, *The Theological Character*, p. 87, note 9.

[100] WOLFF, *Bach*, p. 421.

[101] The letters assigned by Wolff and retained in Table 1, below, p. 418, though not representing the correct sequence of units.

rhetorical *dispositio*. It was obvious that the three-part ricercar (unit B), as the point of departure for the whole cycle – a *principium*-type prelude as defined in the lexicon of Bach's cousin Johann Gottfried Walther – belonged at the beginning, and that, as stated above, unit C with the fullest, 'royal' instrumentation had to come at the end. This left only two possibilities: one had to determine whether the middle units appeared in the sequence DE or ED. And also this question could easily be answered, because unit E bore the engraver's signature,[102] indicating not that it was the very end of the cycle (it concludes with the only piece not in the key of the work, C Minor), but the last of the units in score prepared by him (he delegated unit C, in separate parts, to assistants). Thus it is no accident that Spitta, the Bach-Gesellschaft edition, and now Ursula Kirkendale arrived at the same sequence. It corresponds, of course, to Bach's consignment of the print to the king in two separate instalments, ABD-EC.[103]

We do not think that Bach would have authorized the printing of any one of these units with its pieces in a sequence which was not according to his plan.[104] This means that *his sequence within each printing unit must be respected*, as it was for nearly two centuries. Otherwise we return to the wildly arbitrary rearrangements like those made on subjective, aesthetic (and now, beware, "theological") grounds, or, even worse, exalt a lowly artisan above a great composer, as Wolff and Marissen seem intent on doing.[105] None of the observations on the printing technology presented thus far – they are largely speculative and unconvincing – necessitates a revision of this premise or refutes the 'rhetorical' sequence, which we believe to be consistent with the source, as those of Wolff and Marissen most certainly are not. (Paradoxically, Wolff concedes "that the original sources of Bach's works speak an unmistakable language ...").[106] *Not one* of the "implausible observations on source-cri-

---

[102] Below, p. 423, note 27.

[103] Philipp SPITTA, *Johann Sebastian Bach*, Leipzig, Breitkopf & Härtel, 1873-1880, II, 843f. Also this division renders Wolff's "fascicle 3", with its conflicting formats (vertical and horizontal), impossible. On Spitta's instalment theory, see below, p. 418, note 7.

[104] This obvious conclusion is now sustained also by BUTLER, *The Printing History*, p. 328. Hans T. DAVID, *Bach's «Musical Offering»*, «Musical Quarterly», XXIII, 1937, p. 329, in a fatal footnote, first suggested that the order of the canons may have been altered during the course of printing, possibly because he wished to rearrange these pieces according to his own aesthetic criterion ("symmetry"!). Anatoly P. MILKA, *Über den Autor der Umstellung der Kanons im «Musikalischen Opfer» Johann Sebastian Bachs*, «Beiträge zur Bachforschung», IX/X, 1991, pp. 129-137, is also of this opinion, but, unlike Marissen, he would attribute the alleged "rearangement" to the composer, since it is so unlikely that Bach would have left such important decisions to his engraver.

[105] Cf. MARISSEN, *More ... Research*, p. 24: "Schübler's possible rearranging" of a work dedicated to a king!

[106] *Bach*, p. 267.

tical matters" which Marissen imagined to have found in my wife's article is further specified![107] And the investigations of printing technology were conducted by these writers without regard for the music itself and its content, thus fulfilling Friedrich Blume's prophecy:[108]

A favorite procedure like research on copyists, conducted today with criminalistic sagacity, has become fashionable, even where it is absolutely without interest. There actually exist studies occupied exclusively with paper, ink, staff-liners, and such; and if this continues, then in the year 2000 music history will no longer deal with composers and theorists, but with scribes and copyists, no longer with Masses and symphonies, but with watermarks and staff-liners.

The absolute 'reliability' of the diplomatic method is an illusion, for its limits are reached before one even arrives at the content of the musical work, and, as we have seen, it can lead to serious errors.[109] Wolff referred to his application of it aptly with the medical/philological term "autopsy",[110] apparently unconcerned about the negative implications of a word meaning the dissection of dead matter without the approval of the deceased. In the case of the *Musical Offering*, Marissen's presumed "series [!] of ten austere canons" in succession[111] indeed betrays a lack of musical-artistic sensibility, not to mention an unawareness of the basic principles of rhetoric, which condemned *monotonia* as one of the worst *vitia*, to be avoided by all means. Notwithstanding the variety of the canonic techniques, we can scarcely imagine more unpalatable musical fare than these cerebral canons unrelieved by a different kind of music (ricercar or sonata) – Marissen's "theological character". This is surely one reason why the 'rhetorical' sequence has now found such favor with professional musicians, also for recordings.[112] The five canons which Bach intended to be heard in succession were wisely kept very short, the other group limited to two. This is another reason for the relative brevity and the

---

[107] *The Theological Character*, p. 87, note 9.

[108] *Historische Musikforschung in der Gegenwart*, International Musicological Society, *Report of the Tenth Congress Ljubljana 1967*, Kassel, Bärenreiter, 1970, p. 20.

[109] Pp. 420 and 481. The errors are compounded when the misinterpretation of the source is used as the basis of (intended for?) an implausible 'referential' interpretation, as in the case of Marissen.

[110] Preface to the facsimile edition of the *Musical Offering*, Leipzig, Peters, 1977, p. 11: "the edition of the work in the ... Neue Bach-Ausgabe [VIII/1, 1974], which commendably permitted a comparative autopsy". Here it is unclear whether Wolff is commending himself or his father-in-law, the theologian and ecclesiastical administrator Christhard Mahrenholz, *Reichsobmann* already in 1934, president of the Neue Bach-Gesellschaft 1949-74, and member of the editorial board.

[111] MARISSEN, *The Theological Character*, p. 99.

[112] Cf. *ibid.*, p. 86.

concentration of his 'narratio' and 'argumentatio': rhetorical considerations had to be reconciled with musical ones.

More than that of any other composer, the music of Bach has been abused for subjective and arbitrary theological and numerological interpretations,[113] in some cases perhaps containing a grain of truth, but neither provable nor often even plausibly arguable as hypotheses. Most must be regarded as reflecting more the far-fetched notions of their creators than the intentions of the composer. Since the rhetorical interpretation of the *Musical Offering* seeks to explain the work in a 'referential' rather than 'immanent' manner, drawing upon a very closely related sister discipline, readers who consider music to be nothing more than sound may be inclined to classify it with the above-mentioned types. It does not, however, resort to theological or numerological methods, of which we are sceptical and which we do not wish to encourage. Even the *Musical Offering*, a purely secular instrumental composition originating on a secular occasion[114] and dedicated to a king who always had an intense dislike of music which "smells of the church",[115] has now been subjected to a "theological" interpretation of the most implausible and unfounded nature.[116] Here it is again argued that Bach wrote "ten canons" [*recte*: nine canons and a canonic *fugue*!] with the intention of alluding to the Ten Commandments,[117] as if a musician would presume to give commandments to a king, especially when two of the ten could be interpreted as censures of the monarch's private life ('sexual orientation' in today's jargon). And no attempt whatsoever is made to indicate what canon 'corresponded' to what Commandment and why. If Bach had such an intention, he would hardly have presented a closed group of five numbered canons, one pair, two single canons, and a "Fuga canonica" (where 'canon' is only

---

[113] E.g.: Kees van HOUTEN and Marinus KASBERGER, *Bach et le nombre*, Liège, Mardaga, 1992, pp. 183 and 191, would like us to believe that Bach knew in advance the day of his death and thus could symbolize his lifespan of 23,869 days in his music!

[114] It is not necessary to provide a 'theological' interpretation of Bach's dedication, for a secular, classical one is possible (below, p. 461). MARISSEN, *The Theological Character*, p. 103, bases his argument partly on an inaccurate, pleonastic translation of "den Ruhm ... zu verherrlichen" as "glorifying the glory", rather than "to glorify the fame". The equally irrelevant and implausible 'theological' interpretation of the likewise absolutely secular Brandenburg concertos in Marissen's dissertation has been decisively laid to rest in the review by Michael Talbot in «Music and Letters», LXXVII, 1996, pp. 466-469, which also contrasts its lack of humor with Bach's *Spielfreudigkeit* in these works.

[115] Charles Burney, quoted in W. KIRKENDALE, *Fugue and Fugato*, p. 23.

[116] MARISSEN, *The Theological Character of J. S. Bach's «Musical Offering»*.

[117] The notion is not even original, but was already proclaimed by WOLFF, *New Research*, p. 404, and challenged by U. KIRKENDALE (below, p. 419, note 12).

an adjective!), interspersed with other pieces. Since even the shortest canons (e.g. four measures) of the group of five are now regarded as equivalents to some very extended canonic movements, the 'disproportion' argument would seem to have real validity here. Though no analogies are presented for the individual Commandments, the pious Lutheran motto quoted at the head of the article, "The Cross alone is our theology", is dragged in at the end (note 73), linked to "the apparently conflicting formats of oblong and upright papers in the print"! The diverse formats were, of course, not determined by a "theology of the cross" but by a simple practical tradition. In Bach's time, as in Frescobaldi's, music for keyboard was normally on oblong pages, since the performer had a broad rack on which he could spread them out. Music for melody instruments, on the other hand, had to be in upright format in order to fit onto a much narrower music stand.

Not only the sequence of pieces in the printer's units, but *also Bach's titles of these pieces must be taken seriously*. Both are violated by both Walker and Marissen, for they persist in renaming [!] the two ricercars as "fugues"[118] and the one fugue as "canon". The reasons for this sophistry are abundantly clear. Walker wishes to deny the ricercars the preludial function distinguished with Bach's titles, so he claims that they are "fugues" (see above, p. 99). Both Walker and Marissen would like to legitimize with their new names the sequence of the 'systematic' listings (and hence of Wolff in the *NBA*), listings which were prepared mostly by persons who no longer knew or cared what a ricercar was and therefore substituted the familiar word 'fugue' – another indication of their limited credibility. But both musicologists outdo the imprecisions of the listings (none of which refers to "ten" canons!) by creating a 'round' number of canons: not nine, but ten. This number was already preferred by those who wished to rearrange the components of the cycle according to long since discredited aesthetic, 'symmetrical' criteria. In Marissen's case, the intention is to support a highly implausible interpretation, one which indeed "smells of the church". Bach expressed his intentions with his printed source and its original titles.[119] Walker and Marissen then allow their own wish to become the father of the thought.

Meconi and Walker generally write as professional and responsible scholars, presenting thoughtful arguments and citing contemporary musical and

---

[118] Especially confusing when Marissen's genitive 'fugues' (*sic, More ... Research*, p. 20) cannot immediately be specified as singular (Fuga canonica) or plural (the two ricercars).

[119] These must regarded as definitive, having priority over the formulation "Preußische Fuge" in an informal letter, probably a concession to current parlance; *Bach-Dokumente*, Leipzig, VEB Deutscher Verlag für Musik, 1963-79, I, 117.

theoretical sources, sometimes, but not always, conceding others which could weaken their theses, thus giving the impression of balanced reasoning, though failing to understand the musical-rhetorical processes and, in the case of Walker, also the important liturgical aspects. But such competence and seriousness of purpose cannot be attributed to an organist from Scotland who, while exhibiting a superficial acquaintance with the repertoire, has been incorrigibly hostile to the rhetorical interpretation of the *Musical Offering*.[120] Here, the geographical barriers mentioned at the beginning of this article appear to have been insurmountable: not only the Alps, but also the English Channel and Hadrian's Wall.[121] The few objections by this writer not already answered in our original articles are being addressed in other parts of this one[122] and do not merit specific attention. If someone does not understand that *elaboratio* is a term derived from ancient rhetoric, also when it appears in a musical source, then there is little hope that he will ever understand any of our reasoning. This writer, intentionally or unwittingly, even practiced deceit when he falsified quotations from Ursula Kirkendale, making them appear incorrect by omitting key words.[123] One cannot escape the impression that some writers are determined to cut down a great composer to the dimensions of their own time and experience by demonstrating with every means that he was less educated than he really was. A German musicologist has taken pains to argue that Bach knew little about rhetoric because the school he attended in Lüneburg at one time used a rather poor textbook for this sub-

---

[120] Peter WILLIAMS, *The Snares and Delusions of Musical Rhetoric: Some Examples from Recent Writings on J. S. Bach*, in *Alte Musik: Praxis und Reflexion*, ed. Peter Reidemeister and Veronika Gutmann, Winterthur, Amadeus, 1983, p. 238. Williams – Wolff's key witness (see above, note 79) – revealed his position towards humanistic learning during his aborted term as administrator of an American music department, drastically reducing the requirements of foreign languages and course work in the neighbouring historical disciplines for degrees in a graduate school of arts and sciences! (In a forensic process, it is not only permissible, but necessary to question the credibility of witnesses).

[121] Notwithstanding greatly improved transportation and communication, these obstacles to the transmission of Roman rhetoric seem only to have increased in the second half of the twentieth century, for Britain had already achieved a high degree of Latin literacy in the Middle Ages. Gesner's edition of Quintilian – Bach's 'source' – did, of course, eventually arrive, *inter al.*, as far as England; our parchment-bound copy was sold by the British Museum as a duplicate in 1834. The English antiquarian Albi Rosenthal informed us that the market value of this edition increased substantially in 1980.

[122] Also the more serious misunderstandings in the letter of 12 Sept. 1980 from Alfred Dürr have finally been answered in this article. Yet already in the letter it was conceded, *inter al.*: "That the term 'ricercar' is the musical correlation to proem, I accept as proven".

[123] P. 238, the misquotations: "reserved by Bach for the [omitted: *other*] conclusion of his work" [an error which seems to have influenced Wolff – see above, p. 106], "the only canon to be performed [omitted: *by the king*]"; cf. below, p. 458.

ject, published five years before the composer's birth[124] – as if Bach's intellectual development remained stationary until age sixty-two, by which time he had long been thoroughly immersed in the atmosphere of the Thomasschule, according to his own testimony excellent "in humanioribus",[125] and become closely befriended with eminent rhetoricians!

In pursuing the analogies between Quintilian's teaching and Bach's composition, my wife decided to report all those which she could observe, for what they were worth,[126] fully realizing that some were more convincing than others, that the composer may not have been consciously aware of all of them, and that they might be challenged, especially by readers unfamiliar with Latin and the supreme role of rhetoric in the 16th-18th centuries. However, the sheer quantity of the musical and biographical evidence is so extensive, some of it so persuasive, that the less evident analogies cannot constitute a refutation of the main case. Because there are so many correspondences that it is impossible to imagine that all of them were merely coincidental, I venture the conclusion that the *sum* of the arguments produces no longer an hypothesis, but a fact: that Bach modelled the *Musical Offering* after the *Institutio oratoria*. The analogies do not consist of wild numerological speculations nor vague theological/metaphysical abstractions, but are of a very concrete, musical nature, many of them briefly summarized in the table of 'concordances', pp. 475ff, albeit not intelligible to those who do not understand Latin. Still more direct connections with Quintilian's text are the literary cues provided by Bach himself in the rhetorician's own language and taken from rhetorical terminology and/or, in some cases, probably from specific passages in Quintilian: especially "elaborationes", "Fortuna [and] Gloria",[127] "quaerendo invenietis",[128] and the antiquated word "ricercar", unmistakably linked

---

[124] Arno FORCHERT, *Bach und die Tradition der Rhetorik*, Gesellschaft für Musikforschung, *Bericht über den internationalen musikwissenschaftlichen Kongreß Stuttgart 1985* (with the symptomatic subtitle *Alte Musik und die ästhetische Gegenwart!*), Kassel, Bärenreiter, 1987, I, 169-179 – refuted also, at length, by FLINDELL, pp. 154-160, 181ff, and notes 7, 35, 78. Cf. the much more perceptive article of Z. Philip AMBROSE, *"Weinen, Klagen, Sorgen, Zagen" und die antike Redekunst*, «Bach-Jahrbuch», LXVI, 1980, pp. 35-45, which reconstructs the highly humanistic-rhetorical environment in Weimar during the simultaneous sojourns there of Bach, Gesner, and Salomo Franck, a major purveyor of cantata texts for Bach in those years.

[125] Below, p. 465. Also Gesner's successor as rector of the Thomasschule, Johann August Ernesti, though less appreciative of music, was a classical philologist and editor of works of Cicero.

[126] This applies also to the abbreviated German version, *Bach und Quintilian: Die «Institutio oratoria» als Modell des «Musikalischen Opfers»*, in *Musik in Antike und Neuzeit*, ed. Michael von Albrecht, Frankfurt, Lang, 1987, pp. 85-107.

[127] Cf. below, p. 433, the quotation from Quintilian.

[128] At the beginning of Bach's 'argumentatio'; cf. *quaestiones* as an alternate name for *argumentatio* (above, p. 79, note 222), and Quintilian's "Hortor ad quaerendum et inveniri posse fateor" with

with rhetorical concepts. But the most decisive arguments are the biographical ones: the facts that (1) Bach's old friend and former rector at St. Thomas', Matthias Gesner,[129] published his truly monumental edition of Quintilian – an author whom Frederick the Great wished to be read in the schools –[130] with a long footnote in praise of Bach (see below, ch. 12, Plates XII.1-3),[131] the only contemporary description we have of him as a performing musician. Wolff quoted this only in an English translation and without comment, from *The Bach Reader*.[132] If he had looked at Gesner's edition he would have found not only very copious footnotes, but also a learned 36-page Latin preface and detailed indices of both subjects (169 pp.!) and names (23 pp.) in two columns. The index of subjects was surely for Bach the key to a goldmine of useful information (see below, p. 445, for concrete examples). No other edition supplies so much commentary and critical apparatus. (2) The composer chose to have himself defended from Scheibe's attacks by a rhetorician friend, Johann Abraham Birnbaum, whose well known testimony of 1739 I must quote once again, adding commentaries in brackets, since its full implications still do not yet seem to be universally understood:[133]

He has such perfect knowledge of the parts [i.e. *dispositio*] and merits [rhetorical *virtutes*] which the working out [i.e. *elaboratio*] of a musical piece has in common with rhetoric, that one not only listens to him with satiating pleasure when he focusses his conversations [*inter al.* with the rhetoricians Gesner and Birnbaum][134] on the si-

---

reference to this section (p. 453). Though Bach may have known also the Scriptural version, this alone cannot not explain his use of these words at this point in his cycle.

[129] Cf. Werner BÜRGER and Johannes SCHWINN, *Johann Matthias Gesner (1691-1761): Seine Beziehungen zu Ansbach und J. S. Bach*, in *Bach-Woche Ansbach ... 1991 Offizieller Almanach*, Ansbach, 1991, pp. 122-130. This volume contains also, on pp. 39-59, a reprint of U. KIRKENDALE's *Bach und Quintilian*.

[130] CURTIUS, p. 269. Cf. also above, note 8, the treatise dedicated to Frederick by his teacher Quantz, containing many echoes from Quintilian, both in specific content and general pedagogical tone.

[131] *M. Fabii Quinctiliani De Institutione Oratoria*, Göttingen, Vandenhoeck, 1738, p. 61, note 3; reprinted in *Bach-Dokumente*, II, 331ff; English translation in *The Bach Reader*, ed. Hans T. David and Arthur Mendel, New York, Norton, 1945, p. 231. Our copy contains, on the anterior flyleaf, a handwritten quotation from Edward HARWOOD's authoritative *View of the Various Editions of Greek and Roman Classics*, London, 1782, p. 219: "I have had occasion to examine this edition by Gesner, and can pronounce it to be the *best edition* of Quintilian yet published".

[132] *Bach*, p. 39.

[133] Even WOLFF, *Bach*, p. 393, conceded Birnbaum to be a reliable testimony, but he never pursued the implications of this; on the contrary, he refused to recognize them, merely because they necessitate revision of his own work.

[134] Gesner, in his conversations with Bach on rhetoric, surely mentioned to the composer Aristotle's famous analogy of the forensic exordium and the musician's prelude, one of the relatively few

9

milarities and correspondences [i.e. analogies] of both [music and rhetoric]; but one also admires their clever *application* in his works [!]. His insight into poetry [including Homer? – regarded by Quintilian, X.i.46, as the model and inspiration of all eloquence] is as good as one can expect from a great composer.

What 'harder' evidence can one expect two and a half centuries after the fact than this 'smoking gun'? It renders untenable all attempts to belittle Bach's knowledge of rhetoric (Forchert) and to deny its relevance for his music (Williams). Like great painters of the Renaissance, Bach too undoubtedly had his advisors on literary matters, and we know the identity of two of them: Gesner and Birnbaum. **(3)** The *Musical Offering* served also as Bach's 'membership dues' for Mizler's society, which had declared in its statutes the aim to cultivate "the musical sciences ... [and] what pertains to them in ... rhetoric [!] and poetry".[135] That the society was founded by Bach's pupil the same year in which Gesner published his edition of Quintilian is surely no coincidence. The latter must have provided a stimulus for the former. As is well known, Bach devoted himself with the compositions of his later years less to the responsibilities of his office, and more to his private interests. To these must be counted above all his preoccupation with rhetoric via Gesner's edition.[136]

It was gratifying to see that the article of 1980 soon became itself the subject of *imitationes*.[137] Alan Street ventured to trace the structure of the forensic oration in Bach's Goldberg Variations, using many of the same quotations from Quintilian and likewise appending a table of 'concordances' in two columns. Street combined this interpretation with two others, one as a "mathematical abstraction", the other, more compatible with the first, as a reply to Scheibe's criticism. I do not intend to deal here with all the details of this article, nor to enter into the problems of numerology, of which, in its more arcane forms, we remain unconvinced (also of the gematria presented here),

---

specific references to musical practice in classical texts on rhetoric. In his edition of Quintilian (p. 152) he identified this writer's veiled reference to the passage (III.8.8. "prœmia esse maxime libera existimat") with a footnote: "Aristoteles Rhet. 3.14".

[135] See quotation below, p. 470.

[136] This paragraph was followed, in the original version of this article (1997), by addenda to the article of 1980, now omitted here and incorporated into ch. 12.

[137] Willem ELDERS, *Guillaume Dufay as Musical Orator*, «Tijdschrift der Vereeniging voor nederlandse muziekgeschiedenis», XXXI, 1981, pp. 3-11; Alan STREET, *The Rhetorical and Musical Structure of the 'Goldberg' Variations: Bach's Clavierübung IV and the 'Institutiio Oratoria' of Quintilian*, «Music Analysis», VI, 1987, pp. 89-131; Giuseppe FAGNOCCHI, *Ipotesi per una lettura retorica delle variazioni su 'la follia' opera V,12 di Arcangelo Corelli*, lecture presented at the Conservatorio of Foggia in May 2003 and posted on Internet; Francesco DILAGHI, *Pedagogia, didattica e retorica nelle 'Invenzioni a due voci' di J. S. Bach*, «Studi musicali», XXXIX, 2004, pp. 107-145.

without denying quadrivial concepts in Bach's music. A few general remarks must suffice. The objection of 'disproportion' could be valid here, not so much because most of the variations are assigned to the 'narratio' and the 'argumentatio', but because such radical modification of the proportions would not be expected in a 'forensic oration', which not implausibly is considered here to be Bach's self-defense. Also, although the "ouverture" (Variation 16) by its very title and by its French exordial style is indicated by Bach as an internal exordium, Street, curiously and needlessly, would consider it an *egressus*. The presence of Bach's name (B-a-c-h) and especially of "L'homme armé" would add much wit to the music, but, as often in such interpretations, I suspect that the modern commentator may have gone out of his way to find the notes he desired,[138] where there may be only a very slight, chance resemblance, and that this meaning was not intended by the composer. Having stated these reservations, I must confess that we find many of the article's premises sound, though more difficult to demonstrate than in the case of the *Musical Offering*, where the composer did not constrain himself by a long series of groups of three variations of equal length ending with a canon, but allowed himself full freedom to adapt a variety of musical components completely to the rhetorical *dispositio*. The Goldberg Variations lack also the literary clues of the later work. All of this means that Street's interpretation contains less direct analogies and is of necessity more hypothetical, more difficult to prove. But the author deserves credit for daring to deal with such problems. The composition is an encyclopedic compendium of a great variety of styles, and it is quite possible that Bach wrote it with Scheibe's criticisms of his style in mind. This music is full of rhetoric, and we have little doubt that the composer applied here many things which he had learned from Quintilian, regardless of whether his intentions always corresponded to the interpretations of Street. As always, the composer was free to *select* his rhetorical elements and to apply them when and where he wished, without any obligation to do this so completely and unambiguously as to present watertight arguments for future musicologists. But this only renders the rhetorical approach more challenging; it by no means invalidates it.

When my wife presented her findings on the *Musical Offering*, she received enthusiastic letters which would fill a small book, not only from distinguished colleagues throughout the musicological world, but also from classicists, historians of literature and art, scientists, professional musicians, etc.

---

[138] This, and the preoccupation with numbers, may be conditioned by the author's work on a dissertation in progress on Schoenberg, Berg, and Webern.

Disagreement was expressed only by the editors of the unfortunate edition in the *Neue Bach-Ausgabe*, and later by Walker and Marissen. Even the arch-sceptic Arthur Mendel (whom we never met) wrote on 6 June 1979: "I have now read your paper, with great interest. ... Your hypothesis is indeed striking and, at the least, plausible. ... Your paper is very persuasive". After hearing the paper at the meeting of the American Musicological Society in New York on 4 November of that year (originally Mendel was to serve as chairman of the session, but was prevented by his terminal illness and replaced by Gerhard Herz), Frederick Neumann sent his reaction: "Your lecture was one of the most brilliant essays which I have ever heard or read. ... You received an ovation such as I never heard at such meetings". Colin Slim reported to Edward Lowinsky: "Ursula's paper was not only brilliant, but represented a triumph of human will and spirit over adversity".[139] Gerhard Herz, the Nestor of American Bach scholarship, wrote on 20 May: "Brava – bravissima! I am so absorbed in your most excellent paper. ... I have arrived at page 27 and am simply fascinated by what I have read. It will, of course, demolish the somewhat cavalier-like method by which Christoph Wolff produced his *NBA* edition. But it had to be done and you are doing it"; and on 22 May: "It is almost midnight and I have just finished reading your pathbreaking paper. It will create a tremendous stir and rekindle Bach scholars' preoccupation with the influence of rhetoric. ... I am still stunned. ... Yours is the most exciting paper I have read in years and years. I am overwhelmed by what you have discovered (and what this will imply for the future: your last sentence!) and by the thorough, logical and systematic way you have presented your case. ... Once more my heartfelt congratulations on a stupendous achievement". On 8 June Herz wrote to Alfred Dürr, editor of the *Neue Bach-Ausgabe*: "Not since the surfacing of Bach's Calov-Bible ... has a study on Bach captivated me so much as that of Ursula Kirkendale. ... I came to know Dr. Kirkendale only through this discovery. Thus it is not a matter of doing a favor for a friend, but of truth in scholarship, which is or should be the aim of all research. I am convinced that this work will again point Bach research in the direction opened by Arnold Schmitz.[140] ... I have no doubt that the result

---

[139] The paralyzing apoplectic stroke suffered in 1971, immediately after a brief period as associate professor at Columbia University, resulting in a permanent, moderately severe impairment of speech.

[140] *Die Bildlichkeit der wortgebundenen Musik Johann Sebastian Bachs*, Mainz, Schott, 1950, a book which deserves more attention from Bach scholars. Once the "Bilder" have been identified with the help of the texts of vocal works, they can be recognized also in instrumental music, where they often retain their meaning.

of Dr. Kirkendale's source studies – as sorry as it makes me for Christoph Wolff – will make a new edition of the *Musical Offering* in the *NBA* unavoidable".[141] Edward Lowinsky accompanied an eleven-page commentary on the manuscript with a letter, dated 15 February 1979: "Everything is relative. But your paper is *absolutely* brilliant. With it you have put our understanding of Bach on a new level. ... No one before you has been able to show how a whole, huge, important cyclical work was structured in close harmony with a literary work – and an ancient one at that. It is an immense step forward and you have my whole admiration and gratitude for a momentous and unquestionably successful undertaking. ... With renewed assurances of my admiration for your unprecedented breakthrough in our understanding of Bach ...", to which Bonnie Blackburn added: "Your thesis is absolutely convincing on musical grounds alone, but when toward the end you come to Bach's knowledge of rhetoric and cap it with the quotation from Birnbaum, the effect is stunning. Congratulations on what will surely be the most talked about new contribution of recent years". Similarly Andres Briner of the *Neue Zürcher Zeitung*:[142] "Hardly any musicological study has ever attracted so much attention with us as yours" (letter of 28 Oct. 1980). Or the *Frankfurter Allgemeine Zeitung*, 1 June 1979: "It appears that for the *Musical Offering* the sequence is clarified (and the *Neue Bach-Ausgabe* will again have to revise this work)"; the *Basler Zeitung*, 20 May 1980: "Before the discovery one knew neither the correct sequence of the single movements nor the structure and deeper significance of the work. ... Strong historical arguments ... The thesis will be difficult to disprove"; *Berliner Tagesspiegel*, 12 July 1981: "In principle, the convincing power of Kirkendale's thesis concerns not only musicologists and philologists"; *New York Times*, 125 June 1982: "will, among other things, change the order in which the pieces are usually played". Hildebrecht Hommel, a distinguished professor of Latin at the Universities of Heidelberg and Tübingen, devoted an entire article to the discovery, stating: "[the] work, in its thoroughness and originality as well as abundance can be regarded as epoch-making"; "pathbreaking study; ... a new page has opened for Bach research".[143] In the meantime, the work has gone through eight editions in

---

[141] Translated from the German. Living persons are quoted with their permission.

[142] Referring to the abbreviated version published in the *NZZ* on 25/26 Oct. 1980.

[143] "[Die] Arbeit darf nach Gründlichkeit und Originalität wie nach Ergiebigkeit als epochemachend gelten" "bahnbrechende Abhandlung; ... für die Bachforschung [ist] ein neues Blatt aufgeschlagen" – *Quintilian und Johann Sebastian Bach: Neue Forschungen zum Spätwerk des Thomaskantors*, «Antike und Abendland», XXXIV, 1988, pp. 89-97. Hommel quotes additional, older literature on Gesner, and argues that the philologist surely presented Bach with a copy of his edition of Quintilian. He suggests, like Bürger/Schwinn, p. 128, that Bach may have, *inter al.*, rendered

three languages, one of them a pirated Italian translation, not to mention the extensive reviews broadcast by the BBC, RAI, etc., and the numerous performances and recordings based on this research.

I am grateful to our opponents in this discussion for having stimulated me to return to this subject matter[144] ("Illa vero iucundissima, si contingat aliquod ex adversario ducere argumentum"[145] – *per motum contrarium*) and having given me the opportunity to add some new observations and to clarify some points which we may not have explained sufficiently. In a presentation of this kind, an author is compelled to repeat some arguments which he has made elsewhere, but have been misunderstood or ignored, sometimes willfully. He cannot begin to repeat all of them, so we must beg our readers to refer to our earlier articles with their documentation (*including* the Latin and Italian quotations and the footnotes!) and to the review of the facsimile edition (below, ch. 13). They may draw their own conclusions from what was said there, in the light of the present clarifications, keeping in mind that composers did not necessarily copy rhetoricians to the letter, but freely *selected* their analogies, often indirectly and subconsciously, and that a pedantically exaggerated insistence on positivistic proofs for every last detail would render any explanation of musical compositions going beyond arid structural analyses and qualifying as *Geisteswissenschaft* impossible.[146]

* * *

Writers on music inevitably project their own horizons and backgrounds onto the music and the composers whom they investigate. If their interests are

---

thanks to Gesner by utilizing the volume for his musical composition. Hommel's own copy had been presented by the editor to an obscure friend in 1740, from which Hommel concludes: "erst recht wird [Gesner] auch und vor allem seinem Freund Bach ein Exemplar gewidmet haben" ["all the more and especially, Gesner will have dedicated a copy to his friend Bach"]. The article of Otto L. BETTMANN (founder of the Bettmann Archive and native of Leipzig), *Bach the Rhetorician*, «The American Scholar», LV/1, winter 1985/86, pp. 113-118, though conceived by a layman for laymen, reveals more sense than much 'professional' musicological writing on this composer. It emphasizes also the generally accepted, correct assessment of Bach's cantatas as 'musical sermons', i.e. as affective oratory, fulfilling the function of 'docere, delectare, movere'. In the Baroque, the reverse analogy was equally valid: "quasi ad una musica di comedia si va alla predica per osservare la rettorica" ["One goes to the sermon almost as to an opera, to observe the rhetoric"] – Domenico DE GUBERNATIS, 1672, quoted above, p. 35, note 8). Bettmann's publication inspired, in turn, a third-hand, but likewise sensible article by Donal HENAHAN, in «The New York Times», 24 Nov. 1985, p. 25: *Sonorities do not suffice*.

144 This paragraph was followed, in the original version of this article (1997), by a footnote with addenda and corrigenda to our articles of 1979-80, now omitted here and incorporated, together with its Appendix II, into ch. 2 and 12.

145 "It is truly most delightful if one happens to derive some argument from one's adversary" – Quintilian, VI.i.4.

146 Cf. above, p. 81, the plea of Curt Sachs.

limited to paper, ink, printing technology, textual criticism, or at best to notes and sounds, the image which they create of the composers, the art of music, and the discipline of musicology will not be a flattering or even an accurate one. Thus musicologists and musician-writers can become the denigrators, the worst enemies of the composers and the art which they should be serving,[147] in the case under discussion depriving a great composer of one of his most brilliant feats,[148] accomplished in spite of the limitations of analogies between language and music. It could be argued that the stature of a composer is, *inter al.*, proportionate to the degree to which he transcends such limitations and gives his music meaning by relating it to broader aspects of human experience; and that the most interesting musicological writing is that which reestablishes the multiplex relationships of music with its historical context, with the neighbouring disciplines of the humanities. It is precisely these relationships which should be cultivated rather than denied, for they give music its richness and interest, rather than impoverishing it by rendering it 'impure', as some would imagine.[149] They may not feel at ease in tackling the difficult but central problem of 'meaning' in music, and thus prefer to ignore its existence.[150] Those who have tried to write about it have most often approached it from unprofessional, subjective viewpoints, or from the ahistorical and abstract disciplines of aesthetics, psychology, linguistics, or sociology, thus bringing the problem of meaning into disrepute. But those art historians who have made the most brilliant contributions to their discipline, i.e. iconologists concentrating on the Renaissance, have long realized that the most va-

---

[147] E.g. below, p. 216, note 28.

[148] Christoph WOLFF, *Johann Sebastian Bach: The Learned Musician*, New York, Norton, 2000, in spite of the title, makes no mention of the most striking instance of the composer's erudition.

[149] Cf. CURTIUS, p. 233: "Pure art, which wants to exist only for itself, loses the connection with human beings and things. But in this way, art destroys itself".

[150] WOLFF, *Bach*, p. 422, and WILLIAMS (quoted *ibid.*) do not seem to recognize that a musical composition can have any other 'source' than paper and ink; "excluding any *thought* which may have been a source of inspiration for the work. ... Is there not a danger that by capitulating to diplomatic method we may allow the mere means to become an end in itself and the natural priority of mind over matter to be upset?" (below, p. 421). For abundant examples of concrete 'meaning' in music, see ch. 1 and 15, and articles by Owen Jander on Beethoven's instrumental music. – Deconstructionism, one of the most foolish of the many fads afflicting universities in our time, would deny meaning even to literary works, except for the irrelevant (because anachronistic and subjective) individual response of the unprepared modern reader, who may also be geographically far removed from the author. One could suspect that those who embrace this approach simply do not wish to undertake the hard but rewarding work (learning ancient languages and reading large amounts of old texts and documents), the concrete historical studies necessary for understanding any historical phenomenon such as literature, art, or music. The result is a declaration of bankruptcy for one's own discipline: if literature has no objective meaning, what reason do we have for studying it? Cf. CURTIUS for exemplary method and a wealth of fruitful results.

luable keys to understanding meaning in non-verbal art are language (not in the abstract, but the concrete-historical sense) – the vehicle by which ideas are expressed most explicitly – and literature, particularly that of classical antiquity. A music historian can only be grateful for any literary clues, which a composer of the Renaissance or Baroque provides for his music, and for biographical facts which may help explain it objectively – an aim not to be confused with the amateurish romanticizing biographies written for laymen. We should take these precious indications very seriously and investigate them in their full historical context, in order to approach an understanding of the musical work of art.[151]

---

151 Now that the apologists of the *NBA* have had their day (or, rather, 25 years) in court and their arguments have – hopefully – been refuted, we may again suggest that the *NBA* may someday reissue the *Musical Offering* in its intelligible form.

IV.

FRANCESCHINA, GIROMETTA, AND THEIR COMPANIONS IN A MADRIGAL 'A DIVERSI LINGUAGGI' BY LUCA MARENZIO AND ORAZIO VECCHI

Two of the greatest masters of the Italian madrigal combined their wits in a single fascinating, but unknown piece. Emil Vogel's monumental *Bibliothek der gedruckten weltlichen Vokalmusik Italiens aus den Jahren 1500-1700* does not inform us that Orazio Vecchi's *Selva di varia ricreatione* of 1590[1] contains a miniature madrigal comedy for nine voices, five of which were written by Luca Marenzio and four added by Vecchi.[2] Nor does the original *tavola* reproduced by Vogel give any indication, beyond the title "Diversi linguaggi", that each voice sings a different text and represents a different person.[3] At first glance, such a composition may appear rather confused. Yet the relationship of the components to each other is manifold, intimate, and most natural.

Canto primo, canto secondo, alto, tenore, and basso are designated "del Marenzio", as well as with the names of their roles: Franceschina, Girometta, Zanni, Magnifico, and Tedesco (see Ex. 1). The two girls, however, provide their own texts and melodies: the Italian folksongs "La bella Franceschina" and "Girometta". To these five voices, which constitute a self-contained com-

---

[1] Venice, Angelo Gardano, reprinted *ibid.*, 1595. VOGEL, Berlin, Haack, 1892, II, 268ff, and Pomezia, Staderini, 1977[2], pp. 1761ff.

[2] Ed. in W. KIRKENDALE, *Madrigali a diversi linguaggi von Luca Marenzio - Orazio Vecchi, Johann Eccard und Michele Varotto*, Wolfenbüttel, Möseler, 1975 («Das Chorwerk», 125), together with the compositions of Eccard and Varotto discussed below. The first modern performance took place at the Holland Festival Oude Muziek, Utrecht, 30-31 Aug. 1991, repeated at Trento Musicantico, 8 Oct. 1991, with the Centro di Musica Antica di Padova, directed by Livio Picotti.

[3] A composition with a complete, but different text in each voice corresponds to the first of the three catagories of quodlibets defined by Michael PRAETORIUS, *Syntagma Musicum*, III, Wolfenbüttel, Holwein, 1619, p. 18. Our madrigal is mentioned only very briefly by Angelo CATELANI, *Della vita e delle opere di Orazio Vecchi*, «Gazzetta musicale di Milano», XVI, 1858, p. 92 ["words as strange as they are unintelligible"], and by Gino RONCAGLIA and Charles VAN DEN BORREN, in *Orazio Vecchi, percursore del melodramma (1550-1605)*, Modena, Soc. tip. modenese, 1950, pp. 154, 186. No notice was taken of it in the literature on Marenzio.

Ex. 1. Marenzio/Vecchi: *Diversi linguaggi*, 1590, mm. 1-5.

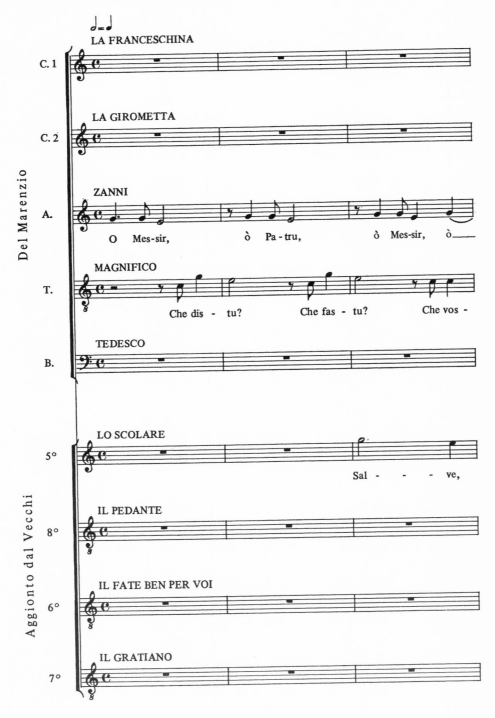

position, Vecchi added middle parts for Scolare, Pedante, "Fate ben per voi", and Graziano, with the designation "aggionto dal Vecchi". Each composer included a dialogue in his share of voices: Marenzio, the dispute between Zanni and Magnifico; Vecchi, that between Scolare and Pedante. In Ex. 1 the voices are so arranged that the partners of a dialogue appear on adjacent staves. The words of each of these four persons become intelligible only in the score, where they are seen in alternation with those of the respective partner. In the texts printed below I have indicated such alternation, but not the extensive overlappings and repetitions.

Our investigation will concentrate to a rather unorthodox extent on the social, literary, and musical traditions of the various character types and of the two folksongs in all their complexity (sections I and II: *Marenzio's Quodlibet* and *Vecchi's Addition*) and then consider briefly the relationship of the voices in this particular piece (section III: *The Ensemble*). The songs, having more or less fixed texts and melodies, unlike the character types, require investigation as entities; and they are all the more deserving of comprehensive documentation as they are among the most popular of the Cinquecento and early Seicento,[4] yet hitherto overlooked in musicological literature. Such groundwork appeared not only worthwhile, but indispensable, for it is on those crossroads of life that we find the keys for our "kleines Welttheater", with townhouse, tavern, school, street, doorsteps, and balcony, and its timeless scale of sounds.

I. MARENZIO'S QUODLIBET

A. Zanni. Del Marenzio. Alto. / Magnifico. Del Marenzio. Tenore

Prima Parte

Z. O Messir.
M. Che distu?
Z. O Patru.
M. Che fastu?
Z. O Messir.
M. Che vostu?
Z. O Patru, à no poss plu canta, perch'à crep de la fam.
M. Ah bestion, fio d'un laro, non t'hastu ben sfondrao?
Z. Mo con que, s'a no g'havì mai pa qua[n]t à vorèf?

Z. O Sir.
M. What are you saying?
Z. O master.
M. What are you doing?
Z. O Sir.
M. What do you want?
Z. O master, I can no longer sing, because I am dying of hunger.
M. Ah, beast, son of a thief, haven't you satiated yourself?
Z. But with what, if I never have as much bread as I would like?

---

4 Nearly 150 musical and literary sources and references could be identified.

M. Poltron, che tutto'1 dì ti è stao à tola. Tirr'in mal'hora.

Z. Andev'à fa impica.

M. Trist'anegao.

Seconda Parte

M. O disgratiao!

Z. Che ve piase Sagnur?

M. Scampao da la galia.

Z. Che bramef, ser minchiu? Cu cu, cu cu, cu cu. Ve ne dispreghi.

M. Ah laro!

Z. Vene disgratio.

M. Te ne disgratio.

Z. Horsù, horsù, via paghem.

M. Mo sù, imbriago! Non dubitar gioton c'hastu d'haver.

Z. E voi al me salari: quara[n]ta tre sesi[5] de bu arze[n]t.

M. Tiò.

Z. U.

M. Tiò.

Z. Do.

M. Tiò tiò.

Z. Tre, quatter.

M. Tirra via, a la mal'hora.

Z. Andè al bordel, am racomandi.

M. Zani.

Z. Messir.

M. O Zani.

Z. O Messir.

M. Mi ti raccomando.

Z. Am racomandi.

M. Idler, who has spent all day at the table. Go to hell.

Z. Go and be hanged.

M. Miserable one!

M. O wretch!

Z. What is your pleasure, sir?

M. Escaped from the galleys.

Z. What do you desire, Mr. Idiot? Cuckoo, cuckoo, cuckoo [i.e. cuckold]. I don't beg you (*also*: I despise you).

M. Ah thief!

Z. I don't thank you (*also*: I wish you misfortune).

M. I don't thank you.

Z. Go ahead, pay me.

M. Come on, drunkard! Don't doubt what you have coming to you, glutton.

Z. And I want my wages: forty-three pennies of good silver.

M. Here.

Z. One.

M. Here.

Z. Two.

M. Here, here.

Z. Three, four.

M. Get out, go to the devil.

Z. Go to the brothel, I take my leave.

M. Zanni.

Z. Sir.

M. O Zanni.

Z. O Sir.

M. I take leave of you.

Z. I take my leave.

Zanni and Magnifico, inseparable since dependent upon each other for their comic effect, were seldom absent from the commedia dell'arte, where they wore masks, being character types rather than individuals.[6] Magnifico

---

[5] Old Venetian coin of very small denomination.

[6] K. M. LEA, *Italian Popular Comedy: A Study in the Commedia dell'Arte, 1560-1620, with Spe-*

first appears by this name in 1559, in a *canto carnascialesco* of Antonfrancesco Grazzini detto il Lasca;[7] he is known also as "Pantalone".[8] An actor who undertakes this role must have "perfected the Venetian language, with its dialects, proverbs, and vocabulary".[9] A remote Venetian descendant of the *senex* of Plautus and Terence, a doting patrician who has lost his dignity in intimacies with his servants – Magnifico usually plays the part of a senile lover or duped parent.

Zanni's name is not derived from the Latin '*sannio*', as Quadrio and others have asserted,[10] but is simply Bergamask for 'Giovanni'. Since the sixteenth century, the *facchini bergamaschi* emigrated to the cities, where they monopolized those services which Garzoni could compare to those of donkeys.[11] They were especially numerous in seaports, and thus the connection of the Bergamask servant with the Venetian merchant was a natural one.[12] (Plate IV.1a).

The dialogue of 'Zanni e Magnifico' was a popular literary genre of the sixteenth century, recited by *montimbanchi* in the streets and included in chapbooks of folk poetry such as Zan Bagotto's *Opera nuova* (n.p. 1576: *Dia-*

---

cial Reference to the English Stage, Oxford, Clarendon, 1934, I, and Günther SCHÖNE, *Die Commedia dell'Arte: Bilder auf Burg Trausnitz in Bayern*, «Maske und Kothurn», V, 1959, pp. 74-77, 179-181, reproduce depictions of Zanni and Magnifico from the frescoes painted for Duke Wilhelm of Bavaria in 1578. Luciano PAESANI, *Per uno studio sui rapporti fra servi e padroni nella commedia dell'arte*, «Trimestre», VII, 1973, pp. 178-204; Ninian MELLAMPHY, *Pantaloons and Zanies: Shakespeare's 'Apprenticeship' to Italian Professional Comedy Troupes*, «New York Literary Forum», V-VI, 1980, pp. 144-151.

[7] *Tutti i trionfi, carri, mascherate ò canti carnascialeschi andati per Firenze*, Florence, s.n., 1559, pp. 461ff.

[8] LEA, I, 18f, mentions four etymologies which have been suggested for the latter name, none of them connected with 'trousers'. See also below, note 19, and p. 193.

[9] "perfetta la lingua Veneziana, con i suoi dialetti, proverbj, e vocaboli" – Andrea PERRUCCI, *Dell'arte rappresentativa premeditata ed all'improvviso*, Naples, Mutio, 1699, p. 246. Cf. also Pietro SPEZZANI, *Il primo repertorio linguistico di Pantalone*, «Atti dell'Istituto veneto di scienze, lettere ed arti», CXX, 1961/62, pp. 549-577, and *Il linguaggio del Pantalone pregoldoniano, ibid.*, CXXI, 1962/63, pp. 643-710.

[10] The etymology is discussed by Orlindo GUERRINI, *La Vita e le opere di Giulio Cesare Croce*, Bologna, Zanichelli, 1879, p. 366, and Domenco MERLINI, *Saggio di ricerche sulla satira contro il villano*, Turin, Loescher, 1894, pp. 130ff. On the role of Zanni cf. Luigi RICCOBONI, *Histoire du théâtre italien*, Paris, Delormel, 1728, pp. 7-20; Francesco Saverio QUADRIO, *Della Storia e della ragione d'ogni poesia*, Bologna/Milan, Agnelli, 1739-52, III/2, p. 212; Vincenzo DE AMICIS, *La Commedia popolare latina e la commedia dell'arte*, Naples, Morano, 1882, p. 63; Maria MAGNI, *Il tipo dello Zanni nella commedia dell'arte in Italia nei secoli XVI e XVII*, «Bergomum», XX, 1926, pp. 111-138, 163-184.

[11] Tommaso GARZONI, *La Piazza universale di tutte le professioni del mondo e nobili e ignobili*, Venice, Somasco, 1585, p. 811.

[12] They flourished also in Bologna, and were ridiculed there by the students during carnival festivities; cf. note 203, and MERLINI, pp. 122, 136.

logo del padrone e del Zanni),[13] the anonymous *Frottola d'un padrone, et d'un servo, intitolata Zanni da Bologna* (n.p. 1577), the *Esordio che fa il patrone al suo servitore Zanni ... con la risposta del detto Zanni* (n.p., n.d.)[14] and *El dialogo de un Magnifico con Zani bergamasco* (n.p., n.d.).[15] It was quickly taken over by composers, such as Orlando di Lasso, in his *Libro de villanelle, moresche ed altri canzoni* (Paris, Le Roy & Ballard, 1581),[16] and Vecchi, in our *Selva di varia ricreatione.*[17] Lasso's dialogue may well have something to do with the commedia dell'arte performed in 1568 for the marriage of Duke Wilhelm of Bavaria and Renata of Lorraine (in his dedication of 1581 Lasso characterizes the *Libro de villanelle* as a collection of youthful compositions).[18] On that occasion Lasso himself played the Magnifico with great success.[19] His pupil Johann Eccard, surely inspired by Lasso's piece, published among his *Newe Lieder mit fuenff und vier Stimmen* a five-part "Zanni et Magnifico".[20] It has the same roles and texts as Marenzio's which followed a year later, except that Girometta is not yet present and Zanni's words are sung by two voices. And it presents only the first strophe of the Franceschina text, repeating it eight times in succession.[21] Whereas Lasso had represented each character by a polyphonic complex (in the manner of Vecchi's *Amfiparnasso*), Eccard, Marenzio, and Vecchi assign roles to a single voice. Marenzio's dialogue, although overlapping the texts of the two persons much more than Vecchi's does, is nevertheless clearer than Eccard's, which presents the two texts simultaneously, one of them in two non-

---

[13] Repr. in Vito PANDOLFI, *La commedia dell'arte*, Florence, Sansoni, 1957-61, I, 187f. Pandolfi does not mention that this text appears also anonymously in the undated *Opera nove nella quale si contiene un lamento di una figliola che non vuolea pigliar il marito vecchio ... con un dialogo del Fortunato et del Zanne su l'aere della bustachina*, *Opera nova dove si contiene un invito de alcuni pastori ...con un dialogo del patrone e del Zanni, di nuovo dato in luce ad instantia di Paolo Emilio Piemontese* (n.p.); *Nuova scelta di vilanelle & altre canzoni ... con un dialogo del patron & del Zanni* (n.p.). These four editions of the same dialogue illustrate clearly the meaning of the word 'nuova' on the title pages of such collections. Cf. also W. KIRKENDALE, *L'Aria di Fiorenza, id est Il Ballo del Gran Duca*, Florence, Olschki, 1972, pp. 24f.

[14] Repr. in PANDOLFI, I, 189ff.

[15] *Ibid.*, I, 174-178.

[16] In Orlando DI LASSO, *Sämtliche Werke*, X, Leipzig, Breitkopf & Härtel, n.d., no. 22, pp. 135-139.

[17] P. 7: *Dialogo a 5*, "Tich toch".

[18] *Op. cit.*, p. XI.

[19] Massimo TROIANO, *Discorsi delli trionfi, giostre, apparati, e delle cose più notabile* [sic] *fatte nelle sontuose nozze, dell'Illustrissimo et Eccellentissimo Signor Duca Guglielmo ... nell'anno 1568*, Munich, s.n., 1568, p. 184: "L'Eccellente Meßere Orlando, di Laßo, fu il Magnifico, Meßer Pantalone, di Bisognosi".

[20] In *Neue geistliche und weltliche Lieder zu fünf und vier Stimmen*, Königsberg, Osterberger, 1589; PäM, XXI, no. 14, pp. 90-96; and W. KIRKENDALE, *Madrigali a diversi linguaggi* cit., pp. 20-25.

[21] In the keys F, B-flat, C, G, and (in the *Seconda parte*) F, B-flat, C, F.

synchronized voices. The language has some affinity to Lasso's – the prover-
bially lazy and gluttonous Zannis were abused by their masters with a vocabulary that had become fairly standardized.

B. Tedesco. Del Marenzio. Basso

In Marenzio's (and Eccard's) bass part is heard the voice of Tedesco, the
drunken mercenary or *Landsknecht*, singing the praises of the bottle in a language that can be called neither Italian nor German:

Prima Parte

Mi star bon compagnon	Me be good fellow
Mi trinchere co'l fiascon	Me drink with the big bottle
Mi piasere moscatelle	Me like muscatel
Mi far garaus di bon.	Me kill good.

Seconda Parte

Mi folentier star fol	Me like to be full [i.e. intoxicated]
Mi far tutt' in un tru[n]ch	Me do everything in a drunk
Mi mangere bon platais[22]	Me eat good dishes
Mi folere star contente	Me want to be satisfied
Mi non esser minchion	Me not be fool
Mi star bon compagnon.	Me be good fellow.

Of all the caricatures of foreigners speaking a language which they are unable to master – the Frenchman in Lessing's *Minna von Barnhelm* being the
most celebrated – none was more widespread than that of the German soldier
(including the Swiss mercenaries) in the Italian literature of the Cinquecento.
He was particularly amusing because he filled at the same time the role of the
drunkard (see Plate IV.1b). His place is above all in the *canti carnascialeschi*
[carnival songs] which flourished especially in Tuscany during the late fifteenth
and early sixteenth centuries,[23] a repertoire assigned to the various trades
and professions, with the often obscene *canzoni dei lanzi* forming a major
component.[24] In the second half of the sixteenth century the Tedesco is repre-

---

22 Cf. I-MOe ms. C.331 (note 26 below), f. 13*v*: "Bon platais stinche di craut".

23 Later he is found also in other literary genres; cf. the comedies mentioned by LEA, I, 126, and
BANCHIERI's *Novella del Tedesco ubriacato* and *Novella del Tedesco insatiabile*, in his *Trastulli della
villa*, Bologna, Mascheroni, 1627, Venice, Giuliani, 1627.

24 Federico GHISI, *I canti carnascialeschi*, Florence, Olschki, 1937, pp. 78-86, and, e.g., the relevant songs in *Tutti i trionfi* ..., and Charles S. SINGLETON (ed.), *Canti carnascialeschi del rinascimento*, Bari, Laterza, 1936. In 1788 Goethe could still see the drunken German mimicked in the Roman
carnival: "Der Fremde muss sich auch gefallen lassen, in diesen Tagen verspottet zu werden. ... Die

sented in the villotta collections and lute books, not only practising his profession in the musical depictions of battles,[25] but also 'off duty', i.e. in the pursuit of alcohol[26] and venal women.[27] In Matthias Hermann's battaglia, incoherent and rather meaningless Teutonic sounds suffice to convey an impression of the German language to a Latin audience. However, the opposite procedure was the normal one: to allow the Tedesco to speak his own brand of Italian. He uses, in the first person singular, "mi" for the nominative case[28] and the infinitive for the verb ("Mi star", etc.); he speaks Italian words with German pronunciation ("folentier" for "volentieri", "folere" for "volere"), or German words written with Italian orthography ("fol"[29] for "voll", "trinchere" for "trinken"). The text used by Eccard and Marenzio is characteristic: its first line is sung again by the Tedeschi in Vecchi's *Veglie di Siena*[30] and Banchieri's *Barca di Venetia per Padova*,[31] the latter with the heading "Aggiunta, il Thedesco con il fiasco" ["Addendum, the German with the bottle"].[32]

---

deutschen Bäckerknechte zeichnen sich in Rom gar oft betrunken aus, und sie werden auch mit einer Flasche Wein in ihrer eigentlichen oder auch etwas verzierten Tracht taumelnd vorgestellt" ["The foreigner must also acquiesce in being mocked in these days. ... The Geman bakers' servants are often distinguished in Rome as drunkards, and they are also introduced in their own or somewhat adorned costume staggering with a bottle of wine in hand"] – *Zweiter römischer Aufenthalt*, in *Sämmtliche Werke*, Stuttgart/Tübingen, Cotta, 1840, XXIV, 221.

[25] Matthias Hermann VERRECOIENSIS, *Die Schlacht vor Pavia*, in Wolfgang SCHMELTZEL's *Guter seltzamer und künstreicher teutscher Gesang*, Nuremberg, 1544, repr. in Matthias's *Battaglia taliana*, Venice, Gardano, 1549. The title in the first edition renders unnecessary Alfred EINSTEIN's doubts on the connction with Pavia – *The Italian Madrigal*, Princeton UP, 1949, II, 744; the *battaglia* of Donino Garsi in the Dusiacki lute book (without text – see below, pp. 144, 161f).

[26] "Trince got è malvasia", in *Villotte alla napolitana a tre voci, con una todesca, non più stampate*, Venice, Scotto, 1566, pp. 25ff, quoted by Stefano ARTEAGA, *Le rivoluzioni del teatro italiano*, Bologna, Palese, 1783-1788, I, 154f, to illustrate "i progressi della poesia musicale"!; "Mi stare pone Toteschе" in I-MOe ms. C. 311 (1574), fol. 13v, text published in *Il Libro di canto e liuto di Cosimo Bottegari, fiorentino*, ed. Luigi Francesco VALDRIGHI, Florence, Giornale di Erudizione, 1891, pp. 63f, text and music in *The Bottegari Lutebook*, ed. Carol MACCLINTOCK, Wellesley College, 1965, p. 38.

[27] E.g. Ghirardo DA PANICO's "Patrone, belle patrone", in [Filippo AZZAIOLO], *Primo libro de villotte alla padoana*, Venice, Gardano, 1557; text published in «Giornale storico della letteratura italiana», XX, 1893, p. 389; LASSO's above-mentioned collection of 1581 (with drastic texts).

[28] Perhaps influenced by the Bolognese dialect: see below, note 296, D-Mbs cod. it. 347, and [Adriano BANCHIERI], *Discorso di Camillo Scaliggeri dalla Fratta, qual prova che la favella naturale di Bologna precede, & eccede la Toscana in prosa & in rima*, Bologna, Mascheroni & Ferroni, 1626, ch. 11: "Che la parola Mi, sia meglio dell'Io".

[29] Misread as "sol" in *The Bottegari Lutebook*, resulting in a meaning diametrically opposed to the character of the "bon compagnon"; "stinche" (for "stinkt") is misread as "schinche".

[30] Venice, Gardano, 1604; Rome, De Santis, 1940 («Capolavori polifonici del secolo XVI», II).

[31] Venice, Amadino, 1605. Modern editions in Carlo DEL FRATI, *I «madrigali accademici» di Adriano Banchieri*, ms. thesis, University of Parma, 1963/64, vol. 2-3 (transcriptions of the editions of 1605 and 1623); Rome, De Santis, 1969 («Capolavori polifonici del secolo XVI», IX); and Bologna, Ut Orpheus, 1998.

[32] Cf. also below, note 145, and the lines "Questi Lanze buon compagne" and "Mi star qui sì

Marenzio, like Eccard and Vecchi, characterizes Tedesco's heavy temperament by a bass melody moving largely in fourths and fifths (cf. Ex. 1). He thus employs the appropriate musical idiom, still recognizable to his audience: that of the *canti carnascialeschi*. And we can assume that the German patrons to whom the edition was dedicated, Jakob and Johann Fugger, were amused by the parody of their countryman.

C. The Folksongs

In the two uppermost voices the melodies of *La bella Franceschina* and *Girometta* alternate with each other as follows:

	Prima Parte	Seconda Parte
Key:		
Canto I, *La bella Franceschina*:	G C a ...	C a G
Canto II, *Girometta*:	G C G	C G C

These voices, unlike those of the two dialogues and three monologues, do not, strictly speaking, represent dramatic roles, since their texts speak of the girls Franceschina and Girometta in the third rather than the first person, with the exception of the second and fourth strophes of the *Girometta* text (see below, pp. 156f). This slight loss of dramatic quality is, however, more than outweighed by the wealth of associations which the traditional songs bring with them, thus adding immeasurably to the meaning of the ensemble. We shall meet here with the milieu of all the character types – especially of Zanni and the drunken soldier, and of the negligent student and the Bolognese doctor whom Vecchi will introduce to us.

The career of *La bella Franceschina* can be traced by means of the following musical sources, which span most of the sixteenth century.

MUSICAL SOURCES OF *LA BELLA FRANCESCHINA*

a) ca. 1520[33]   I-Vm ms. Ital. IV.1227 (= 11699), Italian keyboard music; ff. 2v-3: "La bella franceschina".

---

buon compagne" in texts of Guglielmo detto il Guiggola in *Tutti i trionfi* cit., pp. 242 and 268, the former reprinted by SINGLETON, p. 278. In a letter of 4 June 1576, Orlando di Lasso addresses his Bavarian prince intimately and humorously as "bon Compagnon" – cf. Wolfgang BOETTICHER, *Orlando di Lasso und seine Zeit*, Kassel, Bärenreiter, 1958, p. 440.

[33] These dates, given by Knud JEPPESEN, *Ein altvenezianisches Tanzbuch*, in *Festschrift Karl Gustav Fellerer zum sechzigsten Geburtstag*, Regensburg, Bosse, 1962, pp. 245 and 253, are to be regarded as rough approximations. I-Vm ms. Ital. IV 1227 ed. Jeppesen as *Balli antichi veneziani*, Copenhagen, Hansen, 1962.

b) ca. 1525[33]   CH-SG ms. 463, vocal music, predominately Franco-Flemish; ff. 59 (soprano) and 117 (alto; other parts missing): "La bella Francescina".

c) ca. 1536   Luis Milan, *Libro de musica de vihuela de mano intitulado el Maestro*, n.p., s.n., 1536$_5$, sig. G6: "Pavana".[34] The accompanying note mentions that this pavan was sung in Italy with the text "La bella Franceschina": "Esta pavana que se sigue la sonada della se hizo en Ytalia y canta conella una letra que dizen qua la bella franceschina la compostura que va sobrella es mia y es del otavo tono".

d) ca. 1545   "H.D.", German lute tablature D-Mbs mus. ms. 1512,[35] f. 67: "La bella Franceschina".

e)   1546   Pierre Phalèse, *Des Chansons reduictz en tabulature de luc a trois et quatre parties, livre deuxième*, Louvain, Phalèse, 1546$_{18}$, sig. k4: "La bella franciscana".

f)   1549   *Idem, Carminum quae chely vel testudine canuntur, liber primus*, Louvain, Phalèse, 1549$_8$, f. 7v: "La bella franciskina".

g)   1549   [Matthias Hermann Verrecoiensis (Mathias Fiamengo)], *La Bataglia taliana*, Venice, Gardano, 1549 and 1552, p. 10: "La bella Franceschina" is the last of several folksongs quoted in the cantus of the villotta "Horsu, horsu compagni", Seconda Parte, "Cantar vogl'una canzon".

h)   1568   Sebastian Vredeman, *Nova longeque elegantissima cithara ludenda carmina*, Louvain, Phalèse, 1568$_6$, f. 7v: "La bella franciskina".

i) ca. 1570-75   D-Mbs mus. ms. 1511b, Italian lute tablature, f. 4: "Franciosina".

j)   1589   Johann Eccard, *op. cit.*, Königsberg, 1589.

k)   1590   Luca Marenzio, "Diversi linguaggi" cit., reprinted 1595.

l)   1597   Nikolaus Zangius, *Etliche schöne teutsche geistliche und weltliche Lieder mit fünff Stimmen componiert*, Cologne, Grevenbruch, 1597,[36] no. 5: Quodlibet "Ich wil zu land ausreiten". Reprinted by Paul Kaufmann in *Musikalischer Zeitvertreiber*, Nuremberg, 1609.

The superimposition of the melodies in Ex. 2 reveals an older (b-h) and a newer form (j-l). The newer melody is related to the older only in its first half, where it paraphrases the older structure a third higher – a fact to which we

---

[34] Ed. in Guillermo MORPHY, *Les Luthistes espagnols du XVIe siècle*, Leipzig, Breitkopf & Härtel, 1902, I, 68, and PäM, II, ed. Leo Schrade, 1927, pp. 70f. The method of transcription practised in these editions obscures the melodic line almost beyond recognition. – Dates with subscript numbers refer to listings in Howard BROWN, *Instrumental Music Printed before 1600*, Cambridge MA, Harvard UP, 1967.

[35] On this ms. cf. Kurt DORFMÜLLER, *Studien zur Lautenmusik in der ersten Hälfte des 16. Jahrhunderts*, Tutzing, Schneider, 1967, pp. 15-27.

[36] Ed. Berlin, Merseburger, 1960. PRAETORIUS (see above, note 3) gives "Nicolai Zangij Quotlibet" as the example for his second category of quodlibets, in which each voice has different words, consisting of fragments of text.

Ex. 2. *La bella Franceschina.*[37]

a)
I-Vm
c. 1520
♩ = ♩ (originally a fourth lower)

b)
CH-SG
c. 1525
La bel-la Fran - ce - schi-na, la bel-la Franceschina, e la bel - la Fran - ce - schi-na, la sede sot un pin ri ri rin, la se-de sot un pin.

c)
Milan
1536

d)
H. D.
c. 1545
♭ = ♭

e)
Phalèse
1546
♭ = ♭

f)
Phalèse
1549
♭ = ♭

g)
Matthias
1549
(originally a fifth higher)
E la bel-la Fran - ce - schi-na, la bella Franceschina che la pian-g'e la so - spi - ra che la vorre mari che la vor-re ma - ri.

h)
Vredeman
1568
♩ = ♩ (originally a second lower)

j-l)
Eccard,
Marenzio,
Zangius
1589-97
E la bel-la Fran - ce - schi-na ni - ni - na bu-fi - na la fi-li - bu - sta - chi-na

E che la vor - ria ma - ri - ni - ni la fi - li-bu-sta - chi.

[37] The melodies of 'a', 'i', and the second half of 'j-l' are unrelated to the others and therefore not aligned with them.

shall return later. The vocal sources (b, g, j-l) enable us to trace the development of the folksong text. The two earliest, CH-SG ms. 463 and Matthias, have only one strophe, with only the incipit in common (Ex. 2, b and g). Matthias's text appears again, without music, in a collection of German folksongs from the mid-sixteenth century, demonstrating that it was known in German-speaking countries before Eccard and Zangius employed it.[38]

> La bella franciscina [ij]
> La piange la suspira
> Che la voleva marì.
>
> Beautiful Franceschina,
> She weeps and sighs
> That she wanted a husband.

The next literary source, also without music, gives the most complete version of the text: Zan Bagotto's *Opera nuova di stanze, capitoli, barzelette & altri nuovi suggetti* (n.p., 1576, f. 4v).[39] The first strophe again tells us that the beautiful Franceschina wants a husband,[40] and the following five strophes identify the object of her desire: not the son of the count, to whom her father plans to marry her, but the poor youth who is in prison for her sake. The opening strophe corresponds to Matthias's text, but is expanded by the nonsense syllables forming internal rhymes, so characteristic of this song (printed below in italics), with their implications of 'buxom', 'comic', 'dear'. 'Filibustacchina' may be an Italian cognate of 'filibuster' (obstructionist, pirate).

> La Bella Franceschina
> La bella Franceschina *ninina bufina,*
>   La filibustacchina la piange, e la sospira,

---

[38] CH-Bu ms. F.X.21, p. 115. Cf. Julius RICHTER, *Katalog der Musik-Sammlung auf der Universitäts-Bibliothek in Basel*, Leipzig, Breitkopf & Härtel, 1892, no. 26, pp. 59-68. The ms. contains dates from 1529 to 1575. The song text from this ms. is published, with some inaccuracies, by K. BARTSCH, *Italienische Volkslieder*, «Zeitschrift für romanische Philologie», VI, 1882, p. 414.

[39] This version is reprinted in Vittorio ROSSI, *Le Lettere di messer Andrea Calmo*, Turin, Loescher, 1888, p. 415, and PANDOLFI, I, 188; the first two strophes are quoted without indication of source by JEPPESEN, p. 253, reading "busta ch' estra" for "bustachestra". Marenzio's melody, but with Bagotto's text underlaid, is recorded in *The King's Singers Madrigal History Tour*, EMI, 1983. Bernhard Meier pointed out that this text has a striking similarity to Dufay's three-voice ballata "La belle se siet au piet de la tour" – *Opera omnia*, VI, Rome, American Institute of Musicology, 1964, pp. 27f.

[40] A common subject in folk poetry; cf. "Madre vorrei marito" in the *Opera nuova nella quale intenderai alcune canzoni piacevole, nella prima la figliuola dimanda marito alla madre, nella seconda la madre gli da risposta, nella terza si lamenta che è mal maritata*, n.p., n.d., Florence, 1576, and the "Canzone di una figliuola che vuol marito" in B.R.B.'s *Opera nuova* quoted below, pp. 140f.

Che la vorria marì *ninì*,
La filibustacchì.
Lo suo padre alla finestra *ninestra bufestra*
La filibustachestra,
Ascoltar quel che la dì *ninì*,
La filibustacchì.
Tasi, tasi Franceschina *ninina bufina*
La filibustacchina,
Che te daro marì *ninì*,
La filibustacchì.
Te darogio lo fio del Conte *ninonte bufonte*
La filibustaconte del Conte Constantì *ninì*,
La filibustacchì.
E no vogio lo fio del Conte *ninonte bufonte*,
La filibustaconte del Conte Constantì *ninì*,
La filibustacchì.
Che vogio quel giovenetto *ninetto, bufetto*,
La filibustacchetto, che sta in prigion per mi *ninì*,
La filibustacchì.

[Nonsense sylables omitted in translation].
Beautiful Franceschina weeps and sighs that she wants a husband. / Her father at the
window: Listen what he tells her. / Be quiet, Franceschina, I shall give you a husband. /
I shall give you the son of Count Constantine. / [Franceschina]: I don't want the son
of the count. / I want that boy who is in prison for me.

In Adriano Banchieri's comedy *La Catlìna da Budri overo il furto amoroso*, II.v
(at least eight editions 1613-1650), one of the last literary sources of the text,
Catlìna while baking a cake sings a version in which Franceschina does not
reject, but desires the son of the count.[41]

By Marenzio's time there is some justification for associating *La bella
Franceschina* with the Franceschina of the commedia dell'arte, although the
latter makes her debut only long after the appearance of the song. 'Franceschina' was the stage name of Battista Amorevoli da Treviso, the first actor to
play the role of Zagna, the female counterpart of Zanni.[42] This name soon became the normal appellation of the maidservant in the *scenari*; she is often the
wife of Zanni, and in the employ of Magnifico or Graziano.[43] Thus Vecchi's

---

41 "E la bella Franceschina ninina buffina, / La filibustachina / Che la vorrìa marì, ninì, la filibustachì. / La vorria il fiol del Cont ninot buffont, / La filibustacont, / Del Cont Custantin, ninin la
filibustachin" ["Beauiful Franceschina ... wants a husband, the son of Count Constantine ..."].

42 PANDOLFI, I, 163.

43 Cf. the *scenari* of Flaminio SCALA, *Il teatro delle favole rappresentative*, Venice, Pulciani, 1611,

Magnifico asks, "Zanni, what are you doing with your Franceschina?"[44] Her master's advances naturally lead to conflicts with Zanni, as related in the *Contrasto tra Pantalone & il Zani per amore di Franceschina*[45] and *La gran vittoria di Pedrolino* [= Zanni] *contra il dottor Gratiano Scatolone per amore della bella Franceschina*[46] of the Bolognese folk poet Giulio Cesare Croce (1550-1609).

Eccard's Franceschina text, like that of Matthias, is limited to the first strophe, retaining the nonsense syllables but eliminating "la pianze e la sospira".[47] The strophe recurs in this form in Marenzio's text, where it is followed by four new strophes, quite different from those of Bagotto, ringing the changes on a whole series of girls' names:[48]

La Francesc[h]ina. Del Marenzio. Canto.

Prima Parte

E la bella Franceschina *ninina buffina*
  La filibustachina,
  E che la vorria marì *ninì*
  La filibustachì.

E la bella Nicoletta *ninetta buffetta*
  La filibustachetta,
  E che la và tropp'in frè *ninè*
  La filibustaché.

Seconda Parte

E la bella Marchesetta *ninetta buffetta*
  La filibustachetta
  E che la mi vestirà *ninà*
  La filibustacà.

E la bella Menicarda *ninarda buffarda*
  La filibustacarda
  E che l'è troppo lecca *ninà*
  La filibustacà.

E la bella Ricardona *ninona buffona*
  La filibustacona
  E che la merta corò *ninò* [= merita la corona]
  La filibustacò.

---

passim. "The connotation of the name was the opposite of maidenly or wifely virtue" – Winifred SMITH, *The Commedia dell'Arte*, New York, Columbia UP, 1912, p. 193. Orlando di LASSO, letter of 16 Feb. 1574: "Il Venturino ogni sera ... fa lui solo una comedietta di tre persone: il Magnifico, Zanni e Fransceschina" – *Briefe*, ed. Horst Leuchtmann, Wiesbaden, Breitkopf & Härtel, 1977, p. 70.

[44] "Zanni, che fai con la tua Franceschina?", in the *dialogo a 5* mentioned above, note 17.

[45] In Giulio Cesare CROCE, *Dialoghi curiosi*, Bologna, Cochi, 1629 and n.d.

[46] *Id.*, Bologna, n.d., 1617, 1621; repr. by PANDOLFI, II, 24ff.

[47] In Bagotto's text, these words had increased the length of the first strophe beyond that of those which follow. The statement of Wolfgang ROGGE, *Das Quodlibet in Deutschland bis Melchior Frank*, Wolfenbüttel, Möseler, 1965, p. 33, that Eccard's text and music are "freely invented" cannot be sustained.

[48] Although a fairly consistent evolution can be traced in a chronological examination of the music and especially of the text, we shall, of course, not always conclude that each source took its point of departure from its immediate predecessor. A more recent source may even represent an older version, since we are dealing with an anonymous popular folksong and our knowledge of its musical and literary texts will necessarily remain still less complete than our knowledge of its sources.

Beautiful Franceschina wants a husband. / Beautiful Nicoletta goes too quickly. / Beautiful Marchesetta will dress me. / Beautiful Menicarda is too tasty. / Beautiful Ricardona deserves the crown.

Zangius's quodlibet, seven years later, consists of quotations of a large number of popular songs – mostly German – in the various voices; its quotation from *La bella Franceschina* is limited to the first half of the first strophe as used by Eccard and Marenzio (discant, mm. 35ff).

The texts of both Bagotto and Marenzio illustrate how the *filastrocche*, the nonsense word "bustachina" and its derivatives, take their specific form from their immediate context, in order to form a rhyme (Franceschina – bustachina, finestra – bustachestra, Nicoletta – bustachetta, etc.). The same device is used in Croce's "Contrasto del hosto & del Zani"[49] (incipit "Zuane mi foler cuntare ninare bufare") and the "Dialogo del Padrone, e del Zanni" which immediately precedes *La bella Franceschina* in Bagotto's *Opera nuova*:[50]

> Z. Mi voref o mesir mio caro *ninaro bufaro*
> Che non fossev avaro,
> In darme da magnar *nenar*,
> E no me far stentar.
> P. Zane mio tu sei sì ingordo *ninordo* balordo,
> Che convien far il sordo,
> Se no me voi rovinar *nenar*,
> Con tanto to sfondrar. [Etc.]

Zanni: I should like, my dear sir, that you not be miserly in giving me food, and not cause me difficulty. / Master: My Zanni, you are such a greedy and stupid lout that I must turn a deaf ear if you are not to ruin me with so much gluttony of yours.

Although in this collection the two poems form a single group, the dialogue was published also by itself, in at least three undated, not necessarily later, anonymous editions (see above, note 13). In one of these it is said to be "su l'aere della bustachina", i.e. sung as a contrafactum of either the melody of *La bella Franceschina* or perhaps of a *bustachina* from which this song took the final form of its melody. Since the *bustachina* assumes different forms in different songs, the word was actually used as a plural noun, to indicate this interchangeable poetic component, as in B.R.B.'s *Opera nuova dove si conten-*

---

[49] *Disgratie del Zane*, n.p., n.d.; Bologna, Cochi, n.d. and 1621.

[50] In the remainder of this article, occasional footnote numbers are used merely to locate passages *of the text* to which the diagram on p. 197 refers.

gono alcune bustachine alla bolognese (n.p., n.d., and Venice, 1594).[51] A passage in Croce's "Barzelletta amorosa e piacevole alla bella Fornarina"[52]

> Sì vagamente
> Cantasti, e dolcemente,
> La Pastorella,
> E la Ninetta bella,
> La Mena, la Gambetta,
> Ancor la Gerometta,
> E nella Bustacchina
> La bella Franceschina.

You sang so beautifully and sweetly "La pastorella" and "La bella Ninetta", "La Mena", "La Gambetta", again "La Girometta", and "La bella Franceschina" in the *bustacchina*.

shows that *La bella Franceschina* was one of several texts which could be applied to the ("nella") *bustachina*, i.e. that Croce regards the former rather than the latter as the variable element. However, the *filastrocca* cannot take precedence over the incipit, since it was derived from it by rhyme. As Paolo Veraldo says in his "Testamento del Dottor Gratiano", the real "substance" of the *bustachina* was *La bella Franceschina*:[53]

> Mi faz hered' el più bestial duttor
> Che sipp'al mond' dell'art'oratoria
> Della mia sort', e qualità, e valor.
> ....
> Item, l'humanità d'Orland Lass'
> El contrapunt de Torquat Tass
> Legà stret'in t'un fass.
> ....
> Item, i documenti in barzeletta
> Composti dal sartor della fiametta
> E ancor la Girometta.
> Item, in conclusion la Violina[54]

---

[51] The edition consulted (n.d.) makes use of the bustachina only in the first item, the "Canzone fatta sopra una massarina", and there more sparingly than in other texts of this type.

[52] In *Freschi della villa*, Padua, n.d., Bologna, Cochi, 1612, and at least eight later editions until 1672.

[53] In his *Mascherate et capricci dilettevoli*, Venice, 1672, pp. 42-47; repr. by PANDOLFI, IV, 175-179, misreading "fass" (= "fascio") as "sass" and "sartor" as "fattor". In the reference to Lasso and Tasso, Graziano characteristically has his wires crossed.

[54] A lengthy discussion of this popular song is contained in Severino FERRARI, *Canzoni ricordate nell'incatenatura del Bianchino*, «Giornale di filologia romanza», IV, 1883, pp. 58-79, and *L'incate-*

> E la sustantia della Bustachina,
> La bella Franceschina.

I designate as my heir the world's most bestial doctor in the art of oratory of my kind, quality, and valor. ... Item: the humanity of Orlando di Lasso, the counterpoint of Torquato Tasso, tightly bound in a bundle ... Item: the documents in a burlesque, composed by the tailor of the little flame (or: of Fiametta), and again the 'Girometta'. ... Item: in conclusion 'La Violina'[54] ... and the substance of the bustachina, 'La bella Franceschina'.

The device was associated with children's songs at least since Banchieri's comedy *Il furto amoroso*, 1613 (III.vi: "am arecord quand'ai era una tosa d' sett'anni 'a imparà da mie lola la bustichina tutt'intiera"; "I remember when I was a child of seven years I learned the entire *bustachina* from my grandmother") until the late nineteenth century:[55]

> Una volta c'era una donnetta
> Ninetta buffetta precetta e comina
> Che aveva una gallina
> Piccina buffina precetta e comina; [etc.]

Once upon a time there was a little lady ..., who had a little hen.

Marenzio's Franceschina, we have seen, makes her appearance near the end of the song's long history (ca. 1520-1609).[56] His Girometta, on the other hand, takes her place near the beginning of this song's still longer life (ca. 1552-1710),[56] for, unlike *La bella Franceschina*, the *Girometta* achieved its greatest popularity in the seventeenth century. (It is a nice coincidence that in his score the two songs enter in 'chronological' order, and with the first song in the highest voice, the second in the second highest, as if according to diplomatic protocol).

---

natura del Bianchino (nuove ricerche), «Giornale ligustico di archeologia, storia e letteratura», XV, 1888, p. 124-127.

[55] [A. STRACCALI and S. FERRARI], *Ninne-nanne, cantilene e giuochi fanciulleschi uditi in Firenze*, Florence, 1886, p. 14. Cf. also the children's song quoted in Oreste TREBBI, *Contributo alla storia del teatro dialettale bolognese nel secolo XVII*, «Atti e memorie della r. deputazione di storia patria per le provincie di Romagna», ser. IV, vol. XVI, 1926, p. 25. On *La bella Franceschina* as a children's street song, see below, p. 168, Lasca.

[56] The dates only of extant musical sources, naturally younger than the song itself, not including later literary references (*Franceschina* until 1672, *Girometta* until 1737). The libretto of Pietro Chiari for Ferdinando Bertoni's *La bella Girometta* (Venice, 1761, SL 3884) alludes to the singing of the *Girometta* in the opening terzet and in the final quartet, but does not contain quotations from our text.

MUSICAL SOURCES OF THE GIROMETTA

1552	Giovanni Nasco, *Messa sopra la Gerometa* for CATB, I-TVca ms. 35, destroyed in 1944; transcription by Giovanni D'Alessi as far as "sedet ad dexteram Patris" and brief fragments of "Pleni sunt" and "Agnus Dei", 1935, I-TVca.[57]
ante 1559	[Filippo Azzaiolo, bolognese], *Il Secondo libro de villotte del fiore*, Venice, Gardano, 1559, Scotto, 1564[58] (composed somewhat earlier, since mentioned in the dedication of the *Terzo libro* as "giovanili fatiche"), pp. 7f: Napolitana "Girometta senza te".
1563	Serafino Razzi, *Libro primo delle laudi spirituali da diversi eccell. e divoti autori*, Venice, Rampazetto, 1563; facs. Bologna, Forni, 1969, f. 111: Priego di Fra Serafino Razzi per i novizi, "Torna, torna al freddo cuore"; f. 111*r-v*: Laude di Fra Marco della Casa, "Torna, torna al tuo Signore"; f. 110*v*: music for both lauds (cantus melody, = Ex. 3), with the first strophe of Razzi's text. The text of the first laud, without music, is reprinted in Razzi's *Santuario di laudi, o vero rime spirituali*, Florence, Sermatelli, 1609, p. 213.
1583	*Villotte mantovane a quattro voci* [possibly by Alessandro Striggio], Venice, Gardano, 1583 (only alto and tenor parts extant), pp. 28ff: "Apri hormai l'uscio".
1588	Gioseffo Zarlino, *Sopplimenti musicali*, Venice, De' Franceschi, 1588; facs. Farnborough, Gregg, 1966, p. 284.
1588	Marco Facoli venetiano, *Il Secondo libro d'intavolatura di balli d'arpicordo*, Venice, Gardano, 1588₃, ff. 32*v*-33: Napolitana "Deh pastorella cara" (keyboard piece with text underlaid).[59]
ante ca. 1590	Costanzo Porta (1504/5-1601), I-Bc ms. Q. 38, *Cantiones sacrae diversorum auctorum* (score), ff. 106*v*-112*v*: "Gerometta", for eight instruments.[60]
1590, 1595	Luca Marenzio, "Diversi linguaggi" cit.
1590, 1595	Orazio Vecchi, *Selva di varia ricreatione* cit.: *Battaglia d'amore e dispetto a 10, seconda parte*: "Da l'altra parte", canto, p. 48.

---

[57] The transcription is included in Michele Pozzobon, *La Messa sopra la Gerometta di Giovanni Nasco*, ms. thesis, University of Venice, 1981/82, pp. 121-140 (copy in I-Rvat). Here the tenor is notated an octave too high and no *musica ficta* is applied.

[58] Ed. Bologna 1953. Girometta text repr. in Eugenia Levi, *Lirica italiana nel cinquecento e nel seicento fino all'Arcadia*, Florence, Olschki, 1909, p. XXXVIII.

[59] Ed. in Marco Facoli, *Collected Works*, ed. Willi Apel, «Corpus of Early Keyboard Music», II, Dallas, American Institute of Musicology, 1963, pp. 33f, with text misread.

[60] The first nine measures are quoted by Luigi Torchi, *La Musica istrumentale in Italia nei secoli XVI, XVII e XVIII*, «Rivista musicale italiana», IV, 1897, pp. 604f. Throughout this piece the melody is used rather freely, but generally less freely than this incipit would indicate.

1597	Adriano Banchieri, *Canzonette a tre voci ... Hora prima di recreatione*, Venice, Amadino, 1597, no. 14: villotta "Sentij l'altra mattina".[61] Melody freely varied.
late 16th c.?	I-Fn ms. Magl. VII 618, *canti carnascialeschi* (texts only) and violin tablature,[62] f. 27: "Gierometta" (violin tablature, no text).
late 16th c.?	Donino Garsi, D-Bds mus. ms. 40153 (now in PL-Kj): lute book of Kasimierz Stanislaw Rudomina Dusiacki, "Anno 1620 a Padova": "Battaglia".[63]
17th c.	I-BGi, ms. *Libro di sonate del Signor Rubini per violino o cornetto o flauto*: "Girometta".[63bis]
1600-03	I-SA Bibl. Vesc., ms. Giovanni Lorenzo Baldano, *Libro per scriver l'intavolatura per sonare sopra le sordelline*, Savona, 1600-03, f. 4v: "Gerometta", "In altro modo", "In altro modo".[64]
1603	Jean-Baptiste Besard, *Thesaurus harmonicus*, Cologne, Greuenbruch, 1608, ff. 167v-168: "Bataille de Pavie".[65]
1608	Foriano Pico, *Nuova scelta di sonate per la chitarra spagnola*, Rome, Paci, 1608; plagiarized by Pietro Millioni under the title *Nuova corona d'intavolatura di chitarra spagnola*, Rome, Mancini, 1661, facs. Geneva, Minkoff, 1981, and Florence, SPES, 2002, pp. 24f: "Girumetta" (two pieces).
ca. 1610-35	I-Fn ms. Magl. XIX.30, Italian lute tablature, f. 34v: "Ghierometa".
1614	Giovanni Antonio Cangiasi, *Scherzi forastieri per suonare a quattro voci ... opera ottava*, Milan, Lomazzo, 1614; only alto part extant), p. 16: "La Girometta. (All'Ill. Sig. il Sig. Giovanni Moro)".
1615-	US-SF ms. M 2.1 M 3, lute book of Ascanio Bentivoglio, "cominciato adì 5 agosto 1615", p. 90: "Aria della girometta".[66]
1622	Bellerofonte Castaldi, *Capricci a due strumenti cioè tiorba e tiorbina*, Modena, the author, 1622; facs. Geneva, Minkoff, 1981, and Flor-

---

[61] In Andreas WERNLI, *Studien zum literarischen und musikalischen Werk Adriano Banchieris (1568-1634)*, Bern, Haupt, 1981, pp. 301f.

[62] Cf. Giuseppe MAZZATINTI, *Inventari dei manoscritti delle biblioteche d'Italia*, XIII, Forlì, Borandini, 1905, p. 118. Not listed in Bianca BECHERINI, *Catalogo dei manoscritti musicali della Biblioteca Nazionale di Firenze*, Kassel, Bärenreiter, 1959.

[63] Transcription in Wilhelm TAPPERT, *Sang und Klang aus alter Zeit*, Berlin, Liepmannssohn, 1906, pp. 69ff.

[63bis] Ed. Armando Fiabane, Rome, n.d. (*Musica da suonare*, 4), p. 5.

[64] Facs. ed. Maurizio Tarrini, Savona, Assoc. ligure per la ricerca delle fonti musicali, 1995, p. 234.

[65] Transcription in Oscar CHILESOTTI, *Lautenspieler des XVI. Jahrhunderts*, Leipzig, Breitkopf & Härtel [1891], pp. 210f.

[66] Incipit quoted in Gustave REESE, *An Early Seventeenth-century Italian Lute Manuscript in San Francisco*, in *Essays in Musicology in Honor of Dragan Plamenac on his 70th Birthday*, Pittsburgh UP, 1969, p. 270, no. 73.

ence, SPES, 2002, pp. 4-10: "Capriccio sopra la battaglia", quotes the *Girometta* on p. 9.

ante 1627   Pietro Millioni, *Quarto libro d'intavolatura di chitarra spagnola*, Rome, Facciotti, 1627[2], p. 65: "Girumetta".

1627   *Id.*, *Quinto libro d'intavolatura di chitarra spagnola*, Rome, Facciotti, 1627, p. 65: "Girumetta" (identical to *Quarto libro*, p. 65). Reprinted with minimal variants in his *Corona del primo, secondo e terzo libro d'intavolatura de chitarra spagnola*, Milan, Cerri & Ferrandi, 1631, p. 61.[67]

1635   Girolamo Frescobaldi, *Fiori musicali*, Venice, Vincenti, 1635, pp. 96ff: "Capriccio sopra la Girolmeta", as final component of the third organ Mass.[68] Also in I-Tn ms. Foà 8, ff. 125*v*-129, and I-Vnm ms. It. IV 1299 (= 11068), pp. 95f. Ex. 4.

ante 1639   Alessandro Piccinini, *Intavolatura di liuto libro secondo*, posth. ed. Bologna, Monti & Zenero, 1639; facs. Florence, SPES, 1983, pp. 43-49: "Battaglia"; quotes the *Girometta* on pp. 46 and 48.

1639   Marco Marazzoli, *La fiera di Farfa*, first intermezzo for *Chi soffre, speri* (comic opera by Giulio Rospigliosi [later Pope Clement IX], music by Marazzoli and Vergilio Mazzocchi), I-Rvat ms. Barb. lat. 4386, ff. 200*r-v*, 202*r-v*, and I-Rvat ms. Chigi Q.VIII.190, ff. 20*v*-21, 22*r-v*: *Girometta* quoted freely in the second soprano.

1640   Girolamo Kapsberger, *Libro quarto d'intavolatura di chitarrone*, Rome, 1640, pp. 28ff: "Battaglia", quotes the Girometta on p. 29.

ca. 1640   A-KR ms. L 81, lute book, probably written by Johann Sebastian von Hallwil (1622-1700) while a student in Italy; f. 143*v*: "La Girometa che segue doppo la Trombetta".[69]

1643   Antonio Carbonchi, *Le Dodici chitarre spostate ... libro secondo*, Florence, Sabatini, 1643), p. 43: "Ghirumetta".

1645   Gasparo Zannetti, *Il Scolaro di Gasparo Zannetti per imparar a suonare di violino et altri stromenti*, Milan, Camagno, 1645, pp. 70f: "La Girometta" for CATB (staff notation on p. 70, violin tablature on p. 71).

1645   Giovanbattista Fasolo, *Annuale che contiene tutto quello, che deve far un organista per risponder al choro tutto l'anno, Opera ottava*, Venice, Vincenti, 1645, pp. 247ff: "Girometta fuga seconda".

1648   *Il Primo libro d'intavolatura della chitarra spagnola ... da incerto autore*, Rome, Catalani, 1648, pp. 33f: "Giurmetta per C", "Giurmetta per B". Identical to 1660, below.

1648/49   Stefano Pesori, *Lo scrigno armonico, opera seconda*, n.p., n.d., p. 26: "Chi t'à fatto quelle scarpette", for guitar. Ex. 6.

---

[67] Facs. in Johannes WOLF, *Musikalische Schrifttafeln*, Bückeburg, Kistner & Siegel, 1922-23, Taf. 65.

[68] Ed. in FRESCOBALDI, *Orgel- und Klavierwerke*, V, Kassel, Bärenreiter, 1954, pp. 66-69. Cf. below, p. 463, note 137.

[69] Incipit in Rudolf FLOTZINGER, *Die Lautentabulaturen des Stiftes Kremsmünster: Thematischer Katalog*, Vienna, Böhlau, 1965, p. 87, no. 176.

1649	Marco Uccellini, *Sonate*, Op. 5, Venice, Vincenti, 1649: "Tromba sordina per sonare con violino solo".[70]
mid-17th c.	I-Rvat ms. Chigi Q. IV.28, anonymous keyboard music [1640s?], ff. 62*v*-63*v*: "Girometta".[71] Ex. 8.
mid-17th c.	I-Fr ms. 2774, Italian guitar tablature, f. 78*v*: "La girometta"; f. 82*v*: "La Girometta". Ex. 5.
mid-17th c.	I-Fr ms. 2951, Italian guitar tablature, f. 86: "Ierumetta".
mid-17th c.	Giovanni Battista Ferrini, I-Rvat ms. mus. 569 (*olim* Casimiri Z.VI.104), for keyboard, ff. 26-29*v*: "Trombetta".[72]
mid-17th c.	I-M, *olim* Natale Gallini, Italian guitar talature: "Girometta".[73]
1650	Andrea Falconieri, *Il Primo libro di canzone, sinfonie, fantasie ... per violini, e viole ... con il basso continuo*, Naples, Paolini & Ricci, 1650, p. 27: "Battalla de Barabaso yerno de Satanas", for two violins and basso continuo.[74]
1657	Giuseppe Giamberti romano, *Duo tessuti con diversi solfeggiamenti, scherzi, perfidie et oblighi, alcuni motivati da diverse ariette*, Rome, Balmonti, 1657: "Duo III. Scherzi sopra la Girometta", for canto and alto, without text.[74bis]
1660	Tomaso Marchetti, *Il Primo libro d'intavolatura della chitarra spagnola*, Rome, Moneta, 1660, pp. 33f: "Girumetta per C" and "Girumetta per B". Identical to 1648, above.
post 1660	*Idem*, [tablature for Spanish guitar, published in Rome; copy in I-Rsc with mutilated title page], pp. 24f: "Girumetta" (two pieces, reprinted from Pico, 1608).
1675-1710	Matteo Coferati, *Corona di sacre canzoni o laude spirituali di più divoti autori*, Florence, Barbetti, 1675, Onofri, 1689, Bindi, 1710, pp. 437-440, 499-502, 684ff in the three editions, respectively: "Ghirumetta. Dialogo tra l'anima e Cristo" (with Razzi s text).
ca. 1680-1720	I-PEc rari ms. b-10, Italian lute tablature, f. 27*v*: "Battaglia" with "ghirumetta".

---

[70] *Girometta* quoted in Wolfgang OSTHOFF, *Trombe sordine*, AfMw, XIII, 1956, p. 83.

[71] Ed. in *Seventeenth-century Keyboard Music in the Chigi Manuscripts of the Vatican Library*, «Corpus of Early Keyboard Music», XXXII, Dallas, American Institute of Musicology, 1968, II, 62-65.

[72] Facs. in *Sources Central to Keyboard Art of the Baroque*, XIV, New York, Garland, 1987; ed. in *Roman Keyboard Music of the 17th Century*, Egtved, Edition Egtved, 1981, pp. 18-21. On this ms. cf. W. KIRKENDALE, *L'Aria di Fiorenza*, p. 73, and Arnaldo MORELLI, *Giovanni Battista Ferrini 'della Spinetta' e l'intavolatura cembalo-organistica Vat. Mus. 569*, in *Musicologia Humana: Studies in Honor of Warren and Ursula Kirkendale*, Florence, Olschki, 1994, pp. 383-392.

[73] Parke-Bernet Galleries, *Sixty-six XVII-XXth-Century Italian Music Manuscripts*, catalogue for auction of 3 May 1949, New York, p. 1.

[74] In Luigi TORCHI (ed.), *L'Arte musicale in Italia*, VII, Milan, Ricordi, 1897, pp. 128-142.

[74bis] In Giamberti, *Duetti per due strumenti S. T.*, ed. Giancarlo Rostirolla, Rome, 1976 (*Musica da suonare*, 2, p. 9.

1695	Giuseppe Paradossi, *Modo facile di suonare il sistro*, Bologna, Peri, 1695; facs. Milan, Bollettino bibliografico musicale, 1933, unpaginated: "Girometta". Numerical notation, without indication of rhythm.
late 17th c.	Francesco Provenzale (1627-1704), cantata "Squarciato appena havea" for soprano and b.c., I-Nc ms. cantate 112 (*olim* A 47). Quodlibet, quotes a strophe of the *Girometta* on pp. 42ff.[75]
1703	Anon., "Pro festis solemnioribus librum hunc, in quo plurimi Credo in contrapuncto continentur cum Missa solemni. F. Mez. scrib. 1703", I-Lg ms. 2687, ff. 9*v*-13: Credo "La Girometta", for TT. Copied for the Augustine monastery of Lucca.[76]
1998	Sergio Pallante (b. 1957), *Toccata (con variazioni) sopra la Girolameta*.[76bis]

Like *La bella Franceschina*, the *Girometta* melody exists in two forms, the newer one lying a third above the older.[77] However, in the case of the *Girometta* the newer melody is not merely a paraphrase, but an exact transposition of the older from minor to the relative major (cf. Ex. 3 and Exx. 5, 6, 8). The minor version is found only in the earliest sources: Azzaiolo 1559 (quotes only the second half of the melody, as the second half of the villotta's refrain), Razzi 1563 (Ex. 3), and "Apri hormai" 1583. Without claiming to have found the explanation for this upward shift of a third in both songs, I may present three hypotheses. 1) The change may have been caused by a clef being misread or interchanged – unlikely in view of the wide diffusion. 2) From a homophonic villotta setting, with parts moving in parallel thirds or sixths (cf. below, note 124), a parallel voice rather than the original melody may have been taken as the model for later settings. The possibility of such a procedure its borne out by a modern scholar's interpretation of Azzaiolo's villotta: as an illustration of the *Girometta*, Francesco Vatielli quoted not the tenor, which has the song melody, but the cantus, which doubles it at the sixth above.[78] 3) The change from minor to major might be the result of a process of 'modernization'.

---

[75] Text and melody in Guido PANNAIN, *Francesco Provenzale e la lirica del suo tempo*, «Rivista musicale italiana», XXXII, 1925, pp. 515, 517, and in Teresa GIALDRONI, *Francesco Provenzale e la cantata a Napoli nella seconda metà del Seiceno*, in *La musica a Napoli durante il Seicento*, Rome, Torre d'Orfeo, 1987, pp. 148ff.

[76] Kurt von FISCHER, *Persistence du «cantus binatim» au 18e siècle?*, «Quadrivium», XII/2, 1971, p. 198.

[76bis] *Antichi organi e nuovi musici in Sicilia*, Regione Sicilia, 1998, pp. 115-123.

[77] See note 50.

[78] *Canzonieri musicali del cinquecento: contributo alla storia della musica popolare italiana*, «Rivista musicale italiana», XXVIII, 1921, p. 643. Francesco Balilla PRATELLA, *Primo documentario per la storia dell'etnofonia in Italia*, Udine, Idea, 1941, I, 143, similarly misquotes Vecchi's Girometta melody, transposing it a third lower to the minor and underlaying a different text.

Ex. 3. Razzi: laud "Torna, torna al freddo cor", 1563.

The foregoing hypotheses, suggested in the original version of this article (1972), must be modified in view of the Mass by Giovanni Nasco (1552), which came to my attention only later. In this oldest musical version of the *Girometta* thus far come to light, the musical passages which seem to derive from the popular song, almost always in the canto, correspond indeed to the canto of Azzaiolo, whereas the version of his tenor rarely appears in the Mass: only when the tenor doubles the canto at the lower sixth. These two oldest sources suggest 1) that in its original form, the melody did not yet have the first, characteristic half of the later version, which we find only since 1563; 2) that in the course of the years the second, older half of this song was transposed up a third not only once, but twice, i.e. from beginning on *a* (1552-59: Nasco, Azzaiolo) to *c* (1563-85: Razzi and "Apri"), and to *e* (1588-1703: from Zarlino to ms. I-Lg), respectively.[79]

Of all later sources of the *Girometta* melody, only two do not conform to the major version as used by Facoli, Vecchi, Marenzio, and later composers: Marazzoli's intermezzo quotes it with the beginning freely altered; and Frescobaldi's ingenious "Capriccio sopra la Girolmeta" presents a unique Lydian variant (Ex. 4). This variant has been explained as an imitation of the military trumpet (cf. p. 162) with its eleventh overtone, *f*-sharp.[80] In addition to the modal transpositions, only two slight melodic variants are to be observed: "Apri hormai", Porta, Vecchi, Marenzio, Carbonchi, and Coferati repeat the supertonic for the ninth note (normally it descends to the tonic); Garsi, Zannetti, and I-Fr ms. 2774, f. 78*v* (implied by the harmony) employ the

---

[79] Taking the version on *a* as his point of departure, Pozzobon cites six other pieces (Francesco da Milano, Azzaiolo, Byrd, Sweelinck) which he believes to be related to Nasco's melody. The resemblance is, however, only casual, not significant. These pieces have in common only the range of a fourth (diminished) and the normal melodic curve of ascent-descent. The range of a fourth would correspond to what Giovanni de' Bardi said regarding the melodies of Olympos: "mai più che quattro corde" ["never more than four chords"] – *Discorso mandato a Giulio Caccini*, I-Rvat Barb. lat. 3990, f. 12, and Giovanni Battista DONI, *De' trattati di musica*, Florence, Typis caesareis, 1763, p. 247 – to which Vincenzo Galilei compared the *Girometta* (cf. below, p. 164).

[80] Luigi Ferdinando TAGLIAVINI, *Varia Frescobaldiana*, «L'organo», XXI, 1983, p. 123.

sixth, Cangiasi and Fasolo the fifth rather than the third degree of the scale as the fourth note of the melody.[81]

Ex. 4. Frescobaldi: *Capriccio sopra la Girolmeta*, 1635, mm. 1-6.

The modern editions listed in notes 57-76 illustrate conveniently the use to which the *Girometta* melody was put in more sophisticated music for key-board, lute, and instrumental ensemble. Two transcriptions from Italian gui-tar tablatures may be added here. The popular guitar repertoire of the Seicen-to consists largely of traditional harmonic formulas (Romanesca, Ruggiero, etc.) adapted to the *rasgado* or chord-strumming style and written in the Italian alphabet notation which represents an entire chord by means of a single letter (e.g. Ex. 5a).[82] Such pieces have neither discant nor bass, but consist solely of chord progressions (Ex. 5b). The melodies of folksongs such as the *Girometta* or the *Monica* would be supplied vocally by the player (Ex. 5c).[83] Since the melodies can be harmonized in different ways, the chord progressions vary somewhat in the different sources. A few of the later guitar tablatures (Carbonchi, and Pesori Ex. 6) occasionally revert to the *punteado* numerical notation of sixteenth-century lute music for the two upper strings, thus producing, in combination with the chords notated by letters, the discant melody as well as the accompaniment.

In the nineteenth and twentieth centuries the name "Girometta" was still connected with Italian folksongs and dances, particularly in the backward

---

[81] Fasolo apparently derived his piece from Cangiasi's. Not only is the general style of the two fugal compositions quite similar; the immediate (free) continuation of the *Girometta* melody is iden-tical in each.

[82] This repertoire is dealt with in more detail in W. KIRKENDALE, *L'Aria di Fiorenza*, ch. 2.

[83] Of the Giromettas in the guitar tablatures listed, only that quoted in Ex. 5 has the text un-derlaid. The correspondences between the highest notes of the chords and the *Girometta* melody are merely coincidental (since in alphabet notation there is only one, fixed chord for each major and minor triad), and they are less extensive when the piece appears in other keys.

Ex. 5. I-Fr ms. 2774, f. 82v: *La Girometta*.

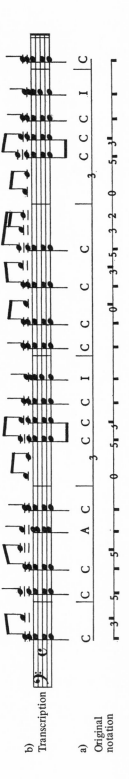

c)
Melody to be
supplied

b)
Transcription

a)
Original
notation

B G   A   D A G B   A B A G B A   B   E B G A G B   A B A G B   A   B

Chi t'ha fat - to le bel - le   scar- pe che ti stan   sì   ben, che ti stan sì ben Gi-ro - met-ta, che ti stan sì   ben.

Ex. 6. Pesori: "Chi t'à fatto quelle scarpette", 1648/49.

b)
Transcription

a)
Original
notation

C | C   C   A   C | C   C C I | C   C   C | C   C   C   I | C   C C C I | C   C   C
    3¹   5¹   3   0   5¹ 3¹   0¹   3¹ 5¹ 3 2   0   3¹ 5¹   3

mountainous regions of Piedmont. The melody of "Giürümeta de la munta-gna" communicated by Costantino Nigra[84] no longer has any resemblance to our folksong, but "Girometta de la muntagna" published by Francesco Balilla Pratella (Ex. 7)[85] still adheres to the old melody. Giromettas from Modena[86] and Brescia[87] retain the second half; "Chi t'à fatto sti be' scarpette" from Pied-mont, the phrase ending of the descending fifth.[88] According to Pratella[89] and Bignami, the *Girometta* is a dance song. Gaspare Ungarelli transcribed quite unrelated instrumental music for a Bolognese dance, "Girumätta".[90]

The text of the *Girometta* has a still longer and more complex history than that of *La bella Franceschina*.[91] Since one of the earliest dated literary sources,

Ex. 7. *Girometta piemontese* (19th c.).

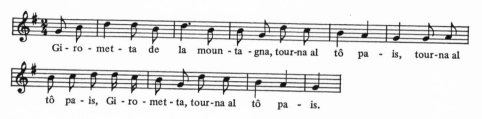

84 *Canti popolari del Piemonte*, Turin, Loescher, 1888, p. 571; repr. in Elisabetta ODDONE, *Canzoniere popolare italiano*, Milan, Ricordi, 1917-23, I, 19f, and in Giulio FARA, *L'anima musicale d'Italia*, Rome, Ausonia, 1921, musical appendix, no. 6; text only repr. in Francesco Balilla PRATELLA, *Saggio di gridi, canzoni, cori e danze del popolo italiano*, Bologna, Bongiovanni, 1919, p. 47, who then sets this later text to Razzi's melody [!] in his appendix to Giuseppe COCCHIARA, *L'anima del popolo italiano nei suoi canti*, Milan, Hoepli, 1929, p. 372. Two variants of the *Girometta piemontese* are given in Riccardo ALLORTO, *I canti popolari piemontesi nelle raccolte di Lione Sinigaglia*, «Ricordiana», n.s. III, 1957, p. 287. Since the 16th century, the bells of the sanctuary of Oropa (Biella) greet the pilgrim with this song.

85 *Saggio*, p. 120 (second strophe of text: p. 47). A longer version is given in Achille SCHINELLI, *Canzoniere dei fanciulli*, Milan, Ricordi, 1927, IV/1, pp. 1ff. The similarity to Nigra's song does not extend beyond the incipit of the melody and text.

86 E. LEVI, p. XXXVIII.

87 Giovanni BIGNAMI, *Danze popolari nel territorio bresciano*, «Lares», XI, 1940, p. 95.

88 G. FARA, musical appendix, no. 9. Characteristic of the reliability of some collections of folk-songs is the treatment of this song, designated here as Piedmontese and reprinted without alteration or commentary in FARA's *L'anima della Sardegna*, Udine, Edizioni accademiche, 1940, p. 89, as a children's song from the Genoese colony of Carloforte in Sardinia.

89 *Saggio*, p. 47.

90 *Le vecchie danze italiane ancora in uso nella provincia bolognese*, Rome, Forzani, 1894, musical appendix II, no. 11; the choreography is described on p. 68. Likewise unrelated is the "Passameggio de la giometrina" in the Fugger lute book of 1562, A-Wn ms. 18821, ff. 8v-9v (DTÖ, XXXVII, 113).

91 The *Girometta* has received practically no attention from musicologists. Treatment of it in Romanistic studies is limited to the quotation, often inaccurate, of small numbers of literary sources.

the anonymous *Canzone di Girometta con altre sette stanze* (Venice, 1587; Plate IV. 2) is at the same time, with 29 strophes,[92] the longest, it may have been written after the text had already undergone considerable development. Indeed, the sixth strophe occurs by itself already in the earliest musical settings (Azzaiolo 1559, Zarlino 1588) and served as the model for Della Casa's religious adaptation of 1563 (see below, p. 172), as it did, much later, for the first strophe of Pratella-Schinelli's "Girometta de la muntagna, / Turne al tò pais".[93]

Canzone di Girometta (1587)[94]

Noi siamo le tre sorelle,
Tutte tre polite, e belle,
Tutte tre d'un gra, Girometta,
Tutte tre d'un gra.
La più bella, e la più gioiosa
La più bella, e la più gioiosa
Venirà con mi, Girometta,
Venirà con mi.
Io metto man al pugnale
Io metto man al pugnale,
Per volerti ferir, Girometta,
Per volerti ferir.

Io ti dono li cento scudi,
Io ti dono li cento scudi,
Stu li fa contar, Girometta,
Stu li fa contar.
La li conta, e li racconta,
La li conta, e li racconta,
Gie ne manca un gra, Girometta,
Gie ne manca un gra.
Torna, torna al tuo paese,
Torna, torna al tuo paese
Tu non fai per mi, Girometta,
Tu non fai per mi.

Little attempt has yet been made to relate these or to draw conclusions from them. *La bella Franceschina* has had no appreciable discussion.

92 Followed by "La Gionta", i.e. the "altre sette stanze" ["six other strophes"], beginning with the same words as the preceding text ("Noi siamo ... belle") but otherwise unrelated.

93 In Nigra's text, Girometta rejects the invitation of a suitor to come down from the mountains ("Giürümeta de la muntagna, / Vös-to vnì al pian?"), remaining faithful to her lover, an alpine shepherd. Notwithstanding this basic difference, Pratella (but not Schinelli) shares the second strophe with Nigra ("Le castagne sun bele e bune"). A considerably different version of Nigra's text, from Savoy and Monferrato, is published by Giuseppe FERRARO, *Canti popolari del Basso Monferrato*, Palermo, Pedone Lauriel, 1888, pp. 44f. According to Ferraro, the song came from Savoy, "da cui escono allo inverno i piccoli montanari coll'organetto e la marmotta a guadagnarsi il vitto" ["whence little mountain dwellers emerge in the winter with the little organ and the marmot to earn their living"]. Another variant was sung in Como by "alcune nutrici ... ai bimbi in culla" ["some nurses ... to babies in the cradle"] – Pietro MONTI, *Vocabolario dei dialetti della città e diocesi di Como*, Milan, Classici italiani, 1845, pp. 100f.

94 The literal meaning of the third strophe is illustrated on the title page (Plate IV.3); the real meaning is, of course, figurative. The odd-numbered strophes 9-27 are identical, except for the change of the object "scarpe" to "pianelle", "calzette", "poste", "vesta", "centa", "scopazzo", "collana", "scuffioto", and "zibillino", and the substitution of other verbs for "stan"; strophe 10 is repeated literally for the even-numbered strophes 12-28, except that the verb "vol" is often replaced by another. The final strophe, 29, is a repetition of the first. The entire text is reprinted in Severino FERRARI, *Documenti per servire all'istoria della poesia semipopolare cittadina in Italia pei secoli XVI e XVII*, «Il Propugnatore», XIII/1, 1880, pp. 455-460 and, corrected, in *L'incatenatura del Bianchino*, pp. 132-137. I shall henceforth refer to this text as the *Girometta* of '1587', without implying that any of it originated at that time.

Mena, mena in qua il cavallo,
   Mena, mena in qua il cavallo,
   Che voi su montar, Girometta,
   Che voi su montar.
Abbandonato ho padre e madre,
   Abbandonato ho padre e madre,
   Per venir con ti, Girometta,
   Per venir con ti.

Io mi compro un par di scarpe,
   Io mi compro un par di scarpe
   Che mi stan pur ben, Girometta,
   Che mi stan pur ben.
Me l'ha pagate il mio amore
   Me l'ha pagate il mio amore
   Che mi vol gran ben, Girometta,
   Che mi vol gran ben. [Etc.].

We are the three sisters, all three clean and beautiful, all three the same size, Girometta. / The most beautiful and joyful one will come with me, Girometta. / I shall take the dagger in my hand to wound you, Girometta. / I shall give you a hundred *scudi* and shall have them counted, Girometta. / Count and recount them, none is missing, Girometta. / Return home, you are not for me, Girometta. / Send the horse here which you wish to mount, Girometta. / I have abandoned father and mother to come with you, Girometta. / I bought myself a pair of shoes, which look so well on me, Girometta. / My love bought them for me, who is very fond of me, Girometta. [Etc.].

The first line belongs to the 'three sister' *topos* common in Italian folk poetry at least from Marchetto Cara's "Le son tre fantinelle" [95] up to folksongs still sung in the twentieth century. [96]

A lengthy and illuminating contemporary discussion of the *Girometta* is to be found in *Il Bottrigaro, overo del nuovo verso enneasillabo* of Ciro Spontone (Verona, Discepolo, 1589), a dialogue on the use of the nine-syllable line in Italian poetry. Introducing the song as his principal example of this meter, Ciro lists the variety of forms in which it could be heard by students in Bologna: as a song, as a dance, [97] and as tower music, played by the many different instruments and ensembles represented in our list of musical sources: [98]

Cir.: ... onde volendo egli [Cav. Hercole Bottrigaro] seguir l'intento suo, gli so-

Cir.: ... whence [Cavalier Hercole Bottrigaro] wishing to pursue his intention, re-

---

[95] In *Canzoni, frottole et capitoli ... libro primo*, Rome, Pasoti & Dorico, 1526, and Fausto TOR-REFRANCA, *Il segreto del Quattrocento*, Milan, Hoepli, 1939, pp. 481f.

[96] Many of these have incipits which are closely related to, some perhaps even derived from, the *Girometta* text; cf. those in E. FISCH and M. VICARI, *Canti popolari ticinesi*, I, Zürich, Hug, n.d.; UN-GARELLI, p. 31, from Bologna; ODDONE, II, 67ff, from Latium, rearranged by SCHINELLI, IV/2, pp. 39f; Vincenzo SPINELLI, *Poesia popolare e costumi calabresi*, Buenos Aires, Mele, 1923, p. 114; PRATELLA, *Saggio* cit., p. 47, and *Etnofonia di Romagna*, Udine, Edizioni Accademiche, 1938, p. 45; *id.*, *Primo documentario*, pp. 222, 257, 271-277, 512-516 ("L'Anello", from Bologna, Arezzo, and Pistoia); Vittorio SANTOLI, *I canti popolari italiani*, Florence, Sansoni, 1940, index.

[97] Cf. above, pp. 143 (Facoli) and 151 (Ungarelli).

[98] Ciro SPONTONE, p. 26.

venne di quella canzone che il Signor Dottore [Francesco Denalio] si ricorderà forse d'haver udito, mentre egli studiava in Bologna, di notte tempo, come spesso avviene, cantarsi da fanciulli, et quando poi su'l lauto, et su la viola, et quando su l'arpicordo, hor con le pive a ballo, et finalmente ridutta a ragione di musica per maggior felicità di quel versificatore essere con tromboni, cornetti, et cornamuse da sonatori eccellentissimi alla ringhiera del palazzo maggiore posto sulla piazza grande della cittade alla solita hora di tal publica honoratissima musica giornale gentilissimamente, et con sodisfattione grandissima del popolo ascoltante sonata in alcuni tempi festevoli.

Mar[chese di Castiglione]: Dev'essere qualche gran cosa; poiché con sì bell'ordine, et con tanto affetto ci andate invaghendo di questa canzone. Qual era ella?

Cir.: Dirollo: ma non paia strano à V. S. Illustrissima se alla prima le parerà diversa dall'aspettatione.

Mar.: Che sarà: dite pure.

Cir.: Incomincia la canzone.

Chi t'hà fatto quelle scarpette
   Che ti stan sì ben
   Che ti stan sì ben Girometta
   Che ti stan sì ben.

Mar.: Ah ah ah, non ne dite più per vita vostra: che vene pare Sig. Dottore: non è riuscito per eccellenza il nostro Spontone cadendo da quella sua magnifica circoscrittione in sì vile soggetto, et plebeo?

Den.: Udij ben' io molte volte questa canzone: ma non haverei mai creduto, che voi, messer Ciro, voleste schermire contro à Dante, et al Minturno con queste armi così deboli.

called that song which Dr. [Francesco Denalio] perhaps will have remembered to have heard while he was a student in Bologna, at nighttime, as often happened, sung by boys, and then sometimes on the lute and on the viol, and sometimes on the harpsichord, now with bagpipes for dancing, and finally – to please that poet – adapted to music with trombones, cornetts, and bagpipes by most excellent instrumentalists at the railing of the *palazzo maggiore* situated on the large square of the city at the usual hour of such daily music, played exquisitely during some festivities, with the greatest satisfaction of the people.

Mar[quis Castiglione]: It must be some great thing, since you with such fine order and so much affection are falling in love with this song. Which was it?

Cir.: I shall say; but let it not seem strange to your illustrious lordship if it at first appears different from your expectation.

Mar.: What will it be? Do tell.

Cir.: The song begins:

   Who has made those shoes for you
   Which look so well on you, Girometta?

Mar.: Ah, ah, ah, say no more of it for your life. What do you think, doctor? Has our Spontone not succeeded excellently, falling from that magnificent sphere to such a low and plebian subject?

Den.: I have often heard this song; but I never would have believed that you, Mr. Ciro, wanted to parry against Dante and Minturno with arms as weak as these.

Denalio's references to authorities can be traced to a passage in Dante's *De vulgari eloquentia* (lib. II, cap. V), paraphrased in Antonio Minturno's *Arte poetica.*[99] Dante states that lines of 3, 5, 7, and 11 syllables are widely used in Italian poetry, but "since the line of nine syllables in fact seemed [to be] three three-syllable lines, it either was never highly regarded, or has fallen into disuse because of its tedious effect".[100] Of the two explanations, the former shows Dante's exclusive concern with courtly literature, since this meter was indeed used in popular Italian poetry; the latter explanation acknowledges that the nine-syllable line had been employed also in the earliest Provencal and French poetry. Ciro cannot contradict his partners' protests regarding the plebian character of the *Girometta*, but he does maintain that the meter could be put to better use. He then describes the wide diffusion and many variants and corruptions of the *Girometta* text, and the manner in which a large number of additional strophes are derived (pp. 26f):

Cir.: Non nego io, che sì com'essa canzone è di concetto vile composta, così con parole baße, et plebee, et con molta rozzezza quello spiegato non sia: ma non habbiamo noi a considerare la maniera, che la forma, poiché buona inventione si può di stile men dalla nobiltà lontano, et con parole più leggiadre vestire, et ornare. Era questa canzone: anzi in gran parte anchora è, poich'ella va tuttavia per le stampe, benché meschine, hora grandemente alterata, et corrotta; composta di versi di nove sillabe insieme con alcuni altri di cinque sillabe ma smozzigati, o tronchi; da' quali ripigliati, ne deriva poi un'altro pur di nove sillabe differente alquanto dal primo, il che si può conoscere da questi.

Cir.: I do not deny that this song is written on a base subject, thus with low, plebian words and much roughness, as described. But we do not have to consider the manner, but the form, since good invention can, in a style less removed from nobility, be dressed more gracefully and adorned with words. This it was, or rather largely still is this song, since it circulates in prints, albeit poor ones, now greatly altered and corrupted, composed with lines of nine syllables together with some others of five syllables, but abbreviated or truncated. Another is then derived from these, likewise of nine syllables, somewhat different from the first, which can be recognized from these:

Me le ha fatte deh lo mio amore;
　Che mi vuol gran ben;
　Che mi vuol gran ben, Girometta,
　Che mi vuol gran ben.

Ah, my lover made them for me,
Who is very fond of me, Girometta.

---

[99] Venice, Valvassori, 1563, p. 185.

[100] "neasillabum vero, quia triplicatum trisillabum videbatur, vel numquam in honore fuit, vel propter fastidium absolvit" – Florence, Le Monnier, 1938, p. 202. SPONTONE, p. 25, objected that neither Dante nor Minturno gave an example of the condemned meter.

Cento scudi ti vuò donare
  Se li sai contar;
  Se li sai contar, Girometta
  Se li sai contar.
	I want to give you a hundred *scudi*
	If you are able to count them, Girometta.

Io li conto, et li riconto,
  Glie ne manca un gran,
  Glie ne manca un gran, Girometta
  Glie ne manca un gran.
	I count them and recount them
	None is lacking, Girometta.

I quai versi sono di quattro stanze delle molte: in che è divisa con pochi versi, et replicati, et riformati stranamente essa canzone.	These verses are four of many into which this song is divided with few, repeated lines, stangely modified.

Finally, the marchese observes that it is precisely the addition of the name "Girometta" which transforms the line of five syllables to one of nine: "intendo il pentasillabo smozzicato riformato replicamente con l'aggiunta sempre di quel nome proprio Girometta" ["I mean the abbreviated five-syllable [line] repeatedly modified, always with the addition of the name Girometta"]. He and Ciro speculate how it in turn could be converted into the respectable *endecasillabo* by the addition of two more syllables at the end or beginning (pp. 38f).

This testimony justifies the derivation of 'Girometta' from the proper name ("nome proprio") 'Girolama', rather than "from the turning [*giro*] or return of the same words".[101] In the strophes spoken by Girometta, the structural function of the "aggiunta" prevails over the sense, as so often in folk poetry, since the girl would not normally invoke her own name. The last two strophes quoted by Spontone correspond, with slight variations, to strophes 4 and 5 of 1587. The first two, related to strophes 9 and 10 of 1587, are the most characteristic. Marenzio uses them as the text of both his *Prima parte* and, changing "scarpette" ["shoes"] to "calzette" ["stockings"] in the *Seconda parte*.

La Girometta del Marentio. Canto Secondo.

Prima Parte

Chi t'hà fatto quelle scarpette Che ti stan sì ben	Me l'ha fatte lo mio Amore Che mi vol gran ben

---

[101] "pel giro o ritorno delle stesse parole" – P. MONTI, *Vocabolario*, p. 101. Cf. also BISCIONI, below, note 103.

Che ti stan sì ben, Girometta,	Che mi vol gran ben, Girometta,
Che ti stan sì ben?	Che mi vol gran ben.

Seconda Parte

Chi t'hà fatto quelle calzette	Me l'hà fatte lo mio Amore
Che ti stan sì ben	Che mi vol gran ben
Che ti stan sì ben, Girometta,	Che mi vol gran ben, Girometta,
Che ti stan sì ben?	Che mi vol gran ben.

With additional strophes formed by the change of a single word, just as the Franceschina text changed the girls' names,[102] these texts belong to that international category of chain-form folksongs familiar, e.g., to English- and French-speaking children from "Old MacDonald had a farm" and *Alouette*. As in *Girometta* and *Alouette*, the interchangeable words often designate a garment or part of the body,[103] but they are not cumulated in the older Italian songs. In actual folk singing, the *Girometta* undoubtedly continued this process beyond the two words included by Marenzio, as in the text of 1587 (see above, note 94). The form of the strophes quoted above is common to all of the *Girometta* texts: alternating lines of nine and five syllables (as described by Ciro Spontone), usually with lines 2-4 identical to each other, except that line 3 adds the word "Girometta". This structure is retained even in the more recent folksongs, such as that communicated by Nigra:[104]

> Giürümeta de la muntagna,
>   Vös-to vnì al pian,
>   Vös-to vnì al pian, Giürümeta,
>   Vös-to vnì al pian?

Girometta of the mountain, would you like to come to the plain, Girometta?

---

102 See note 50.

103 Cf. the definitions of the *Girometta* in Niccolò TOMMASEO and Bernardo BELLINI, *Dizionario della lingua italiana*, II/2, Turin, UTET, 1869, p. 1096, and the *Vocabolario degli Accademici della Crusca*, V, Florence, Tip. Galileiana, 1893⁵, p. 286. They are both taken literally from the *Chiave e note del dottore Antonmaria Biscioni fiorentino sopra le Rime piacevoli di Gio. Batista Fagiuoli*, Florence, Nestenus & Moücke, 1734, p. 52: "Canzone, in lode di tutte le parti del vestire d'una donna, per nome *Ghirumetta*. Il suo principio è questo: 'Chi t'ha fatto sì belle scarpette'" ["Song in praise of all articles of clothing of a woman called *Ghirumetta*. Its beginning is 'Who has made those beautiful shoes for you?'"]. This commentary on the sonnet of Fagiuoli quoted below, p. 163, is apparently based on the *Girometta* text of 1587.

104 This structure is not clearly evident from Nigra's edition, pp. 468f, which does not write out the repetitions after the first strophe.

The "scarpette" text was still sung in the first half of the twentieth century.[105] Like "Noi siamo tre sorelle", the incipit "Chi t'ha fatto" is a very common *topos* in Italian folksong and occurs in songs which have no further resemblance to the *Girometta*; in place of the interchangeable word "scarpette" are found "gunella" (Bologna, 1569),[106] "orecchini", "fazzoletto", "scuffletta" (Piedmont),[107] "oceti" (Venezia Giulia and Dalmatia),[108] "oggitt" (Lombardy),[109] "rizzotoli" (Venezia Tridentina),[110] etc.

* * *

From the foregoing discussion it is clear that there is not a single, 'authentic' version of *La bella Franceschina* or *Girometta*, traceable to a certain time, place, or author, but rather two large families with a widely diffused and varied progeny. Thus the Paduan folk poet Magagnò (Giambattista Maganza) can speak of "a" Franceschina, with the indefinite article: "Ch'à vorne dire, / E far sentire / Na Franceschina".[111] Two of the titles in Croce's humorous catalogue of Dr. Graziano's library, *Indice universale della libraria o studio del celebratissimo, eccellentissimo, eruditissimo & plusquam opulentissimo arcidottor Gratian Furbson da Franculin* (Plate IV.4),[112] allude with the words "compendio", "comento", and "comentati" to the manner in which the traditional texts were varied by different authors: (no. 23) "La Girometta a cinque voci, in compendio, con il comento in forma di statuto, tradotta di burlesco in ridicoloso dall'Academico appetitoso, detto l'Affamato", and (no. 27) "La Bustachina, libri 15, comentati da diversi".

---

[105] LEVI, p. XXXVIII, and FARA, no. 9. However, it is possible that these editors underlaid the old text to the newer melodies. UNGARELLI, p. 68, reported that this text was still sung in Venice and Tuscany; a correspondent of the «Giornale degli eruditi e dei curiosi», III/5, 1884/85, p. 252, heard it in Milan. More recent testimonies that the Girometta survives in Romagna, Tuscany, Veneto (Antongiulio BRAGAGLIA, *Danze popolari italiane*, Rome, ENAL, 1950, p. 252), and Treviso (Emilio LOVARINI, *Studi sul Ruzzante e la letteratura pavana*, Padua, Antenore, 1965, p. 213, note added by the editor of this posthumous edition) do not specify the text or melody. "Chi t'ha fatta sta bella scarpetta" in Vincenzo DE MEGLIO, *Eco di Napoli*, II, Milan, Ricordi, 1877, no. 71, is related to our song only in the text incipit.

[106] Bartolomeo Pifaro bolognese, the napolitana "Chi to fatto quella gunella" in Filippo AZZAIOLO's *Terzo libro delle villotte del fiore alla padovana*, Venice, Gardano, 1569, p. 6.

[107] NIGRA, p. 488.

[108] Alessandro Pericle NINNI, *Ribruscolando*, Venice, Longhi & Montanari, 1890, pp. 37f; Luigi BAUCH, *Le Canzonete de i nostri veci*, Zara, 1913-38, I, 23f.

[109] ODDONE, I, 55f.

[110] SCHINELLI, IV/1, p. 93.

[111] "La Cazza", in *Terza parte de le rime di Magagnò, Menon e Begotto in lingua rustica padovana*, Venice, Zaltieri, 1569, sig. D4.

[112] Bologna, n.d., 1623; title quoted from the latter edition.

Songs as notorious as these naturally provided raw material for the synthetic literary and musical genres which flourished especially in Italy during the sixteenth and seventeenth centuries. Like the German *quodlibet*, the French *fricassée*, and the Spanish *ensalada*, the Italian *incatenatura* or *centone* strung together fragments of different songs, from single words to entire strophes, and the same technique was employed by pieces which make only occasional use of quotation. In the anonymous *Opera nuova nella quale se ritrova essere tutti li principii delle canzoni antiche e moderne poste in ottava rima, cosa piacevole & da ridere* (n.p., n.d.) we have "Dimmi quella scarpetta chi t'ha fatto" and "Le bella franceschina tentalora".[113] The "Segonda parte del Russignuolo" of Menon (Agostino Rava, d. 1583) quotes an entire strophe of the older Franceschina text:[114]

> La bella Franceschina
> La pianze, e si sospira tutt'el dì,
> Che la vorae, che la vorae marì.

In the lines which follow these, *La bella Franceschina* becomes amalgamated with elements of the song "Madre mia, maridème".[115] Similarly, the *Girometta* is combined with *La bella Vendramina*[116] in the anonymous incatenatura "Il cavalier d'amore",[117] and with *Lissandrina* in Lasca's "Pazzia d'un gentilhuomo vicentino, che ha perduto la gratia della sua signora, per non saper far salti mortali".[118] The famous *Opera nuova, nella quale si contiene una incatenatura di più villanelle ed altre cose ridiculose* (Florence, 1613, Verona, 1629)

---

[113] Lines 29 and 48, respectively. The entire text is reprinted in FERRARI, *Documenti*, pp. 434-445. On the *Tentalora* cf. TORREFRANCA, *passim*, and Francesco LUISI, *Il 'Tentalora ballo dei 'tempi passai'*, in *Musicologia Humana: Studies in Honor of Warren and Ursula Kirkendale*, Florence, Olschki, 1994, pp. 75-113. Of the sources subsequently quoted, only those already given in the lists of musical sources include the music of our two songs.

[114] *La quarta parte delle rime alla rustica di Menon, Magagnò e Begotto*, Venice, Donato, 1584, p. 30.

[115] Venice, n.d.; reprinted in FERRARI, *Documenti*, pp. 453ff.

[116] This latter song is contained in the *Libro primo de la fortuna*, Venice, Scotto, 1535; repr. by TORREFRANCA, pp. 275, 571.

[117] I-MOe ms. γ. L. 11. 8, f. 56v-57; only the bass part is extant. This ms. is no. 295 in Raimondo VANDINI, *Appendice prima al catalogo dei codici e manoscritti posseduti dal Marchese Giuseppe Campori*, Modena, Toschi, 1886, p. 112. The text is published in Michele BARBI, *Studi su vecchie e nuove poesie d'amore e di romanzi*, Modena, 1921, p. 278.

[118] *Delle rime piacevoli del Borgogna, Ruscelli, Sansovino, Doni, Lasca, ... e d'altri vivaci ingegni, parte terza*, Vicenza, Barezzi, 1603, ff. 122v-123. This poem has hitherto been attributed to Borgogna and overlooked by the editors of Lasca's works. It quotes the strophe "Chi t'hà fatto quelle scarpette" and follows it with "Me l'han fatte la Lissandrina, / Che tesse sì ben", i.e. substituting "Lissandrina" for "lo mio amore". Cf. the exchange of girls' names in Marenzio's Franceschina text.

of the blind Florentine *cantastorie* Camillo detto il Bianchino[119] gives not only one complete strophe, but also the accompanying instruments, chosen merely to meet the requirements of rhyme: "Ma questa va in sull'arpe: / Chi t'ha fatto le belle scarpe?" ["But this goes with the harps; who made those beautiful shoes for you?"], etc. Of the *napolitane* sung by the four daughters of Cianna in the *Posilecheata* of Pompeo Sarnelli, bishop of Bisceglia, one of Cecca begins: "Chi t'ha fatte ste belle scarpette? / E no l'haje pagate nò?"[120] These 'unpaid shoes', probably fashioned after the 'pagato' strophes of 1587, were still worn by Giromettas in the nineteenth century.[121]

Musical settings of *incatenature* naturally quote the melodies as well as the texts of the component songs. Our earliest source for the *Girometta* melody is indeed one of Azzaiolo's 'quotation villottas'; it cites the second half of the melody with the second half of the sixth strophe of 1587. Augustino Schiopi refers to these same lines in *Le allegre et ridiculose nozze di Zan Falopa da Bufeto* (n.p., n.d.): "Singing that cursed song which says 'not for me, oh Girometta'".[122] A comparison of the text of the serenade "L'aria s'oscura" as set in Alessandro Striggio's *Primo libro delli madrigali a sei voci* (Venice, Gardano, 1560) and Philippe Duc's *Primo libro de madrigali a quattro voci* (Venice, Scotto, 1570)[123] with its *Terza parte*, "Apri hormai l'uscio", in the anonymous *Villotte mantovane a quattro voci* (Venice, Gardano, 1583) reveals clearly the transformation process which the *incatenature* often underwent: the most recent setting omits the *Prima parte*, with the older song "Chi passa per questa strada", and replaces the last three lines of the *Terza parte* with two strophes of the *Girometta*[124] – presumably with the intention of bringing the serenade up to date.

---

[119] Repr. in Wilhelm MUELLER, *Egeria, raccolta di poesie italiane popolari*, Leipzig, Fleischer, 1829, pp. 53-59, and Alessandro D'ANCONA, *La Poesia popolare italiana*, Leghorn, Giusti, 1906², pp. 115-123.

[120] Masillo REPPONE DE GNANOPOLE (anagrammatic pseud.), *Posilecheata*, Naples, Bulifon, 1684, p. 21; the continuation is unrelated to our song.

[121] Cf. the communications in the «Giornale degli eruditi e dei curiosi», V/3, 1884/85, pp. 196, 252, 285, 315. Giovanni Battista ANDREINI, in his *Centaura* (Paris, Della Vigna, 1622, I, v) speaks of a shoemaker: "Chi t'ha fatto ... Me le ha fatte quel ciabattino di Marte al sono di timpani e di gnaccare con tanta melodia che Teucro re di Cipro crepava di doglia di corpo" – Paolo FABBRI, *On the Origins of an operatic topos: the Mad Scene*, in *"Con che suavità": Studies in Italian Opera, Song and Dance*, Oxford, Clarendon, 1995, p. 169.

[122] "Cantando quela canzo la maladeta, / Che dis not fe per mi o Girometa" – repr. in PANDOLFI, I, 231-239.

[123] Text repr. in EINSTEIN, II, 758ff.

[124] Beginning "Chi t'ha compre quelle scarpette" and "Te l'ho compre che son quel gramo / Che ti vuol gran ben", respectively. Although the canto part is lost, it is clear from the alto and tenor that it sang the minor version of the *Girometta* melody, doubled at the lower third by the alto.

Since folksongs constituted a large part of the serenades and matinades presented to ladies by their admirers, it is not surprising to find ours quoted in this literary and musical repertoire. As we have seen, also the serenade which the "cavalier d'amore" brings to "la bella Vendramina" is the *Girometta*; and in Croce's "Barzelletta amorosa", quoted above (p. 141), the *Girometta*, *bustachina*, *Franceschina*, and other folksongs are included in a serenade for "la bella Fornarina". A matinade which identifies its author in its second line[125]

> Deh Pastorella cara ti prego non dormir.
> Senti la matinata del tuo dolce Menon.

Ah, dear shepherdess, I beg you not to sleep. Hear the matinade of your sweet Menon.

quotes after each of its four remaining strophes one strophe of the *Girometta* ("Ascolta ancor quest'altra come è bella canzon, / Chi t'ha fatto quelle scarpette ..." ["Hear again how beautiful is this other song: 'Who made those shoes for you ...'"] – first the two strophes used by Marenzio, then strophes 4 and 2 of 1587.[126] When Marco Facoli writes a keyboard piece on this text by Menon, he employs, of course, the traditional melody for the *Girometta* quotation.[127] From Menon's first strophe he procedes directly to the first strophe of the *Girometta*, which concludes the piece.

Another musical genre which frequently quotes our songs is the *battaglia*. Here they become an almost obligatory component, representing the singing of the opposing troops on the march. Thus Matthias Hermann's *Bataglia taliana* cites the older form of *La bella Franceschina* (Ex. 2g),[128] and the song is

---

[125] The last poem in the *Settimo fiore di villanelle & arie napolitane raccolte a compiacenza de' virtuosi giovani per cantar in ogni stromento* (Venice, n.d., texts only); repr. in Vittorio ROSSI, *Opera nova nella quale si contiene alcune vilanelle & altre cose piacevole degne de ogni spirito gentile*, Bergamo, 1900, no. VI.

[126] A different version, from Genoa, Biblioteca Brignole-Sale Deferarri, ms. D.107.30, f. 4v, is published in Francesco NOVATI, *Contributo alla storia della lirica musicale italiana popolare e popolareggiante dei secoli XV, XVI, XVII*, in *Scritti varii di erudizione e di critica in onore di Rodolfo Renier*, Turin, Bocca, 1912, pp. 943f. Here, among other variants, the order of Menon's second and third strophes is reversed, and the Girometta quotations come one strophe earlier, so that an additional strophe (the fifth of 1587) can be included (between 4 and 2). Menon mentions the Girometta also in the "Mattina de Menon à la Thietta", where he says that his lady is "Pi dolce cha / Miele o bia / La Gerometta" ["sweeter than honey or the Girometta"] – *La prima parte de le rime di Magagnò, Meno, e Begotto in lingua rustica padovana*, Venice, Zaltieri, 1569, sig. E6v.

[127] The quotation and the source and author of the text are not mentioned in Willi APEL's study of Facoli's edition, *Tänze und Arien für Klavier aus dem Jahre 1588*, AfMw, XVII, 1960, pp. 51-60.

[128] Strictly speaking, the villotta containing this quotation does not form part of the *battaglia* (first published in 1544), but was appended to it in its second edition, 1549 (cf. above, p. 135g).

used humorously in the mock battle of the Bavarian wedding festivities of 1568: "two others, at the first run with the legs in the air and the head on the ground, planted in the manner of leeks, remained a short time, and two trumpets mocked them by playing awkwardly *La bella Franceschina*".[129] Besard's lute piece *Battaille de Pavie* (1603) may be harmlessly anachronistic in recruiting the more recent song, the *Girometta*, for a battle fought in 1525. In Garsi's lute *battaglia* the sections designated as "the *Girometta* played by trumpets and drums" and "response of the *Girometta* at the octave, trumpets for the ordinance" follow directly the "response of the German at the octave".[130] The same military instruments are imitated in Piccinini's *battaglia*. This category includes also the battle pieces of Castaldi, Uccellini, and Kapsberger, as well as that in Hallwill's lute book, since this is "La Girometa che segue doppo la trombeta" ["The *Girometta* which follows after the trumpet"]. Falconiero's battle, dedicated to the admiral of the Spanish fleet and fought to the strains of the *Girometta*, may have been won by a descendant of the notorious Barbary pirate Barbarossa, nicknamed 'Satan' – if we assume "Barabaso" in the title to be a corruption.[131] Vecchi cites our camp-follower elsewhere in the *Selva di varia ricreatione*, namely in the "Battaglia d'amore", with the more amorous variant

> Chi t'hà fatto que' tuoi begl'occhi
> Che mi piaccion sì
> Che mi piaccion sì, vezzosetta,
> Che mi piaccion sì?

Who made your beautiful eyes which please me so, pretty one?

alluding to the "beautiful eyes" of Clelia Farnese.[132]

* * *

The key to the associations conveyed by the songs and thus to their meaning in our ensemble lies in the many literary sources which reflect a certain

---

[129] "due altri, al primo corso con le gambe in cielo, e con la testa in terra, a guisa di porri, piantati, poca pezza stettero, e due trombe goffamente la bella Franceschina, a scherno di quelli sonarono", TROIANO, *Discorsi* ..., p. 179. Cf. above, p. 135i (D-Mbs), for two musical sources of this song in Bavaria.

[130] "La Girometta fatta delle trombe et tamburi" and "risposta della Girometta in ottava tamburi per l'ordinanza"; "risposta del todesco in ottava".

[131] Interpretation suggested by Bruce Wardropper.

[132] Francesco VATIELLI, *Battaglia d'amore e di dispetto di O. Vecchi*, «Musica d'oggi», XXIII, 1941, p. 303, errs in believing the song to be "of southern origin". It flourished especially in Bologna, Padua/Venice, and, later, in Piedmont.

social milieu. In 1580 Cesare Caporali characterized with the *Girometta* the idyllic entertainments in Rome during the reign of Augustus:[133]

> E quasi in ogni picciola casetta,
> Accordate le cetere, e le pive
> Si sentiva cantar la Girometta.

And in almost every little house, when the citterns and the bagpipe had been tuned, one heard the *Girometta* sung.

Giovanni Battista Fagiuoli similarly used the song in a sonnet describing the peaceful life of the shepherd: "The body scrapes the cittern, and then the *Girometta* is sung".[134] It is therefore not without justification that Carlo Assonica substitutes "Giromèta" for the "canto" of the three shepherd boys in his Bergamask translation of Tasso's *Gerusalemme liberata* (VII, 6): "and listen to the Girometta [sung] by three boys".[135] When Zarlino wishes to illustrate the manner in which the Ancients sounded melodies over a drone bass, he quotes a modern melody, the *Girometta*. With its compass of a fifth, the song was well suited to such performance by pastoral instruments with drones (hurdy-gurdy, bagpipes):[136]

Gli Antichi cantavano & sonavano in consonanza alcune sorti d'istrumenti antichissimi; com'è la sinfonia o cornamusa, le trombe militari, nelle quali non si può sonare altro tuono che questo che segue; ch'è il primo nel nostro ordine & altri ch'io lascio; ne i quali s'udivano il continuo concerto & l'harmonia, che facevano insieme tre chorde almeno o tre pifferi accordati nella diapason, nella diapente, & nella diatessaron; sopra i quali si modulava o sonava una parte, come si vede esser tra queste della canzone

The ancients sang and played some kinds of very old intsruments in consonance, like the hurdy-gurdy or bagpipes, and the military trumpets, in which one can sound no other tone than this which follows [the separate musical example for the accompaniment gives the chord c-g-c'], which is the first of our order, and others which I omit. In these were heard the continuous concert and harmony, made by at least three strings together or three shawms tuned in the octave, the fifth, and the fourth, above which

---

[133] *Vita di Mecenate*, quoted from the edition of Modena, Gadeldini, 1604, p. 56.

[134] "Alla cetra talora il corpo gratta, / E poi vi canta su la girumetta" – "Sonetti unisoni pastorali', no. LVI: "Ateste a piacer suo pur se la batta", in FAGIUOI's *Rime piacevoli*, VI, Florence, Nestenus & Moücke, 1734, p. 225. These sonnets were begun in Milan in 1711, for Carlo Emanuele d'Este, "Ateste" in the Arcadia.

[135] "E scolta da trí schiegg la Giromèta" for "Et ascoltar di tre fanciulli il canto" – *Il Goffredo del Signor Torquato Tasso travestito alla rustica bergamasca*, Venice, Pezzana, 1670, p. 119. Assonica adds a footnote to the word "Giromèta": "Canzon nota" ["well known song"].

[136] *Sopplimenti musicali*, pp. 283f. On the performance with "trombe militari" see above, p. 162, GARSI.

moderna, posta nel seguente essempio ["Torna, torna al tuo paese"].

one part moved or was played, as is to be seen among those of the modern song placed in the following example ["Torna, torna al tuo paese"].

The pastoral associations and Zarlino's musical example can now explain the unusually primitive style of the keyboard *Girometta* in I-Rvat ms. Chigi Q.IV.28: the only harmony employed throughout the 77 measures of this piece is that of the repeated tonic chord, either as the triad in Ex. 8 or, somewhat more frequently, in the exact arrangement quoted by Zarlino (c-g-c′)![137] The same style is employed in the "Trombetta" of Ferrini, which repeats d-A-D in eighth notes in the left hand throughout the piece (notated only in the first two measures), exactly like the village bassoonist in the scherzo of Beethoven's Pastoral Symphony! Similarily, Uccellini's "Tromba sordina" adheres to a drone (d) and thus has been described as a parody of peasant music.[138] It was probably the continuation and degeneration of this tradition by rustic musicians which led to the Romagnese expression "Zirumlétta" for "trivial music always the same, tedious and fatiguing", "antiquated, monotonous, and boring".[139] Zarlino's pupil Vincenzo Galilei speaks ironically of lutenists who don't even know how to play such a simple song as the *Girometta*, "without the addition of so many strings below the bass",[140] and mentions it as an example of a [modern] melody which corresponds to the ancient style, because it, like the melodies of Olympos, does not exceed the range of a sixth.[141]

Ex. 8. I-Rvat ms. Chigi Q.IV.28, f. 62*v*: *Girometta*.

---

[137] Only the first ten measures employ the *Girometta* melody.

[138] Hermann EICHBORN, *Die Trompete in alter und neuer Zeit*, Leipzig, Breitkopf & Härtel, 1881, pp. 95f; OSTHOFF, pp. 83f.

[139] "musichetta sempre eguale, noiosa e da strapazzo", "antiquata, monotona e stucchevole" – PRATELLA, *Saggio*, p. 47, and *Etnografia*, p. 46.

[140] "senza la giunta di quelle tante corde sotto il basso" – *Il Fronimo*, Venice, Scotto, 1584, p. 105.

[141] I-Fn Ant. di Gal. III, 66*v*; cf. also III, 64*r-v* and Claude PALISCA, *Vincenzo Galilei and Some Links between 'Pseudo-monody' and Monody*, «Musical Quarterly», XLVI, 1960, p. 348.

We have seen that our songs were used as serenades. That such musical offerings are identified particularly with students and *Landsknechte* (German-Swiss mercenaries), who presented them to women of easy virtue, is clear from typical texts.[142] Spontone associated the *Girometta* with students in Bologna. It turns up in lute books compiled by young gentlemen in the Italian university towns[143] (Dusiacki, Garsi, Hallwil, perhaps also Bentivoglio – cf. the list of sources) and, with *La bella Franceschina*, in the Paduan poetry[144] of Magagnò, Menon, Figaro[145] and Orsato,[146] as well as in Azzaiolo's *Villotte alla padovana*. The anonymous comedy *Il parto supposto* (Ascoli, Pinetti, 1583, written 1566)[147] depicts student life in Padua, mentioning, *inter al.*, serenades with the lute and the *Girometta*. Thus the housemaster of the "scolare nobilista" advises:

Siete certo che se Amore molto campo vi pone adosso lo studio vostro sarà il passare per li cantoni, passeggiar per le strade, sedere per le banche, scrivere motti, guardar finestre, sonar liuti, scalare case, destar sviati, & le notte integre, non pur dando loco al sonno, suspirare, ma come vivo argento andarete de cantone in cantone, & li libri terrete in camera per ornamento a guisa de ritratti, & non per altro louri più dalla polvere che dalli dite; andarete alle scuole per compagnia, ragionerete alcune volte con dottori [I.i].	Be certain that if Amor greatly burdens you, your study will be to go about the corners, stroll through the streets, sit on benches, write mottoes, look at windows, play lutes, scale houses, arouse misled persons, and sigh entire nights, giving no place to sleep, but like quicksilver you will go from corner to corner, and you will keep the books in the room as an ornament in the manner of portraits, and worn more from the dust than from the fingers; you will go to the schools for company, and sometimes debate with doctors [I.i].
Credo ... che me vuoi insegnare le Contadinelle o le Gieromette, ... quando saremo la sù cantiamo di coppia la Giero-	[An old companion says to the servant:] I believe ... that you want to teach me the Contadinellas or the Giromettas, ... when

---

[142] Cf. AZZAIOLO, *Secondo libro*, "Bernarde non può stare": "Pero vi priego vengar'a li balcon / Che mi volere cantar une belle canzon"; LASSO, *Sämmtliche Werke*, X, no. 12: the well known "Matona mia cara, / Mi follere canzon / Cantar sotto finestra, / Lantze buon compagnon", etc.

[143] See note 50.

[144] See note 50.

[145] Tuogno FIGARO [pseud. for Alvise VALMARANA], *Smissiagga de sonagitti, canzon e smaregale in lengua pavana*, Padua, s.n., 1586, II, 64: "Co a cantavi con ti la Gierometta".

[146] Sertorio ORSATO, *Raccolta III di lettere in versi*, I-Pci ms. B. P. 1471/111, f. 102: "Già qui parmi veder con la beretta, / Conservata qua su di Tito Livio / Il mio Scarelli a far la girometta" ["Here I already seem to see, with the beret kept here on Titus Livius, my Scarelli (Orsato's friend Gio. Batt. Scarelli) making the *Girometta*"].

[147] Bruno BRUNELLI-BONETTI, *Una commedia padovana del Cinquecento*, R. Accademia di scienze, lettere ed arti in Padova, *Atti e memorie*, n.s. XXXI, 1915, pp. 251-260.

metta, che a dire il vero quest'aria non se impararebbe in dua mesi, & la Gierometta, sta bene cantarla in compagnia [IV.iv].

we are up there [at the beloved's house] we sing as a pair the Girometta, [and] that to tell the truth this melody would not be learned in two months, and it is well to sing the Girometta in company [IV.iv].

In Giulio Cesare Croce's burlesque description of a doctoral examination conducted by animals, *I trionfi fatti nel dottorato di Marchion Pettola*,[148] one of the examiners testifies that the candidate knows how to sing the *Girometta*: "Disse il Zampetta: & io vi faccio fede / Ch'ei sa cantar ancor la Girometta".

Another type of music cultivated by students and soldiers is, of course, the drinking song, and literary sources identify especially *La bella Franceschina* with this repertoire. In Filippo Azzaiolo's *Terzo libro delle villotte del fiore alla padovana* (Venice, Gardano, 1569) we are invited to sing this song and drink in Bartolomeo's cellar: "Let us sing 'La Ramacina'[149] or 'La bella Franceschina', let us drink in the cellar of Bartholomew the cuckhold".[150] Likewise in Croce's *Cantilena gratiosa sopra il primo dì d'agosto* (Bologna, n.d. and 1622) in praise of *ferragosto*, Bacchus, and good wine:

> Vadi dunque il fiasco a torno
> Per memoria di quel giorno
> E cantiam la Franceschina,
> La Simona e la Violina.

Go around, then, with the bottle in memory of that day, and let us sing "La Franceschina", "La Simone" and "La Violina".

Vincenzo Citharedo's *Testamento* (Urbino, 1589) bequeaths the *bustachina* to cooks with the bottle:

> Lascio, che tutt'i mastri di cucina
> Co'l fiasco appresso possan lavorare,
> Cantando sempremai la bustachina.

---

[148] Bologna, Pifarre, n.d.; Padua, 1898.

[149] A passage in the *Ricordi* [1546] of Sabba CASTIGLIONE, Venice, Gherardo, 1555, f. 39, identifies this as a kitchen- and drinking-song: "nella cusina ... cantamo insieme qualche gentil canzonetta da taverna, come è la Ramacina è morta, o fortuna di un gran tempo et altri simili" ["in the kitchen ... we sing together some polite little tavern song like 'La Ramacina è morta' or 'Fortuna di un gran tempo' and other similar ones"]. On the *Ramacina* cf. also NOVATI, *Contributo*, pp. 916ff, and Bianca BECHERINI, *Tre incatenature del codice fiorentino Magl. XIX 164-65-66-67*, in *Collectanea Historiae Musicae*, I, Florence, Olschki, 1953, p. 81.

[150] "Cantarem la ramacina olla bella franceschina / Beverem nella cantina di Bartolome cucu", from the third strophe of "Chi vuol vegni a bergam", p. 7.

I bequeath that all master cooks can work with the bottle at hand, always singing the *bustachina*.

The mention of cooks associates the songs with the European repertoire of *Küchenlieder*, which flourished until the first decades of our century – thus also Banchieri's *Hora prima*[151] and *Catlìna*, Croce's *Fornarina* (cf. above, pp. 144, 138, 141), and his *È tanto tempo hormai tramutato sopra un'amante affamato, et una cuciniera*[152] in which a hungry lover offers to sing "not only the Girometta but also the *bustachina*" in return for food:

> C[uciniera]:
> S'io t'hò promesso trare
> Giù minestra ò boion,
> Io non son per mancare,
> Pur che tu con il son
> De la tua dolce,
> E cara chitarrina
> Cantar la Violina.
> Venghi, ò la Girometta,
> Che ti darò per giunta
> Una polpetta.
>
> B[adile]:
> Non sol la Girometta,
> Ma ancor la bustachina ...

Cook: If I promised you to bring down soup or broth, I shall not fail, if only you, with the sound of your sweet and dear guitar, sing "La Violina". Come, I have the *Girometta*, and I shall give you in addition a meat ball. Badile: Not only the Girometta, but also the *bustachina*.

The identification of the *Girometta* with cooks, shepherds, soldiers, and students made the song proverbial for lazy folk in general. Thus, on an eighteenth-century map of the fabulous *Paese di Cuccagna*,[153] the fools' paradise

---

[151] "Sentij l'altra mattina / In casa d'una vecchia contadina / Cantar mentre faceva le polpette / Chi t'ha fatto quelle scarpette / Che ti stan sì ben Girometta" ["I heard the other morning an old peasant woman singing in her house while she made meat balls: 'Who made those shoes for you which look so well on you, Girometta?'"].

[152] Bologna, n.d.; published also as *Dialogo bellissimo* ..., under the pseudonym of Gio. RIVANO detto Gio. BADILE, Bologna, n.d., 1612, 1623. The frequent culinary references in Croce's works (cf. also above, p. 158, the *Indice universale*) were motivated by the deplorable living conditions of the *popolo minuto* in Bologna at this time.

[153] Reproduced in Francesco NOVATI, *La Storia e la stampa nella produzione popolare italiana*,

with a prison for those who work, a sonnet says that the inhabitants go about thoughtlessly singing the *Girometta*:

> Qui chi manco lavora più guardagna,
> Et chi non è poltron se gli dà bando,
> Qui senza alcun pensier si va cantando
> La Ghirimetta, che d'amor si lagna.

Here the less one works, the more one earns, and he who is not lazy is banished. Here one goes about without a thought singing 'La Girometta', who complains about love.

In a Bergamask idiom, "gira la giromèta" means "to stroll around idly",[154] and the Bolognese say to a good-for-nothing "Go and play the *Girometta*".[155]

Further literary sources confirm the association of our songs with low life and low literature. When Benvenuto Cellini wants to degrade his despised rival, he says that the fellow obtained the favor of the duke either by flattery or by singing *La bella Franceschina*: "This ugly rogue, who knew very well what he did, since, either by means of swelling up or by singing 'La bella Franceschina', he was able to secure that the duke made that purchase".[156] In Croce's *Gran vittoria*, the most humiliating insult which the Zanni Pedrolino can find for Graziano, his rival for the love of Franceschina, is to say "You don't even know how to sing the *bustachina*".[157] In order to cure Piero Cardi of "frenesia poetica", Lasca prescribes various kinds of poems, including one in ottava rima with the lines[158]

> La vita vostra sì gretta e meschina,
> Da goffi ghiribizzi accompagnata,
> Come or si fa la bella Franceschina,
> Sarà da' putti per le vie cantata.

Your life, so mean and wretched, accompanied by awkward whims, will be sung in the streets by the children, as now is done with 'La bella Franceschina'.

«Emporium», XXIV, 1906, opposite p. 192. The country is especially attractive to Zanni and Tedesco. A woodcut of Cuccagna appears on the title page of CROCE's *Nozze del Zane*, Bologna, Cochi, 1631; and in a *canto carnascialesco* the "todeschi" sing: "La udite in l'alte Magne / Queste terre istar cucagne" ["You hear in Germany that these lands are Cuccagne"] – SINGLETON, p. 95.

[154] Antonio TIRABOSCHI, *Vocabolario dei dialetti bergamaschi antichi e moderni*, Bergamo, Bolis, 1873, p. 604.

[155] "Va' a sunèr la girumetta" – FERRARI, *Canzoni ricordate*, p. 86.

[156] "Questo ribaldaccio, che sapeva benissimo quello che lui facieva, perché, se o per via del gonfiare, o per cantare la bella Franceschina, ei poteva ottenere che 'l duca facessi quella compera" – *Vita di Benvenuto Cellini*, Florence, Soc. Editrice Nazionale, 1901, p. 376; written 1558-1567.

[157] "Ti no se pur cantà la bustachina".

[158] "La purga di Ser Piero Cardi", in *Rime di Antonfrancesco Grazzini detto il Lasca*, Florence, Moücke, 1741-42, II, 152.

La bella Franceschina would hardly have been an appropriate melody to play on the carillon for the reception of the Queen of France by Emperor Charles V in Brussels, described by Annibale Caro in a letter of 29 October 1544 to the Duke of Piacenza (Caro does not clearly identify the song with the occasion):[159]

All'entrar di Brusselle, che fu agli 22 a ore 24 fu bel vedere un grandissimo numero di torchi, ed un bel sentire i conserti delle campane. V. Eccell. non si rida ch'io abbia notata questa musica: perché in questo paese le campane suonano fino alla bella Franceschina.

At the entry into Brussels, which was on the 22nd, at midnight it was beautiful to see a very large number of torches and to hear the music of the bells. Let Your Excellency not laugh that I have mentioned this music, because in this country the bells play even *La bella Franceschina*.

As a cure for gout, the sickness which plagues dissolute persons, Giovanni Battista Fagiuoli recommends the *Girometta*:[160]

> Bench'Aulo Gellio scritto abbia lasciato,[161]
> Che la musica opprima una tal doglia:
> ....
> Pure quando un tal mal vi dà la stretta
> Un'altra volta, e voi chiamate tosto
> Un musico a cantar la girometta ...

Although Aulus Gellius[161] recorded that music overcomes such a pain ... Also, when such a malady oppresses you again and you summon immediately a musician to sing the *Girometta* ...

In an extended negative criticism of Italian opera he deplores that diplomats sing such vulgar melodies while dealing with most important matters: "One hears the actors who speak and, while representing monarchs, discuss the most serious affairs of state, singing the *Girometta*".[162] Documentation for this practice is indeed found in Giuseppe De Totis' libretto for Bernardo Pasquini's *Caduta del regno delle Amazzoni* (Rome, Camera Apost., 1690; SL 4348), II.ii:

> Signor, non è più tempo da burlare,
> La regia autorità

---

[159] *Lettere del Commendatore Annibal Caro*, Milan, Classici Italiani, 1807, I, 107f.

[160] *Rime piacevoli*, III, 1732, capitolo terzo: "In lode della gotta" ["In praise of gout"], p. 22.

[161] *Noctes Atticae*, IV.xiii.

[162] "S'odono i recitanti, che parlano, e che in rappresentanza di monarchi ragionano degli affari più gravi del regno, cantando la Girometta" – "Cicalata prima detta nell'Accademia degli Apatisti la vigilia di Berlingaccio", in FAGIUOLI's *Prose*, Florence, Moücke, 1737, p. 62.

Se la siamo giocata alla bassetta,
E Vostra Maestà
Se la passa in cantar la girometta ...

My lord, this is no longer time for jesting; if we have gambled the royal authority at a game of chance and Your Majesty spends the time singing the *Girometta* ...

A Venetian idiom, "cantar la bela Girometa", means "to dupe, deride, make a fool of someone".[163]

The Girometta descends a step further, from the milieu of the lowest social classes to that of animals. Scipione Ammirato appends to his novella *Del maraviglioso avveddimento d'un cane del Re Francesco di Francia* an anecdote about Geronimo Molino's dog, which was able to "sing" the *Girometta*:[164]

Et che direte voi, disse, del mio cane, il qual canta la Ghiremetta? Ogn'huomo si maravigliò. ... Ma egli ci liberò tosto di tal maraviglia, et fece vere le sue parole in questo modo. Era uscita allor per Venezia questa canzone in campagna: et cantavasi da piccoli, et da grandi di giorno, et di notte per le piazze, et per le vie sì fattamente, che ciascuno havea del continuo gli orecchi intronati dal tuono di questa canzone. Hora il cane del Molino, come vediamo tutto dì guaire i cani al suon delle campane, havea incominciato talmente ad abbaiare a quelle note della Ghiremetta, che veramente si potea dire, come le cornette, i pifferi, et gli altri instromenti musicali fanno, che ancor egli la Ghiremetta cantasse.	And what will you say, he said, about my dog, who sings the *Girometta*? Everyone was amazed. ... But he freed us immediately of such wonder and verified his words in this way. At that time this song went out from Venice into the countryside and was sung by young and old night and day on the squares and streets, so that everyone continually had the ears invested with this song. Now Molino's dog, as we see the dogs whining all day at the sound of the bells, had begun to bark at those notes of the *Girometta*, so that one could truly say that he too sang the *Girometta*, as the cornetts, shawms, and other musical instruments do.

Other bestial Giromettas are those of Banchieri's fox, who is too shrewd to be shot like a dog for stealing chickens:[165]

Quando la volpe hebbe veduto il tragico, e sanguinoso esito alla vita dell'infelice cane, tutta la notte pensando a' casi suoi diße cantando, questo paese,

---

163 Giuseppe BOERIO, *Dizionario del dialetto veneziano*, Venice, Santini, 1829, p. 252.

164 *Opuscoli*, Florence, Massi & Landi, 1637, pp. 173f. NOVATI, *Contributo* ..., p. 944, note 1, demonstrates that this story must have been told between 1548 and 1582. TORREFRANCA, p. 136, confuses Molino's dog with the king's, and thus arrives at incorrect dates.

165 "Novelloso discorso volpino", in *Trastulli della villa*, Venice, Mascheroni, 1627, p. 199.

> El non fa per mì,
> El non fa per mì Girometta
> El non fa per mi,

When the fox had seen the tragic and bloody end of the life of the unhappy dog, thinking all night of his affairs, he exclaimed, singing, this place 'is not for me, Girometta',

or his starling or blackbird "who learns to whistle the *Girometta*",[166] and the swan-song mentioned by Fagiuoli in a discussion of carnival masquerades: "whence it will be necessary to agree to appear as Leda, and to converse with certain plucked swans, sweetly singing, without any other sound, the *Girometta*".[167]

Most of our literary references have been drawn from rustic and burlesque poetry, written by the most eminent masters of these genres. Only in a mock epic, such as Francesco Bracciolini's *Scherno de' falsi dei* (VIII.14), could the word "Girometta" be uttered by a god; here a vulgar Venus expresses her determination to take revenge on Vulcan:[168]

> E però ne vorrei, Mercurio mio,
> Far se non si potrà piena vendetta,
> Qualche dimostratione, e crepo,
> Non gl'insegno cantar la ghirumetta.

And, however, I should like, my Mercury, to make, if full revenge is not possible, some demonstration, and [may] I burst [if] I do not teach him to sing the *Girometta*.

In polite society it was taboo, as we have seen from Spontone's dialogue. Thus, in a novella of Celio Malispini a poor wretch provokes laughter because he can contribute nothing better than the *Girometta* to a musical parlor game at the Medici court: "After they made his part for us, and sang those blunders which most entered his imagination, among which there was one, who not knowing what to say, sang 'You are not for me, Girometta'".[169] A reporter writing on 28 August 1677 used the song to express his contempt for the musical life in Rome:[170]

---

[166] "che impara de fischiar la girometta" – *Il furto amoroso*, III.iv.

[167] "onde bisognerà contentarsi di far comparsa da Lede, e far conversazione con certi spelacchiati cigni, dolcemente cantando, senza altro suono, la Girumetta" – "Cicalata seconda" cit., p. 62.

[168] Florence, Giunti, 1618, p. 153.

[169] "Dopo c'hebbero fatto la parte sua, e cantato quei spropositi, che più gli veniva nella fantasia: fra quali ve ne fu uno, che non sapendo che si dire, cantò 'Tu non fai per me Girometta, Tu non fai per me'" – "Affari ridicolosi del Conegiani succeduti in Fiorenza essendo ambasciatore", in his *Ducento novelle*, Venice, Al segno dell'Italia, 1609, II, ff. 122v-123.

[170] D-Mbs Cod. Ital. 192, f. 623v; Thomas GRIFFIN, *Alessandro Scarlatti e la serenata a Roma e a Napoli*, in *La musica a Napoli* cit., p. 352.

Il principe di Palestrina si sta apparechiando per domani a sera per fare una serenata a questo ambasciatore di Spagna, essendoli suoni, e canti a proposito per li romani e forestieri, che dimorano in questa corte, potendo tra quelle armonie andare tutti a cantare la Gierometta.

The prince [Maffeo Barberini] of Palestrina is preparing to make a serenade tomorrow evening for this ambassador of Spain. Instruments and voices are there expressly for the Romans and strangers, who dwell in this court, all able to go about among those harmonies singing the *Girometta*.

When we recall that the compilers of collections of lauds seized even the most notorious melodies as means of popularizing sacred texts and were in no way deterred by the profane associations which accompanied such melodies, then we need not be surprised to find the *Girometta* serving for religious contrafacta, and this, in turn, helps to explain its use in the liturgical organ pieces of Frescobaldi and Fasolo. The laud texts of Serafino Razzi and Marco Della Casa (1563) take as their point of departure the strophe "Torna, torna al tuo paese ... Tu non fai per me" ["Return home ... You are not for me"], which, as we have seen from Azzaiolo, Zarlino, Schiopi, Banchieri, and Malespini (pp. 152, 160, 171), enjoyed a certain independent existence. Razzi substitutes "Giesù mio" for "Girometta"; Della Casa, "animetta", retaining the "-metta" refrain in each strophe.[171]

Serafino Razzi:
Torna, torna al freddo cuore,
   Onde partito se',
   Onde partito se', Giesù mio,
   Onde partito se'.

[Return to the cold heart
   Whence you departed, my Jesus].

[21 strophes]

Marco Della Casa:
Torna, torna al tuo Signore,
   Che farà per te,
   Che farà per te, Animetta,
   Che farà per te.

[Return to your Lord
   It will be good for you, little soul].

[20 strophes]

For such well known melodies it was hardly necessary to include musical notation, and thus Razzi's later edition (1609) gives only the text, as does the "Lauda del Bambino, cantasi come la Gyrometta" in I-MOe ms. γ. F. 6. 9,[172]

---

171 A later strophe of Razzi's laud returns to this text: "Tu non fai per me, cieco mondo" ["You are not for me, blind world"]. Della Casa makes repeated use of the line "Che [here = il Signore] ti vuol gran ben" ["... who loves you dearly"] from the secular text.

172 No. 259 in Luigi LODI, *Catalogo dei codici e degli autografi posseduti dal Marchese Giuseppe Campori*, Modena, Torchi, 1875, p. 170.

f. *2r-v*, beginning "Dhe laudate Jesu meco / Ch'è nato per me" (16 strophes). The reprints of Razzi's laud, now with the melody in the major mode, in the three editions of Matteo Coferati's *Corona di sacre canzoni* (1675-1710), are among the last musical sources for the song. Coferati or his later editor seems to have derived another laud, "Brevità della vita" (Ex. 9) from this melody. It is contained only in his third edition (p. 597f, 8 strophes), and is listed in the index as sung to the "Villan di Spagna".[173] The so profane *Girometta* melody was even used in Mass compositions: in its earliest and second last known musical sources, Giovanni Nasco's *Messa sopra la Gerometa* (1552) and an anonymous manuscript of 1703 from the Augustinian monastery in Lucca, not to mention the third organ Mass of Frescobaldi and Fasolo's fugue. Disapproval of the notorious melody in the religious realm was not lacking, as can be seen from two aphorisms in Francesco Maria Veracini's *Trionfo della prattica musicale* (ca. 1758-62):[174]

Il non far cantare le parole sacre sull'aria della Ghirometta, o della bella Irene sarà cosa santa, ricordandosi che *Domus mea domus orationis*, e però distinguere le parole sacre dalle profane. *Odi profanum volgus et arceo.*

Not letting sacred words be sung to the melody of the *Girometta*, or *La bella Irene* will be a holy thing, remembering that 'My house is the house of prayer' [Luke, 19:46], and, however, distinguishing sacred words from profane. 'I dislike and drive away the profane/uninitiated crowd' [Horace, *Carmina*, III.1.1].

A quella sinfonia intitolata *Lamento pel Venerdì Santo* che debbe essere tutta di stile flebile, non si frameschierano *Romei*, la *Forlana*, il *Trescone*, i *Fantolini*, né la *Ghierometta.*

One will not mix *Romei, La Forlana, Il Tescone, I Fantolini*, or *La Ghierometta* with that *sinfonia* entitled *Lament for Good Friday*, which must be in a plaintive style.

Ex. 9. Coferati: laud "Brevità della vita", 1710.

---

[173] Cf. W. KIRKENDALE, *L'Aria di Fiorenza*, p. 54, note 1, on the harmonic progression of the *Villan di Spagna*, common in Italian guitar tablatures since the early 17th century.
[174] I-Fc F.I.28, ff. 228 and 230, aphorisms nos. 54 and 59.

II. VECCHI'S ADDITION

A. Lo Scolare. Aggionto dal Vecchi. Quinto. / Il Pedante. Del Vecchi. Ottavo.

(In the text of the dialogue printed below I have italicized Latin words and Latin stems with Italian endings, and added quotation marks and most of the punctuation.)

Prima Parte

S. *Salve, Magister*!

P. *Bene veniat*,[175] ti voglio far gustar la *scutica.*

S. Perché?

P. Tu non venisti hier' al ludo literario.[176]

S. Mia madre mi lavò la testa,[177] e 'l zavatino mi conciò le scarpe.

P. Ah *furuncule*, m'hai detto le mendatie. Ti voglio *vapular*, per lo dio Hercule![178]

S. Non più, *Magister*!

P. Vien'a la scola.

S. Ohime, *Magister*!

P. Non far la fuga.

S. Ohime, *Magister*!

P. Ah, tristarello! L'ha' cacciat' un dent'in la cervice a Zambone.[179]

S. *Greetings, Master*!

P. *Welcome*,[175] I want to let you taste the *cane.*

S. Why?

P. You didn't come to school yesterday.[176]

S. My mother washed my hair,[177] and the shoemaker fixed my shoes.

P. Ah *rogue*, you have told me lies. I'll *flog* you, by the god Hercules![178]

S. No more, *Master*!

P. Come to school.

S. Oh, *Master*!

P. Don't flee.

S. Oh, *Master*!

P. Ah, wretch! You bit Zambone in the neck.[179]

---

[175] The same greeting is uttered by the Repetitore in Francesco BELO's *Pedante*, IV.i, Rome, Bresciani, 1529, 1538, and by the pedant Mamphurio in Giordano BRUNO's *Candelaio*, Paris, Giuliano, 1582, f. 45*v*. Latin salutations commonly served to identify immediately the role of the pedant. Cf. also GARZONI, *La Piazza universale*, p. 92.

[176] Cf. below, note 244.

[177] Idiomatic translation: "scolded me".

[178] GARZONI, p. 90, mocks the petty disputes of pedants who invoke "il Dio Polluce et Hercole a ogni tratto" ["continually the god Pollux and Hercules"]. BRUNO's Mamphurio, f. 61, leaves the stage with the words "Eamus dextro Hercule". This god was revered by pedants presumably because of his ancient attribute of 'tutor'; cf. *Paulys Real-Encyclopädie der classischen Altertumswissenschaft*, ed. Georg WISSOWA *et al.*, VIII/1, Stuttgart, Metzler, 1912, col. 593. In ancient Greece he presided over the schools.

[179] The meaning of this sentence became clear to me only from artistic representations of castigation scenes, such as the one referred to below in note 200, and Benozzo Gozzoli's fresco of 1463-64 which depicts no less a spectator than "Sant'Agostino nella scuola di grammatica" (cf. St. Augustine, *Confessiones*, I.ix, P.L. XXXII, 667f) – reproduced by Natale BALDORIA, *Monumenti artistici in San Gimignano*, «Archivio storico dell'arte», III, 1890, p. 51: the head of the person being caned rests on the neck of the student or servant, upon whose back he is hoisted. Zambon is an alternate name for the Bergamask Zanni. There is a slight possibility that it refers here to Zambon da Mosca-

S. *Minimè.*

P. Ah, impudente!

S. *Minimè.*

P. Ah, inurbano!

S. No, a la fè!

P. *Heus, puer.*

S. *Adsum.*

P. Recita la *lectiuncula.*

S. *Nunc:*

"*Iam satis terris nivis atque dirae Gran-dinis misit pater, et rubente Dextera sa-cras iaculatus arces,*[180] *Terruit urbem".*

P. Hor va con Dio.

Seconda Parte

S. O dal gimnasio aprite, o là aprite pre-sto presto, che 'l cane del fornaio non mi piglia.

P. Chi pulsa così nel *diluculo* a le *ianue*?

S. Son io.

P. *Nunc, nunc.* E ch'è quest' 'io'?

S. Muscardino.

P. La voce non mi par già di pubero di tenere *unguicole.*[181]

S. Buon giorno.

P. Hora *surgo* dal *strato; a sterno stravi stratum primitivo derivatur hoc stra-tum strati* il letto.[182]

S. *No.*

P. Ah, impudent one!

S. *No.*

P. Ah, rude one!

S. No, by my faith!

P. *Hear, boy.*

S. *I am present.*

P. Recite your *lesson.*

S. *Now:*

"*The father has already sent enough dire snow and hail upon the earth and smitten with his red right hand the sa-cred citadel*[180] *and terrified the City".*

P. Now go with God.

S. Oh, open the door of the gymnasium, oh, open quickly, so that the baker's dog won't get me.

P. Who is knocking like this in the *dawn* at the *doors*?

S. It is I.

P. *Now, now.* And who is this 'I'?

S. Muscardino.

P. The voice does not appear to be of a boy with tender *fingertips.*[181]

S. Good day.

P. Now I *rise* from the bed; *from 'sterno, stravi, stratum' is derived this 'stratum, strati',* the bed.[182]

---

dello, the famous proprietor of the Hosteria del Chiù in Bologna (cf. Plate IV.4), mentioned in Alessandro TASSONI, *Secchia rapita*, I.31, Paris, Du Bray, 1622, f. 6. The described position of the student being caned was customary already in ancient times – cf. the drawing from Pompei in Theodor SCHREIBER, *Kulturhistorischer Bilderatlas*, I, Leipzig, s.n., 1885, Taf. LXXXIX.3 (surely the depiction referred to in Edward BULWER-LYTTON, *The Last Days of Pompeii*, 1834, III, i, note: "the ceremony of *hoisting* ... is of high antiquity"), and in Arnold von SALIS, *Antike und Renaissance*, Zürich, Rentsch, 1947, plates 26f.

[180] I.e. Jupiter struck by lightening his own temple on the Roman capitol.

[181] BRUNO's Mamphurio, f. 23, identifies himself as "moderator di pueruli di teneri unguicoli".

[182] Cf. Nicolo FRANCO, *Dialogi piacevoli*, Venice, De Ferrarii, 1541, f. lxx: "È costume de pe-danti comentare in ogni parola" ["The pedants are accustomed to comment on every word"]. Absurd etymologies and the recitation of conjugations and declensions are characteristic of pedants' roles. Texts consisting entirely of declinations were set by Tarquinio Merula in his popular "Nominativo hic haec hoc" and "Nominativo quis vel quid" of 1623, and Erasmus Kindermann published settings

S. Cancaro venga a *sterno stravi*, aprit'hormai.

S. Pox on '*sterno, stravi*', open now.

P. Hai troppo fretta.

P. You are in too much of a hurry.

S. Il malan' che Dio vi dia!

S. The curse of God upon you!

P. *Heu, hei*, uha, ahi, ohimè, che non mi bastan tutte l'*interiectiones dolentis*[183] per deprimer l'ira d'un mal educato.

P. *Alas, alack*, oh, ah, woe is me, that all the *interjections of a sufferer*[183] do not suffice to suppress the wrath of an ill-bred person.

S. Ohim' a tua posta, ah Pedante!

S. Alas to you, ah Pedant!

P. Ah *scelesto*!

P. Ah *rogue*!

S. Arcipedante!

S. Archpedant!

P. Nato di *gerulo*![184]

P. Son of a *porter*![184]

S. Pedantissimo!

S. Most pedantic!

P. *Cinedissimo*!

P. *Most lecherous*!

S. Che peggio si puo dir che dir 'Pedante'?![185]

S. What can one say worse than 'Pedant'?![185]

P. *Abis in malis avibus*!

P. *Go to hell*!

Vecchi's Scolare and Pedante, unlike Zanni and Magnifico, belong not to the *commedia dell'arte*, but to the *commedia erudita*;[186] their Latinized language can be fully appreciated – and successfully written! – only by the educated.[187] Humanism, born with the germ of pedantry in its body, had given rise in the sixteenth century to a sizable production of burlesque *poesia pe-*

---

183 In the "Dialogo primo" of Giordano BRUNO's *De la causa, principio et uno*, Venice [*recte*: London, Charlewood] 1584, p. 26, Philotheo quotes the deploration of a pedant: "Quanto tempo è scorso che non s'è trovato ... con che misure et quali ordini vi s'intermesceno quelle interiectione[s] dolentis, gaudentis, heu, oh, ahi, ah, hem, ohe, hui, et altri condimenti, senza i quali tutto il discorso è insipidissimo?" ["How much time has passed since has not been found with what measure and order were interpolated those painful and joyful interjections 'heu', 'oh', 'ahi', 'ah', 'hem', 'ohe', 'hui', without which the entire discourse is most insipid?"].

of Latin grammar lessons in 1655 – Hans Joachim MOSER, *Corydon: Geschichte des mehrstimmigen Generalbassliedes und des Quodlibets im deutschen Barock*, Braunschweig, Litolff, 1933, I, 31-35, II, 43-57; cf. also Giovanni Battista ANDREINI, *Le due comedie in comedia*, V.iii, Venice, Imberti, 1623, p. 89: "nominativo hic, & haec, & hoc".

184 Cf. p. 130, the "facchini bergamaschi".

185 I.e. with the implication of "qual vitio niun altro esse può maggiore" ["that worst of all vices"], associated with this profession – letter of Carlo Sigonio, 17 Nov. 1538, published in «Giornale storico della letteratura italiana», XV, 1890, p. 461.

186 The Pedante did, however, occasionally appear in the commedia dell'arte; cf. SCALA's *scenario* XXXI, *Il Pedante comedia*, in *Il Teatro delle favole rappresentative*, ff. 92-94.

187 Crescimbeni shows little understanding for its wit when he designates it as "prodotto ... da sola ignoranza e temerità" ["product ... of only ignorance and temerity"] – Giovanni Maria CRESCIMBENI, *Commentari ... intorno alla sua istoria della volgar poesia*, Rome, De Rossi, 1702-11, I, 322.

dantesca,[188] peculiar to, but not restricted to Italy.[189] Known also as *poesia fidenziana* after the pseudonym "Fidenzio Glottocrisio Ludimagistro" of Count Camillo Scroffa, who perfected the genre, it was cultivated on the stage by such authors as Francesco Belo (*El pedante* 1529), Pietro Aretino (*Il marescalco* 1533), and Giordano Bruno (*Candelaio* 1582) – to name only the most eminent.[190] Indeed, the *pedante* was a most familiar figure in Italian comedy, as Montaigne recalled at the beginning of his essay *Du pedantisme*: "In my childhood I was often iritated to see in the Italian comedies always a pedant as a joke".[191] A similar observation in Henry Peacham's *Compleat Gentleman* confuses the pedant's dramatic function with that of Graziano[192] (see below): "In Italy, of all professions, that of *pedanteria* is held in basest repute; the schoolemaster almost in every comedy being brought upon the stage to parallel the Zani or Pantaloun. He made us good sport in that excellent comedy of *Pedantius*, acted in our Trinitie Colledge in Cambridge".[193]

Originally the word 'pedant' was synonymous with 'pedagogue' and had no derogatory connotation. However, in comic and satirical literature of the Cinquecento the *pedanti* soon became caricatures of the grammarians or Latin teachers, of which large numbers lived in the university towns of Bologna and Padua during the centuries when grammar and Latin formed the basis for all other studies. The *grammatici*, impoverished wretches, were despised by their higher-ranking colleagues because they lacked the *licentia docendi*. Ridiculed and plagued by their students, they could assert their authority only by use of the cane.[194] Their language is an amusing mixture of Italian words and Latin roots with Italian endings – thus Nicola Villani distinguishes it from the more general category of macaronic, which mixes Latin words and modern vocabu-

---

[188] Cf. Arturo GRAF, *I pedanti*, in his *Attraverso il cinquecento*, Turin, Loescher, 1888, pp. 171-213; Severino FERRARI, *Camillo Scroffa e la poesia pedantesca*, «Giornale storico della letteratura italiana», XIX, 1892, pp. 304-334; Abdelkader SALZA, *Una commedia pedantesca del cinquecento*, in *Miscellanea di studi critici edita in onore di Arturo Graf*, Bergamo, Arti Grafiche, 1903, pp. 431-452.

[189] Cf. Robert BEYERSDORFF's rather polemical *Giordano Bruno und Shakespeare*, Oldenburg, Stalling, 1889, pp. 16-24, on the pedant in the English theatre. Holofernes in Shakespeare's *Love's Labour's Lost* is a distant relative of the Italian type.

[190] Cf. also the titles in Lione ALLACCI, *Drammaturgia*, Venice, Pasquali, 1755, col. 615f.

[191] "Ie me suis souvent despité en mon enfance de voir és comedies Italiennes tousiours un pedante pour badin" – Michele de MONTAIGNE, *Essais*, Bordeaux, Millagnes, 1580, *livre premier*, ch. XXV, p. 167.

[192] As noted by LEA, I, 41.

[193] London, Constable, 1622, p. 27. Peacham was a pupil of Vecchi and acquainted with Marenzio. The Latin comedy *Pedantius* was first acted in Cambridge ca. 1581, published in London 1631, and edited with a commentary Louvain, Uystpruyst, 1905.

[194] Roger ASCHAM, *The Scholemaster*, London, Daye, 1570, preface and book I, *passim*, condemned the use of this educational tool, recognizing that it could lead to hatred of learning.

lary with Latin endings: "macaronic admits only vernacuar and Latin words, both used with the Latin endings and manner; but *pedantesca* admits not only Latin, but also Greek, and Hebrew is not excluded, reducing all of them, however, or the greater part, to the endings and manner of the vernacular".[195] On the one hand a pedant could admit: "I understand the vernacular very well, but don't speak it well";[196] and on the other hand be accused that "The Goths, Vandals, Lombards, and all the barbarians together did not carry as much ruin to the Roman Empire than you to the Latin language".[197] Under these conditions, students "will never know how to write not only a Latin epistle, but also a graceful vernacular letter".[198] Vecchi's Scolare, however, recites the Latin strophe correctly,[199] thus demonstrating that he is linguistically more competent than Pedante.

Ever since the founding of the first Italian universities, the *scolari* were notoriously diligent in the pursuit of gambling, drink, and women of ill repute. In 1360, a wall had to be built in Bologna to separate their living quarters from the red-light district.[200] Croce asks in his *Girandola de' pazzi*:[201]

> Non son pazzi i scolari i quali vanno
> A le parti lontane a studiare
> E in vece d'imparar altro non fanno
> Che starsi con le femine, e a giocare?

Are they not crazy, the students who come to distant parts and instead of learning do nothing but frequent women and gamble?

---

[195] "la maccheronica non ammette se non le parole volgari e le latine; e l'une, e l'altre con la terminatione, e con la guisa de i latini adopera; ma la pedantesca non solamente ammette le latine, ma le greche ancora, e nulla vieta, che l'hebraiche; riducendole però tutte, o la maggior parte di esse alla terminatione e alla guisa della volgare" – *Ragionamento dello academico Aldeano sopra la poesia giocosa de' greci, de' latini e de' toscani*, Venice, Pinelli, 1634, p. 86. Cf. above p. 133, the two procedures for writing 'tedesco'.

[196] "lingua vernacula optime intellego sed non bene loquor" – G. B. ANDREINI, *Le due comedie*, V.iii, p. 90.

[197] "I gotti, i vandali, i longobardi, e tutti i barbari insieme, non portarono tanta rovina all'imperio romano, quanta voi alla lingua latina" – Aonio PALERARIO [pseud. of Antonio DELLA PAGLIA], *Dialogo intitolato il grammatico ovvero delle false esercitazioni delle scuole*, Venice, Marchesan, 1726, p. 34 (a book entirely different from that publshed under the same name and title in Milan, 1557).

[198] "non mai sapranno scrivere non solamente un'epistola latina, ma non pure una leggiadra lettera volgare" – *ibid.*, p. 17.

[199] Unlike the garbled Latin distichs sung in BELO's *Pedante*, V.vii – cf. A. DI PRIMA, *Il Centone di Prudenzio nel 'Pedante' di F. Belo*, «Nuova cultura», I, 1913, pp. 266-272.

[200] On *grammatici* and *scolari* cf. Guido ZACCAGNINI, *La Vita dei maestri e degli scolari nello studio di Bologna nei secoli XIII e XIV*, Geneva, Olschki, 1926, esp. pp. 61f, 86, 92-96, 103; a depiction of a flogging is reproduced in plate XXII.

[201] I-Bu ms. Misc. 3878, caps. LI, t. I, f. 96bis v; Giovanni NASCIMBENI, *Note e ricerche intorno a Giulio Cesare Croce*, «L'Archiginnasio», VIII, 1913, p. 300.

Scenes similar to Vecchi's are contained in the contemporary comedies, such as the anonymous *Pleasant conceited comedie, wherein is shewed how a man may chuse a good wife from a bad*, II.i (London, Lawe, 1602), with the student arriving late for the Latin lesson, making excuses, threatened with flogging by the master; here too the *lingua pedantesca* and the recitation of Latin verbs. Sometimes, as in Bruno's *Candelaio*, it is the pedant who is beaten, for his arrogance and sodomy.[202] The comic schoolmaster remained in music throughout the seventeenth and eighteenth centuries, at least, caricatured in Francesco Maria Bazzani's opera *Il Pedante di Tarsia*,[203] Telemann's *Schulmeisterkantate*,[204] and F. X. Brixi's *Schulmeisterius*.[205]

Our truant Scolare is able to bring Pedante's cane to rest only by reciting hastily the opening strophe of the second ode in the first book of Horace's *Carmina*. This poem, following the dedicatory ode to Maecenas, professes in Sapphic meter Horace's conversion to Caesarism, hailing Augustus as the saviour of the state. The first strophe describes Jupiter's wrath after the assassination of Caesar,[206] here parodied wittily by the wrath of Pedante. The first words, "Iam satis ...", are also appropriate to the situation of Scolare, who has had "enough" flogging.

For further understanding of this passage it is necessary to survey the preceding tradition of musical settings of Horatian odes, particularly those in Sapphic meter.[207]

---

[202] A pedant of Lasca fares still worse: the reader may find the unsavoury details in Antonfrancesco GRAZZINI detto il Lasca, *La prima e la seconda cena*, London, Nourse, 1751, pp. 13-21 – cf. also pp. 279-297.

[203] Bologna 1680 – SL 18300.

[204] Cf. W. KIRKENDALE, *Fugue and Fugato in Rococo and Classical Chamber Music*, Durham NC, Duke UP, 1979, p. 104.

[205] A-Wn ms. 15906; MOSER, *Corydon*, I, 90, II, 199-211. A recording made in Budapest from the German version, H-Bn ms. Mus. IV.349, retains the misattribution to Paisiello.

[206] The ode was later adapted to a comparable historical crisis: the horrors of the French Revolution; cf. Friedrich August Baumbach's setting "An August" for Friedrich Wilhelm II, "als er aus Frankreich zurückkehrte" (Leipzig 1794) and Herder's parody of the first line in "Die Rettung": "Gnug des schrecklichen Hagels" – Johann Gottfried HERDER, *Sämmtliche Werke*, Berlin, Weidmann, 1877-1913, XXIX, 582.

[207] On musical settings of texts of Horace cf. especially Eduard STEMPLINGER, *Das Fortleben der horazischen Lyrik seit der Renaissance*, Leipzig, Teubner, 1906; Günther WILLE, *Musica Romana*, Amsterdam, Schippers, 1967, pp. 234-281; Silvia WÄLLI, *Melodien aus mittelalterlichen Horaz-Handschriften*, Kassel, Bärenreiter, 2002. For settings of Sapphic odes cf. Édith WEBER, *La musique mesurée à l'antique en Allemagne* [Paris], Klincksieck, 1974, *passim*, and *Prosodie verbale et prosodie musicale: la strophe sapphique*, in *Le moyen française*, Montreal, 1980, pp. 159-192. On more recent music for texts of Horace cf. Joachim DRAHEIM, *Vertonungen antiker Texte vom Barock bis zur Gegenwart*, Amsterdam, Grüner, 1981, pp. 41-99, 184-208, and DRAHEIM/WILLE, *Horaz-Vertonungen vom Mittelalter bis zur Gegenwart*, ibid., 1985.

I. MUSIC TO SAPPHIC ODES OF HORACE

a) "Iam satis terris" (*Carmina*, I.2)

11th c.	F-Pn ms. lat. 8214, f. 1*v*. Notation in Aquitanian neumes.
1507	Petrus Tritonius [Peter Treybenreif], *Melopoiae sive harmoniae tetracenticae*, Augsburg, Rimann, 1507, Frankfurt, 1532:[208] Secundum genus.
1515-19	Hans Judenkünig, *Utilis & compendaria introductio*, Vienna, Singriener, n.d.. Subtitle for sig. B1-B4: "Harmoniae super odis Horatianis secundum omnia Horatii genera". Sig. B1*v*: "Ode 2. Iam satis terris".[209] Intabulated from Tritonius for lute, omitting the alto part. Reprinted in Judenkünig's *Schone kunstliche underweisung ... auff der Lautten und Geygen*, ibid., 1523₄, sig. C3*v*: "Saphica".[210] (Only this ode is retained from the previous collection).
1526	Michael [of Augsburg], in Theobald von Billican, *De partium orationis in flexionibus*, n.p. 1526. Reprinted, together with Tritonius's settings, by Petrus Nigidius under the title *Geminae undevigenti odarum Horatii melodiae*, Frankfurt, 1551-52.[211]
1534	Ludwig Senfl, *Varia carminum genera cuibus tum Horatius, tum alij egregii poetae, Graeci & Latini, veteres & recentiores, sacri & prophani usi sunt*, Nuremberg, Formschneider, 1534. New harmonizations of Tritonius's tenors.[212]
ante 1537	Paul Hofhaimer (d. 1537), *Harmoniae poeticae*, Nuremberg, Petreius, 1539.[213]
1546	Johannes Spangenberg, *Grammaticae latinae partes*, Nuremberg, 1546.
1554	Johann Reusch, *Melodiae odarum Georgii Fabricii*, Leipzig, 1554, sig. bb4. One melody for all the Sapphic odes of Horace.
1555	Heinrich Textor, in Joannes Frisius, *Brevis musicae isagoge*, Zürich, Froschauer, 1555. New harmonizations of Tritonius's tenors.
1555	Claude Goudimel, *Q. Horatii Flacci poetae lyrici odae quotquot carminum generibus differunt ad rhythmos redactae*, Paris, 1555 (no copy extant).

---

[208] Ed. in Giuseppe VECCHI, *Dalle 'Melopoiae sive harmoniae tetracenticae' orazione di Tritonio (1507) alle 'Geminae undevigenti odarum Horatii melodiae' (1552)*, Accademia delle Scienze dell'Istituto di Bologna, classe di scienze morali, «Memorie», ser. V, vol. VIII, 1960, pp. 101-124; repr. separately Bologna, A.M.I.S., 1967. Ed. of "Iam satis" in R. von LILIENCRON, *Die Horazischen Metren in deutschen Kompositionen des 16. Jahrhunderts*, VfMw III, 1887, p. 52, and STEMPLINGER, p. 73f.

[209] Ed. in Hans Dagobert BRUGER, *Schule des Lautenspiels*, Wolfenbüttel, Kallmeyer, 1961², p. 73.

[210] Ed. in STEMPLINGER, p. 76, and DTÖ, XVIII/2 (v. 37): *Österreichische Lautenmusik im XVI. Jahrhundert*, Vienna, 1911, p. 7.

[211] Ed. of MICHAEL's "Iam satis" in STEMPLINGER, pp. 75f.

[212] "Iam satis" has Tritonius's tenor in the second highest voice. Ed. in VfMw III, 53; STEMPLINGER, p. 74; Ludwig SENFL, *Sämtliche Werke*, VI, Wolfenbüttel, Möseler, 1961, p. 72.

[213] Ed. of "Iam satis" in VfMw, III, 54; STEMPLINGER, p. 75; and Hans Joachim MOSER, *Paul Hofhaimer*, Stuttgart, Cotta, 1929, II, 112f.

1577 Francisco Salinas, *De musica libri septem*, Salamanca, Gast, 1577, facs. Kassel, Bärenreiter, 1958, pp. 361, 350.

1581 F-Pn ms. fr. 19.098, f. 13.[214]

1582 Ioan. Thoma Freigius, *Paedagogus*, Basle, 1582, p. 216.[215] Underlays "Iam satis terris" to the melody from Glareanus, p. 194 (see below, II, 1547).

1590 Orazio Vecchi, *op. cit.*

b) "Integer vitae" (I.22)

1504 Michael Pesentí, in Ottaviano Petruccí, *Frottole libro primo*, Venice, 1504, f. xliv.[216] Arranged for voice and lute in:

1509 Franciscus Bossinensis, *Tenori e contrabassi intabulati col sopran in canto figurato per cantar e sonar col lauto, libro primo*, Venice, Petrucci, 1509_1.[217]

1518 Bartolomeo Tromboncino, in *Frottole libro tertio*, Rome, Antico, 1518.[218]

1539 Ludwig Senfl, in Hofhaimer, *op. cit.*[219]

1559 Jacques Arcadelt, in *Sixiesme livre de chansons ... par plusieurs autheurs*, Paris, Le Roy and Ballard, 1559.[220]

1582 Martin Hayneccius, *Almansor*, as chorus at end of act IV.[221]

e) "Poscimur si quid" (I.32)

1559 Jacques Arcadelt, *op. cit.*[222]

d) "Nullus argento" (II.2)

11th c. F-Pn ms. lat. 8072, f. 74. Notation in Aquitanian neumes.

e) "Rectius vives" (II.10)

1539 Ludwig Senfl, in Hofhaimer, *op. cit.*[223]

---

[214] Ed. of "Iam satis" in Paul MASSON, *Horace en musique: Contribution à l'étude de l'humanisme musicale en France au XVIe siècle*, «Revue musicale», 1906, p. 357.

[215] Ed. in STEMPLINGER, p. 76.

[216] Ed. in STEMPLINGER, p. 182; Ottaviano PETRUCCI, *Frottole Buch I und IV*, PäM, VIII, 34; *Le Frottole nell'edizione principe di Ottaviano Petrucci*, I, «Instituta et Monumenta», ser. I, no. 1, Cremona, Athenaeum Cremonense, 1954, p. 35; Giovanni Battista PIGHI, *I ritmi e i metri della poesia latina*, Brescia, La Scuola, 1958, pp. 168f.

[217] Ed. in Arnold SCHERING, *Geschichte der Musik in Beispielen*, Leipzig, Breitkopf & Härtel, 1931, p. 71; *Le frottole per canto e liuto di Franciscus Bossinensis*, «Istituzioni e monumenti dell'arte musicale italiana», n.s. III, Milan, Ricordi, 1964, p. 393.

[218] Discant quoted in PäM, VIII, xix.

[219] Ed. in *Werke*, VI, 88.

[220] Ed. in *The Chansons of Jacques Arcadelt*, «Smith College Music Archives», V, Northampton, 1942, pp. 58f.

[221] Ed. in R. von LILIENCRON, *Die Chorgesänge des lateinisch-deutschen Schuldramas im XVI. Jahrhundert*, VfMw, VI, 1890, p. 386; Arthur PRÜFER, *Untersuchungen über den ausserkirchlichen Kunstgesang in den evangelischen Schulen des 16. Jahrhunderts*, diss. Leipzig, Pöschel & Trepte, 1890, p. 235; STEMPLINGER, p. 183.

[222] Ed. in *Chansons*, p. 58.

[223] Ed. in *Werke*, VI, 87f.

f) "Montium custos" (III.22)

    1559   Jacques Arcadelt, *op. cit.*[224]

g) "Est mihi nonum" (IV.11)

    11th c.   F-MO ms. 425, f. 51. Notation in Aquitanian neumes.[225]

II. MUSIC TO SAPPHIC ODES OTHER THAN HORACE[226]

- - - -   "Ut queant laxis", hymn to St. John the Baptist.[227] Text attributed to Paulus Diaconus (8th c.), earliest musical source from 11th c.

1492   Heinrich Isaac, "Quis dabit pacem", motet on the death of Lorenzo il Magnifico.[228] Text after Seneca's *Hercules Oetaeus*, lines 1541-45, 1580-86.

1495   Jacob Locher, *Historia de rege Frantie*, Freiburg, Riederer, 1495, *chorus sapphicus* at end of act I: "Quisquis eternum".[229]

1501   Conrad Celtis, *Ludus Dianae*, chorus at end of act III: "Regis eternas".[230]

1509   Anon., chorus from three eclogues of Pietro Corsi, Rome 1509-10: "Hanc io lucem", I-Rvat ms. Lat. 3441, f. 175.[231]

1511   Johannes Cochläus, *Tetrachordum musices*, Nuremberg, Weyssenburger, 1511; facs. Hildesheim, 1971, sig. Fiiiv: Melos Sapphicum, "Ut queant laxis".[232]

1512   Martin Agricola, *Melodia*, Muhlhausen, 1512, Georgii Fabricii Sapphicum: "Nocte surgentes".[233]

1515   Chelidonius, *Voluptas cum virtute disceptatio*, Vienna, 1515, choruses at end of acts I and II and at beginning of act III: "Veritas summo", "Herculem laetis", "Privates atro".[234]

---

[224] Ed. in *Chansons*, pp. 59f.

[225] Facsimile in Edmond de COUSSEMAKER, *Histoire de l'harmonie au moyen age*, Paris, Durand, 1852, II, plate x, questionable transcription on p. xii; VfMw, III, 37 (second strophe); STEMPINGER, p. 413 (after Coussemaker).

[226] This list makes no claim to completeness; it includes characteristic examples available in modern editions and facsimiles. Cf. also Karl-Günther HARTMANN, *Die humanistische Odenkomposition in Deutschland*, Erlangen, Palm & Enke, 1976, pp. 32-51.

[227] Chant melody in LU 1342. For other melodies cf. R. von LILIENCRON, *Eine alte sapphische Melodie*, «Monatshefte für Musikgeschichte», XXIX, 1897, pp. 32f, and Bruno STÄBLEIN, *Hymnen*, «Monumenta Monodica Medii Aevi», I, Kassel, Bärenreiter, 1956, *passim* (in this volume also many other hymns in Sapphic meter).

[228] Ed. in DTÖ, XIV/1 (v. 28): Heinrich ISAAC, *Weltliche Werke*, Vienna, 1907, pp. 49-52; discussed by Wolfgang OSTHOFF, *Theatergesang und darstellende Musik in der italienischen Renaissance*, Tutzing, Schneider, 1969, I, 170-179.

[229] Facsimile of the beginning in MGG¹ IX, 1845, fig. 3.

[230] Ed. in VfMw, VI, 359.

[231] Ed. in OSTHOFF, II, 64.

[232] Ed. in Johann Nicolaus FORKEL, *Allgemeine Geschichte der Musik*, Leipzig, Schwickert, 1788-1801, II, 160.

[233] Ed. in PRÜFER, p. 11.

[234] Ed. in VfMw, VI, 360f.

1518   Franchino Gaffurio, *De harmonia musicorum*, Milan, Ponzio, 1518, f. lxxxixv: "Musices septem".

1533   *Melodiae Prudentianae et in Virgilium*, Leipzig, Faber, 1533,[235] hymnus VIII from the *Cathemerion liber* of Prudentius: "Christe servorum".[236]

1535   Georg Macropedius, *Rebelles* (music included only in the edition of 1552), chorus before the epilogue: "Laudibus largam".[237]

1541   *Id.*, *Lazarus mendicus* (music only in ed. 1552), chorus at end of act IV: "Cum tibi fidam".[238]

1544   *Id.*, *Josephus* (music only in ed. 1552), chorus at end of act I: "Turbidi plastes".[239]

ante 1547 Nicolaus Listenius, "Ut queant laxis", in Heinrich Glareanus's *Dodekachordon*, Basel, Petri, 1547; facs. New York, Broude, 1967, p. 438.

1547   Heinrich Glareanus, *ibid.*, p. 194: *Ex Prudentio* [see above, Ia, 1582 and II, 1533] "Christe sanctorum".

1585   Statius Olthof, in *Psalmorum Davidis paraphrasis poetica Georgii Buchanani Scoti*, Frankfurt, 1585, and many later editions to 1703, Psalmus V, quintum genus: "O potens rerum".[240]

In the Renaissance and again in the nineteenth century, the view prevailed that the odes of Horace were always sung.[241] From the earliest sources on, the didactic intention, parodied by Vecchi, predominates. The medieval settings of Horace, accompanied by metrical studies, scansions, glosses, translations, etc.[242] have not only their scholastic employment and their meter, but also their melody in common with the well known solmisation hymn "Ut queant laxis" – suggesting that a fixed melody type was used for different texts in Sapphic meter. (It has not yet been clarified whether this melody was first associated with the classical or the Christian text).

The great German humanist Conrad Celtis (1459-1508) and his pupils in Ingolstadt and Vienna, occupying themselves so intensively with ancient meters and recognizing Horace as the unsurpassed master, were quick to utilize mensural notation as an aid for teaching. The numerous musical editions listed above from the first half of the sixteenth century are traceable directly to the pervasive influence of Celtis, the

---

[235] Ed. Bologna, Palmaverde, 1952.

[236] Ed. in PIGHI, p. 168.

[237] Ed. in VfMw, VI, 363.

[238] Ed. in VfMw, VI, 373.

[239] Ed. in VfMw, VI, 374.

[240] Ed. in Benedikt WIDMANN, *Die Kompositionen der Psalmen von Statius Olthof*, VfMw, V, 1889, pp. 298f.

[241] Otto JAHN, *Wie wurden die Oden des Horatius vorgetragen?*, «Hermes», II, 1867, pp. 418-433; Renatus PIRKER, *Beiträge zur Entwicklungsgeschichte der viersimmigen Humanisten-Ode*, «Musicologica Austriaca», I, 1977, p. 137.

[242] Cf. Solange CORBIN, *Comment on chantait les classiques latins au moyen age*, in *Mélanges d'histoire et d'esthétique musicales offerts a Paul-Marie Masson*, Paris, Masse, 1955, I, 109.

'German Horace'. His pupil Tritonius opens the series and establishes the pattern then followed by Michael, Senfl, Hofhaimer, Textor, and probably Goudimel:[243] four-part homorhythmic settings of the first strophe of one ode in each of the nineteen Horatian meters. Such collections provided the repertoire which was sung daily in the *ludus litterarius*, the Latin schools,[244] as mentioned in the school regulations for Zwickau in 1523: "one kind of a song ... of Horace, or something similar, sung harmoniously in four voices".[245] In their selection of odes, Michael, Senfl, and Hofhaimer follow Tritonius. This selection had been determined largely by Horace himself, who began his first book with examples of different meters.[246] The ode to Augustus (I.2) is henceforth not only given by schoolmasters and composers as the model for the Sapphic meter;[247] it was also, as far as I see, more frequently set to music than any other classical Latin poem. Vecchi could not have chosen a more typical, a more obvious text for his *bellum grammaticale*.

Music for Horatian meters is by no means limited to academic exercises in scansion. We find it widely diffused also in the choruses which close the acts of Latin school dramas;[248] occasionally, in editions of *frottole* (Pesenti, Tromboncino), a genre which has a certain affinity to the homorhythmic style of the German humanists; in theorists' discussions of metrics;[249] with neo-Latin religious odes and metrical paraphrases of the psalms (Goudimel, Olthof, etc.); with German chorales (see below); and with French texts written for "musique mesurée à l'antique" (Baïf). The designation of a chorus in Mathias Holzwart's *Saul* (Basle, 1571) as "in der Melodie Jam satis terris" indicates that one setting of this ode, probably Tritonius's, served as a fixed melody type for many texts in Sapphic meter.

With so many of his predecessors occupying themselves with classical meters, it is unlikely that Vecchi would not follow an established practice. An

---

[243] The performance with "cythara" suggested on Tritonius's title page and intended as a revival of ancient performance practice was approximated by Judenkünig's intabulation of the collection for lute – cf. also above, the intabulation of Pesenti's setting by Bossinensis. Tritonius, dissatisfied with his own compositions, hoped to have them reset by Isaac; the latter entrusted the task to his pupil Senfl, who then retained Tritonius's tenors as the first or second voice. On the settings of Tritonius cf. also Manfred Hermann SCHMID, *Musica theorica, practica und poetica: zu Horaz-Vertonungen des deutschen Humanismus*, in *Zeitgenosse Horaz: Der Dichter und seine Leser seit zwei Jahrtausenden*, ed. Helmut Krosser and Ernst A. Schmidt, Tübingen, Narr, 1996, pp. 52-67.

[244] Cf. the formulations on the title pages, such as *Odae cum harmoniis ex diversis poëtis in usum ludi litterari*, Kronstadt, 1548; this collection, edited by J. Honterus, retains the setting of Tritonius for "Iam satis".

[245] "ein genus Carminis ... Horatij oder deß gleichen eintrechtig mit vier stymmen" – PRÜFER, p. 9.

[246] Only with the tenth ode does he return to a meter already employed (Sapphic).

[247] Used for 25 of the 103 odes, this is the most frequent meter in the Roman poet's four books of odes and also the most commonly used Horatian meter in the Middle Ages and Renaissance.

[248] Here too, the Sapphic meter prevails, set occasionally in one or two parts (Macropedius), more often homorhythmically in three (Locher, Celtis, Hayneccius) or four parts (Chelidonius).

[249] Gaffurius in two parts; Glareanus, Salinas, F-Pn ms. fr. 19.098, Freigius, Mersenne (*Harmonie universelle*, Paris, Cramoisy, 1636-37, *livre sixieme*, pp. 395, 418), with unaccompanied melodies.

examination of the repertoire reveals that two rhythms had become standardized for setting the Sapphic meter to music. With very few exceptions, composers chose between a) strictly metrical (quantitative) treatment, with long and short syllables in the ratio of two to one, resulting in melodies which do not fit into a regular musical measure:

and b) the sacrifice of quantitative meter to qualitative 'Vierhebigkeit':[250] the text is forced into duple time by means of the following rhythm, which, although only approximating the quantity of the syllables, gives an illusion of metrical scansion through the regular recurrence of the fixed pattern three and a half times in each strophe (occasionally the sixth note is dotted):

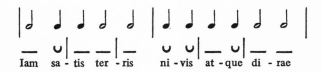

The former, 'academic' solution was adopted rigorously by the Celtis school (Tritonius-Judenkünig-Michael-Senfl-Hofhaimer-Textor), as well as by Chelidonius, Gaffurius, *Melodiae Prudentianae*, Glareanus, Agricola, Freigius, Hayneccius, Olthof, and some German chorales.[251] However, it is generally overlooked that Celtis himself sanctioned the second, 'musical' rhythmization in his *Ludus Dianae* (1501) – i.e. before Tritonius established the humanistic model in 1507 –, taking his place in the series: Isaac, Locher, Cel-

---

[250] Paul EICKHOFF, *Der Horazische Doppelbau der Sapphischen Strophe*, Wandsbeck, Teubner, 1895, believed that Horace constructed his strophe according to both the quantitative and the qualitative principle. This opinion is refuted by Otto SEEL and Egert PÖHLMANN, *Quantität und Wortakzent im Horazischen Sapphiker*, «Philologus», CIII, 1959, pp. 237-280, without mention of Eickhoff.

[251] Johannes ZAHN, *Die Melodien der deutschen evangelischen Kirchenlieder*, Gütersloh, Bertelsmann, 1889-93, I, nos. 966-969, 971, 973; III, nos. 4999-5000, 5009, 5011, 5013. The earliest, listed under no. 966, are the very numerous contrafacta of Tritonius's "Iam satis", one of which survived into the late nineteenth century, at least. Salinas observes the quantitative meter, but adds a rest after the third or fifth note, in the latter position corresponding to the metrical caesura. On the Sapphic meter in German poetry, cf. E. BROCKS, *Die sapphische Strofe und ihr Fortleben im lateinischen Kirchenlied des Mittelalters und der neueren deutschen Dichtung*, «Jahresbericht des königlichen Gymnasiums zu Marienwerder», 1889-90, pp. 3-37.

tis, "Hanc io lucem", Pesenti, Tromboncino, Goudimel,[252] Arcadelt, and some chorales.[253] Isaac's free application of this rhythm is necessitated by the polyphonic (as opposed to homorhythmic) style of the motet, which excludes a strictly quantitative setting.[254] Pesenti and Tromboncino illustrate how Italian composers tend to scan the Sapphic meter as they do its derivative, their own *endecasillabi*.[255] Not only does Vecchi, as to be expected, continue the tradition of his countrymen rather than that, now moribund, of the remote and somewhat esoteric German humanists; the polyphonic style of the madrigal obliges him to choose the declamation in regular musical meter, which will match the duple time of Marenzio's voices. In doing so, he allows his audience to recognize a rhythmic formulation which for at least a century had announced the Sapphic meter in Italy (Exx. 10-11).[256]

Ex. 10. Pesenti: "Integer vitae", 1504.

Ex. 11. Vecchi: "Iam satis terris", *Diversi linguaggi*, 1590, mm. 31-36.

---

[252] SALINAS, p. 435.

[253] ZAHN, I, nos. 983, 991, 994, 996, 1006; III, nos. 5002-5003, 5007, 5012, 5014-5016.

[254] It is mentioned here as an early example of such settings of Sapphic strophes; I have not discussed others since they are not concerned primarily with metrical rendition. Macropedius abandoned quantitative meter in favor of duple time when he increased the number of voices from one to two (second strophe of "Cum tibi fidam"). The chorale melody Zahn no. 969 was transformed later from the first to the second rhythm quoted above.

[255] As observed by Benvenuto Disertori in the preface to PETRUCCI, *op. cit.*, 1954, p. XXIX. PIGHI, p. 169, illustrates this with the incipit of MONTEVERDI's balletto in the same rhythm, "De la Bellezza le dovute lodi", *Scherzi musicali*, Venice, Amadino, 1607; Claudio MONTEVERDI, *Opera omnia*, VII, Cremona, Fondazione Monteverdi, 2002, p. 152. On the derivation of the *endecasillabi* from the Sapphicum cf. John SCHMITT, *La Metrica di Fra Jacopone*, «Studi medievali», I, 1904-05, p. 517. Jacques HANDSCHIN, *Über die Laude*, AMl, X, 1938, p. 18, suggests that endecasyllabic lauds may have been sung to this rhythm. During the Middle Ages, also outside of Italy, the qualitative interpretation of ancient meters prevailed; only with German humanism was there a return to the quantitative principle.

[256] His setting differs from those of his predecessors in its much wider range and invervals. A melodic model is identified below, p. 196, Ex. 12.

Gran - di - nis mi - sit pa - ter, et ru - ben - te

Dex - te - ra sa - cras ia - cu - la - tus ar - ces

Ter - ru - it ur - - bem___.

B. Il Fate ben per voi. Aggionto dal Vecchi. Sesto.

The text of the *sesto* consists solely of the words "Fate ben per voi", re-peated as an ostinato throughout the *Prima* and *Seconda parte*, seventeen times in succession, each time on a monotone[257] (cf. Ex. 14). This style sug-gests a street cry, an exhortation to "Do good", but the definite article in the caption of the *sesto*, "Il Fate ben per voi" (analogous to "Il Pedante" etc.), suggests a specific person. And indeed, I find the exact formulation in con-temporary documents as the nickname of a historical figure. The needle in the haystack turned up in minute descriptions of the spectacular entry of Marc'Antonio Colonna into Rome after the victory of the Holy League (Spain, Venice, and the Papacy) over the Turks at Lepanto, the greatest naval battle of modern times. In this mammoth procession of 4 December 1571 from the Via Appia to the Capitol, modelled after the *triumphi* of the ancient Romans, the interest of the populace was attracted particularly by the Turkish captives. These formed a dividing point in the middle of the procession, being preceded by the militia and followed by the civic dignitaries. Leading them, we are told by Francesco Albertonio, was an eccentric hermit popularly

---

[257] On g' d' c' c' g' d' d'; g' c' g' g' g' d' g' g c' g. As will be demonstrated, this monotone illus-trates that the cultural-historical interest of a musical device need by no means be proportional to its acoustical interest, the mere description of which explains nothing.

known as the "Fate ben per voi", from the words which he was accustomed to cry in the streets:[258]

Quasi capo governator loro giva uno spirituale di professione (che si chiama fate ben per voi, solendo egli così gridare) vestito alla turca, portando su la spalla manca una loro bandiera, e nella destra mano un crocifisso, nella sinistra una scimitarra, il quale tutta via diceva a piena voce: 'Viva la santa lega'.	In command of them [i.e. of the Turks], as it were, marched a member of a religious order (who was called 'Fate ben per voi', being accustomed to cry thus), in Turkish costume, carrying one of their flags on the left shoulder, and in the right hand a crucifix, in the left a scimitar, who continually exclamed in a full voice: '[long] live the Holy League'.

A similar account is given by two Roman students, Domenico Tassolo and Baldassarre Mariotti, in a letter signed "a hore tre di notte" immediately after the event:[259]

... un'altra [bandiera di turchi] ne strascinava ... quel che suol ir per Roma gridando, 'fate ben per voi', vestito anch'egli di spoglie turchesche, portando un crocefisso ne la sinistra, & una storta ignuda ne la destra, seguivano i turchi prigioni in numero di cento settanta.	Another [Turkish flag] was dragged ... by him who is accustomed to go about Rome crying 'Fate ben per voi', he too dressed in Turkish spoils, carrying a crucifix in the left hand and a bared scimitar in the right. The Turkish prisoners followed, numbering 170.

A report of the Venetian envoys Paolo Tiepolo and Giovanni Soranzo to the doge Alvise Mocenigo, written the same day, mentions the Turkish prisoners, but not the Fate ben per voi:[260]

Hoggi si è fatta la solennità della entrata del S.ᵣₑ Marc'Antonio Colonna ...; si facevano andar 170 schiavi, che più non	Today was celebrated the solemn entry of Signor Marc'Antonio Colonna ... ; there were 170 slaves – more were not

---

[258] *L'Entrata che fece l'Eccellentissimo Signor Marc'Antonio Colonna in Roma ... cavata d'una lettera di Francesco Albertonio gentil'huomo romano*, Viterbo, n.d. The letter is dated from Rome, 15 Dec. 1572, and reprinted as "unpublished" in «L'album», III, 1837, pp. 357-360.

[259] *I trionfi, feste, et livree fatte dalli signori conservatori, & popolo romano, & da tutte le arti di Roma, nella felicissima, & honorata entrata dell'Illustrissimo Signor Marcantonio Colonna*, Venice, P.Z.F., 1571, Viterbo n.d. [16th c.]; reprinted in G. B. BORINO – A. GALIETI – G. NAVONE, *Il trionfo di Marc'Antonio Colonna*, Rome, R. Deputazione di storia patria, 1938, pp. 93-103. This publication includes also the texts of the minutes of the relevant council meetings (pp. 43-53; one of the four deputies was the father of Emilio de' Cavalieri) and two *ordini* for the procession (pp. 55-58).

[260] I-Vas Dispacci, Roma, III, ff. 162v-163.

ne sono capitati vivi della portion toccata a S. S.^tà, tutti vestiti a livrea, et per ordine a doi a doi legati, che à fatto assai bella, et honorata pompa; ma si ha lasciata stare qualche altra cosa, che si havea dessegnata, per il risentimento, che pareva, che havessero spagnoli, quasi che con un palese et inusato trionfo, fatto al S.^re Marc'Antonio si volesse diminuir la gloria di Don Giovanni.

captured alive in the share assigned to His Holiness – tied in pairs, in an order which made a quite decorous and honorable pomp. But something else which had been planned was relinquished, because of the resentment which the Spaniards apparently would have had, as if with an overt and unusual triumph, made for Signor Marc'Antonio, one wanted to diminish the glory of Don Juan [of Austria, who had commanded the fleet].

Five days earlier, the Fate ben per voi had presented other Turkish trophies to the pope, according to the *avvisi* in the Vatican codex Urb. Lat. 1042, which also mention his role in the procession (f. 154*v*, 158):

Dì Roma p.° Xmbre [1571]: Avanti hieri il fate ben per voi vestito alla turchesca con turbante in testa andò a basciar i piedi a S. S.^tà con presentarli alcuni pezzi delli stendardi de turchi.

Rome, 1 Dec. [1571]: The day before yesterday the Fate ben per voi in Turkish dress with a turban on his head went to kiss the feet of His Holiness, presenting him with some pieces of the Turkish standards.

Di Roma di 5. Xbre: Inanti andavano li 1020 schiavi turchi vestiti di rosso, et giallo menati per una corda dal fatteben per voi.

Rome, 5 Dec.: In front went the 1020 Turkish slaves dressed in red and yellow, led on a rope by the Fate ben per voi.

Here his nickname is not even explained – which testifies to its familiarity. He had every right to a prominent place in the procession, for he was one of the eight Spanish friars who assisted at the battle, distinguishing themselves with their courageous and untiring care of the wounded.[261] A detailed literary account of Colonna's triumph, such as that of Albertonio or Tassolo/Mariotti, must have served as the basis for the depiction of the event, attributed to Federico Zuccari (d. 1609), which adorns the frieze of a hall of the Castello Colonna in Paliano.[262] So closely does the painting correspond to the literary de-

---

[261] It could not be determined whether he was one of the five whose names have been recorded; cf. Gabriele RUSSOTTO, O. H., *San Giovanni di Dio e il suo Ordine Ospedaliero*, Rome, Fatebenefratelli, 1969, II, 27ff.

[262] Ca. 60 km. east of Rome, the castello has been used as a prison since the 18th century. The fresco (30 cm × 18 m), unfortunately in a poor state of conservation, is reproduced in BORINO/GALIETI/NAVONE, tav. 1-11. The entire procession is depicted also in an engraving – see Plate IV.3b. There is considerable variation between the two depictions, though the components are the same:

scriptions, that it is easily possible to identify the many historical persons. We immediately recognize the Fate ben per voi with his crucifix, scimitar, turban, and Turkish flag – one of the few figures who appear in isolation from a group (Plate IV.3a).

The Romans were not only impressed, but also amused by our stern figure. According to the manuscript *Cose notabili occorse in Roma dall'anno MDLXXVI sin'all'anno MDCXLVIIII di M. Antonio Valena*[263] he was so highly regarded for his charitable work that he had unlimited credit with the pope and princes. This he used to provide dowries and to find husbands for "dangerous girls" – until he took a liking to one of them and married her, whereupon he immediately lost all his credit. He then adopted a new street cry, a confession of his mistake, and became the subject of a popular song warning against the dangers of matrimony:

Vi era un romito chiamato dalle parole che spesso soleva ripetere: 'fate ben per voi'. Era tenuto per santo, et in tal credito appresso il papa e prencipi che tutto quello che domandava non glisi negava niente, e si serviva de denari in maritare zitelle pericolose; ne trovò una, che gli piacque, e se la prese per moglie e perse tutto il credito. Andava poi per Roma con un' paro di bilancie attaccate ad un' bastone incima del quale vi era una testa di morto dicendo che haveva mal' pesato, gli fu cavata una canzona che diceva: 'State attenti che riderete, poi quando saperete, ch'ha preso moglie fate ben per voi'. Andò alla guerra d'Ungaria con Gio. Fran.° Aldobrandino con un crocefisso in mano facendo animo a' soldati e vi fu ferito da turchi. In d.° tempo principiò in Roma la Religione de Fate ben Fratelli, il papa gli diede la chiesa di S. Gio. Colabita nell'Isola di Ponte

There was a hermit named after the words which he was often accustomed to repeat: 'fate ben per voi'. He was regarded as holy, and had such credit with the pope and princes that he was not denied anything which he requested, and he used the money to find husbands for perilous girls. He found one whom he liked, married her, and lost all the credit. Then he went through the streets of Rome with a pair of balances attached to a pole, at the top of which there was a skull, saying that he had weighed badly. A song was made about him which said: 'Be careful what you will laugh about, when you will then know that the Fate ben per voi has taken a wife'. He went to the war of Hungary with Gio. Francesco Aldobrandini, with a crucifix in his hand, encouraging the soldiers, and he was wounded by the Turks. At that time began in Rome the Order of the

---

in the fresco they are more differentiated and detailed, and more architecture is shown, while the engraving is more schematic. It could not be determined which version served as model for the other. In the engraving our man is identified with the subscript "Fate ben per voi". An inferior drawing of the entire engraving was published in Pompo LITTA, *Famiglie celebri d'Italia: Colonna di Roma*, Milan, Giusti etc., 1836, last plate.

[263] Rome, Archivio Storico Capitolino, cred. XIV, t. 9, ff. 2v-3.

quattro capi [= Isola Tiburina].[264] Vi fecero l'ospedale per gl'infermi, andavano la sera per Roma con un campanello dicendo 'fate ben fratelli'.

Fatebenefratelli. The pope gave him the church of S. Gio. Colabita on the Tiber island.[264] There he built the hospital for the sick. In the evening he went through Rome with a little bell, saying 'fate ben, fratelli'.

The cry "Fate ben per voi" occurs at least as early as 1378, when a certain Diego in Cremona begged with these words alms for the poor and the sick.[265] St. John of God (1495-1550) employed a Spanish variant, reported by his first biographer: "Who does good for himself? Do good for the love of God, my brothers in Jesus Christ".[266] The Italian formula was not yet diffused in Rome in 1571, but still associated with a single person; only on 1 January 1572, were the Spanish brothers rewarded in Rome with papal recognition as a congregation, and on 20-24 June 1587, a short time before Vecchi set their motto to music, they could celebrate their elevation to the religious order of St. John of God[267] (Brothers Hospitalers, Barmherzige Brüder, for whom Haydn composed his *Missa Sancti Ioannis de Deo*), active today throughout the world in the care of the sick, and still known in Italy as the Fatebenefratelli. An early historian, who in 1602 explained the origin of the name ("they go [about] dressed with coarse woolen cloth, in the manner of the barefoot hermits, ... saying, almost singing: 'Fate ben fratelli for the love of God'"),[268] at the same

---

[264] The island in the Tiber, where the Fatebenefratelli still have their hospital, was dedicated to medicine since antiquity, when during the plague of 293 B.C. the cult of Asklepios was established there – cf. OVID, *Met.* XV.624f, 741ff: "unde Coroniden [= Aesculapium] circumflua Thybridis alti / insula Romuleae sacris adiecerit urbis"; "Huc se de Latia pinu Phoebeius anguis / contulit et finem specie caeleste resumpta / luctibus inposuit venitque salutifer urbi" ["whence the island flowed around by the deep Tiber added the son [Asklepios] of Coronis to the deities of the city of Romulus"; "Here the serpent of Phoebus left the Latian ship and, resuming his heavenly form, ended the sorrows and came as health-bringer to the city"]. Cf. Karl KERÉNYI, *Der göttliche Arzt*, Basel, Ciba, 1948, ch. 1, and below, p. 237. Here as elsewhere, an island was chosen in order to prevent the diffusion of contageous diseases.

[265] Hieronymo ROMAN, *Republicas del mundo*, Medina del Campo, Del Canto, 1575, I, 318. Cf. also the numerous medieval Latin proverbs beginning with "Fac ben ..." in Hans WALTHER, *Proverbia Sententiaeque Latinitatis Medii Aevi*, Göttingen, Vandenhoeck & Ruprecht, 1963-1969, II, 3, and the text of TROMBONCINO's *canto carnascialesco* "Fate ben gente cortese / A ste povere peregrine" from *Frottole libro VIII*, Venice, Petrucci, 1507.

[266] "Quien haze bien para si mismo? Hazeis bien por amor de Dios, hermanos mios en IESU CHRISTO" – Francisco DE CASTRO, *Historia dela vida y sanctas obras de Juan de Dios*, Granada, 1585, f. 33.

[267] RUSSOTTO, I, 117, 127.

[268] "vanno vestiti d'albagio grosso, in forma di Romiti scalzi, ... dicendo, quasi cantando, 'Fate ben fratelli per l'amor di Dio'" – Camillo FANUCCI, *Trattato di tutte l'opere pie dell'alma città di Roma*, Rome, Facij & Paolini, 1602, p. 70.

time provides an explanation for the musical setting: the cry for alms was uttered in the streets at night "quasi cantando", and Vecchi renders this faithfully as a monotone.

C. Il Gratiano. Aggionto dal Vecchi. Settimo.

Finally, the *settimo* presents another mask of the commedia dell'arte: the ubiquitous Dr. Graziano, caricature of the Bolognese jurist, named after the famous 12th-century canonist of that city (Plate IV.4).[269] In the improvised comedy he often acted as a counterpart to Magnifico: father of the second lover, master of the second Zanni, rival or friend of Magnifico.[270] Even recent literature frequently confuses him with Pedante; that the two characters are quite distinct is clear from our text and the scenari in which they appear simultaneously.[271] Like Zanni, Magnifico, and Tedesco, Graziano was impersonated by students during carneval festivities.[272]

Prima parte (punctuation added)

O zent, o presson, av' do la bona sira, ò Zan. Ah bestiazza selevrad, à son al Duttor Gratian, allias Smursion.[273] Avrev intrar in consortie s'al ve pias, perch'al dis la sentienza di 'Vien' a cena, ch'ogni scimia petna la so scimia'.[274] Un altra si-

Oh people, oh persons, I wish you good evening, oh Zanni. Ah crazy beast, I am Dr. Graziano, alias Smursion.[273] I should like to join your company, if you please, because the proverb says 'Come to dinner, because every monkey combs his

---

[269] This and other woodcuts which adorn the title pages of Italian folk poetry (e.g. those of the numbered series including Tedesco, Plate IV.1b) were used repeatedly for different authors and even by different publishers. Thus our Graziano recurs in Adriano BANCHIERI, *Nobilissima anzi asinissima compagnia della Bastina*, Vicenza, Barezzi, 1597, p. 36, and again, accompanied by a Zanni, p. 48 (new ed. Venice, Amadino, 1611); cf. the reproductions in Arnaldo SEGARIZZI, *Bibliografia delle stampe popolari italiane della R. Biblioteca Nazionale di S. Marco di Venezia*, Bergamo, Arti grafiche, 1913, fig. 265; PANDOLFI, II, opposite p. 289; and Allardyce NICOLL, *The World of Harlequin*, Cambridge UP, 1963, fig. 37. BANCHIERI's account of Graziano's history (*Discorso*, pp. 42 ff) denies the Bolognese origin, but this argument has not been accepted by philologists. The doctor's later career is traced by Carlo SARTI, *Il teatro dialettale bolognese (1600-1894)*, Bologna, Zamorani & Albertazzi, 1894, pp. 131-150.

[270] See note 50.

[271] See note 50.

[272] BANCHIERI, *Discorso*, pp. 48ff, deals with the "Scolare bolognese in habito di Dottor Gratiano in maschera il carnevale" ["The Bolognese student dressed as Dr. Graziano masked during carnival"]. Although Vecchi's text makes some use of rhyme, it is transcribed here as prose, since it does not fit into a poetic meter.

[273] Cf. Graziano's words in CROCE's *Gran vittoria*: "e l'mi calz a Smursion".

[274] "Everyone looks after himself". Cf. Ernst Robert CURTIUS, *Europäische Literatur und lateinisches Mittelalter*, Berne, Franke, 1948, pp. 524f, "Der Affe als Metapher": "About 1200 'monkey' is a fashionable word of the Latin school poetry. ... An unknowing imitator thus could be called

militanza di Diorgano;[275] 'Ch'è con le person è in compagnia'. O zent, o pasturanza.[276]

Seconda parte

Ah, ah, ah, ah, ah, cosa dis q[ue]stor? Al ghe n'è un che dis 'E la bella Franceschina ninina buffina, La fillibustachina'. Es ghe n'è un che dis la me favorida quand'a iera inamorad d'una bella putta, 'Chi t'ha fatte quelle scarpette Che ti stan sì ben?'[277] Al ghe quell'altra bestiazza de Zan che dis 'a voi al me salarie'. E Pantalon ghe dis 'tirra via'. Al ghe po un cert'invriagon che dis 'Mi non esser minchion, mi star bon compagnon'. E dov' lassavi una cera d'Hiporcate[278] chal sta sempr'in s'una vosa gridando 'Fate ben per voi'? Av' do la bona sira, bon sir.

monkey'[274] Another similar one of Diorgano:[275] 'He who is with people is in company'. Oh people, oh herd of sheep.[276]

Ah, ah, ah, ah, ah, what is that fellow saying? There is one of them who says 'E la bella Franceschina ninina buffina, La fillibustachina'. And there is one who says my favorite [song] when I was in love with a beautiful young girl, 'Chi t'ha fatte quelle scarpette Che ti stan sì ben?'[277] Then there is that other beast of a Zanni who says 'I want my wages'. And Pantalon who says 'go away'. And then a certain drunkard who says 'Me not be fool, me be good fellow'. And I almost forgot a face of Hiporcates[278] who is always crying on a monotone 'Fate ben per voi'. I wish you good evening, good evening.

In the *Prima parte* Graziano follows his custom of dropping sententious commonplaces. Especially from the *Seconda parte* it is evident that he is an observer and commentator of the scene, rather than a participant. This is in keeping with the somewhat detached role which he plays in the commedia dell'arte – rarely advancing the action, but often speaking the prologue. In our text he quotes the words and music of all the other voices, except Scolare and Pedante, making a quodlibet out of and within a quodlibet, or a sort of thematic catalogue of the composition. In having Graziano thus introduce and

---

'monkey'", e.g. "monkey of the doctor", "monkey of the orators". Cf. also "simia" in WALTHER, *Proverbia*, index.

[275] Mutilated proper name, perhaps for Diogenes Laertius, who enjoyed a revival in the latter part of the 16th century and as author of epigrams and as biographer of the ancient philosophers would be a natural 'source' for Graziano's travesties.

[276] The characters in the madrigal, or, less likely, "literary academy" (the audience).

[277] See note 50.

[278] *Sic*, not corrected, since Graziano is known for his malapropisms. Cf. the medical term '*facies Hippocratica*' (from HIPPOCRATES, *Prognostikon*, II). Until the late 18th century, the aphorisms of Hippocrates remained the most important text of the medical schools. They possess, in their style if not in their content, great affinity to those of Graziano; cf. *Le Cento e quindici conclusioni in ottava rima del plusquamperfetto Dottor Gratiano*, n.p., 1587, repr. in PANDOLFI, II, 11-18. Our identification of the Fate ben as one of the Brothers Hospitalers explains Graziano's Hippocrates-epithet for him.

explain the various roles to the audience, Vecchi follows an established practice of the popular theatre, as Goethe does in his "Vorspiel auf dem Theater". Could it be that the composer, with a certain self-irony, is depicting himself as the learned commentator?

III. THE ENSEMBLE

The simultaneous use of Bergamask, Venetian, German 'Kauderwelsch', Tuscan, Latin, macaronic (or, rather, 'pedantesque') and Bolognese defines our composition as belonging to the literary and musical genre of *diversi linguaggi*, widely cultivated in Italy at this time, "being nothing else than a tacit accusation of those peoples who speak in such a manner".[279] Limited use of it had already been made in classical comedy (Aristophanes, Plautus)[280] and in the short-lived *greghesche* of Antonio Molino (Venice, Gardano, 1564), more extensive employment in the comedies of Ruzzante (pseudonym of Angelo Beolco, 1502-1542) and Andrea Calmo (1510-1571).[281] It was also a topic of the fashionable parlor games of the Renaissance.[282] But particularly, it characterized the commedia dell'arte, that geographic cross-section of society with its Venetian merchant, Bergamask servant, Bolognese doctor, Tuscan lovers, Spanish *capitano*, and the later Neapolitan types. In *La pazzia*, the commedia dell'arte performed in Florence with the famous intermedi for the Medicean wedding of 1589, the insane Isabella impersonates Zanni, Pantalone, Capitano, and Franceschina in diverse languages.[282bis] The *interlocutori* of Vergilio Verucci's literary comedy *Li diversi linguaggi* (Venice, Vecchi, 1609) speak

---

279 "non essendo ciò altro, che una tacita accusa di quei popoli, che in sì fatta maniera favellano" – N. VILLANI, *Ragionamento*, p. 63.

280 *Ibid.*, pp. 47f, and QUINTILIAN, *Institutio Oratoria*, VIII.3.59. Cf. A. PERRUCCI, *Dell'arte rappresentativa*, p. 244: "La diversità delle lingue suole dare gran diletto nelle comedie, e che sia la verità fin da' tempi de' primi Romani si pratticò" ["The diversity of the languages usually gives great delight in the comedies, truly practised since the time of the earliest Romans"].

281 On the written, not improvised, comedies of Calmo and Gigio Artemio Giancarli, which can be regarded as links between the Paduan dialect comedies of Ruzzante and the *commedia dell'arte*, cf. Giorgio PADOAN, *La commedia rinascimentale veneziana*, Vicenza, Neri Pozza, 1982, pp. 154-183, 'La commedia plurilinguistica', and Richard ANDREWS, *Scripts and Scenarios: The Performance of Comedy in Renaissance Italy*, Cambridge UP, 1993, pp. 144-154, 'Multilingual Comedy'. That polyglot comedy, both written and improvised, flourished especially in Venice is due partly to the multiethnic population of that seaport.

282 Cf. the "Giuoco delle lingue" in Girolamo BARGAGLI, *Dialogo de' giuochi che nelle vegghie sanesi si usano di fare*, Siena, Bonetti, 1572, pp. 80f.

282bis *Diario ... delle feste celebrate nelle solennissime nozze delli serenissimi sposi il Sig. Don Ferdinando Medici & la Sig. Donna Christina di Lorena gran duchi di Toscana*, Bologna, Rossi, 1589, p. 47.

nine Italian dialects and French.[283] However, as explained in the prologue, the author retains only the accents, not an entire dialect, which would be too difficult to write and to understand, "& non usato se non in comedie all'improviso" ["and not used except in improvised comedies"], thus confirming the connection of the polyglot technique with the commedia dell'arte. Off the stage it was cultivated especially by Croce, often with Zanni as the central figure.[284] In music it was applied effectively in the battle pieces of composers such as Jannequin and Matthias Hermann, representing the languages of the opposing forces and their mercenaries.[285] Giovanni Croce uses it in his *Triaca musicale*,[286] as do Vecchi in his *Veglie di Siena*,[287] Banchieri for the motley array of passengers in his *Barca di Venetia per Padova*,[288] and Giovanni Battista Fasolo in his *Barchetta passaggiera*.[289]

The composition which realizes most consistently the principle of *diversi linguaggi* was published shortly before Eccard's and Marenzio/Vecchi's, and probably served Vecchi, at least, as a model (the only copy in Europe is preserved in Vecchi's city of Modena): Michele Varotto's *Dialogo a dieci*, the last piece in the *Fiamma ardente de madrigali et canzoni a cinque voci, con un dialogo a dieci diversi soggetti, novamente raccolt, & datte in luce per Gio. Battista Portio Novarese*.[290] Here again, the *tavola* and Vogel's bibliography (II, 443) give no indication that each of the ten voices represents a different person, who sings his text in his own dialect or language: a Spaniard, Neapolitan, [Bo-

---

[283] They include a Venetian Pantalone, Bergamask Zanni, Sicilian Pedante, and Matriccian Franceschina.

[284] *Opera nova dove intenderete una cavalcata di varij lenguazi* (Bologna, 1590); *Veglia carnevalesca ... et si sentono varij linguaggi, et canzoni* (Bologna, 1620); *Questione di varii linguagi, dove s'intende le ragioni allegate da diversi galant'huomini ... e finalmente come un Todesco gli accorda, con patto di andare tutti insieme all'hosteria* (Bologna, n.d., 1618, 1620, 1628, 1631); *Disgratie del Zane, narrate in un sonetto di diciasete linguazi* (n.p., n.d., Bologna, n.d., 1621); *Le Nozze del Zane in lingua bergamasca nelle quali si vedono sedici linguagi diferenti* (Verona, 1626, Bologna, 1631); *Sogno del Zani in lingua bergamasca, descrito in un sonetto di molti linguaggi* (Bologna, n.d., 1631). Croce's poems however, like Verucci's play, hardly fulfil the expectations of linguistic variety which their titles arouse.

[285] Cf. Rudolf GLÄSEL, *Zur Geschichte der Battaglia*, diss. Leipzig, Thomas & Hubert, 1931, pp. 43, 48.

[286] Venice, Vincenti, 1595. Ed. in «Capolavori polifonici del secolo XVI», III, Rome, De Santis, 1941. *Triaca* is an old folk medicine with a great variety of ingredients.

[287] Cf. the edition listed above, note 30, and VOGEL, II, 275f; also above, note 282.

[288] Editions cited above, note 31.

[289] Rome, Masotti, 1627. *Giovanni Battista Fasolo e la 'Barchetta passeggiera'*, ed. Ottavio Beretta, Lucca, LIM, 1994. Cf. Cesare RUINI, *Edizioni musicali perdute e musicisti ignoti nella 'Notizie de' contrapuntisti e compositori di musica' di Giuseppe Ottavio Pitoni*, in *Musicologia Humana: Studies in Honor of Warren and Ursula Kirkendale*, Florence, Olschki, 1994, pp. 425ff, 433.

[290] Venice, Vincenti & Amadino, 1586; the *Dialogo a dieci*, in W. KIRKENDALE, *Madrigali a diversi linguaggi* cit., pp. 26-38.

lognese] Graziano, Milanese, and gypsy boy in the first choir; a [Venetian] Magnifico, [Bergamask] Zanni, Sicilian, Genoese, and Frenchman in the second.[291] Like Marenzio/Vecchi and unlike Lasso, Varotto forms simultaneous dialogues between single voices rather than between the two choirs. The arrangement of voices may well have influenced Marenzio, for Varotto too leaves the two uppermost parts disengaged from the dialogue of the lower voices, singing two folksongs in alternation: "Cingarin del babo" and "À Paris sur petit pont".[292] In the following diagram the Roman numerals and headings of the ten parts are arranged so as to show the successive entries, at intervals of approximately one measure. The textual content is slight: the Spaniard, Graziano, and the Sicilian each asks whether his respondent knows Isabella, Catharina, and Franceschedda – presumably notorious courtesans – respectively, and Magnifico confesses to Zanni that he is "innamorato". The Frenchman seems to have been a classmate of Scolare (cf. Ex. 11 and 12) – indicating that Vecchi knew this work. Also the declamation in *Amfiparnasso* betrays close affinity to Varotto's motivic structures.

Michele Varotto: *Dialogo a dieci* (1586)

C.		X. Francese solo ....
A.		IX. Genoese risponde al Ciciliano
T		VIII. Ciciliano ....
T.		VII. Zani risponde al Magnifico ....
B.		VI. Magnifico ....
C.	V. Cingaretto solo	
A.	IV. Milanese risponde a Gratiano	
T.	III. Ser Gratiano	
T.	II. Napolitano risponde al Spagnuolo ..	
B.	I. Spagnuolo	

Ex. 12. Varotto: *Dialogo a dieci*, mm. 35f, 68f [these measures are not part of the French folksong].

---

291 See note 50.
292 This text is found also in the *Primo libro de le canzoni francesi*, Venice, Scotto, 1535.

IV.1a. Zanni and Magnifico. From Juvenall Borget, *The Divels Legend*, London, Gosson,
1595, title page. Cf. p. 130.

IV.1b. Tedesco. From Giulio Cesare Croce, *Barcelletta piacevolissima*, Bologna, 1639, title
page. Cf. p. 132.

CANZONE
DI GIROMETTA,

CON ALTRE SETTE STANZE,
Et vna Canzone di Sier Herculano, che
comincia, Donna che fosti la
mia chiara Stella.

In Venetia, In Frezzaria al segno della Regina.
M. D. LXXXVII.

IV.2. *Canzone di Girometta*, Venice, 1587, unicum in I-Bu. Cf. p. 152.

IV.3a. Il Fate ben per voi. Federico Zuccari, detail from triumph of Marc'Antonio Colonna, fresco in Paliano, Castello Colonna. Cf. p. 190.

Fate ben per uoi   Turchi

IV.3b. Il Fate ben per voi. Engraving possibly by Étienne Dupérac from *L'entrata solenne fatta dall'Ec.^{mo} Sig.^r Marcant.^o Colonna in Roma doppo la felicissima vittoria ... contra Turchi l'anno 1571, a iiij dicembre*, Rome, Francesco Tramezzino [ca. 1571/2]. Cf. p. 189, note 262.

INDICE VNIVERSALE
DELLA LIBRARIA

O STVDIO del CELEBRATISS.
Arcidottore GRATIAN Furbson da Fráculin, Opera curiosa, per i Professori delle Sié, Matematiche, e studiosi dell'opere bizzare, e capriciose
Rac. per M. Aquedoto dalle Sanguetole riformatore dell'Hosteria del Chiu.
Di Giulio Cesare Croce

In Bologna, presso l'Erede del Cochi, Con licenza de Superioi., e Prij

IV.4. Dr. Graziano. From Giulio Cesare Croce, *Indice universale della libraria o studio del celebratiss. arcidottore Gratian*, Bologna, n.d. Cf. p. 192.

Marenzio/Vecchi's *Diversi linguaggi* is not merely a random mixture of incongruous elements, as so often found in quodlibets. The threads running from each single part to the others are so manifold that we can tie them together only by means of a diagram (without attributing any 'geometric' intention to the composers). Here the numbers, referring to relevant footnotes and/or adjacent passages in the text of the article, document the continual association of the various character types with each other – in their common social milieu and in the literary and musical sources.[293]

KLEINES WELTTHEATER

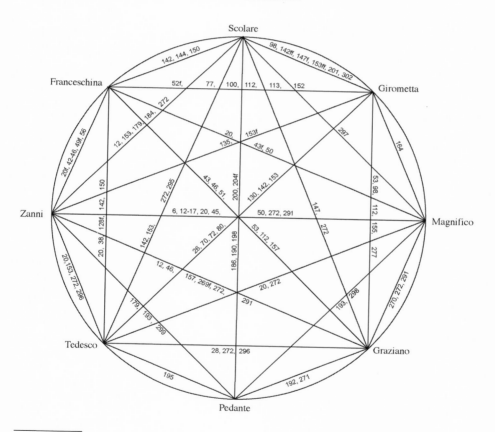

[293] It will be noted that Pedante, remote from life and women, has no relationship to the folksongs. I have not included the historical figure of the Fate ben in the diagram; his connection with soldiers and "perilous girls" has been indicated above.

What may have induced Vecchi to add voices to Marenzio's composition? Above all, he must have been attracted by the dramatic possibilities and the social implications of the five roles and felt challenged to complement them with closely related character types, thus achieving a more representative cross-section of the given milieu. In the stage setting provided by the students' drinking songs he places the appropriate figure of the negligent Scolare, thus bringing the scene to life.[294] Scolare combines just as naturally with Marenzio's other roles. Mutual love of wine brought students together with German mercenaries in the taverns; and another type of Tedesco shared their company: the numerous 'teutonici' who frequented the universities of Bologna and Padua.[295] (One of these introduces himself in an anonymous dialogue of 1567 between "Tedescho et Zanni"[296] with the words "Mi da le studie di Bologna vegne", "I come from the University of Bologna"). Magnifico, in his traditional capacity of a duped parent, could be the father of Vecchi's truant.[297] In the comedy of Verucci mentioned above and in the scenario *Il pedante* of Flaminio Scala, Magnifico indeed employs Pedante as the tutor of his son.[298] The dialogue of Scolare and Pedante, running parallel to that of Zanni and Magnifico, complements the 'poesia villanesca' with its antipode, the 'poesia pedantesca'.[299] The Fate ben per voi, who in real life worked for the conversion of sinners, provides a moralizing commentary on the other persons, urging them to do good, rather than to quarrel, play truant, drink, debauch, etc. If Graziano's commentary is that of Vecchi the intellectual, this one may be that of Vecchi the priest.

By increasing the number of voices from five to nine – or rather from four to seven, since the alternating folksongs were not heard simultaneously and the Fate ben is a mere pedal point –Vecchi adds immeasurably to the rhythmic vitality of the piece. That the master of the madrigal comedy loses no opportunity for dramatic characterization goes without saying. Scolare's "Salve" (m. 3), by beginning with a long note and falling interval, renders in music the gesture of a bow (greeting), recalling also settings of the "Salve Regina". Pe-

---

[294] See note 50.

[295] In the last decades of the 16th century ca. 70-80 members of the 'nazione germanica' graduated each year from the University of Bologna; cf. Luigi SIMEONI, *Storia della Università di Bologna*, II, Bologna, Zanichelli, 1940, pp. 64, 67.

[296] D-Mbs cod. it. 347, f. 4; published by Elia ZERBINI, *Note storiche sul dialetto bergamasco*, Bergamo, Gaffuri & Gatti, 1886, pp. 36f, and PANDOLFI, I, 269ff.

[297] See note 50.

[298] See note 50.

[299] See note 50.

dante's declamation, like his character, is dry and stiff; especially pompous is his etymological pronouncement (mm. 56-61), with its long notes and large leaps (Ex. 13). Vecchi underlines the textual parallelism of the name-calling (mm. 75f: S. "Pedantissimo" – P. "Cinedissimo") by the device of the echo,

Ex. 13. Vecchi: *Diversi linguaggi*, mm. 57-61.

giving the second word the same music as the first. Also in the castigation scene (mm. 15 ff) he suggests Pedante's lack of imagination and originality by making his motive echo that of Scolare. In these same measures, where the quarrel between Zanni and Magnifico reached its climax, Marenzio had very fittingly turned to the unmistakable musical style of the *battaglia: stile concitato*, with short fanfare motives derived from the tonic triad repeated over static harmony. In adopting these motives for his dialogue, Vecchi achieves perfect musical expression for this portion of his text, the *combatti-mento* between Scolare and Pedante (Ex. 14).[300] This correspondence of content suggests that the text of the second dialogue was written to fit that of the first – i.e. either by Vecchi himself or by a poet who collaborated with him. In the latter case the most likely candidate is undoubtedly Croce. He was a personal friend of Vecchi's, and his poetry cultivates the same milieu and situations as Vecchi's works do, as we have seen from our frequent quotations from his poems. Such a collaboration, here or elsewhere, is suggested by lines from the undated *capitolo* which he addressed to the composer: "But first you must send me in prose all the subject [matter] of that which you want".[301]

---

[300] On Vecchi's use of *battaglia* style in other compositions cf. Erich SCHENK, in *Orazio Vecchi ...*, Modena, Soc. Tip. Modenese, 1950, pp. 173f.

[301] "Ma pria bisogna mi mandiate in prosa / tutto il suggetto di quel che volete" – "Del Croce al Vecchi", autograph in I-Bu ms. Misc. 3878, caps. LI, t. I, f. 181, lines 25f; cf. also f. 182, lines 109ff. Published in «Giornale storico della letteratura italiana», XXII, 1893, pp. 383f, and in *Ope-*

Ex. 14. Marenzio/Vecchi: *Diversi linguaggi*, mm. 15-17.

Scolare may give us a final example of the manner in which each role illuminates the others, making the whole greater than the sum of its parts. When he excuses his absence by saying that he had to go to the shoemaker, he does not convince Pedante ("M'hai detto le mendatie" – "You have lied to me"). His companions in the outer voices, Girometta and Tedesco, are singing a commentary which cannot be overheard: in reality, the truant Scolare had been pursuing the pleasures of wine, women, and song; the shoes which he procured (m. 13) were not his own, but those "scarpette" (mm. 8f) which Girometta had received from him, her lover.[302] At the same time the *Girometta* melody recalled to contemporaries not only all its disreputable associations, but also the familiar text of Razzi's laud, with its admonition, echoed by the Fate ben, to return to the Lord and to chastity ("Castità sia in te, figliuolino"; "Chastity be with you, little son") – not entirely inappropriate to the given situation.

Maximum concentration is reached by the simultaneous presentation of texts, effective in music intended more for performers than for an audience: within eighty measures as many words as an entire monotextual madrigal comedy. I may point out the uninterrupted employment of this technique *cum diversis litteris* from the Gothic motet to the operatic ensemble,[303] without implying a direct connection of Marenzio/Vecchi's piece with these phenomena. However, the representation of each role by a single voice comes much closer to the buffo finale than does the choral dialogue of Vecchi's later madrigal comedies, so often and erroneously regarded as 'precursori del melodramma' ['forerunners of opera']. (With Marazzoli's comic intermezzo, *Girometta* indeed survived into opera: one of the idle visitors at the fair, she follows directly the cries of a hawker offering "pettini, specchi, e veli sopra fini", "combs, mirrors, and very fine veils").

In his dedication to Jakob and Johann Fugger,[304] Vecchi explains the title of his *Selva* by comparing the variety of its contents to the variety of botanical

---

rette di Giulio Cesare Croce, I, Bologna, Palmaverde, 1956, pp. 45-48. According to his autobiography, Croce had been exploited in his youth by a "dotissimo pedante" – *Descrittione minutissima delle vita del Croce*, two versions, in the autograph ms. I-Bu Misc. 3878, caps. LI, t. II, nos. 14 (1586) and 13 (1608); in the later version "dotissimo", line 58, is changed to "valentissimo" (cf. f. 97v and 83); published Bologna, 1608 etc., and in *Operette*, I, 11-30.

302 See note 50.

303 This interesting field is surveyed by Reinhold HAMMERSTEIN, *Über das gleichzeitige Erklingen mehrerer Texte: Zur Geschichte mehrtextiger Komposition unter besonderer Berücksichtigung J. S. Bachs*, AfMw, XXVII, 1970, pp. 257-286. On the specific tradition of the quodlibet cf. Kurt GUDEWILL, *Ursprünge und nationale Aspekte des Quodlibets*, in International Musicological Society, *Report of the Eighth Congress, New York 1961*, Kassel, Bärenreiter, 1962, pp. 30-43.

304 Orlando di Lasso had dedicated to the four Fugger brothers a collection of pieces in four languages: *Sex cantiones Latinae, ... sechs teutsche Lieder, ... six chansons françoises, ... sei madrigali*, in four parts, plus an eight-part dialogue in each of the four languages (Munich, Berg, 1573).

species in a forest:[305] "... as in a forest the variety of herbs and plants. ... And likewise having combined in one [work] the serious and the familiar styles, the grave with the facetious and with the dance idiom, from this must result the variety which the world enjoys". The *Diversi linguaggi* achieves this goal of "variety". The diversity of characters is embodied in an infinite variety of simultaneous rhythms. Not only does the work combine "the serious and the familiar styles" (which rhetorical theory since Aristotle, *Ars Rhetorica*, III.7.2, had allowed only for comic effect); it is a veritable compendium of literary and musical styles and genres: from the Horatian ode, regarded by theorists as the most sublime poetic form, to the ridiculous *poesia pedantesca, grazianesca*, and *villanesca*, commedia dell'arte, *diversi linguaggi*, dialogue,[306] madrigal comedy, quodlibet, *canto carnascialesco*, serenade, *battaglia, incatenatura*, villotta, laud, and folksongs from the university, the tavern, and the military camp. This intention is illuminated by the title of Vecchi's collection, for the word 'selva' (Latin 'silva') designated since antiquity the collection of notes which students and men of letters take from their reading, a reservoir of miscellaneous information for their own productions.[307]

Diversi linguaggi joins the hands of two very different masters.[308] With the

---

[305] "... sì come in una selva vi si mirano varietà d'herbe, e di piante. ... Et havendo altresì giunto in uno lo stil serio col famigliare, il grave col faceto, e col danzevole, dovrà nascerne quella varietà di che il mondo gode". Cf. also the title page: *Selva di varia ricreatione di Horatio Vecchi, nella quale si contengono varii soggetti a 3, a 4, a 5, a 6, a 7, a 8, a 9 & a 10 voci, cioè madrigali, capricci, balli, arie, Iustiniane, canzonette, fantasie, serenate, dialoghi, un lotto amoroso, con una battaglia a diece nel fine.*

[306] On the musical dialogue cf. Theodor KROYER, *Dialog und Echo in der alten Chormusik*, «Jahrbuch der Musikbibliothek Peters», XVI, 1909, pp. 13-32, and Don HARRÁN, *Towards a Definition of the Early Secular Dialogue*, «Music and Letters», LI, 1970, pp. 37-50. These writers, however, do not consider the connections with the various species of literary dialogue such as those represented in the editions of folk poetry quoted above.

[307] Thus CICERO advises, "primum silva rerum ac sententiarum comparanda est" ["first a *silva* of topics and phrases must be prepared" – *De Oratore*, III.26.103], and Quintilian criticizes authors who publish such unfinished "lumber" – *Institutio Oratoria*, X.3.17. Cf. also the chapters on notetaking in Orazio LOMBARDELLI, *Gli aforismi scolastici*, Siena, Marchetti, 1603, pp. 94-98, "Dell'utilità e modo di far le selve"; Paolo ARESI, *Arte di predicar bene*, Venice, Giunti, 1611, pp. 831-836, "Di varie selve", perhaps the earliest description of a card file arranged by subjects; and Gio. Battista MANZINI, *Delle meteore rettoriche*, Bologna, Monti, 1652, pp. 243-271, "Dell'apparecchio della materia, da gli antichi chiamato selva, e zibaldone da' moderni". Writers used the word 'selva' also figuratively as the title of a collection of miscellaneous works of a more or less extempore nature (cf. SUETONIUS, *De Grammaticis*, X and XXIV; the practice is mocked by GELLIUS, *Noctes Atticae, Praefatio*). Vecchi follows these ancient traditions.

[308] Agostino MICHELE, in his *Discorso in cui... si dimostra come si possono scrivere ... le commedie e le tragedie in prosa*, published by Ciotti in Venice only two years after the *Diversi liguaggi*, i.e. in 1592, f. 4v, listing what he regards to be the six greatest composers from Josquin up to his own time, mentions for the most recent generation only two: "in questi tempi il Marentio et il Vecchi riescono singolari et illustri, e nientedimeno hanno fra lor maniera di comporre sì diversa, che dalla stessa arte non sieno abbracciati" ["in these times Marenzio and Vecchi have had singular and illustrious suc-

styles and genres mentioned above, Vecchi was in his element; here as else-where he portrays a vigorous cross-section of society, like musical illustrations to Tommaso Garzoni's *Piazza universale di tutte le professioni del mondo e no-bili e ignobili* (Venice, Somasco, 1585),[309] revealing a sympathy for the lower and lowest social classes comparable to that of his great contemporary Shake-speare. Marenzio, on the other hand, the composer of the sophisticated lyrics of courtly madrigals, has not been identified with the styles of this milieu.[310] Yet his quodlibet, possibly modelled on Eccard's, even provided for Vecchi the point of departure.[311] It adds a congenial, human feature, the touch of a smile, to his melancholy portrait.[312]

cess; nevertheless their manner of composing is so diverse that they do not appear to have been embraced by the same art"].

[309] Garzoni's work, pursuing a more serious intention, includes learned historical discussions of the professions represented by Marenzio/Vecchi: "De grammatici, et pedanti", "De' dottori di legge civile", "De mercanti", "Delle meretrici et de' loro seguaci", "Della militia", "De' putti che vanno a scuola & de' dottori di studio", "De' facchini". Vecchi expressed his admiration for this book in his sonnet published among its prefatory material.

[310] One might, for this reason, even question the attribution. Such doubt could be justified if the piece had appeared in a collection of madrigals by various composers, assembled by a careless publisher. However, it forms not only part of a composition, but also part of an edition for which the collaborator makes himself responsible. Vecchi would not have misused the name of his eminent colleague, who was still living. Marenzio did not care to edit his *villanelle* himself, "cose ... tenute in poca stima da lui" ["things little esteemed by him"] – editor's dedication to his *Primo libro delle villanelle*, Venice, Vincenti & Amadino, 1584.

[311] Since it does not appear among Marenzio's publications, Vecchi may have obtained it directly from the composer. In the same year 1590 Gardano published not only Vecchi's *Selva*, but also the large collection of *Dialoghi musicali di diversi eccellentissimi autori a sette, otto, nove, dieci, undici & dodici voci*, containing two dialogues of Marenzio (three reprinted in the edition of 1592; facs. Brussels, Éditions culture et civilisation, 1970) and four of Vecchi.

[312] Addendum. Four additional literary citations of the Girometta could be found in Salvatore BATTAGLIA, *Grande dizionario della lingua italiana*, VI, Turin, UTET, 1970, p. 852: two *Della famosissima compagnia della Lesina* (late 16th c.), one from Ludovico Sergardi (1660-1726), and one from G. B. Marino (1569-1625): "Dante vi [nell'inferno] andò bell'e vivo con la scorta di un altro poeta. Ma non crediate ch'egli fosse nel girometta [= luogo di sofferenza] dove ora sono io".

THE MYTH OF THE 'BIRTH OF OPERA'
IN THE FLORENTINE CAMERATA DEFLATED
WITH THE ROMAN GENTLEMAN EMILIO DE' CAVALIERI:
A COMMEMORATIVE LECTURE

On 11 March 2002, exactly 400 years after the death and burial of Emilio de' Cavalieri, a commemorative marble inscription formulated by the author of these pages[1] was unveiled in the Cavalieri chapel in the church of the S.P.Q.R., Santa Maria in Aracoeli on the Roman Capitoline hill (Plate V.1). It could be translated as:

EMILIO DE' CAVALIERI

ROMAN GENTLEMAN,
INNOVATIVE AND TALENTED COMPOSER,
CREATOR OF THE FIRST OPERAS,
SUPERINTENDENT OF ALL THE MUSICIANS
AND ARTISTS AT THE COURT OF THE MEDICI,
CONSERVATOR OF THE ROMAN SENATE AND PEOPLE.
BURIED HERE 11 MARCH 1602.

* * *

ON THE FOUR HUNDREDTH ANNIVERSARY OF HIS DEATH.

The ceremony, patronized by the Soprintendenza per i Beni Artistici e Storici, included the lecture "Emilio de' Cavalieri e il suo primato nella nascita del melodramma"[2] published here in English translation with the addition of two introductory paragraphs and footnotes, and concluded with an exquisite concert

---

[1] The second in the historical center of Rome; on that for Handel, based on research of Ursula Kirkendale, cf. RIdM, XXI, 1986, pp. 201-205.

[2] In Plate V.1 the Italian word "melodramma" means, of course, "opera", not "melodrama"; and "geniale" means "possessing genius".

of music by this composer performed by the Choro Romani Cantores conducted by Daniela Condemi (excerpts from the *Lamentations* and the *Rappresentazione di Anima e di Corpo* in the church and then the famous *ballo* from the intermedi of 1589 on the illuminated Piazza Campidoglio). The following remarks can be considered as a commentary on lines 3-4 of the inscription and on the commemoration of the "birth of opera" celebrated in Florence in October 2000.

Forty years of research on Cavalieri and on the other composers active in Florence during the last decades of the sixteenth century in Florence[3] have convinced me that the Roman master was not only by far the best and most original of these, but also the most important of all those ever born in Rome. I therefore limited my work on the Florentine composers to bio-bibliographical aspects,[4] having decided that for me personally an extensive study of the music would be worthwhile only in the case of Cavalieri.[5] Also his social position and his high responsibilities at the court of Grand Duke Ferdinando Medici made him a much more important and interesting personality than all the musicians in Florence.[6]

The paternal grandfather of Emilio was a member of one of the oldest, most illustrious of Roman families, the Orsini; he assumed the surname "Cavalieri" from his mother in order to become the heir of her brother. The father of Emilio, Tommaso, if not Emilio himself, is well known to art historians – as pupil and most beloved friend of Michelangelo Buonarroti, recipient of amorous letters and famous poems and drawings by the great artist, which eventually became, with paintings of Raphael, Emilio's property. The Cavalieri, like other families of the minor Roman nobility, participated actively in the government of their city. Both Tommaso and Emilio were councilors, *caporioni*, and even conservators. As Michelangelo's artistic executor, Tommaso supervised the completion of the senators' palace on the Capitoline hill. He directed various archaeological and urbanistic projects and thus had access to ancient sculpture, retrieved especially in his *rione* [district] of

---

[3] I therefore have no reason to downgrade, with this lecture, the merit of that splendid city; it is only a question of historical veracity, *pace* the Florentine Chamber of Commerce.

[4] *The Court Musicians in Florence during the Principate of the Medici, with a reconstruction of the artistic establishment*, Florence, Olschki, 1993. This archival monograph of 752 pages is not listed in the bibliographies of the articles 'Florence' or 'Medici' in NG[2] (2001), although much of this dictionary's undocumented compilations on Florentine musicians is derived from it. (The editor seems to have read p. 15 of the book).

[5] *Emilio de' Cavalieri, "Gentiluomo Romano": His Life and Letters, His Role as Superintendent of all the Arts at the Medici Court, and His Musical Compositions*, *ibid.*, 2001 (henceforth "*EC*"), where Plate 1 shows the Cavalieri chapel, still without the inscription.

[6] More complete documentation, unnecessary in a commemorative lecture, can be found in *EC* (cf. the indices).

Sant'Eustachio. The author of an inventory of his collection (1556) speaks of the "most famous museum" of Tommaso. Important for Emilio's income were also the offices, quasi sinecures, bought by Tommaso for him: that of the customs of the *studio*, which financed the university with taxes on imported wine, and that of the bridges and city gates – both left to his heirs "in perpetuity". The Roman palace of the Cavalieri, mentioned in old guidebooks of the city, was demolished in 1880 during the construction of the Largo Arenula. Emilio owned also one of the more elegant and panoramic villas of Florence, today known as Villa Spelman, the Johns Hopkins Center for Italian Studies in Via San Leonardo.[7] He occupied also an apartment in Palazzo Pitti, directly to the west, where he received visiting cardinals.[8]

When Francesco Medici died suddenly in 1587, his younger brother Ferdinando, residing as a cardinal in Rome, had to succeed him as grand duke of Tuscany. Having little faith in Francesco's Florentine courtiers and "regarding it as dangerous to employ them for great things",[9] Ferdinando summoned to his court Emilio, whom he already esteemed in Rome, for "great things", for a most important function, unique in the history of European courts: superintendent not only of all the musicians, but also of the salaried artists, that is of about a hundred persons. His monthly salary of 25 ducats exceeded that of the two ministers of state – of internal and external affairs – and was more than four times as much as that of the noted Florentine composer Jacopo Peri. Having so many connections with the cardinals of the papal court, Emilio was the most suitable person for Ferdinando to send on diplomatic missions during the conclaves. The grand duke gave him instructions, in code, to offer secret pensions to certain cardinals in return for their votes in favor of a *papabile* acceptable to the Medici.

On Emilio's personality we have positive judgements, such as: "One cannot find a more benign gentleman than this Signor Emilio, who entertains everyone, assists everyone, with infinite kindness, authority, and charitableness" – thus wrote the mother of his librettist Laura Guidiccioni. His most versatile talents – as public official (in Rome), diplomatic agent, *arbiter elegantiarum*, connoisseur of art and organs, dancer, choreographer, theater director, and composer – made him the perfect courtier, in the sense of Baldassare Castiglione's *Cortegiano*.

---

[7] *EC*, Plate 6. The villa is currently (2007) being offered for sale.

[8] The "stanze di Emilio Cavalieri", adjacent to the "salone delle commedie" on the "secondo piano sotto", are identified in the floor plan reconstructed from I-Fas Guardaroba 422 and published in *Palazzo Pitti: l'arte e la storia*, ed. Marco Chiarini, Florence, Nardini, 2000, p. 35.

[9] The Venetian ambassador Tommaso Contarini, quoted in *EC*, p. 86.

Emilio was particularly interested in organ building, beginning with one for the oratorio of San Marcello in Rome, where he was responsible also for music for the Holy Week, and the famous double organ for Santa Maria in Aracoeli 1585-1602, burned by Napoleon's troops in 1798. For Florence and for the cathedral in Pisa he supervised the construction of no less than ten organs, three of them with the tone divided into ten parts in an attempt to revive the enharmonic genus of ancient Greece.[10]

The first music composed by Cavalieri in Florence was for the spectacular intermedi which he directed on the occasion of the wedding of Ferdinando Medici and Christine of Lorraine in 1589. The very first operas followed soon afterward: his *Satiro* and *Disperazione di Fileno* in 1590. A third one, the *Giuoco della Cieca*, based on Battista Guarini's *Pastor fido*, was performed in 1595 and 1599. Neither the music nor the texts of these three pastorales is preserved. For *Fileno* we have a costume design by Alessandro Allori;[11] and of the *Giuoco della Cieca* a contemporary witness confirmed its considerable duration and the use of music throughout: "Everything the actors said was sung to music; ... but it did not last more than a hour and a half".[12] The editor of *Anima e Corpo* said of *Fileno* that the [solo] singers moved the audience not only to tears, but also to laughter. He emphasized the novelty: "a similar manner was never before seen or heard by anyone". These pastorales are the first theatrical works set entirely to music, with affective solo song – as used also in the *Lamentations* for the Holy Week, composed by Cavalieri likewise in the 1590s, ranking among the most expressive music of the period.

Notwithstanding the very high quality of the ballo and the *Lamentations*, I shall speak mostly of the best known work of Cavalieri, the famous *Rappresentazione di Anima e di Corpo*, composed on the occasion of the Holy Year 1600, dedicated to Cardinal Pietro Aldobrandini, nephew of Clement VIII; the libretto, in no. 15, alludes to the pontiff with the words "Il ciel

---

[10] On the enharmonic genus cf. *EC*, pp. 143-158. Pier Paolo DONATI, *Emilio dei Cavalieri: un organologo del Cinquecento*, «Informazione organistica», n.s. XIV, 2002, pp. 185-231, apparently motivated by my chapter "Cavalieri and Organ Building" and the appendix "Documents on Organ Building", *EC*, pp. 121-158, 399-414, promptly presented – with the authority of an organologist – a synthesis, interpretation, and very positive appraisal of Cavalieri's extraordinary importance for the history of organ building, but did not present new documents, nor give evidence of having read my English.

[11] *EC*, Plate 41.

[12] Peter Casal on a revival of 1598: "Alles was die Personen geredet, das ist ... musicaliter gesungen worden" (complete quotation in *EC*, p. 193). This anticipates words written on Monteverdi's *Orfeo* in 1607: "tutti li interlocutori parleranno musicalmente" (Angelo SOLERTI, *Gli albori del melodramma*, Milan, Sandron, 1904, I, 69) – no novelty.

clemente ogn'hor gratia e favore". The opera was heard with the greatest enthusiasm in the oratory of Filippo Neri in Santa Maria in Vallicella[13] by almost all the cardinals present in Rome, and performed in various places as the music most suitable for celebrating the jubilee of 2000. Manuscripts in the Biblioteca Vallicelliana[14] document the impressions of the original audience, including Cardinal Giulio Antonio Santorio, learned in music, who in 1592 had lost the election to the papacy by only one vote. "He stood up and exclaimed in a loud voice: 'Nothing could be said better!'". "Also Cardinal Montalto was extremely pleased". And "the work succeeded with so much applause and so much satisfaction to all who were present". Of the "great gathering of people" there were "many [who] wept from emotion", and "all left as contented as edified". Another witness, Giovanni Vittorio Rossi alias Erithraeus reported many years later the words of a friend: "He had never heard anything which moved the affections so much. ... Nothing more beautiful or more perfect could be made".[15] These testimonies confirm what was said by the editor of the edition of 1600: "This kind of music renewed by him moved to diverse affects, such as to pity and rejoicing, to tears and laughter, and to others similar".[16] He continued: "The *Rappresentazione* ..., with a large audience and applause, [is] a manifest proof of how much this style is suitable to move also to devotion". The obligatory humanistic comparison with classical antiquity is to be taken *cum grano salis*: "compositions resembling that style with which, it is said, the ancient Greeks and Romans on the stage and in their theaters used to move the spectators to various affects".

The libretto, written by Agostino Manni, a pillar of Neri's oratory, emerges from long literary traditions: those of the medieval *contrasto* (dialectic dialogue), of the laud, and of the *sacra rappresentazione*. According to a concept favored by the Counter-Reformation, this text presents the *ecclesia militans* and the *ecclesia triumphans*, depicting life as a contest between evil and good, salvation as achievable only through renunciation of the world. The grand panorama of the blessed and damned souls in the third act can be con-

---

[13] In a letter of 2 Dec. 1606, Peter Paul RUBENS characterized Santa Maria in Vallicella as "undoubtedly the most famous and most visited church in Rome today, located in the very center of the [city]" – *Correspondance de Rubens*, Antwerp, Backer, 1887-1909, I, 354. In these years Rubens was providing the three most important altarpieces for this church.

[14] I-Rv ms. O.58, f. 347*v*; O.60, f. 294*v*; complete quotations in *EC*, pp. 237f.

[15] I-Rv ms. O.57/II, f. 496*r-v*; *EC*, p. 265.

[16] Cf. the continuation: "passing from one affect to the other, contrary"; and [Alexander POPE], *Essay on Criticism*, London, Lewis, 1711, line 375, telling how Timotheus "bid alternate passions fall and rise".

sidered as a modest echo of Dante's *Divina Commedia* and as a translation into words and music of Michelangelo's *Last Judgement* in the Sistine Chapel, begun precisely in the years when the artist exchanged drawings, relevant to this work, with Tommaso Cavalieri, who seems to have been the model for the features of Saint Thomas to the right of Christ.

No manual of music history, not even the most elementary, fails to mention *Anima e Corpo* as a milestone. But biographical information on the composer had been very scant, in the absence of archival research on him. We now have found 460 letters of Cavalieri and innumerable other documents on him and his family, which make his life much better documented than that of every other composer before the eighteenth century. Textbooks have often associated Cavalieri with the 'Florentine Camerata' of Giovanni Bardi or Jacopo Corsi, forming a trio with the composers Giulio Caccini and Jacopo Peri. But Cavalieri never was part of this group, and the grand duke himself defended him against the rival Bardi, esteeming him as "unique in music" and praising his "universal intelligence and great ability". In textbooks of music history, as in musicological publications, the topic 'Florentine Camerata' has received far more attention than it deserves. The only sources which use the word 'camerata' in this sense are the self-promotional prefaces of Caccini and a letter of Giovanni Bardi's son to Giovanni Battista Doni (see below on their prejudices). The word does not occur at all among the abundant music-historical documentation in the Florentine archives.[17]

Probably the most serious and tenacious error in musical historiography is that which attributes the first operas to Jacopo Peri. It is committed even by writers who should know very well the clearly documented dates: the first pastorale of Peri, *Dafne*, which exists only in a few fragments, was performed *eight years after* the first two of Cavalieri and *three years after* the third, as I emphasized in my chapter on the pastorales, prepublished in Italian already in Florence, 1983. Also the first extant opera is not Peri's *Euridice*, as one always reads in philoflorentine writings, but *Anima e Corpo* of Cavalieri, performed *eight months before Euridice* and printed already that year, 1600, i.e. the year preceding the latter. Such writers conceal not only these dates, but also the fact that *both* Peri and Caccini conceded the priority in the composition of operas to Cavalieri. In his well known preface of 1601 Peri admitted:

Although Signor Emilio de' Cavalieri, as far as I know before anyone else, made our music heard on the stage with marvelous invention ...

---

[17] Cf. my *Court Musicians*, p. 33.

And Caccini said, in a letter which I published in 1993:[18]

Signor Emilio de' Cavalieri, a Roman gentleman of honored memory, was the first who here let these Serene Highnesses hear those tales on the stage ...

In spite of these facts, a celebration of the four hundredth anniversary of the so-called 'birth of opera' in 2000 in Florence assigned no space to the legitimate father, but fêted only Jacopo Peri with an atrocious performance of *Euridice*[19] and with hastily compiled writings which produced no new substance on the history of pre-Monteverdian opera.[20] How is this error to be explained? The first indication is to be found in the envy of certain Florentines towards the persons whom Ferdinando Medici had recruited from Rome. In a letter of 11 March 1594 Cavalieri quotes a Florentine functionary as saying: "These Romans, they should leave". The provincial mentality still persists in some who do not pardon the fact that the first operas were written by a lady librettist from Lucca and an Oratorian father, respectively, and set to music by a Roman composer who left their city disgusted by the intrigues, to have his *opus magnum* performed in Rome. Another reason why many writers have not wanted to recognize the priority of

---

[18] Caccini, letter to Virginio Orsini, 6 Sept. 1614, I-Rasc Carteggio Orsini 126/2; *Court Musicians*, p. 157.

[19] Cf. the anonymous review in *La Nazione*, Florence, 8 Oct. 2000: "a feeble and monotonous performance, destitute of tension and theatrical effect". "The director showed the same nonchalance in modernizing the text of Rinuccini with recent content entirely extraneous to the sense of the opera. After the wedding celebrated by a bishop [in ancient Greece!], Euridice does not die, but is raped [by Pluto] up against an olive tree and sent to prostitute herself with a gang of thugs [dressed like Mafia bosses of the 1930s], so that the infernal regions where she is found by Orfeo become a sordid metropolitan scene of street-walkers and drug dealers". Equally brutal were the glaring illumination (like a football stadium or television studio), the ugly cables in full view, and the furies dressed in black and red leather. *De gustibus non disputandum est.* Quite different the enthusiastic reviews of *Anima e Corpo*, performed annually at the Salzburg Festival 1968-73 (quotations in *EC*, p. 285, note 218).

[20] In the catalogue of the exhibition *'Per un regale evento': Spettacoli nuziali e opera in musica dei Medici*, Florence, Centro Di, 2000, the chapter "La prima opera in musica", pp. 145-193, written by the editor, Maria Adelaide Bartoli Bacherini, does not even mention the name of Cavalieri; cf. *EC*, p. 190, note 29, and p. 205. The conference report, *'Lo stupore dell'invenzione': Firenze e la nascita dell'opera*, Florence, Olschki, 2001, offers, in addition to stupor, a new error: a performance of *Anima e Corpo* "in Florence" (p. 6). One of the articles discusses for the nth time the extremely well known prefaces (Solerti, 1903); another occupies itself obsessively with a personal "theory [!] of aulic patronage", without being able to demonstrate concrete results from the "theory"; a third resorts to magic. Very strange for non-Italian readers are the first pages of these two volumes, filled with no less than ca. 80 [!] names of politicians (beginning with the President of the Republic and various *onorevoli*), bureaucratic functionaries, but also musicians and others who have never occupied themselves with the subject matter. Cavalieri might have reacted to this publication with a quotation from his *Anima e Corpo* (nos. 72 and 77): "O gran stupore! / O grav'errore!".

Anima e Corpo is undoubtedly their prejudice against and incomprehension of works of religious content and thus against Rome, the city which during the seventeenth century, under the strong influence of Cavalieri, became the center for religious opera and oratorio, with Carissimi as his greatest debtor. The revival of ancient, 'pagan' culture in the Renaissance, on the other hand, is a topic of such interest and importance that it is not surprising that many secular musicologists have preferred to see the first opera in pseudo-archaeological experiments of a small group of intellectuals in Florence, the city preferred also by foreign musicological tourists. But the tenacious impression created by Jakob Burckhardt that the Renaissance was almost exclusively a secular culture has been revised by historians in recent years. For socioanthropological writers of Marxist ideology, who occupy themselves excessively with propaganda of patronage and the manipulation of works for the 'exercise of power', *Anima e Corpo*, as a moral opera with the intention of edification, is a thorn in the eye, because it does not celebrate an aristocratic festivity (as do so many baroque operas, without this function ever becoming obligatory for the genre).

The principal culprit for the exclusion of Cavalieri was undoubtedly the Florentine music theorist Giovanni Battista Doni (1594-1647), who derived his argument in favor of the Camerata from his friend Pietro Bardi, son of Giovanni. The fact that Giovanni was forced to leave Florence soon after the festivities of 1589 surely did not arouse sympathy in Pietro for the powerful rival Cavalieri. And the musicologists who blindly accepted the judgement of the Florentines did not recognize its chauvinistic motivation, as Charles Burney already had done.[21] The argument presented in favor of the Camerata (Peri and Caccini) is nothing more than a too restrictive and arbitrary definition of 'opera', which would limit the genre to the more severe, declamatory Florentine style (as if to say that Verdi's *Aïda* is not an opera because it is not in the style of Monteverdi), i.e. on the basis of unessential personal differences of *stile recitativo*.[22] Even Peri and Caccini could say no more than that their styles were different from that of Cavalieri. But few musical genres exhibit such a variety of styles as opera. Some

---

[21] Cf. the quotation in *EC*, pp. 288f.

[22] Cavalieri's clear priority is to be claimed for opera, not for recitative. Musicologists (e.g. Nino Pirrotta) have misinterpreted the famous words "recitar cantando" on his frontispiece as a slogan for a new musical style; but these were not intended to mean more than "a theatrical action performed in music". Giulio Caccini could claim to have composed monodies in *stile recitativo* already in the mid-1580s. But *stile recitativo* alone does not constitute opera. Caccini's short pieces belong to the lyric genre – for the chamber, not for the theater. It cannot be reasonably argued that only Peri's *stile recitativo*, not Cavalieri's, qualifies as opera.

EMILIO DE' CAVALIERI

GENTILUOMO ROMANO,
COMPOSITORE INNOVATORE E GENIALE,
CREATORE DEI PRIMI MELODRAMMI
SOPRINTENDENTE DI TUTTI I MUSICISTI
ED ARTISTI ALLA CORTE DEI MEDICI,
CONSERVATORE S.P.Q.R.
SEPOLTO QUI L'11 MARZO 1602.

* * *

NEL QUARTO CENTENARIO DELLA MORTE

V.1. Commemorative inscription by W. Kirkendale, Rome, Santa Maria in Aracoeli, Cappella Cavalieri. Cf. p. 205.

writers, misled by the place of the performance, have called *Anima e Corpo* an "oratorio", a musical designation and genre, that is, which originated only four decades later. They obviously never read the lengthy preface to the original edition of the music, the earliest treatise on the composition and performance of opera. It provides detailed indications for the new genre, leaving no doubt that it is dealing with theatrical works and not distinguishing fundamentally between the pastorales and *Anima e Corpo*. Thus it speaks of scenery, costumes, and gestures: exclusive components of opera, not of oratorio.

The time is more than ripe to eradicate the old clichés dragged on by the writers of elementary textbooks of music history. Musicians, on the other hand, have already made a different judgement, producing *Anima e Corpo* no less than fifty times during the past century,[23] while *Euridice* was almost never performed. Thus *Anima e Corpo* is the earliest opera, the only one before Monteverdi, which has earned a secure place in the modern repertoire, thanks to the fascination of its music, always varied, without the notorious "tediousness of the recitative" found in Florence and later in Rome.[24] This fascination is due partly to popular elements, more or less excluded from the courtly Florentine ambient, and to the composer's complete success in realizing the three aims of Ciceronian rhetoric: to instruct, to move, and to delight – thus avoiding with the rhetorical virtue of variety the worst vice, monotony, which Peri did not succeed in doing.

I cannot disagree with Angelo Solerti, who called Cavalieri "the true animator of the reform after the festivities of 1589"; with the biographer of Palestrina, Giuseppe Baini, who designated him as "a great genius"; and with the great English music historian Charles Burney, who in 1789 defended Cavalieri from the prejudices of Doni and said with regard to *Anima e Corpo* that he was not able to discover any superiority in the *Orfeo* of Monteverdi. If anyone should remain sceptical, it should suffice for him to listen to the good recording by Hans-Martin Linde[25] (not the more recent ones).

---

[23] Cf. *EC*, p. 464, where also six complete recordings are listed (more have appeared since then). I know of only one (good) of *Euridice*. Now that a splendid critical edition of *Anima e Corpo* has appeared (Middleton, American Institute of Musicology, 2007, ed. Murray Bradshaw), it will surely encourage further performances.

[24] In 1600 Cavalieri heard reports judging his rivals' music [*Euridice* and *Il rapimento di Cefalo*] as "tedious", like the recitation tones of plainchant (cf. his letter in *EC*, p. 372; also p. 294). Peri's *Euridice*, if not Caccini's (printed in 1601, not performed until December 1602), might be considered successful in its limited scope (expressive declamation), though it is much less interesting, varied, and pleasing than *Anima e Corpo*. Cf. my positive judgements in *Court Musicians*, pp. 206, 210, and *EC*, p. 211.

[25] Cassette copies filed in the Deutsches Historisches Institut, Rome, and I-Rvat.

* * *

Summing up, I present a list, *salvo errore et omissione*, of Cavalieri's innovations which make him the most original composer of his innovative epoch, between Renaissance and Baroque:

The Ballo of 1589

1. is a work without precedents or followers in its organization of an extensive musical space with unity and variety by means of very consistent application of proportional variations (see diagram, *EC*, p. 172);
2. can be considered the most fertile composition in the history of music, since hundreds of pieces, sacred and secular, vocal and instrumental, were composed upon its bass part in many European countries, for more than a century.[26]

The pastorales 1590-95

3. The two pastorales of 1590 and that of 1595 anticipate by many years the *Dafne* of 1598. These pastorales and not those of Peri *are the earliest operas*, because they present with scenery, costumes, and gesture a theatrical action entirely in music, with a predominance of affective solo song[27] and, in at least one case, with a duration of more than an hour. They established the pastorale as the preferred literary genre for many later operas.
4. The pastorals provide the earliest documentation for the humorous effect characteristic of the future opera buffa, unknown to Peri and Caccini ("laughter", *EC*, p. 259).
5. Cavalieri seems to have composed the earliest music for Torquato Tasso's *Aminta* (*EC*, p. 190), and he surely did this for the first performance of any part of Guarini's *Pastor fido* (*EC*, p. 203) – the two pastorales which soon were to provide texts for so many composers.

The Lamentations

6. composed, at least in part, as early as 1593, are among the very earliest postmedieval collections notated in score, not for the use of theorists or instrumentalists (*EC*, p. 232; the intermedi of 1589 contained only a few pieces in score);

---

[26] Cf. W. KIRKENDALE, *L'Aria di Fiorenza, id est il Ballo del Gran Duca*, Florence, Olschki, 1972, and the addenda in *EC*, pp. 421-431.

[27] I present this as an adequate definition of early opera for anyone who may wish one, although I have always regarded it as the task of the music historian to discover and present new sources and documentation from archives and libraries, thus adding to our concrete knowledge of music history, rather than to sit at a desk and formulate arbitrary abstract definitions in the manner of aestheticians. If one should 'require' also a division into acts and scenes, cf. below, no. 22.

7. are the first musical collection to contain monodies and basso continuo (*EC*, p. 232);
8. apply for the first time monody and basso continuo to liturgical music (*EC*, pp. 224, 232) and to falsobordone (*EC*, p. 225);
9. present, perhaps for the first time, an indication of dynamics ("*f*", *EC*, p. 232; cf. also p. 263);
10. initiate a typically baroque style of frequent alternation of *prima* and *seconda pratica* in the same piece (*EC*, p. 229);
11. employ hitherto unheard harmonies, such as D-flat major, G-flat major, and e-flat minor, to be understood – like the melodic use of the enharmonic genus in these *Lamentations* – in relationship to his construction of enharmonic organs (which divide the octave for the first – and last? – time into 62 parts).

Anima e Corpo

12. is the first completely preserved opera, performed eight months before Peri's *Euridice*;
13. is the first printed opera (1600), in the year preceding the edition of *Euridice*;
14. could be the earliest extant music composed expressly for a Holy Year;
15. was performed before a most illustrious audience ("almost the entire sacred college of the cardinals");
16. is the first score printed in a large, luxurious format (ca. 46 × 33 cm);
17. is the first religious-moral opera;
18. is the first opera performed in Rome;
19. is the earliest edition of monody;
20. has for the first time a libretto, separate from the music;
21. contains the earliest treatise on the composition and performance of opera, with references to scenery, costumes, gestures, etc. leaving no doubt as to the operatic nature of the pastorales and *Anima e Corpo*;
22. divides the libretto for the first time into acts (3) and scenes (5 + 9 + 9), as became normal in the seventeenth century, but is not yet done by Peri (*EC*, pp. 210, 232);
23. presents for the first time an explanation of figured bass (*EC*, pp. 262, 293);
24. has sinfonias and ritornellos which are the earliest extended pieces for instrumental ensemble in an opera and notated in score (*EC*, p. 293);
25. presents in the sinfonias, perhaps for the first time, long passages of sequences – a procedure which was to become typical of the baroque era (*EC*, p. 272).

* * *

As in the case of Carlo Gesualdo, Prince of Venosa, Cavalieri's great originality can be attributed partly to the fact that he belonged to an elevated social class and not to the musical profession. This made him more independent of patrons. As the Venetian ambassador wrote of him in 1588: "He is not so assiduous to the person [of the grand duke] as the others, because he loves liberty" (*EC*, p. 66).

I hope to have demonstrated that Cavalieri had nothing to fear from a comparison with Monteverdi, but surpassed him as an innovator. However, the fascination and pleasant tunefulness of *Anima e Corpo* owe much to the fact that the composer, much more than Peri or Caccini, also preserved idioms of the oldest popular Italian polyphony (laud, villanella, canzonetta). It is not a question of Monteverdi first reintroducing musical interest to the severe *stile recitativo* of the Camerata, but rather of his being much indebted to Cavalieri.[28]

---

[28] POSTSCRIPT. This article already contains refutations of most of the old arguments repeated again in a Florentine rejoinder to it published in RIdM, XXXVII, 2002, pp. 371-383, where we see the curious undertaking of a musicologist to denigrate a very good and important composer (hardly the duty of our discipline), in an attempt to make less successful ones appear better. The questionable method consists largely of compiling an anthology of mediocre and poorly informed writers who do *not* mention Cavalieri – a futile exercise which could be performed on any composer. These north Italian critics and men of letters, who never saw or heard a note of Cavalieri's music, naturally favored Peri and Caccini (in many cases likewise in ignorance of their music), simply because these composers collaborated with a major Florentine poet, Rinuccini. Some of the early writers, like Giovan Battista Magnone, had no reason to mention *Anima e Corpo* because they were presenting only examples of polyphony. The crown witness cited, Francesco Saverio Quadrio – far too remote from Cavalieri in time and place – was certainly no authority on music (least of all Cavalieri's), unlike the great connoisseur of opera Charles Burney, who was competent in music history and studied the scores. Writers on music who ignore the music itself (in this case also the very favorable reactions to *Anima e Corpo* in 1600 and its vigorous performance history throughout the 20th century) do so at their own peril. On denigration cf. above, p. 123, and for a very different recent appraisal of Cavalieri's accomplishments, cf. «Notes», LXI, 2004, pp. 428-430.

VI.

SUL PRIMO ORFEO, FRANCESCO RASI: COMPOSITORE, POETA, CANTANTE, OMICIDA*

Magnificenza, chiarissimi colleghi, cari studenti! Per l'alto onore che mi viene concesso, troppo generosamente, io, sorpreso e commosso, non posso dire altro che grazie infinite. Rivolgo quindi i miei più sentiti e doverosi ringraziamenti all'illustre facoltà dell'Università di Pavia, al suo *rector magnificus* Professor Castellani, alla Scuola di Paleografia Musicale, al suo direttore Professor Monterosso, e, per la cordiale ospitalità, al Signor Sindaco Zaffanella di Cremona. Porgo i saluti del Signor Presidente della nostra Università di Ratisbona in Baviera, Professor Bungert.

La cerimonia di oggi dà lustro alla nostra università ed alla disciplina di musicologia. Non sarebbe stato possibile senza il prezioso aiuto dei miei cari genitori, oggi presenti, del mio scomparso professore Erich Schenk di Vienna, e dei gentilissimi archivisti e bibliotecari italiani, che mi hanno mostrato sempre squisita cortesia. Ciò che mi fa più piacere è ricevere quest'onore dall-l'Oxford lombarda' e dall'istituto di musicologia più antico e più rinomato d'Italia, per il quale ho sempre avuto la più grande stima, sebbene non conoscessi personalmente i professori. Qui si sono perfezionati i migliori musicologi che vanta oggi l'Italia. Né c'è un'inflazione di onori quando l'unica laurea honoris causa finora conferita ad un musicologo in Italia è stata per il benemerito Nestore della musicologia americana, Professor Willi Apel, che ha oggi [1986] 92 anni.

* * *

---

* Lecture delivered in Cremona, 2 June 1986, on occasion of the conferring of the honorary doctorate from the University of Pavia. It appears here in the original Italian because the comprehensive biography of Rasi is published in W. KIRKENDALE, *The Court Musicians in Florence during the Principate of the Medici*, Florence, Olschki, 1993, pp. 556-603, where all of the documentation is to be found. Addendum: Susan PARISI, *Francesco Rasi's* La favola di Cibele ed Ati *and the Cybele Legend from Ovid to the Early Seicento*, in *Music Observed: Studies in Honor of William C. Holmes*, Warren, Harmonie Park Press, 2004, pp. 361-392.

Per questa mia relazione ho scelto un soggetto che ha un rapporto col figlio più celebre della città di Cremona, che ci ospita: Claudio Monteverdi. Da quest'ambiente, come dimostrerò, è arrivata la prima monodia italiana alla nostra antica città sul Danubio, Ratisbona. Francesco Rasi, il più importante alunno di Giulio Caccini e il protagonista dell'*Orfeo* di Monteverdi, è considerato il primo compositore che abbia introdotto la nuova monodia italiana nei paesi oltremontani. Ma della sua vita non si è saputo fin'ora quasi nulla. Con la scoperta di circa 180 sue lettere e molti altri documenti è stato ora possibile ricostruire quasi anno per anno la sua straordinaria carriera. Non ha partecipato solo a quasi tutti i primi melodrammi – *Euridice, Cefalo, Orfeo, Dafne* (del Gagliano), e *Arianna* – ma quale inviato della monodia lirica ha viaggiato come nessun compositore prima di lui: a Varsavia, Vienna, in Fiandra e Lorena, a Praga, Augusta, Monaco, Salisburgo, nonché in quasi tutte le corti dell'Italia settentrionale e centrale. Così ha avuto rapporti con numerosi sovrani, imperatori, papi e cardinali, ed era conosciuto e stimato da personaggi della storia della musica come Bardi e Corsi, Cavalieri, Caccini, Marenzio, Gesualdo, Peri, Monteverdi e Gagliano; il poeta Chiabrera e Galileo Galilei, che ha fatto per lui un oroscopo.

Rasi è nato il 14 maggio 1574 ad Arezzo, quale settimo di 13 figli di Ascanio Rasi, per molti anni capitano di giustizia a Mantova e poi senatore a Casale, uomo infelice che si lamentava sempre dei suoi debiti "per causa dei figliuoli maschi troppo liberi nello spendere", "che per mettermi al fondo, hanno fatto a gara". Ciononostante Ascanio lasciò alla sua morte non meno di 94 pezzi di terra ad Arezzo!

"Francesco Rasi", dice Severo Bonini nei suoi discorsi, "cantò leggiadramente con grandissimo affetto e spirito. Era huomo di bello aspetto, gioviale di voce gradita et soave; faceva apparire con l'allegrezza del volto e maestà il suo canto angelico e divino; fu scolare del Sig.^re Giulio [Caccini]". Già all'età di 14 anni Francesco fu ammesso al ruolo del Gran Duca di Toscana nella classe dei gentiluomini, insieme con Emilio de' Cavalieri e con i poeti Guarini, Chiabrera, Saracinelli e Salvadori. Cinque anni dopo, Virginio Orsini Duca di Bracciano, il Cardinal Montalto a Roma, Carlo Gesualdo a Ferrara e il Gran Duca Ferdinando Medici a Firenze fecero a gara per averlo al loro servizio, come scrive Emilio de' Cavalieri: "Saprà che il Rasi è diventato tanto buono, sì de chitarrone come di cantante; che ne è fatto infinita stima in Roma. ... Oggi non vedo chi canti meglio di lui, et ancho sona bene affatto". Un anno dopo il padre diceva che ancora: "L'Illmo Sr Carlo Gesualdo Principe di Venosa ... usò ogni mezzo per havere Francesco ... appresso di sé".

Nel 1596 il Gran Duca Ferdinando mandò Rasi e Marenzio alla corte di Varsavia. Nelle lettere indirizzate al Re Sigismondo per introdurre questi musicisti, scrisse che il Rasi, "se bene si sia esercitato nella musica, è ben nato" da famiglie nobili in Arezzo – si vede il contrasto fra musico e gentiluomo. Rasi rimase meno di due anni in Polonia ed entrò al servizio del Duca Vincenzo I di Mantova nel novembre 1598. Riceveva 84 lire al mese e diversi *naturalia*. Quando fu messo a disposizione per celebrare le nozze di Maria Medici a Firenze nel 1600, il padre dovette richiedere un salvacondotto per il figlio, allo scopo di proteggerlo da eventuali conseguenze dei debiti contratti in Polonia, "per quella benedetta gita, che fu la ruina di casa nostra". A Firenze, Francesco abitò presso Jacopo Corsi e ottenne da Mantova "licentia alla mia scolare [Sabina] di venire a queste sì belle feste et ad imparare qualche cosa ... Queste occasioni ... vengono ogni cento anni una volta". Non volle, però, che Sabina imparasse lo stile francese, introdotto da Monteverdi a Mantova. Scriveva al Duca di Mantova: "ella perderà tutto il garbo italiano datole da me con tanti stenti in due anni; perché tanto quanto lo spagnuolo aiuta il garbo italiano, tanto il franzese lo toglie, riempiendo molti brutti atti, come di movimento di bocca, di spalle ed altro".

Il 30 aprile 1601 Rasi scrisse al duca di Mantova una lettera eccezionale per lunghezza, immodestia e per il suo contenuto autobiografico. Sua intenzione era di ottenere, come diceva, qualche "nobile titolo", che a Mantova non ricevette mai:

Doppo havere alcuni anni speso a persuasione di mio padre in Pisa inutilmente nello studio delle leggi come in cosa contro al genio mio, deliberai d'arricchirmi di tutte quelle honorate qualità, che possono render chiara la persona d'ogni gentilhuomo, e sopra tutte due ne scelsi, che molte ne comprendono, e queste furono lo studio delle belle lettere e la musica, l'una per adornamento dell'altra.

Scrisse dei suoi viaggi e degli onori ricevuti, p. e. da Papa Clemente VIII, e poi dipinse un quadro poco lusinghiero della vita cortigiana mantovana:

Il primo anno, conoscendo alcuni belli humori ove il mio ingegno m'harebbe potuto condurre, mi furono tanto adosso ... che molte volte fui per irmene con Dio. Il secondo ... fui sì ben trattato dalle beffe di chi sa Vostra Altezza ... fui vicino a perdere il cervello ...; mi viene voglia non solo di fuggire sì crudeli influssi, ma di perdere ancora la memoria e'l nome di Mantova ... conoscendo molti costumi di cotesta corte de i detrattori e mormoratori, trovo che senza una particolar protettione di Vostra Altezza non vi potrei vivere senza disperatione.

Due anni dopo si lamentò con il segretario del duca "che vedendome poi cantare mi danno nome [non di gentiluomo ma] di musico, il quale mai non fu il mio principale scopo né professione, ma loro adornamento".

Nel 1607 ebbe luogo la rappresentazione dell'*Orfeo* monteverdiano, "in quella", secondo un testimone mantovano, "cantando quel Sig. Francesco Rasio, per eccellenza in tal professione così famoso, che ogn'un tiene poter essere al mondo pochi altri, che avanzarlo possano". L'anno successivo Marco da Gagliano scrive della sua *Dafne*, che qui "s'udirono [tutte quelle maggiori leggiadrie] dalla voce del Sig. Francesco Rasi, che oltre a tante rare qualità, è nel canto singolarissimo". Meno fortuna ebbe il Rasi con la sua prima pubblicazione letteraria. Protestò: "Io confidai ad alcuni amici miei di Verona a mesi passati alcune mie chiacchiere poetiche, et essi hanno ardito in questa mia lontananza di farmele stampare da un loro stampatore senza scrivermene né pure una minima parola, sotto pretesto di farmi ... una burla".

Quello che dirò adesso non sarà troppo piacevole. Ma devo andare dove mi conducono i documenti. Ho trovato nell'Archivio di Stato d'Arezzo il protocollo d'un processo d'omicidio contro Rasi. Qui si trovano descritti tutti gli orribili dettagli, che non starò a raccontare qui per non farne un 'giallo'. Dirò solo che dopo la morte del padre di Rasi, la matrigna prese nella sua villa un fattore con giovane moglie "di bell'aspetto". "Dopo alcuni giorni ... Francesco s'invaghì" di questa donna e col suo aiuto ammazzò il marito con 25 coltellate, tentò di strangolare la matrigna e rubò da loro ogni cosa di valore. Per questo furono condannati "nella pena della forca ... et ad essere tutti squartati, nella confiscatione de' beni". Ma in qualche modo Francesco riuscì a fuggire a Torino, e dieci anni dopo fu perdonato "per havere la gratia del Sig.^{re} Duca di Mantova ottenuto gratia ... con conditione che non possa venire in Arezzo".

Un altro protocollo interessante è quello di una seduta dell'Accademia Filarmonica di Verona, dal quale risulta che il Rasi divenne accademico nel febbraio 1612 per *propria* iniziativa. Nell'inverno seguente accompagnò il Principe Vincenzo Gonzaga a Praga per far omaggio al nuovo imperatore Matteo. La continuazione del viaggio per la Baviera fu molto dura. Passando da Norimberga ad Augusta fu maltrattato dai "carrozzieri heretici e nemici d'italiani" e si ammalò dal "freddo acutissimo" e dalla "crudezza di questo vino". Si può bene capire che lasciò i paesi oltremontani "con fermo proponimento di non uscir mai più d'Italia".

Subito dopo il ritorno in patria scrisse una lunga lettera all'amico Galileo, nel quale racconta, fra altro, delle sue amichevoli visite al fratello dell'astronomo, liutista alla corte di Monaco. "Egli ha", diceva, "il più bello puttino e la più bella puttina che siano in quelle parti". Anche colla famiglia Priuli di Venezia il Rasi ebbe per molti anni rapporti amichevoli. Quando Antonio Priuli fu eletto doge nel 1618, il Rasi pubblicò dei versi per l'occasione e fu subito compensato col titolo di Cavaliere di San Marco, un'alta onorificenza conferita dal doge che sicuramente ignorava l'omicidio. Nel dicembre del 1620 finalmente Rasi poté tornare in Toscana e rallegrare con la sua musica il Gran Duca Cosimo II durante la sua ultima malattia, come ricorda il diarista Tinghi:

"Si intrattenne con diverse cose e a sentire sonare et cantare il detto Rasi, al quale sendo bandito dalli stati di Sua Altezza Serenissima li fece grazia libera".

Una delle ultime notizie di questo musicista, che aveva festeggiato tante nozze principesche, è quella del proprio matrimonio. Nel settembre 1621 sposò a Pistoia Alessandra Bocchineri, la cui famiglia era legata da stretta amicizia a Galileo (la sorella di Alessandra divenne sua nuora). Quattro mesi dopo Francesco era già morto e il collega Chiabrera gli scrisse l'epitaffio.

Francesco Rasi merita la nostra attenzione quale capace compositore, colto poeta e celebrato cantante. Essendo lui stesso poeta, rispettò la proprietà letteraria e cominciò già dalla sua prima pubblicazione musicale (1608) la sua insolita abitudine di indicare sempre l'identità degli autori dei suoi testi, anche dei molti propri. Un titolo come quello della sua seconda raccolta, *Madrigali di diversi autori* (1610), si troverebbe normalmente su un'antologia di diversi *compositori*. Rasi, però, volle dire "madrigali di vari *poeti*". La sua terza raccolta, dedicata all'arcivescovo di Salisburgo Marcus Sitticus nel 1612, è rimasta manoscritta. Si trova nella Biblioteca Proske di Ratisbona, tanto ricca di fonti di musica italiana rinascimentale. È uno dei primi autografi musicali che conosciamo e la prima fonte della nuova monodia composta fuori d'Italia. Con la sua ultima raccolta musicale, del 1620, il Rasi presentò composizioni su testi già pubblicati nelle sue *Opere poetiche* del 1614. In queste affermava che "molta differenza di parole ricerca il comporre per recitar cantando, di quel che ricchieggano l'altre maniere di componimenti". Ancora una volta, nel 1619, il Rasi pubblicò opere poetiche, col titolo *La cetra di sette corde*. I sette fascicoli includono poesie con allusioni autobiografiche, altre in lode della bell'Adrianna, prima donna di Mantova, un'"imitazione d'un coro di Sofocle nell'*Aiace*", e due libretti di melodrammi. Per il primo, *Cibele e Ati*, il Rasi diede un lieto fine alla favola di Ovidio (*Fasti*, IV) e compose anche la musica, purtroppo andata perduta. La dedica, con l'invocazione delle autorità greche e romane, esprime idee molto simili a quelle della cosiddetta "camerata fiorentina".

Nel suo triplice talento di poeta, compositore e cantante, Francesco Rasi ha ripristinato l'antica unione personale fra poeta e musicista, e quindi non solo ha cantato, ma ha anche vissuto la parte di Orfeo.

* * *

In conclusione mi sia permesso di indirizzare alcune parole agli studenti, perché il futuro della nostra disciplina è nelle loro mani. Voi avete la fortuna di vivere nel paese più ricco di fonti per la storia della musica. Cito Quintiliano: "Hortor ad quaerendum et inveniri posse fateor". Ma ci sono dei pericoli da evitare, perché i tempi cambiano. Sono convinto che per comprendere il

significato di un opera d'arte del passato dobbiamo acquisire la stessa prepa-
razione dell'artista del passato, cioè studiare le stesse materie, leggere la stessa
letteratura, imparare a pensare come lui e non come un uomo del tardo No-
vecento. Qui si vede la necessità delle lingue (almeno cinque), delle fonti antiche e della paleografia, per leggere non solo la notazione musicale, ma anche i
documenti. Per evitare giudizi anacronistici e quindi sbagliati dobbiamo elimi-
nare sistematicamente attitudini e tendenze che non esistevano in epoche passate e quindi non hanno alcuna importanza per loro. Grande rilevanza per i
compositori del rinascimento hanno p.e. la storia, letteratura e retorica antica,
la sacra bibbia; nessuna, però, ne hanno Marx, Freud, Adorno o Foucault,
che loro non hanno conosciuto. Ci sono degli scrittori che vogliono mettere
la musicologia al servizio non solo della sociologia, ma anche della loro ideo-
logia. Risulta una musicologia abusiva e disonesta, perché perde l'oggettività e
diviene propaganda politica. E la propaganda, tanto di sinistra quanto di de-
stra, non ha mai a che fare con la verità. La parte maggiore della musica per-
venutaci dalle epoche passate è stata destinata o per la chiesa, o per le grandi
famiglie, quindi ci vuole una certa comprensione di queste istituzioni per capire questa musica.

Gli studenti di questa università sanno sicuramente che per diventare un
buon musicologo non è sufficiente studiare solo musicologia, perché ci sono
tanti problemi – appunto i più interessanti – che possono essere risolti solo
con l'aiuto delle discipline umanistiche confinanti, come la filologia antica e
moderna, la storia della letteratura, dell'arte, della chiesa, degli ordini religiosi,
la patristica, l'agiografia, la liturgia, e l'iconologia. Nei nostri studi dobbiamo
sistematicamente nuotare contro corrente, riempire il vuoto lasciato oggi nelle
scuole, dove le materie umanistiche si tralasciano sempre di più a favore del
Master of Business Administration e della tecnologia. L'informatica sicuramente può aiutarci per certi lavori meccanici, ma non sarà mai un'alternativa alle
materie tradizionali e al cervello umano per sviluppare argomenti e trovare
spiegazioni. Spero che appunto in Italia, dove esiste la più grande tradizione
di studi umanistici, si metterà l'*uomo* e non la materia, la parola e non la quan-
tità al centro, e che, come gli iconologi e in contrasto con i positivisti, si avrà il
coraggio di preoccuparsi non solo della forma, ma anche del contenuto, delle
idee, fondate però sempre su fonti concrete.

L'Italia è la mia passione. La saluto, e la ringrazio di cuore per tutto quello
che mi ha dato oggi e negli ultimi trent'anni.

VII.

THE KING OF HEAVEN AND THE KING OF FRANCE: ON A *TOPOS* IN THE MANNER OF LULLY *

"God gives not Kings the stile of gods in vaine".

KING JAMES I, *ΒΑΣΙΛΙΚΟΝ ΔΩΡΟΝ*[1]

As those who have occupied themselves with the instrumental repertoire of the seventeenth and eighteenth centuries well know, composers almost everywhere in Europe imitated the music of Lully,[2] the absolute musical authority of Louis XIV – above all the solemn introductory movements of his overtures (in Germany called "französische Ouvertüren"), which, in his ballets and, later, operas, surpassed in splendour and dignity everything hitherto composed in France. The style seemed simple, yet it was difficult to copy, almost like the 'golden mean' which one never achieves: the melody consisted mostly of scales and triads, the harmony, always in five parts, was never complicated, the rhythm predominantly dotted, the tempo invariably

---

* In memory of my father, August Schöttler (1891-1968).

[1] First line of the prefatory sonnet. Cf. below, notes 17f.

[2] Charles CUDWORTH, *'Baptist's Vein': French Orchestral Music and its Influence from 1650 to 1750*, «Proceedings of the Royal Musical Association», LXXXIII, 1957, pp. 29-47; Rüdiger PFEIF-FER, *Der französische, insbesondere Lullysche Orchesterstil und sein Walten in der deutschen Musikkultur des ausgehenden 17. Jahrhunderts*, in *Der Einfluß der französischen Musik auf die Komponisten der ersten Hälfte des 18. Jahrhunderts: Konferenzbericht der IV. wissenschaftlichen Arbeitstagung Blankenburg/Harz ... 1981*, Blankenburg, Michaelstein, 1982, pp. 15-20; Hans-Joachim SCHULZE, *Der französische Einfluß im Instrumentalwerk J. S. Bachs*, ibid., pp. 57-63; Bernd BASELT, *Einflüsse der französischen Musik auf das Schaffen G. F. Händels*, ibid., pp. 64-76; articles by Hartmut Krones, Peter Andraschke, Eddy Benimedourene, Terence Best, Andreas Waczkat *et al.*, in «Händel-Jahrbuch», L, 2004; NG² IX, 233-236; MGG², *Sachteil*, VII, 1244ff. A French visitor reported that he "found all of Lully's operas" (surely an exageration) in Handel's library – David CHARLTON and Sarah HIBBERD, *"My Father was a Poor Parisian Musician": A Memoir (1756) concerning Rameau, Handel's Library and Sallé*, «Journal of the Royal Musical Association», CXXVIII, 2003, p. 197. Essential for information on Lully's music are Herbert SCHNEIDER, *Chronologisch-Thematisches Verzeichnis sämtlicher Werke von Jean-Baptiste Lully* [LWV], Tutzing, Schneider, 1981, and Jérôme de LA GORCE, *Jean-Baptiste Lully*, Paris, Fayard, 2002.

very slow.[3] Yet the effect was never monotonous. Just as sovereigns great and small outside of France sought in their language, fashions, manners, garden- and palace-architecture, equestrian statues or state portraits a reflection of the Sun King, they adopted Lully's style as representative of the musical Versailles.[4]

At the annual meeting of the American Musicological Society in 1969 in St. Louis (cf. printed abstract) I could already demonstrate that these composers used the same style also for vocal music, when the text spoke of 'majesty', or for instrumental passages which directly preceded or followed such a text. So many did this that this phenomenon became a commonplace, truly a *topos*.[5] Earthly, mythological sovereigns and gods, even the Christian King of Heaven now appear in the musical vestments of Louis XIV, later used also for nobility, *in bono et in malo*, until the nineteenth century.[6] The Appendix identifies a small selection of relevant compositions, illustrated with musical examples.

With the romantic era, the historical model was no longer rationally recognized, due to the limitations of the immanent method. But occasionally

---

[3] With his *Ballet d'Alcidiane* LWV 9 of 1658 (Ex. 1) Lully first presented that type of overture which he maintained with little variation until his death. However, as Jérôme de LA GORCE surprisingly demonstrated, a rival, Louis de Mollier presented already in February of the previous year in the same theater a 'perfect' French overture with his *Ballet des plaisirs troublées*. Its introduction is "a first majestic section, written in duple time with dotted notes", etc. – '*Les plaisirs troublés' de Louis de Mollier*, «Revue inernationale d'études musicales», VIII/IX, 1996/97, pp. 172f. That Mollier had no success with this performance – surely due to the intrigues of Lully's party – is another story. Lully doubtless was victorious, though his paternity of the French overture is now less secure. Cf., however, below, pp. 235ff, the impulses from Classical antiquity.

[4] See below, p. 280 on Caldara's use of the French overture for the "re di Francia".

[5] Ernst Robert CURTIUS employed the term *topos* in his *Europäische Literatur und lateinisches Mittelalter*, Bern, Francke, 1948, as a convenient label for formulations that have become traditional carriers of meaning and rhetorical function. His book offered a wealth of such *topoi* and led to a totally new insight into the continuity of European literature. The method has since been applied to other disciplines, to music first with my monograph *Antonio Caldara: Sein Leben und seine venezianisch-römischen Oratorien*, Graz/Köln, Böhlau, 1966; cf. below, p. 592, note 25. I may mention that the use of the term has been criticized by students of systematic rhetoric as not being in agreement with late classical usage, where it means a reservoir of formulations, rather than the formulations themselves. But in empirical scholarship it can no longer be eradicated. After all, with the English 'commonplace' or the German 'Gemeinplatz' it has its own tradition of several centuries, though burdened with a derogatory accent since the nineteenth-century 'emancipation' from reason and the twentieth-century quest for originality at any price.

[6] My first paper on this topic (1969, see above) already found an echo: a few years later Christoph WOLFF argued that J. S. Bach, in the aria "Es ist vollbracht" in the St. John Passion, used French style as a "conventional *topos* of royal dignity (Christ deceases as king) in this stylized, 'perverse' overture", without mentioning here any modern author. Also his two words "conventional *topos*" are not too well chosen, since they form a pleonasm – *Towards a Methodology of Dialectic Style Considerations*, International Musicological Society, *Report of the Eleventh Congress, Copenhagen, 1972*, Copenhagen, Hansen, 1974, I, 79.

it was perceived on a psychological level, thus by Schweitzer, who assembled examples of J. S. Bach's use of dotted rhythm which "arouses in every musical person the feeling of the solemn; it is found in the *grave* movement of the French overture with the same meaning as in the grail scene in *Parsifal*" (here the premise of a timeless symbolism);[7] or by Abert, who in Mozart's "Rex tremendae majestatis" (Ex. 26) saw "the Lord in all his dark [!] majesty".[8]

I shall attempt to show that the stylistic components of the *topos* had at least three deep roots.

1. SLOW TEMPO AS AN ATTRIBUTE OF 'MAJESTY'

The tempo of the first movement of the French overture and its descendents is normally 'grave' or 'maestoso'. Research on such terminology[9] lists also minor variants of the instrumental type and provides an acceptable answer to the question of how fast the music is to be played. But the full range of meaning in these headings is hardly touched with a quick solution of the technical problem (performance practice). In tracing the history of the concept we reach layers of much deeper human concern – etiquette, ethics, concepts of God – and these, in turn, can enlighten the problem of tempo considerably.

Sébastien de Brossard, his *Dictionnaire de musique*,[10] treated 'grave' and 'maestoso' more or less as synonyms:

GRAVE. Adverbe. Veut dire, qu'il faut battre la mesure & chanter ou jouer gravement, posément, avec majesté, & par conséquent presque toujôurs lentement ...
MAESTOSO ... veut dire, d'une manière majesteuse, pompeuse, emphatique, etc. & par conséquent gravement & lentement, quoy qu'avec une expression vive et bien marquée.

GRAVE. Adverb. Means that it is necessary to beat time and to sing or play slowly, deliberately, with majesty, and consequently almost always slowly ...
MAESTOSO. ... means in a majestic manner, pompous, emphatic, etc. and consequently slowly, with a lively expression and well marked.

He was by no means alone. Since the Middle Ages French dictionaries and literature likewise mention the two as twins.[11] Antoine Furetière preserves

---

[7] Albert SCHWEITZER, *J. S. Bach*, Leipzig, Breitkopf & Härtel, 1909, pp. 484f.

[8] Hermann ABERT, *W. A. Mozart*, II, *ibid.*, 1921, p. 868.

[9] E.g. Irmgard HERMANN-BENGEN, *Tempo-Bezeichnungen: Ursprung, Wandel im 17. und 18. Jahrhundert*, Tutzing, Schneider, 1959, pp. 105ff *et passim.*

[10] Paris, Ballard, 1703, s.v.

[11] Walther von WARTBURG, *Französisches etymologisches Wörterbuch*, Basel, Zbinden, etc., IV,

even the original connection of the figurative meaning with the literal, the motion of the body:[12]

Grave, se dit figurativement en morale de ce qui est majesteux, sérieux, posé, comme si c'estoit un corps pesant & qui eust de la peine à se remuer. Les princes, les prélats, les magistrats doivent estre *graves*.	One says figuratively 'grave' in ethics for him who is majestic, serious, deliberate, as if he were a heavy body which has difficulty moving. Princes, prelates, magistrates must be grave.

Or, in poetry, again on gravity as a majestic, regal attitude by Pierre Ronsard: "The race of kings walked with gravity [i.e. very slowly] in the midst of its troop".[13] Gravity belonged to the sovereign, it was unbearable when assumed by the average mortal. But the Enlightenment brought with it a radical blow to the attitude of gravity and exposed the pretender to fatal ridicule, already embodied in the comic figure of Pantalone, who is "sempre parte grave".[14] The word *gravis* had, of course, belonged since antiquity to the common stock of rhetoric, which had entered other disciplines (philology, poetry, art, music). Some rhetoricians used this word as the name of the most serious of the three *genera dicendi*, synonymously with '*grande*' or '*sublime*'.[15] The retention of this usage for many centuries merely codified what was still a living form of human conduct. Gravity was always prescribed in kings' mirrors (*specula principum*), the traditional collections of maxims on a ruler's virtues and vices compiled by high-ranking educators. (Also the protocols of royal entries belong within this wider frame). The phenomenon of the *genus grave* in the French theatrical exordium indeed comes straight out of rhetoric, where it

1952, pp. 264ff, on the early derivations from the Latin 'gravis'; VI, 1969, p. 54, the following definitions of 'majesty' linked with *gravitas*: "AFr. *majestement* adv. gravement"; "MFr. *maestatique* adj. ... plein d'une gravité imposante"; "NFr. *majestueux* adj. (personne) dont la tenue ou les actions sont pleines d'une gravité imposante". Also Emile LITTRÉ, *Dictionnaire de la langue française*, II, Paris, Hachette, 1873, pp. 1923f, 'grave'; Paul ROBERT, *Dictionnaire alphabétique et analogique de la langue française*, IV, Paris, Robert, 1985, pp. 1031f; Edmond HUGUET, *Dictionnaire de la langue française du seizième siècle*, IV, Paris, Didier, 1950, pp. 364f. Cf. also Charles DU CANGE, *Glossarium Mediae et Infimae Latinitatis*, IV, Niore, Favre, 1885, p. 108, on medieval instances of *gravitas* as honor or "titulus honorarius"; *Thesaurus Linguae Latinae*, VI, Leipzig, Teubner, 1934, pp. 2272ff, "in sensu translato": "auctoritate".

12 *Dictionnaire universel*, The Hague, Leers, 1690, II, 197.

13 "Elle race des rois marchoit en gravité / Au milieu de sa troupe" – "Charité", in *Les œuvres*, Paris, Buon, 1584, p. 267.

14 Piermaria CECCHINI, *Frutti delle moderne comedie*, Padua, Guareschi, 1628, p. 25. "Une gravité étudiée devient comique" – FURETIÈRE, *loc. cit.*

15 Thus Isidor of Seville and still René Bary (1659) – Heinrich LAUSBERG, *Handbuch der literarischen Rhetorik*, Munich, Hueber, 1973², I, 522f.

was associated especially with the orators' exordium.[16] I should like to illustrate 'gravity' in some detail with these kings' mirrors, the more so as scholarly
literature has largely bypassed them.

Age-old etiquette had prescribed that the ruler *in officio* move with the
greatest possible calm. When King James[17] advised his "dear sonne Henry"
in his famous *Basilikon Doron* (1599): "[look] gravely and with a maiestie
when yee sit in judgement, or give audience to embassadours",[18] he echoed
a tradition that, two millennia earlier, made Isocrates [?] say in the mirror
for the young king Nicocles of Cyprus: "Be thou sene to have such wisedome
and gravitee, that nothyng that is done can be hid from thee".[19] Gravity was
but the outer shell of that inner attitude – tranquillity, constancy, amidst the
adverse forces of the outer and inner world, mastery over the passions, meaning freedom and true nobility. The Stoics had postulated it as their principal
dogma.[20] The sage must be without πάθη. Or, as Cicero says, those men in the
highest office (i.e. the sage, in other cultures also the king, the judge) must be
"moreover, totally free from confusion (*perturbatio*), cupidity, fear, then also
too much grief, sensual pleasure, and wrath, so that tranquillity of the mind
and security is [*sic*] present, which brings both constancy and dignity" (*De
officiis* I.xx.69).[21] Since it harboured also perfect reason,[22] *tranquillitas* represented the arrival and fulfilment of all virtue; and if this was so, then man
must be similar to God. And since God is the immutable ground of being,

---

[16] Cf. above, p. 71, note 180: the exordium was not only "grave", but also associated with "majesty" (Daniel Barbaro, 1557).

[17] Still James VI of Scotland, becoming also James I of England only with the death of Elizabeth in 1603.

[18] *Workes*, London, Barker & Bill, 1616, p. 184; marginal gloss: "Arist. 4. eth., Cic. ad At[ti-
cum]". *ΒΑΣΙΛΙΚΟΝ ΛΩΡΟΝ sive Regia Institutio*, London, Norton, 1604, p. 120: "Cum pro tribu-
nali sedeas, aut publicos legatos audias, cum maiestate gravitas".

[19] *The Doctrinal of Princes made by the Noble Oratour Isocrates* [ca. 374 B.C.] *translated out of
Greke into Englishe by Syr Thomas Eliot*, London, Berthelet, 1534, f. 9v, possibly added by Eliot.

[20] Under stoic influence were written such important works as Cicero's *Tusculanae disputationes* and *De officiis*, Seneca's *De tranquillitate animi* and *De clementis*, Plutarch's *De tranquillitate
animi* and *Ad principem ineruditum*. Seneca's last named work was the first *speculum principum*, in
Latin, for Nero. On stoic thought cf. Friedrich UEBERWEG, *Grundzüge der Geschichte der Philosophie*, I, Basel, Schwabe, 1953[13]; Max POHLENZ, *Die Stoa: Geschichte einer geistigen Bewegung*, Göttingen, Vandenhoeck & Ruprecht, 1948-49; Denise CARABIN, *Les idées stoïciennes dans la littérature
morale des XVIe et XVIIe siècles (1575-1642)*, Paris, Champion, 2004; for *tranquillitas*, in the Hellenistic world, cf. *Paulys Real-Encyclopädie der classischen Altertumswissenschaft*, zweite Reihe, XII,
Stuttgart, Metzler, 1937, col. 2138f.

[21] "Vacandum autem omni est animi perturbatione, cum cupidate et metus, tum etiam aegri-
tudine et voluptate nimia, et iracundia, ut tranquillitas animi et securitas adsit, quae affert cum con-
stantiam, tum etiam dignitatem".

[22] "Recta ratio", *Tusc. disp.* IV.xv.34.

He himself is virtue. Tranquillity, then, made the sage memorable, the king truly regal.[23]

Divine calm had of course been a facet of the image of the king in ancient cultures far beyond Greece and Rome. The Persian king of kings, at official receptions, was never seen except seated and motionless, like those sacred Egyptian statues of old. Jewish history, on the other hand, seemed largely dominated by the passionate and angry God;[24] but Jewish thought did not deviate from the belief that God's wisdom, God's council were immovable, and likewise the sage, i.e. the king or judge *in abstracto*. In mythical dawn stood Moses, holding the first of all sets of king's mirrors in ancient history, prototype of the royal judge (up to Bossuet): "that he turn not aside from the commandment, to the right hand, or to the left" (*Deut.* 17:20). The magnificent address to the divine judge: "But you, lord of virtues, judge with tranquillity" (*Wisdom* 12:18) is matched by other passages in the psalms and the [pseudo-]Salomonic books when they speak of the constancy and tranquillity of the just and the sage, or of the stability of a just king's throne.[25] What if the king's disposition changed? I know of no literary passage that foreshadows the catastrophe of king and country as dramatically as the story of Belshazzar:[26]

[there] came forth fingers of a man's hand, and wrote ... upon the plaster of the wall of the king's palace: and the king saw part of the hand that wrote. ... Then the king's countenance was changed (*facies regis commutata est*), and his thoughts troubled him, so that the joints of his loins were loosed and his knees smote one against the other. [When he called in the wise men who could not interpret the characters:] then was the king Belshazzar greatly troubled, and his countenance was changed in him, and his lords were astonished. Now the queen ... came into the banquet house: and the queen spake and said, 'O king, live for ever: let not thy thoughts trouble thee, nor let thy countenance be changed'.

That the king's countenance indeed could change meant at all times to the people revolution, or worse, destruction. In other words, the king's disposition affected directly the well-being of his subjects. It is here, on the cosmic stage, that the antithesis *tranquillitas/tempestas* could reasume, with its metaphorical sense, full powers over the very surface of the earth, as harbinger of

---

[23] René-Antoine GAUTHIER, *Magnanimité: L'idéal de la grandeur dans la philosophie païenne et dans la théologie chrétienne*, Paris, Vrin, 1951, pp. 138ff, 160, 172, *et passim.*

[24] Max POHLENZ, *Vom Zorn Gottes: Eine Studie über den Einfluß der griechischen Philosophie auf das alte Christentum*, Göttingen, Vandenhoeck & Ruprecht, 1909, pp. 1, 8, *et passim.*

[25] Ps. 112:6f; *Prov.* 4:26f, 10:25, 29:14; *Wisdom* 5:1.

[26] *Daniel* 5:5f, 9f.

peace or devastation. Three evangelists gave a well known, unique example with Christ rescuing the apostles on the wildly agitated sea of Genesareth: "and there was a great calm" (*tranquillitas magna* – Matth. 8:26, Mark 4:39, Luke 8:24). Or St. Paul's request to pray "for the kings and for all who are in the highest authority; that we may lead a quiet and peaceable life" (1 *Timothy* 2:2). Though among philosophers, the supremacy of *tranquillitas* could still be a matter of dispute – and stoic *tranquillitas* was certainly not altogether without arrogance, at times reduced to mere decorum – for statesmen it was a dire necessity.[27] How people rejoiced when seeing their ruler move with divine calm can be seen from the (by now famous) description of the entry of Constantine II into Rome, A.D. 357, full of praise for his immobility.[28] In Rome, 'Tranquillus' and 'Serenus' became imperial titles.

Studies on the esoteric ideals of humanism have assumed that with the decline of antiquity *tranquillitas* lost its ground and finally disappeared, and that in the Renaissance the new cult of tranquillity and all that it implies was based on pagan moralistic writings. Yet Petrarch or Erasmus did not have to cross a vast a gulf of ignorance to reach the shores of original stoic writings in order to find the idea. Stoic thought lived on among the hellenized Jews and into the Christian era, pervading the theology of the Greek and later Latin Fathers.

The Christian "immobilitas et tranquillitas animi" (Cassian) now surpassed infinitely the stoic assimilation of an unnamed *ratio*, for it coincides with the revealed kingdom of God, the *pax Christi*. *Apatheia*, the absence of passion, appeared as the only frame of mind that guaranteed a virtuous life (Justinian, Tatian, Clement of Alexandria, etc.), that allowed man to envision God, to become similar to Him.[29] While it was still disputed whether this could be achieved within human life (Cyprian: yes), whether it had characterized the man Jesus (Clement: yes), and whether the total extermination of passion would be desirable (Augustine: no), there was no doubt from the fourth century on that Christ the *logos* and God the Father are without πάθη.[30] And tranquillity was not merely the bastion of monastic asceti-

[27] CICERO, *De off.* I.xx.69, I.xxi.72.

[28] AMMIANUS MARCELLINUS, *Rerum gestarum libri qui supersunt*, Berlin, Weidmann, 1910-15, I, 86.

[29] Cf. Marie J. ROUËT DE JOURNEL, *Enchiridion Asceticum*, Freiburg, Herder, 1936, index, under *apatheia, impassibilitas, pax animae, tranquillitas*, etc.; Michel SPANNEUT, *Le stoïcisme des pères de l'église*, Paris, Seuil, 1957², pp. 242, 248ff, 291ff *et passim*; 'Apatheia', in *Reallexikon für Antike und Christentum*, I, Stuttgart, Hiersemann, 1950, col. 484-487.

[30] *Op. cit.*, I, 486; POHLENZ, pp. 16ff and especially 57ff; also a Protestant, John Kenneth MOZLEY, *The Impassibility of God*, Cambridge UP, 1936, pp. 104-126. JOANNES CLIMACUS (6th c.) saw tranquillity as the penultimate of the thirty steps in the *scala paradisi* of Jacob's dream (P.G. LXXXVIII, 632-1161); but he is only one of many authors who were involved with the subject of *tranquillitas* – see above, DE JOURNEL. The *Nachleben* of his vision in visual art is now well known through John Rupert MARTIN, *The Illustration of the Heavenly Ladder of John Climacus*, Princeton UP, 1954.

cism – it was carried on vigorously throughout the Middle Ages within the strong and uninterrupted, though by nature isolated, tradition of the kings' mirrors, as the core of royal ethics. In Carolingian and later mirrors, this Christian version reappears in classical metaphors. King Louis of Aquitania is advised by the abbot Smaragdus in *Via regia* (ca. 800-814): "with peace arrange what must be arranged, and with tranquillity reign what must be reigned".[31] The erudite Sedulius Scotus, in his *Liber de Rectoribus Christianis* for Lothar II (before 840) weds the pagan *topoi* securely to Christian service. "Let the prudent ruler strive to stabilize his heart in God's grace"[32] if he wishes his transitorial reign to be stable. In Hincmar's treatise *De regis persona et regio ministerio* (before 877) for Charles the Bald, "serenitas maris" is the age-old epithet of the king's justice.[33] Alanus de Insulis, in chapter 42, *Ad principes et judices*, of his *Summa de arte praedicatoria* requires that the king regulate in his body ("in terra corporis sui") the "diversities of three motions: the motion of reason, of the senses, of the flesh; and thus the prince must labor for peace of the material world, i.e. in order to observe the tranquillity of peace".[34] Tranquillity of the mind is no less essential to Hugo of St. Victoire's famous catalogue of virtues and vices, *De fructibus carnis et spiritus*: "fortitude is immobile, its companions are peace, stability, constancy"; "constancy has a dignified, eternal, unmoved mode of life"; "peace is tranquillity of spirits regulated according to the good", etc.[35] In the important *Polycraticus* of John of Salisbury (1159)[36] we read instructions for the king's 'grave' deportment in public (see below); the concept of tranquillity is permeated with Stoic thought, earthly good vs. heavenly good is equated to mobility vs. immobility, or rather, slowest motion. *De principis instructione* of Giraldus Cambrensis, completed 1217, against the sons of Henry II, imitates John when he says that as the glory of God the father is "wise", so "the glory of the prince is peace of the subjects and tranquillity".[37] The *Liber de regimine civitatum* of John of Viterbo (before 1228) speaks wholly with a Ciceronian tongue: tranquillity and serenity as carriers not only of constancy, but also of dignity – the by now well known dictum from Cicero's *De officiis* (see above), quoted here in full in a king's mirror.[38] Guibert of

---

[31] "cum pace dispone, quae disponenda sunt, et cum tranquillitate rege, quae regendae sunt" – P.L. CII, 964A.

[32] "cor suum in Excelsi gratia stabilire studeat" – P.L. CIII, 297D-298A.

[33] P.L. CXXV, 836A.

[34] "rex debet ordinare trium motuum diversitates. Motus rationis, ... motus sensualitatis, ... motus carnis. ... Et sicut ad pacem terrae materialis laborare decet principum, id est ad observandum pacis tranquillitatem" – P.L. CCX, 188D.

[35] "Fortitudo est immobilis. ... Cujus comites sunt ... requies, stabilitas, constantia"; "Constantia ... status suo dignus, perpetuus, et immotus vitae tenor"; "Pax est concordantium in bono animorum ordinata tranquillitas" – P.L. CLXXVI, 1003B-C, 1004D.

[36] P.L. CIC, 379-822.

[37] "principis gloria est pax subditorum et tranquillitas" – London, Her Majesty's Stationery Office, 1891, p. 51.

[38] *Bibliotheca Juridica Medii Aevi*, III, Bologna, Soc. Azzoguidoniana, 1901, p. 220.

Tournai, chaplan of Louis the Saint, King of France, advises in his *Eruditio regum et principum* (1259) that "the sitting [king must have] serenity, the throne, stability"; as a judge he must be "immutable and tranquil". Is it not characteristic of a great mind to be "quiet and tranquil"?[39] Here, as in the writings of John of Salisbury a hundred years earlier, the mental behavior is shared also by the physical: "Who always appears serene, affable in his speech, of easy access, amiable in his features, undisturbed in his mind?"[40] When the ruler has this disposition "neither time may change, power mutilate, necessity break up, nor insolence trample". The unspoiled *habitus* of virtues stipulates "tranquillity of heart, quickness of work, and serenity of countenance".[41] Kings' mirrors by Vincent of Beauvais († 1264) appear around 1250. In his *De eruditione filiorum nobilium* the prince must persuade himself to maintain equinamity,[42] or in *Speculum doctrinale*, vastly extended "according to the philosophers": "patience is a virtue of mind sustaining with tranquillity all attacks of adversity".[43]

This may suffice to fill the 'gap' from late antiquity to Petrarch. Two metaphors may be added: they too show that this 'inner' attitude is always understood as very slow motion. The king's bearing is the "golden mean" (*aurea mediocritas*), that infinitely fine point where the pendulum of the passions nearly comes to rest between too little and too much virtue (each a vice). It is ultimate mastery of the art of living, e.g. according to Hincmar.[44] The king was also often compared to the sun (see below, p. 245) reaching its zenith, approaching almost a standstill, thus by Erasmus of Rotterdam – leaning on Plutarch's authority – in his *Institutio principis Christiani*:[45]

Deus, ut pulcherrimum sui simulacrum in coelo constituit in solem, ita inter homines evidentem ac vivam sui collocavit imaginem regem. ... Deus, cum nullis tangatur affectibus, tamen optime mun-	God placed a most beautiful likeness of himself in the heavens – the sun. So among men He set up a visible and living image of himself – the king. ... Though God is touched by no emotions, yet He

[39] "ad sedentem serenitas, ad sedem stabilitas", "immutabile et tranquillum", "placidum et tranquillum" – Louvain, Université, 1914, pp. 73, 85.

[40] "Qui sermone affabilis, accessu facilis, vultu amabilis, animo imperturbato, serenus semper apparet?" – p. 85.

[41] "nec tempus immutet, nec potentia mutilet, nec necessitas rumpet, nec insolentia exculceret"; "cordis tranquillitas, operis alacritas, et serenitas vultus" – p. 89.

[42] "inter pressuras ac turbines mundi equo animo manere" – Cambridge MA, Mediaeval Academy of America, 1938, p. 68.

[43] "Patientia est virtus animi, cunctus adversitatis impetus, cum tranquillitate sustinens" – *Bibliotheca mundi seu Speculi maioris ... tomus secundus*, Douai, Belleri, 1624, col. 344. Cf. further chapters "De constantia", "De stabilitate animi", "De securitate mentis, et requie", col. 347ff.

[44] P.L. CXXV, 837B. Or JOHN OF SALISBURY, P.L. CXC, 560D, and GUIBERT OF TOURNAI, p. 37.

[45] Venice, Aldus, 1518, ff. 49*v*-50.

dum administrat iudicio. Ad huius exemplum princeps in omnibus, quae gerit, exclusis animi motibus. ... Sol cum altissime provectus est in zodiaco, tum tardissimi motus est, ita quo fortuna te subvexerit altius, hoc oportet animo leniori minusque feroci esse.

rules the universe very well with judgement. The prince [should follow] His example in all his actions, excluding motions of the mind. ... When the sun is at the highest point in the zodiac, then its motion is slowest, so the higher fortune carried you, the milder and less fierce you should be.

Needless to say, gravity was the (once more) outer attitude, e.g. in the cult of the Byzantine emperors who, for many centuries, were the 'slowest' of all mortal beings, then imitated by the Ottonian emperors (see below, p. 244). Or Walther von der Vogelweide, when he could sing to princes: "Let yourselves be seen in dignity".[46] Or in chess, which came from the east to the west around the eleventh century: the king moves in all directions, but he can do so just by one step, thus he is the slowest of all figures.[47] Petrarch resumes the written tradition for *gravitas*, now using heavily stoic thought for the outer deportment: "grace in gesture, ... slowness in laughter, ... gravity in gait".[48] And Francesco Patrizi (1413-92), *Il sacro regno*:[49]

L'equanimità è una certa purezza, e stabilità de l'animo. ... Cotal virtù fu in Socrate, che sempre si vide d'una medesima volontà e fermezza d'anima, non essendo cosa alcuna ... che potesse cavare la sua natura, di modo che ... noi potremmo chiamare stabilità d'animo, la qual molti latini hanno chiamato tranquillità d'animo, e quegli, in cui ella siede, tranquilli: come fu Antonio Cesare, che, essendosi dato a la disciplina de gli Stoici, fu tanto tranquillo, che nessuno mai lo vide una volta, che egli havesse la faccia mutata in modo che vi fusse nessuna differenza da una volta a l'altra. ... Dicono, che [Socrate] sempre stava in

Equinamity is a certain purity and stability of the mind. ... Such a virtue was [found] in Socrates, who was always seen in the same will and firmness of mind, there not being anything which could disturb his nature, so that ... we could call stability of mind, which many Latins have called tranquillity of mind, and those who possess it are tranquil, as was Antonius Caesar, who, having dedicated himself to the discipline of the stoics, was so calm that no one ever saw him to have changed his features so as to make any difference from one time to another. ... They say that he [Socrates] was always in the same being, and

---

[46] "Ir fürsten ... Lât in wirde iuch schouwen", *Gedichte*, Berlin, De Gruyter, 1965, p. 48.

[47] In chess, each of the figures is "en lieu & degré, qu'il convient à son estat" ["in the place and degree which belongs to his rank"] – LOUIS XI (1423-83), *Le rosier des guerres*, Paris, Buon, 1616, p. 8.

[48] "Sit in gestu decor, ... in risu tarditas, ... gravitas in incessu" – second epistle to Nicolò Acciaiolo of Sicily, 1350, *Epistolae de rebus familiaribus et variae*, Florence, Le Monnier, 1862, p. 169.

[49] Venice, Trino, 1547, ff. 131*v*-132.

un medesimo essere, e che mai fu nessuno che gli vedesse mutar color, o faccia
per cagione di perturbatione.

there was never anyone who saw him
change color or facial expression because
of perturbation.

Or Louis XI of France, in *Le rosier des guerres* for his son the Dauphin: "A
man is thus just to prepare peace and tranquillity".[50] Further Erasmus in *Institutio principis* (margin: "True majesty"): "The dignity, grandeur, majesty of
the prince is to be furnished and cultivated not with the noise of fortune, but
with wisdom, integrity, and proper form".[51] And Sir Thomas Eliot, *The Boke
named The Gouvernour*: "In a gouvernour ... the fountaine of all excellent
maners is Maiestie; which is the holle proportion and figure of noble estate,
and is properlie a beautie or comlynesse in his countenance, language and gesture apt to his dignite".[52] Guillaume Budé, *De l'institution du prince* (before
1540), advised François I of France:[53]

Tous Roys sont tenuz (pour conserver la
grandeur & la renommée de leur maiesté) de se maintenir, abstenir, & garder
une certaine contenance bien mesurée.
... [Le roi] ensemble la grace, la maiesté,
le regard plein d'authorité, & sa contenance remplye de gravité. ... Maiesté est
une ample dignité d'estime & de reputation acquise non seulement par grande
puissance & authorité: mais aussy par
gravité & constance.

All kings are obliged (in order to preserve
the grandeur and reputation of their majesty) to maintain themselves, to abstain,
and to keep a certain well measured countenance. ... [The king] unites grace, majesty, the full respect for authority, and
fills his countenance with gravity. ... Majesty is an ample dignity of esteem and
of reputation acquired not only through
great power and authority, but also
through gravity and constancy.

Or Marc'Antonio Natta († 1568): the prince should be "of the greatest gravity
and wisdom";[54] Hieronymus Osorius: "with grace and dignity of mind and
gravity and constancy of virtue";[55] Justus Lipsius: "greatness and gravity of
the highest fortune",[56] or, on Emperor Charles V in great danger: "neither

[50] "Homme est juste ainsi pour aparailler paix et tranquillité" – *ed. cit.*, p. 15.

[51] (Margin: "Vera maiestas"): "Principis dignitatem, amplitudinem, maiestatem, non fortunae
strepitu, sed sapientia, integritate, recte factis, parandam & tuendam esse" – f. 43*v*.

[52] London, Berthelet, 1531, II, 12.

[53] Paris, Nicole, 1547, pp. 40, 79, 154. Cf. also Sebastian FOX MORCILLO, *De regni regisque institutione libri III*, Antwerp, Spelmann, 1556, sig. T4*v*-T5.

[54] "summa gravitate & sapientia" – *De principum doctrina*, Frankfurt, Palthenio, 1603, p. 202.

[55] "in anima decore atque dignitate, & in vitutis constantia & gravitate" – *De regis institutione
et disciplina*, Olysippone, Gondisalvus, 1571, f. 11.

[56] "magnitudinem et gravitatem summae fortunae" – *Politicorum sive civilis doctrinae libri sex
qui ad principatum maxime spectant*, Lyons, Raphelengius, 1589, p. 68. This most influential work
was dedicated to the emperor, kings, and princes of Europe.

his posture nor his countenance changed, ... this constancy, and gravity of his manners and actions ...";[57] Ottavio Durante, *Il prencipe virtuoso*: "he must show some gravity and severity ... the power and majesty of his commands, remaining always immutabile";[58] Andrea Mendo, *Il principe perfetto*: "men change, God does not".[59] In short, at the beginning of the seventeenth century neo-stoic ideas had now reached wide circles, mainly through the books of Justus Lipsius (with 75 editions his *De constantia* was a bestseller of the *ancien régime*). After the dreadful decades of the Huguenot wars, gravity, if not tranquillity, became the social sign of aristocracy. The German poet Paul Fleming (1609-40) summed it up very clearly when he said: "the higher one's rank, the more slowly he moves".[60] A musical movement which was headed "grave" or "maestoso" then reflected the ideal movement of the ruler, and such movement was very slow.

2. DOTTED RHYTHM AS NATIONAL ELEMENT – PAEAN FOR PRAISE AND HEALING/ SALVATION

Between ca. 1650 and 1750 anything French east of the Rhine meant first of all social distinction or pretension. We may not all be aware that well into Goethe's childhood few 'people of quality' spoke or wrote German at all. It was not yet a literary language.[61] Anyone of noble birth or taste used French. Klopstock's *Messias* and Lessing's early works had to be translated into French to find readers.[62] Herder characterized the social gap:[63]

Mit wem man Deutsch sprach, der war ein Knecht, ein Diener. Dadurch also hat die Deutsche Sprache nicht nur den wichtig-	He with whom one spoke German was a menial, a servant. Thus the German language lost not only the most important

---

[57] "nec statum, nec vultum mutavit, ... haec constantia, & morum actionumque gravitas" – *id.*, *Monita et exempla politica qui virtutes et vitia principum spectant*, Antwerp, Moretes, 1605, p. 57; also p. 188, on majesty. The book contains many chapters on *constantia, tranquillitas, modestia, maiestas*.

[58] "è necessario ch'egli mostri qualche gravità e severità, ...la potenza e la maestà de' suoi commandamenti, restando sempre immutabile" – Viterbo, Disceplo, 1614, p. 470.

[59] "si mutano gli uomini, Dio ... non si cambia ..." – Salamanca, Cosio, 1657, p. 10.

[60] "Je höher einer ist vom Stande, je langsamer bewegt er sich" – *Paul Flemings deutsche Gedichte*, Stuttgart, Litt. Verein, 1865, p. 411. Cf. Werner WELZIG, *Constantia und barocke Beständigkeit*, «Deutsche Vierteljahrsschrift für Literaturwissenschaft und Geistesgeschichte», XXXV, 1961, p. 426.

[61] Gottsched's fiancée wrote: "Rien n'est plus plébéian que de se servir de l'allemand dans sa correspondence" ["Nothing is more plebian than to use German in one's correspondence"] – Louis RÉAU, *L'Europe française au siècle des lumières*, Paris, Michel, 1938, p. 45.

[62] *Loc. cit.*

[63] Johann Gottfried HERDER, *Briefe zur Beförderung der Humanität* (1793-97), in *Werke*, VII, Frankfurt, Deutscher Klassiker Verlag, 1991, p. 306.

sten Teil ihres Publikums verloren, sondern die Stände selbst haben sich derge-
stalt in ihre Denkart entzweiet, daß ihnen
gleichsam ein *zutrauliches gemeinschaftli-*
ches Organ ihrer innigsten Gefühle fehlt.

part of its audience, but the social classes
revealed themselves so divided in their
thinking that they lack as it were a familiar organ in common for their most in-
ward feelings.

Or Voltaire, on 1 August 1750 from Potsdam: "Here I am in France. Only
our language is spoken. German is for the soldiers and the horses; it is not
needed except on the road".[64] Also composers, when portraying high society,
resorted, most naturally, to 'French' style (*alla francese*), particularly the
dotted rhythm. Lully himself imposed this rhythm with an iron will on his orchestra from the podium with an enormous staff, which he always struck on
the ground to beat time, until he wounded himself in so doing and died within a few weeks. As is also well known, he used extensively in his overtures also
the *tirada*, often a long note followed by three short ones or vice versa: "These
upbeat flourishes ... are found in many opening sections and were often performed even where not written. They herald the downbeats with an elegance
perfectly suited to the court of Louis XIV".[65] Yet music theorists knew that
this *tirada* is a genuine paean (Dorian παιάν, Lat. *paean*), a poetic foot (*pes*)
which Aristotle and Cicero had already described, in two versions: – *v v v*
used for beginnings and *v v v* – for endings.[66] In late antiquity there were
four, thus in Quintilian, although he explicitly states that only the two from
the Aristotelian tradition were important (IX.iv.47, 89, 96).

When the transfer of verse feet to musical feet took place[67] – long before
Lully – need not concern us here. The paean is mentioned as a rhythmic foot
by such theorists as Francisco Salinas[68] or Marin Mersenne.[69] The eighteenth
century may be represented by Johann Mattheson:[70]

---

[64] "Je me trouve ici en France. On ne parle que notre langue. L'allemand est pour les soldats et
pour les chevaux; il n'est nécessaire que pour route" – *Correspondance*, III, Paris, Gallimard, 1975,
p. 262.

[65] NG² IX, 233.

[66] ARISTOTLE, *Ars rhetorica*, III, 1409a; CICERO, *De oratore*, III.xlvii.183.

[67] Cf. the thorough article 'Rhythmus/numerus' by Wilhelm SEIDEL, in the *Handwörterbuch der
musikalischen Terminologie*, Stuttgart, Steiner, 1980.

[68] *De Musica libri septem*, Salamanca, Gastius, 1577, p. 252.

[69] *Harmonie universelle*, Paris, Cramoisy, 1636-37, *Traitez de la voix et des chants*, p. 179.

[70] *Der vollkommene Capellmeister*, Hamburg, Herold, 1739, pp. 168f (with the four versions in
the same arrangement as Salinas and Mersenne, where the position of the long syllable determines
the numbering). Mattheson asserts, p. 160, that he used the book of "Gerhard-Johann Vossius". But
since this famous work is by the latter's son, Isaac VOSSIUS [*De poematum cantu et viribus rhythmi*,
Oxford, Scot, 1673], the German theorist surely never had it in his hands, but was boasting again.
Nor does the book deal with four-syllable feet (paean).

§ 35. Viersylbige Klang-Füsse

13) Pæon, der erste, – v v v. Von παιών, *hymnus*, weil er den Lobgesängen gewidmet war. Uns dienet er in Ouvertüren und Entreen. Er bestehet aus einer langen und drey kurtzen Noten.

§ 36

14) Pæon, der andere, v – vv. Dessen erster Klang ist kurz, der zweite lang, und die beiden letzten sind wiederum kurtz.

§ 37

15) Pæon, der dritte, v v – v. Dessen beide ersten Klänge kurtz, der dritte lang, und der letzte kurtz.

§ 38

16) Pæon, der vierte, v v v –. Hat erst drey kurtze, und zuletzt einen langen Klang. Diese vier Paeones sind alle zu Lobgesängen gebraucht worden; taugen auch noch sehr wol dazu.

§ 35. Four-syllable feet

13) Pæon, the first, – v v v. From παιών, *hymnus*, because it was dedicated to songs of praise. It serves us in overtures and entrées. It consists of one long and three short notes.

§ 36

14) Pæon, the second, v – vv. Its first sound is short, the second long, and the two last are again short.

§ 37

15) Pæon, the third, v v – v. Its first two sounds are short, the third long, and the last short.

§ 38

16) Pæon, the fourth, v v v –. Has three short, and at the end a long sound. These four pæones are used for songs of praise, and are very useful for these.

From Quintilian it was known that rhetoricians praise the 'heroic' foot (dactyl) and the paean "most highly" (*maxime laudant*). Also, "feet should be mixed ..., taking care that most are pleasing" (*miscendi ... sunt, curandumque, ut sint plures qui placent* – IX.iv.89, 91).[71] But most important for Lully was the twofold distinction of Aristotle and Cicero and their assignment of the first paean to beginnings, hence now for overtures! Our composer must have read the ancient authors or at least listened attentively to counsel from learned members of the Académie de poesie et de musique or from pupils of Mersenne. In any case, his entrées were based on ancient models which were perfect for the royal concept.

The testimonies for the paean as hymn of praise and of supplication to a god, predominately one of healing, extend to the *Iliad*, where it is mentioned

71 Thomas J. MATHIESEN, *Apollo's Lyre: Greek Music and Music Theory in Antiquity and the Middle Ages*, Lincoln, Nebraska UP, 1999, pp. 36-58, presented several fragments of paean songs and indicated in detail their meter.

in four passages: once for Apollo, after the plague (I.473); then, without addressee (but, according to A. Blumenthal, possibly also for this god), after the
last battle (XXII.391ff);[72] both of these passages are translated by Wolfgang
Schadewaldt as "Heilsgesang", since a battle certainly represented life and
death. The other two instances, as a name of a god "Paeon" (Apollo?): Zeus
sent him as healer to Hades and again to Ares, both of whom were wounded
(V.401 and 899f). Whether "Paeon" here stands for Apollo or indeed for another god,[73] I am, of course, unable to determine. However, it is certain that
Apollo appeared already in Homer as 'Phoebus', who 'purified' from guilt
(*katharsis*), later conflated with 'Helios', the sun, who likewise dispells darkness – also the epithet 'paean' was applied to him almost as a title. Passages
refering to Paean, the 'healer', from poetry of Aeschylus, Sophocles, or
Euripides are still famous, above all the paeans of Pindar, surely all addressed
to Apollo,[74] although since the fifth century B.C. gods of his family assisted
him more and more in the function of healer. His son Asklepios seems to have
surpassed him in Epidauros and in Rome.[75] But even in the latter city the ves-
tal virgins invoked "Apollo Medice, Apollo Paean" (Macrobius, *Saturnalia*
I.xvii.15). Until imperial times there was only one temple of Apollo in Rome
(fifth century B.C.; three of its columns can still be seen, next to the Marcellus
theater, 13-11 B.C.). Also here the dedication was "Apollo medicus", after a
dreadful plague (Livy IV.xxv.3). And when Julius Caesar reported from Gaul
that the people there, as everywhere, prayed to Apollo to ward off sickness
("Apollinem morbos depellere", *De bello gallico* VI.17), this was only one
testimony among many.

Also in Christianity, of course, the sick appealled to higher powers for
miraculous healing. We know especially from the excellent research of Marc
Bloch[76] that only the kings of France and their English imitators had the
power to 'heal' by touch people afflicted by scrofula, a tubercular skin disease.
In both countries the earliest documents are from the twelfth century; but the
French very soon argued that their tradition extended back to King Clovis

---

[72] PAULY, XXXVI/1, 1942, col. 2341f.

[73] The latter interpretation has been presented by many philologists.

[74] Stephan SCHRÖDER, *Geschichte und Theorie der Gattung Paian*, Stuttgart/Leipzig, Teubner,
1999, p. 101, and Ian RUTHERFORD, *Pindar's Paeans: A Reading of the Fragments with a Survey of the
Genre*, Oxford UP, 2001, p. 153: "Pindar himself defined the paean as Apollon's genre" – both contrary to Lutz KÄPPEL, *Paian: Studien zur Geschichte einer Gattung*, Berlin, De Gruyter, 1992, and
'Paian', *Der Neue Pauly*, IX, Stuttgart, Metzler, 2000, col. 149.

[75] Karl KERÉNYI, *Der göttliche Arzt*, Basel, Ciba, 1948, and above, p. 191, note 264.

[76] *Les rois thaumaturges: études sur le caractère surnaturel attribué à la puissance royale particu-
lièrement en France et en Angleterre*, Strasbourg, Istra, 1924; also below, p. 249.

(† 511), who, according to legend, already possessed the oriflamme, the holy lilies, the holy ampulla with the chrism, etc.[77] That the kings also later, century by century, fulfilled the ceremony of healing can be assumed, though the sources are sparse. In any case, Louis XIV again attached much importance to it. Immediately after his consacration (Reims 1654, still a youngster) and then during the five major feasts of the ecclesiastical year he 'touched' the sick persons, saying "Dieu te guérit", and gave to each of them a ducat, often more than a thousand persons, occasionally more than 3,000. Shortly before his own death († 15 Sept. 1715), when he left his country in a most miserable condition, Louis 'healed' once again, 1700 persons.

In 1658, as surely in previous years, a poster was printed,[78] announcing the place and time of the event: at the Louvre on Holy Saturday. Only a few weeks earlier, on 14 February, Lully had performed his first overture with an 'Apollonian' paean in the very first measure (Ex. 1). That Apollo was the 'healer' since Homeric times and that for him the paean, the 'song of healing' was sung, was surely not forgotten by the learned advisors of Louis XIV. When the attributes of the sun and Apollo were specified for him, that of "puissance" was coupled with "bienfaisance".[79] The concept of healing/ health is still much alive in many European languages today for forms of address, e.g. "salve" (Latin, in Italy), "salut" (in France), or as attribute of Christ, "salvatore", "Heiland", etc.[80] Also Lully's paean can be understood as what it had been since antiquity, a "salutation" in the literal sense, now for the entry of the Sun King, who still had the mysterious power to 'heal'.

Did at least a few of the composers who adopted Lully's *topos* still know that 'paean' signified also 'healing'? Handel used this foot very frequently, already in Rome, when he, in the overture to his inaugural cantata, "Arresta il passo" HWV 83, saluted his new patron, Marquis Francesco Maria Ruspoli. And for the last cantata which he composed for him he appeared as 'Apollo' in a golden frock.[81] Handel, like J. S. Bach and many others, enjoyed a solid humanistic education, and his father was a prominent physician.

---

[77] Percy Ernst SCHRAMM, *Der König von Frankreich: das Wesen der Monarchie vom 9. bis zum 16. Jahrhundert*, Weimar, Böhlau, 1960, *passim*. Konrad HOFFMANN, *Taufsymbolik im mittelalterlichen Herrscherbild*, «Bonner Beiträge zur Kunstwissenschaft», IX, 1968, p. 12.

[78] Reproduced by BLOCH, fig. 5.

[79] Louis HAUTECŒUR, *Louis XIV Roi Soleil*, Paris, Plon, 1953, p. 3.

[80] The atrocious "Siegheil" and "Heil Hitler", however, show how a tradition can be abused.

[81] Cf. below pp. 401f and note 210.

3. MELODIC AND HARMONIC REGULARITY AND OTHER *VIRTUTES* AS ATTITUDE OF CLASSICISM

Long sequences of verbs, nouns, or other parts of speech would, according to Quintilian, create monotony (*taedium*); one should achieve as much variety as possible (IX.iv.43). But Plato had warned against beginning a musical piece with excessive "complexity or great variety"; "we must observe what are the rhythms of a life that is orderly and brave, and after observing them require the foot and the air to conform to that kind of man's speech and not the speech to the foot and the tune" (*Rep.* III.399E-400A). Thus rhythmic and melodic regularity were also a feature of French classicism. Lully seems intentionally to have avoided variety in the introductions to his overtures, favoring the more solemn ascent and/or descent, simple scales or triads. In Versailles this is the acoustical equivalent of the additive principle in floor and façade plan, the long, straight row of equal elements, as opposed to the Italo-Austrian taste for structures centering around the square, circle, or oval.[82] The analogy is legitimate, for we recognize here the far-reaching influence of the academies, as they brooded over the qualities and tasks of court style. Henri Testelin, Roger de Piles, and other theorists of art expressly demanded 'régularité' for the style of kings and gods. But art theory (and, in general, rhetoric) here only codified what kings' mirrors had postulated as a *live* deportment. Thus, in the century of Louis XIV, Ottavio Durante wrote in *Il principe virtuoso* (1614): the prince who wishes to regulate the state should first reform "everything irregular which he could have in his life and customs".[83] Or Pierre Le Moyne, *De l'art de regner* (1665): "going with measure, acting regularly, ... to distribute with equality, according to the order";[84] Besian Arroy, *Le prince instruit en la philosophie en françois* (1671): he should "pass the time not with precipitation or haste, but with equanimous patience";[85] Jean de La Bruyère, *Les caractères ou les mœurs de ce siècle* (1688): "a perfect equality of temperament";[86] Pierre Nicole (1625-95), *Essais*

---

[82] Also here we find musical analogies (Biber, Schmeltzer, Lotti, etc.): 'king', 'majesty', etc. tend to be set to triads, and not with dotted rhythm, but the older, plain, long notes; 'gloria' to *circulatio* figures – cf. above, p. 17, Exx. 26-29.

[83] "deve cominciare a regolar lo stato da se medesimo, riformando primieramente tutto quello che potesse haver d'irregolato nella sua vita e nei suoi costumi" – *op. cit.*, p. 468.

[84] "Mais allant de mesure, agissant reglément, ... partager avec égalité, selon l'ordre" – Paris, Cremoisy, 1665, p. 6.

[85] "passe le temps sans precipitation, sans haste, & avec une patience égale" – Lyons, Guilimin, 1671, p. 441.

[86] "une parfait égalité d'humeurs" – Paris, Michallet, 1865, I, 388.

de morale: "to lead a regulated life";[87] Jacques Bossuet (1627-1704), *Politique tirée de l'écriture sainte*, for the Dauphin, cites the bad example of King Saul, who "incurs all sorts of irregularity, inconstancy, inequality, bizarrerie, injustice".[88]

We may add other stylistic elements: the lack of *durezze*, the Italian expression for those dissonances which, in the sixteenth and seventeenth centuries, were played on the strong beat (suspended seconds, fourths, sevenths), since not harshness, but mildness (*clementia*) is a virtue of princes. Or the general magnificence of style, the 'pomp' (but see pp. 241f). As single elements, the various stylistic features can all be found elsewhere, far from the time and place discussed here. Only their sum made up the musical image that represented the king at Versailles as unambiguously as the sun in heraldic devices.

I have endevoured to demonstrate that with Lully's *grave* we have a royal, 'high' style in the sense of ancient rhetoric, the *genus grave*, adopted also for the *grande manière* of French painting of the time. Contemporary art theory was conscious of the similarity of methods and goals to those of music, for instance Antoine Coypel:[89]

Enfin chaque tableau doit avoir un mode qui le caractérise. L'harmonie en sera tantôt aigre et tantôt douce, tantôt triste et tantôt gaie, selon les différents caractères des sujets que l'on voudra représenter. On peut suive en cela l'art enchanteur de la musique. ... Il faut prendre, comme les musiciens, un mode qui convienne au sujet.	Finally, each picture must have a mode which charaacterizes it. The harmony will be sometimes shrill and sometimes mild, sometimes sad and sometimes gay, according to the different characters of the subjects which one wishes to depict. In this one can follow the enchanting art of music. ... It is necessary to take, like the musicians, a mode which fits the subject.

"Ut musica pictura" is for these artists as much an axiom as the famous "ut pictura poesis" of Horace had been throughout the age of humanism.[90]

This stylization now becomes understandable from the social function. Text and music in the royal theater had to fulfill the most distinguished task in view of the protocol at the beginning of a piece. The overture accompanied the king at his entrance, and immediately afterwards the prologue was heard.

---

[87] "a mener une vie reglée" – Paris, Desprez, 1730, I, 267.

[88] "entraîne toute sorte d'irrégularité, d'inconstance, d'inégalité, de bizarrerie, d'injustice" – *Oeuvres*, VII, Paris, Le Mercier etc., 1745, p. 378.

[89] *Sur l'esthétique du peintre* (1721), reprinted by Henry JOUIN, *Conférences de l'Académie royale de peinture et de sculpture*, Paris, Quantin, 1883, pp. 238, 301.

[90] Rensselaer W. LEE, *Ut pictura poesis: the Humanistic Theory of Painting*, «Art Bulletin», XXII, 1940, pp. 197-269.

Here the poet exalted the king's divinity. That Lully did not contribute less than the poet may be clear after that which has been said. He too made the initial movement of the overture an authentic apotheosis.

Here I may indicate briefly that also for the caricature of the good king, his antipode the tyrant, a musical *topos* developed: the presto, furioso tempo (the opposite of *grave*), the choleric, abrupt melodies sweeping up and down, the harmonic *durezze* in the arias of all tyrants and Lucifers in opera and oratorio of the baroque. One begins to understand all this if one knows that the bad ruler, in conformity with the tradition of the king's mirrors, is *imago diaboli*. He perverts all royal virtues. As a slave of his passions he is thrown back and forth. Not *tranquillitas, constantia* distinguish him, but *ira, malignitas, inconstantia*, etc. The "calm of the sea" (*serenitas maris*) is now the storm (*procellus, tempestas*), etc. The musical 'storm-topic' is indeed intimately related to the *topos* of the tyrant. Ancient literature already provided the images which became the librettists' cues for the composers. The tyrant is compared to the roaring lion (*Prov.* 19:2, 20:2, 28:15; *2 Timothy* 4:17; Seneca, *De clementia*, I.v.5), the fierce bear (*Prov.* 2:15), the ravenous wolf (*Ezekiel* 22:27, Plato *Rep.* 566A), etc. This vocabulary was retained from Jewish and Greek antiquity at least until the baroque emblems.[91] The tyrant's courtiers are the furies, and whenever they are invoked we can expect an infernal presto, full of large melodic leaps and tremolos (the antitype of *fortitudo*). I have observed only one change in the traditional wording of references to tyrants: in the second half of the seventeenth century the adjective 'pomposo', which until then had been characteristic for their clothing. The king of Persia often served as model.[92] In 1546 Sabba da Castiglione still mentioned this as a *topos*: "the pompous dress of the tyrant",[93] as older writers had done. But with the court of Versailles the rich vestments became essential to the representation of the

---

[91] Visual representations, in Arthur HENKEL and Albrecht SCHÖNE, *Emblemata: Handbuch zur Sinnbildkunst des XVI. und XVII. Jahrhunderts*, Stuttgart, Metzler, 1967, s.v. 'Tyrann', col. 1044f; also 'Bestien' ('Löwe', etc.). For the tyrant the literature is likewise vast, including almost all kings' mirrors. Cf. also Wilfrid PARSONS, *The Medieval Theory of the Tyrant*, «Review of Politics», IV, 1942, pp. 129-143; J. R. DUNKLE, *Study of the Rhetorical Tyrant in Rome of the First Century B.C.*, diss., U. of Pennsylvania, 1965. Regarding music of the renaissance, cf. Sabba da CASTIGLIONE, *Ricordi* [1546], Venice, Gherardi, 1555, ff. 58v-59: "perché l'animo turbato et afflitto ... non gustarebbe le armonie delle gerarchie celesti, non che li canti di Giustino, o di Motone o li suoni di Gioan Maria, et de gli altri eccellentissimi musici" ["because the mind disturbed and afflicted ... would not enjoy the harmonies of the celestial hierarchies, nor the songs of Josquin [?] or of [Jean] Mouton, or the instrumental music of Giovan Maria [da Crema] and the other most excellent musicians"].

[92] Cf. also Andreas ALFÖLDI, *Die Ausgestaltung des monarchischen Zeremoniells am römischen Kaiserhofe*, «Mitteilungen des Deutschen Archäologischen Instituts, römische Abt.», XLIX, 1934, pp. 9ff.

[93] "il pomposo vestire del tiranno" – f. 57v.

monarchy. A French writer insists, on many pages, that "pomps and riches are necessary for the great".[94] Bossuet had written more delicately, cautiously: "I do not call majesty the pomp which surrounds kings, nor the exterior lustre which dazzles the vulgar. This is but the reflection of majesty, not majesty itself".[95] Some composers however, especially Handel, wrote 'pomposo' for royalty, as if they had written 'grave' or 'maestoso', though 'pomposo' was only the first step down towards the outer appearance of it.

* * *

Were our composers careless, irreverant when they identified the King of Heaven musically with the King of France? Hardly, for the very application of a *topos* tells us of their awareness of the rhetoric. And we find among them not a few great masters, much concerned with musical exegesis.[96] What, then, justified such imagery? I shall finally try to sketch the historical forces on which it thrived.

The field we enter is that of 'political theology', which throughout the twentieth century has attracted attention of scholars from various disciplines.[97] The idea that gods could become incarnate in kings or that kings were gods is as old as mankind.[98] It is the most central one, the spinal cord that runs through the religious and political structures of Egypt,[99] Babylonia,[100] Persia,[101] the realm of Alexander and his successors,[102] the Roman

---

[94] "pomps et richesses nécessaires aux Grands" – NICOLE, II, 149.

[95] "Je n'appelle pas Majesté cette pompe qui environne les Rois: ou cet éclat extérieur, qui eblouit le vulgaire. C'est le réjaillisement de la Majesté, & non pas la Majesté elle-même" – p. 429.

[96] Cf. Arnold SCHMITZ, *Die Bildlichkeit der wortgebundenen Musik J. S. Bachs*, Mainz, Schott, 1959, and ch. 1, 11-12, and 15 of this volume.

[97] Not only political historians, but also historians of religion, jurisprudence, art, etc., foremost the profound and brilliant studies by Erik Peterson (early history of theology) and Ernst Kantorowicz (medieval legal history). Also congresses have been held on the subject, thus *La regalità sacra: contributo al tema dell'VIII congresso internazionale di storia della religione (Roma 1955)*, Leyden, Brill, 1959, or *Das Königtum: Seine geistigen und rechtlichen Grundlagen*, Lindau/Konstanz, 1956 (report not published).

[98] Henri FRANKFORT, *Kingship and the Gods*, Chicago UP, 1948; Sigmund MOWICKEL, *Urmensch und Königsideologie*, «Studien zur Theologie», II, 1948/49, pp. 71-89; Berta SEGALL, *Notes on the Iconography of Cosmic Kingship*, «Art Bulletin», XXXVIII, 1956, pp. 75-80.

[99] Hellmut BRUNNER, *Die Geburt des Gottkönigs: Studien zur Überlieferung eines altägyptischen Mythos*, Wiesbaden, Harrassowitz, 1964.

[100] Hans Peter L'ORANGE, *Expressions of Cosmic Kingship in the Ancient World*, in *Regalità sacra* cit., p. 482.

[101] Ivan ENGNELL, *Studies in Divine Kingship in the Ancient Near East*, Uppsala, Almquist & Wiksell, 1943; Cyril J. GADD, *Ideas of Divine Rule in the Ancient East*, London, British Academy, 1948.

[102] Edwin R. GOODENOUGH, *The Political Philosophy of Hellenistic Kingship*, «Yale Classical

empire[103] – to name only those traditions which had some bearing on the idea as it survived in the Christian era.[104] For the theological justification it is not unimportant to see that in the earliest Greek sources Jesus as king is addressed and vested with titles such as 'Christos', 'Basileios', 'Kyrios', 'Soter', derived from late-hellenistic kingship.[105] In some writings He is called 'imperator'.[106] The early Christian descriptions of Christ's entry into Jerusalem and St. Paul's account of His second coming reflect imperial cermonial, and they in turn were imitated in descriptions of a sovereign's entry into a city: the reception of the returning ruler in mid-air by his citizens was in accord with the secular *parousia*, i.e. the custom of going as far as possible out of the city to receive the *Kyrios*.[107] The heavenly cult in the fourth and fifth books of St. John's Apocalypse mirrors the imperial cult in still more detail: the King of Kings is seen between candelabra – reminding us of the imperial cult statue; His feet appear as gold – the ruler's feet were associated with prostration of the subjects; His hand holds seven stars – an imperial symbol; His face shines like the sun – 'sol' was one of the emperor's titles; His habit is richly adorned with gems – a Persian and again Roman symbol of power; He is greeted with acclamations, such as "dignus est" – from Roman constitutional practice, etc.[108] In Byzantium the idea of a heavenly monarchy was fully put to use in the theoretical foundation of a new Christian empire. Liturgy absorbed the imperial acclamations, the ceremonial *silentium*, a wealth of imperial titles, "all of the terms ... which we know from the sovereignty

---

Studies», I, 1928, pp. 55-102; Arthur Darby NOCK, *Notes on the Ruler-Cult*, «Journal of Hellenic Studies», XLVIII, 1928, pp. 21-43; various articles of Ernst KANTOROWICZ, now in his *Selected Studies*, Princeton UP, 1963.

[103] Lily Rose TAYLOR, *The Divinity of the Roman Emperor*, Middletown, American Philological Association, 1931; ALFÖLDI, *op. cit.*, and *id.*, *Insignien und Tracht der römischen Kaiser*, «Mitteilungen des Deutschen Archäologischen Instituts, römische Abt.», L, 1935, pp. 1-158.

[104] Louis BRÉHIER and Pierre BATOFFOL, *Les survivances du cult impérial*, Paris, Piccard, 1920.

[105] Adolf DEISSMANN, *Licht vom Osten: das Neue Testament über die neuentdeckten Texte der hellenistisch-römischen Welt*, Tübingen, Mohr, 1923, pp. 290ff; Heinrich LINSSEN, *ΘΕΟΣ ΣΩΤΗΡ. Die Entwicklung und Verbreitung einer liturgischen Formelgruppe*, «Jahrbuch für Liturgiewissenschaft», VIII, 1928, pp. 1-75; E. von DOBSCHÜTZ, *ΚΥΡΙΟΣ ΙΗΣΟΥΣ*, «Zeitschrift für neutestamentische Wissenschaft», XXX, 1931, pp. 97-123; *Reallexikon für Antike und Christentum cit.*, II, 1954, col. 1257-1262, s.v. 'Christus II (Basileus)'.

[106] E.g. by Cyprian – *Reallexikon, loc. cit.*

[107] 1 *Thess.* 4:17; Erik PETERSON, *Die Einholung des Kyrios*, «Zeitschrift für systematische Theologie», VII, 1930, pp. 682-702; Ernst KANTOROWICZ, *The 'Kings Advent' and the Enigmatic Panels in the Doors of Santa Sabina*, «Art Bulletin», XXVI, 1944, especially pp. 210f, 216, 225.

[108] Erik PETERSON, *Der himmlische Kultus im 4-5ten Kapitel der Geheimen Offenbarung*, «Liturgisches Leben», I, 1934, pp. 297ff; *id.*, *Eis Theos: Epigrammatische, formengeschichtliche und religionsgeschichtliche Untersuchungen*, Göttingen, Vandenhoeck & Ruprecht, 1926, pp. 141ff, on acclamations in general. On Roman practice, particularly, cf. ALFÖLDI, *Die Ausgestaltung*, pp. 9ff.

programs of coins and inscriptions and from the declamations of the panegyrists".[109] Then we have the astonishing 'Liuthar cross' from the time of Otto III, where on the front, at the point of intersection, the superb cameo of Augustus is mounted, and only on the back is the figure of Christ engraved;[110] or the *Codex Aureus* of Saint Emmeran, where the emperor is represented as Christ in the Apocalypse.[111]

In the European power struggle from the twelfth century on, the French kings became predominant, and the splendour of their nimbus increased the more that of the emperor faded. The coronation became an "eighth sacrament" of the French. Saint Louis brought the 'crown of thorns' to Paris[112] and added, as another "symbol of the sacred prerogatives of the crown of France", the device "Christus vincit, Christus regnat, Christus imperat", the motto which had "accompanied the French kings like a shadow".[113] He, "royal crusader and saint, ... enriched that treasure of grace on which all his successors would thrive".[114] It was the popular belief in the sanctity and mission of the king of France which later led Joan of Arc to address the Dauphin as "deputy of heaven who is the King of France".[115] "Rex Christianissimus" became the royal title in France.[116] In this age-old 'religion royale' the legists of sixteenth/seventeenth-century France could construct their doctrine of the divine right of kings:[117] "the king almost a god among

---

[109] *Reallexikon* cit. II, 1261. Cf. also Otto TREITINGER, *Die oströmische Kaiser- und Reichsidee nach ihrer Gestaltung im höfischen Zeremoniell*, Jena, Frommann, 1938; Raymond JANIN, *L'empéreur dans l'église byzantine*, «Nouvelle Revue Théologique», LXXVII, 1955, pp. 55ff; André GRABAR, *L'empéreur dans l'art byzantine*, Paris, Belles Lettres, 1936; Otto G. von SIMSON, *Sacred Fortress: Byzantine Art and Statecraft in Ravenna*, Chicago UP, 1948; Francis DVORNIK, *Early Christian and Byzantine Political Philosophy: Origins and Background*, Washington, Dumbarton Oaks, 1966, especially II, 724ff (influence of monarchial theories on theology, of the emperor on the Church, etc.).

[110] Josef DEÉR, *Das Kaiserbild im Kreuz*, «Schweizer Beiträge zur allgemeinen Geschichte», XIII, 1955, pp. 48ff.; Konrad HOFFMANN, *Taufsymbolik im mittelalterlichen Herrscherbild*, Düsseldorf, Rheinland-Verlag, 1968, pp. 62ff.

[111] HOFFMANN, pp. 53ff.

[112] Allan H. GILBERT, *The Monarch's Crown of Thorns*, «Journal of the Warburg Institute», III, 1939/40, pp. 156-160.

[113] Possibly of Byzantine origin. Ernst KANTOROWICZ, *Laudes Regiae: A Study in Liturgical Acclamations and Medieval Ruler Worship*, Berkeley and Los Angeles, California UP, 1946, p. 3.

[114] *Ibid.*, p. 4. See further, *id.*, *The King's Two Bodies: A Study in Mediaeval Political Theology*, Princeton UP, 1957.

[115] "Vous serez lieutenant du Roi des cieux qui est Roi de France" – Jean de PANGE, *Le roi très chrétien*, Paris, Fayard, 1949, p. 21.

[116] Cf. SCHRAMM.

[117] Most completely expounded by Pierre GRÉGOIRE, *De republica* (1578). Cf. William F. CHURCH, *Constitutional Thought in Sixteenth-Century France*, Cambridge MA, Harvard UP, 1941, pp. 243-271.

men".[118] Bold writers did not shy away from the final step: "As God is by nature the first king and prince, so the king is by creation and imitation. God in every way, here on earth".[119]

In the person of Louis XIV the French, a nation worn out by inner conflicts and tired of being ruled by a foreign prime minister, finally had their sovereign; their expectations of myth and of constitutional thought were fulfilled.[120] The elite knew that Louis had been identified by the very hour of his birth (shortly before noon, 1 Sept. 1638) with the sun in its zenith.[121] The astronomical time was commemorated with a medal which bears on its reverse the inscription "Ortus Solis Gallici". According to Claude-François Menestrier, who was to spend a lifetime laboring over the king's emblems and devices, "This medal represents the disposition of the heavens at the moment of the king's birth".[122] The 'sun'-symbolism now assumed very concrete forms. Already on 7 September 1651 the famous English diarist John Evelyn, witnessing the "cavalcade of the young French monarch Lewis the XIVth passing to parliament, when first he tooke the kingly government on him, as now out of minority & the queene's regents pupilage", could observe that "the king himselfe like a young Apollo was in a sute so coverd with rich embrodry, that one could perceive nothing of the stuff under it".[123] As an actor and dancer, the young king assumed only roles that were befitting. In the *Ballet des noces de Thétis et Pélée* (1654) as Apollo (cf. also Plates VII.2-3), he says: "More brilliant and better made than all the gods together, earth and heaven have nothing that resembles me; my brow is crowned with immortal rays"; or in the ballet *Hercule amoureux* LWV 17 (1662), where he appears as the sun: "This star is not a bad likeness of its creator, and if one didn't have to fear of appearing impious, one could adore this beautiful copy, so much

---

[118] "regem quasi Deum inter homines" – Adam Blackwood after Artistotle, 1581, quoted *ibid.*, p. 254, note 21.

[119] "comme Dieu est par natur le premier roy et prince, le roy l'est par création, et imitation. Dieu en tout, cestui-cy la terre" – Jacques de La Guesle, 1611, quoted *ibid.*, p. 266, note 54.

[120] The Italian cardinal Giulio Mazarini was, of course, the most powerful politician in France from 1642 until his death in 1661. According to a popular saying, he, not Louis XIII, was the father of Louis XIV. Cf. John B. WOLF, *Louis XIV*, New York, Norton, 1968, pp. 68ff.

[121] The metaphor of the sun had already been applied unofficially to predecessors such as Henry IV. Irving LAVIN, *Past – Present: Essays on Historicism in Art from Donatello to Picasso*, Berkeley etc., U. California Press, 1993, pp. 141-144, illustrates that it was applied even in architecture.

[122] "Cette médaille représente la disposition du ciel au point de la naissance du Roy" – *Histoire du Roy Louis le Grand par les médailles, emblèmes, devises ...*, Paris, Nolin, 1691, p. 2. Cf. also the sun on another medal, Plate VII.1.

[123] *The Diary of John Evelyn*, London, Oxford UP, 1959, pp. 306f. An earlier version of this medal (1663) is reproduced in LAVIN, fig. 184.

does it approach its original".[124] Image and person were surely not totally congruent, as later caustically confirmed by Claude Saint-Simon: Louis, "without voice or musical knowledge, ... used to sing, in private, the passages of opera prologues that were fullest of his praise"![125] A contemporary commentator reported that the king himself instituted the academies "expressly for the purpose of being praised as a god".[126] That a particular role belonged to him in this capacity can be illustrated by an example from the fresco of twelve prophets in the chapel of Versailles. The inscription for/from the prophet Malachi, intentionally ambiguous, reads: "statim veniet ad templum suum Dominator" ["the Lord will suddenly come to his temple" – 3:1]. Here, both God and the king of France are meant, because the latter now was also the spiritual sovereign of this realm: from 1673 until 1693 Louis XIV, no longer the pope, appointed the clerics, and until his death he possessed the function of supreme judge. He could reverse sentences without providing justification and condemn persons without court proceedings. A medal of 1667 shows him as judge of judges ("justitias judicanti").[127]

Even two churches are closely connected with the 'hagiography' of Louis. Val-de-Grâce, with its dome, was a celebrity far beyond the city.[128] The founder, Anne d'Autriche, twenty-three years childless since her marriage to Louis XIII, had made a vow to build a church if the Lord would give them an heir. At his birth the son was christened Louis-Dieudonné. In 1645 Anne, by now widowed, began to fulfil her promise: with great pomp, the young Louis laid the first stone.[129] For this event a golden medal was struck by Jean Warin which showed Anne and her son in the pose of a Madonna and child (Plate VII. 4). Twenty years later Michel Anguir's sculpture of Mary, Joseph and the infant Jesus for the main altar emphasized the consacration as a Nativity church.

---

[124] "Cet astre à son auteur ne ressemble mal, / Et, si l'on ne craignait de passer pour impie, / L'on pourrait adorer cette belle copie, / Tant elle approche de son original"; "Plus brillant et mieux fait que tous les dieux ensembles, / La terre ni le ciel n'ont rien qui me ressemble, / De rayons immortels mon front est couronné" – quoted from Louis HAUTECŒUR, *Louis XIV: roi soleil*, Paris, Plon, 1963, p. 10. Louis abandoned such theatrical displays in 1661 when their resemblance to Nero's activities was pointed out.

[125] "Lui-même, sans avoir ni voix ni musique, chantait dans ses particuliers les endroits les plus à sa louange des prologues des opéras" (1715) – *Mémoires*, V, Paris, Gallimard, 1985, p. 480. However, another contemporary, Mme. de Maintenon, testifies that music was "le seul vrai plaisir du Roi", who in his youth had studied voice, lute, clavechord, guitar, and dancing – *ibid.*, p. 1364, note.

[126] Quoted in Hubert GILLOT, *Le règne de Louis XIV et l'opinion publique en Allemagne*, Paris, Champion, 1914, p. 61, note 2.

[127] MENESTRIER, p. 13.

[128] Amédée BOINET, *Les églises parisiennes*, II, Paris, Minuit, 1962, pp. 228ff.

[129] *Ibid.*, II, 256f.

Later arose the grand church of the Invalides, actually two churches in one: the basilica of St. Louis, begun in 1671, and the centrally designed domed church of the veterans, a few years later, mostly by Jules Hardouin-Mansart. The conspicuous similarity between this work and the two projects for the sepulchre of the Bourbons in St. Denis was already observed by Louis Hautecœur.[130] Allan Braham subsequently presented the hypothesis that the Invalides was for a short time intended as a future mausoleum of Louis XIV.[131] In 1677 a very elaborate wooden model had been made by the architect himself and half a dozen prominent artists. Only the king, his immediate family, and a few initiated inspected it in an audience at St. Germain. One artist, Charles de la Fosse, who was later to paint the cupola, wrote a memoire describing in full "the glory of Louis XIV".[132] The model was suddenly locked up and kept secret for years. But two documents shed more light on Mansart's plan. First, his testament[133] includes a publication by Bernardino Amico which describes and precisely illustrates the Holy Land: *Trattato delle piante et imagini dei sacri edificii di Terra Santa.*[134] Second, in 1956 a plan of the Holy Sepulchre was discovered in the masonery of St. Denis. It was immediately recognized as an exact copy of an illustration in Amico's book.[135] Indeed, the Invalides seems to have imitated the most venerated temple in Christendom, the church of the Holy Sepulchre in Jerusalem, since both tombs were placed below the center of the dome, as almost never occurred except in the case of some saint (and later Napoleon!). The tombs of the kings in St. Denis were assigned to the periphery. The projected mausoleum would have broken this tradition: Louis would have been also here the solitary ruler. The architect apparently assumed without inhibition that the king would not resist such a plan. It must have been the Church which rejected such hubris.

Even those who were desperately opposed to Louis' political and social ruthlessness do not seem to have questioned his superhuman stature. The

---

[130] *L'origine du Dôme des Invalides*, «L'architecture», XXXVII, 1924, pp. 353-360.

[131] *L'église du Dôme*, «Journal of the Warburg and Courtauld Institutes», III/IV, 1960, pp. 216-224. This study was scrutenized and expanded by Partick REUTERSWÄRD, *The Two churches of the Hôtel des Invalides*, Stockholm, Norstedt, 1965. A summary of research on this problem is provided by Allan BRAHAM and Peter SMITH, *François Mansart*, I, London, Zwemmer, 1973, p. 254.

[132] First published by REUTERSWÄRD, pp. 114f.

[133] Marie-Antoinette FLEURY, *Les dispositions testamentaires et l'inventaire après décès de François Mansart*, «Bulletin de la Société de l'histoire de l'art française», 1956, pp. 228-253.

[134] Rome, Typ. linguarum externarum, 1609, and Florence, Cecconcelli, 1620.

[135] Jules FORMIGÉ, *Un plan du Saint-Sépulcre découvert à la basilique de Saint-Denis*, «Monuments et Mémoires», XLVIII/2, 1956, pp. 107-130.

anonymous letter to Louis by bishop Fénelon ca. 1694, summing up the most bitter reproaches, begins: "The person who writes this to you, Sire, has no interest in this world. He sees God in you".[136] Pierre Barbier's collection of political chansons provides examples from the streets.[137] And the vast pamphlet literature of the devastated countries east and west of the Rhine (where our *topos* mainly flourished) attests to it everywhere: Matthias Abele, *Tu es Deus qui facis mirabilia* [!] (s.l., Fruchtbringende Gesellschaft, 1670); anon., *Der frantzösische, Deutschland verderbende Greuel und Abgott Ludewig der XIV. König von Franckreich* (s.l., s.n., 1689); *Le monstre de l'apocalypse*, etc.[138] Gottfried Wilhelm Leibniz joined this chorus with his outcry against the *Mars christianissimus* (1684).[139] Did, at last, Louis consider himself 'Dieu en terre'? Few of the great in modern history have left so little in writing that would allow access to the inner person.[140] There is a cryptic answer by Madame Marie de Sévigné's letter of 13 June 1685 to the Chevalier Joseph de Grignan:[141]

Les minimes de votre provence ont dédié une thèse au Roi où ils le comparent à Dieu, mais d'une manière où l'on voit clairement que Dieu n'est que la copie. On l'a montrée à Monsieur de Meaux, qui l'a montrée au Roi disant que Sa Majesté ne doit pas la souffrir. Il a été de cet avis. On l'a renvoyée en Sorbonne pour juger; elle a dit qu'il fallait supprimer. Trop est trop.

The Minorites of your province have dedicated a thesis to the King where they compare him with God, but in a manner where one clearly sees that God is only the copy. One has showed it to Monsieur [Bossuet, bishop of] Meaux, who has showed it to the King, saying that His Majesty must not tolerate it. He agreed. It has been referred to the Sorbonne for judgement; they have said that it should be suppressed. Too much is too much.

For the biography of our *topos* this image could not be surpassed.

During the reigns of Louis' successors court life became lighter, less demanding, finally bourgeois. Louis XVI preferred to walk around among his

---

136 François de Salignac de la Mothe-Fénelon, quoted from William F. CHURCH, *The Greatness of Louis XIV: Myth or Reality?*, Boston, Heath, 1959, p. 16.

137 *Histoire de France par les chansons*, Paris, Gallimard, 1956-61.

138 Cf. Hans von ZWIEDINECK-SÜDENHORST, *Die öffentliche Meinung in Deutschland im Zeitalter Ludwigs XIV. 1650-1700: ein Beitrag zur Kenntnis der deutschen Flugschriften-Litteratur*, Stuttgart, Cotta, 1888, *passim*, and the "Liste des libelles", in GILLOT, pp. 315-363.

139 Cologne, Le Bon, 1684. Cf. also Lionel ROTHKRUG, *Opposition to Louis XIV: The Political and Social Origins of the French Enlightenment*, Princeton UP, 1965; Leon BERNARD, *French Society and Popular Uprisings under Louis XIV*, «French Historical Studies», III, 1963-64, pp. 454-474.

140 Carl HINRICHS, *Zur Selbstauffassung Ludwig XIV in seinen Memoiren*, in *Formen der Selbstdarstellung: ... Festgabe für Fritz Neubert*, Berlin, Dunker & Humblot, 1956, pp. 145ff; Stephan SKALWEIT, *Das Herrscherbild des 17. Jahrhunderts*, «Historische Zeitschrift», CLXXXIV, 1957, pp. 74ff.

141 *Correspondence*, III, Paris, Gallimard, 1978, p. 202.

company as unobtrusively as possible, incognito to the outsider. The king, it is true, still 'healed' the scrofula patients when crowds gathered for this on the great feasts of the church year, though in 1789 he had to give up his old prerogative.[142] In the nineteenth century the 'healing' took place in France only once: in 1825 Charles X appeared, embarrassed, before only 120-130 patients in Reims after his coronation, now changing the traditional "Dieu te guérit" to "Dieu te guérisse"! Of course he was much criticized and ridiculed at the time.[143] For the stylization of genuine majesty (music included), one had to revert to Louis XIV. It should be added that no one needs to frown on J. S. Bach *et al.* for having practised such 'idolatry'. We may recall that even Martin Luther had been well in the main stream of thought with his words on the highest authorities of a just state: "Rightly they are called gods".[144]

Political theology, then, survived the French Revolution by only a few decades. In *Dichtung und Wahrheit* (1808) Goethe still pays tribute to it where he remembers the coronation of Emperor Joseph II in his own youth: "A political-religious solemnity has an infinite attraction. We see the earthly Majesty surrounded by all the symbols of its power; but when it bows before the heavenly majesty, it demonstrates the unity of the two".[145] The sculptor Johann Gottfried Schadow in 1811 could still depict the Protestant Queen Louise of Prussia posthumously as Immacolata in the starry mantle, surrounded by angelic virtues.[146] But the Restoration did not create majesty anew. In 1815, upon the return of the Bourbons, Chateaubriand is said to have greeted Louis XVIII with the acrimonious words: "I believe, Sire, the time of the kings is over", to which Louis replied, "I believe it too".[147]

At that time Charles Bochsa's Requiem was performed in memory of Louis XVI. Its "Rex tremendae majestatis" once more conjures up the family image (*grave*, conspicuous dotted rhythm, scalar melody), which is about all that one can say in its favor.[148] Did the sun begin to set also for the image

---

[142] BLOCH, pp. 397ff.

[143] *Ibid.*, pp. 402f, and on pp. 409ff a critical interpretation of the royal 'miracle'.

[144] "Die selbigen heissen billich Götter" – *Werke*, XXXI/1, Weimar, Böhlau, 1913, p. 201.

[145] "Eine politisch-religiöse Feierlichkeit hat einen unendlichen Reiz. Wir sehen die irdische Majestät vor Augen, umgeben von allen Symbolen ihrer Macht; aber indem sie sich vor der himmlischen beugt, bringt sie uns die Gemeinschaft beider vor die Sinne" – *Sämtliche Werke*, I. Abt., Bd. 14, Frankfurt, Deutscher Klassiker Verlag, 1986, pp. 221f.

[146] On the high altar of the church of Paretz – *Reallexikon der deutschen Kunstgeschichte*, I, Stuttgart, Metzler, 1937, p. 852, Abb. 6: "eine sonderbare Parallele zur Himmelskönigin".

[147] "Je crois, Sire, le temps des rois est passé" – "Je le crois aussi" (apocryphal?).

[148] *Messe de Requiem a trois voix et choeurs avec accompagnement d'instrumens à vent composée et executée pour le service que M. M. Mousquetaires noirs ont fait célébrer le 21 janvier 1815 en mé-*

of the King of Heaven? In Paris of the 'bourgeois' king, Heinrich Heine set a
Janus-faced epitaph for the ancient tradition of political theology. Reflecting
on the "necessity of Deism" he stated: "He [God] and Louis Philippe [are]
necessary – Louis Philippe of heaven".[149] Not much later Friedrich Schleier-
macher, in the name of protestant theology, preached that Christ commands
only the forces of the Church[150] or, as he is interpreted by a later writer, "the
Pantocrator has become the governor of a clearly limited province", "the in-
spirator of a community of souls".[151] It remained only for Baudelaire to level
the sublime with the vulgar, the high style with the perverse, the great prototype, God, with Nothing. The time had come without gods.[152]

Also our musical *topos* faded rapidly with the turn of the nineteenth century, though Schubert (Exx. 29f), born the same year as Heine, carried it na-
ively into the period of romanticism, and Beethoven was still aware of it when
he underlined the words "qui sedes ad dexteram patris" with this *topos*
(Ex. 31), expressing a central concept of political theology, that of 'throne-
sharing', traceable via Bossuet back to Antiquity.[153] But we well know that
Beethoven found his God also in 'the infinite' and 'the eternal', rather than
in orthodox Christian doctrine. By now the rhetoric of the *topos* had been forgotten by the musicians and their audiences. With the growing liberalism in
nineteenth-century theology, fading dogma, dissolution of iconological traditions in art and of rhetorical traditions in literature, the elements of musical
style which had so concretely represented the king (of heaven or of France)
became watered down to pale abstractions such as 'the sublime' or 'the solemn'. In this capacity a shadow of the *topos* vegetated through the rest of
the nineteenth century, and thus it was still recognized by Schweitzer at the
turn of the twentieth, as we have seen (above, p. 225).

---

moire de Louis XVI. Dédée à Sa Majesté Louis XVIII Roi de France et de Navarre. Par N. Ch. Bochsa,
directeur de la musique des Mousquetaires noirs de la garde de Roi. Cette messe est suivie d'un motet
composé pour célébrer l'apothéose de Louis XVI et pour l'heureux retour des Bourbons ...

149 "Notwendigkeit des Deismus – Er und Ludwig Philipp – notwendig – Ludwig Philipp des
Himmels", in *Aphorismen und Fragmente, Werke*, VII, Berlin, Aufbau-Verlag, 1962, p. 402.

150 *Der christliche Glaube*, Reutlingen, Mäcken, 1828, pp. 259f.

151 Willem Adolph Visser't Hooft, *The Kingship of Christ in European Theology*, New York,
Harper, 1948, pp. 25f.

152 Erich Auerbach, *Baudelaires Fleurs du mal und das Erhabene*, in his *Vier Untersuchungen
zur Geschichte der französischen Bildung*, Bern, Franke, 1951, pp. 108ff.

153 On this concept of *condominium* cf. Percy Ernst Schramm, *Das Herrscherbild in der Kunst
des frühen Mittelalters*, Leipzig, Teubner, 1924, pp. 222ff; Arthur Darby Nock, ΣΥΝΝΑΟΣ ΘΕΟΣ,
«Harvard Studies in Classical Philology», XLI, 1930, pp. 1-62; Treitinger, *op. cit.*; Schramm, *Die
Krönung in Deutschland bis zum Beginn des Salischen Hauses (1028)*, «Zeitschrift der Savigny-Stif-
tung für Rechtsgeschichte, kanonistische Abteilung», XXIV, 1935, p. 318; Gilbert, *op. cit.*

But I do not regard *topos* research as an end in itself. It is an extremely useful tool for interpretation. In Mozart's "Rex tremendae majestatis" (Ex. 26) I see the purest, most insistent application of our *topos*. In the earlier repertory, the eighteen strophes of the "Dies irae" were generally through-composed.[154] Mozart adheres to the older practice in the first seven strophes of his "Dies irae". Then he treats the eighth strophe, "Rex", as a separate movement: the King of Heaven appears as isolated as in ancient *majestas* depictions. (A later hand added the word "*grave*" to the autograph for publication, and it was, of course, correct). This piece now gains immensely in perspective and concreteness. The *topos* has straight scales. They are longer and more straight than anywhere else, with the simple dotted rhythm and what I may call the 'mixed paean' with the short notes in dotted rhythm (Ex. 4 and Ex. 26, mm. 7-15). In this form they dominate fifteen long measures. When they first appear they descend from the tonic in the higher octave down to the twelfth below: a tremendous *parousia* of the king who comes from high. Here it is rendered in parallel octaves, i.e. in magnificent solitude. From measure 7 on the instruments branch out and provide emphasis through polyphonic writing. The musical "rex" determines all other, smaller details of the rhetoric. Some are *topoi* themselves: the minor mode was traditional in Italian opera and oratorio for the invocation of deities; there is an instrumental introduction, the prerogative of gods and kings. A chorus appears, a crowd before the king, though the poem implies only a single soul. The "rex", as a single word, is invoked by this chorus three times, likewise contradicting the given text. Could Mozart have known of the ternary structure of invocations in ancient court ceremonial[155] or coronation rites?[156] What was still

---

[154] Also Franz Tuma, Johann Ernst Eberlin, Michael Haydn – direct forerunners of Mozart – in the cantata-type requiem established by Caldara.

[155] The famous Byzantine ceremonial book by CONSTANTINUS VII PORPHYROGENITUS (905-959), *Le livre des cérémonies*, Paris, Les belles lettres, 1935-40, contains in vol. II, ch. 47, numerous ternary acclamations of the people to the emperor. HOFFMANN, *op. cit.*, pp. 21f, mentioned that the ambassador from Constantinople honored Otto III in this manner ("after I honored the emperor three times in prostration, I raised my head"). In the words of the historian Otto bishop of Freising († 1158): "Caesar had been received from the orient in Rome as Augustus with threefold triumph, and on the same day Christ was adored with threefold presents and thus appeared as Augustus and was declared King of Kings" – Leonid ARBUSOW, *Liturgie und Geschichtsschreibung im Mittelalter*, Bonn, Röhrscheid, 1951, p. 20. KANTOROWICZ, *Laudes*, p. 2, communicates threefold invocations in spells and exorcisms, and, pp. 15f, ternary acclamations from the Middle Ages (e.g. three times "Ipsi soli", or "Christe, audi nos").

[156] These were of course largely identical to the ceremonial acclamations. For the West in the earlier Middle Ages cf. Cornelius Adrianus BOUMAN, *Sacring and Crowning: The Development of the Latin Ritual for the Annointing of Kings and the Coronation of an Emperor before the Eleventh Century*, Groningen, Wolters, 1957, pp. 168, 171, 174: three times "vivat rex". Only months before he began work on the Requiem, Mozart attended the coronation of Emperor Francis I in Frankfurt. Could a threefold invocation here have made an impression on him?

left of these in the threefold Kyrie or Sanctus in every Mass must have been enough for him to realize the drama.[157] Between his three invocations there are long rests – certainly a rendering of the ceremonial '*silentium*'.[158] And then, with text repetition, we hear the enormous expanse of "Rex tremendae majestatis, qui salvando salvas gratis" over eleven more measures (mm. 6-16; Mozart's predecessors passed over this passage in one or two measures of syllabic declamation), the polyphonic shouts of all voices, and the large intervals on "tremendae" do justice to the size denoted by this word. The first three words are stated ten times altogether – an acclamation scene as *per definitionem*. It breaks off with syllabic declamation where the invocation ends and the crowd homophonically, laconically finishes the sentence with "salva me, fons pietatis".

Before his death, on 7 December 1791, Mozart had time to write down only what he regarded as most essential. The orchestration had to be left to other hands. His last months are curiously close to those which sealed the fate of the Bourbons. And, more strangely, Mozart wrote "1792" on the title page, in anticipation of the completion. Can the work be seen as the Requiem to an epoch? The kings of France had to die, the King of Heaven "ne meurt pas".

---

[157] Cf. Otto WEINREICH, *Trigemination als sakrale Stilform*, «Studi e materiali», IV, 1928, pp. 198-206.

[158] ALFÖLDI, *Ausgestaltung*, pp. 33ff and especially 38, on Roman emperors, and TREITINGER, pp. 52f, for Byzantine. When Christ sits on his throne in the city of heaven there is courtly *silentium* (Johannes Chrysostomos, in *Reallexikon für Antike und Christentum*, II, 1954, col. 1260). Cf. also Odo CASEL, *Die Liturgie als Mysterienfeier*, Freiburg, Herder, 1922, ch. "Das mystische Schweigen".

APPENDIX

A SELECTION OF WORKS EMPLOYING THE *TOPOS*[159]

Ex. 1. Lully, *Ballet d'Alcidiane et Polexandre* LWV 9 (1658), overture. Paean, dotted rhythm.

Ex. 2. *Id.*, *Bellérophone* LWV 57 (1679), no. 18, prélude le Roy. Paean, dotted rhythm.

Ex. 3. *Id.*, *Persée* LWV 60 (1682), overture. Paean, dotted rhythm.

---

[159] For the examples without musical notation (e.g. p. 258), see the current editions.

Ex. 4. Purcell: Anthem "I will give thanks unto thee, o Lord" (1682-85), symphony. Dotted rhythm, mixed paean.

Ex. 5. *Id.*, Anthem "My heart is indating" (1685), symphony following "The king's palace". Dotted rhythm, paean.

Ex. 6. *Id.*, Anthem "The Lord is King, the earth may be glad" (1688). Dotted rhythm.

Ex. 7. J. S. Bach: Cantata *Himmelskönig, sei willkommen* BWV 182 (1715), no. 1: sonata before the chorus "Himmelskönig sei willkommen". Dotted rhythm.

Ex. 8. *Id.*, Cantata *Der Himmel lacht* BWV 31 (1715), no. 4, aria "Fürst des Lebens". Dotted rhythm.

Ex. 9. *Id.*, Cantata *Was mir behagt, ist nur die muntre Jagd* BWV 208 (1716), no. 7, aria "Ein Fürst ist seines Landes Pan". Dotted rhythm.

Ex. 10. *Id.*, Cantata *Meine Seele rühmt und preist* BWV 189, no. 3, aria "Gott hat sich hoch gesetzet". Dotted rhythm.

Ex. 11. Handel, *Athalia* HWV 52 (1733), no. 17, chorus "Thy mighty pow'r", orch. introduction, mm. 1f, and "give glory to his aweful name", mm. 114f. Dotted rhythm.

Ex. 12 *Id.*, *Saul* HWV 53 (1739), no. 1, chorus "How excellent thy name, o Lord". Dotted rhythm, paean.

Ex. 13. *Id.*, *Messiah* HWV 56 (1742), no. 5, recit. acc. "Thus said the Lord, the Lord of hosts". Dotted rhythm.

Ex. 14. *Id.*, *Semele* HWV 58 (1744), no. 1, recit. acc. "Behold, auspicious flashes", for "Juno accepts our sacrifice". Paean.

Ex. 15. *Id.*, *Belshazzar* HWV 61 (1745), no. 18, chorus "Great Jehovah", mm. 15-22. Dotted rhythm.

Ex. 16. *Ibid.*, no. 38, aria "O God of truth", introduction. Dotted rhythm.

Ex. 17. *Id.*, *Hercules* HWV 60 (1745), no. 5, aria "I feel the god", "pomposo". Paean, dotted rhythm.

Ex. 18. *Ibid.*, no. 13, march and recit. "Thanks to the powers above", following no. 12, recit. "But hark, the victor comes". Dotted rhythm.

Ex. 19. *Id.*, *Theodora* HWV 68 (1750), overture. Paean. No. 1a, aria "Go my faithful soldiers", "pomposo", for "Let the fragrant incense rise to Jove". Dotted rhythm.

Ex. 20. Georg Reutter (1708-72): *Missa Sancti Caroli*, DTÖ 88, Gloria, "Domine Deus, Rex coelestis ... filius patris". Dotted rhythm throughout, paean.

VII.1. Louis XIV (recto) and the sun (verso). Medal by François Warin, 1674. Cf. p. 245, note 122.

VII.2. Louis XIV as the sun in the *Ballet de la nuit*, 1653. Anonymous drawing, F-Pn Coll.
Hennin, tome XLI. Cf. p. 245.

HOC NVMINE FLORET

Hortus Regius.

VII.3. Louis XIV as Apollo. Engraving by Alexis Étienne Rousselet [or Jacques Rousselet]
after a lost drawing by Charles Lebrun (1619-90). Cf. p. 245.

VII.4. Anne d'Autriche with Louis (recto) and Val-de-Grâce (verso).
Medal by Jean Warin commemorating the beginning of the
church, 1645. Cf. p. 246.

Ex. 21. Florian Leopold Gassmann (1729-74): Mass in C, DTÖ 83, Credo, "Et iterum venturus est cum gloria". Dotted rhythm.

Ex. 22. Mozart: *Thamos, König von Ägypten* K. 345 (1779), no. 1, chorus "Schon weichet dir, Sonne" (referring to the priests of the sun), maestoso, mm. 1-7. Dotted rhythm, paean.

Ex. 23. *Id.*, Terzett for TBB, "Gran regno", K. 434 (1783). Dotted rhythm.

Ex. 24. *Id., Le nozze di Figaro* K. 492 (1786), act II, finale, mm. 64-70, imperious command of the count, "Va lontan dagl'occhi miei". Dotted rhythm. Cf. p. 496, Ex. 23.

Ex. 25. *Id., Don Giovanni* K. 527 (1787), act I, no. 8, aria of Donna Elvira "Ah fuggi il traditor". Archaic dotted rhythm indicates that Donna Elvira is no longer the youngest.

Ex. 26. *Id., Requiem* K. 626 (1791), no. 4, "Rex tremendae majestatis" (V. 2 and Va added by Joseph Eybler). Dotted rhythm throughout, mixed paean mm. 7-15.

Ex. 27. Beethoven: *Sinfonia eroica* "geschrieben auf Buonaparte", Op. 55 (1803), Marcia funebre. Dotted rhythm.

Ex. 28. *Id.*, Oratorio *Christus am Ölberge* Op. 85 (1803), final chorus, "maestoso". Paean, double dotted rhythm.

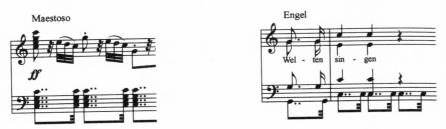

Ex. 29. Schubert: Mass no. 1 in F, D 105 (1814), Gloria, mm. 171-179, "Deus, Rex coelestis".
Dotted rhythm.

Ex. 30. *Id.*, Mass no. 3 in B-flat, D 324 (1815), Gloria, mm. 110-115, "qui sedes ad dexteram Patris". Dotted rhythm.

Ex. 31. Beethoven: *Missa solemnis* Op. 123 (1819-23), Gloria, mm. 269-271, "qui sedes ad dexteram patris"; mm. 312-344, "Quoniam tu solus sanctus, tu solus altissimus, Jesu Christe". Dotted and double dotted rhythm.

Ex. 32. *Id.*, ['French'] overture *Die Weihe des Hauses*, Op. 124 (1822), "maestoso". Double dotted rhythm.[160]

---

[160] Cf. Beethoven's note on an undated sketch, D-BNbh SV 91: "einen maestätischen Menuet mit punktierten Noten" ["a majestic menuet with dotted notes"].

VIII.

THE WAR OF THE SPANISH SUCCESSION
REFLECTED IN MUSIC BY ANTONIO CALDARA
(MANTUA, MILAN, VIENNA, ROME)

On the first of November 1700 King Charles II of Spain died without issue. A few months later the quarrel over his succession became a world war.[1] In contradiction to the Second Treaty of Partition, Louis XIV, husband of Charles' halfsister, now claimed Spain for his second grandson, Philip of Anjou, who was named successor in Charles' lately drafted, much disputed testament. Emperor Leopold I, husband of Charles' younger sister, wished to maintain the Habsburg territories for his second son Charles. While Philip took possession of Madrid as King Philip V, Leopold armed to encounter the French troops that had gathered along the frontiers of the Empire, in the Spanish Netherlands, and in northern Italy. He claimed the Duchy of Milan, the Spanish territory closest to him, as an old fief of the Empire. On 30 May 1701, his generalissimo Prince Eugene crossed the Italian border. Archduke Charles started his expedition against Philip in 1703, entered Barcelona in the late summer 1705, established his headquarters there, and was immediately proclaimed King Charles III of Spain, now rival of Philip until 1711, when he unexpectedly had to succeed his brother Joseph I as Emperor Charles VI.

The Elector of Bavaria and his brother, the Elector of Cologne, had joined the side of Philip, their nephew. The Emperor and the maritime powers formed the Great Alliance. In vain Pope Clement XI had urged the Italian princes to observe a strict neutrality: the Dukes of Guastalla and Modena col-

---

[1] DE LA TORRE, *Mémoires et négotiations secrettes de diverses cours de l'Europe contentant ce qui s'est passé depuis le premier traité de partage de la succession d'Espagne*, The Haag, Moetjens, 1721-25. Carl NOORDEN, *Europäische Geschichte im achtzehnten Jahrhundert*, erste Abteilung: *Der spanische Erbfolgekrieg*, Düsseldorf, Buddeus, 1870. Markus LANDAU, *Rom, Wien, Neapel während des Spanischen Erbfolgerieges*, Leipzig, Friedrich, 1885.

laborated with the Austrians, the Duke of Mantua with the French, likewise the Duke of Savoy, who soon shifted to the Emperor's party. In 1708 Clement himself took action against the Austrian troops. The theaters of operation extended from the English Channel to Gibraltar, from Naples to the upper Danube; the political and economical repercussions were felt even in Canada and South America.

These great waves moved also the history of music and musicians. We know that Charles III made Barcelona a center of Italian opera – engaging the librettists Pariati and Zeno, the stage archictect Ferdinando Galli-Bibiena, the chapel master Porsile, the composers Caldara, Gasparini, Fioré, Astorga, et al.;[2] that the young Handel, who had been a favored guest of the immensely wealthy Marquis Francesco Maria Ruspoli since early December 1706, fled from Rome with other musicians in mid September 1708, when Imperial forces threatened the city with a second *sacco*;[3] that Dall'Abaco and other members of the court chapel of Munich followed their patron Max Emanuel, Elector of Bavaria, to exile in the Spanish Netherlands and France.[4] Dent rightly assumed that for Alessandro Scarlatti "the political disturbances of the kingdom of Naples may very well have been an additional reason" to leave that city in June 1702.[5] The Spanish viceroy's actions of revenge against Austrian-minded Neapolitan princes, the public executions, banishment of families, and destruction of city palaces had driven the people to despair, and Philip V himself, having arrived there on 17 May 1702, already by 2 June preferred to leave the city to escape the public discontent.[6]

The alternate victories resounded many times a year in the *Te deum*. Above the mass of anonymous settings recorded in gazettes and chapel books[7] tower the famous *Te Deum* by Bernier, which after 1700 was much repeated in France,[8] and Handel's *Te Deum* for the Peace of Utrecht (1713). In that year Michel-Richard de Lalande wrote his *Ballet de la paix*

---

  [2] Cf. Josef Rafael CARRERAS Y BULBENA, *Carlos d'Austria y Elisabeth de Brunswick Wolfenbüttel Barcelona y Girona*, Barcelona, L'Anenç, 1902; and now, with new archival documents, Andrea SOMMER-MATHIS, *Von Barcelona nach Wien: Die Einrichtung des Musik- und Theaterbetriebes am Wiener Hof durch Karl VI.*, in *Musica Conservata: Günter Brosche zum 60. Geburtstag*, Tutzing, Schneider, 1999, pp. 355-380.

  [3] Cf. below, p. 399.

  [4] MGG², *Personenteil*, V, 286.

  [5] Edward DENT, *Alessandro Scarlatti: His Life and Works*, London, Arnold, 1905, p. 69.

  [6] DE LA TORRE, III, 333 and IV, 69.

  [7] *Wienerisches Diarium*, 1701ff; *Le Mercure galant*, 1701ff; *Gazetta di Mantova*, 1704ff; Michel BRENET, *Les Musiciens de la Sainte-Chapelle du Palais*, Paris, Piccard, 1910, pp. 267-275.

  [8] BRENET, pp. 375f.

for the king of exhausted France.[9] The Peace of Rastatt (1714) seems to be alluded to in Alessandro Scarlatti's serenata *Pace, Amore, Provvidenza*.[10]

But there are musical events – operas, oratorios, cantatas – that reveal more of the political and human intricacies behind the facades of victories. Some mark the way of the affairs of state by circumstances of their performance. Some, in their musical style, show the influence of a foreign garrison, a partisanship of taste. Others allude in their texts to political events or even have a political mission. An eminent figure is mocked, a prince in his exile dreams of lost splendor, territorial pretensions are presented, the hope of reconciliation is expressed, flattery is a means of propaganda. Thus history is recorded in works of Antonio Caldara (1670/71 Venice - 1736 Vienna), who was employed successively by rival sovereigns involved in the war.

His career, though stormy, was brilliant: until May 1699 he was active principally as harpsichordist, 'cellist, and composer in all genres, especially esteemed for his contrapuntal ability; thereafter, until the end of 1707, court chapel master of the duke of Mantua; from 1708 travel to Rome, Barcelona, Venice; from 1 March 1709 until May 1716 chapel master of (now) Prince Ruspoli in Rome (with an extended one-year leave 1711-12 to Vienna); and the last twenty years of his life as vice chapel master of Emperor Charles VI in Vienna. His works – estimated today at ca. 3,400[11] – already in Venice attracted attention as far as England and France. In Vienna he was left free from the administrative work which so burdened Fux, in order to compose the greater part of the festive operas, church music, etc. for the court, receiving unique favours and a far higher salary than this chapel master or anyone else in the latter office ever had. Telemann, Bach, Leopold Mozart, Albrechtsberger, Beethoven, and still Brahms studied and copied his music as a model.[12]

Shortly after Caldara's appointment as court chapel master in Mantua[13] the war arrived also there. Since little archival material and even less music survived the hostilities, this last chapter of the music history of the Gonzaga dynasty has been rather clouded.[14] It proves, however, to be still worthy of the family's great tradition, although the public affairs of the duchy had already reached their most miserable state.

---

[9] Robert EITNER, *Quellenlexikon*, Leipzig, Breitkopf & Härtel, 1900-16, VI, 19.

[10] DENT, p. 131.

[11] By Angela Romagnoli in MGG², *Personenteil*, III, 1669.

[12] For a more comprehensive evaluation of Caldara's reputation, cf. *AC 2007* pp. 125-134.

[13] Document of appointment in Paola BESUTTI, *La corte musicale di Ferdinando Carlo Gonzaga ultimo duca di Mantova: musici, cantanti e teatro d'opera tra il 1665 e il 1707*, Mantua, Acari, 1989, pp. 83f.

[14] Cf. MGG¹, *loc. cit.*

Along with the preparations for the Italian campaign in January 1701 the main interest of both parties had become directed towards the fortress of Mantua, "one of the principle keys to Italy, a very strong fortress, for the defence of the state of Milan".[15] In vain Leopold reminded the Duke of his obligations as a vassal of the Emperor; the duke even put his capital at the disposal of the French troops. On 7 April 1701, Count Tessé entered Mantua with six thousand men. To the Duke of Bourgogne he declared:[16]

... et c'est le meilleur succès pour les affairs des rois, votre grand-père et votre frère, que l'on pouvoit espérer; c'est même quasi la seule chose qui peut le plus déconcerter les projets et la colère, pour ne pas dire fureur, de Sa Majesté Impériale.	... and that is the greatest success for the affairs of the kings, your grandfather and your brother [Louis XIV of France and Philip V of Spain], that one could hope for. It is even almost the only thing which could most disturb the plans and [arouse] the anger, not to say the fury, of His Imperial Majesty [Emperor Leopold].

Leopold reacted most sharply: he immediately accused the Duke of high treason, banned him, and liberated all subjects from their duties towards their sovereign. From this moment the Duke's chances depended upon the success of the French in Italy. With their defeat in 1706 his fate was sealed.

Ferdinando Carlo Gonzaga (Plate VIII.1), born in 1652 and since 1669 tenth Duke of Mantua and eighth of Monferrato, was mocked as one of the most infamous debtors of his time.[17] His early sponsors, including Venice, had refused for many years to give him further credit – all but France. Louis XIV had indefatigably supplied him with enormous sums and now promised him a monthly pension of 30,000 *scudi* "to be able to continue to live in his pleasures and debauches".[18] Contemporary accounts are unanimous that these pleasures meant ladies, opera, the Venetian carnival.[19] We do not know whether Ferdinando Carlo's passion for the opera was founded on a thorough musical education or, what seems more likely, whether it was just one part of his addiction to the whole theatrical complex. But we have evidence that he

---

[15] "une des principales clefs d'Italie, & un rempart très fort, pour la défense de l'état de Milan" – DE LA TORRE, III, 218.

[16] [Mans Jean Baptiste René De FROULAY, Comte] de TESSÉ, *Lettres du Maréchal de Tessé a Madame la Duchesse de Bourgogne, Madame la Princesse des Ursins, Madame de Maintenon, Monsieur de Pontchartrin, etc. Publiées par le Comte de Rambuteau*, Paris, Calman Lévy, 1888, p. 32.

[17] Giuseppe FOCHESSATI, *I Gonzaga di Mantova e l'ultimo duca*, Milan, Ceschina, 1930², pp. 194ff.

[18] "pour pouvoir continuer de vivre dans ses plaisirs, & ses débauches" – DE LA TORRE, III, 219 and 241.

[19] *Ibid.*, p. 219f. Cf. FOCHESSATI, *loc. cit.*

demanded the highest quality. Muratori tells in his *Annali* of 1690 that the Dukes of Mantua and Modena were the leading Italian princes in the tug-of-war for the virtuosos.[20] Indeed, the most celebrated singers from the 1690s to 1707 were employed by the Duke, in Mantua, Venice, and elsewhere, expressly called "virtuosi del Serenissimo di Mantova" in many libretti:[21] Diamante Scarabelli; Alessandra Scaccia; Margherita Raimondi detta la Salarina; Maria Landini, later the wife of Francesco Conti; Santa Stella, later the wife of Antonio Lotti; Francesca Vanini, who had her greatest triumphs with Handel in London, then married to the famous Giuseppe Boschi; Valentino Urbani, who also was praised by Handel; the celebrated Domenico Cecchi detto Cortona – to name only those whose fame became international. Moreover, documents in the Archivio di Stato in Mantua from July 1700 to the end of 1704 list also the very young Margherita Durastante (b. 1686) and her relatives; she was to become Ruspoli's and Handel's most important singer in Rome.[22]

Ferdinando Carlo adhered to his blissful way of life even during the last seven years. Operas accompany all stages of his exit, throwing uncanny light on it, since they partly cause it. *La Partenope*, performed in the carnival 1701, is the last great musical event in prewar Mantua. The famous libretto names the poet, not the composer, and tells us that the work was previously performed at Naples, in 1699, then dedicated to the Vice-queen, now to the Duchess of Mantua.[23] Partenope is again the mythic foundress, the personified city of Naples.[24] At a time when the duke was already involved in negotiations

---

[20] Lodovico Antonio MURATORI, *Annali d'Italia dal principio dell'era volgare sino all'anno 1748*, XI, Milan, Pasquali, 1749, p. 392.

[21] Cf. the abstracts given by Taddeo WIEL, *I teatri musicali Veneziani del Settecento*, Venice, Visentini, 1897, and the indices of SL.

[22] Paola BESUTTI, *La figura professionale del cantante d'opera: le virtuose di Ferdinando Carlo Gonzaga*, «Quaderni storici», XXII/2, no. 9, 1997, p. 431.

[23] SL 17815. Silvio Stampiglia's text may have been set to music in Naples by Alessandro Scarlatti, and two years later in Mantua by Caldara, whose name is the first to appear in the many libretti dating from different performances (cf. AC 2007 p. 39 and note 86, for a list of the libretti and further argumentation).

[24] "Fu Partenope figlia d'Eumelo Rè di Fera in Tessaglia, la quale partisse da Calcide dell'Isola d'Euboa, oggi Negroponte, seguendo l'augurio d'una bianca colomba, e fece edificare una città appresso le sponde del Mar Tirreno, che fu detta Partenope, e poi fu chiamata Napoli" ["Partenope was the daughter of Eumelos, king of Fera in Thessaly. She departed from Calcide on the island of Euboa, [called] Negroponte today, following the augury of a white dove, and had a city built on the shores of the Tyrrhenian Sea. It was named Partenope, and afterwards was called Naples"] – libretto, p. 3. Alessandro Scarlatti wrote a serenata, *Il genio di Partenope, la gloria del Sebeto, il piacere di Mergellina* in 1696 (cf. DENT, pp. 68 and 211) and an undated cantata *Partenope, Teti, Nettuno, Prote, e Glauco* (ms. US-Wc M 1490 S 28) "celebrating a naval expedition of the Emperor Charles VI against the Turks" – Edwin HANLEY, *Alessandro Scarlatti's Cantate da Camera: A Bibliographical Study*, ms. diss. Yale Univ., 1963, p. 64.

with both of the hostile powers, this glorification of Spanish Naples on the stage of Mantua strongly demonstrated his partisanship with the Spaniards.

The *Opera pastorale*, extant in Caldara's autograph score with his note "Musica di Ant.° Caldara Maestro di Cappella di S.A.S. Ferdinando Carlo Duca di Mantova nell'anno 1701",[25] marks the first stage of the Mantuan war. Was it planned for the carnival 1701/02? This would explain why there is no printed libretto extant. From December 1701 to July 1702 Prince Eugene blockaded the French inside Mantua's walls, among them Tessé and the duke. Hunger and inflation raged,[26] and even the optimistic reports to the French court mention only modest amusements.[27] There was probably no carnival that year and no performance of an opera.[28]

Prince Eugene gave up the siege in July 1702, and the Duke hastened to move to a safer place. He went to Casale, the strongly fortified capital of his duchy Monferrato, close to the friendly borders of France and Savoy, and remained there for three years. He left his wife Anna Isabella at home, but took his whole court with him,[29] and an observer noted especially the inclusion of "part of his male and female music[ians] with his poet to prepare an opera for him".[30] This opera, *Gli equivoci del sembiante*, was composed by "Sig. Antonio Caldara Mastro di Cappella di S.A.S." and performed in the new theater of Casale during the carnival of 1703 with the grand ensemble of singers mentioned above.[31] The contrast between the boundless splendor of the stage and the desperate historical situation is grotesque: the Duke pursued and escaping, lavishing incredible sums, sustained by the inexhaustible King of France, who still needs the lord of Mantua.

A tragicomic episode is reflected in the libretti of two operas which were performed the following year far from Casale, on the stage of Mantua: *Il trionfo d'amore*[32] and *Paride sull'Ida, ovvero gli amori di Paride con Enone*,[33] the

---

[25] A-Wgm III 16124 (A 352).

[26] *Il fioretto delle croniche di Mantova raccolto già da Stefano Gionta, ed in quest'ultima edizione ampliato* [by Federigo Amadei] *colle cose più notabil di essa città succedute fino al presente anno MDCCXLI*, Mantua, Ferrari, 1741, p. 150.

[27] TESSÉ, pp. 79ff.

[28] In Feb. 1711 the *Opera pastorale la costanza in amor vince l'inganno*, SL 6807, appeared in Ruspoli's private theater, probably now performed for the first time – cf. *AC* 1966 pp. 32, 57f = *AC* 2007 pp. 39f, 73.

[29] *Il fioretto*, p. 151.

[30] Cf. FOCHESSATI, p. 230.

[31] SL 8980. The score seems to be lost.

[32] SL 23651.

[33] SL 17784. The score seems to be lost.

first composed by Quintavalle, the second "parte del sig. Antonio Caldara primo mastro di capella di S.A.S. di Mant., parte del sig. Antonio Quintavalle
primo organista di S.A.S. di Mantova".[34] Anna Isabella, Duchess of Mantua,
had died on 19 November 1703 in Mantua. The Duke did not come home for
her obsequies. *Il trionfo d'amore* is dedicated to the general of the French
troops in Mantua Gaston de Choiseul, and this dedication is signed only
one month after Anna Isabella's death.[35] The work was surely planned immediately after the funeral. *Paride* appeared in the spring.[36] It is striking that so
little consideration for the sad event is shown, and there is no doubt that these
operas were commissioned by the French officers who obviously regarded the
ducal theater as their own. In both operas the singers were second class.[37]

Where was the Duke? According to Federigo Amadei, later secretary of
the Duke's prime minister and compiler of the famous *Croniche* of Mantua,
he did not come to the funeral because he was on the point of going to
France. Ferdinando Carlo left Casale with his retinue on 8 March 1704, arrived in Versailles on 10 May, and was embraced by the King.[38] We know
that at least six proposals for a new marriage were then offered,[39] and that
three of them were considered seriously: Susanna-Enrichetta di Lorena Elbeuf, Maria-Enrichetta di Carretto, Duchess of Aremberg, and Louise de
Duras, Duchess of Lesdiguières.[40]

The titles of the Mantuan operas, especially the love affairs of Paris on
Mount Ida fit these events all too well! And indeed, there was a connection.
Marshal de Tessé, whose brilliant letters from Northern Italy to Versailles are
valuable sources for Mantuan history, wrote to the Marquis de Torcy on 23
July:[41]

C'en est un que la conduite de notre Sé-
rénissime, des engagements duquels vous
prenez la peine de m'en mander assez
pour devoire croire que Mademoiselle
d'Elbeuf remportera la pomme. Mais
d'un tel Paris permettez-moi de vous ré-

Regarding the conduct of our Serenissi-
mus, you take pains to write me enough
about his engagements that I must believe
that Mademoiselle d'Elbeuf will carry the
apple away. But with such a Paris, allow
me to repeat, fear is the only motor, ...

[34] Libretto, p. 7.
[35] "Dicembre 19, 1703".
[36] "Da rappresentarsi nella primavera dell'anno 1704" (title page).
[37] Cf. *AC* 1966 pp. 33f = *AC* 2007 pp. 41f. They were obviously those who had stayed in Mantua, in the service of Anna Isabella.
[38] *Il Fioretto*, pp. 152f.
[39] FOCHESSATI, p. 234.
[40] TESSÉ, pp. 175f, editor's note. These persons are discussed by Tessé at different places.
[41] *Ibid.*, p. 191.

péter que la peur est le seul mobile, ... plus certain que l'amour, et que si ce mariage se fait, je croirai que c'est parce que le Roi l'aura agréé et permis. Il n'est pas question de quatre pieds trois pouces, qu'il vent admettre à la taille favorite de ses Dulcinées, il est question de lui dire: 'Je veux', et si Junon, femme de Jupiter, sur le mont Ida, avoit parlé du ton de maîtresse, et dit au berger qu'elle vouloit avoir la préférence, non seulement elle se seroit épargné la honte de montrer son derrière, mais elle auroit évité peut-être de mettre l'Asie en cendres.

more certain than love, and if this marriage takes place I shall believe it is because the king will have agreed to and permitted it. It is not a question of four feet and three inches which he wishes to put on the favorite waist of his Dulcineas; it is a question of telling him 'I want', and if Juno, Jupiter's wife, had spoken to him on Mt. Ida in the tone of a mistress, and told the shepherd [Paris] that she wanted to be preferred, she would not only have been spared the shame of him turning his back on her, but perhaps would also have avoided setting Asia on fire [refers to Venus rewarding Paris with Helen, starting the Trojan War].

Tessé had recommended the Duke to the French court in terms of acrid 'pity':[42]

Le Duc de Mantoue est le seul fidèle, mais il est impuissant; il vous a donné tout, il ne lui reste que trois cent e sept demoiselles; son pays est abimé, il mérite toute sorte de bons traitements.

The Duke of Mantua is the only faithful one, but he is powerless; he has given you everything, he has nothing left but 307 damsels; his country is devastated, he deserves all kind of good treatment.

His letter of 28 December 1703 makes clear that the French were informed about the Duke's new marriage plans immediately after Anna Isabella's death:[43]

Ce prince voluptueux est capable de tout faire par les principes imaginaires de plaisirs, dont la possession le dégoûte dans le moment. Immédiatement après la mort e Madame de Mantoue, il désira passionément Mademoiselle d'Elbeuf sur ce qu'on lui avoit dit qu'elle étoit grande.

This voluptuous prince is capable of doing everything by the imaginary principles of pleasure, its possession disgusts him in a moment. Immediately after the death of Madame of Mantua he passionately desired Mademoiselle d'Elbeuf, because he was told that she is tall.

There is no doubt that the French officers in Mantua were mocking Monsieur de Mantoue with *Paride sull'Ida*. They were very gallant when they had

---

[42] *Ibid.*, p. 102.
[43] *Ibid.*, p. 176, 28 Dec. 1703 [!] from Milan.

treaty of Milan, on 13 March 1707, Austria took over the sovereignty of Mantua. The inhabitants of the disloyal city feared the worst, and sent a deputation to the Emperor to beg for mercy. In these weeks of greatest distress His Serene Highness enjoyed in Venice two operas performed by his own virtuosos at the "famosissimo teatro di San Giovanni Grisostomo": *La Partenope*[52] and *Il selvaggio eroe*.

In the libretto of *La Partenope* the printer says that the old work, only slightly changed, has been restaged by high command. This leads to the suggestion that the Duke brought the score with him from Mantua, together with all his treasures and books, and that in this way Caldara's Mantuan works may have found their way to Venice. With *La Partenope* Ferdinando Carlo recalled once again the glorious days of Mantua which he had now lost forever. A French observer reports: "He is so delighted not to be in Mantua any longer, that he enjoys with more tranquility the pleasures of the carnival".[53]

In the libretto of *Il selvaggio eroe* the composer Caldara is called "Maestro di Cappella del Ser. di Mantova" for the last time.[54] At the latest, he departed at the beginning of 1708 for Rome, where an oratorio of his was performed during Lent.[55] The members of the Gonzaga court retired one after the other, following the Emperor's warning to abandon Ferdinando Carlo or risk the penalty of confiscation.[56] The prime minister left Venice by night, fearing the Duke's revenge, and we also lose trace of Caldara for some months. Ferdinando Carlo was banned and outlawed by the Diet of Regensburg on 30 June 1708. Five days later his sudden, mysterious death "solved the embarrassing case in a natural way" (Noorden). After four hundred years of sovereignty this was the end of the house of Gonzaga in Mantua, that had sheltered Andrea Mantegna, Giulio Romano, Torquato Tasso, Peter Paul Rubens, and Claudio Monteverdi.

French Mantua (and Paris?) has left traces in Caldara's musical style. As far as we know, the only extant operas from these years may be *L'ingratitudine gastigata* and the *Opera pastorale*, for which we have the score but no libretto; and of the surely extensive church music only a few fragments have survived. But some of Caldara's oratorios – *La frode della Castità*, *Le gelosie d'un amore*

---

[52] SL 17817. The score seems to be lost.

[53] "Il se trouve si charmé de n'être plus à Mantoue, qu'il en goûte avec plus de tranquillité les plaisirs du carnoval" – quoted in FOCHESSATI, p. 244.

[54] SL 21475, p. 11.

[55] Cf. *AC* 2007 pp. 48f; also pp. 47f, the discussion of the anonymous *L'ingratitudine gastigata* (1708), with a libretto dedicated to imperial functionaries and again containing malicious allusions to Ferdinando Carlo, but not identical to Caldara's homonymous opera, performed probably in 1702.

[56] FOCHESSATI, p. 249.

utilmente crudele, and *Il trionfo dell'innocenza*,[57] extant in the Santini collection in manuscripts copied by Ruspoli's Roman scribes from February to April 1711 – might be assigned to the early Mantuan years because of their French characteristics and their antiquated physiognomy as compared to works from 1708 to 1711. Here, the scale-like themes in dotted rhythm, so familiar from Lully's music, are used in arias of tyrants referring to a violent death (for example, "Pensa ch'il vivere, e il morir da te dipende" and "Vanne a morir").[58] Later too, Caldara employed French styles, more rarely, but still consciously. Of his seventeen oratorios written before 1716 only one begins with a French overture. It appropriately announces "le roi très chrétien": *La conversione di Clodoveo re di Francia*.[59]

Returning to the war in Italy, 1707 – now to Rome and Ruspoli. Until the middle of the year he commissioned works from Alessandro Scarlatti and Handel which clearly reflect the troubled times and where he intervened himself.[60] Naples fell on 10 July, and although it was a defeat for the Spanish lands, peace, it seemed, returned to Italy. The conquest was celebrated in Vienna with Carlo Antonio Badia's serenata *Napoli ritornata a' Romani* [i.e. Naples restored to the Holy Roman Empire] on King Charles' birthday, 1 October 1707.[61]

During Lent 1708 Caldara's oratorio *Il martirio di Santa Caterina* was performed for Cardinal Pietro Ottoboni in the Roman *cancelleria*. The composer surely did not miss the opportunity to appear personally in this prestigous venue of his fellow Venetian, at a time when brilliant musicians were present: not only Corelli and Cesarini (the chapel masters of Ottoboni and Pamphilj, respectively), Alessandro and Domenico Scarlatti, and other Italians, but also, attracting the most attention, the young Handel, who at Easter had his oratorio *La Resurrezione* performed five times in the splendid Bonelli palace.

But soon Caldara must have departed for the north, where an 'enemy' now gave him a highly important commission: *Il più bel nome nel festeggirsi il nome felicissimo di Sua Maestà Cattolica Elisabetta Cristina de le Spagne*.

---

[57] D-MÜs Hss. 743, 744, and 745. Chronology and style are discussed in *AC* 1966 pp. 223-238 = *AC* 2007 pp. 282-301. The earlier date is supported by the news of a Florentine performance of *Il trionfo dell'innocenza* in 1704.

[58] *La frode della Castità*, aria of Clearco (no. 12); and *Il trionfo dell'innocenza*, aria of Melantia (no. 21). On the style, cf. also above, p. 241.

[59] D-MÜs Hs. 741. First performed 14 April 1715, in Palazzo Ruspoli, Via del Corso.

[60] Cf. below, ch. 11.

[61] Ludwig Ritter von KÖCHEL, *Johann Josef Fux*, Vienna, Hölder, 1872, Beilage VIII, no. 439.

Componimento da camera per musica. Poesia del Dottor Pietro Pariati. Musica di Antonio Caldara.[62] I could recently demonstrate that this music belonged neither to the actual wedding of Charles III and Elizabeth Christina of Braunschweig-Wolfenbüttel on 2 August 1708 – as I had once assumed[63] – nor to one of the various namedays of Elizabeth (19 Nov.), but was performed in June in Milan during the bride's voyage from Vienna to Barcelona.[64] Shortly before departing from Vienna, she had been married *per procurationem* to Charles represented by his brother Emperor Joseph I. From Milan it is quite possible that Caldara and Pariati continued with the retinue to Barcelona, since another *componimento* of theirs may have been produced there, *Il nome più glorioso*[65] for Charles' nameday (4 Nov.), though not only the place, but also the year is uncertain. Incidentally, one of the five roles in *Il più bel nome* is already Hercules, but he does not speak of his 'Spanish' labor, the theft of the golden apples from the Hesperides. Only in later works for Charles do we find this myth, where the emperor is compared to Hercules. It has been assumed that this has something to do with the pretensions to Spain.[66] Of course they claim the whole of the peninsula from the Pyrenees to the pillars of Hercules – not only by a free allegorical figure. Charles took the two columns into his emblem and seal with the inscription *Constantia et Fortitudine*.[67] He officially assumed the figure of the mythic hero. The two columns in front of the church of Saint Charles (after 1716) in Vienna have been proven to be a translation of this idea into architecture,[68] and Fux's opera *Costanza e Fortezza* in 1723 for Charles' Bohemian coronation still echoes the old pretensions.[69]

In the spring of 1708 the peace still seemed to prevail in southern as well as in northern Italy. But in the early summer hostilities flaired up once more. Emperor Joseph had sent his troops into the Papal territories to force Pope Clement XI to acknowledge his brother Charles. Roman princes had to mobilize troops for the pope. Ruspoli supplied a regiment of 550 men, marshalled on Sunday, 9 September 1708 on the Piazza Santi Apostoli. And for this occasion

---

[62] Title page of the score, ms. B-Bc 584 (the only source).

[63] *AC* 1966 pp. 41f.

[64] *AC* 2007 p. 52ff.

[65] Ms. A-Wn 18238.

[66] John Henry VAN DER MEER, *Johann Josef Fux als Opernkomponist*, Bilthoven, Creighton, 1961, I, 99.

[67] Gustav HERAEUS, *Inscriptiones et Symbola*, Vienna, 1723, p. 23.

[68] George KUNOTH, *Die Historische Architektur Fischers von Erlach*, Düsseldorf, Schwann, 1956, p. 145.

[69] Charles VI never gave up his title "Hispaniae Rex".

Handel performed his serenata *Olinto* ("O come chiare e belle" HWV 143)[70] to the text of this patron, named 'Olinto' in the Arcadia, here as assistant to "Gloria", who will restore her ancient splendor on the banks of "il Tebro", under the light of the "astro Clemente" ["Clement star"];[71] the warrior's laurel will then miraculously become a branch of the olive tree, announcing peace. This festive day was commemorated also in an enormous painting by Alessandro Piazza, now in the Palazzo Ruspoli in Via del Corso.[72]

At last, on 15 January 1709, under utmost pressure, Clement signed the treaty obliging him to demobilize his troops and recognize Charles as the Catholic King of Spain. The French ambassador left Rome in uproarious protest.[73] (It surely meant a demonstration of sympathies for France when a few weeks later, during Lent, Maria Casimira Queen of Poland presented Domenico Scarlatti's oratorio *La Conversione di Clodoveo re di Francia* in her Roman palace).[74] Reconciliation was slow. When Charles was crowned Emperor Charles VI, on 19 December 1711, Clement did not hasten to recognize him. It was not until February 1714 that he gave his *confirmatio electionis*.[75]

On 5 February 1709, soon after the truce, Ruspoli had been made prince of Ceveteri by the pope. And immediately thereafter he, as we know, summoned Caldara as his chapel master. The Venetian had already composed 'royal' music, and now that hostilities had subsided, there was no obstacle to his appoimtment. For him began another brilliant and prolific period. An an amusing aside in the account books informs us that in February 1711 the prince still employed some of his soldiers: "sargenti e soldati della compagnia colonnella Ruspoli" ["sargeants and soldiers of the Ruspoli regiment"] were paid for their assistance in Caldara's opera *L'Anagilda*,[76] presumably as mute supernumeraries.

But the documents also reveal that Caldara obtained a leave of absence from the prince in May 1711 with the obligation to send back further com-

---

[70] It is mentioned by Ruspoli's copyist Antonio Giuseppe Angelini in a bill receipted 10 September 1708 – cf. p. 342, Doc. 27, and p. 401. Edited in «Hallische Händel-Ausgabe», Ser. V, Bd. 4, Kassel, Bärenreiter, 1995, pp. 227-256. Cf. Percy ROBINSON, *Handel and his Orbit*, London, Sherratt & Hughes, 1908, p. 173.

[71] Allusion to the star in the pope's coat of arms – cf. *AC* 2007, Plate 12.

[72] Reproduced below, ch. 11, Plates XI.10-12.

[73] Leopold von RANKE, *Die römischen Päpste in den letzten vier Jahrhunderten*, Cologne, Phaidon, n.d., p. 732.

[74] SL 6541.

[75] Ludwig Freiherr von PASTOR, *Geschichte der Päpste im Zeitalter des fürstlichen Absolutismus*, XV, Freiburg, Herder, 1930, p. 69.

[76] *AC* Doc. 100.

positions.[77] He stayed in Milan with King Charles who had come back from Barcelona, and may have accompanied him to the coronation in Frankfurt in November. After Charles' entry into Vienna Caldara is soon found at the Imperial court, favored with the most honorable commissions. In the middle of June 1712 he, with his wife and infant daughter Sofia Giacobina Maria (baptized on 9 May), embarked upon the return to Rome and then to Albano. In November Ruspoli summoned him back to Rome. On the first Sunday of Lent, 5 March 1713 the *Oratorio Santo Stefano primo re d'Ungheria* was heard in the Bonelli palace.

I find testimony of Charles' efforts to reconcile the pope in this oratorio, extant in score in the Santini collection.[78] It differs from the other sixteen oratorios which Caldara composed before 1716[79] by its complete lack of action.[80] Stefano, the first king of Hungary, and his court praise unanimously their happy relations with the Pope. Towards the end of *Parte seconda* Stefano describes his gloomy vision of Hungary that is rent by sanguinary revolts and unbelief. Yet "nel gran soglio di Piero ... un'anima Clemente" ["a Clement soul on the great throne of Peter"] will restore peace and belief in this country. The Pope's name then is alluded to in several numbers ("a piè della Clemenza," "la Clemenza assisa in soglio", etc.). The last four lines of the final recitative make Stefano say that he longs to adore the reigning Clemency on the banks of the Tiber and to see reborn the triumphs of Augustus on the Capitol.[81] Since this part, in the manner of a *licenza*, projects the relations between emperor and pope into the present, we are allowed to presume Stefano to be the Emperor, who was also King of Hungary and had Saint Stephan's crown in his treasury. Here we are reminded of paintings of ancient historical events ordered by secular sovereigns and popes who had accomplished similar feats and had their ancient counterparts depicted with their own features (e.g. Raphael's *stanze* in the Vatican).

Archival documents enable us to date the oratorio precisely. The score was copied by Francesco Lanciani, Caldara's main scribe in Rome. Lanciani's

---

[77] The documents of Caldara's years are published in *AC* 1966 pp. 350-378 = *AC* 2007 pp. 445-479.

[78] Hs. 736.

[79] Bibliography and discussion of political content and style in *AC* 1966 pp. 118, 161, 277-280 = *AC* 2007 pp. 153, 210f, 348-351.

[80] This seems, in general, typical for occasional oratorios, cf. the *Occasional Oratorio* composed by Handel in 1746.

[81] Allusions to the name of Clement XI in Roman compositions of the time are rather frequent (cf. the above-mentioned cantata "O come chiare e belle" by Handel, and *AC* 1966 pp. 49, 68, 161ff = *AC* 2007 pp. 62f, 85, 210f), like those to his namesakes in earlier centuries. In Caldara's libretto of Rome, Komarek, 1726, "un'anima Clemente" is replaced by "una celeste mente".

bill for the parts, in the Ruspoli archive, is dated 17 March 1712.[82] At this time Caldara was in Vienna, composing for the Emperor. Yet during his leave of absence from Ruspoli he continued to send works to Rome. Several compositions completed and dated in Milan and Vienna are mentioned a few weeks later in the bills of Ruspoli's copyists.[83] In Vienna, Caldara seems to have worked on *Santo Stefano* no later than January. Charles had then been crowned only several weeks, and was waiting impatiently for the papal confirmation – we know of the obstinate negotiations of his ambassador;[84] later he probably became accustomed to waiting. The libretto, which had already been set by Flavio Carlo Lanciani in 1687,[85] was modified – surely according to the emperor's wishes – with the intention of winning the Pope for the imperial cause. Stefano's vision of "unhappy Hungary" ("sventurata Ungheria") and the flattering passage on the shielding "Clemenza" seem to refer to Clement's first benevolent gesture towards the house of Austria: in a brief to the primate of Hungary, on 17 August 1709, Clement had officially damned the Hungarian revolution.[86] Ruspoli, however, did not make himself the instrument of Viennese politics. *Stefano* was not performed in his palace until 1713,[87] when the tension had somewhat relaxed.

Why was the work sent to him and not to one of the cardinals? We know that he had already given splendid peformances. After being made prince he did not slacken in his ambition to offer the most exquisite and lavish musical events of the city. Maria di Piedz, Agnese Corsie, Giuseppe Valentini, Silvestrino Rotondi, Giuseppe Peroni, Domenico and Pietro Castrucci were then among his virtuosos.[88] The music expenses often equalled and sometimes exceeded those for the whole household of eighty to ninety persons. In 1715 the German Baron von Uffenbach reported that Ruspoli's concerts were then regarded as the finest in Rome.[89] Immense financial resources guaranteed a regularity that those of Pamphilj and Ottoboni no longer had after 1710.[90] It was

---

[82] *AC* Doc. 148.

[83] Cf. *AC* 1966 pp. 64, 118 = *AC* 2007 pp. 80f, 153. Caldara used to sign each autograph with the place and day of its completion.

[84] LANDAU, pp. 450ff.

[85] Gloria STAFFIERI, *Colligite fragmenta: la vita musicale romana negli 'Avvisi Marescotti' (1683-1707)*, Lucca, LIM, 1990, pp. 23, 76; Arnaldo MORELLI, *Il tempio armonico: musica nell'oratorio dei Filippini in Roma (1575-1705)*, Laaber, Laaber Verlag, 1991, doc. 408.

[86] LANDAU, p. 438f.

[87] *AC* Doc. 187.

[88] *AC* 1966 pp. 350-355 etc. = *AC* 2007 pp. 437-444 etc.

[89] *AC* 1966 pp. 74f = *AC* 2007 pp. 92f.

[90] The extracts from Pamphilj's *giustificazioni* given by Lina MONTALTO, *Un cardinale in Roma*

in Ruspoli's palace where the Roman aristocracy and the lords of the curia assembled every Sunday night, and even travellers were admitted without introduction.[91] At this marketplace of music and opinions the Emperor's intentions would not have fallen on deaf ears.

To Caldara the Emperor's commission once more meant much honor, before the appointment in Vienna. Probably in the fortifications of Barcelona Charles' extraordinary affection for Caldara had begun. It lasted for more than thirty years, even after Caldara's death, as is shown in the letter of Luca Antonio Predieri to Padre Martini, 15 March 1738. Predieri writes that several composers had tried in vain to obtain the position of vice chapel master during the fifteen months after Caldara's death. He, Predieri, who had submitted works of Martini as his own, was the first who was able to please the Emperor to some extent. His success "stupified everyone, since no one could believe that after Caldara a composer would ever again please the emperor".[92]

barocca, Florence, Sansoni, 1955, pp. 338f, seem to indicate a negligence of the house music then. Ottoboni is known to have been in considerable financial difficulties (cf. below, p. 394).

[91] Uffenbach's report is confirmed by continuous information from Ruspoli's *giustificazioni* concerning the weekly copies, refreshments, etc. for the *conversazione*. The names of the distinguished guests are preserved in the lists of *mancie* paid to their servants.

[92] "ha fatto stordir tutti poiché nessuno poteva mai credere che doppo Caldara altro compositore potesse piacergli" – I-Bc Ep. mart. I.3.126; Adelmo DAMERINI, *Luca Antonio Predieri e il suo "Stabat"*, in Accademia Musicale Chigiana, *Musicisti della Scuola Emiliana*, Siena, Ticci, 1956, p. 36.

IX.

THE RUSPOLI DOCUMENTS ON HANDEL*

The first sojourn in Italy, "it was a period of glorious uncertainty for Handel".[1] Was it? No one knows [1967]. Perhaps a period of glorious uncertainty had overcome the biographer when he wrote this. Few chapters in the lives of major eighteenth-century composers are still as dark as this one. Few also are as fascinating. We know some of its components, but very little about their composition. There are fabulous ones, as provided by Mainwaring:[2] princes and cardinals rivaling to house the young genius; in Naples a palace, coaches and lackeys; in Florence a princely china set and the favor of a grand ducal prima donna; diamonds in Rome; recognition. And, significantly, it is these fabulous components that seem to be backed by the weightiest authority, by Handel himself (one knows that Mainwaring had his information from Handel's confidant, the younger Smith). This was what the old master remembered best. Through the distance of half a century, his Italian years must have appeared to him in a rosy dawn, the aurora of his art and career: "Et in Arcadia ego". To reconcile the eighteenth-century sources – Mainwaring's account, Mattheson's *Ehrenpforte* sketch, Hawkins' interview, Pseudo-Coxe's *Anecdotes*, and the few datable compositions – has proved impossible. Chrysander's version[3] was long ago discarded by Ademollo[4] and Streatfeild,[5]

---

* [**PS**: The text of 1967 is presented here more or less intact, with revisions indicated by "**PS**" in square brackets, often with references to *HR* = below, ch. 11. The time for my work in Rome almost half a century ago was limited by a student budget. After acquiring a domicile in Trastevere in 1983 the work could benefit from longer experience and removal of time limits for the continual checking which archival work requires, now done not in a few weeks, but in several decades. Most of the addenda and corrigenda are supplied in *HR*. Consultation of ch. IX and XI is now facilitated by the listing of HWV numbers on pp. 347ff and 617f].

[1] Sir Newman FLOWER, *George Frederic Handel, His Personality and His Times*, Boston and New York, Cassell, 1923, p. 64.

[2] John MAINWARING, *Memoirs of the Late George Frederic Handel*, London, Dodsley, 1760.

[3] Friedrich CHRYSANDER, *G. F. Händel*, I, Leipzig, Breitkopf & Härtel, 1858, pp. 147-251. We can still admire in this pioneer work the amount of material on contemporaries and institutions – to mention here only the information on Roman patrons and on the Arcadia.

which did not prevent it from setting the pattern for nearly all the following monographs.[6] Robinson shrewdly demonstrated that we knew next to nothing.[7] A summary of the few facts known in the 1930s was given by him in tabular form as a reply to Dent.[8] The fog of legend can indeed be dispelled only if we refrain from further speculation on the anecdotes. The Italian journey has to be reconstructed by documentary and bibliographical evidence, which then, in turn, may confirm an old report here and there.

Since Robinson's time considerable information has been added. Montalto presented the copyist's bill for *Il Trionfo del Tempo* and *Il delirio amoroso*.[9] Fabbri traced some of Handel's movements between Lent 1709 and September 1709 by means of three letters in the Archivio Mediceo del Principato.[10] Zanetti published the first preliminary catalogue of Handel's 'Italian' works.[11]

---

[4] Alessandro ADEMOLLO, *G. F. Haendel in Italia*, «Gazzetta musicale di Milano», XLIV, 1889, pp. 257ff, 283ff, 303ff.

[5] R. A. STREATFEILD, *Handel in Italy*, «Musical Antiquary», I, 1909/10, pp. 1-14.

[6] Chrysander built Handel's itinerary on the encounters with Prince Gian Gastone de' Medici, the Duke of Manchester, and Agostino Steffani, as reported by Mainwaring, generously adding Prince Ernst August of Hanover to this list. In Rolland's, Leichtentritt's, and many others' biographies his hypotheses became part of the tale. Flower's chapter on "The Italian Journey" is for the most part unscrupulously invented, the route not only fixed, but enlivened by alliterations and astonishing details: "The Prince welcomed the wanderer. He was considerably startled by *Rodrigo*. ... Throughout the run of the opera Prince Ernest of Hanover sat in a box. He never tired of the work, it possessed some extreme fascination for him". Fortunately, the prima donna who "swept through her country, a queen of song without morals or pity, to die as such women so often die", had nothing to do with Flower's hero.

[7] Percy ROBINSON, *Handel and his Orbit*, London, Sherratt & Hughes, 1908, largely concerned with the Italian period; *id.*, *Handel's Journeys*, «The Musical Antiquary», I, 1909/10, pp. 193-200, a reply to Streatfeild; *id.*, *Handel's Early Years and Mainwaring*, «Musical Times», LXVI, 1925, pp. 814-816, 820.

[8] *Id.*, *Handel up to 1720: A New Chronology*, «Music and Letters», XX, 1939, pp. 62f. This, however, includes the hypotheses which he had advanced in *Handel, or Urio, Stradella, and Erba*, «Music and Letters», XVI, 1935, pp. 269-277.

[9] Lina MONTALTO, *Un mecenate in Roma barocca: il Cardinale Benedetto Pamphilj (1653-1730)*, Florence, Sansoni, 1955, pp. 325 (facsimile), 335. Untenable are Montalto's statements that these works were "immediately printed" (p. 335), that Handel's cantatas *con stromenti* were published in the years 1708-09 (p. 538, n. 78), and that Handel returned to Rome in 1711 as the guest of Prince Ruspoli (p. 335).

[10] Mario FABBRI, *Alessandro Scarlatti e il Principe Ferdinando de' Medici*, Florence, Olschki, 1961, p. 24 (letter from Prince Ferdinando to Prince Karl von Neuburg in Innsbruck, 9 Nov. 1709); pp. 25f (Karl's reply, 9 Mar. 1710); p. 26 (Johann Wilhelm, Prince Elector in Düsseldorf, to Ferdinando, 13 Sept. 1710).

[11] Emilia ZANETTI, *Le musiche italiane di Haendel*, «L'approdo musicale», III, no. 12, Oct./Dec. 1960, pp. 41-46, as an appendix to her *Haendel in Italia*, *ibid.*, pp. 3-40. This latter article expands information presented in her *Roma città di Haendel*, «Musica d'oggi», II, 1959, pp. 434-441. English locations of cantata mss., without specifying titles, are given by William C. SMITH, *Catalogue of Works*, in *Handel: A Symposium*, ed. Gerald Abraham, London, Oxford UP, 1954, pp. 296ff; the

(This catalogue does not list manuscript sources of serenatas and smaller secular cantatas – the bulk of the Italian music – but does contain such sources
for the oratorios, operas, and sacred works). Another contribution to a future
bibliography of Handel's Italian works is Ewerhart's description of the Handel manuscripts in the Santini collection, Münster (D-MÜs).[12] A large number of these, it was shown, originated in Rome; a few even bear headings that
point to definite performance days. Also Hall's attribution of Handel's Latin
Vesper works to the feast of the Madonna del Carmine, sponsored by the Colonna family in Rome on 16 July 1707, is very likely, though it will remain an
hypothesis as long as its nineteenth-century source, a note of Edward Goddard on the Egerton ms. of "Saeviat tellus" HWV 240, has not been tested
for reliability.[13] [**PS**: On the connection of "Dixit Dominus" HWV 232 with
the Colonna family, its date and place of performance, etc., cf. *HR* 318 = below, p. 377ff].

    Here are the known facts [before 1967] of Handel's whereabouts and ac-
tivity after the performance of *Almira*, 'early' 1705 in Hamburg:[14]

[handwritten margin note:] } Colonna

---

same in «Händel-Jahrbuch», II, 1956, pp. 151f. [**PS**: These publications are now now superseded by
HWV].

  [12] Rudolf EWERHART, *Die Händel-Handschriften der Santini-Bibliothek in Münster*, «Händel-
Jahrbuch», VI, 1960, pp. 111-150. See also his *New Sources for Handel's La Resurrezione*, «Music
and Letters», XLI, 1960, pp. 127-135.

  [13] James S. HALL, *The Problem of Handel's Latin Church Music*, «Musical Times», C, 1959,
pp. 197-200. Goddard exchanged manuscripts with Santini (cf. a note on the last page of Caldara's
cantata "La viola mammola", GB-Lbl ms. add. 34291: "Presented by the Abate F. Santini, the eminent musician of Rome, to his friend the Rev. Edward Goddard ..."). Goddard's information may
thus have derived from Santini. Cf. also EWERHART, *Die Händel-Handschriften*, p. 120, on Santini's
knowledge of the Vesper pieces. Ewerhart assigned two more sacred works, "Donna che in ciel"
HWV 233 and "O qualis de coelo sonus" HWV 239, to Rome and to their places in the church year
from the copies in D-MÜs (*ibid.*, pp. 120, 123): the former, according to the title page, commemorated the "Anniversario della liberatione di Roma dal / terremoto nel giorno della purificatione della
Beat.^ma Vergine"; the latter, as evident from its text, was for a Pentecost service. For neither work is
the year certain. [**PS**: The dates and places have now been determined – cf. *HR* 308f and below,
pp. 368f]. A final piece of evidence for 1707 is an entry of 14 Jan. in the diary of Francesco VALESIO
(*Diario di Roma*, Milan, Longanesi, 1977-79, III, 754f) on a "Sassone", musician and composer, who
had lately arrived and played the organ in San Giovanni in Laterano. Most writers have followed
Flower, p. 62, in identifying this person with Handel. There may have been a number of musical
Saxons in the city (cf. below, Doc. 37, the note on a composing "Sig.^r Giovanni Sassonese" at the
Ruspoli court in April 1711, perhaps Johann Heinichen). Of course, the virtuosity on the organ plus
his certain presence in Rome a few months later speak for Handel [**PS**: subsequently proven – see
below, ch. 10].

  [14] [**PS**: In reporting that Handel left Hamburg for Italy only in 1709, Jacob Wilhelm Lustig
merely propagated an error of his teacher Mattheson – CHRYSANDER, II, 364, note 38, and below,
p. 395. We now know that a "Pianto di Maria" by Handel was not performed in Siena on Good
Friday 1709, as asserted by FABBRI, *Nuova luce sull'attività fiorentina di Giacomo Antonio Perti, Bartolomeo Cristofori, e Giorgio F. Haendel*, «Chigiana», XXI, 1964, pp. 148f (according to which Francesco Maria Mannucci met with Scipione Maffei on 14-15 Feb. and recorded such an event and

1707: before May 14	at Rome	*Il delirio amoroso* HWV 99 and *Il trionfo del Tempo* HWV 46ᵃ copied for Cardinal Benedetto Pamphilj.[15]
April [**PS**. "4" *deest*]	»	"Dixit Dominus" HWV 232 finished.
June 13 [**PS**. 14]	»	"Coelestis dum spirat aura / In festo S. Antonij de Padua ... 1707" HWV 231 performed.[16]
July 8	»	"Laudate pueri" HWV 237 finished.
July 13	»	"Nisi Dominus" HWV 238 finished.
September	»	Handel seen as virtuoso in the houses of the Colonna and Cardinal Pietro Ottoboni (letter of Merlini).[17]
1708: March 3		"Lungi dal mio bel Nume" HWV 127ᵃ finished.
mid-March	»	Marquis Francesco Maria Ruspoli rents bed and other things for Handel.
April 8	»	*La Resurrezione* HWV 47 performed at Ruspoli's.
ca. April 30	»	Bed, etc., given back.
June 16	at Naples	*Aci, Galatea e Polifemo* HWV 72 finished at the house of the Duke of Alvito.[18]
July 12		"Se tu non lasci amore" HWV 201ᵃ finished in Naples.

---

date). See Juliane RIEPE, Carlo VITALI, and Antonello FURNARI, *"Il pianto di Maria"* (HWV 234): Rezeption, Überlieferung und musikwissenschaftliche Fiktion, «Göttinger Händel-Beiträge», V, 1993, pp. 270-296.

[15] The date of the copyist's receipt by no means testifies for a performance of these works in May, as Zanetti assumed (*Le musiche italiane*, p. 41). Bills were not always paid immediately. *Il Trionfo del Tempo* was very probably performed during Lent [**PS**: no – cf. *HR* 320 = below, p. 381: 2 May 1707], the season in which nearly all oratorios were performed during this decade in Rome. An exception can be seen in I-Rvat, Urb. Lat. 1706, ff. 1-4*v*: "Oratorio esposto al publico e fatto rappresentare nel cortile della cancelleria con sontuoso apparato intitolato *Il regno di Maria assunta in cielo* dall'em.ᵐᵒ Card. Pietro Ottoboni" ["Oratorio entitled *Il regno di Maria in cielo*, with a sumptuous apparatus, presented to the public and performed in the courtyard of the *cancelleria* by the most eminent Cardinal Pietro Ottoboni"] on 23/24 Aug. 1705 with music by A. Scarlatti (SL 19727, anon.).

[16] D-MÜs Hs 1887; see EWERHART, *Die Händel-Handschriften*, p. 119.

[17] STREATFEILD, p. 6.

[18] On the 'missing' final pages of the autograph see William BARCLAY SQUIRE, *Catalogue of the King's Music Library*, part I: *The Handel Manuscripts*, London, the Trustees, 1927, p. 1.

1709: ca. Nov. 9	from Florence	Handel leaves the Medici court with a letter of recommendation to Prince Karl von Neuburg in Innsbruck.
Dec. 26 - through carnival 1709/10	at Venice	*L'Agrippina* HWV 6 performed 27 times at the theater of San Giovanni Grisostomo.
1710: March 9	from Innsbruck	Prince Karl writes to Ferdinando Medici that Handel did not have use for his assistance.
June 16		Handel is appointed chapel master of Elector Ernst August of Hanover.
Sept. 13	from Düsseldorf	Elector Johann Wilhelm writes a letter of thanks to Ferdinando Medici, mentioning that Handel had been staying with him for some weeks.

The largest lacunae [before 1967] are the date of the arrival in Italy, the time up to the spring of 1707, all winters preceding the one of 1709/10, and the time between July 1708 and Lent. Contrary to Fabbri's assumption, the time between Lent and November 1709 must also be seen as a gap, as long as evidence for a continuous Florentine activity is missing (though such an activity is probable).[19] There are other questions to be asked. Did Handel serve an apprenticeship with an outstanding Italian composer? Was he treated everywhere as a favored guest only, or did he have some regular employment? Were the works which we regard as the Italian ones all produced in Italy: where, when, and for whom? And do they represent the complete production of the Italian years?

Here new biographical and archival material will be presented that provides a partial answer to these questions: documents from the Fondo Ruspoli in the Archivio Segreto Vaticano. A few fragments of these documents have appeared in Flower's *Handel* (pp. 70-73), translated and paraphrased. They were referred to as "from the household books" and concern payments for *La Resurrezione* (the composer's bed and food, part of the decoration, and

---

[19] Robinson's note that Prince Gian Gastone was back in Florence not only from June 1705 to Nov. 1706, as traced by Streatfeild, but again from summer 1708 on, through 1709 (*Handel's Journeys*, p. 196) may speak in favor of Handel's activity there. And a passage from the *Memorie fiorentine* of Francesco Settimani (I-Fas Ms. 141, f. 442) could include a reference to Handel. It states that on 28 Sept. 1709 a thanksgiving service for Ferdinand's recovery was held in the church of the SS.ma Annunziata "con solenne e squisita musica e ricche sinfonie, composta de' primi virtuosi di Firenze e d'altri musici forestieri" ["with solemn and exquisite music and rich symphonies, composed by the first musicians of Florence and other foreign musicians"].

the number of the performers) between 18 March and 30 April 1708. A perusal of this group of papers brought surprises: it appeared that Flower's 'documents' had been corrupted and misinterpreted, and that the volume from which they were taken and the adjoining volumes yield a wealth of hitherto unknown material on Handel.[20] These papers can establish his whereabouts during most of 1707-08; the character of his agreement with Ruspoli; the kind, number, and performances of pieces written for this patron; and relative dates for some 50 undated compositions.

Between 16 May 1707 and 10 October 1711, thirty-eight entries concerning Handel are traceable. I publish them in chronological order, in their entirety, except for nos. 18 and 19, very lengthy bills of craftsmen, which had to be reduced to what is here relevant. Omitted are the payments which mention only a helper (e.g. the carrier of refreshments, or someone paid for 'aiuto') or which do not refer to Handel directly, but to the regular musical affairs of the court.[21] The Handel documents represent payments: a) to a lender of furniture, the purser, and the ice merchant for the guest (nos. 8, 9, 14, 15, 20, 22, 23, 26, 30, 31); b) to the stationer for music paper (10), and to copyists for scores and parts of cantatas (1, 2, 5-7, 24, 25, 27, 33-38) and the oratorio *La Resurrezione* (included in 11); c) to printers for librettos (13, 28); d) to the master mason, the carpenter, the decorator, the painter of the ornaments and coats-of-arms, and the painter of the canvas and the "cartellone" of the house theater erected for the performance of *La Resurrezione* (4, 12, 16-19); e) to 'borrowed' musicians for the performance of cantatas *con stromenti* (3, 21, 29, 32) and of *La Resurrezione* (11).[22]

This material falls into four distinct chronological groups. The first group, nos. 1-6, records various activities for Ruspoli from May through October

---

[20] Flower did not examine the documents himself, but had a few extracts made for him by Mr. Sheppard from the British Museum. Otto Erich DEUTSCH, *Handel: A Documentary Biography*, New York, Norton, 1955, pp. 21ff, took over Flower's notes almost literally.

[21] These latter documents have been presented and discussed in *AC*. For information on Ruspoli as a patron, the reader is referred to details given in this study and in ch. 11, below. The copyists' bills for Caldara's cantatas, of which, for reasons of space, only the dates could be given, have been added by W. Kirkendale to *AC* 2007. Compilations of information from the German edition and from the original version of the present article have been published by Roberto MATTIA, *Haendel e Caldara a Palazzo Valentini*, «Rassegna del Lazio», XXII, Dec. 1975, pp. 33-49; and *id.*, *Feste musicali a Palazzo Bonelli*, in *Palazzo Valentini*, ed. Gennaro Farina, Rome, Editalia, 1985, pp. 213-228.

[22] Flower refers to our Doc. 9, 10, 11 (from the latter only the number of performers and the receipt, misquoted as from two different sources; hence 'two' documents quoted by Deutsch, p. 22), 14, 18 (only the heading). An entry from Valesio's diary, IV, 57, is quoted by Flower as a Ruspoli document (p. 71: "Sunday April 8 ... This evening ..."). The heading of Doc. 17 is then given by Deutsch (p. 21: "As for the decorations ..."); the statement that the "following description" includes a picture of the Resurrection is incorrect; this "picture" is described in our no. 16. ZANETTI, *Haendel in Italia*, mentions Doc. 16 and gives an extract of Doc. 17.

1707; the second, nos. 7-20, a continuous period of work at the Ruspoli court from the end of February to the end of April 1708; the third, nos. 21-33 – and this is unexpected – another highly prolific period with Ruspoli from mid-July into September or even November 1708, the latter time limit not being definable yet; a fourth group, nos. 34-38 comprises isolated entries from February 1709, after the employment had ceased, to October 1711. [**PS**: For a revision of the date of Handel's arrival and of the eight cantatas in Doc. 1, see *HR* 303-316 = below, pp. 363-376].

A. 26 May to 14 October 1707

The first document which can be traced with certainty to Handel is a bill of the copyist Antonio Giuseppe Angelini, receipted 16 May 1707 (Doc. 1). Here, as in all later documents of this year, Handel's name is not yet mentioned, but the text incipits are familiar from his works. Angelini is known as a collaborator of Handel not only from a list for Cardinal Pamphilj, dated 14 May 1707; a large number of extant Handel manuscripts have already been identified as copies from the pen of this scribe.[23] It will be demonstrated that they are the manuscripts mentioned in these documents. Two cantatas "con stromenti" and five continuo cantatas are listed in this earliest bill. For the first one Angelini leaves us without the incipit; his indications "della caccia" and "con tromba" do not allow us to identify the work with any of the published cantatas. [**PS**: This is HWV 79, cf. *RD* 518 and *HR* 301, 309ff = below, pp. 361, 370f].

Knowledge of procedures at Ruspoli's court during Caldara's tenure helps to clarify the origin and performance circumstances of these cantatas. From the fall of 1705 the Marquis Francesco Maria Ruspoli lived in the Palazzo Bonelli, today seat of the Provincia di Roma, at the south side of the Piazza Santi Apostoli. The documents from Caldara's time testify minutely that Ruspoli, at least since March 1709, presented one cantata every Sunday during the *conversazione*, the official period of entertainment which filled the evening until midnight. The cantatas with basso continuo were performed by his house musicians; cantatas *con stromenti* normally, but not always, required a larger ensemble. Singers and instrumentalists who were then 'borrowed' in addition to the house musicians are mentioned in special bills. From their wages the number of rehearsals and performances can be deduced. Through-

---

[23] Cf. note 9 and EWERHART, *Die Händel-Handschriften, passim.*

out the first two decades of the eighteenth century a rehearsal ("*prova*") was paid with 50 *baiocchi*, i.e. half a *scudo*, a recital ("*funtione*") with one *scudo*.[24] (Occasionally the first violinist of a large group received considerably more, this to be explained by his additional duties as soloist and, probably, his 'star' qualifications and demands). Often two or three violinists were hired, all of them renowned virtuosos. Steadily employed, from 1708 on, were one to two lady singers, two to three violinists, one 'cellist, and one bass violist. The documents prior to that year do not yet show the regularity and affluence of the later musical life at the court – probably to be explained by the fact that only in the fall of 1706 did Ruspoli inherit the two valuable estates of Vignanello and Cerveteri [**PS**: *recte*: with the death of his father, 1703; cf. *HR* 302 = below, p. 362, and Valesio, II, 538]. However, we do find several years earlier (at least since the beginning of 1705) the violinists Silvestro Rotondi and Pietro Castrucci[25] employed, both celebrated in contemporary reports as eminent virtuosos, and with them Pietro's father Domenico Castrucci, who possibly played the harpsichord. [**PS**: Both Castruccis appear already before 1700 with Ruspoli – cf. *HR* 345, note 230 = below, p. 406, note 230]. These three appear in the *ruolo* as *camerieri*, high-ranking valets – which illustrates the original meaning of *musica da camera*, music to be played informally for the patron's private delight, by his own domestic staff. The first singer makes her appearance only shortly before Handel, in January 1707: the famous soprano Margarita Durastante (Plate XI.4). It is not until November 1707 that she receives a monthly salary, of 20 *scudi*; but numerous services for her are listed throughout the year, beginning in January 1707 with a payment "al facchino per porto del credenzone, e libri di musica in casa della Sig.ʳᵃ Margherita" ["to the porter for transport of the large buffet and books of music to the house of Signora Margherita", *Lista di spese* – hereafter abbreviated as "Sp." – Jan. 1707, item 7]. In 1708 the two violinists, as required for the *sonate a tre* of the time, were joined by the 'cellist Giuseppe Peroni, possibly a relative of the brothers Giuseppe Maria and Giovanni Perroni of

---

24 Sven HANSELL, who communicated parallels from the music at the *cancelleria* (*Orchestral Practice at the Court of Cardinal Pietro Ottoboni*, JAMS, XIX, 1966, pp. 398-403), finds that "performers were generally paid" only "50 baiocchi" per performance (p. 401; when was this? – Ottoboni lived here from 1689 until 1740); see *ibid.* for the relative value of the *scudo*.

25 For the documentation on the musicians mentioned in this paragraph see *AC* 1966, pp. 46ff and Appendix 1 = *AC* 2007, p. 59 and Appendix 1. Contrary to FLOWER (pp. 69f) and DEUTSCH (p. 22), Ruspoli was not made Prince of Cerveteri until 3 Feb. 1709; the old Ruspoli palace was not the present Palazzo Ruspoli in Via del Corso, but the present Palazzo Pecci-Blunt on the Piazza di S. Maria in Aracoeli. The palace in the Corso was not acquired until 1713; this one, not the Bonelli palace, is described by Flower when he writes of "a marvellous palace of marble pillars and Grecian statuary" (p. 69).

Novara who were much applauded for their virtuosity on violin and violoncello, respectively.[26] And at least regularly on Sundays the bass viol was played by Bartolomeo Cimapane. Though in 1707 no monthly payment for the latter two can be traced, they must have served frequently, as their names appear already in a pay list for Lenten services. We can assume that the cantatas in our bill Doc. 1 served for the *conversazione* on the Sundays before the date of the receipt, and that they were performed by "Signora Margarita" and Handel himself, plus the house musicians. Certainly they were all new pieces: Handel had not been there long, and Ruspoli was too ambitious to present during his official concert hours works that had been heard elsewhere. And since only the parts of the first of the two cantatas *con stromenti* were prepared, we can be sure that the autograph score stood on the *leggio* of the harpsichord, and the composer was present. Score copies – designated as "l'originale" not only in the bills of Ruspoli's scribes, but also on the original covers of the corresponding scores – were often made considerably later, for a second performance, or for the library. Still, the scribe then found time to write both parts and score for "Tu fedel?" HWV 171. Here as later we find one *foglio*, i.e. four sheets or eight pages, of normal sized paper ("carta reale") [**PS**: *recte* "royal paper", i.e. "in octave format"; cf. *HR* 319, note 112 = below, p. 380, note 111] billed with one *giulio*, i.e. ten *baiocchi*. Of course the *fogli* of continuo cantatas refer to scores; one copy of a continuo cantata was enough to serve the singer and the continuo players.

[**PS**: The following two paragraphs on the cantata *Diana cacciatrice* HWV 79 and the *villeggiatura* in Vignanello are superseded and have been completely revised. This cantata was performed not in Vignanello in May, but in Cerveteri on 23 Feb. 1707 – see *HR* 301f, 309ff, 321-324 = below, pp. 361f, 370f, 382ff, and Appendix II]. The cantata "della caccia" finds its appropriate background in a number of entries during April, May, and June that concern "polvere", "munitione", "cacciatori", and porters of hunting equipment sent to Cerveteri and Vignanello. Ruspoli's first lengthy sojourn at his newly acquired castello in Cerveteri ended on 6 April. The last weeks of Lent were spent in Rome, and on Easter Sunday, 24 April, Alessandro Scarlatti's oratorio *Il giardino di rose* was performed. It must have been a new work, since all the parts were now copied.[27] On 2 May the large sum of 200 *scudi* is consigned to a Signor Constanti for distribution among singers, instrumentalists, the messenger, Ruspoli himself (he needed silver and gold piasters for gratu-

---

[26] Cf. *AC* index.

[27] The score is preserved in D-MÜs Hs. 3861; cf. below, p. 375f.

ities), and the copyist "Panstufato" alias Angelini. The latter, in his appended bill for 13.20 *scudi*, unfortunately does not specify his work, but says that it was for cantatas, etc., of the preceding months. It is not unlikely that cantatas of Handel are already included here. The cantata "della caccia", billed on 6 May, was in any case copied after 2 May and thus can hardly be assigned to Cerveteri. Was it performed in Rome? On 14 May a payment was made "al cimbolaro per accomodatura del cimbolo per Vignanello" ["to the harpsichord maker for adjusting the harpsichord for Vignanello" – Sp. May-June, item 25], and during the following weeks the whole household, with cooks, huntsmen, and musicians, moved to Vignanello. On 9 June (*ibid.*, item 86) Cavalier Piscitelli received 1.30 *scudi* for "rinfresco delli musici che manda a Vignanello" ["refreshment of the musicians which he sends to Vignanello"]; on 21 June (*ibid.*, item 130), Signor Pitoni 12 *scudi* as a final payment for the musicians who had been sent to Vignanello. On this or the next day everyone returned to Rome. A payment on 21 June for five drapes "per la Sig.ra Margarita" in Rome (*ibid.*, item 132), and one on 22 June to the cook for 22 days spent in Vignanello (*ibid.*, item 135) illustrate this. With regard to the calendar we may then consider the cantata "da caccia" as composed for and performed in Vignanello. This village, some fifty miles north-northwest from Rome, halfway between Civita Castellana and Viterbo, is today still dominated by the magnificent Ruspoli castle.

The next bill (Doc. 2), for cantatas copied "in Vignianello", indicates that not only the musicians were in Vignanello, but also Handel himself. The copyist would not have had to be summoned if the compositions were not originating there. The pieces of which the incipits are listed are all known as Handel's. May we for the unnamed "mottetti" suspect the same author? This bill is of great interest, not only because it dates the famous *Armida* HWV 105 once copied by J. S. Bach, but also because of those mysterious sacred works. These can be illuminated by entries of other expenses. A payment on 24 May for the gold decoration of a "baldachinetto ... per esporre il SS.mo, e mandarlo a Vignanello" ["a small canopy ... for exhibiting the Host, and to send it to Vignanello" – Sp. May-June, item 32] already suggests a church feast. More vividly speaks an entry of 4 June for a thousand little prints with the picture of Sant'Antonio of Padua, sent to Vignanello: "A dì 4 giugno pagati per n. 700 santi stampati in mezzo foglio a b. 30 il cento e n. 300 in carta di foglio con [a]rabesche intorno a b. 60 il cento d'imagini di S. Ant.° di Padova, e mandati a Vignanello come per riceuta S 3.90" ["On 4 June paid for 700 saints printed in half folio at 30 *baiocchi* per hundred and 300 in folio, paper, with a border of arabesques at 60 *baiocchi* per hundred, with images of S. Antonio of Padua, and sent to Vignanello according to receipt, *scudi* 3.90"] – *ibid.*, item 74.

These were followed by two large candle holders, a wooden crucifix, and other pious objects (*ibid.*, item 75). A payment of 41.10 *scudi*, a large sum, to "Padre Benedetto Marcioni [?] guardiano di S. Sebastiano di detto loco" (*ibid.*, item 97) clarifies the destination of these objects. Finally, the focus of the festival is mentioned, a new altarpiece by Michelangelo Ceruti for Vignanello, $9\frac{1}{2}$ *palmi* high, $5\frac{1}{4}$ palmi wide, depicting Sant'Antonio above the clouds, holding the lily and the book, surrounded by other clouds and by "splendor" (Doc. 4). The feast of Sant'Antonio, 13 June, was the climax of our Vignanello calendar. In 1707 the 475th year of his canonization was celebrated. This was doubtless the day on which Ceruti's painting was consecrated. And for this occasion Handel composed his "Mottetto ... In festo S. Antonij de Padua ... 1707" "Coelestis dum spirat aura" HWV 231 [**PS**: but for 14 June – see p. 408]. June 12, 1707, was Pentecost Sunday. There can likewise be no doubt that this was the feast for which he had written his Pentecost work "O qualis de coelo sonus" HWV 239. Both pieces have come down to us only in Angelini's manuscripts, the only Roman works by Handel (aside from one of 1729) that bear the designation "mottetto" on the title pages.[28] The third sacred piece mentioned in Angelini's bill, the "Salve Regina" HWV 241 was probably performed during one of the two feasts at Vespers, in any case in Vignanello, before 21 June 1707 [**PS**: at Compline on 18 June – see below, p. 410]. It is identical with the celebrated work first published by Chrysander. The old thesis that only the Roman cardinals, especially Carlo Colonna (see above), were the instigators of Handel's Roman sacred music can thus no longer be defended. In a payment of 5 June "per pro[visione] di due anelli mandati a Vignanello d'ord. di S. E. al Sig.^r Cavaliere ... cioè uno con pietra amatista in mezzo, e n. 6 diamantini dalle bande, et un altro con pietra giacinto ... S 14. –" ["compensation for two rings sent to Vignanello by order of His Excellency to the Cavalier ... i.e. one with an amethyst stone in the middle and six small diamonds on the bands, and another with a hyacinth stone ... *scudi* 14" – *ibid.*, June, item 77] we may see Handel and Durastante [**PS**: No, Vittoria Tarquini and probably Handel – cf. *HR* 322ff = below, pp. 382ff] rewarded with jewelry.

Back in Rome, during the *conversazione* on Sunday, 26 June, the house musicians were joined by the violinists Alfonso Poli and Lorenzo Bononcini for a cantata *con stromenti* (Doc. 3), doubtless one of those by Handel which are listed in the neighboring bill of Angelini (Doc. 2).

The next bill of Angelini (Doc. 5), receipted on 22 September, mentions six new cantatas of Handel, together with the score of the earlier *Armida*. The

---

[28] See above, notes 13 and 16.

"cantata francese" can be identified as "Sans y penser" HWV 155, the "cantata Spagniola" as "No se emenderá jamás" HV 140. Their extant manuscripts from Angelini's pen bear a peculiar stamp of authenticity, as in both Handel underlaid the text himself,[29] obviously not thinking too highly of Panstufato's linguistic abilities. Margarita's confirmations below this and the preceding bill tell that she was the singer to present these pieces. Indeed, all cantatas mentioned thus far are for soprano. [**PS**: On the history, dates, and texts of these cantatas see *HR* 324 = below, pp. 384f].

As no other composer but (indirectly) Handel is named throughout the remainder of 1707, I am inclined to connect also Angelini's bill of 14 October for an obviously very lengthy "Cantata a tre con violini" (Doc. 6) with our composer, the more so as such an oversized work exists in an Angelini copy: the "Cantata a tre con stromenti di Monsù Hendel" HWV 96 with the incipit "Cor fedel", in two volumes, of 232 and 332 pages respectively.[30] The ten round *scudi* of this bill would have covered 800 pages, first of all parts. [**PS**: See, in addition, *HR* 325 = below, p. 385]. On 31 October Angelini again received six *scudi* (Sp. Sept.-Nov., item 162), but unfortunately he says only: "sono per rest. saldo e final pagamento di tutte le copiature et altre da me fatto ... sino al presente giorno" ["they are for the remaining balance and final payment for all the copying *et al.* done by me ... up to the present day"]. We shall have to suspect cantatas of Handel to be included here too.

For the rest of 1707 only a few meager, unspecific bills for copies by Pietro Castrucci [**PS**: No, he only authorized payment for them. In the following his name is eliminated from the copyists] are to be found. Around 7 November Margarita Durastante was at Ruspoli's "casino" in Albano (*ibid.*, items 179 and 180). Handel was then certainly not at the palace in Rome.

B. 26 FEBRUARY 1708 TO THE END OF APRIL 1708

Handel's name appears for the first time[31] in a bill of 26 February 1708 for the copy of an unnamed cantata, below the list of musicians who performed the oratorio *Il giardino di rose* (Doc. 7). The date is the first Sunday in Lent, the opening day of the oratorio season. The oratorio mentioned is the

---

[29] D-MÜs Hss. 1898 and 1899; cf. EWERHART, *Händel-Handschriften*, pp. 141 and 132.

[30] D-MÜs Hss. 1900/I and II; cf. EWERHART, pp. 128-132.

[31] [**PS**: Already since Feb. 1707 he is mentioned in the *giustificazioni* as "il Sassone" – cf. *HR* 310, note 62 = below, p. 371, note 60 etc.].

previous year's work by Alessandro Scarlatti. It was the main concert of the day, surely heard in the evening, during the latter part of the *conversazione*. Though only the copy of Handel's cantata is mentioned, not the performers, we suspect that it may have been heard the same afternoon, during the first hours of the *conversazione*, since payment for the copy of a single piece was often made on the day of the recital [**PS**: Delete this sentence]. No extra musicians were to be hired, since it was a cantata "in 2 fogli", a solo cantata with basso continuo, doubtless for Durastante.

About 15 March 1708[32] we find those entries on bedding for the guest Handel which were referred to by Flower (Doc. 8 and 9). The payment "per nolito d'un mese di d. letto" ["a month's rent for the said bed"], however, is not for the month to come, as has been freely assumed;[33] a second sum, paid for the rent of the same items "per l'aprile scorso" ["for last April" – Doc. 20], makes it clear that the first one covers the month of March, possibly a 'short' month retroactive from the 15th – cf. the smaller amount compared to that of April. Services rendered to the court were paid only after they were completed. Handel thus had moved into the Bonelli palace before the end of February, and his little cantata for soprano marks the new beginning of his activity there.

Handel's music, then, opened Ruspoli's copious concert programs for Lent of 1708, and it was Handel's music that concluded the season on Easter Sunday in a most spectacular performance: the oratorio *La Resurrezione*. Whether the young master contributed music to other Lenten concerts is uncertain,[34] for most of the pay lists do not mention a composer. This was the calendar: on 4 March 1708 the tenor Vittorio Chiccheri and two violinists were hired, certainly for a cantata *con stromenti*;[35] on 11 March, the contralto Pasqualino and again Vittorio, with the violinists Carlo Guerra and Alfonso Poli, for an unidentified oratorio; and, in addition, two unidentified fiddlers (for a cantata?);[36] on 18 March, the same four names for the *Oratorio di San*

---

[32] The date is derived from the *lista delle spese*.

[33] FLOWER, p. 71.

[34] On the Bavarian ambassador's report (below, note 53) "Dal March.ᵉ Ruspoli si sono sentiti buoni oratori per lo più la compositione della musica del virtuoso sassone" ["Good oratorios have been heard at Marquis Ruspoli's, mostly with music composed by the Saxon virtuoso"]. EWERHART (*New Sources*, p. 128) comments: "The words 'per lo più' suggest that Handel had produced several works for Ruspoli". They should be translated, however, as "mostly" or "especially".

[35] *Giustificazioni*, B 45, *lista delle spese* Jan.-March, item 162: "A dì 4 marzo pag. al Sig.ʳ Vittorio e 2 violinisti S 4.40".

[36] *Ibid.*, item 184: "A dì 11 d.° pag. per li musici e istromenti per la conversazione S 9.40"; plus bill of Domenico Castrucci:

Clemente, a work likewise anonymous, but through its title an eloquent testimony to Ruspoli's efforts to please Pope Clement XI;[37] on 25 March, its proper day in the Church year, Alessandro Scarlatti's *Oratorio per la SS.*[ma] *Annunziata* was presented with Vittorio, the soprano Pippo, and a larger ensemble that included also violas and bass viols.[38] From the bill of the copyist An-

---

A dì 11 marzo 1708. Nota di quelli che si pagano per l'oratorio che si fu per la conversazione di S. E. Padrone.

Al Sig.[r] Pasqualino	S 3.–
Al Sig.[r] [cancelled: Cristofano basso] Vittorio	S 2.40
Al Sr Carlo Guerra violino	S 1.–
Al Sr Alfonso violino	S 1.–
Somma	S 7.40
E più per altri due violini	S 2.–
	S 9.40

[37] *Lista delle Spese*, 18 Mar. - 8 May 1708, item 1: "A dì 18 marzo pag. a musici e sonatori per l'oratorio di S. Clemente S 7.40"; plus bill of D. Castrucci: A dì 18. marzo 1708. Per l'Oratorio di S. Clemente fatto nella conversazione di S. E. Padrone.

Dato al Sig.[r] Pasqualino	S 3.–
Al Sig.[r] Vittorio	S 2.40
Al Sr Carlo Guerra violino	S 1.–
Al Sig.[r] Alfonso violino	S 1.–
Somma	S 7.40

Cf. *AC* 1966 pp. 160-163 = *AC* 2007 pp. 62f, 85, 210f for other textual homages presented to Clement by Ruspoli in these years.

[38] *Lista delle spese* cit., item 18: "A dì 28 d.° pag. a Panstufato per copia di musica come per lista S 1.35"; plus Angelini's bill: Conto delle copiature fatte nell'oratorio del SS.[ma] Anunnziata.

Un basso continuo	fogli 6
Due violini del concerto grosso	fogli 7½
In tutto	fogli 13½

[Ruspoli:] F. M. Ruspoli 28 [?] marzo 1708.
[Angelini:] Io Antonio Giuseppe Angelini ho riceuto [per] li sudetti fogli scudi uno e baiochi cinque [*sic*] 1.35.
Ibid., no. item: "A dì 11 aprile pag. per una lista passata da Sua Ecc. per l'oratorio dell' 25 scorso a Silvestrino S 13.–"; plus bill of Silvestro Rotondi:
Lista delli stromenti che hanno sonato l'oratorio della SS.[ma] Anuntiata di Scarlatti in casa dell'Ecc.[mo] Sig.[re] Marchese Ruspoli di 25 Marzo 1708.

Violini	Carlo Guerra	S 1.–
	Alfonzo	S 1.–
	Bartolomeo di Giustiniani	S 1.–
	Bononcini	S 1.–
	Giuseppe Valentini	S 1.–
	Giuseppe il Rosso	S 1.–
Viole	Pietro della De Rossi	S 1.–
	Gio. Francesco	S 1.–
Contrabbasso		
	Trauaglia	S 1.–
		S 9.–

[D. Castrucci:]
E più per Vittorio tenore che canto nel sud.° oratorio S 2.40
[Another hand, added later:]

gelini it appears that the work was not new: only the basso continuo and two violin parts of the concerto grosso had to be copied.

Palm Sunday, 1 April, was already filled with the preparations for the great event to come, *La Resurrezione*. This performance is indeed without parallel in Ruspoli's musical affairs for the splendor of the decoration, the number of performers, and the size of the audience. Speculating on the circumstances under which it was composed, Flower stated that it was the pope's displeasure at Ruspoli's intentions of having comedies improvised at his country residence Vignanello during carnival that gave Ruspoli the idea of staying at home and hearing oratorios instead: [39]

As the Prince had so shortly before been raised from the Marquisate to a princeling, he could not incur the Papal displeasure. Therefore he decided to remain in Rome and employ Handel. This probably accounts for Handel having written *La Resurrezione* in such a hurry. A religious work, even if it were shaped like an opera, would provide the prince with all the diversion he required, and at the same time escape the wrath of the pontiff. It was another instance of Handel's growing characteristic of grasping impulsively at opportunity.

We must reverse the situation. Since Ruspoli had planned to spend carnival, not Lent, in Vignanello (the papal note reached him before 2 February, three weeks before Ash Wednesday), there is no evidence that he had to change his plans for Lent; he always returned to Rome for the Lenten concerts. There was no new "princeling" concerned about escaping the "wrath of the pontiff", but the marquis who wanted to become a prince and offered oratorios as demonstration of his devotion to the Holy See.[40] Handel cannot have written the work in a hurry, but must have known long before of his task – Ruspoli used to plan his programs much in advance.[41] Living in the house for at least the preceding seven weeks, Handel was certainly expected to spend much of his time on this composition. On 20 March we glance through the keyhole: the *cameriere* Domenico Castrucci, who regularly looked after the

---

E più al S.re Pippo soprano della Regina per d.° oratorio   S   1.60
[D. Castrucci:]

                   Somma in tutto   <u>S 11.40</u>
                                        S 13.–

[Ruspoli:] M.se F. M. Ruspoli.
The score is preserved in D-MÜs Hs. 3881.

[39] FLOWER, p. 70.

[40] *AC* 1966 pp. 48f = *AC* 2007 p. 62.

[41] *AC* 1966 p. 57 (the long-term planning for the carnival of 1711); p. 76 (the *ottavario*, 1715) = *AC* 2007 pp. 72f, 94f.

"corde e penne del cimbalo" ["strings and quills of the harpsichord"], now provides music paper (Doc. 10).

We should dwell for a moment on evidence for the artistic framework (Doc. 32 and 16-19). The bill of the master mason Francesco Pagnacelli (Doc. 19) describes extensive mural preparations for the woodwork of the theater; that of the carpenter Crespineo Pavone (Doc. 18) in 20 pages, the whole complex of stage and decoration. The stage in the hall for the academies ("Stanzione delle Accademie")[42] on the second [**PS**: ground] floor had been expensively remodeled, but had to be transferred at the last minute to the great hall on the main floor [**PS**: *piano nobile*] for a larger audience. Here between Monday and Saturday of Holy Week a new stage with scaffolds for large-scale decorative effects was built. This 'stage' appeared as a "teatro a scalinata" (Doc. 18, pp. 1 and 9), with four rows of seats for the orchestra, 55 *palmi*[43] wide (Doc. 18, p. 3; Doc. 12 says that "tre ordini" were decorated), slightly curved towards the audience, the ranks ascending to the back wall. It was separated from the audience by a barrier, with a higher center piece to hide part of the view of the orchestra (Doc. 18, p. 5). The carpenter's bill mentions also 28 music stands with carved racks and legs in the shape of fluted cornucopiae (*ibid.*, p. 6). On fourteen of these Giuseppe Rossi painted the coat-of-arms of the marquis, on the other fourteen those of his wife, Isabella Cesi del Duca d'Acquasparta, in golden *chiaroscuro* (Doc. 12). Three rows of the orchestra seats were given yellow color and an illusionary cornice. Above the ranks there was a raised podium for the "concertino de' violini" (Doc. 18, p. 12) – another testimony for the original spatial conception of concertino and ripieno.

One of the two main pieces of the decoration was a large canvas measuring 18×18 *palmi*, in the central background of the stage. This is how the painter, Michelangelo Ceruti, describes it (Doc. 16): within the square a round frame in yellow chiaroscuro; the Ruspoli coat of arms (Plate IX.1) in the four corners, with square frames in similar coloring; within the frame, painted "al naturale", the resurrection of our Lord with a "gloria" of *putti* and cherubim, and the angel sitting on the tomb announcing the resurrection to Mary Magdalene and Mary Cleopha, with John the Evangelist in the vicinity of a mountain, and demons plunging into the abyss. The latter part of

---

[42] MONTALTO notes that the Palazzo Doria Pamphilj had a hall set up especially for anatomical academies (p. 155).

[43] The *palmo romano* corresponded to about 22 cm.; the *oncia*, mentioned below, to about 1.86 cm. – Angelo MARTINI, *manuale di Metrologia*, Turin, Loescher, 1883, p. 596.

Ceruti's bill refers to the other major component of the decoration: a large cartoon, 30 *palmi* wide at the base, 20 at the top, 14 *palmi* high. With much inconvenience the carpenter's staff fixed it to a wooden bridge that crossed the full width of the hall (64 *palmi*) above the proscenium (cf. also Doc. 18, p. 8: "bocca del sud.° teatro a scalinata"). This *cartellone* represented an ornamented frontispiece, cornices, volutes, a cherub, tablet, foliage, and palms, in yellow and crimson chiaroscuro, and on the tablet the title of the oratorio (the painter says "motto"; cf. Doc. 18, p. 8: "il titolo di detto oratorio") in four lines and 46 letters, each letter ten *oncie* high.[44] These letters, cut out and backed with transparent paper, were illuminated from behind by 70 light pans, carefully watched by two of the carpenter's helpers during "tre sere" ["three evenings"] (Doc. 18, p. 9).

All this was but the bare skeleton. To complete the *apparato* the draper added his art (Doc. 17): two widths of damask above the stage, trimmed with velvet, in crimson, yellow, and red; the canvas in the center framed with crimson taffeta and velvet formed into rosettes; a "sky" ("cielo") of trimmed damask across the full width of the stage; and the entire "church or hall" (Doc. 17, p. 1: "chiesa dico sala") lavishly decorated with red and yellow taffeta and velvet fringed with gold, and illuminated by sixteen candelabra – the whole aimed at leading the listener into the ecstatic, heavenly spaces we enter when looking up to the airy painted ceilings in baroque churches. A final detail: there was also a curtain. The carpenter billed seven wooden wheels which lifted the taffeta forming the "telone da calare et alzare" ["large curtain to lower and raise"] (Doc. 18, p. 5).[45] For an example of such oratorio decorations one may compare the designs of Filippo Juvarra in one of the Turin sketchbooks, also prepared in 1708, for Ottoboni's oratorio "nella settimana

---

[44] Possibly in this arrangement: ORATORIO / PER LA RESURREZIONE / DI N.° SIGNOR / GIESÙ CRISTO (cf. Plate IX.1, title page of the libretto, which differs from this only with the word "Resurretione").

[45] ZANETTI, *Haendel in Italia*, p. 11, rightly interprets such decoration as compensating for "the absence of acting in oratorios, when these were differentiated from the operatic genre". Paul Henry LANG's statement that "many of the [Italian] works, whether cantata, festa, or oratorio, clearly demanded staged performance" and that there is "documentary proof that the oratorio *La Resurrezione* was staged in the Ruspoli palace" (*George Frideric Handel*, New York, Norton, 1966, p. 64) seems to result from a misinterpretation of Flower's documents. We now know that not a single oratorio in Italy before 1750 was acted. The only thing sometimes to be seen on a 'stage' was an altarpiece or a decoration, and, of course, the performers. Those pieces for which SCHERING once assumed staging (*Geschichte des Oratoriums*, Leipzig, Breitkopf & Härtel, 1911, pp. 46, 116, 123, 126) were either not oratorios, but sacred operas, or, as in Florence, simply gave scene divisions and descriptions of the scenes in the librettos to aid the listeners' imagination. The performances of oratorios with such librettos are described in the diaries of several Florentine confraternities of the earlier 18th century – cf. also *AC* 1966 pp. 148f = *AC* 2007 pp. 193f.

santa".[46] This oratorio was Alessandro Scarlatti's *Passione*.[47] The *apparati* lift these two works out of the common, modest frame of Lenten oratorios; and it will be seen that the two productions were indeed closely connected. For Ruspoli the whole *apparato* must have been designed by Giovanni Battista Contini, architect of the school of Bernini, builder of the library of prints in Montecassino and the parish church of Vignanello (through Ruspoli's patronage), specialist in church interiors and fountains. Contini worked with Ruspoli for many years; he now assessed the bills of the artists.

The immense labor was for the splendor of a moment. As soon as the performances were over, the carpenter's staff dismantled "tutto d.° teatro" and carried the materials into the cellars of the palace to preserve them for other occasions (Doc. 18, pp. 18-19).

One feature of oratorios held special attraction for the audience: the intermission. Originally, in Roman prayer halls, *Prima parte* and *Parte seconda* had framed the sermon; now they framed the pleasant interlude described by Uffenbach: "Approximately halfway through the music an intermission was made, and then a quantity of liquors, frozen things, confection, and coffee was carried around and presented to everyone".[48] On the occasion of *La Resurrezione*, such *rinfreschi* were served in the *stanzione delle accademie* which had been lavishly redecorated for this purpose. In the adjoining chamber Contini had even installed a waterfall that sprang nimbly down into a "bagno" scene painted by Giuseppe Rossi (cf. Doc. 12, 18, 19).

The number of performances is stated in the highly informative list of hired musicians (Doc. 11). On 14 April the instrumentalists were paid for three rehearsals ("prove") and two performances ("funtioni"). As testified by the carpenter, the first rehearsal was held on Palm Sunday, 1 April, in the *stanzione delle accademie*, after which date the move was made to the *salone al piano nobile*;[49] the second rehearsal on the following Monday (Doc. 18, pp. 16-17); the third on Holy Saturday, 7 April, in the *salone*, already within the completed new decoration (Doc. 19, p. 1: "il Sabbato Santo, e giorni se-

---

[46] A. E. BRINCKMANN, *Filippo Juvarra: i disegni*, Turin, Oberdan Zucchi, 1937, pl. 188f.

[47] See VALESIO, IV, 55, 4 Apr. 1708; *AC* 1966, p. 39 = *AC* 2007 p. 50; and *RD* note 63 = below, note 65 for the libretto.

[48] "ohngefähr in der helffte der musiq machten sie eine pause, und da wurden liqueurs, gefrohrene sachen, confect, und caffé in quantität herumb getragen und jedermann pressentirt" – Eberhard PREUSSNER, *Die musikalischen Reisen des Herrn von Uffenbach*, Kassel, Bärenreiter, 1949, p. 78, and *AC* 1966 pp. 74f = *AC* 2007 p. 92 on oratorios at Ruspoli's in 1715.

[49] The note on the title page of the libretto saying that the work was performed "nella sala dell'Accademia" obviously was printed before the decision was made to move to the "salone al piano nobile".

guenti"; cf. in Doc. 18 the statement on the illumination for three evenings). The main concerts then took place on Easter Sunday and Monday, 8 and 9 April. The Sunday performance is recorded in many of the bills, in the libretto, and by Francesco Valesio, whose lines may be given here in their original wording: [50]

Dom. 8 Pasqua di Resurrezione [1708] – Questa sera il marchese Ruspoli fece nel palazzo Bonelli a' SS. Apostoli un belliss.[mo] oratorio in musica havendo fatto nel salone un ben'ornato teatro per l'uditorio, si intervenne molta nobiltà et alcuni porporati.

Easter Sunday, 8 [April] – This evening Marquis Ruspoli had performed in the Bonelli palace at SS. Apostoli a most beautiful oratorio in music, having made in the great hall a well decorated theatre for the audience. Many aristocrats and some cardinals were present.

Once more the number of performances and, in addition, the size of the audience appear from the bill of the Roman printer Antonio de' Rossi for the libretto (Doc. 13 and Plates IX.1-2). For Scarlatti's *Annunziata* (SL 17273), performed two weeks earlier, 250 ordinary librettos plus fifty bound in "carta dorata" are billed; then five times as many, 1500, for *La Resurrezione* (SL 17271), dedicated to Filippo Antonio Gualtieri (1660-1728, cardinal since 17 May 1706). We can be sure that for all five performances, the rehearsals and the *funtioni*, visitors were expected. It was recently shown that in Rome, in 1708 and 1709, when operas were still forbidden by papal decree, many operas as well as *commedie in prosa* were performed under the pretence of being rehearsals ("sotto titolo di prova"), even in monasteries and theological seminaries.[51] The fact that Ruspoli's *stanzione delle accademie* proved to be too small at the first *prova* tells of the crowds that had been thronging in.

Turning to the performers, we remember that on Easter Monday Valesio mentioned a papal admonition issued to a Roman nobleman for having employed a female singer in the oratorio of the preceding evening: "Lunedì 9 [April 1708] ha fatta S. B. fare una ammonizione per haver fatto cantare

---

[50] IV, 57. FLOWER was concerned about a 'discrepancy' between Handel's autograph date for "la festa di Pasqua" (according to him "held at the Marchisa [*sic*] di Ruspoli on the 4th April 1708" – p. 70) and Easter Day [= *Pasqua*], reported in another source (*loc. cit.*, not mentioning that this is Valesio); repeated by DEUTSCH, p. 21: "According to Carlo Sigismondo Capece's word-book, it was performed on Easter Sunday 'nella sala dell'accademia del Signor Marchese Ruspoli'; but according to Handel's manuscript it was written for 'la festa di Pasqua dal Marchese Ruspoli'". No difficulty then but one of Italian vocabulary. On Capeci cf. Manuela DI MARTINO, *Oblio e recupero di un librettista settecentesco: Carlo Sigismondo Capeci (1652-1728)*, «Nuova rivista musicale italiana», XXX, 1996, pp. 30-55.

[51] *AC* 1966 p. 50f = *AC* 2007 pp. 63f.

nell'oratorio della sera precedente una cantarina".[52] A letter of the Bavarian ambassador confirms that it was Ruspoli who was cited to Cardinal Fabrizio Paolucci for his misbehavior, and informs us that the virtuosa lived in his house.[53] Now the names of the five singers are preserved in the performers' list (Doc. 11). Yet there is no woman among them. Filippo, certainly identical to "Pippo soprano della Regina" (i.e. borrowed from Maria Casimira, Queen of Poland, who lived then in the 'palazzino' Zuccari) and Matteo[54] were the sopranos; Pasqualino our well known contralto; Vittorio [Chiccheri] the tenor; and Cristofano identified by an earlier entry (Doc. 7) as bass. Here the wages solve the riddle. Pasqualino is seen to receive almost twice as much as each of the sopranos, although a first soprano always earned slightly more than a contralto. The first soprano normally would have received 20 *scudi*, Pasqualino 18. We can thus be sure that Filippo sang only at the second *funtione*, on Easter Monday, replacing the virtuosa, Margherita Durastante. She was, then, the first Maddalena, the singer who established the fame of the popular aria "Ho un non so che nel core". It is no wonder that this piece was taken over into *Agrippina* where it was hers again, in the title role! [**PS**: But the opera now appears to be the earlier work – cf. *HR* 336f = below, p. 398]. In this way Handel insured his Venetian success in advance: he not only presented a number of pieces which had proved successful but also brought with him the singer who had premiered them.

It is well known that Corelli was the maestro of the orchestra. This was even larger than has been assumed from the number of instrumentalists in Doc. 11 (as extracted by Sheppard for Flower), since only the hired performers are listed. We must add the musicians of the house. The numbers as given by Flower and Deutsch[55] must therefore be corrected to at least 22 (or 23) violins, 4 "violette", 6 "violoni", 6 "contrabassi", 2 trumpets, 1 trombone, 4 oboes. This mammoth orchestra was unique among Ruspoli's productions.[56] As for the types of instruments, however, they were all well established in Rome.[57] (We miss the viola da gamba demanded by the score

---

[52] IV, 57.

[53] D-Mbs Cod. It. 198, f. 127*v*; EWERHART, *New Sources for Handel's La Resurrezione*, p. 128; ZANETTI, *Haendel in Italia*, pp. 22f.

[54] Not "Marco", as given by DEUTSCH, p. 22.

[55] Pp. 71 and 22, respectively.

[56] Contrary to ZANETTI, *Haendel in Italia*, p. 10. Cf. the paylists in *AC* Appendix 1.

[57] Until ca. 1715 the terms 'violette' and 'viole' as well as 'violoni' and 'violoncelli' are used interchangeably at Ruspoli's, in both scores and bills, always accompanied by 'contrabbassi'. Known 'virtuosi di violoncello' appear among the 'violone' players, 'viola' players among the 'violette', and for performances of the same works in different years the bills use different terms. Some oratorios by

– an instrument, though, that never appears in a Ruspoli account or a Caldara score). [**PS**: Neverthless, a gambist did participate in the performance, as kindly called to my attention by August Wenzinger].[58] The perfect balance between the numbers of the violins and the total of other stringed instruments, observed in Ottoboni's ensembles[59] and to be encountered also at Ruspoli's as the normal practice, is here distorted in favor of the violins; these constitute half the orchestra. Apart from its value for performance practices, Doc. 11 is to be welcomed as a biographical source for 48 Italian musicians, including among the violinists Valentini again, Carlo Guerra, Alfonso Poli, and Lorenzo Bononcini; among the violetta players the Roman composer Giuseppe Pertica, and Lorenzo Gasperini, probably a member of Francesco's family; and among the 'cellists the celebrated Pippo. Not yet identified is the first violinist Antonio, who is mentioned in another document as the highly paid "Sr Antonio del Cardinale Colonna".[60] The last and probably youngest of the violinists was a pupil of Rotondi's ("scolaro di Silvestro"). Rotondi and the mysterious Antonio may have played the violins of the concertino. Finally, below the musicians there appears the copyist's name, "Panstufato" (not "Pastufato"),[61] the nickname for the now familiar Angelini. [**PS**: On this name cf. *HR* 2004, p. 353 = below, p. 397]. His handwriting was found in the D-MÜs copy of *La Resurrezione*; this was therefore assumed to be the Roman original, dating from the first performance.[62] It is indeed *l'originale*. Angelini's reimbursement of thirty *scudi*, for some 300 *fogli* or 2400 pages, certainly includes not only the score in two volumes, to be used by Corelli, but also the parts distributed to the 28 music stands. The total expenditures for the production exceeded 1000 *scudi*. Besides the above-mentioned items the master of the household reckoned the *rinfreschi*, the rental of chairs for the audience, the purchase of a violoncello, and the candlesticks.

We must not forget the music: a magnificent work, undeservedly neglected through two and a half centuries, until it made its resurrection in 1961.[63] Moreover, the splendid components of this day can be related to a

---

Caldara, dating from ca. 1700 (Venice or Mantua), still employ two staves and clefs, alto and tenor, for the 'violette'. Cf. HANSELL, pp. 399f.

[58] Cf. August WENZINGER, *Die viola da gamba in Händels Oratorium 'La Resurrezione'*, «Österreichische Musikzeitschrift», XLII, 1987, pp. 80-83.

[59] HANSELL, p. 399.

[60] *AC* Doc. 24.

[61] As in DEUTSCH, p. 22.

[62] EWERHART, *Die Händel-Handschriften*, p. 116.

[63] Conducted by Rudolf Ewerhart and recorded by Vox Productions.

greater concept: Alessandro Scarlatti's *Passione*, performed on Wednesday of Holy Week at Cardinal Ottoboni's, in the *cancelleria*, and Handel's *Resurrezione* must have been planned together, as a sequence.[64] Ottoboni and Ruspoli were intimate friends, seen in contemporary reports as united in their musical enterprises, and Alessandro Scarlatti and Handel appear surprisingly often not only in the same city, but together at the same court. Passion oratorios, though much more frequent in Italy than Pasquetti once assumed, were still very rare in Rome at the beginning of the eighteenth century.[65] And the sequence of Passion and Resurrection in this genre is, as far as I see, unique. Scarlatti's work is furthermore notable for its location: never before do we find a Passion sung in a palace. Whenever Christ's death was commemorated through oratorios, it was in the churches or prayer halls of confraternities devoted to the service of and prayer for the sick and the dying, thus by the Confraternita della Morte in Bologna, or, in Rome, by the Arciconfraternita del Crocifisso. With the cyclic concept it seems that now for the first time the oratorio was given a task that had been fulfilled by the *sacra rappresentazione* two and three centuries earlier. Passion and Easter plays, traceable everywhere from western through middle and southern Europe since the later Middle Ages, had produced in Rome a species worthy of the exceptional historical role of this city: the plays of the Passion on Good Friday in the colosseum followed by those of the Resurrection on Easter Sunday in San Giovanni in Laterano. These grandiose spectacles, with costumes, scenery, machinery, and musical intermezzi, were staged by the Confraternita del Gonfalone from at least 1486 into the pontificate of Paul III.[66] In Handel's time the memory of those plays may have been still alive, at least among the members of this confraternita, whose statutes, generations after the interdict, still recall that "rappresentare la Passione di N. S. Gesù Cristo" was once

---

[64] This hypothesis was first advanced in *AC* 1966 p. 150 = *AC* 2007 p. 196.

[65] Guido PASQUETTI, *L'oratorio musicale in Italia*, Florence, Le Monnier, 1914, pp. 289-299. A more comprehensive bibliography was given by Karl NEF, *Beiträge zur Geschichte der Passion in Italien*, ZfMw, XVII, 1935, pp. 218f; however, nothing could be added to Pasquetti's small list of four Roman works between 1689 and 1725. It is, moreover, doubtful whether Pasquetti's reference to one of the four, a Passion by A. Scarlatti of 1707, is trustworthy. It relies on Dent who gives the date 1708, like the libretto SL 18468 and like Valesio's diary, IV, 55. As a corrective to Pasquetti's generalizations on the fear of messianic themes throughout the Counter-reformation cf. the works listed by Kurt von FISCHER, *Zur Geschichte der Passionskomposition des 16. Jahrhunderts in Italien*, AfMw, XI, 1954, pp. 189-205; cf. also Ala BOTTI CASELLI, *Parafrasi e meditazioni sulla Passione nell'oratorio romano del Seicento*, in *Percorso dell'oratorio romano*, ed. Saverio Franchi, Rome, IBIMUS, 2002, pp. 51-53.

[66] Cf. Vincenzo BARTHOLOMAEIS, *Laude drammatiche e rappresentazioni sacre*, II, Florence, Le Monnier, 1943, pp. 117-120.

their principal task. Who was responsible for the revival of such a concept of pre-reformation time? The thread could lead to Ottoboni, who was also arch-priest of Santa Maria Maggiore where the Confraternita del Gonfalone was seated. (It may also not be pure speculation to think that Handel's being a Protestant might have had something to do with it). The concept was now transplanted into a quite different social and artistic medium: from the am-phitheatre into the *salone nobile*, from a public act to high-society entertain-ment, from a spoken and acted drama to a purely musical one, from epic grandeur to elegance and fashion.

The documents following *La Resurrezione* give an approximate date for Handel's departure for Naples. Bed, bed-curtain and other things, rented un-til the end of April (Doc. 20), were given back to the owner after 1 May (Doc. 14), and Ruspoli's *dispensatore* Francesco Maria de Golla (not Tolla)[67] had his food expenses reimbursed (Doc. 15). [**PS**: Cf. *HR 333*, note 174 = below, p. 393, note 173]. The latter bill is another testimony for Handel's gargantuan appetite. If – scholarly, but indiscrete – we must prosecute the innocent eater this far, we cannot help but marvel at the payment of 38.75 *scudi* for the food ("spese cibarie") consumed by Handel and his companion ("comp.°" – von Bienitz?).[68] Measured against the monthly salary of 23.50 for the first noble-man of the *famiglia alta*, 20 for the prima donna, 10 for the later *maestro di cappella* Caldara (20 from 1 March 1710 on), down to 10 per year for the bass violinist – this sum, devoured in two months, conjures up mountains of fruit, pheasants, nectar and ambrosia, making the marble tables bend.

One is always tempted to explain a famous man's action through a motive centered in him: 'Handel now decided to go ...', in our case combined with the pressure of political disturbances.[69] The *giustificazioni* reveal that Ruspoli was the one who decided to go. In the first half of May the marquis left for his country residence Vignanello, as usual around this time of the year. Handel thus was free, and he travelled to Naples. [**PS**: Ruspoli was now occupied in Vignanello with the recruitment of soldiers for his regiment; he may have sent Handel on a commission to Naples – cf. *RD 242* = below, pp. 313f].

---

[67] As in Deutsch, p. 22.

[68] The gentleman whom Johann Mattheson reports to have travelled with Handel to Italy – *Grundlage einer Ehren-Pforte*, Hamburg, Verfasser, 1740, p. 95.

[69] The political motive was first suggested by Chrysander and has often been repeated, e.g. by Zanetti, *op. cit.*, p. 13, and by myself, above, p. 270. It is quite probable that the general mood among the Roman populace had something to do with the departure. In fact, the political tension was highest just before 15 Jan. 1709, when Pope Clement XI signed under pressure the treaty with Vienna. Cf. below, p. 400.

C. 14 July to 24 November 1708

Payments starting 14 July 1708 (Doc. 21ff) show that Handel was free only a short time; he soon returned from Naples to his former patron. I doubt whether he was still at Naples for the Duke of Alvito's wedding on July 19, which Flower vividly described.[70] A sizable bill for food consumed by him at Ruspoli's during the month of July (Doc. 23) suggests that he was back by the middle of that month. His autograph date, 12 July in Naples, on "Se tu non lasci amore" HWV 201ᵃ must mark one of the very last days of his sojourn there. His presence at the Bonelli palace is then once more confirmed by a payment for two large, used, lined curtains for the windows of "M. Endel" on 31 July, when the sun must have shone hot on Rome (Doc. 22).

An undated note by Silvestro Rotondi on the payments due to Giuseppe Valentini and Giovanni Ciambelli for their playing "nella cantata 'Fiamma bella' di Monsù Hendel" is matched by an entry in the *lista delle spese* on Saturday, 14 July (Doc. 21), thus dating the recital. As neither copies nor hired performers had been mentioned since April, we can be sure that "Fiamma bella" was featured as the first cantata *con stromenti* after Ruspoli's return from Vignanello, i.e. after 17 June 1708. Our date marks a new beginning, also traceable from payments to the violinist Alfonso Poli, who played (probably instrumental music) for Ruspoli every Sunday from 15 July 1708 to 16 June 1709.[71] "Fiamma bella", to be found neither as title nor incipit in any of the extant manuscripts of Handel's cantatas, must be identical with the lengthy cantata "Arresta it passo" (Aminta, Fillide) HWV 83, of which the second aria begins "Fiamma bella che al ciel s'invia". A violinist, like Rotondi, was certainly not pedantic over titles. Or, on that day, the performance may have begun with this aria. I find no bill for copies of the parts. [**PS**: The bill is Tarquinio Lanciani's of 29 Dec. 1706 – cf. *HR 305* = below, p. 365]. Was it an older work? Had Handel, who was still in Naples on 12 July, rushed to Rome to direct the performance? From the extant copy in Angelini's handwriting two Roman performances are suggested, for the scribe later inserted eleven more *fogli* into fol. 22; five measures of these appear in Handel's own hand.[72] Here the text comes

---

[70] Pp. 74ff. Thus the sojourn in Naples shrinks to about 10 weeks, i.e. not "nearly a third of his time in Italy" (LANG, *Handel*, p. 87), but roughly a twentieth. So far no other visit to Naples has been traced.

[71] The payment "Per 10 funtioni in più volte" in Doc. 29 refers to the ten Sundays from 15 July to 16 Sept.; in 1708 Poli is paid for the Sundays after 23 Sept. 1708 – *AC 1966* pp. 351, 353 = *AC 2007* p. 438.

[72] EWERHART, *Die Händel-Handschriften*, pp. 127f.

to our assistance, revealing this cantata's peculiar function at a festival of the Arcadia which had now to take place in early summer. Aminta's passion is not of earthly nature, he desires to kindle his frigid mistress with a heavenly flame; and it is "il Dio bambin col strale suo divin" ["the Christ child with his divine arrow"] who then wounds Fillide's heart. The subject, the characters, the imagery are all too familiar from the Roman Christmas cantatas to allow "il Dio bambin" to be interpreted simply as the pagan Amor. These shepherds are the "shepherds abiding in the fields" of Bethlehem. The Arcadians were indeed concerned about their brotherhood with these more humble herdsmen since they had chosen the *bambino Gesù* for their protector. Therefore, as Crescimbeni informs us, they celebrated the Nativity every year with great pomp. However, they did so not on the day "when it is celebrated by all the faithful", for the winter season did not allow them to meet in their *bosco*. Since it was only here, where they spent their official season, from 1 May to 7 October, that they could feel like true shepherds, they had placed the festival on the first of the seven general assemblies that were then to be held:[73]

Io ho detto di sopra, che l'Arcadia non ha protettore temporale; ma non però priva dello spirituale, essendosi messa sotto la tutela del Santissimo Nostro Signore Gesù Nascente, la cui festa non potendo ella celebrarla nel dì, che si celebra da tutti i fedeli, perché la stagione d'inverno non permette esercitarsi nel bosco, soleva già solennizzarla ogni anno nella prima adunanza generale, che si faceva nello stesso bosco.

I have said above that the Arcadia does not have a worldly protector; however, it does not lack a spiritual one, being placed under the guardianship of our most holy lord the infant Christ, whose feast cannot be celebrated on the day when it is celebrated by all the faithful, because the winter season does not permit it in the forest, it was already customary to celebrate it every year during the first general assembly which took place in the said forest.

I have no doubt that "Fiamma bella", which we may label 'Christmas cantata', was the composition which crowned the Arcadian 'Christmas' when it was still celebrated in the summer, at the first *adunanza generale* in 1708. Ruspoli was the host of the Arcadians at that time; his little garden southwest of San

---

[73] Giovanni Maria CRESCIMBENI, *Breve Notizia dello stato antico, e moderno dell'adunanza degli Arcadi pubblicata l'anno 1712*, in his *Istoria della volgar poesia*, VI, Venice, Basegio, 1731³, pp. 313f. He goes on to say that the festival was later moved back to its proper day in winter and celebrated in an eminent member's townhouse (during the off-season the Arcadians used to meet alternately in each other's *capanne*), and that thus it was done "this year", at the *cancelleria*. Whether this news, published at the end of 1712, refers to Christmas 1712 or to the preceding year, does not need to concern us here too much; it has the flavor of a novelty.

Matteo in Merulana had become their *bosco parrhasio* in September 1707, succeeding that of Prince Giustiniani. That the concert took place on a Saturday, supports this thesis, as Saturday seems to have been the day reserved for their official meetings.[74] No singers were hired. [**PS**: The cantata was, in fact, first performed as his Handel's Roman debut, Christmas 1706 – *HR* 305ff, = below, pp. 365ff, with the bill of the copyist Tarquinio Lanciani].

Already by 9 August (Doc. 24; Plate IX.3) the copyist Angelini received his *scudi* for eleven cantatas, of which ten are well known as Handel's; the eighth in the series, *La Marciata* could not be identified. The first, second, and fourth have been encountered already in 1707; they may have now been copied to be given away. The third cantata listed here is the well known "Hendel non può mia musa" HWV 117. Though Cardinal Pamphilj is the poet, it is now clear that the work was composed and first performed at Ruspoli's. (Two more copies were made at Ruspoli's expense – cf. Doc. 35f – and the autograph is preserved in the Santini collection, surely of Ruspoli provenance). The cardinal was a frequent guest. Since Ruspoli apparently did not write poetry himself [**PS**: He seems to have written some poetry, both in Italian – cf. HWV 143, *HR* 340 = below, p. 401 – and, according to a verbal communication from Saverio Franchi, in Latin], he presented the composer with poems of his house poet or of his friends. (Thus we find Cardinal Pietro Ottoboni and Pietro's father Don Antonio delivering texts to Caldara during his employment with Ruspoli). The date of the bill could clarify the situation of the poem. Pamphilj says that his muse cannot in a twinkling sing verses worthy of Handel's lyre, but feeling in himself such sweet harmony, he was impelled to sing like this (there follows the 'Orfeo' aria, etc.). This was a reply, in a tone which shows a little resignation. In addition to the oratorio *Il trionfo del Tempo* Pamphilj certainly had given Handel other texts during 1707 and the first half of 1708. Then Handel had gone to Naples, and now, immediately after his return, he had approached his former patron for more poetry. Evidently Pamphilj's muse was just then somewhat tired, so that he wisely took refuge in this personal address, describing his situation. His use of the Orpheus metaphor should not be taken too seriously, as a monumental apotheosis of Handel,[75] but rather as a nice compliment paid by the old gentleman to the young one.

---

[74] Cf. below, note 107. The garden can be located as no. 28 in Giambattista NOLLI's *Pianta di Roma*, Rome, 1748, reproduced in Amato Pietro FRUTAZ, *Le piante di Roma*, Rome, Salomone & Saderini, 1962, III, tav. 408.

[75] It was MAINWARING (p. 63) who first interpreted this as Handel having been "exalted above the ranks of mortals".

Handel's presence at the court in August is testified by another impressive food bill, receipted 31 August (Doc. 26). Angelini had to be diligent to keep pace with Handel's fast quill. As he states in the heading of his next bill, Doc. 25, he again delivered "molte carte di musiche", from 11 August to 3 September. However, he signed the receipt for the full sum on 28 August, and we may assume that the date in the heading circumscribes the time for which the music was planned [**PS**: probably already performed]. Two large cantatas *con stromenti* and five cantatas with basso continuo and are included, among them "Se pari e la tua fé" HWV 158ª in two copies, "Ditemi o piante" HWV 107 and "Clori, vezzosa Clori" HWV 95, as duplicates. The unidentified "Cantata a voce sola con VV" seems to have been performed on Sunday, 2 September, when for the second time after Ruspoli's return violinists were hired (cf. Doc. 29, first part) and no additional singer is traceable.

A brilliant event took place the following Sunday, 9 September. There is Angelini's bill for the parts of the "cantata a tre con stromenti *Il Tebro*", receipted on Monday, 10 September (Doc. 27; Plate IX.4). This is no other than the famous cantata with the roles Olinto (soprano), il Tebro (alto), and la Gloria (soprano), known under the text-incipit "O come chiare e belle" HWV 143. It can be connected at once with Doc. 29 (Plate IX.5), a note on the payments to three additional violinists and the trumpet player Gaetano,[76] who performed Monsù Hendel's "seconda cantata con stromenti" (i.e. the second in September, the third since 22 July) on Sunday, 9 September, for HWV 143 is the only known cantata [**PS**: after *Diana cacciatrice*] by Handel to employ a trumpet. (The text requires it; Olinto says at the end of his last recitative: "voglio altro stile, cangiare in tromba la zampogna umile" ["I want another style, to replace the humble bagpipe with the trumpet"], then begins his D-major aria, accompanied by trumpet and violins; thereafter comes the final "Viva" terzet, still with trumpet, plus violins and *bassi*). The trumpet is employed expressly for its traditional task: to announce the hero, to proclaim his fame. It had to praise Ruspoli the warrior, who had been a shepherd until then, and now exchanges the rustic bagpipe for the trumpet. One remembers that Ruspoli, whose Arcadian name was "Olinto",[77] had glorified with this text his patriotic and well calculated deed in the service of Pope Clement XI, the establishment of the "colonella Ruspoli" for the defense of

---

[76] Gaetano is known also from Doc. 11.

[77] Giovanni Maria CRESCIMBENI, *Prose degli Arcadi*, Rome, De' Rossi, 1718, III, p. CI: "Olinto Arsenio. Il Conte Francesco Maria Capizucchi Romano. Poi Marchese Ruspoli, e ora Principe di Cerveteri".

Ferarra.[78] New evidence from the documents is the date. Robinson suggested March 1708 for general historical reasons. Our date, however, 9 September 1708, fits into the diplomatic events and illustrates them vividly, for it was in September that Clement held a secret consistory to solve the hopeless problem of financing the mobilization.[79] (An aside from a contemporary may show Ruspoli's 550 men in the proper light: when the Pope's own soldiers were given the choice of either marching toward Ferrara or staying at home with only half of their normal salary, only six of six hundred did not prefer to stay where they were).[80] Document 28 then presents the bill of the Roman printer Luca Antonio Chracas for 300 libretti "della cantata" with his receipt dated 15 September, certainly referring to this extraordinary work. Very rarely were librettos printed for secular cantatas, only twice in a decade at Ruspoli's. [**PS**: cf. *HR* 340 = below, p. 401, Plate IX.9, and *AC* 2007, Plate 10].

Although the singers are not mentioned in our pay list (Doc. 29), it is possible to trace their identity. One of the soprano parts was, as always, sung by Durastante. The contralto's name is handed down incidentally, in an entry for the cleaning of his room when he left, shortly after 15 September 1708: "Pag. per sgom[bra]re le stanze per la Sig.^ra Marg.^a e Sig.^re Ursini [*scudi*] –.50".[81] Mentioned here in one line with the prima donna, the gentleman can be only one, the great contralto Gaetano Orsini. He was perhaps a native Roman.[82] That "Ursini" refers to a contralto is the more probable, since the second soprano, Anna Maria di Piedz, was [**PS**: may have been] already present.

Another witness for Handel's very presence, and a relief from 'dry' documents, is the bill of the *nevaiolo* for 45 pounds of "snow" or ice delivered to Monsù Endel during the hot month of September to cool his bottles (Doc. 31). A final food bill, however, limits this period to the first eleven days (Doc. 30). Handel had thus departed from the court on 12 September, about the time that the singers left. Whether he then still remained in Rome or with Ruspoli in the country, we cannot say. Margarita, though she had moved out, was still employed.

---

[78] The connection Olinto-Ruspoli was first mentioned by CHRYSANDER, I, 209. For the political implications see ROBINSON, *Handel and his Orbit*, p. 173.

[79] Vat. Lat. 8629, ff. 486-488*v*: "Scrittura d'autor anonimo a papa Clemente XI per le presenti emergenze di guerra 1708"; ff. 490-493: "Concistorium secretum super defensione status ecclesiastici & super extractione pecuniarum in erario Arcis S. Angeli", 24 Sept., signed "Ottobono"; ff. 494-499*v*: "Romana extractionis pecuniarum ab aerario ...", 4 Sept.

[80] DE LA TORRE, *Mémoires et negociations secrettes de diverses cours de l'Europe*, V, The Hague, Moetjens, 1725, p. 125.

[81] *Giustificazioni* A 46, *Lista delle spese*, 10 July - 19 Sept. 1708, no. 161.

[82] Carlo SCHMIDL, *Dizionario universale dei musicisti*, II, Milan, Sonzogno, 1938, p. 199.

The fourth and last cantata *con stromenti* of this season[83] was performed on 28 October, traceable through the performers' list receipted on 31 October (Doc. 32). The presence of the contralto Pasqualino would suggest a cantata either for contralto or for soprano and alto with violins. The former does not exist among Handel's Italian works. A duo could have been provided by Angelini, with his parts waiting for two months: *Il duello amoroso* in Doc. 25 was copied before 28 August 1708 (see above; not to be confused with either *Il delirio amoroso* HWV 99 or "Dalla guerra amorosa" HWV 102). [**PS**: Only the terrible events of the war could have delayed the performance]. This work, HWV 82, not known from Chrysander, is mentioned and described for the first time by Ewerhart, under the text-incipit "Amarilli vezzosa", from a score by Angelini in Münster.[84] It contains 11 *fogli*, and may have been included in the 24$\frac{1}{2}$ *fogli* listed in our bill, though only the "*cavate*" ["parts"] are mentioned. The contralto Pasqualino, as Daliso the shepherd, may have joined the soprano Durastante, the nymph Amarilli, to be honored with three silver *scudi*. The three hired violinists received one ordinary *scudo* each. It has been pointed out that Amarilli's aria "Piacer che non si dona" and Daliso's "E vanità" occur again in *Agrippina*, there sung by Poppea and Ottone respectively[85] – two more examples of Handel's careful strategy with regard to his Venetian debut. Here an aria first introduced by Durastante was presented later [**PS**: possibly the second performance – cf. *HR* 336f = below, pp. 398f] by her co-actress Diamante Maria Scarabelli. At Ruspoli's we can assume a particularly festive arrangement, for the messenger Ascanio delivered special invitations (Doc. 32). This was the custom for only the most splendid events.[86] Once more Angelini adds new copies to Ruspoli's repertoire: two continuo cantatas "di Monsù Hendel ... in sei fogli", paid for on 24 November 1708 (Doc. 33).

D. 28 February 1709 to 10 October 1711

After 24 November 1708, the chain is interrupted: there is no reference to Handel until we find an isolated bill for copies of three cantatas, known as his, receipted on 28 February 1709 (Doc. 34). As to performances and the com-

---

[83] On the possible identity of this cantata, cf. also below, note 106.
[84] *Die Händel-Handschriften*, pp. 125ff.
[85] Ewerhart, *loc. cit.*
[86] See *AC* 1966 p. 48 = *AC* 2007 p. 60.

poser's presence, we are on less solid ground. The interpretation of this document is doubtful, depending upon the meaning of "per il baron tedescho". Is this Handel? The bill shows the handwriting of Pietro Castrucci who very probably, like everyone in the house, would have called him "Monsù Endel" or "Hendel", and not used "per" to point to the composer. It more likely designates a person who ordered these copies, possibly a German guest unknown to us.[87] Handel's occupation in Tuscany in the latter half of March diminishes the probability that he was in Rome now.

Half a year later we find another isolated bill, receipted on 31 August 1709, in the handwriting of Francesco Lanciani (Doc. 35; Plate IX.6 and *AC* 2007, Plate 16). There is no doubt that these solo cantatas with basso continuo were not copied for immediate performance. At least ten of the 21 pieces are duplicates (see below, pp. 318-322). And the cantatas used during the second half of 1709 were provided by Caldara.

Again two years go by until, with three small copies, billed by Francesco Lanciani on 15 March, before 22 May, and on 10 October 1711, Handel's name appears for the last time in the master of the household's *giustificazioni* (Doc. 36ff). By this time his presence is with certainty to be excluded.[88] Doc. 36 is interesting as it lists a new copy of "Hendel non puo mia musa" (the third copy mentioned in these documents) and states expressly "doppo partito il Sig.ʳ Antonio Caldara" – only after Caldara had left did Ruspoli dare to revert to Handel. Doc. 37 spins threads far across the continent, to England. Here "Ho un non so che nel cor" from *La Resurrezione* is copied separately. It was in these spring months of 1711 that Francesca Vanini-Boschi on the London stage crazed the audience with the aria that had once been transferred into *Agrippina* [**PS**: vice versa – cf. PS to *Agrippina* on p. 315] then, in London, into Alessandro Scarlatti's *Pirro e Demetrio*, now into *Rinaldo* – a craze that produced mocksongs on the melody.[89] Perhaps they had heard in Rome that it was so much in fashion now, and someone asked for it. Final-

---

[87] Could it be Agostino Steffani? Long domiciled in Germany, he was in Rome from 7 Oct. 1708 until the end of February 1709 on a secret diplomatic mission for the Elector of Hanover which was instrumental in creating the truce between the pope and the emperor during the War of the Spanish Succession (cf. STREATFEILD, *Handel in Italy*, p. 11; Colin TIMMS, *Polymath of the Baroque: Agostino Steffani and his Music*, Oxford UP, 2003, pp. 90-92). Thus he came as a 'tedesco', and, of course, a 'baron'; he may have visited the performances at the Bonelli palace [**PS**: Timms has confirmed our impression that this hypothesis should be withdrawn].

[88] From the documents in DEUTSCH, pp. 43-46, it appears that Handel was still in Düsseldorf on 17 June, in Hanover in July, and in Halle on 12 Nov. for the baptism of his niece (no proxy was registered for him).

[89] Cf. William C. SMITH, *Handel's First Song on the London Stage*, «Music and Letters», XVI, 1935, pp. 286-292; DEUTSCH, pp. 40ff.

ly, on 10 October 1711, there is a bill for the copy of the score of "Ah crudel" HWV 78, a large cantata *con stromenti* (Doc. 38). This certainly does not indicate the first performance (parts would have been prepared instead). The work may have been heard again now, since the same note mentions a payment to "Sig.ʳ Ignatio", an oboist,[90] and this work requires two oboes. Caldara was in Milan at the time, and although he sent a number of compositions to Rome, Ruspoli may have had to fall back on older pieces in his library.

* * *

We shall now try to define the time limits, the amount, and the character of Handel's work for Ruspoli. Without imposing fixed conclusions on the obviously problematic, isolated documents from February 1709 on, we can say that they cannot possibly have issued from a regular employment. Indeed, we know that after 1 March 1709 Antonio Caldara was employed as Ruspoli's chapel master – his cantatas fill the bills from then on – and that sometime during Lent 1709 [**PS**: at least before winter 1709] Handel had again joined the court of the Medici in Florence. Although, after the 'snow' bill of September 1708, there is no entry from which to conclude his presence or departure from Rome, we can be sure that by 1 March 1709 (Doc. 34), at the latest, Handel had left. [**PS**: Handel's cantatas billed during 1709ff were certainly not performed in his presence].

His activity for Ruspoli may well have ceased between 12 September and the end of October 1708 [**PS**: Doc. 32 – not proof of Handel's presence]. Between his return from Naples, around 15 [**PS**: by 14 – Doc. 21] July 1708, and the last payment for Angelini's copies, on 24 November 1708, "Fiamma bella" was performed and fifteen new cantatas were copied (duplicates we must leave aside), and the calendar shows exactly sixteen Sundays up to 28 October. Even more precisely: after the performance of "Fiamma bella" the scribe wrote [**PS**: was paid for] three large cantatas *con stromenti*, and there are three bills for borrowed musicians, permitting the assignment of these large works to their performance days. The exact recital dates of the small cantatas with basso continuo cannot be traced, and speculation does not lead very far. The pieces mentioned in Doc. 24 could be placed any time after 22 July 1708; those in Doc. 25 after 11 August 1708, according to Angelini's heading. By 28 August (cf. the receipt in Doc. 25) there was an ample reserve of pieces from which to choose, so that we by no means have to assume that they were then performed in the order in which they appear in

---

[90] *AC* 1966 p. 355 = *AC* 2007 p. 444.

the bills. [**PS**: The first performances cannot be dated with such exactness, though also here Angelini seems to have respected the chronology].

How close are the dates of the copies to those of the compositions? Were the cantatas copied for Ruspoli all composed for him? This is doubtless the case for those copied [**PS**: receipted] before 24 November 1708: first, no work is included which was evidently written for another patron (this argument is supported by the fact that the two cantatas finished in Naples, i.e. immediately before Ruspoli's fall season, do not appear in Rome); second, the cantatas were copied for scheduled performances; and last but not least, Handel was there not merely to dine at Ruspoli's table but to deliver music. Thus we can generally assume that the copyist's work was then done only days or weeks after the composer's. [**PS**: Still, Ruspoli at first was not in a hurry to pay the bills; he must have waited for the musicians to have established a 'track record'. Only after four or five months were payments punctual, also for Caldara].

Age and destination of the cantatas 'newly' copied in 1709 and 1711 cannot be determined with such directness, since, as stated above, the pieces of 1709 were not copied for scheduled Sunday concerts, and the one of October 1711 was obviously copied for a second performance. Here the dates from the bills must be taken with more caution, as *termini ante quos*. In this group 23 cantatas are mentioned, 12 of them for the first time, 11 for the second or third time [**PS**: numbers now corrected; the aria from *La resurrezione* not counted] (cf. the chart below, pp. 347ff). While the duplicates are of proven Ruspoli origin, we face many (theoretical) possibilities for the new titles: were these cantatas composed at Ruspoli's, ordered by Ruspoli while Handel was elsewhere, sent to this court as presents, by Handel or by other patrons?

A glance at the titles reveals that in this group, too, the cantatas for Cardinal Pamphilj and for Naples do not appear. One may be startled to find the famous *Lucrezia* HWV 145 included in Lanciani's bill of 31 August 1709 (Doc. 35), a work that has been supposed to have originated in Tuscany ever since Chrysander learned from Quadrio that the Florentine court employed a virtuosa Lucrezia d'André, called Madama Caró.[91] This lady, dear to many a biographer and recently exhumed once more,[92] can now be laid to rest. Her position was already weakened when Ademollo noted that the Grand Duke

---

[91] CHRYSANDER, I, 162.

[92] LANG, p. 63: "Several cantatas can be traced to Handel's first Florentine visit, among them *O numi eterni*. ... *La Lucrezia* ... lends some credence to the rumored love affair with Lucrezia d'André".

counted two more Lucrezias among his virtuosas: "Lucrezia Pontissi, la lucchese" and "Lucrezia Storni, veneziana".[93] I may add that Lucrezia d'André is traceable also at Ruspoli's,[94] which means that even if her connection with the piece had been established, this would not prove Florentine origin. It has not even been ascertained whether she was a soprano. [**PS**: She has now been identified as a contralto – cf. *HR* 329f = below, p. 390]. Once her shadow has faded out of the picture, we see that all roads lead to Rome. The heroine is, first of all, 'romana'. Celebrated by poets and painters of many nations and generations as the personification of marital virtue, her involuntary role in Rome's becoming a republic endeared her especially to the Romans. Painters seem to have been occupied with the theme in Rome, Bologna, the republics north of the Apennines, Venice and the Netherlands, and everywhere else more than in ever-jealous Florence, where it seldom appears outside of the intimate, private realm of the bridal *cassoni*, and, significantly, seldom after the beginning of the Grand Duchy.[95] As a cantata text this theme is once more traceable in Rome. Cardinal Benedetto Pamphilj himself wrote the lyrics for a *Lucrezia romana* cantata which was set to music by Alessandro Scarlatti.[96] In 1690 the poet had a gift copy sent to Cardinal Francesco Maria Medici.[97] (It is rather improbable that the Medici would have ordered a Lucrezia story from their own chapel master; music at the court level was never a private, but always a representative matter). There is little similarity between the Pamphilj text of 1690 (incipit "Lasciato havea l'adultero superbo") and Handel's (incipit "O Numi eterni, o stelle, stelle") with the exception of roughly equal length and the notable correspondence of the recitatives containing the invocation of father and husband as the recipients of the sacrifice (Pamphilj: "Voi, genitor, consorte"; Handel's poet: "A voi, padre, consorte"). The parallel treatment does not necessarily suggest that Handel's poet knew Pamphilj's text, or that Pamphilj wrote this one too: we may have to do with a *topos* familiar to the time from the numerous dramas on the subject.[98] Still,

---

[93] *Haendel in Italia*, p. 283.

[94] *AC* Doc. 53.

[95] Cf. the lists in A. PIGLER, *Barockthemen*, II, Budapest/Berlin, Akadémiai Kiadó, 1956, pp. 386-390 and 415ff.

[96] ZANETTI, *Roma città di Haendel*, p. 440; Edwin HANLEY, *Alessandro Scarlatti's Cantate da Camera: A Bibliographical Study*, ms. diss., Yale, 1963, pp. 291f. Marcello's Lucrezia cantata, with the text used by Handel, has not yet been traced back to time and place of origin – Eleonor SELFRIDGE-FIELD, *The Music of Benedetto and Alessandro Marcello: A Thematic Catalogue*, Oxford, Clarendon, 1990, p. 140, no. A229.

[97] MONTALTO, p. 330.

[98] Renowned Italian Lucrezia plays of the late 17th century were those by Cardinal Daniello

that it was Pamphilj who was engaged in this subject should not be over-looked. Finally, it is time to recall Mainwaring's remark that Handel's *Lucrezia* was composed in Rome[99] – a remark which Chrysander felt obliged to 'correct'.

More evidence comes from the extant manuscripts. Here only some general results can be given. Only two of the scores of the thirteen 'new' cantatas bear the date of origin or a remark on the provenance. Both these manuscripts lead to Ruspoli. "Lungi da te mio nume", in Lanciani's bill of August 1709, is surely identical with the well-known "Lungi dal mio bel nume" HWV 127[a] (throughout these bills the titles seem to have been written down hastily, probably partly from memory). The autograph is dated by Handel "Roma, il dì 3 di marzo 1708".[100] By that time Handel was already living in the Ruspoli house. An English copy of "Ah crudel nel pianto mio" HWV 78 in the hand of the copyist "S 13", seemingly taken from a copy in the hand of "S 2", bears the remark "composto a Roma per il S.^{gr} Marchese Ruspoli da G. F. Handel".[101] Both scribes are, as Larsen has proved, collaborators of Smith the elder and thus close enough to the most reliable source of information: Handel himself. The formulation, omitting the title "Sig." for Handel's name, and giving the English spelling of this name in an Italian context, comes closest to what we are familiar with from his autographs.

These few notes on the provenance have come down to us by chance. For a balanced picture, all extant copies of Handel's Italian cantatas have to be considered. By good fortune a large number of the very copies listed in our bills has been preserved in Fortunato Santini's collection. On the basis of works written for Ruspoli by Caldara, F. Gasparini, and A. Scarlatti, it has been demonstrated that this collection contains the patron's music library more or less in the state as it was when Santini acquired it from the Ruspoli in the nineteenth century.[102] Here we meet all but six of the forty copies listed in Angelini's bills from May 1707 to September 1708. "Tu fedel?" (Hs. 1913 and Hs. 1910 ff. 7-50) and "Mentre il tutto" (Hs. 1899 ff. 28-35 and Hs. 1910

Marco Delfino and Bonnicelli, mentioned by Barthold Feind in the *Vorbericht* of his libretto to Keiser's opera *Die kleinmüthige Selbstmörderin Lucretia*, Hamburg, 1705 (see Oscar George Theodore SONNECK, *Catalogue of Opera Librettos Printed before 1800*, Washington, Government Printing Office, 1914, I, 671), a work, by the way, that Handel must have known. Its influence on the cantata can no longer be pursued, since the score has survived only in small fragments.

99 MAINWARING, p. 200.

100 GB-Lbl ms. add. 30310, ff. 2-12*v*.

101 GB-Lk ms. R.M.19.d.10. The activities of these copyists are defined by Jens Peter LARSEN, *Handel's Messiah: Origins, Composition, Sources*, London, Black, 1957, pp. 265f and 272f.

102 *AC* 1966 pp. 103-107 = *AC* 2007 pp. 136-140.

ff. 169-176) from Doc. 25 are present twice in Angelini's writing (we shall have to explain this); "Aure soavi" (Hs. 1898 ff. 68-72) from Doc. 1 and 24 with two pages added in Handel's own hand;[103] "Manca pur" (Hs. 1898 ff. 89-95) and a second copy of "Quando sperasti" (Hs. 1898 ff. 101-106) from Doc. 24 by an anonymous collaborator of Angelini's [**PS**: Alessandro Ginelli – cf. *HR* 306, note 32 = below, pp. 365f, note 30] (the other copy, Hs. 1910 ff. 1-6, is by Angelini); in the copy Hs. 1899 of "Mentre il tutto" Angelini wrote the music, this anonymous scribe the words; "Ditemi o piante" from both Doc. 24 and 25 once by Angelini (Hs. 1899 ff. 17-24) and once by a Roman scribe who is very close to the Castrucci family [**PS**: *recte*: by Cosimo Serio – cf. *HR* 316f and Plates 7a-b = below, pp. 376f and Plates XI.8a-b] (Hs. 1910 ff. 159-167). Only Angelini's "Hendel non può mia musa" from Doc. 24 is missing; but the autograph is there (Hs. 1898 ff. 1-4), and a copy which was doubtless made in the closest proximity to Ruspoli's *cameriere* Pietro Castrucci (Hs. 1910 ff. 189-192). [**PS**: I now designate the still anonymous copyists with the sigla assigned by Watanabe,[104] this one as Mü XI]. However, when we now look for copies from Doc. 34 and Lanciani's from Doc. 35, 36, and 38, we are surprised to find nothing. Of the three cantatas paid by Castrucci, *Armida abbandonata* and "Poiché giurarò amore" are present here in Angelini's [!] hand (Hs. 1894 ff. 1-22 and Hs. 1899 ff. 83-90, respectively), "Ninfe e pastori" by the same 'Castrucci neighbour' [Serio] who wrote "Ditemi o piante" (Hs. 1898 ff. 49-56). Of the 21 cantatas billed by Lanciani in August 1709 only "Dalla guerra amorosa" shows up in Francesco's handwriting (nor does Tarquinio Lanciani, who worked with Francesco, appear); nine are in copies written by Angelini, two more by his collaborators; "Lungi dal mio bel Nume", composed at Ruspoli's, is copied once by Angelini (Hs. 1898 ff. 23-33) and once by an anonymous [Mü II] who is probably identical [**PS**: no] with Pietro Castrucci (Hs. 1910 ff. 141-151). Nor is the "originale" present which Francesco Lanciani wrote of "Ah crudel" in 1711 (Doc. 38); but the autograph is there – a case similar to the above-mentioned "Hendel non può mia musa" – confirming now that the first performance was accompanied from the autograph. This cantata may well be the "cantata a voce sola con VV" of which the parts were copied before 28 August 1708 – see Doc. 25 – and which was then certainly

---

[103] EWERHART, Die Händel-Handschriften, p. 135.

[104] [**PS**: Keiichiro WATANABE, *Die Kopisten der Handschriften G. F. Händels in der Santini-Bibliothek, Münster*, «Journal of the Japanese Musicological Society», XVI, 1970, pp. 231-236. Here Ginelli is designated as Mü I, Serio as Mü VIII, and Franesco Lanciani as Mü III, but none is identified by name. Could also Mü XI be Serio?].

performed on 2 September 1708. [**PS**: Delete the preceding sentence; the following one has been modified]. To sum up: the copies billed by Angelini until 1708 are present in Münster; those by Castrucci and Lanciani since 1709 are lost, but about half of them had already been copied by Angelini

At this stage [1967] of my investigation of handwriting and text variants it seems that the manuscripts of 'Ruspoli' cantatas outside of the Santini collection are altogether younger. There is little doubt that the Santini copies were the first which were taken from the autographs. The Ruspoli collection is indeed fairly intact in this library – if diminished at all, then only by a very few manuscripts which Santini presented to collector friends. The absence of copies "per il barone tedescho" (Doc. 34) confirms that these were all duplicates sent out by Ruspoli as gift copies. The same goes for the 21 Lanciani copies of August 1709 (Doc. 35), of which ten could be proved to be duplicates. The bill itself had the character of a 'gift-copy' bill. These copies must have been bound together as a large collection, otherwise single pieces would have come to light. The models from which copies for the "German baron" and by Francesco Lanciani were taken must have been present at Ruspoli's. Again, there is no doubt that these were the Angelini copies in the Santini collection.

Still, how can we explain that some of these 'first copies', by Angelini, do not appear in Ruspoli's accounts? Were they themselves gift copies, presented by Ottoboni, Pamphilj, or Colonna? (Angelini worked also for Cardinal Pamphilj, and the Santini collection does contain pieces of Pamphilj- and Colonna-provenance). Let our considerations start from cantatas which were with certainty composed for Ruspoli. There is no Ruspoli bill for the two extant Santini copies of "Lungi dal mio bel nume" HWV 127^a, a genuine product of the Ruspoli house, and likewise there is no bill for one of the extant twin copies of "Mentre il tutto" HWV 130. For "Lungi dal mio bel nume", composed in March 1708 [**PS**: F. Lanciani may have corrupted the title in Doc. 35], a clue may be found in the fact that one of the two copies was written by the scribe who seems to be identical with Pietro Castrucci [**PS**: *recte*: Mü II]. It is quite probable that during the busy Lenten weeks of 1708 the house musicians had to help copying. They may have then received a general compensation for their 'overtime', as was the case in 1711.[105] Angelini had his hands full with the copies for *La Resurrezione*; the 2400 pages for which he was paid must have kept him and his relatives and/or employees busy for weeks, and the round sum of 30 *scudi* may have included also some small items such as continuo cantatas (hence it is possible also that Handel contrib-

---

[105] See the special payments to the two *camerieri* after the opera season, listed in *AC* Doc. 79.

uted more cantatas than appear in the bills for the Sunday concerts between 26 February and his departure for Naples). It is equally probable that some of the 11 'new' cantatas in Doc. 35 were already included in those earlier Angelini bills of 1707 that do not specify the titles. After all, it is unlikely that a patron as ambitious as Ruspoli would include in a gift collection pieces that had not originated under his auspices.

From the documentary evidence it seems almost certain that also the twelve cantatas which are 'new' in Ruspoli accounts after 1708 were composed for this patron. Altogether there are 48 secular cantatas (4 of them not identified) and three sacred cantatas mentioned. There is no doubt that Ruspoli continued to perform cantatas by Handel until Caldara arrived.[106]

The function of "Fiamma bella" may rouse a question as to whether this was the only cantata that served the purposes of the Arcadia. It is not impossible that other *cantate con stromenti* were heard at subsequent general assemblies, as no such cantatas were copied or performed after October, during the Arcadian off-season. Since the first general assembly of 1708 was not held before July, one may wonder whether the last one was not equally late, and identical with our event on 28 October (see above), and thus the normal season, from 1 May to 7 October, delayed as a whole. But it should be kept in mind that the Arcadian meetings, in Ruspoli's garden on the Esquiline, had nothing to do with Ruspoli's weekly *conversazione*, though they may at times have made the latter superfluous.[107] If, in this context, we must return once more

---

[106] Only one cantata mentioned before March 1709 is not by Handel: a "cantata ... in $5\frac{1}{2}$ fogli" by Caldara, paid on 11 Oct. 1708 – AC Doc. 1. Could this piece have served the festive event on 28 Oct. (*RD* 243 = above, p. 315)?

[107] A note on the confusion in Handel literature between the Arcadia and certain patrons' academies may not be out of place. The frequent statement about Handel having appeared "in the academy" – a suspect place – is echoed and elaborated in MGG[1] V, 1236: "Cardinal Ottoboni assembled about himself artists and friends of arts for sociable cultivation of the arts. The circle was called Arcadia". Also LANG, p. 53: "The principal circle of cultivated intellectuals met in the academy called Accademia Poetico-Musicale, usually in the palace of Cardinal Pietro Ottoboni, and occasionally at the residence of the Marquess [*sic*] Francesco Maria Ruspoli". When Merlini in 1707 referred to Ottoboni's gathering as to an "accademia poetico-musicale", he simply characterized the meeting, not referring to the name of an institution. The term *accademia* was used interchangeably with *conversazione*; it could mean the event as well as the assembly, and covered a wide range of quasi-intellectual and more elevated activities (see MONTALTO, pp. 152-157), most of which were by no means regulated by statutes. The Arcadia, on the other hand, the literary academy founded in 1690 by followers of Christina of Sweden, was strictly organized (as so immortally ridiculed by Goethe, by chance one of its honorary members) and completely independent of those social gatherings, with the exception that its members and visitors were largely the same. For the *conversazione*, each patron had his day reserved, not interfering with those of his friends: Ruspoli Sunday, Ottoboni Wednesday (not Monday), Pamphilj (in these years) Friday. It appears from a number of Ruspoli papers in 1712 that the Arcadians then met on Saturdays in Ruspoli's new *bosco* on the Aventine.

to the old question why Handel was not made a member of this solemn circle, there is no need to maintain Chrysander's theory that he could not be admitted since he had not reached the required age of 24 – a theory reported piously as fact through all of the monographs. The Arcadia was primarily a literary society, then largely limited to members of the aristocracy, though the statutes liked to veil this fact. (The famous admission of three musicians – Corelli, Alessandro Scarlatti, and Bernardo Pasquini – was a unique occurrence, and afterwards partly 'justified' by nobility bestowed on them; on the other hand, Benedetto Marcello, as a *nobile veneto*, had no difficulty in entering).[108] There is a commentary in the statutes, hitherto overlooked, which makes it clear that the age limit of 24 was no serious barrier: "to enter in this assembly there are three prerequisites: first the age of 24 years, *but this can be waived by the assembly*".[109] Finally, by 23 February 1709, Handel was 24 years old, and still not made a member. He was then [probably] staying in Tuscany and could have been accepted by the Arcadians of the Florentine colony, if they had so desired.

Summing up the evidence on the nature of Handel's work with Ruspoli, we can state that although our composer was treated as a favored guest – and no official salary was paid to him –[110] his activity had the character of a clearly regulated employment. A definite number of compositions was expected from him; by (probably informal) agreement he was obliged to remain and do his duties. This has to be said expressly, to correct the romantic picture of the pampered youngster who wrote music or appeared "in the academies" only when the spirit moved him. It confirms Mainwaring's remark, "Handel was desired to furnish his quota",[111] a remark which does not have the flavor of an anecdote. In this position Handel was Caldara's immediate predecessor, no chapel master having been employed before March 1709.

The importance of this period within the whole of the Italian sojourn is obvious: not only one of the two oratorios of this time, but a large percentage of all the 'Italian' cantatas were composed for Ruspoli.[112] That Handel had to

---

[108] The same arguments apply to Caldara – see *AC* 1966 p. 83 = *AC* 2007 p. 106.

[109] "Per entrare in questa conversazione si richieggono tre requisiti: il primo, l'età d'anni 24, *ma questo può dispensarsi dall'adunanza*" – CRESCIMBENI, p. 311 (my italics).

[110] This would have appeared in the *giustificazioni*, where the monthly payments to the regular court members as well as to temporary employees are carefully registered, together with their receipts.

[111] MAINWARING, p. 55.

[112] "While he was in Rome [!] he made a kind of oratorio entitled *Resurrectione*, and one hundred and fifty cantatas, besides sonatas and other music" – MAINWARING, p. 65. The exact number of the extant cantatas is not yet known. ZANETTI, *Le musiche italiane*, lists 25 *con stromenti*, 65 with basso

deliver his 'Sunday cantatas' compels us to an analogy with J. S. Bach: here the Italian, secular genre, there the German, Protestant one. This period is the more worthy of our attention as Handel, in assimilating the patterns of Italian style, had now achieved mastery. The large number of early copies of "Sento là che ristretto", "Sarei troppo felice", "Se pari è la tua fé", "Oh numi eterni" (*La Lucrezia*)[113] show the esteem in which these works were held by contemporaries. One may wonder, then, why Ruspoli isn't mentioned at all by Mainwaring, but we can take it as one more proof that this author's information is rather sketchy. [**PS**: For the answer to this question, see *HR 339* = below, p. 400. I have become more and more convinced that Mainwaring is a reliable witness – cf. *HR 335* = below, p. 396].

Details on Ruspoli's role as a patron of the arts may help to clarify the picture of the society to which Handel was admitted. Though many of Ruspoli's social and artistic undertakings before February 1709 were obviously directed to the goal of becoming a prince, his ambitions were not limited to this. Then and later he made his court a shelter of arts and artists, by no means restricting his favors to music. The eighty members of his court included such illustrious men as the aforementioned Giovanni Battista Contini, and, by the end of 1710, Girolamo Gigli, the eminently learned, sarcastic, rebellious mind who after 1717 became notorious for his daring *Vocabulario Cateriniano*, a pious philological pretext for attacks on contemporary men and institutions. In Italian literature he has been given a place as one of the three foremost comedy writers of the Settecento before Goldoni. He was employed as house poet and tutor of Ruspoli's eldest son, Bartolomeo, a fact which indicates that a bold, free spirit prevailed at this court. Ruspoli was 34 years old when the 22-year-old Handel first arrived [**PS**: 33 and 21, respectively] – an age when ardour and audacity usually have not yet completely cooled down. Handel's lifelong interest in painting may have been much stimulated in 1708: in the cloisters of San Salvatore in Lauro, where annually on 10 December exhibitions of old masters were held, Ruspoli showed 194 paintings from his collec-

---

continuo, plus second versions of some of the latter. W. C. SMITH, *Verzeichnis der Werke*, «Händel-Jahrbuch», II, 1956, pp. 151f, gives from Chrysander's edition the numbers 28 and 72, respectively, not including duets and trios in the first number. [**PS**: These numbers are superseded by HWV which lists solo cantatas as nos. 77-177, "Kammerduette" as 178-199, and "Kammertrios" as 200f].

[113] "Sento là" leads with seventeen 18th-century copies, five ahead of *Lucrezia*, of which MATTHESON said that it was "in vieler Leute Händen" ["in many people's hands"] – *Grosse Generalbaß-Schule*, Hamburg, Kissner, 1731, p. 355. [**PS**: 28 copies of "Sento là" have now been identified, including later transpositions – cf. Graydon BEEKS, *The Curious History of a Handel-Cantata: 'Sento là che ristretto' and its Various Versions*, in *Florilegium musicae: Studi in onore di Carolyn Gianturco*, Pisa, ETS, 2004, pp. 303-306 – and 25 of *Lucrezia*].

tion, an exhibition shared with only 23 paintings owned by another collector.[114]

Handel seems to have left friends at Ruspoli's. No less than four of the musicians with whom he had worked here followed him later to London: in 1715 Pietro Castrucci who afterwards became a celebrity as concert master in Handel's opera orchestra; in 1719 Pietro's father Domenico, then reported as being "sick in London"; with these two the famous 'cellist Filippo Amadei alias "Pippo" who had participated in *La Resurrezione*, active also as composer; and during later years (1720-24 and 1733f) Margarita Durastante.[115]

The documentary/biographical information is here presented in the hope of providing a more solid foundation for further studies on Handel's style. First, it is now possible to establish a chronology for the hitherto undistinguished mass of Italian cantatas. Secondly, through the fog of the 'Italian' influence we may begin to trace the actual music Handel could have heard from 1707 to 1709 [**PS**: from Dec. 1706 to the end of 1708]. This will go beyond an arbitrary listing of masters who may have made an impact. For music performed in Rome between March and September 1707, between February and May 1708, and between July and November 1708 one can draw on established work lists of Caldara, Cesarini, and Alessandro and Domenico Scarlatti. Finally, one must consider that the fruits of the encounter of North and South were gathered not only by Handel. His genius also left traces in Italy. There is a musical passage where the Sassone is remembered in a 'diabolical' banter. When Caldara composed the *Oratorio per la SS.^{ma} Annunziata* for Ruspoli in 1713 and had to present the figure of Lucifer, he invoked the Lucifer that had disturbed the same house five years earlier, in *La Resurrezione*. He used the same long, descending, anapestic scale, in the same key, that was once sung by Handel's Lucifer in his first aria, now for Lucifer's words "Col pensar all'altrui pene",[116] "thinking of the pains of others" – of his predecessor Handel.

ADDENDUM 1967

I should like to add here some information on Handel's activity in Vignanello, which I could obtain only during travels last summer when my article *The Ruspoli Documents on Handel* was already in press.

---

114 Francis HASKELL, *Patrons and Painters: A Study in the Relations between Italian Art and Society in the Age of the Baroque*, London, Harper & Row, 1963, pp. 128f.

115 Cf. DEUTSCH, *Handel, passim*, for these four.

116 For the musical examples see *AC* Exx. 201f.

My thesis that "Coelestis dum spirat aura in festo S. Antonij de Padua ... 1707" was composed for Vignanello could not be confirmed more simply than by a passage in the second recitative where "Julianelle" is addressed and declared happy for having St. Anthony as patron. The name does not refer to a person;[117] 'Julianellum' was the medieval Latin name of the *borgo* Vignanello, derived either from a legendary founder Giuliano, head of a group of fugitives who escaped from the Goths, or, more probably, from a 'fondo Giuliano' that preceded the foundation of the castello.[118] In Vignanello I searched in vain for Ceruti's altarpiece of S. Antonio. The convent of S. Sebastiano for which it was destined has been suppressed; the church, now a parish church, has been crudely renovated. Yet a modern statue of S. Antonio is there. The castello Ruspoli, dating from the later Middle Ages and impressively reconstructed in 1537 by Antonio da Sangallo, has been in the possession of the Marescotti-Ruspoli ever since the middle of the sixteenth century, when Sforza Marescotti acquired it through his marriage with Beatrice Farnese's daughter Ortensia Baglioni. Handel's secular cantatas from Doc. 1-2 were probably heard in the gallery of ancestors on the first floor or on the wide terrace at the southwest end of the garden that extends east of the castello, offering a magnificent view into the valley. [**PS**: The rest deleted, since now superseded, *inter al.*, by the discussion of *Diana cacciatrice*, and Vignanello, below, pp. 370ff and Appendix II].

---

[117] As assumed by EWERHART, *Die Händel-Handschriften*, p. 119.

[118] Plinio MARCONI, *Il territorio della media valle del Tevere*, Facoltà di Architettura, Università di Roma, «Quaderni dell'Istituto di Ricerca Urbanologica e Tecnica della Pianificazione», III, 1966, p. 116.

THE DOCUMENTS

Documents for many months are bound together as one thick *filza* of the *giustificazioni di Roma*. The *filze* in question bear the following shelf numbers: A 43-44 for 1707, A 45-46 for 1708, A 47-48 for 1709, B 51-52 for 1711 (there are no Handel documents from 1710). At irregular intervals of approximately two months each, after 1708 every month, Ruspoli's *maestro di casa* Angelo Valerij summarized the expenses in numbered fascicles: at the beginning of each such accounting period a lengthy list with short, numbered entries for each payment is given (the *lista delle spese*), followed by the original bills and receipts, in more or less arbitrary order. For smaller items in the list there is often no bill preserved. I quote the entries from the lists as "Sp.", with the accounting period and item number, and immediately thereafter, designated by "+", the relevant bill with receipt. The latter occasionally shows different handwriting. In such cases, and in anonymous bills I have indicated the name of the writer, if traceable, in square brackets at the beginning of the lines. Most bills of the copyists were approved with Ruspoli's autograph signature in the lower left corner. The original edition of this article presented quasi-diplomatic transcriptions of the documents. Now they are edited for greater legibility. The various, often indistinguishable abbreviations for "Signore" (Sig.^{re}, Sig.^{r}, S.^{re}, S.^{r}) have been transcribed uniformly as "S.^{re}".

1707 (vol. A 44)

1

Fasc. 71, Sp. May-June 1707, item 40: A dì 16 detto [maggio] pagato ad alias Pan-stufato per un conto di copie di cantate diverse come per riceuta S 3.50.

+   [Angelini:]

Conto dell'Ecc.^{mo} S.^{re} Marchese Ruspoli

Una cantata della caccia con VV e tromba	fogli	$6\frac{1}{2}$
Una cantata "Sei pur bella e pur vezzosa"	fogli	2
Una cantata "Se per fatal destino"	fogli	$1\frac{1}{2}$
Una cantata che dice "Udite il mio consiglio"	fogli	2
Una cantata che dice "Aure soavi e lieti" [*sic*]		$1\frac{1}{2}$

E più una cantata con stromenti con parte cavate [*sic*] che dice "Tu fedel":

E più la parte che canta	sono fogli	$4\frac{1}{2}$
E più il concertino	fogli	$2\frac{1}{2}$
E più l'originale	fogli	$8\frac{1}{2}$
E più la sinfonia	fogli	2
E più una cantata "Nella stagione"	fogli	2
E più una cantata "Poi che giurarò Amore"	fogli	2
[Ruspoli:] M.^{se} F. M. Ruspoli		35

[Angelini:] Io sotto scritto ho riceuto ... scudi tre e baiocchi cinquanta moneta per saldo del presente conto questo dì 16 maggio 1707. Io Antonio Giuseppe Angelini.

2

Sp. *ibid.*, item 166, June 30: Pag. ad Ant.° Gios.ᵉ Angelini per una lista di spese di copie di musica in Vignanello conto per ricevuta 3.05.

+ [Angelini:]
Conto dell'Ecc.ᵐᵒ S.ʳᵉ Marchese Ruspoli.
Scritti da me Antonio Giuseppe Angelini in Vignanello:

Per una cantata che dice "Un Alma innamorata" parte, originale e VV.	fogli 9¹/₂
Per due mottetti parte con VV.	fogli 9¹/₂
Per una "Salve" parte e VV. e violone	fogli 4
Una cantata d'*Arminda* cioè concertino, concerto grosso e la parte	7¹/₂
	In tutto fogli 30¹/₂

[Durastante:] Margarita Durastante affermo questo sopra.
[Ruspoli:] M.ˢᵉ F. M. Ruspoli.
[Angelini:] Io sotto scritto ho riceuto ... scudi tre e baiochi cinque ... questo dì 30 giugno 1707. Io Antonio Giuseppe Angelini.

3

Fasc. 88, Sp. July-Aug. 1707, item 6, July 6: Pag. al S.ʳᵉ Castrucci per una lista di due violini passata da Sua Ecc.ᵃ 2.–

+ [Domenico Castrucci:]
A dì 26 giugno 1707.
Per una cantata fatta nella conversazione del S.ʳᵉ March.ᵉ padrone, dove furono presi due violini di più del solito, cioè:

Alfonzo	1.–
Bononcino	1.–
[Ruspoli:] M.ˢᵉ F. M. Ruspoli	2.–

4

Sp. *ibid.*, item 52, July 31: a Michelangelo Ceruti pittore per hauer dipinto il S. Antonio di Padoa per Vignanello come per conto e riceuta 2.70.

+ [Ceruti:]
Conto.

Per avere fatto tirare una tela alta palmi 9¹/₂ et larga palmi 5¹/₄ et averla fatta e incollare et ingessare di gesso fino da potersi involtare per mandare fori	S –.30
Per avere fatto comprare, e mulinare tutti li colori necessarij per d.ᵗᵗᵃ pittura	S –.60

Per avere dipinta in d.^{tta} tela S. Ant.º da Padova con giglio, e libro in mano sopra le nuvole, e splendore, et altre nuvole attorno il tutto colorito al naturale   S 2.50

Tutto importa S 3.40

Io infrascritto ho riceuto ... scudi 2 b. 70 moneta per saldo dell' sud.º conto in fede questo dì 31 luglio 1707. Io Michel Angelo Ceruti.

5

Fasc. 100, Sp. Sept.-Nov., item 39, Sept. 22: per copie di musica come per ordine e ricevuta 2.15

+ [Angelini:]
Conto dell' Ecc.^{mo} S.^{re} Marchese Ruspoli di molte copie di musiche copiate da me Antonio Giuseppe Angelini.

Per l'originale dell' [sic] cantata dell'*Arminda*	fogli 5½
Una cantata francese	fogli 1½
"Qual or legre pupille"	fogli 2
Una cantata spagniola	fogli 4½
"Sarei troppo felice"	fogli 3
"Mensogniere [sic] speranze"	fogli 1
"Ne tuoi lumi"	fogli 4
	21½

[Durastante:] Margarita Durastante affermo quanto sopra.
[Angelini:] Io Antonio Giuseppe Angelini ho riceuto ... scudi due e baiochi quindici moneta per saldo del detto conto questo dì 22 setembre 1707.

6

Sp. *ibid.*, item 115, Oct. 14: ad Ant.º Gius.^e Angelini d'ord. a voce di Sua Ecc.^a a conto di copie di cantate come per riceuta 10.–

+ [Angelini:] Io sotto scritto ho ricetto dall'Ecc.^{mo} S.^{re} Marchese Ruspoli ... scudi dieci moneta quali sono per una cantata a tre con violini e parte cavate ... questo dì 14 ottobre 1707 – scudi 10. Io Antonio Giuseppe Angelini mano propria.

1708 (vol. A 45-46)

7

Fasc. 27, Sp. 7 Jan. - 14 Mar. 1708, item 137, Feb. 26: per li musici e sonatori per l'oratorio come per lista S 10.60.

+ [Domenico Castrucci:]
A dì 26 feb.^{io} 1708.
Dati per ordine di S. E. per la cantata seu oratorio *Il giardino di rose*

Al S.^{re} Pasqualinetto	S 3.–
E più al S.^{re} Cristof.° basso	S 2.40
E più al S.^{re} Vittorio	S 2.40
Al S.^{re} Carlo Guerra violino	S 1.–
Al S.^{re} Alfonso	S 1.–

E più dato a Panstufato per una cantata consist.^e in 2 fogli di Monsù
Endel

	S –.20
Somma	S 10.–
Pag. a quel che cantava da rosignolo	S –.60
	S 10.60

Al S.^{re} Pasqualinetto ... [values as above]

8

Fasc. 30, Sp. 18 Mar. - 8 May, item 4, Mar. 18: per porto del letto et altro per Monsù
Endel S –.10.

9

Sp. *ibid.*, item 5, Mar.18: all'ebreo per nolito d'un mese di d. letto e cuperte di tela
S –.60.

10

Sp. *ibid.*, item 10, Mar. 18: per carta di musica, penne, e corde di cimbalo come per
lista S –.60.

10bis

Sp. *ibid.*, item 43, Mar. 31: per spese cibarie di companatico per Monsù Endel e com-
p.° 19.35.

11

Sp. *ibid.*, item 72, Apr. 14: a virtuosi e sonatori per l'oratorio della Resurr.^e come per
lista distinti ordine di S. E. ... S 252.50.

+ Lista delli vertuosi, che hanno operato nell'oratorio della Resuretione di N.^{ro} S.^{re}
Giesù Christo nel palazzo dell'Illmo et Ecc.^{mo} S.^{re} Marchese Ruspoli nell'anno
corrente 1708.

Violini:

S.^{ri} Antonio due funzioni e tre prove	S 4.50
Ferrini due funtioni e tre prove	S 3.50
Tibaldi due funtioni e tre prove	S 3.50
Dom.° due funtioni e tre prove	S 4.50
Andrea due funtioni e tre proue	S 3.50
Giovannino due funtioni e tre prove	S 3.50
Alfonso due funtioni, e tre prove	S 3.50
Budassi due funtioni e tre prove	S 3.50
Carlo Guerra due funtioni e tre prove	S 3.50

Ciambelli due funtioni e tre prove	S	3.50
Bartolomeo de monte due funtioni e tre prove	S	3.50
Paolo due funzioni e tre prove	S	3.50
Valentini due funzioni e tre prove	S	3.50
Bononcini due funzioni e tre prove	S	3.50
Gioseppe Bolognese due funzioni e tre prove	S	3.50
Bonazzi due funzioni e due prove	S	3 –
Aim due funzioni e una prova	S	2.50
Luigi due funzioni e una prova	S	2.50
Battistino di Sacchetti due funzioni et una prova	S	2.50
Scolaro di Silvestro due funtioni et una prova	S	2.50

Violette:

Bartolomeo due funzioni e tre prove	S	3.50
Pertica due funzioni e tre prove	S	3.50
Pietro due funzioni e tre prove	S	3.50
Gasperini due funzioni e tre prove	S	3.50
Somma, e segue	S	81.50

[Page 2:]

Somma a tergo e segue	S	81.50

Violoni:

# Gio: Ant.° Aim due funtioni e tre prove	S	4.50
Pippino due funtioni e tre prove	S	3.50
Lazzaro due funtioni e tre prove	S	3.50
Lauretti due funtioni et una prova	S	2.50
Giovannino due funtioni et una prova	S	2.50

Contrabassi:

Travaglia due funtioni e tre prove	S	3.50
Bandiera due funtioni e tre prove	S	3.50
De Carolis due funtioni e tre prove	S	3.50
Franchi due funtioni et una prova	S	2.50
Pietrino una funtione e una prova	S	1.50

Trombe:

# Gaetano due funtioni e tre prove	S	4.50
# Cammillo due funtioni e tre prove	S	4.50

Trombone:

Andrea due funtioni e tre prove	S	3.50

Obuè:

# Ignatio due funtioni e tre prove	S	4.50
Giovanni due funtioni e tre prove	S	3.50
Valentini due funtioni e tre prove	S	3.50
Nicolo due funtioni e tre prove	S	3.50
Ascanio mandataro per portatura di tutti li strumenti et inviti per tutte le funtioni	S	4.40
	S	144.50

Angelo Valerij nostro maestro di casa pagarete al S.^{re} Arcangelo Corelli li sudetti scudi centoquarantaquattro e b. 50 moneta ad effetto li paghi alli descritti sonatori ad ogniuno la sua rata per loro intiero e final pagamento de tutte le operationi
[Page 3:]
da loro date a tenore dalla presente lista, che con prenderne solamente ricevuta del d.° S.^{re} Arcangelo saranno ben pagati questo dì 11 aprile 1708. S 144.50.
Io Dom.^{co} Castrucci di commissione del S.^{re} Arcangelo sud.° ho ricevuto la sud.^a somma, e consegnata di suo ordine al S.^{re} Almerigo Bandiera per farne il sud.° pagamento mano propria.
[Unknown scribe:]
E più pagato d. ordine di S. E. alli sottoscritti cioè:

Al S.^{re} Arcangelo Corelli	S 20.–
Al S.^{re} Matteo	S 10.–
Al S.^{re} Filippo	S 10.–
Al S.^{re} Pasqualino	S 18.–
Al S.^{re} Vittorio	S 10.–
Al S.^{re} Cristofano	S 10.–
A Panstufato per copiatura	S 30.–
	S 108.–

E per la somma delli sonatori di sopra scritti in tutti consegnati al
S.^{re} Arcangelo   S 144.50
                                                                                               S 252.50
In tutto pagati d'ord.^e di S. E.
E più pagati alli sottoscritti per provisione delli sottoscritti anelli come dalle ricevute consegnate al maestro di casa da S. E. S 116.–

anello rosetta con rubino e diamanti	12.–
altro con diamanti con acquamarina	18.–
altro con diamanti di forma [?] grande	38.–
altro con diamante grosso, 16 piccoli	S 35.–
altro con smeraldo e 6 diamantini	S 13.–
[Ruspoli:] M.^{se} F. M. Ruspoli	S 116.–

12

Sp. *ibid.*, item 79, Apr. 21: a Gios.^e Rossi pittore per lavori fatti per l'oratorio tassato dal S.^{re} Contini S 12.90.
+ [Giuseppe Rossi; figures in left margin by G. B. Contini:]
Conto delli lavori di pittura fatti per servitio del sontuoso aparechio del oratorio del Ecc.^{mo} S.^{re} Marchese Ruspoli da me Giuseppe Rossi pittor come segue:
        Prima per havere dipinto numero 14 armi di S. E. sopra le tavole intaliate dipinte di chiaro e scuro color d'oro lumegiate di gialolino
2.80   considerando tempo spesa fattura inporta giuli tre caduna sono   S 4.20
        E più per haverne dipinte 14 altre nel medemo modo e forma ma l'ama [*sic*] duplicata con quella della S.^{ra} considerando la più fattura

3.50   inporta tre giuli e mezo l'uno sono   S   4.90

        E più per haver dipinto 28 cornucopij per sostenimento delle md.^e pur nel medemo modo e con folie e scanelature la metà diferenti alti palmi 6 con havervi mesoli cartoncini fini del mio considerando

4.90   spese fature inporta 27½ baiochi l'uno sono   S   7.70

        E più per haver datto di gialo e scorniciato il sottopiede delli seditori a tre ordini lunghi quelche 55 palmi in circa considerando come sop.^a

1.80   inporta giuli 12 l'uno sono   S   3.60

        E più per haver datto due mani di geso con bona colla al telarone della escritione et a tutte le tavole delli ageti inporta

– 90   S   1.50

        E più per hauer datta di meza tinta di chiaro e scuro alla porta che si è chiusa al altra sala con hauerli dipinto il pilastro scanelato con parte di una bugna fatto supre le scale molto scomodo considerando

1.–   come sopra inporta   S   1.80

14.90   Somma S 23.70

[G. B. Contini:]

Si tassa questo conto in S.^di quattordici e b. 90 m. dico S.^di 14.90. Gio. Batta Contini.

[Page 2, G. Rossi:]

Io sotto scritto ho ricevuto dal Ecc.^mo S.^re Marchese Rospoli per le mani del S.^re Angelo Valerio suo maestro di casa scudi dececi [sic] e ba.^ci novanta moneta sono per pagamento finale ... questo dì 21 aprile 1708. Io Giuseppe Rossi mano propria.

13

Sp. *ibid.*, item 96, Apr. 27: al S.^re Ant.° de Rossi stampatore per l'oratori stampati [SL 17271], rame et altro come per conto ... S 100.–

+   [Antonio de' Rossi:]

        Adì 12 aprile 1708 in Roma.

        Conto dell'Illmo et Ecc.^mo S.^re Marchese Fran.^co Maria Ruspoli con Ant.° de' Rossi stampatore, cioè:

        Per duecento cinquanta oratorij della SS.^ma Annuntiata legati in carta ondata di Germania a ragione di scudi cinque il cento così d'accordo importano scudi dodeci, e b. cinquanta: dico   S   12.50.–

        Più per cinquanta oratorij sudetti legati in carta dorata da un grosso il foglio importano scudi quattro e b. cinquanta: dico   S   4.50.–

        Più per mille e cinquecento oratorij della Resurrezione legati in carta ondata di Germania a ragione di scudi cinque, e mezzo il cento, essendo questo oratorio più lungo un foglio e mezzo del sud.° importano scudi ottantadue, e b. cinquanta dico   S   82.50.–

        Più per haver fatto intagliare il rame della Resurrezione per servitio del sud.° oratorio, spese nell'intagliatore   S   06. – –

Più per stampatura del sud.° rame per i detto 1500 oratorij, spesi
collo stampatore di rame   S   04.50.–
Più per haver fatto legare un'oratorio in cordoano de levante, coll'ar-
ma dell'Em.ª [Filippo Antonio] Gualtieri et altri ornamenti scudo
uno e b. 20. Dico   S   01.20.–
                 Somma in tutto S 111.20.–
[Angelo Valerij:] Concordato per S cento m.ta Ang.° Valerij m.ro di casa 100.–
[Antonio de' Rossi:] Io sottoscritto ho ricevuto dall'Ecc.mo S.re Marchese Fran.co
Maria Ruspoli per le mani del S.re Angelo Valerij suo maestro di casa scudi cento
m.ta saldo e final pagamento del sud.° conto, chiamandomi contento e sodisfatto.
In fede questo dì 27 aprile 1708. Antonio de' Rossi stampatore mano propria.

14

Sp. *ibid.*, item 101, Apr. 30: per riporto del letto delli Ebrei presosi per Monsù Endel
S –.10.

15

Sp. *ibid.*, item 119, Apr. 30: al sud.° [= Francesco Maria Golla dispensatore] per cibarie per Monsù Endel e comp.° come per lista S 38.75.

16

Sp. *ibid.*, item 147, May 8: al S.re Mich. Angelo Ceruti per saldo di un conto tassato
dal S.re Contini del quadro grande della resuretione per l'oratorio S 27.–
+ [M. A. Ceruti pittore:]
Conto di pittura.
Per avere tirato una tela sul telaro di palmi 18 per ogni verso   S   –.15
Per avere dipinto una cornice in d.ta tela in tondo di chiaro scuro
giallo   S   3.–
Per avere dipinto nelli angoli di d.ta tela quattro imprese dell'arme di
S. E. con sue riquadrature atorno a chiaro scuro giallo   S   2.–
Per avere lumegiato di mordentino da cornice   S   1.20
Per avere lumegiato le d.te 4 imprese di S. E. con suoi riquadri atorno   S   –.80
Per avere dipinto in d.° vano tondo di d.ta tela la resuretione dell'
Sig.re con gloria di putti e cherubini, e l'angelo a sedere sul sepolcro,
che anuncia la resuretione sud.ta alle S. Maria Madalena e M. Cleofe,
con S. Giovanni Evangelista in contorno dell' monte, e la caduta delli demonij nell'abbisso il tutto dipinto colorito al naturale   S 24.–
Per avere dipinto un telone largo da piedi palmi 30, e da capo p. 20
et alto p. 14: con riporti rapresentante un frontispitio ornato di cor-
niccione volutoni e cherubino, cartella, fogliami, scuro giallo, e cremisino   S 12.–

Per avere compartito il motto in d.^{ta} cartella in quatro rige con n.º 46
lettere alte oncie dieci l'una, e dipintole, et intagliatole, et agiustatoci
la carta trasparente al di dietro   S   3.45
Per auvere tinta cremisi la fune dell lampadaro   S   –.20
                                                                                                                          S 46.80

[Page 2, G. B. Contini:]
Il retroscritto conto visto e ben considerato da me vien tassato in S.^{di} ventisette
monete e così dico
S.^{di} 27.–. Gio. Batta Contini.
[M. A. Ceruti:]
Io sottoscritto ho riceuto dall'Ecc.^{mo} S.^{re} Marchese Ruspoli ... scudi ventisette ...
questo dì 8 maggio 1708.
Io Michel'Angelo Ceruti mano proprio dico S.^{di} 27.– moneta.

17

Fasc. 21. Conto dell'apparato fatto nella sala dell'Illmo et Ecc.^{mo} S.^{re} Marchese
     Ruspoli per l'oratorio fatto per la Resurettione del Sig.^{re} a dì 8 aprile 1708.
Per mia manif.^{ra} di haver apparato sopra il palco dove stavano li sonatori a due altezze di damasco, e messoci il fregio di velluto da
capo, e messo il quadro in mezzo, et attorno fattoci un festone di taffettano cremisino, e fattoci le rossette, e messoci le trine attorno, e
messoci un fregio di velluto attorno d.º quadro per tutto li versi,
che faceva cornice, e fatto il cielo di damasco trinato quanto teneva
la larghezza del palco, e messo il fregio di damasco davanti a tutti li
seditori delli sonatori, et apparato davanti il palco, e esso diverse fi-
lagne per fare il sudetto apparato   S   6.–
E più per haver apparato tutto il restante della chiesa dico sala di
taffett.ⁿⁱ rossi, e gialli a due altezze con il fregio simile da capo, e
messo il fregio di damasco per tutto il cornicione, e fatto uno scenario di taffettani con il fregio simile da capo con sue cord' e girelle per
alzare e bassare, et attaccato, 16 lustriere attorno, e messoci e torcie
per tutto   S   .50
E più per nolito del sup.º pezzo di tenda sevita come sopra   S   1.50
                                                                                         Somma, e segue   S 12.–0

[Page 2:]
                                                                                 Somma di là, e segue   S 12.–
E più per nolito di n. 96 teli di damasco trinati d'oro serviti per ap-
parare sopra il palco, et il cielo, e d'havanti a b. 10 il telo   S   9.60
E più per nolito di n. 205 teli di fregio di damasco serviti attorno per
tutto il cornicione, e d'avanti alli seditori sopra il palco a b. 2½ il telo   S   5.12½
E più per polito di n.º 87 teli di fregio di velluto serviti da capo alli
damaschi, attorno al quadro, che faceva cornice, e d'havanti il palco
a b. 4 il telo   S   3.48

E più per nolito di n. 234 teli di taffettani rossi e gialli serviti per ap-
parare tutta la sala, il proscieno, e festone attorno il quadro a b. 2½
il telo   S   5.85

E più per nolito di n. 112 teli di fregio di taffettano rosso e giallo
serviti da capo alli taffettani   S   1.80

E più per nolito di n. 15 trine d'oro staccate servite dove bisog.º   S   .30

E più per haver attaccato il quadro grande della Resuretione, et il
cartellone sopra d.º quadro in sala, e due quadri grandi   S   1.–

E più per haver apparato tutto il sud.º lavoro come sopra   S   3.–

E più per danno delli damaschi macchiati, con sego, et essere stati
tagliati li damaschi del cielo, conforme ha veduto il S.ʳᵉ Gio. Btta
Contini.   S   2

Somma tutto   S 44.15½

[A. Valerij:] Concordato il tutto per S trenta. Angelo Valerij maestro di casa.

18

Fasc. 168. [20 unnumbered pages, detailed bill of the carpenter, C. Pavone, specifying measurements, materials, etc., of the components for the theatre on the *piano
nobile* of the Bonelli palace. Only the lines that give the most essential particulars
are transcribed here].

A dì 11 aprile 1708.

Misura e stima delli lavori di legname et altro fatto a tutta sue spese, e fatture da
Mas.º Crespineo Pavone falegniame per servitio dell'Ecc.ᵐᵒ S.ʳᵉ Marchese Ruspoli in haver fatto il teatro a scalinata in occasione dell'oratorio sacro in musica che
S. Ecc.ᶻᵃ a fatto fare nel salone del suo palazzo nella piazza di S. Appostoli con
suo palco e seditori per commodo de sonatori di diversi strumenti, e fatto altri
commodi e lavori in occasione della medesima funtione come seguono misurati
e stimati da me sotto scritto.

[Page 3:]

Per le tavole di castag.º rustiche addrizate poste per formare li n. 4 seditori con sotto
piedi del sud.º teatro centinate per d'avanti ...

[Page 4:]

Per ... li due filagnioni aggiunti insieme posti per traverso sopra la bocca di detto teatro da un cornicione all'altro di detta sala long' assieme p. 64 tirati in opera con
incommodo ...

[Page 5:]

Per haver spartito e posto in opera le n. 7 girelle che alzavano il taffettano che for-
mava il telone da calare, et alzare ...

Per una tavola d'alb.º rustica addrizzata per di sotto e centinata per di sopra posta nel
mezzo di detto parapetto per coprire la veduta di parte del seditore delli musici
log. p. 12½, larg. p. 1, g. p. ⅛ fermata con tre traversette dietro ...

Per haver fatto n. 28 legivi per posarci le

[Page 6:]

carte di musica e per coprire li lumi con piede di legname d'albuccio tagliato stor-
to ad'uso di cornucopia alt. p. 5$^{1}/_{2}$ l'uno larg. p. $^{1}/_{4}$, g. p. $^{1}/_{6}$ puliti con tavola con-
tornata per di sopra dove si è dipinto l'impresa di S. E. log. l'uno p. 3 alt. p. 1$^{3}/_{4}$
di tavola ordinaria con legivo per di dietro log. p. 2 alt. p. 1 di tavola simile pulita
con suo regoletto sotto ... et alli 4 che restano isolati nel palco postoci le traverse e
saettoni dalle bande per fermarli isolati ...

[Page 7:]

Per haver fatto il telaro del quadro della resurettione di nostro Sig.^{re} che si è posto nel
mezzo di detto teatro alt. p. 18, larg. p. 18 fermato in pendenza con fette d'albuccio, e rampini per di sotto e per di sopra con scommodo e più huomini ...

Per i regoli ... posti attorno detto quadro per imbollettarvi il fregio di velluto che faceva cornice attorno detto quadro post[o] in opera con scommodo ...

[Page 8:]

Per haver fatto un altro telaro per il titolo di detto oratorio che si è posto sopra il
traversone alla bocca del sud.° teatro a scalinata ... con riporti di tavole d'albuccio
... sotto li cartoni delle palme volute e del cherubino di cima ... Per haver tirato in
opera detto telaro doppo dipinto e collocato sopra il sud.° traversone ...

[Page 9:]

Per haver illuminato le littere trasparenti del suddetto titolo per tre sere con n. 70
coccioli di grasso a spese del mas.° e fattoci stare dui huommini di continuo ...

[Page 11:]

Per l'armatura fatta ... per li coccioli che illuminano il titolo dell'oratorio ...

[Page 12:]

Per haver rialzato e dato le giunte allo scabbellone che serviva per posamento delli
legivi del concertino de' violini sopra il palco ...

[New heading:]

Lavori fatti nella gallaria dove si fanno le ricreatione [sic] e dove si voleva fare l'oratorio.

Per haver schiodato e calato abbasso il telaro con la tela dipinta che fa sof-

[Page 13:]

fitta allo stanzino in testa a d.ª gallaria dove si era fatta la scala per entrare nel
palco che doveva servire per l'Em.^{mi} / S.^{ri} cardinali log. p. 18, larg. p. 10 ...

Per aver fatto un telaio per la cateratta che si è fatta nel sud.° taglio del solaio log. 7,
lg. p. 4$^{2}/_{3}$ ...

[Page 15:]

Per haver fatto n. 8 colonne d'arcaucciotti di castagno lavorate ad ottangole e pulite
che dovevano servire per mettere dentro li chiusini per l'Em.^{mi} SS.^{ri} cardinali ...

[Page 16:]

Per haver messo in opera li n. 10 cavalletti in gallaria ... e fermato il palco per provare
l'oratorio e fatto attorno li parapetti come furno ordinati da S. E. e dal ministri
[sic] e poi per esser bassi rifatti di novo li pezzi im piedi di detti parapetti e levato
n. 4 cavalletti dalle bande perché quella domenica non volse il palco così grandi
per provar l'oratorio ...

[Page 17:]

Per haver disfatto il lunedì seguente li parapetti ... e fatto il palco grande quanto era
larga la stanza e rifattoci di novo li parapetti d'avanti e sopra detto palco fattoci
n. 11 squadre a tre altezze de' seditori ... e fermato il telaro a scalinata e fattoci li
legivi per modo di provisione per provare l'orat.º in d.º palco e teatro così termi-
nato e poi per essersi mutato pensiero di farlo nella sala suddetta disfatto tutte
dette squadre scalinate e pavimento e preso tutto d.º legniame portato in detta
sala ...

[Page 18:]

Per aver disfatto tutto d.º teatro doppi che fu finito di fare l'oratorio per con ponti
ripiani armat.ᵉ e squadre con diligenza per potersene servire in altre occasioni con
sei huomini e portato tutto il

[Page 19:]

medemo legniarne nelli cantinoni del palazzo ...

[Page 20, G. B. Contini:]

Sommano in tutto li retroscritti lavori fatti per servitio dell'Ecc.ᵐᵒ S.ʳᵉ Marchese
Francesco Maria Ruspoli padrone in occasione del solenne oratorio nel giorno
della SS.ᵐᵃ Resurrettione del Sig.ʳᵉ 1708 in S.ᵈⁱ duecento trentadue, e b. 55 m.,
dico S.ᵈ 232.55. Gio. Batta Contini.

19

Fasc. 244. [Slightly abridged]

Adì 12 aprile 1708.

Misura e stima delli lavori ad uso di muratore, et altri simili fatti a tutte sue spese, e
fatture da mastro Franc.º Pagnacelli capo mastro muratore per servitio dell'Ill.ᵐᵒ
et Ecc.ᵐᵒ S.ʳᵉ Principe Don Francesco Maria Ruspoli in occasione di fare il teatro
per l'oratorio fatto il Sabbato Santo e giorni seguenti ad honore della resuretione
del Sig.ʳᵉ nel palazzo su la piazza de SS.ᵗⁱ Apostoli dove Sua Ecc.ᵃ abita. Visti,
misurati, e stimati da me sotto scritto come seguono e pagata.

Lavori fatti nello stanzione delle accademie e nelli gabinetti contigui dove si doveva
cantare al sudetto oratorio per fare la scaletta e palco per commodo delle SS.ʳᵉ
dame dovevano intervenire a d.ᵃ cantata che poi non servì per essersi trasportato
nel salone.

Per haver rotto il muro del ramello di una testa di mattoni tra d.º stanzione, et il ga-
binetto e fatto il vano di una porta per entrare nel palchettone delle dame ...

[Page 2:]

Per haver disfatto un pezzo di mattonato con suo astuco sotto acciò il falegname potesse tagliare il solaro per fare la bocca della scala da salire a detta porta ...

Per haver messo e murato il telaro della cataratta a capo la scala di legno fatta di nuovo lg. p. 6³/₄, larg. p. 5 e tagliato p. 2 di muro da una banda di detta e costo, e
mettitura da n. 37 mattoni rossi rostati con acqua attorno d.ᵃ ...

Per haver rotto il mattonato nello stanzione sudetto dell'accademie e fatto le bughe e
messo e murato con gesso li n. 4 chiusini di marmo tutti di un pezzo traforati per

mettervi le colonne di legno dell'armatura principale del sudett.° palchettone delle dame ...

[Page 3, new heading:]
Lavori fatti nel salone al piano nobile dove fu trasportato il teatro e cantato il suddetto oratorio per maggior capacità di persone.

Per aver rotto il muro di una finestra smurato sopra il cornicione dell'imposta della volta di detto salone che corrisponde al piano dell'appartamento di cima e smurato detta finestra acciò si potesse godere la cantata del sud.° oratorio ...

Per n. 5 giornate di mastro e garzone impiegate per far bughi ponti e per tirar sopra e mettere in opera l'armatura de' legni che fumo fatte e cavate fuori delle dui vani delle finestre

[Page 4:]
che dal piano dalla sala dell'appartamento di cima corrispondono in detto salone del piano nobile per reggere il filagnone sopra la bocca del teatro di d.° oratorio dove fu fermato il cartellone con il titolo, telone, et altre armature del cielo del med.° teatro ...   S 3.50

Per altre dui mezze giornate da mastro e garzone servite per mettere in ordine per le sere che si cantò d.° oratorio seguono tre nottate di mastro e garzone servite per assistere nel tempo che ci cantava d.° oratorio.   S 2.80

[G. B. Contini:] Somma in tt.° S.di dieci et 59 m. dico S.di 10.59. Gio. Batta Contini.

20

Fasc. 96, Sp. 10 May – 7 July 1708, item 7. May 10: all'ebreo per nolito del letto di M. Endel portiere et altro per l'aprile scorso S –.80

21

Fasc. 133, Sp. 10 July – 19 Sept. 1708, item 15, July 14: Silvestro per una lista di due sonatori di violino S 2.–
+ [Silvestro Rotondi:]
2 violini che sonarono nella cantata "Fiamma bella" di Monsù Hendel
S.re Giuseppe Valentini   S 1.00
S.re Gio. Ciambelli   S 1.00
[Ruspoli:] M.se F. M. Ruspoli.

22

Sp. *ibid.*, item 48, July 30: per due store grandi usate foderate con suoi bastoni per le finestre di M. Endel per ordine del S.re cavaliere S 3.90.

23

Sp. *ibid.*, item 63, July 31: al detto [Francesco Maria de Golla] per cibarie del Sassone S 13.37.

24 (Plate IX.3)

Sp. *ibid.*, item 78, Aug. 9: a Gios. Angelini per copie di cantate S 2.75.

+ [Angelini:]

Conto dell'Ecc.^{mo} S.^{re} Marchese Ruspoli.

"Tu fedel" con VV.	fogli	8
"Aure soavi e liete"	fogli	2
"Hendel"	fogli	2
"Sarei troppo felici" [*sic*]	fogli	2½
"Manca pur"	fogli	2
"Ditemi ò piante ò fiori"	fogli	2
"Lungi da voi che"	fogli	2
La Marciata	fogli	1½
"Clori vezza Clori"	fogli	2
"Quando sperasti ò core"	fogli	1½
"Stanco di più sospire"	fogli	2

[Ruspoli:] M.^{se} F. M. Ruspoli.　　　　　　　　　　In tutto 27½

[Angelini:] Ho riceuto li sudetti scudi due e baiochi settanta cinque moneta questo dì 9 agosto 1708. Io Antonio Giuseppe Angelini.

25

Sp. *ibid.*, item 110, Aug. 28: a Panstufato per una lista di copie di musica S 4.80.

+ [Angelini:]

Conto dell'Ecc.^{mo} S.^{re} Marchese Ruspoli di molte carte di musiche scritte da me Antonio Angelini dall'ii agosto sino alli 3 di Sett.^{re} 1808 [*sic*].

Due cop.^e della can.^{ta} "Se pari e la tua fé"	fogli	4
"Dite ò piante ò fiori"	fogli	2
"Clori vezzosa Clori"	fogli	2
"Lungi lungi n'andò Fileno"	fogli	2
"Mentre tutto in furore"	fogli	2
Una cantata a voce sola con VV cavate	fogli	11½
Il Duello amoroso cantata a 2 con VV cavate	fogli	24½

[Ruspoli:] M.^{se} F. M. Ruspoli　　　　　　　　　　In tutto 4.80

[Angelini:] Io ho riceuto scudi quatro e baiochi ottanta alli 28 agosto 1708. Io Antonio Angelini.

26

Sp. *ibid.*, item 127, Aug. 31: al detto [De Golla] per spese cibarie del Sassone 16.89

27 (Plate IX.4)

Sp. *ibid.*, item 145, Sept. 10: ad Ant.º Angelini per copie di musica per riceuta S 4.–

+ [Angelini:]

23

Conto dell'Ecc.^{mo} Sg.^r Marchese Ruspoli per una cantata con stromenti e parti cavate che dice a 3 con strumenti *Il Tebro* sono fogli S 4.0.
[Ruspoli:] M.^{se} F. M. Ruspoli.
[Angelini:] Io riceuto scudi quatro moneta. Io Antonio Angelini alli 10 sett.^{re} 1708.

28

Sp. *ibid.*, item. 152, Sept 15: al S.^{re} Cracas per la stampatura d'una cantata in quaderni 13 e n. 300 libretti ligati e cuperti di carta ondata per ricevutta. S 7.60.
+ [L. A. Chracas:]
Conto della stampatura e legatura della cantata per il S.^{re} Marchese Ruspoli.

Carta francese per num. 300, quaderni 13, compresovi il calo,	S 1.30
e qualche poche di più tiratura, e furono tirate due volte quattro forme	S 1.20
Composizione, inghiostro, sbuturra di caratteri, et altro	S 2.–
Carta ondata per le coperte	S 1.30
Per legatura	S 1.80
[Ruspoli:] M.^{se} F. M. Ruspoli.	S 7.60

[Chracas:] Io sotto ha ricevuto li sud.^{ti} scudi sette e b.ⁱ settanta moneta per l'effetto come sopra questo dì 15 settembre 1708 per le mani del S.^{re} Angelo Valerio maestro casa. Luca Ant. Chracas.

29 (Plate IX.5)

Fasc. 165, Sp. 24 Sept. – 9 Nov., item 8, Sept. 25: Silvestrino per violini ... S 10.–
+ [Silvestro Rotondi:]
Prima cantata con stromenti di Monsù Hendel dì 2 7.bre 1708.
Violini:

Carlo Guerra	S 1.00
Gio. Ciambelli	S 1.00

2.ª cantata con stromenti dì 9 7bre 1708.
Violini:

Gio. Ciambelli	S 1.00
Carluccio ragazzo del Sr Olm essendovi stato tutte due le funtioni	S 1.00
Gaetano della tromba	S 1.00
Alfonso per 10 [cancelled: 9] funzioni in più volte	S 5.–

[Ruspoli:] M.^{se} F. M. Rus.
[Rotondi:] Io Silvestro Rotondi ho ricevuto li sudd.ⁱ scudi dieci moneta dì 25 7.bre 1708.

30

Sp. *ibid.*, item 30, Sept. 30: al d.° [De Golla] per cibarie al Sassone per giorni 11: ... S 6.03.

31

Sp. *ibid.*, item 86, Oct. 22: al nevarolo per neve 30.85.

+   L'Ecc.^{mo} S.^{re} Marchese Ruspoli deve dare l'app[osit]a neve consegnata come per taglia.

lb.^e 1845 neve consegnata per tt.° il mese di sett.^{re} 1708		S 29.52
E più lb.^e 50 consegnta al S.^{re} Raffael		S .80
lb.^e 45 d.° neve consegnata per Monsù Endel		S .54
		S 30.86

Credenza	lb	53	S 84
Buttaglieria	lb	1792	S 28.67
Confettaria	lb	50	S 80
Monsù Endel	lb	45	S 54
	lb	1940	S 30.85

Ang.^{lo} Valerij nostro maestro di casa pag.^{to} a Gio. Batta Mattei nevaiolo scudi trenta, b. 85 moneta ... 8 ott.^{bre} 1708. ...

Ho riceuto li sud.ⁱ scudi ... 22 ott.^{bre} 1708. Gio. Batta Mattei mano propria.

32

Sp. *ibid.*, item 97, Oct. 31: al S.^{re} Castrucci per una lista de sonatori S 6.40.

+   [Domenico Castrucci:]

Il Sr Pasqualino contralto	S 3 di argento
Viol. per l'accademia:	
Carlo Guerra	S 1
Giusep. Bolognese	S 1
Giusep. Valentini	S 1
Somma in tutto	S 6 – –
Per Ascanio mezzo festone	S .16.1
[Ruspoli:] M.^{se} F. M. Ruspoli	S 6.16.1
[Another hand:]	
Pasqualino	S 3.24
Ascanio	S –.16.1
3 violini	S 3. –
M.° da cam.^a	S 6.40.1

33

Fasc. 193, Sp. 13 Nov. – 8 Dec., item 41, Nov. 24: per due cantate in sei fogli d'ord. di Sua Ecc. come per lista S –.50.

+   [Angelini:]

A dì 24 nov.^{re} 1708

Per 2 cantate di Mr Hendel consist.^e in 6 fogli. S –.50

1709 (vol. A 47)

34

Fasc. 38, Sp. Feb. 1709, item 89, Feb. 28: al S.^{re} Castrucci per copie di cantate di musica come per lista S –.90.

+ [Pietro Castrucci, delegated to pay the copyist:]

Cantata *Arminda* con violini	fogli cinque e mezzo	5
Cantata senza stromenti "Poiché giurarò Amore"	fogli due	2
Cantata "Ninfe e pastori"	fogli due	2
		9

per il baron tedesco
[Ruspoli:] M.^{se} F. M. Ruspoli.

35 (Plate IX.6)

Fasc. 113, Sp. Aug., item 87, Aug. 31: al S.^{re} Lanciani per copie di musica ... S 4.5.

+ [Francesco Lanciani:]

In carta reale:

"Da sete ardente"	2
"Se pari e la tua fé"	2
"Chi rapi la pace"	1½
"Ninfe e pastori"	2
"Aure soavi e liete"	1½
"Nella stagione"	2
"Del bell'idolo mio"	2½
"Ne' tuoi lumi a bella"	4
"Se per fatal destino"	1½
"Hendel non può"	1
"Sei pur bella pur vezzosa"	2
"Fra tante pene e tante"	2
"Poiché giurarò Amore"	2
"Filli adorata e cara"	2½
"Dalla guerra amorosa"	2
"Sento là che ristretto"	3
"Lungi da te mio nume"	3½
"O numi eterni"	3½
"Lungi da me pensier tiranno"	2½
"Aurette vezzose"	1
"Sans penser" francese	1½
In tutto	f. 45½

[page 2:]

Io sotto scritto ho ricevuto ... scudi quattro e b. cinquanta cinque questo dì 31 agosto 1709 S 4.55. Io Francesco Lanciani.

1711 (vol. B 51)

36

Fasc. 74, Sp. May 1711, item 23, May 22: al S.^{re} Lanciani ... per copie di musica ... S 18.55 [includes payment for doc. 37].

+ [F. Lanciani:]

A dì 3 maggio 1711.

Daliso et Irene, cantata a 2 con VV. del S.^{re} Antonio Caldara originale f. 8

Daliso f. 3

Irene f. $2\frac{1}{2}$

Concertino f. $2\frac{1}{2}$

In tutto fogli sedici. Importa scudi uno e baiocchi sessanta 1.60 f. 16

[Caldara:]

Antonio Caldara

[F. Lanciani:]

A dì 15 maggio 1711. Doppo partito il S.^{re} Antonio Caldara.

"Hendel non può mia musa" f. 1

e più arie sedici, otto dell'*Anagilda* e otto della *Pastorale* [both by Caldara] con stromenti per servitio di S. Ecc.^{za} in tutto f. $18\frac{1}{2}$

In tutto fogli trenta cinque e mezzo f. $35\frac{1}{2}$

Importa scudi tre e baiocchi cinquanta cinque.

Io sottoscritto ho riceuto ... questo dì 22 maggio 1711. Francesco Ant.º Lanciani. S 3.55.

37

Ibid. [See above, doc. 36]

+ [Tarquinio Lanciani.]

Nota delle copie fatte per l'ecc.^{mo} S.^{re} Prencipe Ruspoli dell'oratorio *La frode della castità* [= Caldara] cantato la domenica di pasqua 5 aprile 1711.

Originale	f. $50\frac{1}{2}$
Parte di S. Eufrasia	$08\frac{1}{2}$
Parte di Meraspe	07
Parte di Clearco	04
Parte della Fede	$03\frac{1}{2}$
Parte del Testo	04
Concertino	17
Violini concerto grosso	24
Viola	$11\frac{1}{2}$
Contrabasso	$06\frac{1}{2}$
"Ho un non so che nel core", aria della Madalena oratorio di M. Hendel	$\frac{1}{2}$
Parte di Elpino	07
e parte di Filli della cantata del S.^{re} Giovanni sassonese	06
	150

In tutto sono fogli centocinquanta, e sono scudi quindici S 15.

[Caldara:] Ant.° Caldara
[F. Lanciani:] Io sottoscritto ho ricevuto questo dì 22 maggio 1711 Francesco
Antonio Lanciani S 15.

38

Fasc. 164, Sp. Dec. 1711, item 72, Dec 31: al S.^{re} Castrucci ... per ... virtuosi di musica
e copie di musica S 11.

+ [F. Lanciani:] A dì 10 ottobre 1711.
Originale della cantata con stromenti del S.^{re} Hendel "Ah crudel nel pianto mio"
f. dieci e mezzo f. 10$^{1}/_{2}$
Importa scudi uno e b. cinque S 1.05
E più a dì 3 X.^{bre} [Antonio Caldara:] *La Zenobia* a voce sola con VV.
La parte   f. 2
Violini concertino f. 2$^{1}/_{2}$
In tutto e per tutto importa scudi uno e b. cinquanta S 1.50
[Ruspoli:] F. M. R.
[Pietro Castrucci:]
S.^{re} Mom.° 2 accademie   S 6.50
S.^{re} Igniatio 2 accademie   S 3. –
                                                                    S 11. –

Revised 2007. Titles are listed in the order of their first appearance in the copyists' bills. The dates in the heading are those of the receipts for payment. See below, pp. 365f. for additional information. The period given there as "early Dec. 1706 - 21 Feb. 1707" is simplified here as "Winter '06/7". The symbol "~" in the last column signifies "probably".

Abbreviations: A = Angelini.
FL = Francesco Lanciani.
TL = Tarquinio Lanciani.
o = parts.
x = score.

HWV / Document numbers:	1706	1707						1708						1709		1711			Performed
	* TL: 29 Dec.	† A: 2 May	1. A: 16 May	2. A: 30 June	5. A: 22 Sept.	6. A: 1 Oct.	† A: 31 Oct.	7. A: 26 Feb.	11. A: 14 Apr.	24. A. 9 Aug.	25. A. 28 Aug.	27. A. 10 Sept.	33. A. 24 Nov.	34. 28 Feb.	35. FL. 31 Aug.	36. FL. 15 May	37. FL: 22 May	38. FL: 10 Oct.	
120b "Arresta il passo"	x																		Rome, Bonelli, Christmas '06; garden at S. Matteo in Merulana, 14 July '08, beginning with "Fiamma bella"
79 Cantata della caccia [*Diana cacciatrice*] con VV e tromba			o																Cerveteri, 23 Feb. '07
160a "Sei pur bella, pur vezzosa"			x																Cerveteri, ~ 27 Feb. '07
159 "Se per fatal destino"			x												x				Cerveteri, ~ 6 Mar. '07
172 "Udite il mio consiglio"			x												x				Civitavecchia, 18 Mar. '07
84 "Aure soavi e liete"			x												x				Cerveteri, ~ 20 Mar. '07
171 "Tu fedel? tu costante?" con VV.			ox							x									Cerveteri, ~ 27 Mar. '07
137 "Nella stagion che di viole e rose"			x							x					x				Massa, ~ 3 Apr. '07
148 "Poiché giurarò amore"			x												x				Rome, Bonelli, ~ 10 Apr. '07
173 "Un'alma inamorata"				x										x					Vignanello, ~ 6 June '07
239 "O qualis de coelo sonus"				o															Vignanello, 12 June '07
231 "Coelestis dum spirat aura"				o															Vignanello, 14 June '07
241 "Salve Regina"				o															Vignanello, 18 June '07
105 *L'Armida* [*abbandonata*, = "Dietro l'orme fugaci"] con VV				o	x									x					Vignanello, 19 June '07
155 "Sans y penser"					x										x				Rome, Bonelli, ~ 3 July '07
152 "Qualor l'egre pupille"					x														Rome, Bonelli, ~ 10 July '07
140 "Nò se emenderá jamás"					x														Rome, Bonelli, ~ 17 July '07
157 "Sarei troppo felice"					x					x									Rome, Bonelli, ~ 24 July '07
131 "Menzognere speranze"					x														Rome, Bonelli, ~ 31 July '07
133 "Nè' tuoi lumi, o bella Clori"					x										x				Rome, Bonelli, ~ 7 Aug. '07

---

* See below, pp. 365f.

† Unspecified cantatas – see above, pp. 295f.

Table — payment and performance record of Handel cantatas

HWV (Document numbers:)	Paid — 1706	1707						1708						1709		1711			Performed
	TL: 29 Dec. *	A: 2 May †	1. A: 16 May	2. A: 30 June	5. A. 22 Sept.	6. A. 1 Oct.	A: 31 Oct. †	7. A: 26 Feb.	11. A: 14 Apr.	24. A. 9 Aug.	25. A. 28 Aug.	27. A. 10 Sept.	33. A. 24 Nov.	34. 28 Feb.	35. FL: 31 Aug.	36. FL: 15 May	37. FL: 22 May	38. FL: 10 Oct.	
96 Cantata a tre ["Cor fedele"]						o													Rome, ~ Cancelleria, Sept. '07
– Cantata con b.c.																			
117 "Hendel non può mia musa"								x							x	x			Rome, Bonelli, before 9 Aug. '08
129 "Manca pur quanto sai"										x									Naples or Rome, May – mid-July '08
107 "Ditemi o piante, o fiori"										x	x								”
126a "Lungi da voi che siete poli"										x									”
– La Marciata																			
95 "Clori, vezzosa Clori"										x	x								”
153 "Quando sperasti, o core"										x									”
167b "Stanco di più soffrire"										x									”
158a "Se pari è la tua fè"										x	xx								Rome, Bonelli, before 28 Aug. '08
128 "Lungi, lungi n'andò Fileno"											x								”
130 "Mentre il tutto è in furore"											x								”
78? "A voce sola con VV. [= "Ah crudel"?]											o								
82 Il Duello amoroso ["Amarilli vezzosa"] a 2 con VV.											o								Rome, before 28 Aug. '08, ~ garden at S. Matteo in Merulana
143 Il Tebro ["O come chiare e belle"], a 3 con VV. e tromba												o		x					Rome, Bonelli, 9 Sept. '08
– Cantata con b.c.													x						
– Cantata con b.c.													x						
139a "Ninfe e Pastori"															x				Rome, Bonelli, winter '06/7?
100 "Da sete ardente afflito"														x	x				”
90 "Chi rapì la pace al cuore"															x				”
104 "Del bell'idolo mio"															x				”
116 "Fra tante pene e tante"															x				”

HWV	Paid 1706 * TL: 29 Dec.	1707 † A: 2 May	1. A: 16 May	2. A: 30 June	5. A. 22 Sept.	6. A: 1 Oct.	† A: 31 Oct.	1708 7. A: 26 Feb.	11. A: 14 Apr.	24. A. 9 Aug.	25. A. 28 Aug.	27. A. 10 Sept.	33. A. 24 Nov.	1709 34. 28 Feb.	35. Fl: 31 Aug.	1711 36. Fl: 15 May	37. Fl: 22 May	38. Fl: 10 Oct.	Performed
114 "Filli adorata e cara"															x				”
102b "Dalla guerra amorosa"															x				”
161a "Sento là che ristretto"															x				(After HWV 161b – see below, p. 389)
127a "Lungi da te mio nume" [recte "Lungi dal mio bel nume"]															x				Rome, Bonelli (autogr. Rome 3 Mar. '08)
145 "O numi eterni" [La Lucrezia]								?											
125a "Lungi da me, pensier tiranno"									x						x				Rome, Bonelli, ~ Dec. '06
177 Aria "Aurette vezzose" [from "Zeffiretto, arresta il volo"]															x				Rome, Bonelli, winter '06/7?
47 Aria "Ho un non so che nel cor" [from La Resurrezione]											o?				x		x		”
78 "Ah crudel nel pianto mio" con VV.																		x	”

Document numbers:

ORGAN PLAYING IN THE LATERAN
AND OTHER REMEMBRANCES ON HANDEL:
A REPORT IN THE *VOIAGE HISTORIQUE* OF 1737

"There arrived in this city a Saxon, an excellent harpsichord player and composer of music, who today has displayed his splendid ability to play the organ in the church of San Giovanni to the amazement of everyone".[1] This report of 14 January 1707 by the Roman diarist Valesio has been for two generations a favorite *topos* of Handel biographies,[2] but some knew that the "Saxon" did not necessarily have to be identical with our composer.[3] Although the original text has been easily accessible since 1975,[4] translations still bear not innocuous fruit.[5] When Valesio's words are rendered as "In Rom

---

[1] "È giunto in questa città un sassone eccellente sonatore di cembalo e compositore di musica, quale oggi ha fatto pompa della sua virtù in sonare l'organo nella chiesa di S. Giovanni con stupore di tutti" – Francesco VALESIO, *Diario di Roma*, ed. Gaetana Scano, Milan, Longanesi, 1977-79, III, 754f. The extremely important ms. of the *abbate* (1670-1742), preserved in eleven volumes in the Archivio Storico Capitolino, contains autograph entries from 1700 (and surely earlier – cf. I, ix) until his death, with a gap from 1711 to 1724. The editor's brief, but well founded introduction mentions Valesio's activity as hagiographer, his friendship with antiquarians, etc. Yet the purpose served by the ms. is hardly demonstrated. Did the diarist write it only for himself, or on commission, did he intend to publish it, at least in part, etc.? In any case Pope Benedict XIV Lambertini could present it to the archive of the S.P.Q.R. in 1745, only three year's after the author's death.

[2] Newman FLOWER first published the notice, in English translation – *George Frederic Handel: His Personality and His Times*, Boston and New York, 1923, p. 62. He had received it from L. A. Sheppard of the British Museum, who conducted researches for him in Rome.

[3] On p. 289 above, note 13, I expressly recommended caution in this question. How often we have been tricked by the real, infinitely more manifold history? One need only think of "Giovanni sassone" with Ruspoli in 1711, who likewise was a composer (cf. p. 345). With due caution only 'probability', not 'certainty' for Handel's appearance in this notice was expressed by Winton DEAN, article *Handel* in NG[1], VIII, 84 (misread as "Valerio") and the editors of the *Handel-Handbuch*, IV, Kassel, Bärenreiter, 1985, p. 26.

[4] Hans-Joachim MARX, *Ein Beitrag Händels zur Accademia Ottoboniana in Rom*, «Hamburger Jahrbuch für Musikwissenschaft», I, 1974 (1975), p. 70.

[5] That as late as 1980 Ellen HARRIS, *Handel and the Pastoral Tradition*, Oxford UP, p. 149, still 'quoted': "A German prince [!] arrived in this city" [allegedly from Flower] already astonished

sei an diesem Tage ... ein Sachse eingetroffen, ... der in der Chiesa S. Giovanni ... geglänzt hat" ["in Rome this day ... a Saxon arrived"],[6] this is not only a free turn of expression – the meaning is at stake. The diarist presented in his long period not one, but two indications of time: "è giunto" = "[a Saxon] has arrived"; then, in a relative clause, "hoggi ha fatta pompa" = "has displayed today ...". In both cases, the perfect tense is used, but unqualified with an adverb the first time. The "has arrived" thus hardly refers to "today", but rather "recently" or even "some time ago", i.e. possibly weeks, if not months before the performance of 14 January.

Of course much would suggest that the diarist meant our composer. (That Handel, as a Lutheran, would not have played in a catholic basilica, is already contradicted by his Roman liturgical music, especially that for the Virgin Mary). The bill of delivery by the copyist Alessandro Ginelli of 12 February 1707 for *Il delirio amoroso* HWV 99 in the Pamphilj household[7] can be regarded as the earliest document with Handel's *name* in a Roman archive (others already referred to him without mentioning him by name – cf. pp. 364f and 371, "the Saxon"). Since he must have composed this cantata "at the end of January or the beginning of February",[8] with a text written by Pamphilj himself, and since the organ playing of the "Saxon" had just taken place, it seems probable that the 'two' German musicians were identical.

The organist in the Lateran church on 14 January was indeed Handel, as I may now demonstrate. But first two bits of circumstantial evidence. The literature on Handel has overlooked that the archpriest of San Giovanni in Laterano was Cardinal Pamphilj himself, for more than 30 years (1699-1730), until his death. (Montalto described this powerful position in the last chapter of her book).[9] In this sublime house of God, seat of the popes until the Avignon exile and to this day the Roman cathedral, much, including organs and organ playing, was under the protection of the archpriest. (Thus the cardinals Ottoboni or Colonna could not have been Handel's patron in San Giovanni, as sometimes asserted). A second consideration – it may at first appear

MARX, who defended the biographer – *Händel in Rom: Seine Beziehung zu Benedetto Cardinal Pamphilj*, «Händel-Jahrbuch», XXIX, p. 116, note 4.

[6] MARX, p. 107.

[7] MARX, pp. 108f and 113. Lina MONTALTO, *Un mecenate in Roma barocca: il Cardinale Benedetto Pamphilj 1653-1730*, Florence, Sansoni, 1955, p. 504, had already dated this cantata correctly Feb. 1707 (incipit quoted as "Da quel giorno felice" [*recte*: "... giorno fatal"], confused with the preceding cantata in her list), without commentary. On p. 325, however, she reproduced only the later bill of the copyist Angelini for this cantata, 14 May 1707.

[8] MARX, p. 108.

[9] "La Colomba Pamphilj della Basilica Lateranense fra il 1699 e il 1730", pp. 433-450.

trivial, yet is not unimportant: Valesio begins his entries always with the days of the week, on 14 January 1707 with "Friday". And Pamphilj always held his *conversazione* on Friday, surely on occasion as here with the organ in San Giovanni. The long list of musicians for Pamphilj's palace[10] was likewise dated on a Friday, 18 February, and Roman musicians were almost always paid on the evenings of the performances. Handel thus, if identical with the famous "Saxon" at the Lateran organ, may already have been patronized by Pamphilj.

But the trump card for a possible Lateran concert of Handel was dealt to me by a Roman friend, Patrizio Barbieri. He called my attention to an extremely rare work of an anonymous author,[11] where a performance at the harpsichord by Handel during his Roman sojourn is mentioned: *Voiage historique et politique de Suisse, d'Italie, et d'Allemagne* (Frankfurt/M., Varrentrapp, 1736-43, 3 vol.).

An anonymous editor prefixed a dedication to Landgrave Wilhelm von Hessen.[12] There he writes:[13]

Je l'ai tiré des mémoires qu'un de mes amis avoit faits dans le cours de ses voiages, et je n'y ai d'autre part de les avoir mis en ordre. Comme j'y ai trouvé beaucoup de choses nouvelles et une heureuse variété de matières, jointes à un choix fait avec goût, je me suis flatté que le public me saurait bon gré d'avoir tiré ce recueil de l'obscurité, auquel la modestie de l'auteur le condamnoit.

I have drawn this [publication] from the memoires that one of my friends had made during the course of his travels, and I have merely participated in putting them in order. Since I found in them many new things as well as a felicitous variety of material, combined with a tastefully made choice, I am flattered that the public would appreciate that I have withdrawn this collection from the obscurity to which the author's modesty would have condemned it.

This "friend" – we may designate him as the real, doubtlessly older author[14] – indeed remembered very well his personal contact with the young Handel in Rome, where the latter played the harpsichord; but – and this is more inter-

---

[10] MARX, p. 114.

[11] Now identified by Jean-Daniel Candaux as Denis Nolhac (1679-1746) – cf. Werner BRAUN, *Händel und der 'römische Zauberhut' (1707)*, «Göttinger Händel-Beiträge», III, 1987, pp. 71-86.

[12] "A son Altesse Serenissime Monseigneur Guillaume, Landgrave de Hesse, Prince de Herszfeld, Comte de Catzenelnbogen, Dietz, Ziegenhain, Nidda, Schaumburg, et Prince Regnant de Hanau &c, &c" (f. 2r-v).

[13] Fol. 3v.

[14] The editor mentions at the beginning of vol. I (p. 7) that the author first visited Geneva on his travels, in 1687. This is the earliest date which I have found from his life. In the year following the first publication of this article, Werner BRAUN, *op. cit.*, provided further information on him and on Handel.

esting – he tells also of his organ virtuosity in San Giovanni, of a visit of the composer in Florence, and finally his sojourn in England, so that the hitherto oldest biographical sketch results.[15] Here is the entire passage:

Histoire du Musicien Haindel.

[P. 176:] Pendant le sejour que j'ai fait à Rome, le fameux Haindel Musicien Allemand y vint, dont la réputation à la vérité n'étoit pas encore établie au point quelle l'a été depuis; j'eus occasion de le voir chez les fameux Musiciens du Pape nommez *Pasqualini*; comme ils avoient été [p. 177:] long temps à Paris au service du Duc d'Orleans, ils étoient charmez quand ils rencontroient des François ils leur faisoient mille honnêtetez; ils venoient même quelque fois chez moi manger la soupe à la Françoise. Monsieur Haindel rendoit visite à Rome à tous ces Messieurs Musiciens qui avoient quelque réputation, il vint par consequent chez ceuxci, qui m'invitèrent à cette occasion. M'y étant rendu, j'y trouvai tout ce qu'il y avoit à Rome d'habiles Musiciens tant pour les voix que pour les instrumens. Nous y fumes d'abord regalez de *Rinfreschi*, comme on dit. Après une petite conversation, Monsieur Haindel s'étant approché d'un Clavessin, le chapeau sous le bras, dans une figure fort génante, il toucha cet intruments d'une maniere si savante, que tous en furent surpris, & comme Monsieur Haindel étoit Saxon, par concequent *Lutèrano*, celà les fit entrer en soubçon, que son savoir jouer étoit plus que naturel. J'entendis même quelques [p. 178:] uns qui disoient, qu'il ne gardoit pas pour rien son chapeau. Je

Story of the Musician Haindel

During my sojourn in Rome, the famous German musician Haindel, whose reputation truly was not yet as well established as it has become since, came there. I had the occasion to see him with the pope's famous musicians, called 'Pasqualini'. Since they had been in the service of the Duke of Orleans in Paris for a long time, they were charmed when they met Frenchmen and gave them a thousand honors. They even came to my house sometimes to eat French soup. Monsieur Haindel visited in Rome all of those musicians who had some kind of reputation and consequently came to those gentlemen who invited me on this occasion. Having gone there, I found there all of the most able musicians of Rome, both for voices and for instruments. We were first treated to *rinfreschi*, as they say. Following a brief conversation, Monsieur Haindel, having approached a harpsichord, his hat under his arm, in a very awkward position, touched this instrument in such a knowledgeable manner that all were surprised by it, and since Monsieur Haindel was a Saxon, consequently Lutheran, it caused them to suspect that his ability to play was more than natural. I even overheard some of them say that it was not for nothing that he guarded his hat. I laughed to myself at this amusing idea,

---

15 Ludwig SCHUDT, *Italienreisen im 17. und 18. Jahrhundert*, Munich, Schroll, 1959, describes the *Voiage* as an entertaining guidebook which reports much new information on the society of the time (pp. 122f *et passim*), yet he mentions our composer with only one sentence: "At a social gathering he met also Handel, who was then in Rome" (p. 123). My *Orgelspiel* 1988, p. 4, reproduces two pages of the *Voiage*.

ris en moi même de cette plaisante idée, & m'étant approché de Monsieur Haindel pour le voir jouer, je lui dis en Allemande, afin qu'ils ne m'entendissent pas, le ridicule soupçon de ces *Signori Virtuosi*. Un moment après il laissa, comme par hazard, tomber son chapeau, se mit à son aise & joüa beaucoup mieux qu'auparavant. Le lendemain il fut à Saint Jean de Latran, pour jouer des Orgues, où il y eut un concours extraordinaire, sur tout des Cardinaux, Prélats & de la Noblesse. En passant à Florence pour retourner en Allemagne, le gran Duc l'arrêta quelque tems, il y composa un Opera qui fut généralement applaudi. Du depuis sa réputation a beaucoup augmenté, & il passe à présent avec justice pour le plus habile Musicien de l'Europe. Il est actuellement à Londres.

Ce qui arriva au fameux Monsieur Haindel, me fait revenir dans l'idée, [p. 179:] combien les Italiens sur tout les Romains sont dans des préjugez sur le pouvoir du Diable & des sorciers.

and having approached Monsieur Haindel in order to see him play, I told him – in German, so that they would not be able to hear me – [about] the ridiculous suspicion of these *signori virtuosi*. A moment later, as if by chance, he dropped his hat, made himself comfortable and played even better than before. The next day he was at St. John in Lateran to play the organs, where there was an extraordinary crowd, especially of cardinals, prelates, and aristocrats. As he was passing through Florence, returning to Germany, the Grand Duke detained him for some time. There he composed an opera which was applauded by all. Since then his reputation has greatly grown and he is now rightfully considered the most able musician of Europe. He is currently in London.

What happened to the famous Monsieur Haindel brings back to my mind how much the Italians, especially the Romans, are [immersed] in prejudices about the powers of the devil and of sorcerers.

That the author was indeed in Rome during Handel's first sojourn there and was not merely bragging is evident from his personal acquaintance with the learned François Deseine († 1715), book dealer and author of several of the most useful guidebooks for Italy 1690-1713, or with the sculptors Pierre Legros († 1719) and Jean-Baptiste Théodon († 1713), who, like him were French and worked in Rome, e.g. together on the altar of St. Ignatius for the church of Il Gesù.[16] A later sojourn of Handel in Rome is thus excluded for this report.[17]

Although one can derive no direct date from the *Histoire*, its author does provide a sequence of some of the events. The most important is, of course,

---

[16] *Voiage*, II, 95, 99, and 104; more in SCHUDT, *passim*.

[17] Handel returned to Rome only in 1729, as reported in [John MAINWARING], *Memoires of the Late George Frederic Handel*, London, Dodsley, 1760, p. 113. The author's information on Handel's early years derived very probably from Handel himself, via his adjunct, John Christopher Smith jr. – cf. Donald BURROWS, *Handel and Hanover*, in *Bach – Handel – Scarlatti*, Cambridge UP, 1985, p. 37, and Gerhard POPPE, *Beobachtungen zu 'Georg Friedrich Händels Lebensbeschreibung' von John Mainwaring und Johann Mattheson*, «Händel-Jahrbuch», XXXVI, 1990, p. 181, note 41; also below, p. 396.

the description of how, after an amusing encounter of the two in the company of Vatican musicians (to be discussed below), on the following day ("lende-main") Handel played organs in the Lateran, whereby there was "an extraor-dinary assembly, particularly of cardinals, prelates, and nobility". The author apparently found this concert with the large audience so important that he mentioned only this, no other public performance of our composer in Rome. Since Valesio too reported only once on the magnificent organ playing in San Giovanni during these years – for the diarist surely wrote down only that which was of interest to the clerus and the aristocracy – we no longer need to doubt that his report and that of the *Voiage* refer to the same day, 14 January 1707. Thus this moment can henceforth enter Handel's biography as one of the first appearances of the young genius in the eternal city. That the Roman high so-ciety crowded into San Giovanni is reported also by Valesio, though very briefly. Both authors had probably not often experienced such a musical event before. But fame as a virtuoso, which may have preceded Handel's entry, can hardly, by itself, have accounted for such an "extraordinary assembly". [**PS**: I recently demonstrated that Handel arrived in Rome from Venice with Mar-gherita Durastante in early December 1706, as house guest of the now very wealthy Marquis Francesco Maria Ruspoli and composed/performed weekly cantatas for him].[18] A strong recommendation, possibly from Grand Prince Ferdinando Medici, crown prince of Tuscany, may also have been effective here. Ferdinando's former (?) mistress, the powerful intrigant and singer Vit-toria Tarquini, may likewise have been involved. Only a few months later she was featured at Marquis Francesco Maria Ruspoli's country estate Vignanel-lo.[19] Thus Cardinal Pamphilj hastened to receive the young Handel in princely style and to have him perform before a large audience.

Back to the preceding day, 13 January. Then, at the beginning of our story, we found the young composer moving in the company of papal musi-cians, i.e. hosted by the "Pasqualini". The anonymus first describes their French connections: "since they had long been with the Duke of Orleans in Paris, they were now charmed to meet Frenchmen, to whom they offered a thousand reverences", possibly in gratitude for past favors; they "sometimes even visited him to eat French soup". One could pass over this if a biographi-cal detail on at least one Pasqualino were not supplied: the celebrated soprano castrato Pasqualino Tiepoli, for he not only belonged to the papal chapel, but was visiting singer at the court of the Duke of Orleans in Paris from April

---

18 Cf. pp. 317, 367f, 387, 390.
19 Cf. below, pp. 356f.

X.1. Organ of Luca Blasi and Giovanni Battista Montani, 1599, in San Giovanni in Laterano. Photo courtesy of the Fondazione Pro Musica e Arte Sacra, Rome.

1703 until July 1705 and was just now, in January 1707, promoted to master of the papal chapel.[20] Also here the report proves credible. At Christmas 1706 a large-scale cantata was performed at Ruspoli's starring the very expensive "Pasqualino soprano" (doubtless Tiepoli) and the 'house' soprano, surely Margarita Durastante: the unusual work for two [!] sopranos "Arresta il passo" HWV 83. Ruspoli as host of the Arcadia had it performed again for the academy's summer 'Christmas' on 14 July 1708,[21] but not for the first time, as the Ruspoli score clearly proves. From the *Histoire* we must conclude, however, that more than one Pasqualino is meant here. A second one on that evening, namely 13 January, could have been Pasqualino Betti, although he did not enter the papal chapel until 14 April 1707.[22] His name appears already in the above-mentioned musicians list of Pamphilj.

The *Histoire* thus introduces us to a kind of *conversazione*, where, of course, there is no lack of refreshments. What follows is obviously the main attraction of the evening, the story about the superstition of Handel's audience: how the composer went to the harpsichord and played; that everyone was surprised by this; why they began to become suspicious that something was not kosher, if only because Monsieur Handel was a Lutheran; that they regarded the hat, which he held in an uncomfortable position under his arm, as supernatural, until it suddenly fell to the floor (the anonymus had already whispered that something was brewing in the audience); that the listeners were then relieved and could breathe more easily, and Handel played bet-

---

[20] Enrico CELANI, *I cantori della cappella pontificia nei secoli XVI-XVIII*, «Rivista musicale italiana», XVI, 1909, p. 72, provides biographical notes on Tiepoli, who came from Udine; *inter al.*: 19 March 1690 admission to the papal chapel, 1725 hermit at Monteluco (Spoleto), 24 Nov. 1742 notice of his funeral. He was employed also by Ottoboni – cf. Hans-Joachim MARX, *Die Musik am Hofe Pietro Kardinal Ottobonis unter Arcangelo Corelli*, «Analecta Musicologica», V, 1968, p. 176 (index, under "Tiepoli"), with date for the visit in Paris given incorrectly as 1704 instead of 1703. Tiepoli is likewise included in Pamphilj's list of musicians of 18 February 1707 (see above), as Marx explicitly comments. Questionable, however, is his conclusion from this document: a "premiere" of *Il delirio amoroso* with Tiepoli as the only singer (p. 109). Is Pasqualino present for only one rehearsal and four concerts, while the soprano Checchino is there for various rehearsals and seven concerts? At least from statistical considerations one might give precedence to Checchino. This singer may have been the idolized Francesco de Castris alias Checchino de' Massimi – until June 1703 intimus of crown prince Ferdinando in Florence, then in exile in Rome because Vittoria Tarquini had intrigued against him (see Warren KIRKENDALE, *The Court Musicians in Florence during the Principate of the Medici*, Florence, Olschki, 1993, pp. 441-444) – and/or Ruspoli's "Checchino" (here "De Grandis" or "de' Paolucci", at least the latter only the name of a patron, since the singer for a time was in the service of Cardinal Fabrizio Paolucci). In any case, Checchino repeatedly received princely compensation also from Ruspoli – *AC* 1966 pp. 53, 55, 61ff, 351 = *AC* 2007 pp. 67, 70, 77f, 439; Doc. 8, 23, 46, 215.

[21] That the Arcadia indeed celebrated Christmas in the summer is reported by the academy's secretary Crescimbeni – cf. above, p. 311 and below, p. 366.

[22] MARX, *Händel in Rom*, designates him as "contralto?", probably because he regards him to be identical to "Pasqualino contralto", who repeatedly appears with Caldara (cf. *AC*, index).

ter than before. Our author told this story because it illuminated not so much Handel himself as the psychological background of this society. (Before and after our story he presents other anecdotes of devils, magic, etc., and reveals that he, as a Frenchman, is superior by virtue of his reason).

The incredulous wonder of the audience at Handel's "diabolical" playing in Italy was described also by two other authors. According to Mainwaring,[23] "He was first discovered there [in Venice] at a masquerade, while he was playing on a harpsichord in his visor. Scarlatti happened to be there, and affirmed that it could be no one but the famous Saxon, or the devil". And Johann Christoph von Dreyhaupt from Halle, in his very brief biographical sketch of his famous compatriot, 1750: the composer is[24]

ein Schüler des damals berühmten Zachow, [der ihn] im Clavierspielen und der Composition getreulich [unterwiesen habe], so daß er es in beyden sehr hoch gebracht, und auf seiner Reise in Italien wegen seiner großen Fertigkeit und Manieren im Spielen des Claviers selbst von den Italiänern sehr bewundert, ja von einigen Abergläubigen solches geheimen Teuffelskünsten zugeschrieben worden.	a pupil of the then famous Zachow, who instructed him faithfully in harpsichord playing and composition, so that he became very accomplished at both; and during a trip to Italy, because his great ability and manners in playing the harpsichord, he was much admired even by the Italians; indeed, some superstitious people attributed [to him] such secret diabolical arts.

As is evident from a comparison of this report with the *Histoire*, the author in Halle cannot possibly have known the latter. Not only is he silent on the other Italian episodes in our *Histoire*, he believes also that Handel was "in Hamburg" after his Italian sojourn. He may not have known that the composer had lived in Hamburg for some years before going to Italy. But since he reports from the Italian visit only that which we have read in the *Histoire*, of course with more liveliness and detail – from the harpsichord playing and the "diabolical arts" – he must have been somewhat informed about this episode. One might assume that this amusing story came to his ears in Halle itself, possibly from friends or from Handel's relatives whom we know by name. In any case, we must now take this report more seriously than hitherto. Hardly any of its statements are far-fetched, not even "in Hamburg", since the author merely placed this city after instead of before the Italian journey. Handel surely told

---

[23] Pp. 51f.

[24] *Pagus Neletici et Nudzici, oder: Ausführliche diplomatisch-historische Beschreibung des ... Saal-Creyses*, zweiter Theil, Halle, 1750, p. 625, quoted in *Händel-Handbuch*, Kassel, Bärenreiter, 1978-85, IV, 446.

his mother about Italy, also about his triumphs on the harpsichord and organ, of the astonishment of the Italians at such virtuosity, until they suspected that ... [etc.] – and both probably laughed heartily. (We always knew that he revered his mother, though distant from her, was kind to her and also sent money, up until his last visit, when she, long since blind, was close to death. The clumsy, but honest poem which his cousin, the theologian Christian Roth sent to Handel in London shortly after the death of the mother recollects drastically: "The most faithful mother shed many tears of joy when she felt the strange hand in the dark".[25]

Once again [for us], Handel's harpsichord playing must have been 'infernally' good. At Ruspoli's he surely used the unique harpsichord with "seven" [?!] registers which Ferdinando Medici had presented to the marquis's wife in 1703.[26] And the audience in the Vatican already knew – as we may conclude from the *Histoire* – that the performer was a Lutheran.[27] Also lesser particulars in the *Histoire* are not insignificant, e.g. that Handel "visited in Rome all musicians of reputation".[28]

We cannot conclude this story without asking whether Handel composed specific music for the most important organ in Rome. This instrument was donated for the Holy Year 1600 by Clement VIII and had been built between 1597 and 1599 by Luca Blasi of Perugia, for which the pope knighted him.[29] In the eighteenth century it was described:[30]

Dirimpetto a questo altare, cioè nella testa destra, vi sono le tre porte laterali della chiesa, sopra le quali v'è l'organo fattovi dallo stesso Clemente VIII il quale è il migliore e il maggiore di quanti ne sono in Roma; e in esso si legge il nome dell'artifice nella sequente guisa *Lucas Blasii*	Opposite the altar, that is on the right wall, there are three lateral doors of the church, and above them is the organ installed there by Clement VIII himself, which is the best and the largest of all those in Rome; and on it can be read the name of the builder in this form: "Lucas Blasii

[25] "Die treuste Mama vergoss viel Freuden-Thränen, da sie bei Finsterniss die fremde Hand bekam" – *Händel-Handbuch*, IV,183.

[26] VALESIO, II, 479.

[27] Cf. below, p. 400, how this operated to Handel's disadvantage.

[28] First of all Corelli and Cesarini, then surely many others, as to be seen today in the payment lists of the leading Roman patrons ca. 1707, which Marx (*Handel in Rom*) and myself (above, ch. 9) have published. In my *Orgelspiel* (1988) this paragraph was followed by another which has been superseded by ch. 11.

[29] Adriano BANCHIERI, *Conclusioni nel suono dell'organo*, Bologna, Rossi, 1609, pp. 12f: "per lo cui valore, da Papa Clemente 8 ottenne ordine cavaliero".

[30] [Alessandro BALDESCHI and Gio. Maria CRESCIMBENI], *Stato della SS. chiesa papale Lateranense nell'anno MDCCXXIII*, Rome, S. Michele, 1723, p. 89. On Montani, cf. Warren KIRKENDALE, *Emilio de' Cavalieri: Gentilhuomo Romano*, Florence, Olschki, 2001, index and plate 30.

Perusinus fecit Anno D. MDXCIX; il disegno però, e il lavoro dell'intaglio messo a oro in campo azzurro, è di Gio. Batista Montano milanese, unico ... in quei tempi nel suo mestiere".

Perusinus fecit Anno D. MDXCIX"; the design, however, and the [wood] carving in gold on a blue background is by Gio. Batista Montani from Milan, unique in his craft at that time.

The organ had 59 keys, 26 pedals, and 16 registers. The second keyboard with its registers was probably added only after 1730. Today little original substance of Blasi's masterpiece is left, although the instrument was restored in 1984-87. Montani's splendid facade remains.[31] Can we find in the third volume of the *Händel-Handbuch*, which catalogues the instrumental music, extended, virtuoso organ pieces from these years? Perhaps, in addition to a few preludes, fugues, chaconnes, and sonatas, also suites which sometimes end with a chaconne? Could, for example, the partita in c-minor HWV 444, which sustains some long notes like pedal points have been played here? All this needs to be considered. It is quite possible that Handel, as a great organist, also improvised here.[32] (In the eighteenth century this still was regarded as the culmination of the art). In any case, Valesio and our anonymus both provide their testimony of this Lateran concert, of music unheard of, for the applause of the audience must have been immense, even if only, as customary in catholic churches, "with a coat folded several times between their hands, so as not to be heard, since that would have been disrespectful and is allowed only in theaters".[33]

---

[31] Cf. Alberto CAMETTI, *Organi, organisti, ed organari del senato e popolo romano in S. Maria in Aracoeli*, «Rivista musicale italiana», XXVI, 1919, pp. 461 and 480f; Renato LUNELLI, *Der Orgelbau in Italien*, Mainz, Rheingold, 1956, pp. 135-141 and Abb. 26; *id.*, *L'arte organaria del rinascimento in Roma*, Florence, Olschki, 1958, pp. 29-36; Francesco Saverio COLAMARINO and Furio LUCCICHENTI, *L'organo di Luca Blasi nella basilica di S. Giovanni in Laterano, Roma*, Amici dell'organo, «Bollettino», II, 1971, pp. 20-26; Arnaldo MORELLI, *I Testa celebri organari romani*, «Note d'archivio per la storia musicale», n.s. I, 1983, p. 124 (on Celestino Testa and Ugo Annibale Traeri, who extended the organ after 1730).

[32] As we know, Johann MATTHESON did not neglect to mention this strength of the young Handel during these years, when they were together in Hamburg: "Er war stark auf der Orgel: stärker als Kuhnau, in Fugen und Contrapuncten, absonderlich ex tempore" ["He was strong at the organ: stronger than Kuhnau in fugues and counterpoint, especially *ex tempore*"] – *Grundlage einer Ehren-Pforte*, Hamburg, der Verfasser, 1740, p. 93.

[33] "auf dem dazwischen gelegten viel mahl doppelten mandel, damit man nicht hörete, in dem solches gegen den respect wäre und nur in theatris erlaubet ist" – Friedrich Armand Freiherr von Uffenbach, who visited Ruspoli's concerts since the end of March 1715 (quoted in *AC* 1966 p. 75 = *AC* 2007 p. 99).

XI.

HANDEL WITH RUSPOLI: NEW DOCUMENTS FROM THE ARCHIVIO SEGRETO VATICANO, DECEMBER 1706 TO DECEMBER 1708

In the summer of 1985, the 300th anniversary of Handel's birth, Don Sforza Ruspoli very kindly invited us to an exquisite dinner with his elderly father Don Francesco Prince of Cerveteri and family in the Ruspoli palace in Via del Corso, to celebrate again the patronage extended to the young 'Sassone' by their ancestor Francesco Maria Ruspoli (then marquis, soon to become the first Prince of Cerveteri; Plate XI.1 and *AC* 2007, Plate 8). But afterwards he took me aside and indicated that he did not quite agree with one of the dates suggested in my article *The Ruspoli Documents on Handel*:[1] May 1707 for the performance of the cantata *Diana cacciatrice*. We know that this work appears as the first of eight cantatas for which Handel's principal copyist Antonio Giuseppe Angelini (alias "Panstufato" – see below, p. 397) was paid on 16 May 1707.[2] Since the patron and his retinue departed from Rome the next day for his country estate in Vignanello, where he also used to hunt, I had assumed that the cantata on the divine huntress was performed there. But Don Sforza had his doubts, pointing out that the main event in this pastime was the hunting of the stags, which in his family always took place in late winter in Cerveteri, never in the spring in Vignanello, where smaller game was hunted.[3] In central Italy the deer hunt indeed finished in early March, when, unknown to me, the stags lose their antlers and thus their interest as trophies.

---

[1] JAMS, XX, 1967, pp. 222-273, 518; ch. 9, above.

[2] Above, p. 328, Doc. 1.

[3] I am grateful to His Excellency Don Sforza Ruspoli Prince of Cerveteri for this not unessential correction. If he had remained silent, this article might never have been written. My thanks to him also for access to the paintings reproduced in Plates XI.1, 6, and 10-12.

My error was taken over by the facsimile edition of the cantata,[4] and until now has been stated as fact in the literature on Handel. (But for me, this was a lesson, for a maggiordomo did not pay for work at a court until it was concluded, unless, exceptionally, an advance was authorized in writing, e.g. to pay for travel expenses; thus a copyist often received his fee months after the immediate musical performance). In 1992, at the conference *La musica a Roma attraverso le fonti d'archivio*, I showed that Handel was indeed a guest at Ruspoli's stag hunt already in February 1707 in Cerveteri, where his cantata *Diana cacciatrice* was performed. In March 1707 he was found in the nearby seaport of Civitavecchia – a place absent from his biographies – again in Ruspoli's retinue. There the patron not only held important political discussions, but even put a new ship at the disposal of the papal fleet, and Handel once more composed a particular cantata for the occasion. In May-June he can be further documented at the religious functions and secular entertainments in Vignanello. But I did not want to publish these results before examining all relevant volumes in the Archivio Ruspoli-Marescotti. In addition to the expense lists, bills, and receipts in the *giustificazioni* etc., I have now consulted the huge *libri mastri*, i.e. records of income and expenses kept only for the patron and bound in precious Morocco. Also here "Monsù Endel" appears repeatedly.

Today I can sketch Handel's sojourn in Rome and Latium from the beginning – early December 1706 – with new documents and facts relating to Ruspoli and his friends. The very first documents do not mention Handel by name, but they reflect the situation so clearly that only the composer, his lodging, and at least one of his large cantatas can be meant.

* * *

Ruspoli could engage in continuous and extensive patronage of music only after he concluded successfully on 22 September 1705 the legal action which put him in possession of an immense fortune. At that time he was still living in the palace of his uncle Cardinal Galeazzo Marescotti "nella isola della Madonnina di Santa Casa di Loreto" (see below, Appendix I). In late October he rented the Palazzo Bonelli,[5] today Palazzo Valentini, seat of the government of the Province of Rome (Plates XI.2, 3 [no. 273], and 11). But for many

---

[4] Georg Friedrich HÄNDEL, *Diana Cacciatrice: Cantata a voce sola* [and chorus] *con strumenti* (HWV 79); *Faksimile nach dem Partituautograph ... mit einer Einführung von Bernd Baselt ...*, Leipzig, Zentralantiquariat der DDR, 1985. Likewise Hans-Joachim Marx, in *Hallische Händel-Ausgabe*, V/3, Kassel, Bärenreiter, 1994, p. x, and critical report, V/5, p. 115.

[5] Saverio FRANCHI, *Il principe Ruspoli: l'oratorio in Arcadia*, in *Percorsi dell'oratorio romano*, ed. S. Franchi, Rome, IBIMUS, 2002, p. 286, note 93.

months masons and carpenters were occupied with renovations.[6] Under these conditions Cardinal Pietro Ottoboni had performed for Ruspoli an oratorio, dedicated to him, in the *cancelleria*,[7] and for more than a year, until Advent 1706, the marquis presented hardly any music in his residence, with the exception of a few unidentifiable cantatas.[8] In March 1706 a harpsichord was transported there,[9] possibly the "bellissimo cembalo a sette [!?] registri" which "il gran prencipe [Ferdinando] di Toscana" had presented to Ruspoli's wife Isabella in 1703.[10] A priest from S. Agnese was paid in July for adjusting "i cimboli".[11] On 4 October the marquis settled personally debts of the singer Lucrezia d'André alias Madame Carò,[12] the once famous virtuosa of Ferdinando Medici.[13] (Although she was no longer young, she occasionally received wine and poultry for *ferragosto* and Christmas at least until 1710).

The arrival of Handel in Rome can be established safely before 1707. Not only did the composer date his manuscript of duets by Steffani "Rome 1706".[14] We know also that he must have arrived some weeks before his organ debut in the Lateran, which according to biographical allusions in Francesco Valesio's diary and the *Voyage historique* took place on 14 January 1707.[15] Im-

---

[6] Francesco VALESIO, *Diario di Roma*, ed. Gaetana Scano, Milan, Longanesi, 1977-79, III, 567 (7 March 1706). On this palace cf. *Palazzo Valentini*, ed. Gennaro Farina, Rome, Editalia, 1985, and below, Appendix I.

[7] FRANCHI, *loc. cit.*

[8] Mentioned in the accounts 30 Jan. and 31 Aug., Archivio Segreto Vaticano, Archivio Ruspoli-Marescotti, *Giustificazioni di Roma*, vol. A 42, after list 94 (28 Jan. - 10 March 1706), and vol. A 43, list 177 (12 Aug. - 13 Sept. 1706), item 63. The folios of the *giustificazioni* are not numbered. For each year there are one or two volumes: 1706 = A 42-43, 1707 = A 44, 1708 = A 45-46. Each volume contains several expense lists with their items numbered consecutively, followed by the relevant bills, with many of the major ones bearing consecutive numbers. See my *Ruspoli Documents*, 1967, p. 253, where the letter 'B' for this series of volumes should be corrected to 'A'. Records of monthly salary payments, with their receipts, are contained in a volume of their own (*ruolo*) only until 1705 (vol. 383); thereafter they appear on large, folded folios for single months dispersed among the *giustificazioni*. The name of Handel does not appear in the *ruoli*.

[9] Vol. A 42, list 95 (13 March - 14 Apr. 1706), item 20, 23 March.

[10] VALESIO, II, 479, possibly exaggerated.

[11] Vol. A 43, list 154 (14 June - 10 Aug. 1706), item 51, 28 July.

[12] Vol. A 44, list 3 (Jan. 1707), item 34.

[13] Francesco Saverio QUADRIO, *Della storia e della ragione d'ogni poesia*, III/2, Milan, Agnelli, 1744, p. 536.

[14] Colin TIMMS, *Handel and Steffani: A New Handel Signature*, «Musical Times», CXIV, 1973, p. 374.

[15] VALESIO, III, 754f; above, ch. 9; Werner BRAUN, *Händel und der 'römische Zauberhut'*, «Göttinger Händel-Beiträge», III, 1989, pp. 71-86, identifying the author of the anonymous *Voyage* as Denis Nolhac. That the performer was Handel is not merely a "likelihood" (Ellen T. HARRIS, *Handel as Orpheus: Voice and Desire in the Chamber Cantatas*, Cambridge MA, Harvard UP, 2001, p. 42), but a certainty.

mediately after New Year's day the name of the singer Margarita Durastante (Plate XI.4; she signed her last name always with 'e', not 'i', as still is often written in the north) appears for the first time in the household books: a porter was paid for bringing a large buffet and music books into her house,[16] a task surely performed before Christmas 1706. But an arrival was being prepared by Ruspoli already by 13 October, when he ordered, for no less than 20 *scudi*, "una muta di bandinelle di damasco cremisi per la carrozza della cantarina" and "una sella ... coperta di felpa verde" ["a set of strips of crimson damask for the carriage of the female singer" and "a saddle ... covered with green plush"], to be ready by December.[17] A census of [March] 1707 locates the 21-year-old Margarita with her relatives in a nearby house of Ruspoli "alle tre cannelle",[18] where I had found other singers in later years.[19] Beginning in November 1707 she received the monthly salary of 20 *scudi*, the second highest at the court.[20]

From Ruspoli's accounts we see that already on 24 December 1706 a painter/gilder with four assistants was paid more than ten *scudi* for several days' work on – again – a large buffet, a harpsichord [!], three sedan chairs, two large drawings for a creche, etc.[21] – in time for Advent. This was all for the old Ruspoli palace, a building which is seldom mentioned in the following years and is now known as Palazzo Pecci-Blunt (Plate XI.5).[22] On the map of Giovanni Battista Nolli, 1748,[23] it is still identified with the name Ruspoli

---

16 List no. 20 (Jan. 1707), item 7, Jan. 3; above, p. 294.

17 *Libro mastro* 2, opening 202 right.

18 Rome, Archivio del Vicariato (I-Rav), SS. Apostoli, *Status animarum* 1700-1711, f. 133*v*, 1707: Margarita, her mother, and aunt; also f. 152*v*, 1708. Cf. also *Libro mastro* 2, opening 313 right: her "pigione della sua casa alle tre Cannelle". Handel's name does not appear in the *status animarum*, perhaps because, as a not only foreign, but also Lutheran [!] guest, he was never registered among the *anime*, not because he was absent from Rome at the time, as suggested by Juliane RIEPE, *Händel in Neapel*, in *Ausdrucksformen der Musik des Barock: ... Bericht über die Symposien der internationalen Händel-Akademie Karlsruhe 1998-2000*, ed. Siegfried Schmalzriedt, Laaber, Laaber-Verlag, 2002, p. 109, note 28. From July 1700 until at least the end of 1704 the very young Margarita, with her mother, uncle, and servants, was receiving a salary from the Duke of Mantua – Paola BESUTTI, *La figura professionale del cantante d'opera: le virtuose di Ferdinando Carlo Gonzaga*, «Quaderni storici», 22/II, no. 95, 1997, p. 431. Thereafter she and her relatives no longer appear in Mantuan documents. That she established herself in Venice is likely, especially since she was already fêted as singer. In any case, she did not stay with the Duke of Mantua, who in January 1707 "fled to Venice, taking his court with him" – above, p. 278.

19 In 1710 Caldara's future wife Caterina Petrolli was given quarters there – *AC* 1966 p. 54 = *AC* 2007 p. 68.

20 Vol. A 44, list 44 (12 Nov. - 31 Dec. 1707), item 57, 30 Nov.

21 Vol. A 43, list 309 (5-31 Dec. 1706), item 37, and following bill of 24 Dec.

22 On this palace see below, Appendix I.

23 Reproduced in Amato Pietro FRUTAZ, *Le piante di Roma*, Rome, Salomone & Staderini, 1962, III, plate 410. A photograph of the palace, before its restoration, can be seen in Maria Celeste COLA, *Scelte dinamiche residenziali di una famiglia fiorentina a Roma: i Ruspoli*, in *Il sistema delle*

and the number 985 (Plate XI.3), located at the foot of the two long flights of stairs leading up to the church of Santa Maria in Aracoeli and the Piazza Campidoglio, respectively, at the northwest end of the ancient forum. The buildings and streets on the northeast side of the Piazza d'Aracoeli, including the parish church SS. Venanzio ed Ansuino, were sacrificed in 1927-28 to the enlargement of the Piazza Venezia.

Were the furnishings mentioned in this bill destined for Handel? Much, including the analogy to Durastante ("large buffet"),[24] points to him, the more so as he said, according to Mainwaring: in "Naples, ... as at most other places, he had a palazzo at command, and was provided with table, coach, and all other accommodations".[25] Ruspoli must have put part [certainly not all!] of this palace at Handel's disposal immediately.[26] The composer surely lived there from December 1706 until October 1707, when he left Latium for the first time. He moved into the Bonelli palace in February 1708,[27] after an absence of several months from Rome, and remained there, except for a visit to the Campania, until he left the city for good on 12 September of that year.[28]

Margarita and Handel seem to have arrived in Rome about the same time, very probably from Venice, accompanied by their servants and Margarita's relatives. Their association with each other thus made it possible for them to appear together in performances soon after their arrival.

On 29 December 1706 the copyist Tarquinio Lanciani was paid for no less than 160 pages of "una cantata nuova" – *parts* for singers [plural!] and concertino violinists.[29] Only the cantata "Arresta il passo" HWV 83, for the unusual combination of *two* sopranos, violins and continuo, fits this description perfectly. Angelini, with two other scribes, copied the *score*,[30] which

---

residenze nobilari: Stato pontificio e granducato di Toscana, ed. M. Bevilacqua and M. L. Madonna, Rome, De Luca, 2003, p. 130.

[24] For Caldara Ruspoli provided even "tre buffetti usati" (*AC*, Doc. 2).

[25] *Memoirs of the Late George Frederic Handel*, London, Dodsley, 1760, p. 65.

[26] The *piano nobile* was rented to the powerful Cardinal Carlo Agostino Fabroni and his household (*libro mastro* 2, ff. 16, 174; cf. I-Rav SS. Venanzio e Ansuino, *Status animarum* 1687-1721, ff. 72, 76*v* (1707-8, without identification of the palace). – Contrary to HARRIS, pp. 80, 271 and 25f, Handel's first patron in Rome was not Cardinal Pamphilj, nor did I "imagine" that the cantata "Hendel, non può mia musa" HWV 117 was performed in Ruspoli's palace; this is proven by bills for no less than three copies of it, 1708-11.

[27] Above, p. 299.

[28] Above, p. 314.

[29] Vol. A 44, after list 20 (Jan. 1707): "A dì 29 Xbre 1706 / Pagato ... al S.ʳ Tarquinio Lanciani copista per avere cavato le parti che cantano e concertino per li violini da una cantata nuova con esse in fogli 20. – Sc. 2". Recorded again on 4 Jan. 1707 – list 20, item 15. Cf. *AC 2007*, Pl. 17.

[30] D-MÜs 1912. The other scribes are Alessandro Ginelli (*olim* "copyist I") and copyist II

extends to over 300 pages, albeit with large writing and later interpolations. He was paid only on 2 May (see below, p. 379). In July 1708 the cantata was heard, surely not for the first time, in the Arcadia's belated 'Christmas' celebration, now held outdoors in the summer.[31] The first performance may well have taken place at Christmas 1706, perhaps on 25 December, a Saturday, the day which was always reserved for the Arcadia. In any case, this was Handel's formal debut in Rome. [**PS**: In the summer 1708 the first aria was omitted, perhaps according to Ruspoli's instructions, since the text was no longer relevant, as we shall soon see]. The text, possibly by Abbé Francesco Mazziotti, tutor of Ruspoli's eldest son Bartolomeo, certainly does not present a homosexual theme, as one reads in a recent book on Handel's cantatas obsessed with this topic – currently so fashionable in America – ignoring archival documents.[32] The piece appears as a playful dialogue ('scherzo', 'gioco') between the patron and his composer, but this subtext is a serious musical 'contract'. Ruspoli, disguised as the shepherd Aminta, detains the nymph Phyllis, representing Handel.[33] This occurs already during the unusually virtuoso French overture: the majestic introduction with trochaic and paean rhythm followed by a "furioso", continuous thirty-second-note runs in a wide ambitus. Aminta "arrests" these innumerable "steps": "Arresta il passo!" – Phyllis should remain with him, in one of his palaces. Thus the voice enters without a seam. The nymph is still "free" (the words "libera" and "libertà" are clearly emphasized; Handel was not a court employee,

---

– Keiichiro WATANABE, *Die Kopisten der Handschriften G. F. Händels in der Santini-Bibliothek, Münster*, «Journal of the Japanese Musicological Society», XVI, 1970, pp. 231-236. Later Ginelli worked also for the confraternity of Santa Cecilia and its church San Carlo ai Catinari (= of the makers of basins), not "San Catinari", as WATANABE and Hans Joachim MARX, *Händels italienische Kopisten*, «Göttinger Händel-Beiträge», III, 1989, p. 197, believed.

[31] Not in Ruspoli's palace (as stated in WATANABE/MARX, p. 205), but in their 'Bosco Parrhasio', at that time his garden southwest of S. Matteo in Merulana. Cf. above, pp. 310 and 340, Doc. 21, where the cantata is listed by the incipit of the second aria, "Fiamma bella".

[32] HARRIS, *Handel as Orpheus: Voice and Desire in the Chamber Cantatas*. The writer's 'politically correct' penchant for homosexuality determines the method: assumption of an excessive number of homoerotic meanings through alleged, sometimes forced multiple readings, subtexts, and codes, where in a large number of cases these are neither necessary nor justified, but distorting. She defends the more implausible such interpretations with the facile claim that discretion and secrecy had to be observed in such a sensitive matter – a verdict of homosexuality unless proven otherwise. Although the writer takes immense pains to make Handel 'gay', her conclusions seem inconsistent when she hedges her bets by sitting on the fence, avoiding an unequivocal statement that Handel practiced homosexuality. Reviewers will surely deny that she succeeded with her innuendoes; cf. «Early Music», XXX, 2002, pp. 608-612, and MGG², *Personenteil*, VIII, 599: "more than questionable".

[33] As HARRIS correctly observes (p. 84), men sometimes speak with the voices of women in cantatas.

but the son of an "eminent surgeon and physician").[34] The well-bred Phyllis is at first shy, but then begins to sing long melismas on the word "cant*a*ndo, cant*a*ndo". Finally she admits defeat ("Vincesti"). The two swear constancy ("costanza") and fidelity ("fedeltà") to each other and conclude with a prayer to the gods. These virtues were especially important for the patron, who had now become one of Italy's most wealthy men. Handel, after the ouverture, responded again with his best: e.g. the aria "Fiamma bella", characterized by its legato motion in 9/8 time as Christmas cradle music, such as is still played by Italian shepherds from Advent until Epiphany in the streets of Rome;[35] or the aria "Se vago rio", a Venetian villotta,[36] surely a homage to Ruspoli's closest friend Cardinal Pietro Ottoboni, of whom everyone knew that he with his great-uncle, the deceased pope Alexander VIII, came from Venice. (Handel may have become acquainted with the family, especially with Pietro's father Antonio, there in March 1706).[37] The Romans must have been carried away by this debut. Years later Handel remembered its success: also the first composition which he presented on the London stage was the solemn introduction to this overture![38] The role of Aminta was doubtless sung in 1706 by the soprano Pasqualino. In January the Ruspoli accounts record payments to him for two undated performances.[39] Apparently only he could sustain the high b-flat for more than three measures of 6/8-time, depicting the word "cost*a*nte". Phyllis alias Handel was sung, of course, by Margarita.

If we calculate the time for composing and copying the music, Handel must have arrived in Rome before mid-December. On 31 August 1709 a bill of Francesco Lanciani still listed 21 cantatas,[40] certainly for gift copies, since

---

[34] MAINWARING, p. 1. Cf. the composer's own words: "des Weyland Edlen Hochachtbahren und Kunsterfahrnen ... Chur Fürstl. Brandenb. auch Fürstl. Sächsischen Cammer-Dieners"; and the tombstone inscription: "der vormalige H.F.S.M. auch Churf. Brandenburg. geheimder Cammer-diener, auch Leib-Medicus ..." – *Händel-Handbuch*, Kassel, Bärenreiter, 1978-85, IV, 15f. Also Werner PIECHOCKI, *Die Familie Händel in der Stadt Halle: Der Wundarzt Georg Händel (1622-1697)*, «Händel-Jahrbuch», XXXVI, 1990, pp. 201-221.

[35] Handel is known to have 'borrowed' the melody from Reinhard Keiser, and did not hesitate to present it as his own. Cf., *inter al.*, John H. ROBERTS, *Handel's Borrowings from Keiser*, «Göttinger Händel-Beiträge», II, 1986, pp. 65f.

[36] Not a "Spanish dance", as suggested by HARRIS, pp. 160 and 399, note 39; the music has none of the characteristics of the folia. On Caldara's (and Mozart's) use of the villotta style for its Venetian associations, cf. *AC* 1966 pp. 190ff = *AC* 2007 pp. 243ff.

[37] Anon. *avviso* of 20 March from Venice, I-Rli ms. 35.A.18, f. 133, referring to a Requiem celebrated for Pietro's great-uncle "con bellissima musica". Pietro remained in Rome – VALESIO, III, 574.

[38] *Rinaldo*, HWV 7, 1710/11.

[39] List 20, item 99, Jan. 31, mentions the "sonatori" and provides the date for payment of the undated bill.

[40] Above, p. 344, Doc. 35.

Handel had long left Rome. Eleven earlier pieces (including the very early *Lucrezia* cantata – see pp. 318ff and 387) appear only here. With one per week, they fit perfectly in the period from early December until the departure for Cerveteri on 22 February. A coincidence? We shall see that Handel provided not only the usual cantatas for Sunday evening, but at the same time also music for important occasions.

The cantata "Donna che in ciel" (with chorus) HWV 233, known only from Angelini's copy, is defined on its title page as for one of the annual commemorations of the "Anniversario della liberatione di Roma dal terremoto" ["anniversary of the liberation of Rome from the earthquake"], which had occurred on the day of the Purification of the Blessed Virgin Mary, 2 February 1703.[41] The piece was dated 1708 by Rudolf Ewerhart and even 1709, without arguments, by Reinhold Strohm.[42] But Anthony Hicks, for stylistic reasons, then Watanabe, again without comment, suggested February 1707.[43] They were right. Here Angelini was again assisted by the same two scribes who had collaborated with him already for "Arresta il passo" at the end of 1706[44] and now for *Il delirio amoroso* HWV 99[45] (consigned by the scribe Alessandro Ginelli to Cardinal Pamphilj on 12 February 1707).[46] From the fall 1707 until late February 1708 and after 12 September of this year Handel is no longer traceable in Rome until two decades later. As a plea for peace, the text of the final chorus reflects the conditions of both 1707 and 1708: "Maria, salute e speme del mondo afflitto, ... pace e gioia sia a noi qua giù" ["Mary, salvation and hope of the afflicted world, ... may peace and joy be to us here below"]. But only for Sunday, 6 February 1707 – not in 1708 or 1709 – did the very thorough Roman diarist Valesio[47] describe a solemn Mass with a concluding *Te Deum*, celebrated by an archbishop in Santa Maria in Aracoeli, the

---

[41] VALESIO, II, 505-517, 519, 522.

[42] Rudolf EWERHART, *Die Händel-Handschriften der Santini-Bibliothek in Münster*, «Händel-Jahrbuch», VI, 1960, pp. 120f (followed by HWV). Reinhard STROHM, *Händel in Italia: nuovi contributi*, «Rivista italiana di musicologia», IX, 1974, p. 172.

[43] Anthony HICKS, *Handel's Early Musical Development*, «Proceedings of the Royal Musical Association», CIII, 1976/77, pp. 87f; Keiichiro WATANABE, *The Music-Paper used by Handel and his Copyists in Italy 1706-1710*, in *Handel Collections and their History*, ed. Terence Best, Oxford, Clarendon, 1993, p. 209.

[44] See above, p. 366 and note 31.

[45] The group of three – Angelini, Ginelli, and no. II – appears again only in "Oh come chiare e belle" (see below, p. 401). For "Donna che in ciel" a fourth scribe was also involved (no. VI, in WATANABE, *Die Kopisten*, pp. 241ff).

[46] MARX, *Händel in Rom – seine Beziehung zu Benedetto Card. Pamphilj*, «Händel-Jahrbuch», XXIX, 1983, p. 113, and *Die 'Giustificazioni della Casa Pamphilj' als musikgeschichtliche Quelle*, SM, XII, 1983, p. 177.

[47] III, 765.

church of the S.P.Q.R. on the Capitoline hill (Plate XI.3, no. 917), decorated with precious tapestries, silver lamps, etc. Also the Roman magistrates and three cardinals participated in this thanksgiving for the delivery of Rome from the earthquake. The petition which had been submitted to the pope in February 1703 had requested that this solemnity take place on the Sunday after 2 February, the day of Purification of the Virgin:[48]

Facciano celebrare nella chiesa d'Aracæli da un prelato romano una Messa solenne, con predica, e che lo stesso si continui a pratticare per il corso d'anni cinque, ogn'anno nella domenica dentro l'Ottava della Festa della Purificatione.	Let a *Missa solemnis* be celebrated by a Roman prelate in the church of Aracoeli with a sermon, and that the same continue to be practiced annually for five years on the Sunday within the octave of the feast of the Purification.

That the *devozione* of the same day employed festive music goes without saying, and it was the cantata of the composer living at the bottom of the stairs below Aracoeli, introduced by Ruspoli and perhaps also by Cardinal Pamphilj. The work was surely commissioned by the Roman senate: the petition of 1703 had been signed by Ruspoli's half-brother Sforza Marescotti as prior of Rome.[49] But how did a Protestant composer come to write Marian music? From 1542 until 1676 the Nobile Collegio dei Catecumeni, the only Roman institution especially for conversions, was located directly to the left of the parish church of SS. Venanzio ed Ansuino (see above, p. 365). Thereafter the Collegio was transferred to the church of S. Maria dei Monti.[50] That Handel firmly resisted the attempt of at least one cardinal (his closest neighbor Fabroni? – secretary of the Propaganda Fide! – cf. note 26) to convert him[51] is of no importance here. For more than half a year he composed music for the Roman liturgy.

---

[48] Petition *Alla Santità di Nostro Signore Clemente XI, die 15 februarij 1703*, Rome, Camera Apostolica, 1703, p. [1] (inserted by Valesio in his diary, II, 531f). For these five years "siano nella città di Roma in ogni tempo, anche di carnevale, totalmente proibite le maschere, corse de pallij, festini, balli, e recite, così di comedie, come di tragedie, rappresentationi e simili, benché in musica, & anche nelli collegij, seminarij, monasterij, e luoghi pij e profani" ["be completely prohibited in the city of Rome at all times, also during carnival, the masquerades, horse races, festivities, dances, and theatrical performances, both of comedies and tragedies etc., also with music, in the colleges, seminaries, monasteries, and sacred and profane places"].

[49] See also Lucantonio CHRACAS, *Racconto istorico de terremoti sentiti a Roma ... la sera de' 14 di gennajo, e la mattina de' 2 di febbrajo dell'anno 1703*, Rome, G. F. Chracas, 1704, pp. 56f, and VALESIO, II, 505f: the edict which prohibited women from receiving instruction in music. On Marescotti, see below, p. 382 and Appendix I.

[50] Carlo PIETRANGELI, *Rione X: Campitelli*, I, Rome, Palombi, 1992, p. 24.

[51] MAINWARING, pp. 64f: "one of these exalted ecclesiastics".

The accounts for February contain many bills for ammunition transported by oxcart for the hunting season in Cerveteri, Ruspoli's estate in the Etruscan settlement on the Tyrrhenian coast, famous today for its ancient necropolis.[52] Also the harpsichord maker Mattia [di Gand] received his fee: he furnished a new, costly keyboard which he took to Cerveteri and back, obviously for a musical performance.[53] On 22 February[54] Ruspoli arrived with relatives, friends, and retinue at his castle for the deer hunt the next day on the extended slopes and ravines of the northern hills.

It was surely a *parforce* hunt, on horseback with hounds (the account books mention saddles, nets for the game, etc.).[55] The chef presented a long list of food for six days.[56] For 23 February the list is not only much longer than for other days – the antlers of a stag are mentioned ("cimatura di corno di cervo")! The antlers were surely exhibited in the great hall. It was a prize trophy, from a *cervo nobile*, traditionally reserved to be shot by the patron. And on that day the cantata *Diana Cacciatrice* HWV 79 was certainly performed during the traditional *conversazione* towards midnight, not, as I once assumed, in the early morning, since no hunter would have had the patience to listen to music before the hunt, least of all a cantata amounting to 52 pages in Angelini's copy, not merely the eleven pages of the autograph, which Baselt did not recognize as a fragment, repeatedly dismembered by early owners[57] as gifts. The text begins, of course, with the departure for the hunt: Diana summons her nymphs to pursue "wild boars and every kind of game" ("cingnali [for "cinghiali"] alla preda ed'ogni belva"). The events which followed, such as the sighting and shooting of the stag, probably were depicted on the lost pages. Also J. S. Bach's cantata, "Was mir behagt, ist nur die muntre Jagd" (BWV 208 and 208a) consists of many arias, with duets, a chorus, etc. But it was sung on the name- or birthday of a patron, after a "Kampff-Jagen ... bei einer Tafel-Music", not *before* a hunt.[58] Handel's cantata employs not

---

[52] List 33 (5 Feb. - 6 Apr. 1707), "Per l'andata a Civitavecchia e per la villeggiatura in Cerveteri", *passim*.

[53] *Ibid.*, item 35, Feb. 20, and bill.

[54] *Ibid.*, item 40.

[55] Bill after list 33.

[56] "Lista della spesa di Cerveteri", after list 33. The dates are given in list 33, item 62: the payment to the "offitiali e sala ... per sei giornate dalli 23 a tutto li 28 [Feb.]".

[57] Aloys Fuchs and Fortunato Santini, who designated himself, on the first page of the autograph, "al servizio di S[ua] Em[inen]za R[everendissi]ma il Sig. Cardinale Odescalchi"; the familiar title of a cardinal is garbled beyond recognition in Baselt's facsimile edition, p. 6 ("Emp. Rm.") and in Donald BURROWS and Martha J. RONISH, *A Catalogue of Handel's Musical Autographs*, Oxford, Clarendon, 1994, p. 265 ("Emja Rine"). The facsimile comprises 13 pages with music, one of them crossed out.

[58] I thank J. Riepe for this reference. Cf. Josef PÖSCHL, *Jagdmusik*, Tutzing, Schneider, 1997,

hunting horns but trumpets. It was perhaps Ruspoli who prescribed these instruments. This is suggested by the original incipit of the first aria, "Guerriera la tromba".[59] As I shall presently demonstrate, Ruspoli was already providing military assistance to the pope against the emperor in the ongoing War of the Spanish Succession, and he let also these politics be reflected in music.

Not mentioned are the names of the guests who were invited to the six-day party, but only those of their servants:[60] one of the 'Saxon', one of Abbé Mazziotti, possibly the librettist, and one of Duke Federico Pierdonato Cesi (1664-1752), head of the house of Acquasparta, Ruspoli's brother-in-law. A final amusing detail: on 1 March Ruspoli sent a "gift of little wild boars" to three Cardinals – Pietro Ottoboni, Joseph La Trémouille ("Tremoglie" in the documents), and Francesco Del Giudice.[61] These three belonged to his closest friends and regularly joined him late Sunday night to play cards ("da ombra").[62] La Trémouille was de facto ambassador of Louis XIV to the Holy See,[63] brother of the all-powerful Anne Orsini (widow of the Duke of Bracciano), who almost single-handedly directed Spanish politics in Madrid; Del Giudice, Philip V's Spanish-speaking viceroy of Sicily (1701-05).[64] All three cardinals turn up, via Ruspoli, in musical relationships with Handel, as will be seen.

Immediately after Cerveteri, Handel appears in the ancient seaport Civitavecchia, again with his servant ("servatore del Sassone") and Margarita Durastante. The lengthy food bill for Civitavecchia mentions tasty fish and oysters for everyone and extra bread and wine for the singer and the Saxon ("la cantarina e sassone") from 17 to 19 March.[65] Ruspoli indeed arrived in the city by land on 17 March with a large retinue and 40 horses.[66] On 18 March he gave

---

pp. 65ff, on the so-called "Festjagd" in the baroque era: the hunt was, as ever, in the early morning, but the music was heard at a much later time of day.

[59] Handel altered it later to "Foriera la tromba"; also this was overlooked by Baselt and Marx.

[60] Bill after list 33: "Servatore del Sassone" etc.

[61] List 33, item 67.

[62] MONTALTO mentions this game as being played by Cardinal Pamphilj and aristocratic friends, but also Pope Clement XI's strong disapproval of such pleasures – Un mecenate in Roma barocca; il Cardinale Benedetto Pamphilj (1653-1730), Florence, Sansoni, 1955, pp. 111 and 518, notes 51, 53.

[63] VALESIO, III, 606 and 706: "la soprintendenza de' negozii della Francia"; "rappresenta le veci dell'ambasciatore di Francia".

[64] Id., I, 565, III, 452.

[65] After list 33.

[66] List 33, item 100: "l'arrivo di S. E."; item 109: "40 cavalli". Ruspoli's brigantine, already moored in Civitavecchia, could not come to bring him from Cerveteri because of bad weather (ibid., item 96: "Pagato ad un marinaro venuto a posta da Palo che il bregantino non veniva a causa del tempo"; VALESIO, III, 780: "fu la giornata con pioggia, indi si levò una fredda tramontana e la notte precedente era caduta neve con acqua").

a banquet for the governors, officials, and sponsors of the galleys.[67] Here I must fill in the background.

Civitavecchia, with its harbour founded by Emperor Trajan and its mighty fortification built by Michelangelo, belonged since 1431 to the Papal State. Its jurisdiction by land and sea was thus subordinated to the Pope.[68] The warships employed in the Mediterranean states until ca. 1700 were generally galleys. Though they were very maneuverable, they had often suffered shipwreck because of their shallow draught. Already during the first years of the War of the Spanish Succession this type of ship was gradually replaced by sailing vessels, and in France they were already obsolete by the time Louis XIV died. Only the pope retained them in Civitavecchia; the last ones were said to be still in use there during the second half of the eighteenth century.[69] Large galleys had 25 long oars on one side, 26 on the other, each pulled by five or six men, often chained there for the rest of their lives. Our fleet consisted of five galleys. The largest and best equipped was the admiral's ship, called 'la capitana' or 'la reale', with more than 500 men under a *commendatore*. This gentleman was the military governor; a prelate served as governor of the city – a division of power calculated by the pope.[70] From May until September the galleys were at sea; during all other months they lay at anchor in the harbor. And it was normally during this period of rest that a *commendatore* received visits from prominent guests on his galley.

Returning to 18 March: Ruspoli gave his feast that evening as thanks for an event which had occurred the previous day. In the long food bill appear gratuities paid on 17 March for the boat ("mancia alla barchetta") which ferried him with a few retainers to the state galley, where he was surely received with all honors by the military governor. This high position was held since 1696 by Francesco Maria Ferretti, who was described by Labat as a venerable personage, but caricatured by Ghezzi.[71] That Ferretti and Ruspoli were not

---

67 List 33, item 103: "banchetto che Sua Ecc. fece alli governatori et officiali delle galere et assentisti".

68 Towards the end of World War II it was demolished, so that little historical substance remains, apart from the reconstructed fortification.

69 We are informed about the first decades of the century already by the eye-witness Jean-Baptiste LABAT, *Voyages du P. Labat ... en Espagne et en Italie*, vol. 4, Amsterdam, Delespine, 1731; cf. also Vittorio VITALINI SACCONI, *Gente, personaggi e tradizioni a Civitavecchia dal Seicento all'Ottocento*, Civitavecchia, Cassa di Risparmio, 1982. One can find there the information which I do not supply from Ruspoli documents. On the galleys specifically, cf. especially LABAT, pp. 144f, 192; VITALINI SACCONI, pp. 283, 285.

70 LABAT, pp. 182, 186.

71 *Id.*, pp. 167, 186, 210; Carlo CALISSE, *Storia di Civitavecchia*, Florence, Barbèra, 1936, p. 526 (capitano 1700-21); VITALINI SACCONI, I, 287f, 320 (*governatore* 1696), 352.

alone during this first reception is clear from the expense list of the next day. With his banquet Ruspoli thanked those who had invited him. His advice was desired, especially now that the war was moving still closer to Rome. Thus the visit on the state galley, the aim of his trip, was not merely a holiday outing, but an important meeting where precarious matters were discussed.

It can be taken for granted that, after his banquet the last evening, Ruspoli had music performed by Handel and Margarita. The question is only: what music? Since the fourth week after the performance of *Diana cacciatrice* had now almost past, it may well have been the fourth cantata in Angelini's bill,[72] "Udite il mio consiglio" ("Listen to my advice", HWV 172). The cantata's text is indeed so full of allusions, that it can have belonged only here. I may briefly demonstrate that the vocal part – who else but Ruspoli? – gave advice on a matter which was being discussed in these very days. The incipit already alludes subtly to the proud coat-of-arms of Civitavecchia,[73] where, since the early Middle Ages, the two letters 'O' and 'C' stood for "ottimo consiglio". The legend reports that after the destruction of the city by the Saracens the desperate people gathered under a large oak to deliberate whether they should ever go to sea again; whereupon an old salt named Leandro stood up to encourage them, so that his advice was really an "ottimo consiglio".[74] I quote and translate the cantata's first recitative (with my italics):[75]

Udite il mio consiglio, / *Inesperti* d'amor pastori, udite; / Se incontraste giammai / Qui dove suole / Guidar *l'errante greggia* / Dal colle al piano, o dalla selva al *fonte*, / Picciola pastorella, / Di *membra agili* e pronte, / D'atti languidi e schivi, / Che ha *nero ciglio in bianco volto* / E fregia della guancia / Il pallor labbro vermiglio, / Fuggite, ah! fuggite, / Que' suoi furtivi sguardi, / E quelle sue semplicità mentite.	Hear my counsel, shepherds *inexperienced* in love. If you ever meet the little shepherdess here, where she is wont to guide the *flock going astray* from the hill to the plain or from the woods to the *spring*, the shepherdess with *agile limbs*, ready for languid and shy acts, who has *black eyebrows on a white face* and the pale red lip adorns the cheek: flee, ah yes, flee those furtive glances of hers and her false simplicity.

There follows the first aria: a warning against the falsehood and cunning of the shepherdess. The text becomes clear when we eliminate the embellish-

---

[72] Above, p. 328, Doc. 1.

[73] Reproduced on the front cover of CALISSE.

[74] CALISSE, p. 74, note 1, and p. 72.

[75] The text of the cantata, with some variants (including the alteration of the allusive first line to "O pastori io v'aviso"), was set to music also by Benedetto Marcello and Nicola Porpora; see Eleonor SELFRIDGE-FIELD, *The Music of Benedetto and Alessandro Marcello: A Thematic Catalogue*, Oxford, Clarendon, 1990, pp. 140f, nos. A230[a-b] and Z231.

ment of the Arcadian metaphors. The shepherds who love the shepherdess are the gentlemen who still prefer the galleys, without knowing ("inexperienced") what the future will bring. Some of the Muslim prisoners ("the flock going astray")[76] may hopefully arrive at the "spring", the font of baptism. The galleys were very maneuverable, had "agile limbs" (= oars), but a shallow draught and were thus less useful for trade and warfare than for "languid and shy acts", though their appearance was beautiful. The text would seem to allude to the female figure which often adorned the prow of a galley ("black eyebrows", "white face", etc.; see below, the "testa intagliata").[77] The simplicity of the shepherdess is deceptive. The lesson: She ruins you, gentlemen, financially and perhaps even with shipwreck. (No less an authority than Torquato Tasso had recommended "navi converse in ninfe" as a *topos* of the miraculous for early modern epics).[78] At the end of the cantata the voice reveals itself as "Fileno", expressing pain and even contempt. Fileno again appears to be Ruspoli, in his military role.[79] All this could seem an implausible hypothesis if not, at the end of March, the mandate of one of the two so-called "assentisti" had expired.[80] These were very wealthy gentlemen, who served as sponsors of the galleys, supplied clothing for the prisoners, etc. At the time of their appointment, they often provided a new galley.[81] Ruspoli may have hoped to assume this function, for he brought with him a brigantine, a different kind of warship, which was probably smaller than the galleys, but still faster and more manageable, certainly with a deeper draught. It may well have been a precious gift from Ruspoli to the pope, via his governors. In the castello of Cerveteri hang several paintings showing a brigantine (Plate XI.6), a sailing ship with two masts, without oars or prisoners. Ruspoli not only advised against galleys: he proposed an alternative. Thus he again entered the political arena, in the interest of better efficiency of the papal fleet against the emperor. His banquet was doubtless given on this ship. The account books document expenses for its

---

[76] Not "wandering flock", as HARRIS, *Handel as Orpheus*, pp. 154 and 360, translates.

[77] Many such figures, largely from the 19th century, are reproduced in Eigel WIESE, *Galeonsfiguren*, Königswinter, Heel, 1999.

[78] *Discorsi dell'arte poetica*, Venice, Vassalini, 1587, f. 3.

[79] Cf. STROHM, p. 171, on the cantata "Mentre il tutto è in furore" HWV 130, already identifying Ruspoli with Fileno and clearly implying the war with the emperor.

[80] Cristofaro Felice's, subsequently renewed – Antigono FRANGIPANE, *Istoria dell'antichissima città di Civitavecchia*, Rome, Pallade, 1761, p. 221. On the 'assentisti' (from 'assenso' = 'agreement', in this case a contract awarded to the highest bidder) see LABAT, pp. 146, 172ff, 192, 196, 198f; CALISSE, p. 487.

[81] FRANGIPANE, p. 220.

rich furnishings[82] and for the instrumentalists ("forzati che sonorno",[83] from the galleys?). The ship had also "una testa intagliata al naturale fatta per porla in cima allo sperone del detto bergantino" ["a carved head, made *al naturale*, to be placed on top of the prow of the said brigantine"].[84] Handel's cantata reflected only Ruspoli's wishes. The text may well have been provided by Mazziotti, who had again come with his servant. Clearly, it was not written overnight, but planned in advance according to Ruspoli's order, as was Handel's music, which contains corrections, both in the autograph and in Angelini's copy. The tenacious hypothesis that this cantata and others from the Roman bills were written earlier for Florence[85] could never be sustained.

It is by now known that on Easter Sunday, 24 April, Alessandro Scarlatti had his oratorio *Il giardino di rose* performed in Ruspoli's Roman palace. But three weeks earlier, on Laetare-Sunday, 3 April, the patron gave a sumptuous banquet for "cardinali, dame, principi, prelati e cavalieri" on his estate in Massa ca. 20 km. northeast of Rome.[86] Also this place has remained hitherto unknown to musicologists. Since a man who imitated a bird in an oratorio ("uno che contrafa la voce e canto d'uccello nella prova dell'oratorio") was paid already on 19 April,[87] and in this oratorio a "nightingale" indeed sang between a recitative and an aria,[88] the music must have been performed before then, disguised as a "prova" ("rehearsal"), as often with performances during Lent.[89] Only Laetare-Sunday in Massa can be considered for the date. Since the pontificate of Gregory I, this fourth Sunday of Lent was the day

---

[82] E.g. vol. A 44, list 33, item 96, 10 March 1707; and especially vol. A 45, no. 22, before the first list (no. 27) for 1708: "Conto de lavori fatti di pittura, e indoratura per un bergantino fatto a Civita Vecchia" occupying several painters and artisans over a longer period of time. Also *Libro mastro* 2, opening 326 left-right, for "pitture, doratura", "tele", "bandiere", the "testa intagliata", etc., recording late payments for work largely done in 1707.

[83] After list 33, 18 March 1707.

[84] *Libro mastro* 2, opening 326 right.

[85] Ellen HARRIS, *Händel in Florenz*, «Händel-Jahrbuch», XXVII, 1981, p. 49; *Le cantate romane di Händel*, in *Le muse galanti: la musica a Roma nel Settecento*, ed. Bruno Cagli, Rome, Enciclopedia Italiana, 1985, p. 60; *Handel as Orpheus*, p. 272. See also below, pp. 386ff.

[86] List 33, items 202 and 204. On this estate of Ruspoli, cf. Giuseppe TOMASSETTI, *La campagna romana antica, mediovale e moderna*, VI, Banco di Roma, 1977, pp. 226f, 273f. I-Ras Catasto Alessandrino, cartella 431, f. 17 (ca. 1660) shows a single building (*casale*) on this *tenuta*.

[87] List 34 (Apr. 1707), item 22. On 24 Apr. he was paid for the performance in Rome: once more "homo che fece canto di rosignolo nell'oratorio al palazzo di ordine di S. E." (item 44).

[88] D-MÜs 3861, p. 315: "Si sentirà il canto d'un rosignuolo".

[89] E. g. also three performances of Handel's *Resurrezione*, each with at least 300 libretti, were disguised as '*prove*'; cf. above, p. 304. For '*prove*' of oratorios which Caldara composed for Ruspoli, cf. *AC* 1966 pp. 59f, 70, 73 = *AC* 2007 pp. 76, 87, 91.

when the pope honored a sovereign or other exalted personage with a golden rose; beginning with the sixteenth century this was most often a lady, such as an incumbent empress or queen.[90] Scarlatti's oratorio is full of political allusions. The rose garden must withstand the north wind (the bass role Borea, i.e. the emperor) and the large eagle ("aquilone", his emblem), finally vanquishing him with the help of the Virgin Mary (and the sovereigns of the Mediterranean states allied against the house of Hapsburg). Handel's cantata "Nella stagion che di viole e rose" HWV 137 may well have been composed for this same occasion (precisely at the time when the first violets and roses bloom in Latium), also because it is the seventh title in Angelini's bill paid on 16 May 1707 – again reading the bill 'chronologically' with one cantata for each of the seven weeks, from 20 February (*Diana cacciatrice*, 23 Feb.) to 3 April. It is surprising that also Cardinal Pamphilj was involved with Massa, even at the same time: on 17 April Ginelli had copied two unidentified cantatas which he sent there "per ordine di Sua Eminenza",[91] though we know only that Pamphilj was aware of Ruspoli's, Scarlatti's (and Handel's?) presence in Massa.

Their lordships assembled in Massa surely discussed the difficult political situation, for imperial troops were now advancing to central Italy. Cardinals Del Giudice and La Trémouille were doubtless present, perhaps also the Spanish ambassador, Pacheco Tellez, Duke of Uçeda.[92] All three met very frequently in Rome for deliberations.[93] And the Spaniard is found also in Ruspoli's accounts, again in a list for playing cards.[94]

Watanabe and Marx assumed that the score and parts of Scarlatti's oratorio and many other manuscripts were copied by Domenico Castrucci. Massive corrections are needed here.[95] Domenico was not a copyist, but a musi-

---

[90] Elisabeth CORNIDES, *Rose und Schwert im päpstlichen Zeremoniell*, Vienna, Geyer, 1967, pp. 24, 116. Cf. also Antonio BALDASSARRI, *La rosa d'oro che si benedice nella quarta domenica di Quaresima dal sommo pontefice*, Venice, Poletti, 1709.

[91] MARX, *Die 'Giustificazioni'*, p. 178, no. 160.

[92] MARX, *Händel in Rom*, p. 117, transcribed incorrectly "[g]l'Ambasciatori Cattolici" [plural] (cf. VALESIO, III, 788). Only the Spanish ambassadors, like their sovereigns, were designated as "catholic", and there was only one of them in a state at any time.

[93] VALESIO, III, *passim*.

[94] Vol. A 46, after list 199 (10-31 Dec. 1708): bill of Dec. 1708 for cards including "1 mazzo per Ecc.^{za} Amb. c[attolic]o".

[95] WATANABE/MARX, pp. 198, 220 (notes 8, 10), 222f (note 23), 216, and Abb. 7. They misattribute a large number of manuscripts of important composers to this alleged "copyist", designated first as "anon. Mü VIII" by WATANABE (*Die Kopisten*, p. 244), and later confused with a different scribe (*The Paper used by Handel and his Copyists during the Time 1706-1710*, «Journal of the Japanese Musicological Society», XXVII, 1981, p. 131), whom I regarded as close to Pietro Castrucci (*RD* 248), referring to HWV 117 in D-MÜs 1910, designated by Watanabe as Mü XI.

cian and head *cameriere* of the patron.[96] The oratorio was copied not by him, but by Cosimo Serio,[97] who signed the receipt on his bill for *parts* (Plate XI.8a; cf. *AC* 2007, Pl. 18). A bill for the *score* was not to be found, but the words for this (D-MÜs 3861) were written in the same hand as the receipted bill, as is particularly evident from a comparison of the words "concertino" and "concerto grosso" on the first page of the score (Plate XI.8b). Fortunately I could also locate his lodgings, with the Scarlatti family in Via Frattina.[98] The notion that freelance music copyists fulfilled important commissions on a large scale in their own shops is another lapse of Watanabe and Marx.[99] Ruspoli took care that music remained secret from the time of its composition until its performance. Angelini had no choice but to live under Handel's close supervision, in order to safeguard against clandestine diffusion of new music.

By 6 or 7 April Ruspoli and his retinue had finally returned to Rome.[100] We know that this same month Handel concluded his "Dixit Dominus" (Ps. 110) HWV 232 with the words "S[olo] D[eo] G[loria] / G. F. Hendel / 1707 / li [lacuna] d'aprile / Roma". Fortunato Santini noted on an anonymous Roman copy: "esiste in Casa Colonna" (i.e. the palace no. 281 in Plate XI.3).[101] In 1959 James Hall presented the interesting, widely accepted hypothesis that

---

[96] Domenico was on the Ruspoli payroll since May 1698 with a monthly salary of 7, later 6.5 *scudi* (vol. 383 and the various pay lists in vol. A 43-44 etc., respectively). He lived since 1700 with Ruspoli in the Loreto palace (see Appendix I), then, since 1706, in the Bonelli palace – I-Rav SS. Apostoli, *Status animarum* 1700-1711, f. 144*v*, 1707. The bills of copyists in the *giustificazioni* (series 'A') include none by him. He is mentioned frequently in the expense lists, but only as a *delegate* for payments to copyists, musicians, harpsichord makers, playing cards, etc. List 71 (May-June 1707), item 10, for example, reads: "a dì 7 maggio pagato al Sig.^re Castrucci per copiar una parte di cantata come per lista – 45 [baiocchi]", specified on a following page as "dato al copista del Sig.^re [Carlo Francesco] Cesarini per avere cavata una parte della sua cantata" (same date and amount). A sample of his own handwriting can be seen in line 7 of Plate XI.7, among the receipts for the very substantial clothing allowance of the *camerieri* (20 *scudi* each), after list 20, 5 Jan. 1707, or in his confirmation of payment on a bill of "Monsu Mattia cimbalaro" [for Vignanello], after list 71, 4 May 1707. WATANABE/MARX allege to have compared copies of music to Castrucci's hand in the "Filze delle Giustificazioni B 44-46" (p. 198), but these shelf numbers do not exist. They are an error taken over from *RD* 253 (cf. above, note 8).

[97] Cf. list 34, item 12, Apr. 14, payment to Castrucci [for Serio or his collaborator]; the corresponding bill: "In carta reale grande per copia delle parti dell'oratorio a 5 con strumenti ... [scudi] 4.45". The oratorio is clearly identified here not by its title, but by the specification of the single roles (Speranza, Religione, Borea, Penitenza). Item 19, Apr. 17: "pagato a Cosmo Serio copista di musica ... 6.20", i.e. for his bill for the rest of the parts (Carità and the remaining instruments, Plate XI.8a).

[98] I-Rav S. Lorenzo in Lucina, *Status animarum* 1704, f. 8*v*, and 1705, f. 11*v*: "Sig.^r Alessandro Scarlatti maestro di cappella", "Domenico f[iglio]", "Cosimo Serio copista", etc. In 1707 nine Scarlattis, including an Alessandro, were living in Palazzo Grassi (I-Rav SS. Apostoli, *Status animarum* 1707, f. 134*v*).

[99] P. 196.

[100] See above, note 52.

[101] D-MÜs 1924, f. 1*v*.

the work was composed for Carlo Cardinal Colonna, who had it performed, with other Vesper pieces,[102] on 16 July for the Feast of the Madonna del Carmine. But this occasion has not convinced everyone. Since I cannot here produce a Ruspoli document, we must take a brief look at the dates and this grandiose work itself.

First: in Rome neither Handel nor his successor Caldara ever composed music to lie unperformed in a drawer for three months. Patrons in the eighteenth century wanted brand new music, and since important composers were paid very well, they had to comply. That explains also why Handel, under such pressure, 'borrowed' music from himself and others. Second: this music can hardly have been intended as decor for a Marian feast. It is not innocuous, charming, but, now composed as a *psalmus in tempore belli*, conjures up terrifying military elements – beginning with the words "ponam inimicos tuos scabellum pedum tuorum" ["I shall make thine enemies thy footstool"], measures dominated by Pyrrhichius rhythm, or, the climax, "conquassabit capita in terra multorum" ["He will shatter the heads of many on earth"]: suddenly (mm. 210ff) the voices, now in triple time, become homophonic and deadly monotonous, intensify continually in gruesomely heavy strokes in remote keys, like God at the Last Judgement. The music is so disturbing that I can connect it only with an extraordinary Sunday of the Spaniards, already on 1 May 1707, the nameday of their King Philip V. It was the feast of the apostles Philip and James.[103] On 20 April the Spanish ambassador, fearing the imperial troops, had fled with his family and retinue from Rome to his country estate in Frascati,[104] ca. 25 Km. southeast of Rome, renowned already in antiquity as a summer resort. And he invited ca. fifty persons, of whom Del Giudice and La Trémouille arrived first, on 26 April.[105] Then on 1 May he gave a festive banquet for Saint Philip and the king.[106] "Dixit Dominus" must have been heard there during the second Vesper, probably in the cathedral, where also Philip and James were patrons. Indeed it was a gift for a sovereign. And also this music did not come from nowhere. Without doubt Ruspoli knew of Handel's

---

[102] "Laudate pueri" HWV 236, "il 8 Julii Roma", and "Nisi Dominus" HWV 238, "gli 13 di Giulio Roma" (autograph lost). James S. HALL, *The Problem of Handel's Latin Church Music*, «Musical Times», C, 1959, pp. 197-200, followed by HARRIS, *Le cantate*, p. 61, and *Handel as Orpheus*, p. 275.

[103] Until 1960. The Second Vatican Council moved them to 11 May.

[104] VALESIO, III, 769.

[105] *Libro manuscrito que contiene noticias sobre visitas, fiestas, etc.*, archive of the Spanish Embassy to the Holy See, leg. 126 (now removed to the Archivo General del Ministerio de Asuntos Exteriores, Madrid), f. 251v.

[106] VALESIO, III, 802.

composition performed in Frascati, perhaps he even initiated it, since he was the host of the 'summit meeting' in Massa. In any case, he gave full support to the catholic ambassador, who was now in a desperate situation. Filippo Colonna, the 'conestabile', had dedicated in 1704 the huge fresco of the two apostles Philip and James in his Church of Santi Apostoli (Plate XI.3, no. 283) adjacent to the Palazzo Colonna on the square facing the palace where Ruspoli was living. His brother Carlo was not only *maggiordomo* of Pope Clement XI, but in these years also governor of Frascati.[107] (A *colonna* stands before the old bishop's palace in Frascati with an inscription referring to *his* activity in office). He may have paid for the music. All this would explain both the date of April on the autograph and the name Colonna on the Roman copy.

Ruspoli may well have been present at the premiere of this work, for on that day his accounts record no expenditures for the usual Sunday music. These we find only for the next day, 2 May: the unusually large sum (more than 134 *scudi*) to seven well-known singers, twenty instrumentalists, and the factotum Ascanio, who transported the instruments, for "oratorios" [plural!] and "cantatas" which were heard in the *conversazioni* of the marquis.[108] Since also some goldpieces were needed by His Excellency as presents (for more than 50 *scudi*), and Angelini alias "Panstufato" now finally obtained his first payment, certainly for work already done before Cerveteri, the disbursements for music were increased to a total of no less than 200 *scudi*! This surely included the rehearsals and performances of *Il giardino di rose* in April. But what oratorio was heard on 2 May, which must have been the major event? Contrary to the usual practice, a title is quoted neither here nor later, although this payment for oratorios is mentioned again a few times.

On 14 May Angelini delivered to Cardinal Benedetto Pamphilj his statement for copies of the cantata *Il delirio amoroso* HWV 99 and the oratorio *Il trionfo del tempo e del disinganno* HWV 46ª, altogether 287 folios, with Handel's signature.[109] It was overlooked by Marx that he was not yet paid, since *these* documents, and also earlier and later ones, were not proof of payment. They are merely lists with the number of folios which the copyist submitted to a patron after completing some work. Often he had to wait for months for his fee.[110] Only on 5 July did Handel receive payment from Pamphilj's *com-*

---

[107] *Id.*, II, 244.

[108] List 71 (May-June 1707), item 1, + bill.

[109] MARX, *Händel in Rom*, p. 115. HARRIS, *Le cantate*, pp. 61f, and *Handel as Orpheus*, pp. 37 and 388, note 109, curiously states that this document precedes any mention of Handel in those of Ruspoli and that its date is that of a performance of *Il trionfo*.

[110] Since the separate parts for *Il delirio* had been copied by Alessandro Ginelli already by 12

piutista: the very substantial sum of 84 *scudi*. He gave Angelini exactly one third, 28 *scudi* (without *baiocchi*). At the usual rate of one *scudo* for ten folios (with 8 pages per folio),[111] that is the amount of the full *scudi* which corresponds to the number of folios copied. Handel retained twice as much, 56 *scudi*, for himself. That very large payment of 84 *scudi* – more than four months' salary of a first class prima donna (Durastante) – was misunderstood by Marx as compensation merely for Handel's cantata "Tra le fiamme" HWV 170, which has a duration of only ca. ten minutes.[112] No records have been found for payments to the musicians who performed *Il trionfo del tempo*, nor has it been known when and where it was heard.[113] I shall argue that this oratorio of Handel to Pamphilj's libretto was indeed heard on 2 May 1707, in either the Palazzo Bonelli or the Collegio Clementino, performed by Ruspoli's musicians.[114]

The text belongs to a long tradition of a genre which deals with the contest between the world and heaven, vices and virtues, whereby the latter of each pair are, of course, always victorious.[115] This conflict, favored by Jesuits

---

Feb. (see above, note 30), the "originaletto" of this cantata in Angelini's list of 14 May must also have been copied by then. (The term "originaletto", of course, designated a copyist's *score*, not an autograph).

111 "Royal paper" ("carta reale", heavy paper in octavo format) was used, not "normal paper", as I stated in *RD* 229.

112 While it is true that the bookkeeper did write, carelessly, "per haver fatto una cantata [*sic*] di Sua Eminenza Padrone", he was not a musician and must not be judged by the criteria of modern systems, where every piece of music is assigned to a category and placed in its own drawer. Thus a mason's bill for the performance of the *Resurrezione* designates this work as both "oratorio" and "cantata", and even the musician Domenico Castrucci referred to Scarlatti's *Giardino di rose* as "la cantata seu oratorio" – above, pp. 339 and 330, Doc. 19 and 7.

113 WATANABE/MARX, p. 223, note 34: a performance "is not traceable and also improbable". But nine years later Marx returned to the assumption that *Il trionfo* was performed, in the early summer of 1707 (on the basis of Angelini's list of 14 May), in the theater of the Collegio Clementino, "although no documentation ... has survived"; he argues that already in previous years oratorios were heard there under Pamphilj's patronage – *Händels Oratorien, Oden und Serenaten*, Göttingen, Vandenhoeck & Ruprecht, 1998, p. 244. *Il trionfo* seems indeed to have been performed [also?] in the Clementino, possibly as a repetition. Cf. Arnaldo MORELLI, *"Un bell'oratorio all'uso di Roma": Patronage and Secular Context of the Oratorio in Baroque Rome*, in *Music Observed: Studies in Memory of William C. Holmes*, ed. Colleen Reardon and Susan Parisi, Warren, Harmonie Park Press, 2004, note 85.

114 The absence of flutes (prescribed in the scores of the two oratorios) in the list of 2 May for the performances indicates only that musicians did not have to be paid to play them (the oboists or house employees may have done this) – not that the list is not connected with these oratorios, the only ones which can be associated with these dates. Also the lists of performers for the *Resurrezione* (above, pp. 331ff, Doc. 11) and the bill for the copy of *Il delirio* (MARX, *Händel in Rom*, p. 113, doc. 1) do not mention the flutes employed in these scores. MARX, p. 111f, assumes: "die Oboisten [waren] zugleich auch Flötisten". At least in 1698-1700 Ruspoli had the famous flautist Jacques Hotteterre on his payroll (FRANCHI, pp. 280f, notes 78f).

115 Warren KIRKENDALE, *Emilio de' Cavalieri, "Gentiluomo Romano"*, Florence, Olschki, 2001, pp. 251-257.

during the Counter-Reformation, is a Leitmotif of religious literature, also oratorios, of the Baroque. Each work, however, was conceived for a specific
audience – something which needs more investigation.

Thus also *Il trionfo del tempo*, with its allegorical personages. When
"Beauty" is flattered by "Pleasure", when "Time" and "Truth" demonstrate
to her that only divine beauty is lasting, and she finally repents and begs God
for forgiveness, then a particular class of people is covertly addressed: painters, sculptors, and architects, whose ideal was precisely 'beauty'. Within a
few days, on 6 May, the annual competition of their Accademia di San Luca
was to be held on the Capitoline hill, to determine who was the best in each of
the three categories. First they held the election and put their ballots, each for
three candidates, into an *urn*, then the winners were celebrated with music.[116]
This is anticipated in Pamphilj's text. Concretely, the "mirror" is mentioned
seven times in arias and recitatives, at first by Beauty ("fido specchio"), who
believes it reflects the truth, and then the real "specchio del vero", which en-
dures forever, held up to her by Time and Truth. After the third aria, the four
decide to measure their strengths in a *contest*. In the fifth aria ("Urne voi")
Tempo looks into the *urn*, to see if he finds there votes for Beauty – he discovers only ashes. I cannot discuss further details here, but believe that these
indications of a reflected image of beauty and of a contest decided by the urn
suffice to suggest a connection. Pamphilj himself, an honorary member of the
Accademia di San Luca,[117] had, on 25 February 1702, already written a cantata text for the same occasion and for the same artists in the academy ("Per la
nuova Accademia eretta nel Campidoglio sotto gli auspicij della Santità di
Nostro Signore Clemente XI.°"):[118]

> Qui dove aveano i Domator dei Regni
> Teatro di *Trionfi* al genio audace,
> Guerreggian fra di lor nobili Ingegni
> E modesta Virtù combatte in pace.
> Linee, Marmi, Colori, Opre, Disegni
> Illustre Poesia, Cetra loquace ...
> Erudito *trionfi* il Campidoglio ...

[116] On music for these competitions, organized by Corelli from 1702 until 1713, cf. *AC* 1966
pp. 56f = *AC* 2007 pp. 71f, and Franco PIPERNO, *"Anfione in Campidoglio": presenza Corelliana alle
feste per i concorsi dell'Accademia del Disegno di San Luca*, in *Nuovissimi studi corelliani*, Florence,
Olschki, 1983, pp. 151-209; *Musica e musicisti per l'Accademia del Disegno di San Luca (1716-
1860)*, in *La musica a Roma attraverso le fonti d'archivio: atti del convegno internazionale (Roma 4-
7 giugno 1992)*, Lucca, LIM, 1994, pp. 553-563.

[117] Since 1687 (Ottoboni since 1695); *Il centesimo dell'anno MDCXCV celebrato in Roma
dall'Accademia del Disegno*, Rome, Buagni, 1696, p. 40.

[118] I-Rvat Barb. Lat. 3890, f. 103 (my italics).

Also with the performance of *Il trionfo del tempo* His Eminence must have remained in command and felt very flattered. Thus the event is not to be regarded as rivalry between patrons, but as a 'joint venture', if this expression may be permitted. For Easter 1708, Handel could even use the overture again for his oratorio *La resurrezione*, surely with Ruspoli's permission, since the audience had been so impressed with it the previous year. Ruspoli had probably already given him compensation similar to that of Pamphilj two months later, since he withdrew almost the same amount in *piastre* and gold (cf. above, p. 379).

Ruspoli's sojourn in Vignanello during the spring 1707 can now be more precisely described. His party left Rome on 17 May, arrived the next day, and departed for Rome on 21 June, as revealed by thick lists of persons, food and drink for the "Villeggiatura di Vignanello".[119] Since the 475th anniversary of the canonization of St. Anthony, 13 June, coincided with Pentecost Monday, its celebration, strictly according to the liturgy, had to be postponed to the next day (hence "quindici messe ... celebrate nelle *tre* feste della Pentecoste").[120] Handel's two *motetti*, "O qualis de coelo sonus" HWV 239 and "Coelestis dum spirat aura" HWV 231, were thus heard on Pentecost Sunday, 12 June and on 14 June, respectively. **[PS**: See below, p. 410, a correction of the date for the "Salve Regina" to 18 June].

Of course we would like to know who was present. The long lists include all the names of guests and court personnel, beginning with the marquis and his family, his half brothers Count Sforza Marescotti, mentioned above in connection with the earthquake, and Count Mario Capizucchi (on both see Appendix I); Isabella's brother Federico Pierdonato Cesi, Duke of Aquasparta, with the duchess etc. and – Cardinal Ottoboni, with a small retinue. He was present for supper on 6 June until after lunch the next day.[121] But also Abbate Mazziotti, "Sassone" (now in person), and Durastante were all admitted to the "ecc.^ma tavola". "Panstufato", "camerieri", musicians borrowed from Rome, and again the servants of Mazziotti and Handel had their place in the "tinello".[122]

Still another, surprising name turns up: "Sig.^ra Vittoria". She appears only once in the lists, right between the musicians "Sig.^ra Margarita" and "Sassone", without date. From a Roman census (see p. 364) we know that also Margarita's

---

119 After list 88, July-Aug. 1707. On the visit to Vignanello see App. II.

120 See below, note 232.

121 *Ibid.*, between the two groups of pages: 6 June "a cena" and 7 June "partì ... dopo pranzo".

122 Undated pages after list 88 (July-Aug.!) and the rubric "Villegiatura di Vignanello" from 18 May 1707 (Handel, Durastante, and other musicians), and three pages dated 8-20 June (Handel's servant and Angelini).

mother was named Vittoria, but I find her in no Ruspoli document for Rome, Cerveteri, or Civitavecchia. Is the mysterious lady in Vignanello the celebrated singer Vittoria Tarquini, nicknamed "la Bambagia", who for some time was the favorite of Prince Ferdinando Medici in Florence?[123] She is found there as early as 1699, and in May 1703 was involved in a feud with another favorite, the castrato Checco De Castris, who was then forced into a comfortable retreat to the Palazzo Madama in Rome.[124] But two witnesses, independent of each other, are known to have alluded to a love affair between Vittoria and Handel. One is the Electress Sophie of Hanover, in a letter of 14 June 1710: "la medisance dit qu'il a esté amant de la Victoria" ["gossip says that he was Victoria's lover"];[125] the other, Mainwaring, half a century later, mentions Vittoria's leading role in Handel's opera *Rodrigo* (see below, p. 395) and continues:[126]

She was a fine woman, and had for some time been much in the good graces of his Serene Highness. But, from the natural restlesness of certain hearts, so little sensible was she of her exalted situation, that she conceived a design of transferring her affections to another person. Handel's youth and comeliness, joined with his fame and abilities in music, had made impressions on her heart. Tho' she had the art to conceal them for the present, she had not perhaps the power, certainly not the intention, to efface them.

Likewise in connection with her performance in Handel's next opera:[127]

At *Agrippina* her inclinations gave new lustre to her talents. Handel seemed almost as great and majestic as Apollo, and it was far from the lady's intention to be so cruel and obstinate as Daphne.

---

[123] Vittoria was not "of noble family" (the nobility did not practice music professionally), nor did Ferdinando became infected with his fatal disease, syphilis, from her, as HARRIS would like to believe (*Handel as Orpheus*, p. 39). The error, committed also by other modern writers, is the result of conflating two *separate* statements about two *different* women by Gaetano PIERACCINI, *La stirpe de' Medici di Cafaggiolo*, Florence, Vallecchi, 1924-25, II, 723. Here it is asserted only 1) that Ferdinando became infected in Venice in 1696; and 2) that he brought his lover Vittoria from Venice to Florence that year. Pieraccini's source, I-Fas Misc. Med. 781 (*olim* 458), int. 12, ff. [7v-8v] likewise does not connect these two facts: the "bellissima signora, e nobile" had honestly warned Ferdinando that an intimate relationship with her would be very dangerous, and she tried, in vain, to dissuade him from it. "L'incauto prencipe nel vaso di Pandora si dissetò di tal veleno ... che lo condusse al sepolchro" [17 years later]. "Partì di ritorno per Firenze, e condusse con li suoi guai una bella musica nominata Bambagia, ma il suo nome proprio era Vittoria Tarquini".

[124] See Warren KIRKENDALE, *The Court Musicians in Florence*, Florence, Olschki, 1993, pp. 652, 441-444. Contrary to HARRIS, p. 39, Checco was not "Venetian", but Roman, and Vittoria's nickname, "la Bombace" (= "la Bambagia", *loc cit.* [both from the Latin *bombax*]), does not mean "bombshell" (p. 179), but something much softer, 'cotton wadding'.

[125] *Händel-Handbuch*, IV, 45.

[126] Pp. 50f.

[127] *Ibid.*, p. 54.

For Vignanello Handel composed before the "mottetti" only the cantata "Un'alma innamorata" HWV 173,[128] which indeed fits his situation. It may have been written by Abbate Mazziotti. Was it a prank from the *famiglia alta*, to see how the 'Sassone' would react? A lover, says the text, is like a slave, has only grief, jealous fear, torment, etc. "I [and this is surely the composer speaking] enjoy myself, I laugh, I hope, I love more than one heart ... when I despise the strict rules of love" ("dell'amore le severe leggi et il rigore") – the "Vittoria" in Vignanello was certainly "la Bambagia", who was married to a musician named Tarquini. Handel seems to have escaped from the risky game elegantly, again with light, exuberant music, for also here a cantata had to entertain, never to create brooding atmosphere. "Aquavita per il Sassone" had been purchased on 26 May.[129] The cantata was performed probably no later than Monday, 6 June. Ottoboni had to depart the next day for Bologna, where he participated in the celebration of the anniversary of St. Anthony, patron saint of the Accademia Filarmonica.[130] But Ruspoli must have entertained him – close to the pope in the ecclesiastical hierarchy – only with the best musicians in Italy. Vittoria seems to have left with the cardinal, for she was detained by imperial troops a week later near Ferrara.

On the last Sunday in Vignanello the cantata with instruments *Armida abbandonata* ("Dietro d'orme fugaci") HWV 105 must have been first performed. It was the last piece which Angelini listed in his bill of 30 June containing all five items "scritti ... in Vignianello". (See Appendix II for further information on Vignanello).

On 22 June Ruspoli and his retinue were back in Rome, and on Sunday 26 he may well have had Handel's *Armida* heard again, since the Roman audience did not yet know the piece – on this evening his musicians plus two violinists played in a large, unknown cantata.[131] In Angelini's bill of 22 September *Armida* is listed again, no longer as parts, but as a score.[132] It stands there in the first place, and if one considers Angelini's chronology (he nearly always had to deliver one cantata per week), then the six following cantatas were performed by 7 August, including the French and Spanish ones on 3 and 17 July.

---

128 As seen above, p. 329, Doc. 2.

129 Above, note 119.

130 Ottoboni was thus no longer present for the performance of "Coelestis dum spirat aura" (see below, and above, p. 297). He was *cardinale protettore* of the academy from 1713 until his death in 1740 – Nestore MORINI, *L'Accademia filarmonica di Bologna (1666-1966)*, Bologna, Tamari, 1967, p. 91.

131 Above, pp. 297 and 329, Doc. 3.

132 Above, p. 330, Doc. 5.

To whom did Ruspoli address these cantatas, if not to his very close friends, the cardinals La Trémouille and Del Giudice, the highest representatives of France and Spanish Sicily/Naples, respectively (see above, p. 371)? They needed support now more than ever. On 7 July the imperial troops marched into Naples and on the same day toppled the statue of Philip V, which was then gleefully dragged through the streets by the populace and the soldiers. Also the house of a French printer, who apparently had collaborated with the old regime, was plundered. Cardinal Vincenzo Grimani, now in charge of the city, informed "tutti gli cardinali e baroni romani" of the city's occupation; only the cardinals Ranuccio Pallavicini (archbishop of Naples) and Del Giudice were ignored (a *damnatio memoriae*?).[133] In the text of the French cantata the lover is betrayed by the damsel and therefore seizes the bottle. Also the music is light, playful (never sad), as the Frenchman probably wanted. The text and music of the Spanish cantata, on the other hand, are melancholy. The singer will never abandon his loved one, though the "sins of reason" increase every day; he is consoled by longing for her (Spanish Naples?). This mood is captured in the rhythm of the Spanish saraband with accompaniment for guitar. The composer wrote the texts in large, elegant letters, with only eight staves on most pages, also in the copy, because Angelini knew neither French nor Spanish.[134]

As we know, Angelini was paid in October 1707 for his copy of the gigantic cantata *a 3* "Cor fedel" HWV 96.[135] But it was surely not performed at Ruspoli's because there is no payment recorded for the musicians. Very probably it was heard in Ottoboni's *cancelleria*, as Ruspoli's thanks to the cardinal for the oratorio which had been performed for him there the previous year (cf. above, p. 363). Ruspoli had already presented musical offerings to two of his card-playing companions, and the most important one was not to be overlooked. In these months Handel had performed at Ottoboni's with a child prodigy who played the archlute,[136] and he now composed for him the aria with archlute, "Come la rondinella" in this cantata. The three roles – Clori, Tirsi, and Fileno – seem to represent Isabella (Ruspoli's wife), Ottoboni, and Ruspoli himself. The two men woo Clori in vain. Tirsi is for Fileno the "amico e compagno". Both consider abandoning their sighs. But in the final terzett they all agree that life without love is not possible.

---

[133] VALESIO, III, 846ff, reporting three days later.

[134] The text of the Spanish cantata and a translation of it are likewise omitted from HARRIS, *Handel as Orpheus*, Appendix 2.

[135] Above, pp. 298, 330 (Doc. 6), 348.

[136] Merlini's letter of 24 Sept. 1707 (below, note 172).

* * *

Further information, especially on the *Resurrezione* HWV 47 (1708), until Handel's final departure from Rome, is provided above, ch. 9. The cantata *Il duello amoroso* HWV 82, which I dated 28 October 1708, after Handel's departure, was surely heard before 28 August, when Angelini was paid for it.[137] But many of the interpretations have now become facts.

In her article *Händel in Florenz*, Ellen Harris already attempted to assign five of the cantatas from the Ruspoli bills to 'Florence 1706': "Chi rapì la pace" HWV 90, "Fra tante pene" HWV 116, "O numi eterni" (*Lucrezia*) HWV 145, "Tu fedel" HWV 171, and "Udite il mio consiglio" HWV 172. But not one of the four criteria cited by her – "watermarks, handwriting, style, and text" (p. 49) – demonstrates Florentine provenance. Thus her assertions were rejected by Watanabe/Marx (p. 201) and the *Hallische Händel-Ausgabe* (Ser. V, Bd. 3, p. IX). The four cantatas HWV 90, 116, 145, 172 and "Dixit Dominus" HWV 232 all exhibit, with minor variants, the same **watermarks** (Venetian, three crescents)[138] and rastra (10 staves per page).[139] They thus form a coherent, early group among Handel's Italian autographs.[140] Since I could assign HWV 172 to Civitavecchia, March 1707, and the

---

[137] The "cantata a voce solo con VV" in the same bill may well be "Ah crudel" HWV 78, possibly performed on 2 Sept. 1708 (above, pp. 313, 321f). Handel's use of a discarded sheet from HWV 150 for this autograph does not indicate that the cantata was written in 1707 (HARRIS, *Handel as Orpheus*, p. 281), because for HWV 150 "an exact dating is not possible" (Bernd BASELT, *Händel-Handbuch*, II, 572).

[138] HARRIS, *Händel in Florenz*, notes 12 and 15, cites Heawood's plausible identification of this watermark with Venice (likewise Aldo CHEMELLI and Clemente LUNELLI, *Filigrane Trentine*, Trent, Alcione, 1980, p. 198: heavy Venetian paper, used especially for "music manuscripts or administrative documents"), yet assigns it not to this city, but to Florence (pp. 45f, following an old and unfounded assumption of Chrysander). This error invalidates also the subsequent elaboration of her views regarding cities and dates, compromising her 'chronological' discussion of musical styles in *Le cantate* and *Handel as Orpheus*. For very detailed studies of the scribes and the watermarks in the Italian autographs and copies of Handel's music, cf. WATANABE, *Die Kopisten* (cit., 1970), and *The Paper* (cit., 1981). WATANABE/MARX, *Händels italienische Kopisten* (cit., 1987) and WATANABE, *The Music-Paper* (cit., 1993) are largely revised versions of Watanabe's two earlier articles, repeating much of their useful information. But the occasions of the compositions are not taken into consideration. Very incomplete in all four articles are the references to the dated copyists' bills and, in WATANABE/MARX, pp. 204f, the list of extant copies (including only seven of the very numerous cantatas!) from Ruspoli's collection. (Such copies of Caldara's cantatas are identified by W. Kirkendale in *AC* 2007, Appendix 2a). In *The Paper*, p. 134, the date of the bill of 28 Aug. 1708 is misprinted as "1707". Contrary to WATANABE/MARX, p. 226, the handwriting of the text in their Abb. 4 is not that of the copyist Francesco Lancani, as is evident from the bills and the many copies of Caldara's music written by this scribe, e.g. GB-Lbl Add. 34056 and *AC* 2007, Plate 16.

[139] A bill for harpsichord strings, quills, and paper of 18 March 1708 specifies "carta da musica a 10 tirata lunga tre giulij", as Domenico Castrucci had ordered (vol. A 45, after list 30 [18 March - 8 May 1708]). Such paper was still being purchased for Caldara in 1712 (*AC* 1966 p. 67 = AC 2007 p. 84). In each case, the composer decided in advance how many lines he needed for his score and instructed the stationer accordingly.

[140] Together with HWV 113 and 156 (absent from Ruspoli bills). Thus these six cantatas are placed by WATANABE at the beginning of his approximately 'chronological' list (*The Music-Paper*, p. 205; only HWV 116 was not included in Harris' "first group" of five cantatas, note 35). The

autograph of HWV 232 is dated Rome, April 1707, it can now be assumed that all five works in this group of autographs were composed in Rome during the first months of Handel's sojourn there. Would Handel's **handwriting** have changed so suddenly that it could be a criterion for distinguishing between works composed only months apart (in this case 'Florence, 1706' [!], rather than Rome, winter 1706/07), as Harris believed?[141] In the two operatic scores from these years Handel even employed two styles of handwriting in alternation (see below, p. 399). Nor does musical **style**, of course, permit such accurate dating.[142] The subject of the *Lucrezia* **text** of HWV 145 is clearly Roman (possibly a first homage to the *genius loci* of the new patron on the Tiber), not Florentine, and Mainwaring's location of it "at Rome" (p. 200) carries more authority than Chrysander's assumption for Florence, based not on the text, but on a singer's name. (For these and further arguments, see above, pp. 318ff). HWV 90, 116, and 145 are included in what I suggest constituted a series of one cantata per weekly *conversazione* during eleven weeks between December 1706 and February 1707 (see above, p. 368). Since also for "Tu fedel" HWV 171 (Harris, p. 48: "Roman paper"!) no proof against Roman provenance is presented, not one of the titles appearing in the Ruspoli bills can be assigned, as Harris imagined, to Florence.

Harris fails also to provide the slightest archival documentation (so abundant for Rome) to sustain her 'Florentine' speculations.[143] Recent research has demonstrated that Prince Ferdinando Medici was less supportive of Handel than hitherto presumed. It was not he, but his German-speaking brother Gian Gastone in Prague who met Handel in Hamburg.[144] The composer may have been alienated from Fer-

---

use of double hyphens in this group of seven autographs indicates the early date, as does the German signature "Händel" (only in HWV 145, 156, and 196), rather than the Italian "Hendel". The HWV-numbers for the cantatas are, of course, not chronological, but alphabetical.

[141] *Handel as Orpheus*, pp. 380f, note 1, misattributes to Watanabe an assignment of "Hendel, non può mia musa" HWV 117 to 1707 rather than to the year of its earliest bill, 1708, "on the basis of handwriting". In general, Watanabe wisely refrained from assigning specific years or cities to cantatas through handwriting or watermarks.

[142] Only if little or no biobibliographical/archival documentation were available, might one, as a last resort, have attempted a *hypothetical* chronology on the basis of style, as in HARRIS, *Le cantate*, tav. 1 (somewhat revised in *Handel as Orpheus*, pp. 90-106), where cantatas are even removed from their context in the bills (cf. the no less than 15 [!] groups on pp. 269-287, confused by misinterpretations of watermarks) – let alone the assignments to cities or patrons – for a period of less than three years is too indistinct and the groups are too small (only 4-5 works each) to admit convincing conclusions. In many cases the musical style will depend more upon the specific text and occasion than upon a 'stylistic chronology' of such a brief period.

[143] She repeatedly cites as authority for information on the Medici ("modern scholarship"; p. 385, notes 64, 66ff, 70, 74f) "especially" the muck-raking scandal-monger Christopher HIBBERT who churned out innumerable thrillers on subjects as diverse as the Medici and Mussolini, and informed us that Prince Ferdinando (1663-1713) patronized not only Handel, but also Jacopo Peri (1561-1633): "He corresponded with Jacopo Peri, Bernardo Pasquini and Handel, all of whom were invited to Florence to collaborate with him" (*The Rise and Fall of the House of Medici*, London, Penguin Books, 1974, p. 300)!

[144] Contrary to STROHM, *Händel in Italia*, pp. 154ff. Cf. Werner BRAUN, *Georg Friedrich Händel und Gian Gastone von Toskana*, «Händel-Jahrbuch», XXXIV, 1988, pp. 109-123, where a presence

dinando as recipient of affection from the prince's beloved virtuosa Vittoria Tarquini (see p. 383, Sophie of Hanover and Mainwaring). Ferdinando recommended him in a letter of 9 November 1709 only lukewarmly as "più che mediocre nella musica" ["more than mediocre in music"],[145] and did not entrust to him a single of the many operas he had performed in Pratolino.[146] Almost nothing is yet known of an involvement of Ferdinando with cantatas,[147] a genre so widely cultivated in Rome.

Handel left Rome for Naples at the beginning of May 1708, still dated the *cantata a 3* HWV 201 there on 12 July, and had returned to Rome (with express coaches?) by 14 July.[148] No other visit of his to Naples is known. The four cantatas written on 'Neapolitan' paper ("Mentre il tutto" HWV 130 Angelini, "Quando sperasti"

---

in Hamburg for Ferdinando is rightly excluded and for Gian Gastone is securely documented only for Oct.-Dec. 1703. There is no evidence that Gian Gastone heard Handel's opera *Nerone* in Hamburg in 1705, as Harris, *Handel as Orpheus*, p. 40, would like to believe. He returned from Prague to Florence in June or July of that year, and according to Mainwaring, p. 49, Handel arrived there soon afterwards. (The date of 1706 in Harris *et al.* thus should be corrected).

[145] Mario Fabbri, *Alessandro Scarlatti e il Principe Ferdinando Medici*, Florence, Olschki, 1962, p. 24.

[146] Carlo Vitali and Antonello Furnari, *Händels Italienreise – neue Dokumente, Hypothesen und Interpretationen*, «Göttinger Händel-Beiträge», IV, 1991, pp. 60f, 64. Cf. also Rainer Heyink (editor of *Rodrigo* for the *Hallische Händel-Ausgabe*), *Georg Friedrich Händels 'Rodrigo': Anmerkungen zur Entstehungsgeschichte, Quellenlage und Rekonstruktion*, «Händel-Jahrbuch», XLIX, 2003, pp. 332f: for a sojourn in Florence exist "astonishingly few documentary traces". Heyink believes: "There is no question ... of continual free access to the court" – which may be true for 1707. "It still cannot be documented that Handel ever composed for Ferdinando Medici. Thus is lacking every testimony for the assumption, repeatedly converted into fact in the Handel literature, that the commission for *Rodrigo* came from Ferdinando personally. ... Ellen T. Harris also lacks corresponding proof; ... nevertheless, the writer presented the hypothesis ...". However, Handel may well have heard operas performed in Pratolino, since later in London five of his own new operas – HWV 19, 30, 33, 36, 38 – were based on libretti of Antonio Salvi for Pratolino (1703, 1707-10). Thus Riepe's categorical rejection (p. 95) of Strohm's reasonable hypothesis is not fully justified – cf. Reinhard Strohm, *Handel's Italian Journey as a European Experience*, in his *Essays on Handel and Italian Opera*, Cambridge UP, 1985, p. 11. This would provide a better explanation for Handel's absence from Rome during the winter 1707/8 and after 11 Sept. 1708 (i.e. to hear operas in Pratolino/Florence) than the two visits to Hamburg suggested by John H. Roberts, *A New Handel Aria, or Hamburg Revisited*, in *Georg Friedrich Händel – ein Lebensinhalt: Gedenkschrift für Bernd Baselt (1934-1993)*, Halle, Händel-Haus, 1995, pp. 113-130, and traceable to a certainly inaccurate statement of Johann Mattheson. The conditions of modern American jet-setting did not apply to travel in the 18th century. The means for long-distance transportation were stage coaches, which one normally rode for 6-7 hours per day. Since the trip from Augsburg to Venice consumed no less than 17 days, Rome to Hamburg – approximately three times as far – might have taken ca. 50 days, the return trip more than three months, at great expense! (cf. Ludwig Schudt, *Italienreisen im 17. und 18. Jahrhundert*, Vienna/Munich, Schroll, 1959, p. 155). Not only was travel across the Alps avoided in the winter (when it would be slower, more dangerous, and uncomfortable), but Handel is documented in Italy still until 19 Oct. 1707 and again on 26 Feb. 1708 (as mentioned by Roberts, p. 126).

[147] Only one cantata manuscript which can be connected with Ferdinando, I-Bc DD.50, containing, *inter al.*, a single piece by one of the musicians of the Medici court (Martino Bitti), has come to light. Cf. W. Kirkendale, *The Court Musicians*, p. 436. Contrary to *Ruspoli Documents*, 1967, p. 225, the *Pianto di Maria* HWV 234, which Mario Fabbri associated with Handel and Ferdinando, is now known to have been composed not by the Saxon, but by Giovanni Battista Ferrandini (1710-91!) – cf. «Göttinger Händel-Beiträge», V, 1994, pp. 276-283.

[148] Above, pp. 309f.

HWV 153 autogr., "Sento là che ristretto" HWV 161[b] autogr., "Stanco più di sof-frire" HWV 167[b] Angelini) were hardly destined for a Neapolitan patron, but rather for the marquis who paid for the copies[149] (HWV 153 and 167[b] on 9 August, HWV 130 on 28 August 1707 [PS: *recte* 1708], HWV 161[b] on 31 August 1709, as part of a [gift?] collection) and expected work to be rendered by Handel in return for the long-term hospitality, just as Caldara had to fulfill his quota for Ruspoli even when he was given leave to travel to Lombardy and Vienna.[150] HWV 161[b] may be merely a transposition of the 'Ruspoli' soprano cantata HWV 161[a] for contralto. [PS: It has been argued, not without some justification, that HWV 161[b] probably preceded 161[a] and was written during Handel's visit to Naples].[151] The paper of the autograph [PS: *recte*: copy] of HWV 130 could have been brought by Handel from Naples to Rome, as indicated by Angelini's bill of 28 August.[152] If Angelini had copied this cantata by 9 August, he would have included it in his bill of that date.

Of cantatas existing in versions for different voice ranges, it was assumed by Har-ris[153] – again without proof – that the soprano versions, especially the Ruspoli copies in Münster, were transpositions for Durastante of earlier works, possibly composed for other patrons. In the absence of dated sources, of course, it is rarely possible to estab-lish with full certainty in which direction a transposition occurred, i.e. which was the earlier version.[154] Of the seven cantatas from the Ruspoli bills having transpositions

---

[149] *RD* Doc. 24f, 35.

[150] *AC* 1966 pp. 63ff, 69 = *AC* 2007 pp. 80ff, 86.

[151] [PS: HWV, p. 587; Graydon BEEKS, *The Curious History of a Handel Cantata: 'Sento là che ristretto' and its Various Versions*, in *Florilegium Musicae: Studi in onore di Carolyn Gianturco*, Pisa, ETS, 2004, pp. 294f. But when it is stated here that "it is not readily apparent" why I included An-gelini's copy of HWV 167b among the cantatas written on Neapolitan paper, it was overlooked that its paper is the same as that used for the autograph of *Aci, Galatea e Polifemo* – cf. WATANABE, *The Music Paper*, p. 166, and *HR* 330 = below, p. 390].

[152] Above p. 341, Doc. 25. The (ubiquitous) soprano range of this cantata and HWV 153 does not provide the slightest argument for an association with Naples, as HARRIS suggested, nor does the paper prove that Handel wrote cantatas "for opposite sides of the War of Spanish Succession" (*Han-del as Orpheus*, pp. 23, 177, 209, 280, 396). Handel did not compose music for the imperial occu-piers of Naples, but for friends of Ruspoli residing there, who now were obliged to make certain compromises with the Austrians. The Duke of Alvito was not "austrofilo" (STROHM, *Händel in Italia*, p. 169) but, like Ruspoli, raised a regiment *against* the Hapsburgs and swore an oath of allegiance to them only when forced to do so in order to avoid confiscation of his property – RIEPE, p. 91, contrary also to STROHM, *Handel's Italian Journey*, pp. 5 and 9 ("supporter of the Emperor"). Cf. also Anto-nello FURNARI, *I rapporti tra Händel e i Duchi d'Alvito*, in *Händel e gli Scarlatti a Roma*, ed. Nino Pirrotta and Agostino Ziino, Florence, Olschki, 1987, pp. 76ff (also p. 78: "There is no basis for sustaining that ... the cantatas composed by Handel in Naples ... were written for the Gallio", dukes of Alvito – contrary to HARRIS, p. 145). Furnari suggests that the words "d'Alvito" at the end of the Ms. of the serenata *Aci, Galatea e Polifemo* HWV 72 could refer to the place rather than to a ded-icatee, and, that, on the basis of the unsuitable text, the work might not have been performed for the wedding of Tolomeo Saverio Gallio (pp. 73, 75), though commissioned by the bride's aunt. Cf. also VITALI/FURNARI, pp. 56f.

[153] *Op. cit.*, p. 285, and *Le cantate*, p. 64.

[154] Tangible proof of the direction of transpositions does not yet seem to have been presented. Only for HWV 167, EWERHART, p. 144, suspected that in the scribe's "Vorlage" the cantata was a

(HWV 102[a-b], 125[a-b], 126[a-c], 127[a-b], 139[a-c], 161[a-c], and 167[a-b]), only one has autographs for more than one version (161[b-c]), and these are of little use for an absolute chronology because the earliest version does not seem to have survived in autograph. Significantly, with the only other of these cantatas extant in autographs, HWV 127[a] and 139[a], it is the soprano versions which are presented there, and the alto versions exist only in copies (HWV 127[b], 139[b]); also the much later versions HWV 127[c] and 139[c] are for soprano, perhaps reflecting an original preference. The HWV assigns the letter 'a' also to the soprano versions of HWV 125, 126, and 161. This evidence – from the autographs in the only relevant cases where original manuscripts can be confronted with obviously later copies – would seem more convincing than the greater diffusion of some of the alto versions in copies, which could be merely coincidental.[155] Be that as it may, the argument that the alto cantatas were not composed for Ruspoli simply because this patron was known to have had only a soprano in his service must be laid to rest, since I can now demonstrate that he had also Lucrezia D'André at this time (see pp. 363, 402) and that she was a contralto. The cast list in the libretto of Alessandro Scarlatti's *Eraclea* (Parma, 1700) identifies her with the role of Irene, which was set for this voice range. The smaller number of Handel's cantatas for alto is consistent with the less active part played by this older singer in Ruspoli's house.

It is unlikely that someone of Ruspoli's wealth and ambition would have been satisfied by collecting music which had been composed for other patrons. Since Angelini presented no bill during Handel's sojourn in Naples, but one for eleven cantatas on 9 August, soon after his return to Rome, I believe that these represent Handel's accumulated 'obligatory quota' of one cantata per week for eleven weeks' absence. Angelini may very well have accompanied him to Naples. All these assumptions are confirmed also by the fact that the two works known to have been composed in Naples, not for Ruspoli – the serenata *Aci, Galatea e Polifemo* HWV 72, finished on 16 June 1708 in Naples, and the cantata "Se tu non lasci amore" HWV 201[a], dated 12 July [i.e. in Naples] – do not appear in Ruspoli bills.[156]

In her most recent publication on Handel's cantatas, Ellen Harris again has devoted much effort to provide a chronology, assign patrons, and reduce radically the Ruspoli 'canon' (now from more than 50 to ca. 25 works!).[157] She draws upon the

---

third lower, i.e. not in d-minor, but b-minor. The reason for this assumption lies in a few (senseless) sharps placed before the notes 'e' in the d-minor version, possibly retained from a b-minor version with a key signature of one sharp, where they would have been necessary before the notes 'c'. [PS: It is surprising that HARRIS should state that "of the eight cantatas in the Santini collection ... composed for alto or, in one case, for bass, all but one are transposed into the soprano range" – *Handel's London Cantatas*, «Göttinger Händel-Beiträge», I, 1984, p. 88. A glance at the HWV readily shows that of all the Ruspoli-Santini cantatas, only HWV 161b and 167a can be suspected of having been preceded by a version for alto; for all the rest, the earliest sources are clearly for soprano].

155 Cf. Peter Allsop, quoted in JAMS, LV, 2002, p. 537.

156 Cf. above, p. 318.

157 *Handel as Orpheus*, p. 89 (reducing *all* Roman cantatas to 28 – contradicted by her note 4) and Appendix I: "Cantata Chronology", which unfortunately creates more confusion than clarification and thus flaws her attempts at 'chronological' discussions of musical style. Likewise *eadem, Le cantate*, p. 65.

diplomatic studies of Burrows/Ronish, while fatally disregarding their wise caveats. They understood:[158]

Handel's autographs from the Italian period do not relate watermarks to specific locations for composition, [but reflect only] different sources of paper supply within Italy. ...
Paper characteristics of Handel's Italian-period autographs do not seem to be very closely tied to specific places or dates of composition. ... There is no simple chronological or geographic sequence to be derived from the paper types. On the present evidence, it seems either that Handel carried supplies of manuscript paper around with him during his Italian travels or that the principal paper types were available to him in different places.

Stationers' products were by no means limited to local providers, but often imported from foreign countries. Thus a long series of bills of Giuseppe Fiorese,[159] "cartolaro dell'eccellentissima casa Ruspoli", for 1707 includes "penne d'Olanda", "cera di Spagna", "carta francese" ["quills of Holland", "wax of Spain", "French paper"].[160] (There is only a very slight possibility that these designations refer not to provenance, but to Italian products 'in the manner of'). Since the bill of the printer Giovanni Francesco Chracas for the libretti of Handel's *serenata* "Oh come chiare e belle" HWV 143 specified "carta francese",[161] it was possible for us to identify the watermark of this paper, which occurs not only in the libretti, but also among Fiorese's bills of 1707: a dove above three 'monti' within a circle.[162] But this watermark does not appear among Handel's manuscripts, and thus the composer did not use Fiorese's "French" paper. Much more relevant is an entry among the expenses for the hunting party in Cerveteri: on 28 February 1707 the *scalco* noted "carta fiorentina quinterni sei"! It is well known that the paper most used by Handel in Rome (also for *Diana cacciatrice*) has the watermark of a lily within a double circle.[163] Both the expense account and the lily, the familiar emblem of Florence, suggest that the paper might have been produced in the Tuscan capital. But since very little documentation

---

[158] Pp. XXIV, XXVI.

[159] One of the most important stationers in Rome, with his shop on Piazza S. Pantaleo, patronized by Ruspoli for at least 39 years. Cf. Saverio FRANCHI, *Le impressioni sceniche: dizionario bio-bibliografico degli editori e stampatori romani e laziali di testi drammatici e libretti per musica dal 1579 al 1800*, Rome, Edizioni di Storia e Letteratura, 1994-2002, I, 530n, 577n, 835n; II, 51, no. 28. On Fiorese's activity for Ruspoli, see *AC*, index.

[160] Vol. A 44, after list 129, no. 153. The same formulations occur in Fiorese's later bills, e.g. still in vol. B 87, no. 177 (for Jan.-Dec. 1724). In 1708 Ruspoli's printer Antonio De' Rossi used "carta ondata di Germania" for the libretti of the *Oratorio per la Santissima Annunziata* of Ottoboni/Scarlatti (SL 17273) – see above, p. 334, Doc. 13.

[161] Above, p. 342, Doc. 28, contrary to *HR* 331.

[162] Edward HEAWOOD, *Watermarks Mainly of the 17th and 18th Centuries*, Hilversum, Paper Publications Society, 1950, no. 162, located an almost identical watermark in Rome 1685. In the libretto the letters "M" and "T" within the circle (no. 162) are missing, as is the "F" above it (some of Fiorese's bills and Heawood's no. 161, found in Rome 1646).

[163] Cf. HEAWOOD, plates 203-270 (especially nos. 1636f, found in Rome in 1693 and 1705), and Gerhard PICCARD, *Wasserzeichen Lilie*, Stuttgart, Kohlhammer, 1983 (especially Abb. 950-965, found in Rome, 1561-80).

exists for determining where papers were *manufactured*, even the most comprehensive repertoires of watermarks – Briquet, Heawood, Piccard, etc. – generally had to limit themselves to indicating where and when papers were *used*, on the basis of both manuscripts and printed books bearing dates and names of cities. Literature on Handel sometimes designates the paper with the lily as 'Roman', after the city where he used it.[164] One can no longer assume that this paper was manufactured in Rome (it was certainly used also in other places) any more than one can argue that Handel's music written on "carta fiorentina" must have been composed in Florence. Still, Ruspoli surely supplied him with this paper for his precious autographs, of a heavier quality than the ordinary "French" paper used for bills etc. His preference for the highly regarded Florentine product may have been conditioned by family tradition: his mother, née Corsini, was a granddaughter of Prince Ottaviano Medici; his paternal ancestors came from Florence; to this day a portrait of Cosimo I de' Medici hangs as the sole painting on one wall of the reception room in the Palazzo Ruspoli – to mention only the most obvious Florentine connections.

Another untenable assumption is that Handel waited until finishing a batch of one type of paper before beginning another.[165] This most certainly does not apply to his Italian years, since no less than six autographs of this period begin with one type of paper and continue with another.[166]

Work employing exclusively diplomatic methods can create an illusion of absolute reliability, since these are cautiously limited to the physical description of paper, watermarks, rastra, scribal hands, etc. In the interest of objectivity, such work (Watanabe, Burrows/Ronish) [167] will often avoid drawing conclusions from such descriptions, however desirable this may be. Harris, on the other hand, adds extensive hypotheses to the diplomatic work of Burrows/Ronish, and the 'paper arguments' she presents are almost entirely speculative and often incorrect. The scholars mentioned give very little or no consideration to the content of the works or to the important historical-biographical facts which can sometimes better determine the date, place, patron, and occa-

---

[164] Thus HARRIS, *Händel in Florenz*, pp. 46, 48, and *Handel as Orpheus*, pp. 267, 270.

[165] HARRIS, p. 267: her "premise that Handel acquired his music paper in batches and worked through a single lot before requesting or purchasing more". BURROWS/RONISH admit that this assumption might have some validity for Handel *only* after he settled in London (p. XXVI). But the well known satirical depictions of Handel in London still show him amidst a mess of papers, food, drink, etc.

[166] HWV 5, 90, 116, 145, 172, and 232 all begin with the 'Venetian' watermark of three crescent moons, then continue with the fleur-de-lis used in most of Handel's subsequent Roman autographs. Cf. WATANABE, *The Paper*, p. 132, on "Dixit Dominus" HWV 232: "In all probability Handel had brought with him the 'Three Crescents' paper – from Florence or Venice, at any rate from North Italy, to Rome to finish his composition, supplying the Roman paper for the last part". But since Handel arrived in Rome several months earlier than Watanabe assumed, he had ample time to compose all of this work in that city. The patronage would exclude for HWV 232 not only Florence, but also Venice (suggested by WATANABE/MARX, pp. 201, 205).

[167] It is strange that BURROWS/RONISH should designate their work as "pioneering" (p. IX), when so much of it duplicates (and expands) the patient labors of Watanabe, more or less ignored also by Harris.

sion.[168] Thus we have seen that "Udite il mio consiglio" cannot be connected with Florence, nor the French and Spanish cantatas with Ottoboni on the basis of the paper.[169] Also: no documents indicate that Handel ever resided with the cardinals Pamphilj, Ottoboni, or Colonna, contrary to the suggestions of Marx for January-May and Harris for the summer 1707.[170] And no composition of Handel has yet been convincingly attributed to Ottoboni's patronage.[171] Of course the composer *improvised* brilliantly on the harpsichord at *conversazioni* of three cardinals and even during an evening with the Vatican castratos.[172] But only for Ruspoli was he obliged to *compose* large amounts of vocal music, in return for room, board, a coach, sedan chairs, copies, etc. during the better part of two years. We need no longer be concerned that the radical reduction of his works for this patron be taken seriously.

* * *

In *libro mastro* 2, expenses of delegates for musicians, also for Handel, are to be found from the end of 1708. But since he had long left, they add little to his biography.[173] More important is what emerges from the first pages of this volume.[174] These reveal that Ruspoli's wealth amounted to more than two million *scudi*. Of particular interest to us is information we find on one of the highest debtors, Cardinal Ottoboni, who had been Ruspoli's *amicissimo* since their

---

[168] For a particularly serious negative result of the narrow diplomatic perspective, see ch. 12-13.

[169] As done by HARRIS, *Handel as Orpheus*, pp. 275f.

[170] MARX, *Händel in Rom*, p. 133, and HARRIS, *Le cantate*, p. 63. Handel's name is mentioned nowhere in the extant accounts of Ottoboni.

[171] Cf. RIEPE, p. 79: "In fact as of now not a single composition by Handel can be proven to have been written for Ottoboni". The cardinal's importance for Handel was "surely tendentiously exaggerated" by Marx (*eadem*, p. 107, note 17). The note of Aloys Fuchs on the autograph of HWV 150 after 1834, associating this work with Ottoboni – probably influenced by Mainwaring – is far too late to have any value as a source (contrary to HARRIS, p. 276).

[172] R. A. STREATFEILD, *Handel in Italy*, «The Musical Antiquary», I, 1909/10, p. 6, letter of Annibale Merlini to Ferdinando Medici, 24 Sept. 1707; above, ch. 10.

[173] The payments are irregular, and not itemized, but lumped together. Opening 313 left: 31 May 1708, "[al maestro di casa Angelo Valerij] pagati alla S.ra Margarita Durastante Cantarina per sua provisione" and "vitto al Sig.r Giorgio Endel compositore di musica, sonatori, e musici per diversi oratori", the large sum of 177.31 *scudi*; on the same day "al [dispensatore Francesco Maria] De Golla a pane ... per la tavola del S.r Giorgio Endel nelli mesi di marzo et aprile ... 3.65"; 24 Oct., "al Valerij" for various musicians and "al suddetto De Golla, rinborso di spese fatte per la tavola del Sassone e a libretti copie di cantate et altro", again for the very high sum of 291.05 *scudi*; 3 Nov., "al Valerij inconto a denari in maggiore somma ... per la tavola di Monsù Endel, alla Cantarina per provisione di settembre et ottobre" and "a sonatori et altro speso in occasione delli conversationi fatte nelle domeniche ... 64.96"; 9 Dec., "[al De Golla] vino ... et aceto ... per la tavola del Sassone et altro ... 12.70". Opening 313 right: "al De Golla a pane ... date a diversi che hanno lavorato in cucina per pasti fatti di S. E. per la tavola di Monsu Endel, et a diversi servitori presi per supplemento in occasione delle villegiature ... 7.43". For other, less specific references to music see openings 224 left-right, 238 right, 240 left, 312f left-right, 415 left.

[174] *Ibid.*, opening 1, 25 Sept. 1705.

youth and was still present when he died. On 21 October 1700 he received, for 21 years at 3% interest, the large loan of 11,300 *scudi*,[175] roughly four times the annual salary of a cardinal. This means that also for Handel the relationship Ottoboni-Ruspoli must be seen in a new light. That the cardinal was "the most powerful patron" in Rome, as one often reads,[176] is an illusion, for his own purse had long been empty. The debts which he left at his death were enormous.[177]

With Saverio Franchi's bibliographical study of the oratorios connected with Ruspoli[178] we begin to realize the true dimensions of this gentleman's patronage. For oratorios alone no less than 71 productions could be identified with him (or his wife) from 1695 until 1727, some of the earliest ones hypothetically. Adding Ruspoli's subvention given to Ottoboni, the creditor rather than the cardinal might be regarded as the most important patron of music in Italy during the late baroque era and surely for Handel there. We now know that our composer *lived with Ruspoli for almost two years*, not for merely "two months".[179] Subsequently Caldara was the prince's chapel master for more than seven years, eventually with lodging in the Ruspoli palace in Via del Corso, not to mention the earlier and later services of Alessandro Scarlatti, Francesco Gasparini *et al.* for him. This patron, whose "perfect knowledge of musical art" ("perfetta cognizione ... nell'arte della musica") was praised by Bernardo Gaffi already in 1700 and whose concerts, featuring music of Caldara, were rated by Uffenbach in 1715 as the best in Rome ("die besten allhier"),[180] should now be rated according to his merits[181] and no longer reduced to an appendix to Roman cardinals.[182]

---

175 *Ibid.*, openings 5, 89, etc.; the notary's deed in *Istromenti* 62, fasc. 195. Repayment occurred on 24 Dec. 1721 (*Libro mastro* 3, opening 436: 18,860.84 *scudi*, including interest). Since the loan was made precisely during the weeks between the death of Innocent XII on 9 Sept. and the election of Clement XI on 23 Nov. 1700, it was probably a move to gain Ottoboni's vote for Ruspoli's *papabile* uncle, Cardinal Galeazzo Marescotti.

176 E.g. MARX, *Händel in Rom*, p. 108.

177 VALESIO, VI, 356, mentions the sale of Ottoboni's property to pay debts of 170,000 *scudi*.

178 *Il principe Ruspoli*. This work contains also much information on the family.

179 *Hallische Händel-Ausgabe*, V/3, p. IX, possibly connected with his notion that "except for the indications [compilations!] in the *Händel-Handbuch* there is hardly any literature worth mentioning on the cantatas" (*ibid.*, p. VII); at that time we had one dissertation and sixteen articles dealing with Handel's cantatas, to which six more have subsequently been added. The hypothesis of MARX "that Handel lived in the Pamphilj palace during the months January to May 1707" (*Händel in Rom*, p. 113) cannot be taken seriously. In our commemorative inscription in the Bonelli palace, referring only to this location, the words "diversi mesi" can now be regarded as understated (cf. RIdM, XXI, 1986, pp. 201-205).

180 Quoted in *AC* 1966 p. 47 = *AC* 2007 pp. 59f. Gaffi appears in the Ruspoli payroll with a monthly salary of 3 *scudi*, at least from Sept. 1695 until July 1707 (vol. 383).

181 That BASELT wrote scornfully of Ruspoli can be forgiven, for he still lived in a communist state – *Der spanische Erbfolgekrieg, Italien und Händel*, in *Aufklärerische Tendenzen in der Musik des 18. Jahrhunderts und ihre Rezeption*, ed. Bernd Baselt and Siegfried Flesch, Halle, Martin-Luther-

It would be interesting to know what led Ruspoli to admit Handel and Durastante into his *famiglia*. That they were, for him, at that time still unknown personalities is unlikely (we have seen, p. 364, that he incurred considerable expenses for the singer even before she arrived in Rome). In the absence of firm documentation, we can, of course, hardly even speculate on the source and nature of his knowledge of them. But if he had heard that Handel's operas *Rodrigo* and *Agrippina* had been performed with great success in Florence and Venice, respectively, this could have justified his decision to accommodate the two musicians, with their servants and Durastante's relatives, immediately upon their arrival in Rome. We must return to Mainwaring's account: [183]

Florence ... was his first [!] destination. ... At the age of eighteen he made the Opera of *Rodrigo* [there], for which he was presented with 100 sequins [= *scudi*], and a service of plate. This may serve for a sufficient testimony of its favourable reception. Vittoria [Tarquini], who was much admired as an actress, and a singer, bore a principal part in this opera.

The veracity of the statement on *Rodrigo* has been questioned ever since Mattheson's [malicious] threefold assertion that Handel did not leave for Italy before 1709 and then travelled to Venice for the performance of *Agrippina* in 1710.[184] But the "age of eighteen" can have been derived ultimately only from

---

Universität, 1987, p. 28 (reprinted in «Analecta Musicologica», XXX, 1998). On pp. 20-30 this article 'borrows' extensively, quasi literally, from Reinhard STROHM (*Handel's Italian Journey*). In an equally astonishing and rare lapse, Strohm's abusive judgement of Ruspoli in the style of the vituperative propaganda of the German Democratic Republic, is heightened even further here. Handel's Roman patron is hardly mentioned in Strohm's *Handel in Italia* and not at all in Marx's *Händel in Rom*.

[182] Harris seems to have been inspired by the bisexuality of Ferdinando Medici and an alleged homosexuality of Pamphilj and even of Ottoboni (who is known to have had several mistresses) when she downsizes Ruspoli with revisionistic speculations in favor of these three. Ruspoli, with a wife and eight children, decisively contradicts her assumption of "homoerotic context of the entire [!] cantata repertory" (p. 239), a repertoire composed by Handel overwhelmingly for him. There have been attempts, on the other hand, to give Ruspoli more than his due. According to BURROWS/RONISH, p. XIV, Tobia Nicotra forged 'Handel' autographs, including 'dedications' to Ruspoli. And a *Gloria* for solo soprano, recently touted promotionally by journalists as an unknown 'masterpiece' of Handel, has been connected with Ruspoli's patronage in Vignanello (notwithstanding my contrary recommendation in a letter to Marx of 14 May 2001) by an incorrect definition of the voice range and by instrumentation not limited by Handel to that place (cf. «Early Music», XXIX, 2001, p. 348, and XXX, 2002, pp. 254-260, where the attribution to Handel is seriously challenged, and again by John ROBERTS in a paper at the conference of the Handel Institute, London, 23-24 Nov. 2002). All works known to have been composed by Handel for Ruspoli appear in the accounts, as this piece does not.

[183] Pp. 49-50.

[184] MATTHESON's annotated translation of Mainwaring's biography, *Georg Friedrich Händels Lebensbeschreibung*, Hamburg, 1761, notes on pp. 37, 45, 61 ("1709 war er noch nicht aus Hamburg weg")!

the composer, who remembered that this was his age in 1703 when he met Gian Gastone de' Medici in Hamburg and was probably then encouraged to compose an opera for Florence, at least begun before he left for Italy, not performed until Gian Gastone returned to Florence in June (or – less likely – in July) of 1705. The identity of Gian Gastone, rather than Ferdinando Medici, and the dates are established in the excellent article of Werner Braun (cf. note 144), still overlooked by some writers. Handel indeed accepted the invitation and, as Mainwaring testified, came to Florence *"soon after* the Prince of Tuscany"* arrived. From today's perspective, this must have been in the early summer of 1705, and *Rodrigo* could have been performed not long afterwards – little more than a year and a half after the invitation. That it was full four years later (see below) exceeds all plausibility. Not only would the novelty of a 'child prodigy' have been diminished – the ambition of a young artist was always to be at the immediate disposal of a patron, as we know from the complimentary closes of the letters offering their services, during a century when life expectancy was much less than today. My recent researches confirm more and more Mainwaring's credibility.[185] He obtained his information from reliable sources: not only from two of Handel's closest associates, his amanuenses and copyists Smith, father and son, but, as also Donald Burrows pointed out: "the accuracy of these details lends support to the hypothesis that one of the main sources of the *Memoirs* was Handel himself, ... the only person in London who could have known as much about [his] early years" (further arguments follow).[186]

When Strohm found an anonymous libretto *Vincer se stesso è la maggior vittoria*, an opera performed "in Firenze nell'autunno dell'anno 1707 sotto la protezione del Serenissimo Principe [i.e. Ferdinando!] di Toscana", and observed that its content corresponded to *Rodrigo*, he believed that this libretto was for the first performance of Handel's opera, even though he noted considerable divergences between this text and the score. Variant versions of complete librettos, of course, were set innumerable times by different composers, and anonymous ones were often for pasticcios. Nevertheless, Strohm's opinion was immediately accepted, also by myself,[187] and is still stated as an unqualified fact at the very beginning of Heyink's article on *Rodrigo*. But Winton Dean and John Merrill Knapp, though still assuming the date

---

185 I must apologize to him for my judgement in *RD* 251. His authority, resented by Mattheson, was certainly much greater than that of a non-commital anonymous libretto.

186 Donald BURROWS, *Handel and Hanover*, in *Bach – Handel – Scarlatti*, ed. P. Williams, Cambridge UP, 1985, p. 37.

187 *Orgelspiel* 1988, p. 7.

1707 in their discussion of this opera, regarded the work as very naïve and arrived at devastating judgements of it, which could not be made of the music Handel composed during the years with Ruspoli: "numerous signs of immaturity", some arias "stunted", others "disproportionately long", coloraturas "at disastrous cost to dramatic consistency", "not ... without triviality", an "exquisite tune out of place in the mouth of [a] graceless tyrant", etc.[188] Today I believe that the autograph, deviating so much from *Vincer se stesso*, may represent a pre-Roman version, probably the first performance of Handel's earliest opera for Italy. Handel seems to have written the nine-movement [!] overture (with many dances), on three-moon paper, immediately after (or before?) his arrival in Italy, as a Franco-Germanic orchestral suite. The handwriting, almost calligraphic, is that of a very young person. May he not have used, for the rest of the score, the "carta fiorentina" with the lily already in Tuscany? And may he not have enlisted Angelini's services already in Florence (the last aria of Act I in the autograph contains several pages written by his hand) and then brought his trusted copyist with him when he moved from one city to another, in order not always to have to search for another one? Angelini is not documented in Rome in the earlier years of the eighteenth century. (His nickname "Panstufato" was probably applied sarcastically by the Romans. It means 'bread soup', made from warmed-up leftovers. This may indicate that Angelini was not only an outsider, but also collaborator of a composer who already was known for 'warmed-up' music or 'borrowings'). That he later in Rome copied two arias which appear only in the libretto[189] suggests that the score is the earlier source, for the premiere. We know that the last aria of Act I, "Per dar pregio all'amor mio", shares music with the first one from the cantata for Pamphilj, *Il delirio amoroso*: "Un pensiero voli in ciel", also copied by Angelini and dated 12 February 1707. Here, however, in the B-section, there is a new text with a splendid rhetorical figure for the underworld, "Averno": a *katabasis* after upward leaps of a minor ninth and even tenth. Thus it would seem that Handel's 'self-borrowing' in this case proceeded from the opera to the cantata, rather than in the opposite direction, as hitherto assumed. Another argument: the libretto's list of cast *does not include* Vittoria Tarquini, so admired by Mainwaring for her performance in Handel's opera. Strohm dismissed her quickly as a legend of 1707, putting the cart before the horse.[190] Also here, Mainwaring was probably right when

---

[188] *Handel's Operas, 1704-1726*, Oxford, Clarendon, 1987, pp. 100-107. On the overture, which possibly did not originate with the opera, cf. below and DEAN/KNAPP, p. 108.

[189] HEYINK, p. 337, nos. 7 and 38.

[190] *Händel in Italia*, p. 158. Also HEYINK, p. 329, still accepts the date 1707 (citing Mainwaring

he said that Handel had his opera performed with Vittoria during his first visit to Florence and was generously rewarded by the Grand Duke.

Also *Agrippina* must be examined briefly. Mainwaring continues:

He stayed near a year in Florence. ... Venice was his next [!] resort. ... He was strongly importuned to compose an opera. But there was so little prospect of either honour or advantage from such an undertaking, that he was very unwilling to engage in it. At last, however, he consented, and in three weeks finished his *Agrippina*.[191]

As we have seen, Mainwaring testified also that Vittoria [Tarquini] sang a lead role in *Agrippina*, which must have been *before* the performance with Margarita Durastante and Diamante Scarabelli as Agrippina and Poppea, respectively, in the winter 1709/10 (SL 508); this could be a revival. Here too, the libretti for an earlier performance could be lost, possibly as a result of the confusion of the war. Often opera research assumes that every performance must have had a printed libretto. But we still know too little about those which did not, or have none extant, although a good number of such cases have been documented.[192] Libretti were generally printed only in several hundred copies. Of three hundred printed for Handel's serenata *Olinto*, only one survives, and of the 1,500 [exceptional!] for the *Resurrezione*, only six.[193]

The applause which Mainwaring describes for *Agrippina* ("with shouts and acclamations of '*viva il caro Sassone*' and other expressions of approbation too extravagant to be mentioned")[194] savors of that for a newly arrived quasi-child prodigy assisted by a virtuosa such as Vittoria, not for a composer who had already been in the country for three or even four and a half years and in the opera metropolis at least twice for several months without composing an opera.

The handwriting in the autographs of *Rodrigo* and *Agrippina* is "very early", as already observed for the latter by Watanabe, who could not reconcile this with the accepted later dating. It has "a few double hyphens", used "until about the beginning of May 1707", "short-stemmed notes" and "quavers of this type, but with somewhat oval note-heads" in most arias here and in Venetian cantatas.[195] Yet he then conforms obediently to the 'facts' of the secondary

---

only as an "amorous anecdote") and seems to have overlooked the independent confirmation by Sophie of Hanover (above, p. 8).

[191] Pp. 51f.

[192] See, for example, W. KIRKENDALE, *The Court Musicians in Florence*, pp. 476, 486, 491, 507, 509, 517, 532f (Giuseppe Maria Orlandini, a creditor for Handel's borrowings).

[193] Plate XI.9, pp. 342, Doc. 28, and pp. 334f, Doc. 13.

[194] P. 53.

[195] *The Music Paper*, pp. 201, 203.

literature. I may add that in the arias of these operas most of the note-stems are vertical, the flags curved and narrow, almost always carefully and legibly, though very densely written, with a thick pen. However, Handel seems to have used a different, thinner pen for most recitatives. Here the notes are almost always slanted, very hastily written, almost as if by another hand (thin lines, flags on eighth notes are straight and widely separated, etc.). The writing of the 'hit' aria "Ho un non so che nel cor" seems still rather pedantic, with the violin part written out, instead of being simply indicated "colla voce" (it doubles the voice). The aria was in any case composed before the performance of *Agrippina* in 1709/10, because it appeared already in Carlo Sigismondo Capece's libretto and Handel's score for the *Resurrezione*, 1708. Did Ruspoli know of a still earlier success of this aria when he was planning the *Resurrezione*? He may well have expressed the wish to Capece, secretary of his friend the queen of Poland, to have this aria included, to guarantee applause in advance. For *Agrippina* of 1709/10 he may have inserted at the last minute Poppea's aria "Per punir che m'ha ingannata". The text is not yet contained in the libretto.[196] Could Handel in this aria have depicted his own situation – that he had nothing more to gain from Ruspoli and therefore would soon leave the country?

Handel certainly did not remain idle between Hamburg and Rome. Hypothetically I offer a schedule: departure from Hamburg during the spring 1705, via Halle (visit with mother) and Weißenfels; arrival in Florence during the second half of June, where Gian Gastone had just arrived;[197] premiere of *Rodrigo* there in the fall at the latest; to Venice no later than the end of January 1706, discovered there during carnival by "Scarlatti" (Ash Wednesday was on 20 February); meeting with the Ottoboni family there in March; premiere of *Agrippina* in a yet unidentified theater in November with Vittoria and Margarita; Handel's and Margarita's departure very soon thereafter and their arrival in Rome about the first week of December.

Why did Handel leave the eternal city? Here we must again consider the historical situation, too often ignored, in which Handel found himself in the fall of 1708, when people were terrified by the approach of the imperial troops, fearing a new sack of Rome, and fleeing from the city in droves.[198] Also Durastante left during the same week as Handel,[199] accompanying Ru-

---

[196] Contrary to BASELT, *Händel-Handbuch*, I, 89.

[197] BRAUN, *Händel und Gian Gastone*, p. 112, where the conflicting testimonies are cited.

[198] Musical reflections of this turbulent time are presented also above, ch. 8.

[199] Above, p. 314: "per sgomberare le stanze per la Sig.ra Marg.a".

URSULA KIRKENDALE

spoli's family to Frascati. Only in January 1709, a cease-fire was reached between pope and emperor. Immediately after being made Prince of Cerveteri on 5 February, Ruspoli appointed as his *maestro di cappella* Antonio Caldara, who had recently distinguished himself by composing music for the bride of King Charles III, the future Emperor Charles VI. A large cantata of his had already been copied by Angelini in Rome before 17 October 1708.[200]

When Handel heard of Caldara's appointment by Ruspoli, he must have resented it very much, having hoped that the marquis, now prince, would welcome him back after the hostilities subsided. I believe this is the reason why he apparently did not speak later about his major patron and that Mainwaring thus failed to mention him. I do not think that Handel's flight was 'religiously' motivated, but suspect that this generally accepted Protestant explanation was merely a rationalization on his part. His pride made him unwilling to admit that he really would have preferred to remain in what must be considered one of the most important musical centers of Europe, if only he could have lived there in security. But Ruspoli, after having been made prince by the pope, could not consider appointing a protestant chapel master.

With this article I believe to have introduced the date, the place, and the occasion of the first performance of a dozen important works. "Arresta il passo" was Handel's formal debut in Rome, probably on 25 December 1706, marking his official entry into the service of Ruspoli; "Donna che in ciel" was performed on 6 February 1707 in Santa Maria in Aracoeli for the commemoration of the liberation from the earthquake; *Diana cacciatrice* on 23 February in Cerveteri during the first day of the annual deer hunt; "Udite il mio consiglio" on 18 March in Civitavecchia at the banquet which Ruspoli held on his brigantine for the governors of the city; "Dixit Dominus" on 1 May in Frascati for the Spaniards' feast of King Philip's nameday; Pamphilj's *Trionfo del tempo* the following day with Ruspoli's musicians in Palazzo Bonelli or the Collegio Clementino, alluding to the forthcoming contest of the Roman artists; "Un'alma innamorata" probably 6 June in Vignanello; the French and Spanish cantatas in July in Rome for La Trémouille and Del Giudice; "Cor fedel" September or early October in the *cancelleria* for Ottoboni. Also the first performances of Scarlatti's oratorio *Il giardino di rose* and, possibly, of Handel's cantata "Nella stagion che di viole e rose" could be located: at Massa on 3 April, Laetare Sunday, the festival of the *rosa d'oro*. All of these performances had interesting liturgical, biographical, and/or political signifi-

---

[200] *AC* 1966 pp. 43 and 356 = *AC* 2007 pp. 55 and 446, Doc. 1. In *HR* 338f the paragraph above was followed by an excursus on Caldara, extensively revised in *Handel mit Ruspoli*, pp. 356ff, now transferred to *AC* 2007 pp. 52ff.

— 400 —

cance. This must be explicitly stated – otherwise Handel's so dramatic music will continue to fall on deaf ears.

I may conclude with an iconographical discovery. Once Ruspoli was blessed with the huge inheritance in 1705, his ambition was, of course, to have his title upgraded from marquis to prince. He eventually achieved this by recruiting and equipping a fully armed regiment of 550 men[201] which he put at the disposal of the pope for the defense of Ferrara. Sunday 9 September 1708, three days before Handel's definitive departure, was an exciting event for Rome, recorded, for instance, not only by Valesio,[202] but also in an enormous painting now in the Palazzo Ruspoli, measuring no less than 1.95 × 5.06 m. (Plate XI.10). I could identify the painter as Alessandro Piazza from documents of 1710.[203] Here Ruspoli's regiment is displayed on the large Piazza SS. Apostoli, shortly before its mobilization. It was led by his eldest son Bartolomeo, who was then only eleven years old. The Ruspoli family looked on from the balcony of the Bonelli Palace (Plate XI.11). Many dignitaries were present as the troops marched up to receive the pope's blessing from the balcony of his palace on the Quirinal. Again that evening[204] music was heard: Handel's serenade "Oh come chiare e belle" HWV 143, a setting of a text, possibly by Ruspoli, for three voices, one of which represents the marquis under his Arcadian pseudonym of Olinto (unicum in the Biblioteca Vaticana; Plate XI.9).[205] Also this music was thus connected with a definite historical event. But of particular interest to us are the two groups of people likewise in a conspicuous position directly in front of the palace. They are surely those from the top of the Ruspoli payroll and distinguished houseguests.[206] I believe the lady in the left group is Handel's young virtuosa Margarita Durastante; beside her, three clerics (probably the secretary Abbate Giuseppe Lari, Abbate Giacomo Buonaccorsi,[207] and Abbate Mazziotti, who after August 1707 was no longer in the *ruolo*);[208] behind them, the judge Francesco Mancia, the physician Michel-

---

[201] Not 1200, as stated in *RD* 242. Fifty of the 550 men were officers.

[202] V, 150, 155.

[203] *AC* 1966 p. 46, note 14 (the year incorrectly indicated as "1709") = *AC* 2007 p. 58, note 207.

[204] Not "in ottobre" (HARRIS, *Le cantate*, p. 64) or in "August" (*Handel as Orpheus*, pp. 117, 128).

[205] This *serenata* is not mentioned in MARX, *Händels Oratorien, Oden und Serenaten*.

[206] Vol. A 46, after list 165 (24 Sept. - 9 Nov. 1708): "Rolo a denari e pane della famiglia".

[207] On Buonaccorsi's activity as librettist cf. *AC* 1966 p. 52, note 60 = *AC* 2007 p. 66, note 254; Giancarlo ROSTIROLLA, *Un compositore di oratori 'celeberrimo', ma 'vario di cervello': Quirino Colombani da Correggio*, in *Percorsi dell'oratorio romano* cit., p. 222; and FRANCHI, *Il principe Ruspoli*, notes 45, 49, 93. With Durastante, D'André, and Mazziotti, he is one of the favored few who received generous allowances of wine and poultry from Ruspoli (see above, p. 363).

[208] He is found there for the last time in vol. A 44, after list 88 (July - Aug. 1707), possibly because his pupil Bartolomeo then may have entered the Collegio Clementino.

angelo Paoli, the *maestro di casa* Angelo Valeri, etc., all with hats on their heads. In the group on the right (Plate XI.12), surely the elderly singer Lucrezia d'André, alias Madama Caró, discretely withdrawn, since encumbered by debt,[209] and the five literate *camerieri* (their signatures in Plate XI.7, lines 7-11) who functioned also as musicians, including Domenico Castrucci, with his hands outstretched, palms up, thus indicating that all in this group merit praise, though he is their master (his gesture is like that of conductors today, who after a concert raise their hands to give *all* the musicians their share of applause). Next to him is his son Pietro, who points to his father. The small man with the blond wig must be Silvestrino Rotondi, the star violinist. And I am convinced that the tallest (15.5 cm.), well nourished young man, very conspicuous through his golden gala suit and central position is no other than Handel – the earliest depiction of him. Not only the small, down-turned mouth and already a trace of his double chin are visible, as clearly seen also in the later realistic portrait by Denner. Unlike the other persons, he, imitated by his fiddler, holds his hat firmly under his arm, as he did, according to the author of the *Voyage historique*, when he played the harpsichord miraculously while standing up, soon after his arrival in Rome, leading superstitious Romans to suspect that the Lutheran was in league with the devil.[210]

---

[209] See above, p. 363.

[210] On the hat, cf. above, pp. 354f, 357, and BRAUN, *Händel und der 'römische Zauberhut'*. The golden color of Handel's clothing could have been associated with the sun god Phoebus Apollo, mentioned at the very beginning of the serenata ("Febo i suoi raggi d'or"). Also, as Mainwaring suggested, Vittoria may have compared Handel with Apollo (cf. the quotation above, p. 383). And the reference to the devil does not stand alone. When Handel, masked, played the harpsichord during the carnival in Venice, "[Domenico] Scarlatti happened to be there, and affirmed that it could be no one but the famous Saxon, or the devil" (MAINWARING, pp. 51f).

A sensible article (*Haendel: la révolution*, «Diapason», no. 520, Dec. 2004, pp. 68-71) and a one-hour French radio broadcast (21 Dec. 2004) by Ivan A. ALEXANDRE were based on ch. 9-11. – Olaf Brühl made a 45-minute documentary *Händel in Rom*, transmitted from Berlin (3Sat, 24 Dec. 2006, plus seven repetitions in 2007, including the Hallische Händel-Festspiele and the D.H.I. – see below). In spite of my appearance in the film and its dedication to me, I am not responsible for the errors – not few – of other persons involved, not having seen the text before its transmission. That the sequence of Handel's sojourns 1705/6 in Florence and Venice is now reversed, and that – still asserted here as a fact – *Rodrigo* was not performed until the fall of 1707 in Florence, "voller Einfälle aus seinem römischen Fundus", notwithstanding its immense inferiority to the splendid works composed in the eternal city, borders on the fabulous (cf. above, p. 397, the scathing judgements of Dean and Knapp, painfully confirmed by the sound track). Less harmful, but still strange is the alleged 'portrait of Handel' (relic in Halle after Christoph Platzer) recurring throughout the film: the elongated, narrow face, large almond eyes, wide, straight mouth, feminine features – irreconcilable with the true portraits of Handel. But one scene in the film was gratifying: the famous policeman directing the chaotic traffic on Piazza Venezia, like a very elegant conductor of Handel's music – a joy to behold and to hear. (We identified his surname: "Buffon" – *nomen est omen*). Now Sabine Ehrmann Herfort is organizing a conference commemorating "Händel in Rom" for October 2007 in the Deutsches Historisches Institut. As she stated in her circular invitation of 18 Sept. 2006, "Händels römische Zeit ist, insbesondere was die in Rom entstandenen Kompositionen betrifft, noch verhältnismäßig wenig erforscht",

APPENDIX I

NOTES ON RUSPOLI'S RESIDENCES[211]

In the late sixteenth century the Palazzo al Campidoglio belonged to Mario Fani, who had once served as *conservatore*. He had it renovated by the architect Giacomo Della Porta, chief architect of the S.P.Q.R. since 1564 and director of the *fabbrica di S. Pietro* since 1573. In 1632 it was sold to Bartolomeo Ruspoli (1595-1681).[212] Until recently an inscription "BART. MARCHIO RVSPVLVS" was to be seen in the entrance hall, now transferred to the right wall of the courtyard.[213] It was Bartolomeo who had acquired during his long life the tremendous wealth. His paternal grandfather Bartolomeo (son of a niece [ward] of Emilio de' Cavalieri), a Florentine financier who had settled in Rome, and uncle Alessandro, treasurer of Pope Paul V, had paved the way for him.

Since the younger Bartolomeo soon became a widower, without children, he bequeathed his estate to his nephew Francesco Marescotti,[214] who now assumed, with his wife Girolama Bichi, the name Ruspoli and moved into the Palazzo al Campidoglio. Also he died without issue. With his will (opened 2 Dec. 1687) he had directed that his widow retain a life interest in the palace before it passed to his universal heir,

---

and then requested a paper from me on "Händel und Ruspoli". I declined. For the same month the Accademia Nazionale di Santa Cecilia has scheduled a conference on "Monsù Endel in Italia".

[211] On the 'Romanization" of the Florentine family Ruspoli and their various early residences in the eternal city, cf. COLA, cited. above, note 24. Further information on the family is provided in *AC* 1966 pp. 45f = *AC* 2007 pp. 56ff.

[212] Archivio Ruspoli-Marescotti, vol. 60 (*istromenti*), no. 106, 18 Feb. 1632: "Copia pubblica della vendita fatta da Fabio Fani d'una casa e palazzo nella piazza sotto le radici delo Campidoglio ... a favore del Marchese Bartolomeo Ruspoli ... per prezzo di scudi 18000".

[213] PIETRANGELI, p. 20.

[214] Son of Bartolomeo's sister Vittoria and Sforza Marescotti, who lived in the Marescotti palace, Via Campo Marzio 69 (I-Rav S. Nicola de' Prefetti, *Status animarum, passim*). From this marriage issued nine children, including Cardinal Galeazzo (1627-1726; see below) and Alessandro (1641-1703), prominent knight of the Order of Malta and father of our Francesco Maria. Alessandro, however, must have assumed the name Capizucchi already before 1670 and have moved into the Palazzo Capizucchi (Plate XI.3, no. 987) on the east side of the Piazza S. Maria in Campitelli, one short block from the Palazzo al Campidoglio, long before his inheritance from his cousin Francesco Capizucchi, who died in 1678 – contrary to FRANCHI, *Il principe Ruspoli*, p. 283, note 83. This is confirmed by the baptismal record of Francesco Maria, where the father is named Conte Alessandro Capizucchi: "Die 5 mensis Martij an. 1672. Franciscus Maria Dominicus Gaspar natus die 10 Februarij proximi preteriti hora circiter 23 ex Ill.° D. Comite Alexandro Capizucchi et Ill.ᵐᵃ D. quondam Anna Maria Corsini coniugibus hodie in me est baptizatus, quem in sac. fonte susceperunt Eminentissimus et Reverendissimus D. Flavius Cardinalis Chisius et Excellentissima D. Principessa D. Catherina de Alterijs" – I-Rav S. Marco, *Battesimi*, V, 269v, and copy in Archivio Ruspoli-Marescotti, vol. 56, no. 21, f. 16. Thus the child was baptized almost a month after his birth, three days after the death of his mother. Pompeo LITTA, *Famiglie celebri italiane*, Milan, Giusti, etc., 1819-1883, *Marescotti di Bologna*, tav. IV, mistook the date of baptism for the date of birth, and this error was retained by me in *AC* 1966, p. 45.

the son of his brother Alessandro, young Francesco Maria, "quale [ha] sempre amato", but not without provisos. (It is curious to see how far Bartolomeo and Francesco differed already in the first sentences of their wills. The former had instructed: "Il mio cadavere voglio sia portato di notte con doi sole torcie e sepolto subito nella nostra cappella della Chiesa nuova ... senza funerale, o segno d'armi, lutto, o dimostratione alcuna".[215] Francesco, on the other hand, must have feared the worst, since he ordered "che l'infrascritta mia erede in termine di tre giorni subito seguita la mia morte facci dire tre mila messe per la mia anima").[216]

After Francesco's death in 1687 Francesco Maria's family assumed for him, already during his minority (age 15), the name Ruspoli.[217] But when Girolama died, on 16 January 1704 in the Palazzo al Campidoglio, she had eliminated Francesco Maria from her testament and declared her nephew, Cavaliere Alessandro Bichi, as universal heir. Only on 22 September 1705, after a very bitter lawsuit in the Sacra Romana Rota[218] (with twelve lawyers, ten in favor, one opposed, one absent) Francesco Maria won, "con generale applauso e giubilo di Roma", as the *prologo* of the *libro mastro* asserts.[219] The last lines are a *laudatio* of the uncle Cardinal Galeazzo Marescotti, who had played a decisive role behind the scenes; to him Francesco Maria owed everything. (In 1706 he commissioned a costly marble bust of his uncle from the sculptor Lorenzo Ottone).[220]

Since 1689, long before the lawsuit, Girolama's brother Cardinal Carlo Bichi was residing with her and younger relatives in the Palazzo al Campidoglio.[221] For decades he had been the archenemy of Galeazzo. Both had been *papabili* (Marescotti 1670 and 1700, Bichi 1689), but each time one thwarted the hope of the other for this highest office in Christendom.[222] And it is clear that not only political rivalry deter-

---

[215] Vol. 63/64 (testamenti), no. 18, f. 3.

[216] Vol. 56 (alberi), no. 21, f. 6*v*.

[217] His halfbrother Sforza, six (not eight – FRANCHI, *op. cit.*, p. 274) years younger (from Alessandro's second wife, Prudenzia Gabrielli), retained the name Marescotti. The youngest halfbrother, Mario, who since his birth bore the name Capizucchi, remained the head of this family. Also these two sons were born and raised in Palazzo Capizucchi. After age ten in 1682, however, Francesco Maria disappears from the *Status animarum* of Campitelli (vol. 1682-99, p. 38), to appear in that of S. Nicola dei Prefetti in 1688 (see below, note 229). In the meantime he lived probably in the Collegio Clementino, where his uncle Galeazzo had been an alumnus.

[218] *Romana attentatorum pro illustriss. D. Marchione Francisco Maria Ruspolo contra illustriss. D. Equitem Alexandrum Bichium*, Rome, Camera Apostolica, 1704.

[219] Vol. 2, p. [I]; cf. also VALESIO, III, 459f.

[220] *Libro mastro* 2, openings 201 left etc. to 273 left (13 Oct. 1707).

[221] I-Rav SS. Venanzio ed Ansuino, *Status animarum* 1687-1721, f. 10, 1689, until f. 62*v*, [March] 1705 (here "Cardinal Carlo Bichi 69 [years of age], ... Abbate Francesco Bichi 27", altogether 17 souls).

[222] Valesio mentions all three cases. First on 15 Oct. 1700, regarding the conclave of Clement XI: "Dicesi essere in conclave nato dissapore fra il cardinale Bichi et Ottoboni per gli avanzamenti di Marescotti" (I, 83). Then at the end of the year, where he mentions those cardinals who were *papabili* in earlier conclaves and reciprocally criticized: Marescotti in 1670 during the conclave of Clement X by "l'opposizione della Francia" [long before the War of the Spanish Succession, when Marescotti sided with the French] and "la contrarietà del cardinale Bichi"; Bichi in 1689 during the conclave of Alessandro VIII by Marescotti: "L'aderenza con la Francia" (I, 207).

XI.7. Receipts of *camerieri* for clothing allowance, 5 Jan. 1707. Line 7: sample of Domenico Castrucci's handwriting. Archivio Segreto Vaticano, Archivio Ruspoli Marescotti, *Giustificazioni di Roma*, A 44, after list 20. Cf. p. 377, note 96, and p. 402.

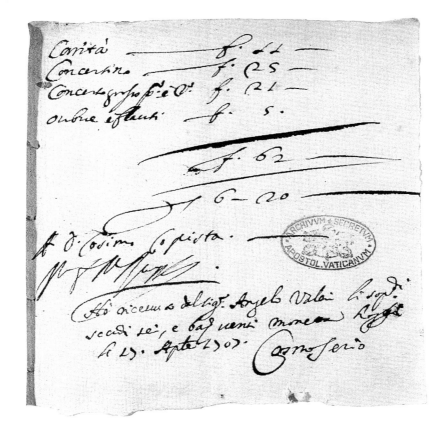

XI.8a. Bill and autograph receipt of Cosimo Serio, 17 Apr. 1707, for copying music for Alessandro Scarlatti's oratorio *Il giardino di rose. Ibid.*, after list 34, Apr. 1707. Cf. p. 377 and note 97.

XI.8b. Sample of Cosimo Serio's handwriting from Alessandro Scarlatti's oratorio *Il giardino di rose*, D-MÜs 3861, p. 1. Cf. Plate IX.8a and p. 377.

OLINTO

PASTORE ARCADE
ALLE GLORIE DEL TEBRO

Serenata à trè Voci.

Fatta cantare dal Sig. Marchese RUSPOLI
la sera delli 9. Settembre 1708.

IN ROMA MDCCVIII:
Nella Stamperia di Gio: Francesco Chracas.
✳✳s✳✳✳s✳✳✳ ✳✳✳✳✳✳✳✳✳✳
Con licenza de' Superiori.

XI.9. Libretto of Handel's serenata "Oh come chiare e belle" HWV 143. Text
very probably by Francesco Maria Ruspoli. © Biblioteca Apostolica Vaticana.
Cf. pp. 314, 401.

XI.10. Colonella Ruspoli on the Piazza Santi Apostoli, 9 Sept. 1708. Alessandro Piazza, oil on canvas, 1.95 × 5.06 m., 1708. Rome, Palazzo Ruspoli in Via del Corso. Cf. p. 401.

XI.11. Ruspoli's own family on the balcony of the Palazzo Bonelli and the more important members of the court below. *Ibid.*, detail. Cf. p. 401.

XI.12. Handel (in the gold frock) in front of the Palazzo Bonelli. *Ibid.*, detail. Cf. p. 402.

mined their animosity: the future inheritance was immense. With the *expediatur* of this patrimony – pronounced shortly before 8 June 1705 – arrived finally a turning point for Francesco Maria: Cardinal Bichi moved in all haste out of the "palazzo spettante a detta eredità" and into Palazzo "Landi" [= Lante], near the Sapienza.[223] However, Francesco Maria, after his legal victory, established himself not in the Palazzo al Campidoglio, but in the palace rented from Bonelli. Perhaps he feared the old palace because of the endless malice of its former inhabitants towards his family.

But we must still ask where he had lived until now. From Valesio we know that on 1 April 1704 (i.e. soon after the beginning of his lawsuit) he had the anonymous oratorio *San Clemente papa e martire* performed "nel suo palazzo ... con invito di molti personaggi e in specie di tutta la famiglia [of pope Clemente] Albani".[224] And a year later the *Avvisi Marescotti* record that again in March "un bell'oratorio" was heard "in sua casa coll'invito de cardinali e nobiltà".[225] From this Saverio Franchi assumed that Francesco Maria resided "nel palazzo della sua famiglia d'origine (Marescotti) in via di Campo Marzio".[226] This might have been true if the sources did not often mention another domicile, the Palazzo Pallavicini, occupying the northwest corner between Via dei Prefetti and Via di Campo Marzio[227] and housing in the south parterre since 1867 the elegant textile shop 'Il Tebro', with large show-windows from the nineteenth century.[228] Here resided as tenant Cardinal Galeazzo, not only with his own court: soon after the opening of his brother's testament he saw that his nephew Francesco Maria lived with him under one roof, until the spring 1706, marriage to Isabella Cesi (1695) and children included.[229] Perhaps not irrelevant for the cardinal was the location, that is in the block ('isola') dedicated to the "Madonnina di Santa Casa di Loreto". The "Madonnina" can still be seen behind the fountain in the courtyard, a much older relief figure with a crown and the cape characteristic of Loreto, girded by three horizontal chains, each with a pendant (medallion, pearl in an open shell [?], cross). Had Galeazzo, thinking of the future, already selected the Bonelli palace for his nephew because directly to the south of this building stood the church of the Madonna of Loreto (Plate XI.3, no. 274), protection for his house after the difficult legal action? (To this day a club of nobility from the Marches, where Loreto is

---

[223] VALESIO, III, 404f.

[224] III, 57.

[225] Gloria STAFFIERI, *Colligite fragmenta: la vita musicale romana negli 'Avvisi Marescotti' (1683-1707)*, Lucca, LIM, 1990, p. 163.

[226] NOLLI, no. 342; FRANCHI, *Il Principe Ruspoli*, pp. 283, note 83; 284, 286. Another 'Palazzo Marescotti' (Via della Pigna, NOLLI, no. 867) came into the family's possession only in 1746.

[227] Cf. Pietro ROMANO, *Il rione Campo Marzio*, Rome, Tip. Agostiniana, 1939, II, 105f, and *Strade e piazze di Roma, ibid.*, 1939-40, II, 77f.

[228] "Palazzo della S. Casa di Loreto", no. 437 on Nolli's map (FRUTAZ, III, 413).

[229] I-Rav S. Nicola dei Prefetti, *Status animarum* 1682-1703, f. 57*v*, 1688: "Sig.ʳ Francesco Maria Capizucchi d'anni 17" [16?], with the *famiglia* of the cardinal and his own servants. From 1686 until 1692 Galeazzo was absent, only his court of ca. sixty persons remained there. Francesco Maria is listed every year, since 1696 (f. 142) with his wife etc.

located, is still lodged in the Palazzo Pallavicini – the town remains its geographic and spiritual home). Of the two portals in the Via Campo Marzio, the northernmost (no. 30), "verso S. Lorenzo in Lucina", was for the young family Ruspoli.[230] Also a number of the court personnel already lived here, such as Domenico Castrucci[231] or the Abbate Giuseppe Lari, secretary of Ruspoli. The two oratorios mentioned above were performed in this palace, surely in its most elegant hall, entered through the Via dei Prefetti 46. In the spring of 1706 the family still lived and slept ("abitano e pernottano") here.[232] It was only a stone's throw to the Palazzo Fiano on Piazza S. Lorenzo in Lucina, home of Ottoboni's uncle (Marco Ottoboni, duke of Fiano) and aunt. The cardinal Pietro must have frequented this palace.[233] Francesco Maria's lifelong friendship with Pietro Ottoboni must have begun here, in the immediate neighborhood. When Ruspoli in 1713 acquired the Gaetani palace in the Corso (Nolli, no. 434), on the north side of this square, he would have felt at home with his friend.

APPENDIX II (2007)

HANDEL IN VIGNANELLO

When Handel joined Marquis Ruspoli in *villeggiatura* at Vignanello from 18 May until 21 June 1707, he fulfilled his quota, as had surely been agreed with his patron: five pieces in five weeks. But if we examine the lists of persons who were present, we can see why in the first three weeks only the cantata "Un'alma inamorata" was performed and only thereafter, beginning with Pentecost, the four others in a single week. The first period of this calendar must have been reserved for Vittoria, the queen of song who, moreover, had been the favorite of crown prince Ferdinando Medici. Her very presence suggests that she brought successful numbers with her from Florence, where Handel surely had accompanied her with keyboard instruments built by Bartolomeo Cristofori. And since he was already celebrated as an extraordinary harpsichordist, their music must have been divine. Must not Ruspoli have put at their disposal an excellent instrument? The one serviced by Mattia di Gand,

---

[230] *Ibid.*, f. 177*v*, 1699, with two children and 17 other persons "in detto palazzo [f. 177: "della Santa Casa di Loreto"] verso S. Lorenzo in Lucina". And one year later, "nell'istesso palazzo per la porta che entra nel vicolo che va a S. Lorenzo", are listed Francesco Maria, his wife, and 28 others, including "Domenico Castrucci cameriere" (f. 190).

[231] Between 1700 and 1706 (*ibid.*, f. 190, and *Status animarum* 1704-24, f. 27*v*); "Domenico Castrucci Cameriere" and "Pietro figlio sonator di violino", age 50 and 20, respectively, in 1704 (f. 6).

[232] *Ibid.*, 1704-24, f. 33.

[233] Still in 1727 he had a close relationship with his widowed aunt: he presented a cantata with a text of Metastasio in the *cancelleria* in honor of the *gran principessa* of Toscana. The invitation came from the Duchess of Fiano – VALESIO, IV, 890.

just before it was transported from Rome to Vignanello,[234] was in all probability the harpsichord with seven [?] registers which Ferdinando Medici had given to Ruspoli's wife Isabella Cesi in 1703 (see above, p. 359). The faithful Mattia was not only paid for this work on 14 May; he travelled with Ruspoli's retinue to Vignanello and remained there for at least eleven days. On 30 May he and a *cavalcante* of Federico Pierdonato Cesi, Isabella's brother, dined with Ruspoli. On 9 June the duke departed, accompanied by Mattia and three lackeys. (Three days later, at Pentecost, the duke is again present at dinner in Vignanello).[235] His close contact with Mattia indicates that he was not indifferent to music.

The climax of this *villeggiatura* was of course the feast of Pentecost, followed immediately by the celebration of the 475th anniversary of the canonization of S. Antonio of Padua. The Franciscans venerated this saint as much as their own patron, the Seraphicus of Assisi. Not only did he become a member of their order – he was one of the most powerful preachers of his time and was renowned as no other for the working of miracles. Since Ruspoli himself was named 'Francesco' and the church of S. Sebastiano in Vignanello belonged to the Franciscans, he was especially linked to it and made it a principle venue for his festivity. The feast of S. Antonio is normally on 13 June, the anniversary of his death, beginning with the first Vesper of the preceding evening. But since in 1707 this eve of S. Antonio corresponded with Pentecost Sunday, the main feast of the saint had to be postponed to Tuesday 14 June.

11 June: vigil of Pentecost
12 June: Pentecost Sunday
13 June: Pentecost Monday and eve of S. Antonio
14 June: S. Antonio

We have seen that fifteen Masses were celebrated by the fathers and three by their guardian "during the *three* days of Pentecost" [i.e. 12-14 June, including S. Antonio].[236] In addition to the baldachin, the thousand printed images, Ceruti's new altarpiece with San Antonio, the candle holders, crucifix, and other pious objects (above, p. 297), Ruspoli purchased also for a substantial sum (*scudi* 19.37) candles and torches used for the *expositio* of the Host in the church, the statue of the saint in the procession, etc.[237]

---

[234] "Per accomodatura di un cimbalo, cioè linguette, saltarelli, saldato il bancone allentato con sue fortezze, incollato il fondo panni, penne, leggio, pezzetti alla mazza, e mutata la metà delle corde in tutto 1.50. Per serratura e chiave –.40. Per porto e riporto –.20. Somma [scudi] 2.10" – *Giustificazioni di Roma*, vol. A 44, fasc. 71 (Sp May-June 1707), no. 25, May 14 + bill. Domenico Castrucci confirmed below that "Monsù Mattia cimbalaro" received this sum. On 15 May was paid "a Pietro Fochetto andato a Roma col suo cavallo a portare il cimbalo scudi 1.20" – *Giustificazioni di Vignanello*, vol. 15 (1703-11), fasc. 87 (Sp May-June 1707), no. 13.

[235] *Giustificazioni di Roma* cit., after fasc. 88.

[236] "Alli RR. Padri di S. Sebastiano e per essi al Padre Marieni guardiano scudo uno e baiocchi cinquanta per la solita carità di quindici messe da essi celebrate nelle tre feste della Pentecoste 1.50" and "Al sud.° padre guardiano per haver cantato tre messe nelle d.ᵉ tre feste –.45" – *Giustificazioni di Vignanello*, cit., fasc. 87, item 43, June 17. See above, p. 382.

[237] *Ibid.*, no. 35, June 19: "Ad un mercante di Viterbo ... per lib. trentasette e mezzo [di cera] ...

The diarist Valesio provides information on the feast of S. Antonio in Rome for three decades, more detailed in the first years of the century, with the two successive days. Here we learn that already for the first Vesper altars were adorned with statues or pictures of the saint, always illuminated, sometimes only below the Capitol, but often in "quasi tutta la città" ["almost the entire city"], with a large number of people and coaches.[238] Today we can better understand the events of 1707 in Vignanello. On the Saturday before Pentecost, after the Missa post nonum, the Host was displayed in S. Sebastiano with the new baldachin and extensive illumination. Since the text of Handel's motet "O qualis de coelo sonus tamquam advenientis spiritus vehementis totam replet domum amore" corresponds almost literally to the epistle of the Mass for Pentecost Sunday (*Acts* 2:2): "[... erant omnes discipuli parituri in eodem loco] et factus est repente de caelo sonus, tamquam advenientis spiritus vehementis: et replevit totam domum", its performance can have taken place only in this Mass, at the Offertory. On Monday evening, to introduce the celebration of S. Antonio, the church and the whole village were again illuminated with innumerable lights, and Ceruti's new painting was carried in the procession to the church of S. Sebastiano. The entry was probably accompanied by organ music improvised by Handel (S. Sebastiano does not seem ever to have had a permanent organ; on such occasions, portable organs were commonly used). The new crucifix and altarpiece were then consecrated in the Antonius chapel,[239] the thousand prints of the saint distributed among the large crowd in- and outside the church, the Vesper celebrated with psalms, followed, outdoors, by a night of merry-making. Finally, on 14 June, "Coelestis dum spirat aura" was heard in the Mass, analogous to the first motet. Angelini, as we know, added to the title page the designation "in festo S. Antonii de Padua". Since his first name was 'Antonio', he may have derived a pious satisfaction from this. On 15 June Ruspoli paid further expenses of 26 *scudi* for instrumentalists who performed during the four "festini" (1. "chitara" and "violino", 2. "teorba è [*sic*] citara", 3. "citarino", and 4. "per li strumenti").[240] The violinist was certainly Silvestro Rotondi, the guitarist probably a close relative, identical with the Cintio Rotondi who was to appear as composer, guitarist, and lutenist in the service of Cardinal Pamphilj in October-November 1707.[241]

---

servita per l'esposizione di S. Sebastiano nelle feste di Pentecoste et il rimanente servita per la Compagnia del S. Angelo Custode per la cappella di S. Antonio e processione solenne fatta in dette feste con il trasporto in processione della statua di d.° santo Sc. 19.37".

[238] I, 402, II, 183 and 621, III, 101 and 621, IV, 289.

[239] *Giusificazioni di Vignanello*, cit., no. 4, June 19: "pagato a maestro Biagio Zani muratore ... per lavori fatti nella cappella di S. Antonio scudi 13.83"; no. 6, May 1: "Pagato ad Antonio Butij ... per la cappella di S. Antonio nella chiesa di S. Sebastiano ... scudi 1.27"; no. 36, June 19: "A Michel Angelo [Ceruti] e Ricciotto pittori ... per spese cibarie ... scudi 7.20" and "A Francesco Corallo ... per dicidotto libretti d'oro e ... per colori per la nuova cappella di S. Antonio in S. Sebastiano ... scudi 3.80". The chapel must have been within this church, at the north wall, but at some later time demolished to make room for more people. Cerruti's altarpiece is surely lost.

[240] *Giustificazioni di Roma* as above in note 119.

[241] MARX, *Die "Giustificazioni"*, p. 180, 182f.

I may finally add some information from four unnoticed bills for food and drink which are all dated 14 June and contain the word "saracino".[242] They might easily be overlooked, but without them the celebration cannot be completely understood. They reveal that on this very day Ruspoli held a tourney, where aristocratic young horsemen (cavalieri) charged upon a wooden saracino who bore a metal shield and turned upon his own axis when struck by their lances. (A noble lady always bestowed a prize upon the victor). Ruspoli then provided a banquet for the cavalieri. The time of day and number of participants for the tournay followed Roman tradition. It must have been held in the morning, immediately after the Mass – in 1634 a famous tourney took place likewise in the morning on the Piazza Navona, "with cavalieri in the presence of important personages, ambassadors of princes, titled ladies and gentlemen who were admiring it from those palaces, houses and platforms". Our timing is evident also from the mention of the departure of Ruspoli's two half-brothers "dopo il pranzo" ("after the mid-day meal"). For the repast – which included pullets, mortadella, wine – 24 loaves of bread distributed to as many cavalieri. Also in 1634 there were 24: "6 squadriglie di 4 cavalieri per ciascuna".[243]

More difficult to determine is where in Vignanello the tourney took place, since the documents do not reveal this. Such courses normally consisted of two long, straight, parallel sections, as can be seen in the well known painting of Andrea Sacchi in the Museo di Roma (17th c.), this too set on the Piazza Navona.[244] I suspect that the tourney in Vignanello may have taken place in the park behind the castello, in the famous formal garden consisting of twelve parterres (3 × 4) with two central long, straight paths, ideally visible from the windows of the *piano nobile* (as in 1634). Within the first parterre, plants form the proud, large initials "FMR" (Francesco Maria Ruspoli), still to be seen, but, again, only from above, also from horseback.

Saracen tournaments were held in Italy surely since the high Middle Ages when the Moslems, who had devastated also much of Latium and Rome, had been driven out. A 'saracino' was an infidel and thus a mortal enemy, though the word is documented only later.[245] Tournies with a *saracino* still take place today, e.g. on 2 August in Ascoli Piceno. But what did this have to do with the life of S. Antonio? Born in 1195 of a noble family in Lisbon, he changed his name, domicile, and religious order, from an exclusive Augustine to a humble Franciscan. When he heard – still in

---

[242] *Giustificazioni di Roma*, cit., 14 June: a long list of food, including "pollastre per li cavalieri del Saracino n. 20, scudi 1.50"; a list with "pane ... per quelli che corsano al Saracino n.° 24"; a list of "spese diverse" with "Mortadella per quelli del Saracino scudi 3". *Giustificazioni di Vignanello* cit., fasc. 87, "Entrata di vino del mese di giugno 1707 ... per detta villeggiatura": "tinello, musici e cavalieri del Saracino e camerieri ... barili 13.20", "cantarina e sasso[ne] ... barili 3.13.3", and "Abbate Mazziotti ... barili 2.19".

[243] Antonio MARTINI, *Il secolo XVII*, in Luigi Fiorani *et al.*, *Riti, ceremonie, feste e vita di popolo nella Roma dei papi*, Bologna, Cappelli, 1970, p. 208.

[244] Reproduced, *ibid.*, fig. 96.

[245] Salvatore BATTAGLIA, *Dizionario della lingua italiana*, VII, Turin, UTET, 1994, p. 569, beginning with Boccaccio.

Portugal – that the king of Marocco had "beheaded with his own hand" five Franciscans, he embarked for North Africa "to preach to the Saracens" and, if God willed, to attain the crown of martyrdom. Fortunately he became sick at sea and landed on the coast of Sicily – thus according to the legend entwined with history.[246] During the last third of the seventeenth century half of Europe was in danger of being overrun by the Turks. By 1683 they had advanced as far as Vienna; only the king of Poland, Jan Sobieski, saved the city. Shortly thereafter Austria, Poland, Venice, and later Russia formed an alliance against Turkey: the 'Holy League' under the protection of Pope Innocent XI. The decisive victory of the Christians took place at Salankemen in 1691 under Margrave Ludwig von Baden (the 'Türkenlouis'), with 47,000 men against 100,000 Turks. He attributed it largely to the energetic support of St. Anthony, whom he always venerated and now invoked before and during the battle![247] When Ruspoli scheduled the tourney on the feast of this saint, he can have done this not merely as a popular entertainment. The Saracen was still a danger. But the marquis must have included also *hilaritas* in his tourney. The magistrates of the Capitol had recommended this expressly for papal tournaments.[248] In Vignanello, artisans, illuminators, painters, sculptors, the composer, musicians and many others had labored by the sweat of their brows to commemorate the saint – now they were also to relax and be entertained. According to the ancient rhetoricians, gayety normally came at the end of an epideictic oration. Thus the tourney crowned the festivity, followed only by the banquet – surely awaited eagerly by Handel. All *per devotionem*.

Here I must revise the date given in *HR* 348 to the "Salve regina", which, of course, was not a "mottetto", but a Marian antiphon. I had assigned this piece to the evening of 13 June, but it now appears unlikely that it was connected with the festivities for S. Antonio. The long season in which the "Salve Regina" was sung at the end of Compline began and still begins with the eve of *Dominica Trinitatis* (LU 276), i.e. on Saturday, 18 June in 1707, ending with Advent.[249] Also here, Angelini must have been correct with his usual 'chronological' listing: first the two motets for the festive Masses, and then the "Salve Regina", for a later day, 18 June.

Northern musicologists have not always been friendly towards the "Salve Regina". They were disturbed by the unusual agitation in Handel's setting, such as chromaticism, the powerful leaps of more than an octave in the voice, etc. But here too the opera *régisseur* Handel was at work, as skilled rhetorician, who quickly

246 P. Beda KLEINSCHMIDT OFM, *Antonius von Padua: In Leben und Kunst, Kult und Volkstum*, Düsseldorf, Schwann, 1931, pp. 22-28.

247 *Ibid.*, p. 364.

248 Pio PECCHIAI, *Il secolo XVI*, in *Riti, ceremonie* cit., p. 141ff.

249 Thus the date given by Marx must be revised from *Dominica Trinitatis* to the evening before – Hans Joachim MARX, *Händels lateinische Kirchenmusik und ihr gattungsgeschichtlicher Kontext*, «Göttinger Händel-Beiträge», V, 1993, pp. 110, 122. Cf. LU 276: "A primis Vesperis [i.e. Saturday] Festi SS. Trinitatis usque ad Nonam Sabbati ante Adventum".

learned his art from the Venetian theaters: the customary rests for "suspiramus"; tremolo for "gementes et flentes", fear of death, also in opera for storms (literal and figurative) and underworld; *katabasis* for "in hac lacrimarum valle", the "valley of tears", etc. The last and shortest section can be counted among Handel's finest – "O clemens, o pia, o dulcis virgo Maria". The voice, with a very simple falling melody to the tonic, and the basso continuo become silent. But the solo 'cello and the two violins, pianissimo, procede, until also they, on g-g', disappear. There may be few passages in music where a composer withdraws so elegantly and inconspicuously (quite the opposite of the massed performers – up to 4000 – for presentations of Handel's oratorios in England in the nineteenth century). The audience in Vignanello must have been grateful, for all feared the worst, the war with the emperor. On 15-16 June the duke and duchess of Acquasparta, Abbate Mazziotti (as probable poet, see *HR* 306 = above, p. 366), *et al.* travelled to Otricoli (some 30 km. by poor roads from Vignanello) and back to see the imperial "armata" recently encamped there.[250] On these very days Valesio reported on the troops and diverse damages to the roads at Otricoli.[251] Handel's "Salve Regina" must have reflected the deep concerns.

As we know, in the third section of the *Salve Regina* the organ plays a brilliant part, accompanied by the orchestra. Already Merrill Knapp believed that this could hardly have taken place in Vignanello.[252] He assumed that it was in Rome. But only about one mile from the castello Ruspoli is the church of Madonna del Ruscello in Vallerano, with a magnificent organ by Giulio Cesare Burzi of 1635-44, said to be the second largest in Italy.[253] Surely Handel played this instrument when he was in Vignanello.

Could Margarita indeed have sung in the three liturgical works, as I long assumed?[254] If Ruspoli had allowed this before such a large assembly, the pope would have learned of it and issued a censure, as he was to do even in the case of the non-liturgical *Resurrezione*. Of course Margarita did perform the secular cantata *Armida* HWV 105 in Ruspoli's Sunday *conversazione* of 19 June. But few conclusions for the three liturgical works can be drawn from her signature on Angelini's bill for the five pieces for Vignanello[255] – Handel seems to have delegated this formality to her.

---

[250] *Giustificazioni di Roma, loc. cit.*

[251] III, 826f.

[252] *Handel's Roman Church Music*, in *Händel e gli Scarlatti* cit., p. 23.

[253] Renzo GIORGETTI, *Un 'Ercoli' storico*, «Tuscia», XX, no. 55, pp. 8f (article kindly brought to our attention by Arnaldo Morelli).

[254] And as Marx incorrectly assumed for the Gloria which he attributed to Handel – cf. above, note 182.

[255] On the cantata "Un alma innamorata" HWV 173, performed probably already on 6 June, see above, p. 384.

Appendix III

REVISIONS FOR THE *HÄNDEL-WERKVERZEICHNIS* (HWV)

My table above, pp. 347ff, provides not the dates of the *copies* themselves, but only the (later) dates of the copyists' *receipts* of payment, i.e. the last step in the production sequence: composition – copy – performance – receipt of payment. That distinction was ignored by HWV, Harris *et al.*; for this reason many corrections are needed, not specified below but evident from the table. Although the receipts furnish only secure *termini ante quos*, specific performance dates for some works could now be provided in this article. In the original bills the works appear always in chronological order of copying and performing, mostly with one cantata for each Sunday *conversazione* (above, pp. 328 and 330, Doc. 1 and 5). *Suggested* dates of first performances derived from such listings are indicated below in square brackets after "Doc. 1" and "Doc. 5". "Doc. 24" refers to the cantatas to be assigned to Handel's visit in Naples, from early May to mid-July 1708, some composed perhaps before his departure from Rome. I believe that those cantatas which appear for the first time in the bill of August 1709 for gift copies, "Doc. 35", may well belong to Handel's earliest months in Rome, December 1706 to 21 February 1707 (see above, pp. 367f). The frequent formulations "wöchentliche *conversazione*" and "vermutlich für Ruspoli" in HWV should be corrected to specify "sonntägliche *conversazione*" and "für Ruspoli". All of the works listed below, with exception of HWV 5, 6, 91ᵃ, 110, 113, and 141, can be regarded as composed for him. A more complete list is included above, pp. 347f, where very few, if any, items might be assignable to another patron. Also the lists of Handel's works in NG², X, 786, 789-792, and MGG², *Personenteil*, VIII, 547f, 552ff, and especially 516, "Händels Kompositionen aus seiner italienischen Zeit" need to be corrected in the light of the following revisions.

HWV	Page	Revision
5	p. 66	First performed in Florence, fall 1705?
6	p. 77	First performed in Venice, November 1706? In this case the direction of 'borrowings' listed on p. 89, col. 2, would have to be reversed.
46ᵃ	pp. 20, 35	First performed ["UA"]: Rome, 2 May 1707, Palazzo Bonelli or Collegio Clementino. Composer paid by Pamphilj, performers by Ruspoli.
78	pp. 463f	Doc. 35: [Dec. 1706 - 21 Feb. 1707].
79	pp. 465f	First performed in Cerveteri, 23 Feb. 1707. Source fragmentary: only 11 pp. extant in autograph; bill of copyist Angelini was for 52 pp.
82	pp. 469, 471	First performed before 28 Aug. 1708, in the garden at S. Matteo in Merulana.

83	pp. 471, 474f	Text possibly by Abbate Francesco Xaverio Mazziotti (also for other Roman cantatas). First performed: very probably Christmas 1706 for the Arcadia. On 29 Dec. 1706 Tarquinio Lanciani was paid for parts. Angelini copied the score much later. Cancel the paragraph "Daß diese Erweiterung ... entnahm".
84	p. 476	Cerveteri. Doc. 1: [20 March 1707].
90	p. 484	Composed probably at the beginning of Handel's sojourn in Rome. Doc. 35: [early Dec. 1706 - 21 Feb. 1707]. Possibly included among the unnamed cantatas mentioned in the bill of 2 May 1707 (above, p. 379).
91[a]	p. 485	Composed probably before Dec. 1706, not in Rome.
92	p. 487	Undated copy by Angelini for Ruspoli's wife (= Clori).
95	p. 489	Before 9 Aug. 1708. Doc. 24: [May – mid-July 1708].
96	p. 494	Handel lived with Ruspoli not merely in "Juli-September 1707". Performed probably in the *cancelleria*, Sept. 1707 (bill receipted by Angelini before 14 Oct.).
99	p. 499	Replace "Rechnungsdatum" and "Kopistenrechnung" (Marx) with "eingereicht am ...". On 14 May Angelini consigned the score to the cardinal. Only on 5 July was he paid for this work and HWV 46[a]. Nothing is known of a payment to Ginelli; he may have been a salaried employee of Pamphilj's court.
100	p. 500	Doc. 35: [early Dec. 1706 - 21 Feb. 1707].
102[b]	p. 503	Composed in Rome. Change no. 102[b] to 102[a], 102[a] to 102[b] ("Sopranfassung" = "Originalfassung"). Doc. 35: [early Dec. 1706 - 21 Feb. 1707].
104	p. 505	Doc. 35: [early Dec. 1706 - 21 Feb. 1707].
105	p. 506	Doc. 2: [first performed "in Vignanello" on 19 June and again in Rome on 26 June 1707].
110	p. 513	Not written "in Florenz". The paper is not "florentinisch", but north Italian.
113	p. 515	Probably composed not "in Florenz", but in Venice (cf. above, HWV 110).
114	p. 516	Doc. 35: [early Dec. 1706 - 21 Feb. 1707].
116	p. 517	Composed in Rome. Doc. 35: [early Dec. 1706 - 21 Feb. 1707].
117	pp. 518f	Composed for Ruspoli before 9 Aug. 1708, as a favor for Pamphilj, who wrote the text in praise of Handel.
125[a]	p. 533	Doc. 35: [early Dec. 1706 - 21 Feb. 1707].
126[a]	p. 535	Doc. 24: [May – mid-July 1708].
128	p. 540	The text may allude to Ruspoli's [= Fileno's] absence, his extended stay in Vignanello, May-July 1708, making preparations for his regiment.

129	p. 540	Doc. 24: [May – mid-July 1708].
130	p. 542	Composed probably in Campania, early summer 1708.
131	p. 543	Doc. 2: [31 July 1707].
133	p. 547	Doc. 5: [7 Aug. 1707].
137	pp. 553f	First performed very probably 3 Apr. 1707 in Massa.
139[a]	p. 557	D-MÜs Hs. 1898, ff. 49-56 not copied by Pietro Castrucci, to whom only the payment was delegated (Doc. 34). Doc. 35: [early Dec. 1706 - 21 Feb. 1707].
140	p. 558	Composed [at Ruspoli's request as a homage] for Cardinal Francesco Del Giudice, performed very probably 17 July 1707. For the occasion, see above, p. 385.
141	p. 559	Composed not in "Florenz, Herbst 1707", but probably Venice, 1706.
143	p. 563	The libretto has now been found – see Plate XI.9.
145	pp. 565f	Composed probably (in Venice?) for presentation in Rome, Dec. 1706. Doc. 35: [early Dec. 1706 - 21 Feb. 1707].
148	p. 569	Doc. 1: [10 Apr. 1707].
152	p. 574	Doc. 5: [10 July 1707].
153	p. 575	Doc. 24: [May – mid-July 1708].
155	p. 577	Composed [at Ruspoli's request as a homage] for Cardinal Joseph La Trémouille, performed very probably on 3 July 1707. For the occasion see above, p. 385.
157	p. 580	Doc. 5: [24 July 1707].
159	p. 582	Cerveteri. Doc. 1: [6 March 1707].
160[a]	p. 584	Cerveteri. Doc. 1: [27 Feb. 1707].
161[a]	pp. 585, 587	[PS: After HWV 167[b]].
167[b]	p. 593	Doc. 24: [May – mid-July 1708].
171	p. 597	Cerveteri. Doc. 1: [27 March 1707].
172	pp. 599f	First performed 18 March 1707 in Civitavecchia. See above, p. 373.
173	p. 601	First performed probably 6 June 1707 in Vignanello. First item in Doc. 2.
177	p. 605	Doc. 35: [early Dec. 1706 - 21 Feb. 1707].
231	pp. 649f	First performed 14 June 1707 in Vignanello. See above, p. 408.
232	p. 650	Composed for the Spaniards' feast of St. Philip and the nameday of King Philip V in Frascati, 1 May 1707.
233	p. 653	First performed on 6 Feb. 1707 in S. Maria in Aracoeli. See above, pp. 368f.
239	p. 667	First performed (not "vermutlich") on Pentecost Sunday, 12 June 1707 in Vignanello.
	p. 668	Delete "HWV 232" from col. 1.
240	p. 667	Rome 1707.
241	p. 669	First performed on Pentecost Monday, 13 June 1707 in Vignanello [PS: The vigil of *Dominica Trinitatis*, 18 June 1707].

Note on Plates XI.1 and XI.6

[Plate XI.1]. The portrait of Francesco Maria, inscribed "FRANCISCUS M. MARE-SCOTTI PRIMUS EX PRINCIPIBUS RUSPOLI MDCCIX", was painted on the occasion of his elevation to the principate. He is in dark gala dress, his white lapdog sits on a table covered with red damask. I can now identify the unsigned painting as the work of Antonio David, born in Venice as son of the painter Lodovico David from Lugano, known for his polemical writings against the Accademia di San Luca etc., but also for some of the first research on Leonardo da Vinci. Antonio was sought after as a portraitist of eminent persons, including popes Clement XI-XII and Innocent XIII, Louis XV of France, and Elector Clemens August of Bavaria.[256] His original paintings, with exception of Ruspoli's portrait and one of Cardinal Neri Corsini in a Roman private collection, seem to be lost and survive only in engravings, such as the one of Ruspoli in armor (inscribed "PRINCEPS ANTIQUAE URBIS AGYLLINAE ITALIS. CERVETERI EXCELLENTISSIMUS FRANCISCUS MARIA RUSPOLUS", Rome, Arnaldus van Westerhout, 1710).[257] Between 20 Dec. 1708 and 20 Dec. 1710 he received no less than 155 scudi for "diversi ritratti fatti dell'Ecc. padrone e figliuoli".[258] Two copies of this portrait, in rectangular frames, dated 1731 (shortly after Ruspoli's death), are in the castello and in the apartment of the parson of S. Maria della Presentazione in Vignanello.

[Plate XI.6]. Prominent among the artists and craftsmen who decorated Ruspoli's brigantine was Girolamo Giacobbi, the "pittore ed indoratore" who painted "tutte le facciate della barca, e riquadri di sopra la poppa e proa" etc., receiving 82 scudi for this.[259] He could be the author not only of the ship's figurehead, but also of the five paintings in Cerveteri showing a brigantine.

---

[256] Cf. Ulrich THIEME and Felix BECKER, *Allgemeines Lexikon der bildenden Künstler*, VIII, Leipzig, Engelmann, 1913, p. 449.

[257] Reproduced in *AC* 2007, Plate 8.

[258] *Libro mastro 2*, opening 380, and *giustificazioni* A 48-49, *passim*.

[259] *Giustificazioni*, A 45, no. 22; A 47 after list 41 (Mar. 1709); *Libro mastro 2*, opening 326. Giacobbi died about two years later (B 51, list 73, item 14: posthumous payment on 11 Apr. 1711).

XII.

THE SOURCE FOR BACH'S *MUSICAL OFFERING*: THE *INSTITUTIO ORATORIA* OF QUINTILIAN*

The external genesis of the *Musical Offering* is so familiar that only the briefest summary need be given here. From several early sources[1] we know that Bach, during his audience with Frederick the Great on 7 May 1747, improvised a three-part fugue on a theme given to him by the king (the *thema regium*; below, p. 492, Ex. 14), much to the delight of all persons present. Bach scholars regard this fugue as the embryo of the *Musical Offering*, later notated as one of its two ricercars. Also the other ricercar of the completed work, in six parts, has been associated with the visit to Potsdam, for Bach had improvised a six-part fugue there as well, though on a theme of his own choosing. Soon after returning to Leipzig he must have begun work on what became a cycle of thirteen pieces – the two ricercars, a trio sonata, a canonic fugue, and nine canons – each based on a version of the *thema regium*. Within a few months he had completed his musical homage to the king, for a Leipzig newspaper announced on 30 September that it had just been published.[2]

But the internal genesis and the state of the sources have been a riddle. Here we are faced with one of "the most discussed and most difficult problems of Bach-philology", as Christoph Wolff observed when he published a new edition in the *Neue Bach-Ausgabe*.[3] Autograph manuscripts, except for the six-part ricercar, have not survived. We are thus almost entirely depen-

---

* This chapter is a continuation of ch. 2, and is continued in ch. 3. The chapters are best read in the sequence 2, 12, 13, 3.

[1] *Bach-Dokumente* (quoted hereafter as *Dok.*), ed. Werner Neumann and Hans Joachim Schulze, Kassel, Bärenreiter, 1963-72, II, 434-5, III, 666, 276. Johann Nikolaus FORKEL, *Über Johann Sebastian Bachs Leben, Kunst und Kunstwerke*, Leipzig, Hoffmeister & Kühnel, 1802, pp. 9f. See also *Dok.*, II, 436f, 454; I, 241ff, 117f.

[2] *Dok.*, III, 656 (see below, note 20).

[3] J. S. BACH, *Neue Ausgabe sämtlicher Werke*, Ser. VIII, Bd. 1: *Kanons, Musikalisches Opfer*, Kassel, Bärenreiter, 1974 (hereafter NBA) and its *Kritischer Bericht*, *ibid.*, 1976 (hereafter KB), p. 99.

dent upon the original edition, consisting of five printer's units of bifolios and folios in differing formats. Since these were never all bound together, even such an essential question as the correct sequence of movements has to this day remained without a convincing answer. To avoid further complications I shall retain Professor Wolff's letter designations for the printer's units,[4] though I shall show that not his sequence, but that of Philipp Spitta and the old Bach-Gesellschaft edition is the correct one[5] (see Table 1). The three nineteenth-century editions[6] placed units A and B at the beginning, C at the end. Only for the intermediate units D and E was there disagreement. Spitta was the first to examine critically the original, if only the dedication copy and a few others. He followed A and B with the unit, D, which was appended to them in the dedication copy and elsewhere. According to his 'instalment' theory,[7] this complex ABD was sent to the king in July 1747. Since he regarded everything else as composed later but advocated no new position for C, only one place remained, between D and C, for unit E.

Table 1 - PRINTER'S UNITS IN THE *MUSICAL OFFERING*

Spitta and the Bach-Gesellschaft edition	Format of first edition	Wolff[8]	
Title. Dedication	Horizontal bifolio	A	"Fasc. 1"
Ricercar a 3. Canon Perpetuus super Thema Regium	3 horizontal folios	B	
Five canons (numbered 1-5). Fuga canonica	Vertical bifolio	D	"Fasc. 3"
Ricercar a 6. Two enigmatic canons (a 2, a 4)	4 horizontal folios	E	
Engraver's signature			
Trio Sonata. Canon Perpetuus	3 vertical parts: bifolio cover and 3 bifolios	C	"Fasc. 2"

---

[4] *New Research on Bach's Musical Offering*, «Musical Quarterly», LVII, 1971, pp. 382f; KB, pp. 48f. See also Wolff's facsimile of the original edition, Leipzig, Peters, 1977 (hereafter Facs.), pp. 11f, and my review, below, ch. 13.

[5] Philipp SPITTA, *Johann Sebastian Bach*, Leipzig, Breitkopf & Härtel, 1873-80, II, 843f. *Johann Sebastian Bach's Werke*, XXXI/2, ed. Alfred Dörffel, Leipzig, Bach-Gesellschaft, 1885. This sequence was accepted also by Alfred OREL, *Johann Sebastian Bachs 'Musikalisches Opfer'*, «Die Musik», XXX, 1937, pp. 83-90, 165-171; Heinrich HUSMANN, *Die 'Kunst der Fuge' als Klavierwerk*, «Bach Jahrbuch», XXXV, 1937, pp. 53-60; Erich SCHENK, *Das 'Musikalische Opfer' von Johann Sebastian Bach*, Österreichische Akademie der Wissenschaften, phil.-hist. Klasse, «Anzeiger», XC, 1953, pp. 51-66.

[6] Breitkopf & Härtel, 1831 (ABEDC); Peters, 1867 (ABE²DE¹C); Bach-Gesellschaft, 1885 (ABDEC).

[7] Questioned by Hans Theodore DAVID, *J. S. Bach's 'Musical Offering'*, New York, Schirmer, 1945, pp. 94f (followed by WOLFF, *New Research*, p. 389), but now vidicated, with a modification, by Gregory BUTLER, *The Printing History of J. S. Bach's 'Musical Offering': New Interpretations*, «Journal of Musicology», XIX, 2002, p. 315.

[8] *New Research*, KB.

But Spitta had already characterized the *Musical Offering* as "a curious conglomeration of pieces, lacking both outer typographical and inner musical coherence. Since it was not a finished unity, everyone copied whatever and as much as he pleased, in random arrangement".[9] And since the 1920s, musicians have rearranged the order of the components according to their own notions, shifted pieces from one unit to another, disregarded also Bach's prescribed sequence of the five numbered canons, and in one case even inserted a canon between two movements of the sonata. Between 1831 and 1964 at least fourteen different 'solutions' had been proposed by as many persons.[10] Then, in a series of five publications between 1967 and 1976, Wolff alone presented some sixteen different arrangements, thereby increasing the grand total to well over two dozen.[11]

It is sufficient at this point to illustrate the 'Neuordnungen' with just one of their authors' criteria, that of 'symmetry'. At first sight it could appear convincing, and it has therefore found the most extensive application. David regarded it as the *summum bonum*, and was fascinated by an arrangement with the two ricercars at the beginning and end and the sonata in the middle, dividing the 'ten' canons (actually, nine canons and a *Fuga canonica*!)[12] into two groups of five each, in spite of their very disparate lengths (4 to 78 mm). Ger-

---

[9] "ein sonderbares Conglomerat von Stücken, denen sowohl der äußere typographische als auch der innere musikalische Zusamenhang fehlt. Denn da es kein abgeschlossenes Ganzes war, so schrieb jeder ab, was und wieviel ihm gefiel, und in beliebiger Anordnung" – II, 845. Cf. Heinrich HUSMANN, *Die Form in Bachs Spätwerken*, in *Bach-Gedenkschrift 1950*, Zürich, Atlantis, 1950, pp. 185f: "not conceived as a unit", "senseless to look for a logical or artistic plan for the whole".

[10] E.g. Hans Joachim MOSER and Hermann DIENER, *Bachs 'Musikalisches Opfer' und 'Kunst der Fuge'*, «Jahrbuch der Staatlichen Akademie für Kirchen- und Schulmusik Berlin», II, 1928/29, pp. 56-62; DAVID, *op. cit.*; Rudolf GERBER, *Sinn und Ordnung in Bachs 'Musikalischem Opfer'*, «Das Musikleben», I, 1948, pp. 65-72. To the ten arrangements tabulated by Wilhelm PFANNKUCH, *J. S. Bachs 'Musikalisches Opfer': Bemerkungen zu den bisherigen Untersuchungen und Neuordnungsversuchen*, «Die Musikforschung», VII, 1954, p. 445, may be added those of Breitkopf & Härtel 1831, Peters 1867, Pfannkuch himself (p. 453), and Joel SHEVELOFF, *Quaerendo invenietis*, ms. M.A. thesis, Brandeis University, 1964 (revised 1969), p. 17.

[11] *Der Terminus 'Ricercar' in Bachs Musikalischem Opfer*, «Bach-Jahrbuch», LIII, 1967, p. 72 (Spitta's 'instalment' theory); *Ordnungsprinzipien in den Originaldrucken Bachscher Werke*, in *Bach-Interpretationen*, ed. Martin Geck, Göttingen, Vandenhoeck, 1969, pp. 157f (3 versions); *New Research*, p. 407; NBA, 1974; when the three different new arrangements of units D and E (KB, p. 125, nos. 1, 2, 4) are applied to his previous six for the work as a whole, about 16 possibilities emerge. Some of these are intended as a sequence of movements in performance, others merely as an arrangement of the original print or the new edition. It will be shown that such distinctions are unnecessary.

[12] Not only the unique title and length, but also Bach's [?] newspaper announcement (see below, note 20) underline the independence of the fugue (*sic*: "canonica" is only an adjective). Since, as will be further shown, no grouping of 5 + 5 can any longer be upheld, we must reject also the assumption that Bach 'symbolized' here the Ten Commandments, an assumption irrelevant to a secular work – WOLFF, *New Research*, p. 404; KB, p. 124.

ber, still more picturesquely, compared the sonata to the "richly adorned middle tract of a baroque palace" and arranged the canons in what he regarded as "mirror-like symmetry".[13] But all acoustical systems, including musical, take their form and content from time, not space. Musical form, like that of a drama, sermon, or forensic speech, should therefore not be confused with optical categories.[14]

But Wolff conducted also extensive diplomatic studies. Could they perhaps remedy the subjective aesthetic speculation? His construction of three "fascicles" from the five printer's units, with the bifolios A and D serving as "covers" for B and E respectively (analogous to the first bifolio of C forming a cover for the rest of C), must be regarded as a bookbinder's nightmare, with 1) the title page (f. 1 of A) separated from the dedication (f. *2r-v* of A) by the insertion of B before the dedication; 2) a vertical bifolio D as a "cover" for the horizontal folios E; and 3) the *Fuga canonica* (f. *1v*-2 of D) torn asunder by the insertion of E between f. *1v* and 2 of D.[15] Wolff then interprets some conflicting evidence as "mutilation".[16] From his investigation of the source he arrives at a negative judgment of the work as a whole, denying categorically that Bach himself conceived a cyclic order.[17] "Considerations of printing technology" are given priority over any artistic purpose, the original position of the canons is explained by the availability of empty space, which might have been 'wasted' if it were not filled out with these

---

13 P. 68. Variants of this scheme were provided also by PFANNKUCH and WOLFF, *Ordnungsprinzipien*, p. 158, the latter by analogy to three other works of Bach, which, however, lack even an optical axis in the "middle." See above, p. 79.

14 Cf. «Bach Jahrbuch», XXXVI, 1939, p. 47. Even in the textbook example of 'symmetrical' form, the da-capo aria, the two A sections are never mere satellites of the B section; on the contrary, the second A supplants B and confirms the supremacy of the main section at the end of the linear form.

15 See the diagrams in WOLFF, *New Research*, p. 395, and KB, pp. 48f. If D served as cover for E, one might wonder why only seven extant copies have both units, while eight have only one of the two (KB, p. 96). Wolff must have realized that his 'fascicle' structure could be used neither for binding nor for performance. According to my enquiries, none of the extant copies is bound in this manner. Only the units in horizontal format (A, B, E) are bound together (KB, p. 96); the fold along the top of A is, of course, cut open. Unit C could not be bound, but for a valid reason: it consisted of separate parts for three instruments. The unconventional pagination of its bifolios (4-1-2-3) was to allow 2 double pages of continuous music, separated by a single turn of the page. Pp. 2 and 4 therefore end with a completed movement, while music from pp. 1 to 2 and from pp. 3 to 4 is continuous. Wolff's "fascicle" or "wrapper" theory, not surprisingly, has been refuted also by BUTLER, pp. 319-321.

16 *New Research*, p. 390: in all but one copy, bifolio A was cut open, "thus destroying the original layout", and in some copies bifolio D "suffered the same mutilation".

17 *Ordnungsprinzipien*, p. 160; *New Research*, pp. 403f, 407; KB, pp. 106, 121f, 125; facs ed., p. 13. But at the same time he continues the aesthetic-speculative constructions which characterized the earlier subjective literature – *Ordnungsprinzipien*, pp. 158f; KB, p. 124.

shorter pieces.[18] His edition then presents "a systematic sequence of movements ... [which] implies no cyclic order of the work",[19] a sequence corresponding to a contemporary newspaper advertisement which merely summarized the
components for brevity's sake and was never intended as a table of contents.[20]

But is it not more likely that a mature work of J. S. Bach, dedicated to a
king and consisting of such carefully contrived components as the elaborate
canons of the *Musical Offering*, would have been conceived also as a sophisticated and meaningful sequence? My study, unlike previous ones, accepts the
premise that the original edition presented the various movements in the order intended by the composer. Though this edition seems to have been produced hastily, Bach, after all, supervised it himself and made sure that errors
were corrected by hand after printing. We see no justification for altering the
position of pieces within the printer's units. Since units A and B obviously belong at the beginning and, as will be shown below, E and C must be in fourth
and fifth position, respectively, D falls into place after AB: ABDEC.

The foregoing survey has revealed that even a thorough description of the
source does not bring us very far toward a solution of the problems. Could
this not suggest that we today sometimes adopt a too narrow conception of
a composition's 'source', limiting it to paper and ink,[21] excluding any thought
which may have been a source of inspiration for the work and thus might
throw light on the composer's intentions? Is there not a danger that by capitulating to diplomatic method we may allow the mere means to become an
end in itself, and the natural priority of mind over matter to be upset? In this
article I shall show concretely that the prime source of the *Musical Offering* lay
in classical antiquity.[22]

---

[18] *Ordnungsprinzipien*, p. 160; *New Research*, pp. 407f; KB, p. 106, 122; Facs., p. 12. The notion is derived from DAVID, pp. 93f, where the wish that the 'Neuordner' could discover the optimal
arrangement was father to the thought. Wolff is led by his 'cover-fascicle' theory to assume that no
canons were placed on the last page of D because music there might become soiled; but he does
assign the dedication to such an exposed position, at the back of another 'cover' (A).

[19] KB, p. 45. Once the composer has been denied intentions, conception, and disposition, it is
difficult to understand how "the NBA utilizes a maximum of the original intentions with regard to
conception and disposition of the work" – KB, p. 126.

[20] «Extract der eingelauffenen Nouvellen», XXXIX, Leipzig, 30 September 1747, p. 156: "Die
Elaboration bestehet 1) in zweyen Fugen, eine mit 3, die andere mit 6 obligaten Stimmen; 2) in einer
Sonata, a Traversa, Violino e Continuo; 3) in verschiedenen Canonibus, wobey eine Fuga canonica
befindlich" ["The elaboration consists of 1) two fugues, one with three, the other with 6 obbligato
parts; 2) a sonata for traverse [flute], violin, and continuo; 3) various canons, where is found also a
canonic fugue"] – *Dok.*, III, 656; facsimile in KB, p. 46.

[21] WOLFF designates his diplomatic investigations as an "autopsy" (Facs., p. 11). While I by no
means deny the importance of diplomatic studies, I regard them as preliminary.

[22] Some of the methods employed here were developed in my *AC* 1966 (and *AC* 2007). They are

As is well known, Bach in his life's work never used the archaic designation 'ricercar' except for the two pieces in the *Musical Offering*. Throughout the age of humanism, a large number of literary sources compare and indeed identify a specific section of the orator's speech, the exordium (proem) or introduction, with an equally specific part of a musical performance, the preludial ricercar.[23] All of these could be traced back to a passage in the third book of Aristotle's *Ars rhetorica*, where the proem is compared to the freely improvised *proaulion* or prelude (translated invariably as 'ricercar' by the sixteenth-century Italian authors), consisting of whatever the performer can execute skillfully, and not connected with what follows. But even more influential in humanistic rhetoric was Cicero's reaction to this passage, demanding coherence with the rest of the speech, dignity and gravity rather than external brilliance. For he distinguished two types of exordia: one, the *principium*, is direct, plain, like an improvisation; the other, the *insinuatio* or 'subtle approach', steals upon the listener's mind unobtrusively, by indirection, with all the resources of the orator's art, and is used to captivate a hostile audience.[24] The all-powerful sixteenth-century movement of Ciceronianism did not remain without effect on music, especially in Venice, where major composers formed their preludial pieces according to Cicero's twofold distinction. Music theorists such as Dressler, Burmeister, Herbst, or Kircher also apply Cicero's categories, sometimes his very words, when they write about the musical 'exordia'. The dichotomy between the contradictory styles of the free and the ingeniously contrapuntal ricercar, which had hitherto eluded explanation in purely musical terms and now emerges as a rhetorical phenomenon, finds a late exemplification in the *Musical Offering*; for Bach here provides one essay in each of the two types. Their use and position in his work can be explained only by the theory and practice of dual exordia in classical rhetoric: the *principium* (here the three-part ricercar) occurs at the very beginning and the *insinuatio* (the six-part ricercar) marks the beginning of a major internal division; they correspond to the exordia which introduce the two main sections of the oration, the *narratio* and the *argumentatio*, respectively.[25] Since the ri-

---

based on the fact that music, instrumental as well as vocal, was not an abstract pattern of sounds, but possessed content and conveyed meaning. Once the text has provided the clue for our understanding of musical formulations in the vocal repertoire, the same formulations can easily be recognized when they occur in instrumental music, with the same or similar meaning – e.g. Exx. 6 and 5, below.

[23] Documentation for this and the following remarks on the ricercar is given above, ch. 2.

[24] *De inventione*, I.xv-xviii.

[25] Multiple exordia were common in German baroque rhetoric, but adversely criticized by Gottsched and others – cf. Ursula STÖTZER, *Deutsche Redekunst im 17. und 18. Jahrhundert*, Halle, Niemeyer, 1962, pp. 152f. Bach employs internal exordia also in the *Goldberg Variations* (sixteenth

cercar was still understood both as an initial and internal prelude in the baroque era,[26] contemporary musicians would have realized that each of Bach's ricercars (in units B and E) would have to be followed by another unit of music, and that unit E therefore must have been the fourth one: ABDEC.[27]

But music theorists from Gallus Dressler (1559/60) to Mattheson (1739) did not stop with comparing the opening of a musical performance with the exordium; they wanted the entire composition to correspond to an oration.[28] Mattheson even applies to the 'Klang-Rede' all the divisions of classical rhetoric: *exordium, narratio, propositio, confirmatio, confutatio,* and *peroratio*. His use of the words *confirmatio* (proof) and *confutatio* (refutation) rather than *probatio* and *refutatio* for the two sections of the *argumentatio*[29] derives from the pseudo-Ciceronian *Rhetorica ad Herennium*,[30] which, together with Cicero's *De inventione*, had been the standard rhetorical textbook ever since

---

of the thirty variations BWV 988, = "Ouverture") and in the *Klavierübung*, I (fourth of the six partitas BWV 825-830, = "Ouverture").

[26] Cf. ch. 2 and 3, *passim*.

[27] The only other possibility, ABCED, will be eliminated below. An argument advanced for placing E at the end is that it concludes with the signature of the engraver Johann Georg Schübler – WOLFF, *New Research*, p. 407, and KB, p. 49, where it is incorrectly stated that the "fascicle" DED concludes with the signature, rather than with the *Fuga canonica*. However, E cannot form the end of the *Musical Offering*, not only because it contains a prelude, but also because its last piece, the four-part enigmatic canon in G minor, is the only piece in a key other than c-minor. Its key, chosen for notational reasons (DAVID, pp. 176f), is not "an infallible [!] sign that Bach cherished no cyclic intentions" (KB, p. 122) but, rather, it disqualifies this canon, and unit E, as the conclusion of an otherwise tonally unified cycle. Schübler placed his signature here, on the last page of the horizontal units with score notation, subsequently bound together. Unit C, in vertical format, was not suitable for this purpose, since it consisted of separate parts for flute, violin, and continuo, not engraved by him, but delegated to assistants. He would have been faced here with the uncomfortable alternative of having to sign his name either three times, to work not done by himself – which modesty or even the composer might have prevented – or else on only one third of the whole. Thus the name of the engraver does not mark the end of the work, but unit C can fulfil this function. FORKEL, p. 52, realized this ("Endlich ist ... ein Trio ... beygefügt"; "Finally ... a trio ... is added"), though he reversed the position of units D and E.

[28] See Hans-Heinrich UNGER, *Die Beziehungen zwischen Musik und Rhetorik im 16.-18. Jahrhundert*, Würzburg, Triltsch, 1941, pp. 46-62, ch. III b: *Die musikalische Dispositio und Elaboratio*.

[29] Johann MATTHESON, *Der vollkommene Capellmeister*, Hamburg, Herold, 1739, reverses their positions in his discussion on p. 236, after listing them correctly on p. 235. Jacobus KLOPPERS, in his otherwise useful dissertation, *Die Interpretation und Wiedergabe der Orgelwerke Bachs*, U. Frankfurt, 1966, bases some of his conclusions on this error (pp. 63, 68, 74, 77, 84-90), as did UNGER, when he illustrated the six *partes orationis* with the first movement of Bach's third Brandenburg Concerto (pp. 53f). Such analyses had already been attempted by MATTHESON, pp. 237ff (aria of Benedetto Marcello), and Carl DREGER, *Die Vokalthematik Johann Sebastian Bachs*, «Bach-Jahrbuch», XXXI, 1934, pp. 40f, 50 (arias BWV 52.3 and 70.8). The method of the present study was adapted to two pieces by Dufay by Willem Elders in 1981, to the *Goldberg Variations* by Alan Street in 1987, to Corelli's *Follia* by Giuseppe Fagnocchi in 2003, and to Bach's three-part inventions by Francesco Dilaghi in 2004 (see above, p. 118, note 137).

[30] I.iii.4.

the Middle Ages. On the other hand, his inclusion of the *propositio*, which was generally regarded not as a separate section but as part of the *probatio*, is indebted to Quintilian's *Institutio oratoria*.[31] It is to this latter work that Bach owes his concept of the *Musical Offering*.

Marcus Fabius Quintilianus was born in Spain, taught rhetoric in Rome, and died about 96 A.D. His only extant work, the *Institutio oratoria* (ca. 92-95 A.D.),[32] largely an enthusiastic elaboration of Cicero's teachings, is the most extensive ancient treatise on rhetoric. It comprises all aspects of literature (composition, style, criticism, poetics), also philosophy, pedagogy, etc., so that Ernst Robert Curtius could compare it with Castiglione's *Cortigiano* as a handbook for the education of an ideal gentleman.[33] It had an immense influence in the Renaissance and Baroque, and went through a very large number of editions after its first printing in Rome, 1468 (over a hundred in the sixteenth century alone!). As the model for his detailed discussion of the sections of the oration in his books IV, V, and VI, Quintilian chose the forensic speech. The other two rhetorical *genera*, the epideictic and the deliberative, he treats only briefly, in book III:

Nor will any [genus] be found ... in which we must not praise and blame, advise and dissuade, prove or refute. These are also common [to all three genera]: to reconcile, narrate, instruct, expand, extenuate, to shape the minds of the audience by exciting or tranquilizing their passions (III.iv.15).

Thus one cannot carelessly separate the three genera, "for all three kinds rely on the mutual assistance of the other" (III.iv.16). "Just as panegyric applied to practical matters requires proof, so too a certain semblance of proof is at times required by speeches composed entirely for display" (III.vii.4). Humanist orators, who had little occasion to practice any rhetorical genus other than the epideictic, took their topics and persons from this *genus*, but followed more or less the forensic model in constructing the speech and decided themselves how

---

[31] III.ix.1.

[32] An introduction to Quintilian is given by George A. KENNEDY, *Quintilian*, New York, Twayne, 1969. Claude PALISCA finds that "there is hardly an author on music in the last half of the sixteenth century who does not dip into Quintilian's *Institutio Oratoria*" – *Ut oratoria musica: The Rhetorical Basis of Musical Mannerism*, in *The Meaning of Mannerism*, ed. F. W. Robinson and S. G. Nichols, Hanover NH, New England UP, 1972, p. 39. Much of the tenth chapter of Quintilian's first book deals with the importance of music for the orator. The translations in my article are literal, by Warren Kirkendale, based on the Latin text of the Loeb edition, London, 1933-36. For the edition undoubtedly used by Bach, see below, p. 466.

[33] *Europäische Literatur und lateinisches Mittelalter*, Bern, Franke, 1948, p. 436. Martin LUTHER esteemed and recommended Quintilian very highly – *Briefe*, 1. Theil, Berlin, Reimer, 1825, p. 385, letter of 1519.

long each section was to be. Bach does the same. His imitation of Quintilian is not limited to vague or chance elements; it is very concrete and systematic, extending even to the rubrics and to smallest details.[34] And, most astonishing, it is perfectly integrated with his homage to the king's person. The enigma of the work is thus discovered: the various pieces represent the successive sections of an oration. Bach writes no fewer and no more than those described by Quintilian, and in the proper order. I shall now comment on them, always confronting the music with the relevant passages in Quintilian's text.

Exordium I (Principium) = Ricercar [A 3]

The opening piece is a fugue with extended, quasi-improvisatory episodes which altogether are about twice as long as the fugal sections. Wolff rightly relates this to one of the two types of ricercar described by Bach's friend and cousin Johann Gottfried Walther:[35] "a kind of prelude or fantasy ... such as is normally realized extempore and without preparation, and thus requires strong ability".[36] These words, however, which merely translate Brossard,[37] are ultimately derived from Quintilian's description of an exordium which creates the effect of an "extemporalis oratio" because it has "nihil praeparati", yet "summae artis est" (IV.i.54, 57; see full quotation below).

The function of both types of exordium, as formulated by Cicero and repeated in virtually all later treatises on rhetoric, was to make the listener "benevolum, attentum, docilem" ["benevolent, attentive, and ready to learn"] – Quintilian IV.i.5, from Cicero, *De Inventione*, I.xv.20. With a ricercar, traditionally exemplifying the 'learned style',[38] Bach fittingly expresses the idea of 'instruction' contained in "docilis" (from *docere*). Quintilian advises the orator, moreover, to arouse in the exordium the impression that he has "undertaken the case out of duty to kinship or friendship, or especially ... to the state,

---

[34] One could rightly object that Quintilian's divisions of the oration were taught also by Cicero and other earlier rhetoricians. However, none of these provides the wealth of details corresponding so closely to Bach's work.

[35] *Der Terminus 'Ricercar'*, p. 79.

[36] "eine *Praeludien-* oder *Fantasie-*Art. ... Solches geschehe *ordinairement ex tempore* und ohne *praeparation*, und erfordere folglich einen starcken *habitum*" – *Musicalisches Lexicon*, Leipzig, Deer, 1732, p. 526.

[37] Sebastien DE BROSSARD, *Dictionnaire de musique*, Paris, Ballard, 1703, s.v. 'ricercar': "un espèce de prélude ou de fantaisie ... ordinairement sur le champs & sans préparation, et par conséquent cela demande beaucoup d'habilité" ["a kind of prelude or fantasy ... normally improvised and without preparation, consequently demanding much ability"].

[38] E.g. for a 'philosopher' in an oratorio of Caldara (1708 – cf. *AC* 1966 p. 258 = *AC* 2007 p. 325), or still for 'Wissenschaft' in Richard Strauss's *Also sprach Zarathustra*. See also above, p. 76.

or at least to some significant consideration" (IV.i.7). Bach, of course, took his subject dutifully from the head of state.

But the 'instruction' must not be overdone: "We shall find it useful also for rousing the attention of the listeners if they discern that we shall not dawdle" ("nos necque diu moraturos. ... Docilem ...; sed ... breviter" – IV.i.34). "We shall derive some silent support if we say we are weak, unprepared, and no match for the talents of our opponents. ... For there is a natural partiality to the underdog. ... Hence the pretence of the ancients of concealing their eloquence" (IV.i.8f). Bach, too, acts as if he were totally unprepared, still improvising in Potsdam. An exordium

acquires conviction also from the appearance of simple speech taken from common usage, so that, even if the rest has been written out and elaborated, the whole oration will generally appear improvised (videatur tota extemporalis oratio), when its beginning clearly has no signs of preparation (nihil praeparati). ... One must take care to avoid any display in the exordium, since any art of the speaker seems to be directed at the judge. But to avoid that itself requires consummate art (summae artis est) – IV.i.54-57.

Here, too, Bach fulfills the requirements of the *principium*, adhering throughout the three-part ricercar to "simple speech" and "common usage", the Ovidian "ars est celare artem" as understood by Quintilian. Simple eighth notes, mostly in conjunct motion, pervade the entire piece, passing smoothly from one voice to another.

But what about the details? Spitta was at a loss to explain what he called the "strange episodes".[39] The first of these short passages interpolates triplet eighth notes, measures 38-41, 46f, 87-90, 95f, 124, 127f (Ex. 1). Quintilian admits, somewhat ruefully, that nowadays "the judges themselves demand rousing and careful speeches ... and want not only to be instructed, but also to be charmed (*delectari*). It is difficult [to find] the happy mean here which can be so tempered that we seem to speak carefully but not cunningly" (IV.i.57f). Since Bach's dedicatee was a judge of music, it is not surprising that the composer finds the "happy mean": here, as always in Bach's vocal music, the interpolation of triplet passages, usually rising, in a context of binary eighth notes, expresses joy[40] and produces pleasure.

---

[39] SPITTA, II, 673.

[40] E.g. the triplets in BWV 30ª/3, "Willkommen im Heil, willkommen in Freuden"; BWV 36/1, "Schwingt freudig euch empor" (instruments); BWV 36/5, "Willkommen, werter Schatz" (instruments); BWV 83/3, "Eile, Herz, voll Freudigkeit"; BWV 94/6, "Die Welt kann ihre Lust und Freud". Arias expressing joy in triple time are too numerous to require mention.

Ex. 1. *Musical Offering*, Ricercar a 3, mm. 38f.

Ex. 2. *Ibid.*, mm. 42f.

Second, the triplet rhythm leads directly into alternating *alla zoppa* and Pyrrhichius rhythm, measures 42-45, 90-94 (Ex. 2), for the rhythm of each of these measures is perceived clearly as ♪ ♩ ♪ + ♫♫, with the complementary rhythm in adjacent parts creating the effect of a succession of eighth notes in the second half of each measure. Music theorists of Bach's time testify that the *alla zoppa* rhythm was then in high fashion, and Spiess remarks, only two years before the *Musical Offering*, that it has an eager and driving effect ("was eifriges und treibendes an sich").[41] The Pyrrhichius, the warlike foot of ancient poetry, "flies rather than runs", "at most suitable for expressing rapid motions".[42] It had been used by Monteverdi for the *stile concitato*;[43] and in the heroic arias of Venetian opera and oratorio[44] this rhythm, consisting solely of short notes, was much favored, "for the circumstances of war leave no place for inaction, either in fleeing or in pursuing the enemy".[45] Again Bach is listening to Quintilian's words on the exordium, those saying that the mind of the judge "must be stirred (*agitandus est*) by hope, fear, admonition, entreaty"

---

[41] MATTHESON, p. 168; Meinrad SPIESS, *Tractatus musicus compositorio practicus*, Augsburg, Lotter, 1745, p. 164; Franz Xaver RICHTER, *Harmonische Belehrungen*, ms. B-Br II.6292, pp. 189f.

[42] "volat potius quam currit", "aptus duntaxat ad celeres motus exprimendos" – Isaac VOSSIUS, *De poematum cantu et viribus rythmi*, Oxford, Sheldonian Theater, 1673, p. 5.

[43] Preface to *Madrigali guerrieri et amorosi*, Venice, Vincenti, 1638.

[44] *AC* 1966 p. 312 = *AC* 2007 p. 389.

[45] MATTHESON, pp. 164f; also SPIESS, p. 164: "tauglich zu flüchtigen und Kriegs-Wesen ["useful for flighty and war-like character"].

(IV.i.33f). These measures could be understood also in the light of the dedication, which alludes to Frederick's knowledge of both military science and music, "dessen Grösse und Stärke, gleich wie in allen Kriegs- und Friedens-Wissenschaften, also auch besonders in der Musik, jedermann bewundern und verehren muss" ["whose greatness and strength, just as in all sciences of war and peace, thus also especially in music, everyone must admire and revere"].

Ex. 3. *Ibid.*, mm. 107-111.

Third, the traditional 'sighs', measures 107-118 (Ex. 3), which combine all means for expressing profound sorrow, pain: suspensions, rests on the downbeat (*suspiratio*, *tmeses*), stepwise, often chromatic descent – the latter, of course, already present in the second half of the *thema regium*, but not yet formulated with the pathos motives as a sigh. Here Bach applies the entire arsenal, even achieving a bold chromatic descent in parallel minor sixths (Ex. 4, mm. 117f). "For pity (*miseratio*) alone moves even an honest judge. However, it should be only tasted in the exordium, not worn out. The person of our opponent is usually attacked by nearly these same means, but inverted" (*e contrario ductis*) – IV.i.14. Bach portrays the adversary relationship not only by using again the Pyrrhic rhythm, but also by opposing chromatic descent with chromatic ascent, i.e. "inverted" (mm. 115-123; Ex. 4).[46] "It is useful to give the impression that, just as our fate will be deserving of pity if we lose, ... our adversaries will be arrogant if they win" (IV.i.29). The rising chromatic line, expressing this insolence, collides with the falling one in a veritable

---

[46] Cf. above, p. 76, on the relationship of melodic inversion to rhetoric.

Ex. 4. *Ibid.* mm. 117-121.

Pyrrhic *combattimento*, until it finally succumbs, yielding to the 'joy' of the returning triplets.

Once again, let us hear Quintilian on the exordium. His counsel to create the impression "that we shall not delay long" now explains one of the more puzzling features of the piece: the brevity of the passages for '*docere*', '*delectare*', and '*movere*' (*agitare, suspirare*). "We give briefly and lucidly a summary of the case ..., which Homer and Virgil do at the beginning of their works" (IV.i.34). Bach has done just this, given a brief summary of rhythmic, melodic, and harmonic devices all of which we shall find elaborated later, in the trio sonata.[47]

NARRATIO BREVIS = CANON PERPETUUS SUPER THEMA REGIUM

The *narratio*, the section of the oration which follows the exordium, was classified in rhetoric as either short or, if long, divided into short sections (*partitio*). This latter *narratio* is of course hardly designated as 'long', for that would be a *vitium*, but euphemistically as 'ornata' or 'repetita', since in some cases the two types might be used in the same oration: "There is a certain repeated *narratio* ..., albeit belonging more to declamation than to forensic oratory, but invented (since the *narratio* should be brief) to enable the facts to be set forth at greater length and with more ornament" (IV.ii.128). We shall see that Bach's *Canon perpetuus* is a *narratio brevis*, while the five numbered canons which follow it are a *narratio ornata*, a *repetita narratio*.

---

[47] SPITTA already noticed that the "strange episodes" discussed above return in the sonata – II, 673, 676.

In the *narratio brevis*

we must be content with giving the conclusions from which the rest can be understood. ... [But] our brevity must not be without elegance. ... The syntax should be unobtrusive, yet as attractive as possible; the figures must be neither poetical nor contrary to the usage of speech, even if retained by authority of antiquity (for our language must be as pure as possible), but should avoid tedium with variety and lift the spirit with alterations; nor should we cut up [the speech] into equal sections (*ne pares ... tractus*) delivered with the same terminations and similar syntax. ... The more dignified and serious (*gravius ac sanctius*) [our style], the more weight it will lend ... to our assertions (IV.ii.40f, 46, 117f, 125).

In his *Canon perpetuus* Bach places the *thema regium*, in diminution, between the two other voices, which form with each other a two-part perpetual canon at the lower double octave and at the distance of one measure. It is indeed the shortest, with only five measures. But it surprises us with great metrical and rhythmic variety. The meter, underground, could be indicated as: $2 \times 4/4$, $2 \times 3/4$, $1 \times 2/4$, $1 \times 4/4$ (the long notes, dotted or tied, have the effect of beginning a measure) – "ne pares ... tractus". In their first measure the canonic voices pay tribute to the royal theme with dotted rhythm, descending stepwise. It is the 'king'-topos, "dignified and serious", which Lully used especially in his overtures as homage to the Sun King and was imitated throughout Europe, particularly in Germany and England, not only in instrumental, but also in vocal music (by Bach of course in both repertoires) whenever the text speaks of royalty.[48] The second measure moves entirely in running (Pyrrhic) sixteenth notes, the third and fourth introduce still another rhythm, the 'heroic' dactyl, in interpolated (not notated) 3/4 time, and the fifth finally holds back the motion with the longest note in the canon (2 beats). The first half of the *thema regium* is, moreover, separated from its continuation by rests, which gives it the effect of a heading, like the *Devise* or motto in baroque arias.

Characteristic of the *narratio brevis* is the *oratio perpetua*,[49] which, like Bach's infinite canon proceeds straight ahead, without an end in sight.[50] When Quintilian comes to deal with this in a later book, he finds that he can do no better than to bring an extensive quotation from Cicero: "In the *oratio perpe-*

---

48 See above, ch. 7.

49 Uninterrupted speech, as opposed to dialogue and dialectic debate; see QUINTILIAN, II.xx.7, and below, note 150, and Plate XI.2: "perpetuo commentario".

50 ARISTOTLE, *Ars rhetorica*, III.ix.2; HEINRICH LAUSBERG, *Handbuch der literarischen Rhetorik*, Munich, Hueber, 1973², p. 457.

tua ... there is often a rapid summary (*percursio*), suggesting more than you said; there is distinctly concise brevity and extenuation; and to this irony (*illusio*) is added" (Quintilian, IX.i.26ff, from Cicero, *De oratore*, III.lii.201-liii.202). Cicero excelled in the use of such *percursiones* in the *narratio brevis*. They present a condensation of events, which touches briefly the most important points, like "headings of omitted chapters; essential for this figure is that much more could be said about each of these themes, but this is relinquished".[51] Just as the orator fills out the "headings of omitted chapters" in the *repetita narratio*, so Bach fully elaborates the characteristic features of his *percursio* later in the *Elaborationes canonicae*, the five *canones diversi*. The French rhythm, used here in only one measure, will pervade the entire fourth canon; the running sixteenth notes, likewise in only one measure, will dominate the first canon (the doubling of note values of both the *thema regium* and the canonic parts is only visual, since the time signature is changed from c to ¢); the 'heroic' dactylic rhythms (♩♪♪) will return in the second half of the fifth canon; and the strict, literal imitation of the first canonic voice by the second (here at the double octave) will be used again for the second canon (there at the unison). Also the *thema regium* contributes rhythms to the canons of the *narratio ornata*: its diminution form is taken over by the third canon, its paean-rhythms in measures 4 and 5 contribute to the grand style of canons 4 and 5.

NARRATIO ORNATA (REPETITA NARRATIO) =
[5] CANONES DIVERSI SUPER THEMA REGIUM
(THEMATIS REGII ELABORATIONES CANONICAE)

[**PS**: The discussion of the five numbered canons has now been revised]. The famous acrostic "**R**egis **I**ussu **C**antio **E**t **R**eliqua **C**anonica **A**rte **R**esoluta" ["The theme and the rest resolved by canonic art, according to the command of the king"] was, as we know, not included in the original printing phase of the *Musical Offering*, but added to it afterwards, in two ways: 1) in the dedication copy it is written by hand in large, calligraphic letters on f. 1 of unit B,[52] i.e. directly before the three-part ricercar; 2) in the other copies it is printed on a strip of paper end pasted on f. 1 of unit D, preceding the *canones diversi*.[53] There can be little doubt that the second arrangement represents

---

[51] LAUSBERG, p. 435.

[52] Contrary to KB, p. 59, where the position of the two facsimiles is reversed – an error which, if undetected, could have had no little consequence for our conclusions.

[53] Whether or not one regards the acrostic as an afterthought (as WOLFF did in *Terminus*,

Bach's definitive intention, since the dedication copy, where it was not yet printed, would be the first one released, and in any case the acrostic refers to the canons of unit D ("reliqua"). But why did Bach decide to place an acrostic here?

Whenever we have employed the exordium, whether we intend to proceed to the *narratio* or directly to the *probatio* [i.e. the first section of the *argumentatio*], it must end with something which can be easily joined to the beginning of the next section. In the schools there is indeed a frigid and childish affectation that the transition (*transitus*) itself at least forms some epigram (*sententiam*) as if one seeks approbation for this trick. Ovid often plays with this in his *Metamorphoses*, which, however, can be excused by the necessity of uniting the most heterogeneous elements (*res diversissimas*) to a sort of single body (IV.i.77).

Although Quintilian does not recommend the insertion of an epigram in forensic orations, he allows the possibility in cases, like Ovid's *Metamorphoses*, where diverse elements must be given unity. Bach thus follows the example of Ovid (via Quintilian) and places his epigram between the three-part ricercar (exordium) and the "*canones diversi*[ssimi]" (*narratio ornata*). The acrostic recalls the former, by spelling out the word 'ricercar', and anticipates the latter ("reliqua canonica arte resoluta"), thus forming the a *transitus*. The presence of the *Canon perpetuus* between the three-part ricercar and the acrostic does not speak against this interpretation, for it will be remembered that the *narratio brevis* was also an alternative to the *narratio ornata*. Bach was therefore quite justified in placing the acrostic before his *narratio* proper, as a heading for the new printer's unit containing even more "heterogeneous elements" than the single *Canon perpetuus*. Only here are these elements fully *elaborated*, in keeping with the technique of the *narratio ornata*. For this reason Bach had added to f. 1 of unit D in the dedication copy (i.e. where the printed acrostic appears in the other copies) the handwritten heading "Thematis Regii Elaborationes Canonicae". Also the term *elaboratio*, used again in the newspaper announcement, is, of course, taken directly from rhetoric.

Speaking of the detailed *narratio*, Quintilian says, "Division (*partitio*) relieves tedium" (IV.ii.49). Then he advised how such a *narratio* is to be made credible, stressing especially five forensic qualities (*virtutes*): naturalness, mi-

---

p. 77, and *Ordnungsprinzipien*, p. 159, but not in *New Research*, p. 394, and KB, p. 47), and whether or not one accepts the technological explanations in the latter two publications – these considerations do not affect our conclusions on the position and function of the acrostic. Wolff explains its position in the dedication copy by his 'fascicle' theory – *New Research*, p. 395; KB, p. 60. But the caption is as suitable for 'D plus E' as for 'D covering E'.

micry, illusion of simplicity, magnificence, and palpability. Also Bach divides his *repetita narratio* into five canons which, as we shall see, correspond precisely to these five forensic qualities. But Quintilian had already discussed also *virtutes* of the epideictic genus. For the praise of a person one can derive them from his ancestors, character, etc.:

Ipsius vero laus hominis ex animo et corpore et extra positis peti debet. ... Nam et pulchritudinem interim roburque prosequimur honore verborum, ut Homerus in Agamemnone atque Achille, et interim confert admirationi multum etiam infirmitas, ut cum idem Tydea parvum sed bellatorem dicit fuisse. Fortuna vero tum dignitatem adfert, ut in regibus principibusque (namque est haec materia ostendendae virtutis uberior), tum quo minores opes fuerunt, maiorem bene factis gloriam parit ... (III.vii.12f).	The [topics for] praise of the individual himself must be sought in his mental and physical characteristics and in external circumstances. ... For we sometimes accompany manly excellence[54] and strength with laudatory words, as Homer does with Agamemnon and Achilles; sometimes even weakness may confer much admiration, as when Homer says that Tydeus was small but a courageous warrior. Sometimes *fortune* in fact produces dignity, as with *kings* and princes (for this subject is more fertile for the display of virtue); another time, where the resources are less, it brings forth greater *glory* with good deeds ... (III.vii.12f).

We shall see that these five epideictic virtues – manly excellence, strength, overcoming weakness, fortune (bringing dignity), and gloria – are indeed combined by Bach with the five forensic ones, in a single series of five canons, endowing each piece with human content. These are the only components of the *Musical Offering* which the composer numbered. We shall examine them separately, each one for its form and style ("[f]" = forensic quality), then for its content ("[e]" = epideictic quality). On such application of epideictic content to forensic form, see above, pp. 104, 424. The discussion will be clarified by reference to Table 2, p. 448.

1. *Canon a 2* [*cancrizans*]

[**f**: Naturalness]. As the first forensic virtue Quintilian proposes "not to say anything contrary to nature" (IV.ii.52).[55] Bach fulfills this brilliantly with

---

[54] Here "pulchritudo" should be translated not simply as "beauty", with its connotions of femininity.

[55] E.g. one should not use the figure of *adynaton*, illustrated by CURTIUS, pp. 102-106 ("verkehrte Welt").

a crab (retrograde) canon, for the crab is one of the very few natural phenomena which has a terminological and technical equivalent in music.[56] That it walked backward (*adversum*) was believed[57] to be part of its nature. Thus the composer need say nothing which is not already contained in the single staff of the crab canon. All of the other *canones diversi* say more, by adding a second staff. (Those who are at all acquainted with Frederick's private life may find the words "contrary to nature" not irrelevant). Like most crab canons, this one is for two voices, one reading the part forwards, the other starting at the end and reading it backwards. The first half combines the *thema regium* with a counterpoint in running eighth notes, the second presents this material in retrograde motion with the roles of the voices exchanged. Bach could have found the rhetorical model for his crab canon in the *redditio contraria*, where a simile (*similitudo*) directly precedes, rather than follows, the subject which it illustrates and stands in an exactly reciprocal relationship to it: "it is attached to the subject which it illustrates, corresponding in turn by analogy, which is produced by going back in the opposite direction" (VIII.iii.77). He presents here the *genus humile*: half and quarter notes for the *thema regium* and running eighth notes for its continuation, entirely free from effeminate embellishments. Only the five suspensions in the *thema* create a strange delay.

[e: Strength]. Of the epideictic virtues the rhetorician mentions first "manly excellence" and "strength". Since the two heroes are syntactically equivalent, Bach could choose freely their sequence. He preferred to begin with Achilles, whose "strength" had for so long lain dormant, but now becomes active, as we know from the famous lines of Homer, familiar to every schoolboy:

---

56 Crab imagery is, of course, not limited to music. Some ancient coins combined on their two sides a crab and a sovereign – see below, note 58. In astronomy and astrology cancer (♋) marks the solstice, the time of year (21 June) when the length of the days begins to move backward, becoming shorter. This is depicted musically in Gregor Joseph WERNER's *Neuer und sehr curios- Musicalischer Instrumental-Kalender, Parthien-weiß mit 2 Violinen und Basso o Cembalo in die zwolff Jahrs-Monat eingetheilet*, Augsburg, Lotter, 1748, where the length of the two sections of the [non-canonic] menuets is in proportion to the length of the days and nights. Baroque authors employed the cancrizans idea for emblems ("Simul retroque", "Orbis iter", etc.), poems (e.g. as an encomium which, read backwards, produced a libel), or retrograde 'concetti' (such as a river flowing toward its source) – cf. Alfred HENKEL and Albrecht SCHÖNE, *Emblemata*, Stuttgart, Metz, 1967, cols. 722-729; Giovanni da LOCARNO, *Saggio sullo stile dell'oratoria sacra nel seicento*, Rome, Inst. Storicum, 1954, p. 172; Théophile de VIAU, quoted in CURTIUS, p. 105. All such usages convey a positive and/or negative idea; also Bach does this, as will be seen.

57 Not only by composers or astronomers, but in general. Nowadays zoologists will tell us that it walks sideways.

There was no one who would lead the men into the ranks. For swift-footed, godly Achilles lay among the ships, angered on account of the fair-haired maiden Briseïs, whom he had taken out of Lyrnessus after great toil, when he had laid waste Lyrnessus and the walls of Thebes and struck down Mynes and Epistrophus, the spear-wielding sons of King Evenus. On her account he lay grieving, but soon he was to rise up (*Iliad*, II.685-694).

The *thema regium* too is indeed 'idle', with the chromatic descent delayed by its suspensions. But the second half of the canon (or the second voice in the first half) is just the opposite: with the steady eighth notes often found in Bach's vocal music to express walking or running, it is equivalent to the Homeric epithet for the "swift-footed" Achilles (II.688), who is now reactivated. (We are reminded of the association of the crab with the butterfly in emblematic art, illustrating the slowness and speed, respectively, of the motto "festina lente").[58] Since the eighth notes are grouped into fours by usually changing direction every half measure, they produce also the Pyrrhic effect for the warrior. The rise through the tonic chord in quarter notes at the beginning of the second voice is a typical heroic incipit: Achilles "rises",[59] just as God does in Schütz's "Es steht Gott auf".[60]

2. Canon a 2 violini in unisono

[**f**: Mimicry]. Secondly (*deinde*), Quintilian recommends that "we make the roles of the persons agree with the facts we desire to be believed, ... [and give] a certain air of credibility, as in comedies and pantomimes (*in comoediis etiam et in mimis*). For some things follow naturally and are coherent, so that, if only your preceding remarks are made well, the judge himself will be eager to hear what you have to say next" (IV.ii.52f). And Bach? He adapts this canon to the stage. The two-part canon at the unison at the distance of one measure over the *thema regium*, moves in declamatory style, largely in eighth notes, while the *thema regium* is inconspicuous, without ornament, like a *basso continuo*. The two upper parts are notated for violins (only here), the

---

[58] W. DEONNA, *The Crab and the Butterfly: A Study in Animal Symbolism*, «Journal of the Warburg and Courtauld Institutes», XVII, 1954, p. 47.

[59] Whether the figures following the initial *anabasis* are also 'translated' from Homer I shall not determine, but it is not impossible that Bach meant to depict Achilles' famous shield with the *circulus* in mm. 1-2 and the motion of his arm (back-forward) hurling the spear with the large leaps in the first half of m. 3.

[60] *Symphoniarum sacrarum secunda pars*, Bautzen, Klemm & Herring, 1647; *Neue Ausgabe sämtlicher Werke*, XVI, Kassel, Bärenreiter, 1965, p. 29. In his preface, Schütz acknowledges that he derived the *stile concitato* of this piece from Monteverdi's *Madrigali guerrieri et amorosi*.

'royal' bass part remains in the keyboard instrument. The slow harmonic rhythm in **c** (rather than **¢**), the long, precipitous descent at the beginning, then the upward transposition of short motives which flow three times into a musical 'question' (the so typical rise to a long note on the second or fifth degree) and one 'answer' with gigantic leaps and a broken triad at the end – all this makes this canon not only 'gallant', modern, but dramatic, operatic. It is a typical three-part [!] *duetto* as Mattheson described:[61]

... von kleinen Fragen und noch kleinern Antworten Gesprächs-Weise zusammen gesetzet. ... [Der Baß könne] selten grosse Sprünge machen, noch sich sonderlich hervorthun. ... [Er soll] nur gantz einfältig, doch edel einhergehen, und sich mehrentheils, als ein Gefährte und Geleitsmann, nach den Ober-Stimmen richten. ... Steffani war hierin unvergleichlich. Ich habe selbst Sachen von ihm in dieser Schreib-Art auf der Schaubühne gesungen. ... Es kehren sich die beiden Singstimmen nicht das geringste an den Baß. Daher führet auch diese Gattung den Nahmen der Duette, obgleich ... eine dreistimmige Harmonie vorhanden ist: gerade, als ob der Baß, weil er nur auf Instrumenten gespielet wird, bloß zur Ziefer da wäre. ... An etlichen Orten macht der Baß ... eine *Tenuta*, hält eine Zeitlang in einem Tone aus, und wartet gleichsam auf die Singstimmen, bis sie sich gemächlich aus einander gewickelt haben.

... composed of questions and even smaller answers in the manner of a conversation. ... [The bass can] rarely make large leaps or distinguish itself particularly. ... [It should] only proceed quite simply yet nobly, and, for the most part, as a companion and escort, conforming to the upper parts. ... Steffani was incomparable at this. I have myself sung pieces by him in this style on the operatic stage. ... The two vocal parts don't pay the least attention to the bass. Hence also this genre bears the name of 'duet', even though ... a three-part harmony is present: precisely as if the bass, because it is played only on instruments, were there only as a number. ... At some places it makes ... a *tenuta*, sustains a note for some time, and waits as it were for the voices, until they have leisurely untangled themselves.

Bach thus presents the *stylus theatralis* in the *genus medium*, that *genus* most suitable for fulfilling the rhetorical function of *delectare* (XII.x.59), which was traditionally assigned to comedy, with milder affect (*ethos*) and a wealth of figures (VI.ii.9, 19f, XII.x.60) – in this canon: *mimesis* (strict imitation), *katabasis* (long scalar descent), *subjectio* (question-answer), *circulus* (sine curve), etc.

[**e**: Manly excellence]. When Quintilian alluded to Agamemnon's excellence, he surely had another memorable passage of Homer in mind (*Iliad* II.474-483):

---

[61] Pp. 348-351.

And just as goatherds separate easily the wide-ranging flocks of goats, when they mingle in the pasture, so the leaders marshalled them [the troops] on this side and that to enter into battle, and among them mighty Agamemnon, his eyes and head like Jupiter who delights in thunder, his waist like Mars, and his chest like Neptune. He was like a bull pre-eminent by far over all the herd, since he was conspicuous among the gathering cattle. For such did Jupiter make the son of Atreus on that day, conspicuous among many and pre-eminent among heroes.

Bach, too, must not only have read, but fully understood these lines, before he wrote his second canon.[62] The first 'question' (cf. above, p. 436; Ex. 5, mm. 1f)

Ex. 5. *Musical Offering,* Canon a 2 violini in unisono.

in this 'duet' must refer to Jupiter. The high and powerful head motive, with the falling fifth in quarter notes, can be identified with the impressive 'head' of the god, for immediately follows a long *katabasis*, first descending abruptly, then abating, as he hurls down his thunder-bolt, the attribute which identified him since Homeric times. If a reader should doubt the objectivity of this interpretation, he need only look at Monteverdi's setting of Jupiter's thunder-bolt ("Giove ... tenga ... il fulmine") in Act I of *Il ritorno d'Ulisse in patria* (1641, Ex. 6),[63] the "thunder" in Purcell's *Dido and Aeneas,*[64] David hurling

---

[62] He could have identified the passage with the help of a gloss in an edition of Quintilian, such as those of Lyons 1549, Geneva 1580, London 1641, or Paris 1736. The passage on Achilles, however, is given incorrectly in the latter edition and many of the following ones (consistently misprinted as "II.180" instead of "II.680ff"), up to and including Loeb, 1933.

[63] *Tutte le opere,* Asolo, Malipiero, 1926-43, XII, 38.

[64] *Works,* London, Novello, 1878ff, III, 57.

Ex. 6. Monteverdi, *Il ritorno d'Ulisse in patria*, Act I.

Ten-ga e-gli a vo-glia sua nel - la gran de-stra il ful - - - mi-ne

a stone at Goliath in one of Kuhnau's biblical sonatas (a rapid run, set off rhythmically from its context),[65] or still the lightening in Mozart's *Thamos*.[66] Bach would not need to have known Monteverdi (though he surely knew the publication of Kuhnau, his predecessor in Leipzig), for such imagery was still universally understood.[67] The next 'question' (mm. 3f) can represent with its Pyrrhic rhythm the war god Mars. Its four-note motive is repeated at widely separated pitches, suggesting the words "separate easily the wide-ranging flocks" and "marshalled the troops on this side and that". (Similar classical imagery is applied to Frederick the Great in letters by his contemporaries. Kammerdirektor Christoph Werner Hille wrote in 1731: "It is astonishing how much he [Frederick] sometimes resembles *Juppiter tonans*";[68] or Voltaire, in 1752: "He would prefer to mount his horse and exercise the soldiers of Pyrrhus").[69] And the motive itself – three times descending a minor third in legato, followed by a staccato note – could it perhaps imitate the bleating of the goats?[70] The third 'question', with three *circulus* figures in succession (mm. 5f), can depict with its wave-motion the sea god Neptune, while retain-

---

[65] *Musicalische Vorstellung einiger biblischer Historien ... auf dem Claviere zu spielen*, Leipzig, Tietz, 1700; «Denkmäler Deutscher Tonkunst», IV, Leipzig, Breitkopf & Härtel, 1901, p. 129.

[66] «Neue Mozart-Ausgabe», Serie II, Werkgruppe VI/1, Kassel, Bärenreiter, 1956, pp. 228f. Cf. also the elaborate coloraturas for the words "il ciel tonante e di fulmini armato" in the first recitative of Borea in Alessandro Scarlatti's oratorio *Il giardino di rose*, D-MÜs 3861. By this time such a device was not always appreciated; Stefano ARTEAGA, not favoring musical depictions of single words, gives as an example "le [parole] precipitano sul *fulmine*" ["the words are precipitated on lightening"] – *Le rivoluzioni del teatro musicale italiano dalla sua origine fino al presente*, Bologna, Trenti, 1783, I, 75.

[67] This rhetorical *ratio* of the Renaissance and Baroque is not to be confused with the 'sound effects' of 19th-century program music (Wolff). See the study by Arnold SCHMITZ, *Die Bildlichkeit der wortgebundenen Musik Johann Sebastian Bachs*, Mainz, Schott, 1950.

[68] "Es ist erstaunlich, wie er zu gewissen Zeiten dem *Jupiter tonans* gleicht" – *Friedrich der Grosse im Spiegel seiner Zeit*, ed. Gustav Berthold Volz, I, Berlin, Dobing, 1926, p. 32.

[69] "il voudrait monter à cheval et exercer les soldats de Pyrrhus" – letter of 22 Apr. from Potsdam, *Correspondance*, III, Paris, Gallimard, 1975, p. 669.

[70] Bach's wit has been well documented (e.g. by Schweitzer), thus in the *Bauernkanate* BWV 212 or the *Kaffeekantate* BWV 211, where even in the chorus "Die Katze läßt das *Mau*sen nicht" – with the syllable "Mau-" a quick motion rising through a minor third to a sustained note – the 'miaowing' can be heard.

ing the Pyrrhic rhythm, now pairing the eighth notes across the beat by alternating staccato and legato to emphasize the 'floating' and 'rocking' – a rare instance of detailed articulation in this work. But what is the significance of the 'answer', the last two measures with their huge leaps, extending to two octaves? Surely they depict Agamemnon himself, like "a bull, ... conspicuous among many and pre-eminent among heroes". For this the Pyrrhic rhythm continues, and the canon closes with the same 'heroic' rise through the tonic chord which introduced Achilles in the first canon. The questions and answer permit us to imagine an unspoken text, such as: "Who is like Jupiter? like Mars? like Neptune? That am I, Agamemnon".[71]

Quintilian's allusion to Agamemnon thus identifies the actors in this miniature operatic scene. Here beings of unequal rank are compared, a human with gods. The musical means correspond to the rhetorical *emphasis*, which has a deeper meaning than the words themselves (VIII.iii.83-86; IX.ii.3). Violins are used here exceptionally to depict persons in operatic style, three gods and a king, just as the return of this instrument in the trio sonata and the final *Canon perpetuus* will be explained by King Frederick's participation as a performer. "Et in mimis" provides also the clue for the contrapuntal structure of the second canon. *Mimesis* is defined by Quintilian as "imitation of other persons' characteristics" ("imitatio morum alienorum" – IX.ii.58), and in music theory it designated canonic imitation.[72] In Bach's canon, the gods, of course, enter first; the second voice, beginning one measure later, is already their 'imitation', Agamemnon, who then imitates himself at the end. We see now why Bach here writes a canon at the unison: this most literal form of imitation depicts most perfectly the hero 'mimicking' the gods. The entire canon is a courtly masquerade or 'Wirthschaft', such as often included gods. Gottsched confirms that this genre was still fashionable at the German courts.[73]

---

[71] On the appearance of Mars and Neptune in courtly *Aufzügen* cf. above, p. 108, and Julius Bernhard von ROHR's important *Einleitung zur Ceremoniel-Wissenschaft der großen Herren*, Berlin [!], Rüdiger, 1733 [!], p. 745 (kindly brought to my attention by Juliane Riepe). WOLFF's reference to my interpretation (*Bach: Essays on his Life and Music*, Cambridge MA, Harvard UP, 1991, p. 422) fails to identify the Pyrrhic rhythms with Mars, whom he lists separately, omitting Neptune, identified by *cirulationes* (waves). Like most composers of the Baroque, Bach consistently employed the *circulatio* to depict waves or water – cf. the conspicuous examples from his works quoted above, pp. 7f, Exx. 10ff.

[72] Cf. Johannes Frosch (1532) and Johannes Stomius (1537), quoted above, pp. 66f, note 155. BURMEISTER seems to have been unaware of this usage, for he uses 'mimesis' to designate homophonic imitation: the repetition of a *noema* at a different pitch (p. 59).

[73] *Versuch einer critischen Dichtkunst*, Leipzig, B. C. Breitkopf, 1751[4], pp. 756-771 ("Von Wirthschaften, Mummereyen, und Balletten").

3. Canon a 2 per motum contrarium

[**f**: Illusion of simplicity]. According to Quintilian's third forensic quality, the best kind of preparatory remarks will be those which are concealed. ... [Cicero's] most effective device is his very cunning feint of simplicity: 'Milo, however, having been in the senate that day until it adjourned, went home, changed his shoes and clothes, and waited a short time, while his wife was getting ready, as happens'. How Milo's action appears without haste or premeditation! The most eloquent man attains this not merely with the facts themselves, with which he depicts the delay and slow departure, but also with ordinary, everyday speech, concealing the art. ... That sort of thing appears dull to most people, but by just this it is shown how he deceives the judge because he is scarcely detected [even] by a reader. It is these things which make the *narratio* credible (IV.ii.57ff, with quotation from Cicero, *Pro Milone*, X.28).

Bach again gives us a musical model for one of the three *genera dicendi*, now the *genus humile/subtile* or plain style,[74] moving in simple eighth and quarter notes, in high, narrow range (SSA), like boys' or womens' voices, corresponding to the rhetorical *apheleia*, i.e. "simple and unaffected", with "a certain purity which is admired also in women" (VIII.iii.87). He presents the *thema regium* in the upper part, unadorned and in diminution (now in quarter notes) – a *ratiocinatio* relationship, where "one thing is wont to be magnified by allusion to another" and "attenuation is effected by nearly the same method" (VIII.iv.20 and 28). The two lower voices form a two-part canon by inversion at the distance of half a measure, moving simply in eighth and sixteenth notes, largely alternating in complementary rhythm. But Bach conceals his art (*arte occulta* – IV.ii.58) by writing this canon in contrary motion, so that the listener does not readily perceive the canonic structure. The use of exclusively high ranges may represent also *acumen* ('peak', hence 'keenness'), which Quintilian mentions as necessary for *docere*, the function best fulfilled by the plain style (XII.x.58f).

[**e**: Overcoming weakness] Since Bach endows his third canon with the *genus subtile*, *simplicitas*, 'smallness', and diminution, he accepts, again with a smile, Quintilian's third epideictic virtue, overcoming *infirmitas*: "Sometimes even weakness may confer much admiration, as when Homer [*Iliad*, V.801] says that Tydeus was small but a courageous warrior". These words fit also Frederick perfectly, for his physical stature was unusually small for

---

74 The Latin adjective '*subtilis*' as used in classical rhetoric means 'plain', 'simple', 'unadorned'. The term '*ars subtilior*' for the highly sophisticated French music of the late 14th century is probably derived from the alternate meaning: 'finely woven', 'slender'.

a king, so much so that all Europe knew it, and he sometimes compared himself to a monkey. Of over 900 portraits, only about half a dozen show him in the vicinity of other persons, none of these more 'to scale' than *Die Wachtparade* by his famous engraver Chodowiecki: on his horse, at the very front of the picure, but tiny.[75]

4. *Canon a 2 per augmentationem, contrario motu*

[**f**: Magnificence]. The fourth forensic quality – "To these three qualities of narration some add ..." – is admitted by Quintilian only with reservations: *magnificentia*. One cannot apply it "in all cases (for what place can a language rising above the normal level have in most civil suits – certain loans, leases, hirings, prohibitions?)" (IV.ii.61). Thus he indicates that it is to be used only for the highest authorities – the emperor, his family, the senators. But since Bach is paying tribute to a king, he can make this entire canon 'magnificent', in the *genus grande*. Even without reading Quintilian, we cannot fail to recognize the magnificent 'royal' style. All three voices have the majestic 'French' rhythm with dotted notes and paean, the style of the first movements of Lully's overtures, which emanated from the court of the Sun King. The style was, however, derived in part from meters of antiquity, where the paean signified praise of the ruler.[76] "Lofty passages ... are fond of the dactyl's and also the paean's amplitude" (IX.iv.136). This was doubtless understood by Lully's imitators throughout Europe, including Mattheson: "Paeon, ... from παιών, hymnus, because it was dedicated to songs of praise".[77] Since the 'first' paean (long plus three short) was regarded also as especially "suitable for beginnings" (IX.iv.96),[78] baroque composers used it extensively "in overtures and entrées".[79]

But Bach pays further tribute to the king's magnificence with the two figures most characteristic of epideictic rhetoric and the *genus grande*: augmentation and hyperbole. Augmentation had of course been applied by panegyrists since antiquity, in all rhetorical degrees, to praise the virtues of patrons.

---

[75] Cf. Reinhold KOSER, *Die Berichte der Zeitgenossen über die äussere Erscheinung Friedrichs des Grossen*, «Hohenzollern Jahrbuch», 1897, pp. 90-94, 103.

[76] Cf. above, pp. 236f.

[77] "*Pæon* ... von παιών, *hymnus*, weil er den Lobgesängen gewidmet war" – p. 168.

[78] Cf. also ARISTOTLE, III.viii.6.

[79] "Uns dienet er in Ouvertüren und Entreen" – MATTHESON, *loc. cit.* Cf. SPIESS, p. 164: "zu Ouverturen und Entreen fleissig gebraucht" ["used diligently for overtures and entries"].

It "is most effective when even inferior things appear great" (VIII.iv.3).[80] With the fourth canon, the *thema regium*, now rhythmically ornamented, is presented in the middle voice, framed and crossed by two canonic voices, the higher imitating the lower strictly in both augmentation and contrary motion (see Appendix I). This manner of augmentation – simultaneous with the normal theme – corresponds to Quintilian's second category of *amplificatio*: through *comparatio*, the *locus* "a minore ad maius",[81] since "augmenting ... that which is below, it is necessary to raise that which is placed above" – VIII.iv.9].

The hyperbole is, in rhetoric, the intensification of augmentation beyond the limit of credibility (VIII.vi.67, XII.x.62). It too was amply employed for the praise of rulers. In music it is not necessarily related to the technique of augmentation, but designates, according to Burmeister, a voice rising above the upper limit of its ambitus. His one example is, significantly, a setting by Lasso of the words "semper laus eius" ["always his praise"].[82] Bach places the hyperbole in the tenor voice, with its gigantic range of a thirteenth requiring ledger lines even in the original notation.[83]

Yet, after eight measures, at the end of the non-augmented canonic voice and half of the augmented one, we must pause. Of the three attempted solutions[84] we can immediately exclude that of the old Bach edition (Dörffel) with the augmented voice continuing recklessly to the end, since this yields intolerable dissonances and "a senseless harmonic structure".[85] We can for-

---

[80] UNGER, p. 78, and Martin RUHNKE, *Joachim Burmeister*, Kassel, Bärenreiter, 1955, p. 154, have suspected that the definition of *auxesis* used by Burmeister in 1599 shared a common source with Gerardus Vossius. We can now identify this source as Quintilian's description of *augmentatio*, which continues with the words "uno gradu ... pervenit ... ad summam", repeated almost verbatim by the two later authors. Burmeister, however, no longer retains this formulation in his revised definition of *auxesis* in his *Musica poetica*, Rostock, Myliander, 1606, and he never associates this figure with increased note values.

[81] LAUSBERG, pp. 218, 222f.

[82] P. 64: "Hyperbole ... est melodiae supra supremum ejus terminum superlatio. Exemplum est in Orlandi 'Benedicam' ad textum: 'Semper laus ejus'" ["Hyperbole ... is rising beyond the upper range of a melody ...", as in Lasso's motet "Benedicam Dominum" from his *Hieremiae prophetae lamentationes et aliae piae cantiones*, Munich, Berg, 1585].

[83] NBA, p. XIV. The six-part ricercar (score) and the four-part canon (G minor) are deliberately notated in a manner to avoid ledger lines – see DAVID, p. 177, and KB, p. 111.

[84] By Johann Christoph Oley (1738?-1789), Alfred Dörffel, and Friedrich Smend. The last two in KB, p. 114.

[85] KB, p. 114; also DAVID, p. 98. Astonishingly, this absolutely unmusical solution (together with Dörffel's rhythmic alteration of the lowest voice in m. 7), already rejected also by DAVID, p. 98, is retained in Peter WILLIAMS' edition, London, Eulenburg, 1986, pp. 50f, where the sequence of the pieces likewise has no justification and the untenable "wrapper" theory is still taken seriously.

get also Oley's solution, which ends already with the first half of the augmented voice and then only repeats what was already heard.[86] But as Friedrich Smend pointed out,[87] Bach himself has given us his own solution in a very similar case: in the two-part canon *per augmentationem contrario motu* in the *Art of Fugue* BWV 1080.14. Here, after the first half of the augmented voice, the composer does not present a simple repetition, but exchanges the two voices in double counterpoint at the octave. He probably intended a similar solution for our canon, especially since his device of the hyperbole only then could be fully effective (see Smend's solution, reprinted below, Appendix I).[88] When Dörffel continued with the augmented, inverted voice, he produced in the second half an inversion (*al rovescio*) of the hyperbole, i.e. a *hypo*bole – a descent *below* its ambitus – the opposite of a figure intended for praise of a ruler. Of course that must be excluded, after all that has been said regarding the *magnificentia*. Quintilian speaks even of a double hyperbole, where one is added above the other: "sometimes the hyperbole grows with another added above" (VIII.vi.70). Here Quintilian provides a clue for the solution of a canon, for Bach presents indeed a double hyperbole: first in the lower voice, then "insuper", in the upper, as in Smend's solution which thus should replace the one in the *Neue Bach-Ausgabe*, where the double hyperbole is omitted.

[**e**: Fortune bringing dignity]. In the paragraph on Agamemnon, Achilles, and Tydeus (quoted above, p. 433), Quintilian did not mention other persons for the fourth and fifth epideictic virtues, but referred only to rhetorical figures discussed in his later books. He assigns the last of these, the hyperbole, to the "summo loco", because of its boldness:

Hyperbole is, then, a virtue, when the subject on which one must speak is abnormal. For it is permitted to amplify, because the magnitude cannot be expressed, and it is better for the speech for go beyond than to fall short (VIII.vi.76).

Two of his examples present a double hyperbole; the second he regards as a "truly exquisite figure" ("exquisitam vero figuram"). Here the rhetorician paraphrases a hymn of the "prince of lyric poetry", Pindar (VIII.vi.71):

for when he [Pindar] describes the attack of Hercules against the Meropes, ... he says the hero was not like fire, wind or ocean [the single hyperbole], but like light-

---

[86] Wolff used this solution for his edition in the NBA, without mentioning Oley.

[87] *Der Kanon 'per augmentationem in motu contrario' in Bachs 'Musikalischem Opfer'*, ZfMw, XI, 1928/29, pp. 252-255.

[88] Since Smend replaced Bach's tenor clef with the alto clef, the hyperbole is less evident in his edition than in the original print.

ening [the double hyperbole], as the former were too little, the later, equivalent (VIII.vi.71).

Also with the fourth canon, now in *genus grande*, with the 'royal' French rhythm and even the double hyperbole, Bach truly communicates content. The all-powerful, hyperbolic Hercules appears in paean rhythm and royal pomp. And he is not only twice as fast as his adversaries, who lament in chromatic harmonies: he distributes his blows "like lightening"![89] Since Quintilian's text is the only known reference to this hymn, lost since antiquity, it was surely Bach's source (see p. 445). Moreover, one might mention that in France up to the eighteenth century Hercules was regarded, because of his exploits in Gaul, as 'French' – thus in royal panegyrics since Henry IV.[90] Also here Bach paid homage to Frederick's French preferences.

5. *Canon a 2 [per tonos]*

[**f**: Palpability]. After *magnificentia*, Quintilian considers only two further qualities: *iucunditas* (attractiveness) and *evidentia* (palpability). The former he rejects as a typical quality of the *narratio*, for it is equally suitable for all parts of the oration (IV.ii.63). *Evidentia* is thus the last of the five qualities which Quintilian recommends here: "In the *narratio*, palpability ... is indeed a great virtue, when some truth must not only be told, but also be displayed in a certain way" (IV.ii.64). Later on he elaborates on what he means by this: "Palpability is more ... than clarity; the latter lies open, the former somehow thrusts itself upon one's attention. ... [The facts are] to be expressed and displayed to the mind's eyes" (VIII.iii.61f). Quintilian then adds examples from Cicero: vivid depiction of a luxurious banquet, the sacking of a city, etc.

With the fifth, last canon of this group the *thema regium* again appears in the upper voice, embellished at the beginning. The two lower parts form a canon at the upper fifth at the distance of one measure. After eight measures the whole canon repeats itself a tone higher – a procedure which could go on *ad infinitum* were it not for the limitations of human ears and instruments: c-d-e-f♯-g♯-a♯-b♯, etc. But since the *Musical Offering* was conceived for tempered keyboard instruments, this canon returns after six modulations to its initial key (b♯ = c). Could Bach have made the *evidentia* more palpable than

---

[89] Cf. above, pp. 437f.

[90] Marc-René JUNG, *Hercule dans la littérature française du XVIe siècle*, Geneva, Droz, 1966; Corrado VIVANTI, *Henry IV, the Gallic Hercules*, «Journal of the Warburg and Courtauld Institutes», XXX, 1967, pp. 176-197; Karl MÖSENEDER, *Zeremoniell und monumentale Poesie*, Berlin, Mann, 1983, p. 87.

he does in this canon, where the *thema regium* rises like reliefs on a triumphal column, twisting higher and higher and seen from all sides until their figures transcend the limits of human eyesight?[91] By the fourth repetition almost every note is chromatically altered with an accidental – Bach may have chuckled when he read Quintilian's statement that *evidentia* can be achieved "ex accidentibus" (VIII.iii.70)! The entire canon is a strict application of the figure of the κλίμαξ (Greek *klimax*, 'ladder' = Lat. *gradatio*, stepwise intensification; cf. below), which the composer of course also found in Quintilian (IX.iii.54-57; also VIII.iv.3-9). And he formulates the rhythm not only with the heroic dactyl, but also again with the paean, this time the 'fourth' one (three short + one long),[92] "which is assigned to the end" (IX.iv.96), now for the last canon of the group.

[e: Gloria]. Quintilian gives only one example of a six-step *gradatio* (his others have fewer steps), the famous one of Homer (*Iliad*, II.101) where the scepter is passed consecutively from Hephaistos to Zeus, from Zeus to Hermes, from Hermes to Pelops, from Pelops to Atreus, from Atreus to Thyestes, from Thyestes to Agamemnon (IX.iii.57; see Table 2, last column and bottom, "5 e"). Bach presents this figure splendidly. (The *abbreviatio* of the *thema regium*, i.e. the omission, only here, of its last three measures, may be explained not merely by his need to modulate a step higher, but also by Quintilian's association of "lesser resources" with "gloria" – above, p. 443). Since the *thema regium* is now inscribed with "gloria" (see below) and the sceptre symbolizes sovereignty and honor, and Bach like Homer constructed an exceptional *gradatio* with six steps, there is hardly any doubt that these six heroes served as his model. They bring the series of five musical *exempla* to its culmination and conclude it.

The two terms 'hyperbole' and 'gradatio' for two of the more common rhetorical and musical figures were of course familiar to German composers from music-theoretical literature since Burmeister. Bach could find them *et al.* immediately in his copy of Quintilian (see below, p. 466), *where they are both identified in the enormous index*, with only two (main) entries for *hyperbole* and one for *gradatio* (κλίμαξ) – both in the rare forms (double and six-step) used in the two canons – leading directly to the key references to Pindar and Homer![93]

---

[91] The relevance of *evidentia* (ευάργεια) for the visual arts did not escape humanist authors – cf. Pomponius GAURICUS, *De sculptura*, Florence, Giunta, 1505; ed. André Chastel and Robert Klein, Geneva, Droz, 1969, pp. 179, 197.

[92] Cf. above, p. 236.

[93] This observation has been taken from p. 364 of the original version (1997) of ch. 3, above. It removes the doubt expressed by FLINDELL, note 69 (cited above, p. 93, note 21).

The identification of Quintilian's allusions to Homer's descriptions of Achilles, Agamemnon, and Tydeus (canons 1-3) would hardly have been any more difficult, since these are among the best known passages in all ancient literature; the editors and commentators of Quintilian identify his references in footnotes and indices, citing the books and lines of the epic.

The *Sententiae* for the Fourth and Fifth Canons

To the last two of the five *canones diversi* Bach added, in the dedication copy of the *Musical Offering*, the well known handwritten inscription:[94]

Notulis crescen-	Ascendenteque Modula-
tibus crescat	tione ascendat
Fortuna	Gloria

regis.

"As the notes grow may the fortune of the king grow" and "As the modulation rises may the glory of the king rise", wishes for the fortune and fame of the king, are equated with the augmentation in the fourth canon and the rising spiral of modulations in the fifth.[95] But why did Bach insert again an inscription here? The ancients, says Quintilian, used *sententiae* to express a feeling or opinion. When we wish someone good fortune ("gratulantes ... dicimus"), we do it "ex sententia". Such phrases could be appended especially at the conclusion ("in clausulis posita sententias" – VIII.v.1f).[96] Following his mentor and innumerable other precedents, Bach could thus insert the congratulatory *sententiae* and place them at the end of his *narratio ornata*.

As for the details: Bach took his key words "Fortuna", "Gloria", and in between "regis" directly from Quintilian's "fortuna ... in regibus ... gloria" quoted above (p. 433) for the last two epideictic virtues. Only here does the rhetor discuss these together! And that the composer also put them in their proper places, fourth and fifth, need no longer surprise us. With his op-

---

94 See facsimile in NBA, p. XIV.

95 Edward LOWINSKY has observed apropos these canons that augmentation occurs in some of the earliest 'Fortuna' pieces and that "if descending modulation symbolizes the evil aspects of *Fortuna desperata*, ascending modulation may well be equated with Fortuna bringing glory" – *Matthaeus Greiter's Fortuna: An Experiment in Chromaticism and in Musical Iconography*, «Musical Quarterly», XLIII, 1957, p. 77. He adds a footnote from Howard R. PATCH, *The Goddess Fortuna in Medieval Literature*, Cambridge MA, Harvard UP, 1927, p. 1, observing that Fortune and Glory "are at all times closely associated", especially in warfare.

96 Here I must correct myself: in 1980 I had designated these *sententiae* as *epiphonemata* (concluding epigrams).

tative *sententiae*, Bach's praise of the king overflows into the margins of his composition, from notes into words, which, in turn, leave no doubt about the meaning of his music, as interpreted above.

— - -

We have seen that in the five *canones diversi* Bach applies concretely devices almost in the same sequence as Quintilian describes them abstractly in his eighth and ninth book: *redditio contraria* (VIII.iii.77-81), *emphasis* (VIII.iii.83-86), *apheleia* (VIII.iii.87), *ratiocinatio* (VIII.iv.15-28), *comparatio* (VIII.iv.9-14), *hyperbole* (VIII.iv.29, VIII.vi.67-76), *klimax* (IX.iii.53-57) – see below, our index of subjects. He arranges his canons as *exempla* of the classical *genera dicendi*, with a twofold intensification from a simpler to a higher style (1-2, 3-4/5; see p. 448, Table 2). Like his mentor he begins with the *genus humile* and concludes with the *genus grande*; in between, for the *delectio* of his audience, the *genus medium*, associated with the ever popular theater, and again the *genus humile*, throwing into still higher relief the following two canons in *genus grande*, celebrating amply the king. Thus the *canons diversi* could not have been better 'disposed', implied by Quintilian's sequence of forensic qualities. Bach could indeed combine these qualities with the epideictic ones in a single series of five pieces, for in each canon the two respective elements and their genus are closely related. That he communicated also human content, we shall by no means reject as 'extramusical'.

And Bach's 'librettist' Homer? He himself

says how the source of all springs and rivers is taken from the ocean, he gave us a model and orientation for all aspects of eloquence. ... No one will have surpassed him in the sublimity for great things, in the propriety for the small ..., most eminent not only in poetic, but also in oratorical excellence (nec poetica modo sed oratoria virtute eminentissimus). ... In every branch of eloquence he truly leaves everyone far behind him (Quintilian, X.i.46, 51).

Also Bach must have felt comfortable in this "ocean", for he formulated as *similitudines* according to Homer (the acknowledged master of such *exempla*)[97] and Pindar all five *canones diversi* and of course the *sententiae*, equating royal virtues from ancient mythology and contemporary history with musical devices. Such poetic *exempla* were universally esteemed in literature until the end of the *ancien régime*, employed by authors whenever they could assume that the audience was familiar with the classics.

---

[97] Cf. LAUSBERG, p. 232f and index, pp. 699, 812f on *similitudines* and *exempla*. "Homer is a master of the *similitudo* (Quint. X.i.49)".

Table 2 - Canones diversi (narratio ornata)

Form and Style (f = forensic quality) and *Content* (e = epideictic virtue)

Genus	Canon 1	Canon 2	Canon 3	Canon 4	Canon 5
grande				f: Magnificentia e: Fortuna (**Hercules**)	f: Evidentia e: Gloria (**Hephaistos** – **Zeus** – **Hermes** **Pelops** – **Atreus** – **Thyestes** – **Agamemnon**)
medium		f: Mimus e: Pulchritudo (**Jupiter, Mars,** **Neptune, Agamemnon**)			
humile	f: Natura e: Robur (**Achilles**)		f: Illusio simplicitatis e: Infirmitas (**Tydeus**)		

Arrangement of 5e, Homer's *gradatio* (Greek *klimax*)

```
                            f ........ g
                    e ........ f
              d ........ e
        c ........ d
     b ........ c
a ........ b
```

Egressus = Fuga Canonica in Epidiapente

The *thema regium*, which hitherto has not participated in the canonic writing – except in the crab canon – now appears in the upper voices as a strict two-part canon at the upper fifth at the distance of ten measures.[98] The second entry thus forms the *comes* of a fugue. Later, in measure 38, the first voice again presents the *thema regium*, this time in the subdominant, so that its imitation in the following voice results in an entry in the tonic. Finally, in measure 59, the otherwise free bass voice [continuo] also lets the *thema regium* be heard in the tonic. As David observed, "we seem to hear

---

[98] ¢, not **C**, as in NBA, p. 75.

a two-part accompanied fugue while the strict canon is at no place interrupted. The second group of entries is ingeniously extended by a third entrance, in the bass; thus the two-part canon seems to broaden into a three-
part fugue".[99] A piece which is both a canon and a fugue is surely a very
rare accomplishment; I know of no other example, and have not yet found
the term 'fuga canonica' used in this sense by theorists, not even in Mattheson's extended canon-battle with Bokemeyer[100] or in Marpurg's thorough
treatise.[101]

At the end of his discussion of the *narratio*, Quintilian speaks of the *egressus* (*excursus*; Cicero: *digressio*):

Most are accustomed to digress immediately after the narratio to some pleasant
and praiseworthy topic, to obtain as much favor as they can. This originated in rhetorical ostentation and now has entered the courts, after it has been discovered how to
conduct trials not for the benefit of the litigants, but for advocates to show off (*ad
patronorum iactationem*) . ... I admit, however, that this kind of digression can be ad-
vantageously appended not only to the *narratio*, but also to the *argumentatio* ... if the
subject demands or at least permits; and that the speech can even be illuminated and
adorned to the highest degree with it, but [only] if it is coherent and follows logically.
... For there is no closer connection than between the *narratio* and the *probatio*, unless
that digression is either a sort of end of the *narratio* or beginning of the *probatio*.
There will therefore sometimes be room for it" (IV.iii.1-5).

Such an egressus "serves as a peroration" to the first main section of the
speech (IV.iii.11f). It was, then, Quintilian who authorized Bach to insert at
this point his contrapuntal *tour de force*, which shows all his artistry ("advocates show off") and "illuminates and adorns" the *Musical Offering*. The most
astonishing achievement, however, is that this *iactatio*, in spite of its ingenuity,
is very "pleasant" – much more so than the canons which preceded it. Not
only is it smooth, elegant, almost gallant; with its adherence to the ever-pre-
sent *thema regium* "it is coherent and follows logically".

---

[99] P. 28.

[100] See the *Canonische Anatomie* in his *Critica Musica*, Hamburg, Herold, Jan.-Apr. 1723,
pp. 237-354, and Werner BRAUN, *Bachs Stellung im Kanonstreit*, in *Bach-Interpretationen*, cit.,
pp. 106-111.

[101] Friedrich Wilhelm MARPURG, *Abhandlung von der Fuge*, Berlin, Haude & Spener, 1753f, I,
10, 16, defines the *fuga canonica* simply as a strict canon (which earlier theorists such as Tinctoris
designated as 'fuga' and Walther calls "fuga in consequenza"), as opposed to the *fuga periodica*
(fugue in the modern sense). He does not mention a canon such as Bach's which presents successive
entries of a subject in the manner of a fugue. His example of a "canonische Doppelfuge", the g-min-
or fugue from the *Well-Tempered Clavier* II (I, 140 and table XLI, 1), is canonic only in the exposition.

Exordium II (Insinuatio) = Ricercar a 6

The six-part ricercar has two complete entries of the *thema regium* in each voice. As stated above, it corresponds perfectly to the (optional) second exordium, which may be used to introduce the second and last main section of the oration, the *argumentatio* (IV.iii.9). Of the two types of exordium distinguished by Cicero – *principium* and *insinuatio* – it was the *insinuatio* which was employed in this place. Quintilian's description of the *insinuatio* is based on Cicero's: "Some therefore divide the exordium into two kinds, the *principium* and the *insinuatio*, so that there is in the former a direct appeal to goodwill and attention. Since this cannot be [used] in scandalous [or: difficult] cases, the *insinuatio* should creep upon the minds [of the listeners]" (IV.i.42). Quintilian uses the verb 'surrepo' ['creep or crawl up to from below'] more or less as Cicero used 'dissimulo': to disguise one's argument by means of indirection.[102]

Since the middle of the sixteenth century, the Ciceronian *insinuatio* had found its musical equivalent in the strictly imitative ricercar, in which the voices enter unobtrusively in succession.[103] The six-part ricercar is a model of such an *insinuatio*, for Bach uses every means to camouflage his entries of the theme. Unlike the three-part ricercar, where the successive entries are separated (and thus marked) by short interludes, the first note of the *thema regium* is now sounded simultaneously with the last note of the preceding entry, so that the seam is concealed (mm. 5, 9, 13). New entries are further camouflaged by being placed in an inner voice (especially mm. 13, 58, 73) and by forming with their first note a unison with an adjacent part (mm. 19, 48, 73, 86). In measures 65f, the note immediately preceding the new entry in the same range is closer to that voice (a melodic whole tone) than to its own notated continuation (minor third), so that the new entry is heard as the actual continuation, not as a new voice. In the second half of the movement the roles of *dux* and *comes* are exchanged, almost beyond recognition, for the *comes*, which now enters first, as it were disguises itself as *dux* (mm. 48, 66, 86), and likewise the *dux* as *comes* (mm. 58, 73, 99). Once (m. 66) the *comes* even abandons the minor mode, almost always obligatory for the *thema re-*

---

[102] The words 'Insinuation' and 'insinuieren' in the most general sense were current in baroque German. Christian WEISE's widely used etiquette book, *Politischer Redner*, Leipzig, Ritz, 1681, has an entire chapter "Von der Insinuation" (pp. 182-205), and Bach himself writes in a letter of 18 Aug. 1736, "meine ... gehorsamst insinuirte Beschwerden" ["my most obediently insinuated complaints"] – *Dok.*, I, 88.

[103] See above, pp. 61, 63.

gium. The most thoroughly disguised entry occurs in measure 48, after a series of abbreviated three-note entries in measures 45ff, each of which, with its third note, forms a unison with the next fragmentary entry (Ex. 7). The full entry is thus smuggled in surreptitiously (see above, 'surrepo') in the second-lowest voice in what would initially be perceived as just another fragmentary entry in the sequence. A somewhat similar effect is created by the two

Ex. 7. *Musical Offering*, Ricercar a 6, mm. 45-48.

tenors in measures 72f. These features of the musical *insinuationes* (i.e. Italian ricercars) clearly contradict the north German, late baroque fugal theory, which recommends that subject entries be clearly marked by being placed in a new range and/or after rests. It must be emphasized that, as Bach surely understood, the *insinuatio* techniques are fully effective only on a keyboard instrument, where the different voices are not distinguished by tone color. He used only two staves for the autograph notation of this ricercar; by deciding upon the less crowded score notation for the printed edition, he merely followed an Italian keyboard tradition (see below, Frescobaldi). The various attempts to 'improve' this piece by "analytical instrumentation" for an ensemble[104] must be regarded as contrary both to the tradition and to the composer's intention, and therefore misguided.

Argumentatio (Probatio + Refutatio) = Canon a 2 + Canon a 4 (Quaerendo Invenietis)

Like the other canons in the *Musical Offering*, these two indicate the number of parts in their titles, and the pitch and direction of imitation by multiple clefs in the original notation: the two-part canon is by contrary motion (one clef inverted), the four-part one is at the double octave (and unison).[105] But they show neither by *signa congruentiae* nor by fermatas the time interval at which the imitation(s) must begin, unlike the other canons (except the crab canon, which of course needed no *signum*, and the second *Canon perpetuus*, which is written out in parts). Bach's heading "quaerendo invenietis" ["by seeking you will find"] applies to the pair, for both pieces are 'riddle' canons.[106] Of the various solutions which have been attempted, only those at the distance of $2^1/_2$ and 7 measures, respectively, are satisfactory.[107]

But why does Bach introduce riddle canons only at this point? Surely it is because the *argumentatio*, our next section of the oration, was designated in rhetorical terminology also by the alternate name of *quaestiones*,[108] a word

---

[104] DAVID, p. 51, and those listed in PFANNKUCH, p. 441, note 6; also Carl DAHLHAUS, *Analytische Instrumentation: Bachs sechsstimmiges Ricercar in der Orchestrierung Anton Weberns*, in *Bach-Interpretationen* cit., pp. 197-206.

[105] NBA, p. 54.

[106] Cf. KB, pp. 131, 157.

[107] KB, pp. 115f. A computer solution of the first enigmatic canon with "next-to-maximal harmonicity [!]" resulted in unacceptable parallel fifths and octaves, overlooked by George W. LOGEMANN, *The Canons in the Musical Offering of J. S. Bach*, in *Elektronische Datenverarbeitung in der Musikwissenschaft*, ed. Harald Heckmann, Regensburg, Bosse, 1967, p. 73.

[108] QUINTILIAN, IV.iii.4; LAUSBERG, p. 190; above, p. 79, note 222.

which Bach, like Quintilian, uses in the gerund form. There are two canons because the *argumentatio* was always divided into two parts, the *probatio* and the *refutatio*. The heading "quaerendo invenietis" has its precise correspondence in Quintilian's discussion of the *probatio*: "hortor ad quaerendum et inveniri posse fateor" ["I urge that one search and I bear witness that discoveries can be made" – V.xii.1],[109] the source of Bach's heading.

Quintilian distinguishes between the *probatio* and *refutatio* as follows:

The basis of the arguments in this section [*refutatio*] may not be sought in places other than the *probatio*, nor is the arrangement of the topics or thoughts or words and figures different. This section has for the most part milder emotions. ... Yet defence has always been considered ... more difficult than prosecution. In the first place accusation is simpler, for it is put forward in one manner, [but] refuted in many ways, since it is generally sufficient for the accuser that his charge be true, [whereas] the defence attorney may deny, justify, object, excuse, deprecate, soften, extenuate, avert [the charges], express contempt or derision. Therefore the accusation is usually straightforward and ... clamorous (*clamosa*); [but] the defence needs a thousand deviations and arts (V.xiii.1f).

Bach derives the thematic material of his *refutatio* (second canon) from "no places other than the *probatio*" (first canon), for, unlike the first *Canon perpetuus* and numbers 2-5 of the *canones diversi*, these two canons both introduce the *thema regium* canonically, at the beginning of each voice. Since there are no other voices, these two canons could be notated on one line (NBA, p. 54). Nor are their "words and figures different", for in each canon the *thema regium* begins with the same upbeat of two ascending eighth notes and fills out its rising thirds with stepwise motion (chromatic and diatonic, respectively). Since "accusation is simpler", the first canon has not only half as many voices but also less than half the length of the second. And because "defence needs a thousand deviations and arts", the second canon is not only the longest one in the *Musical Offering* (excluding the *Fuga canonica*), but also the only one in four parts, and thus it also has the greatest variety of simultaneous rhythms and melodies. The imitation by contrary motion in the 'accusation' canon may be intended to represent the adversary relationship ("Our opponent is usually attacked by nearly the same means, but inverted" – IV.i.14). The

---

[109] WOLFF, KB, p. 106, mentions the biblical "Quaerendo [*recte*: Quaerite et] invenietis" (MATTHEW 7:7), which should be regarded as just one version of a familiar ancient maxim. While it is likely that Bach knew both passages, the one from Quintilian is more relevant to his compositional plan. The *inventio* is, of course, the first of the five *partes artis*, the skills exercised by the orator (cf. above, p. 82). On the complementary conceptual relationship of 'seeking and finding' to the musical terms 'ricercar' and 'invention', cf. above, p. 73.

groups of three eighth notes (γ $\int\int\int$, mm. 15f, 18f – "clamorous"?) were already included in the preliminary "summary of the case" given in the first ricercar (mm. 109-112). To refute the opponent's statements, the second canon translates the "deviations" (*flexus*) with winding figures (mm. 3f) and expresses 'negation' traditionally with the subdominant sequence,[110] used probably also to 'soften, extenuate'.

PERORATIO IN ADFECTIBUS =

SONATA SOPR'IL SOGGETTO REALE A TRAVERSA, VIOLINO E CONTINUO

The trio sonata and the final *Canon perpetuus* remain. Up to this point, instruments had been specified only for the second of the *canones diversi*, where violins represented gods in theater style. It is generally agreed that the flute part in the sonata and final canon was intended for performance by the king himself. And we now see that this was planned as a fitting climax at the end of the work, never at the middle as has often been asserted since the 1940s, since any such position would have produced an anticlimax. "Finis coronat opus" for all great literature, also musical, had been an unwritten law since ancient times. Frederick appears, as is proper, with his entourage, with the richest instrumentarium in the *Musical Offering*: flute, violin, and basso continuo [clavier and 'cello].[111] Unlike the other pieces, these are both notated in separate parts.

Mattheson had required of the peroration, "the conclusion of our musical oration ..., more than other pieces a particularly emphatic motion", and he observed that "it has become custom that we close almost with the same passages and sounds with which we have begun, which then after our exordium substitute for the peroration".[112] But Quintilian had already implied this with other words: the appeal to the emotions in the peroration is "similar to the exordium, but with greater freedom and fullness" (VI.i.9). "Certain things which needed only to be revealed there [in the exordium] must be treated fully in the peroration" (VI.i.12). Bach's idea for fuller instrumentation in his peroration thus was conditioned directly by Quintilian rather than by

---

110 *AC* 1966 pp. 183, 244, *AC* 2007 pp. 235, 308.

111 One arrangement favored by Wolff, with the sonata in the center for the sake of "axial symmetry", must thus give way to considerations not only of rhetoric, but also of court protocol: the royal ensemble assumes the place of honor as a grand finale.

112 "der Ausgang oder Beschluß unserer Klang- Rede ... vor allen andern Stücken eine besonders nachdrückliche Bewegung"; "Die Gewohnheit hat es so eingeführet, daß wir ... fast mit eben denjenigen Gängen und Klängen schliessen, darin wir angefangen haben: welchem nach unser Exordium auch alsdenn die Stelle einer Peroration vertrit" – p. 236.

the mediocre theorist. With the sonata he achieves 'fuller treatment' also by the only multi-movement component of the *Musical Offering*.

But why would Bach write two pieces, sonata and canon, for the peroration? Quintilian explains that there is a choice of two kinds of peroration, "based either on facts or on emotions" ("Eius duplex ratio est posita aut in rebus aut in adfectibus" – VI.i.1). Since the two types are equated here with "aut . . . aut", Bach is free to determine the sequence of the two. Just as, with 'German thoroughness', he included both types of exordium (*principium* and *insinuatio*) and *narratio* (*brevis* and *ornata*), here too he presents both alternatives, a *peroratio in adfectibus* (sonata) and a *peroratio in rebus* (the final *Canon perpetuus*).

Quintilian repeatedly compares the peroration with the exordium and shows that in the latter the emotions should be expressed only "rather sparingly and modestly" ("parcius et modestius"), whereas in the former they may pour out freely ("liceat totos effundere adfectus" – IV.i.28). "Here [in the *peroratio in adfectibus*], if anywhere, one can open all the floodgates of eloquence" ("totos eloquentiae aperire fontes licet" – VI.i.51). He therefore continues with a discussion of *pathos* (Lat. *adfectus*) and *ethos*: "The more cautious writers ... stated *pathos* to be the violent emotions and *ethos* the calm and gentle ones, ... a distinction as sometimes [is found] in the perorations, for *ethos* generally calms the violent emotions aroused by *pathos*" ("quae πάθος concitavit, ἦθος solet mitigare" – VI.ii.9, 12). How could one better describe Bach's sonata, which has long been recognized as employing a much more affective style than the other components, as his single concession in the *Musical Offering* to the 'modern' style of the Prussian court? Only here did the composer provide tempo indications. And only here is found deep, disturbing *pathos*,[113] which is then dispersed by *ethos* in the fourth move-

---

[113] Though musicologists have realized the importance of Kircher's formulation "musica pathetica" for the new baroque style, they have not traced it to ancient rhetoric – Rolf DAMMANN, *Der Musikbegriff im deutschen Barock*, Cologne, Volk, 1967, pp. 222ff; Ulf SCHARLAU, *Athanasius Kircher (1601-1680) als Musikschriftsteller*, Marburg, Gorich & Weiershäuser, 1969, pp. 234-238. DAMMANN, p. 223, calls it merely "eine latinisierte Wortschöpfung". BROSSARD includes the concept in his dictionary and applies it to the fugue (s.v. 'Pathetico', 'Fuga pathetica'), hence WALTHER, pp. 466, 267: "Passiones erreget", "Affekt exprimiren" ["It arouses the passions", "express the affect"]. The *fuga pathetica*, associated erroneously by Walther with the *fuga gravis*, is employed by Bach very rarely: the B-minor fugue in Book I of the *Well-Tempered Clavier* and the 15th Goldberg variation (i.e. canon). These pieces are not only characterized by "the sighing suspensions of a semitone, the augmented and diminished intervals, and the lamenting character" (Stefan KUNZE, *Gattungen der Fuge in Bachs Wohltemperiertem Klavier*, in *Bach-Interpretationen* cit., p. 77), but – and here too the resemblance to the trio sonata is significant – also here they are the only pieces in the collection with a tempo designation, and they both serve as a conclusion (Variation 15 to the first half, followed by an "overture" which opens the second half). Kunze, pp. 77 and 81, confuses *pathos* with *ethos*. His additional examples from the *Well-Tempered Clavier* qualify less as *fugae patheticae*, since they lack the sighs, tempo designation, etc.

ment. The requirements of a *peroratio in adfectibus* caused Bach to abandon, only in the sonata, the strict contrapuntal style of canon and ricercar, which does not lend itself easily to affective expression. Here, where there is "a particularly emphatic motion" (Mattheson) and "liceat totos effundere adfectus", "it is this [rhetorical power] which dominates the courts of law, this eloquence reigns supreme" ("haec eloquentia regnat" – VI.ii.4). That Bach makes room not only for the musical eloquence which now "reigns" supreme, but also for a real king, a royal flautist (who, incidentally, often designated his own compositions "affettuoso") – all this climaxes the homage *ad personam*. Moreover, in all four movements the ambitus of the flute is very high (to e♭'''): "the eloquence should increase most [H. E. Butler translates, less literally, "be pitched higher"] in this section, since, if it does not add anything to what has preceded, it seems even to diminish" (VI.i.29).

The sonata, then, gives free rein to the emotions only hinted in the first ricercar. The sighing sixteenth notes in its first movement (Largo, e.g. in the violin, mm. 3, 6, Ex. 8) remind us of the 'sospiri' motives there (mm. 113-118). The bass in the minor mode and with the harmonic rhythm of the saraband, rising slowly in throbbing eighth notes derived from the opening of the *thema regium* (mm. 1-4) and the wide, pathetic gestures dramati-

Ex. 8. *Musical Offering*, Sonata a 3, first movement, mm. 1-4.

cally articulated in the upper parts are clearly in the style of the heroic lamentos of late baroque vocal music.[114] But why is it used here? Because the peroration was traditionally associated with weeping and lamenting. Here "pity prevails most of all" (VI.1.23). The orator may even "dress the characters with fictitious speeches and raise the dead [to life]" (IV. 1.28) as the two declamatory upper voices (violin and flute) do with their lamento. The second movement (Allegro), a ternary fugue in which the *thema regium* eventually appears as a countersubject, takes its cue from the 'agitare' sections of the first ricercar, for the peroration will excite even more the emotions ("concitare adfectus" – VI.i.11). The syncopations (closely related to the *alla zoppa* rhythm) and the persistent Pyrrhic figures, especially when concertizing in the upper parts (e.g. mm. 77ff), all contribute to this effect. The warlike associations of the Pyrrhic meter are thus heightened by those of "konzertieren", with its still widely disseminated derivation from classical Latin 'concertare' ('contend', rather than from Italian, 'agree', 'accord').[115] The third movement (Andante) is dominated throughout by sighs, no longer of a mourner, as in the first movement, but of a passionate lover, in the gallant style, with major mode, slow harmonic rhythm, and echo dynamics. "Just as lovers cannot judge beauty because the mind instructs the eyesight, so the judge, overcome by emotions, abandons every plan to investigate the truth" (VI.ii.6). According to Mattheson's characterization, Bach's key, E-flat, "is distinguished by much pathos".[116] The movement ends suddenly, in keeping with Quintilian's advice to "break off at the height of emotion" (VI.i.29), imitated by Mattheson's *peroratio ex abrupto*.[117] With the final movement, a free fugue (Allegro) in gigue meter, the 'delectare' triplets which seemed strange in the first ricercar now fall into their natural place. The opening theme is, of course, derived from the *thema regium*, but some passages are closer to the triplets of the ricercar (e.g. bass, mm. 78ff). The piece fulfills the function of the peroration "not only to arouse pity, but also to disperse it … with wit" ("urbane dictis" –

---

[114] Similar examples by Bach: "Und wenn der harte Todesschlag" BWV 124/3, "Ich will auch mit gebroch'nen Augen" BWV 125/2, "Crucifixus" BWV 232/16. Only the stagnant bass: "Ich wünschte mir den Tod" BWV 57/3, "Ich will leiden" BWV 87/6, "Es ist vollbracht" BWV 159/4, "Wenn der Ton zu mühsam klingt" BWV 201/7, "Qui tollis" BWV 232/8, "Erbarme dich" BWV 244/47, "Wir sitzen mit Tränen nieder" BWV 244/78, "Zerfliesse, mein Herz" BWV 245/63. Further contemporary examples in *AC* 1966 and *AC* 2007, Exx. 140, 165, 224.

[115] Cf. Michael PRAETORIUS, *Syntagma Musicum*, III, Wolfenbüttel, Holwein, 1619, pp. 5, 126: "mit einander scharmintzeln", "untereinander … streiten" ["to skirmish with each other"].

[116] "hat viel pathetisches an sich" – *Das neu-eröffnete Orchestre*, Hamburg, Verfasser, 1713, p. 249.

[117] *Der vollkommene Capellmeister*, p. 237.

VI.i.46).[118] But wit produces laughter, which "often ... convulses the whole body with its power" (VI.iii.9). This could explain the wild, breathless quality of the movement. As countless instrumental works of the seventeenth and eighteenth centuries testify, composers were well aware that in a finale "brevity in wit gives greater point and speed" (VI.iii.45), though few knew how ancient this tradition was.[119]

PERORATIO IN REBUS = CANON PERPETUUS

The flute and violin, over a free figured bass, present an embellished version of the *thema regium* in a strict canon by inversion at the interval of two measures. The second half repeats exactly and in their entirety the canonic voices of the first half, but with the inversion now preceding rather than following the opening theme. The piece is thus a mirror canon, combining two different solutions to a single canon, without the slightest modification of the given melody. It is the most extraordinary contrapuntal coup in the *Musical Offering*, reserved by Bach for the other conclusion of his work, the only canon to be performed by the king. Yet, as in the *Fuga canonica*, the difficulties of the strict procedure are concealed from the listener, and, in spite of them, the piece assumes a light, gallant, 'modern' style. Similarities between these two pieces were recognized correctly by David.[120] We now see that they are due in part to their analogous function as conclusions to the two halves of the musical oration.

The factual peroration (*peroratio in rebus*) is, then, quite different from the emotional one (*peroratio in adfectibus*):

The repetition and grouping of the facts (*rerum*), which ... is called the enumeration by certain Latin [authors], both refreshes the memory of the judge and at the same time places the whole of the case before his eyes. ... That which we repeat here must be said as briefly as possible, ... for if we delay, no longer an enumeration would be made but a sort of second oration. However, anything to be enumerated must be said with some weight, enlivened with suitable thoughts and at least varied by figures. Otherwise there is nothing more odious than that straight repetition (*recta repetitione*). ... But the most attractive [enumeration] is ... when we have an opportunity of drawing some argument from our opponent (VI.i.1-4).

Bach accordingly formulates his alternative peroration as a *recapitulatio in rebus*, drawing upon the first canon of his *argumentatio*, since the *probatio* or

---

[118] Is it mere coincidence that Quintilian's two examples of such urbanities, "Date puero panem ne ploret" and "Quid faciam?", fit perfectly to the first thirteen notes (10 + 3) of the theme?

[119] Cf. also Giovanmaria MEMO, *L'oratore*, 1545, quoted above, p. 71, note 180.

[120] Pp. 36f, used, however, to construct a "symmetrical frame".

accusatio is the most crucial section of an oration. Here, as there, imitation by contrary motion not only depicts the adversary relationship ("aliquod ex adversario ducere argumentum"), but also avoids "recta repetitio", for in the terminology of music theory 'contrarius' ('inverted') is the opposite of 'rectus'. Bach thus recapitulates the two basic forms of the *thema regium*. But, as Quintilian suggested, he varies the theme by presenting it in still another embellished version ("figuris utique varianda"), thus avoiding 'repetition' of the earlier canon. His return to *alla breve* time provides the "weight". Other 'facts' of the *probatio* 'enumerated' here include the chromatic quarter notes in measures 8 (flute) and 10 (violin), taken from the opening of the 'probatio' canon but now no longer forming part of the *thema regium*; and the six eighth notes moving scalewise and followed by a quarter note in measures 6f (flute) and 8f (violin), recalling measures 11f and 14f of the other canon.

Why does Bach entitle only the first and last canons "perpetuus", though all except the crab canon and the finite *Fuga canonica* return to their point of departure (transposed only in the canon *per tonos*) and thus could be regarded as perpetual? In the case of the first canon, I suggested that this may be because he associates *oratio perpetua* with the *narratio*. Another clue, which would apply particularly to the concluding piece of the work, was observed by Erich Schenk[121] in another collection of canons composed as homage to a sovereign: Giovanni Battista Vitali's *Artificii musicali* (Modena, Cassani, 1689). In the dedication to Francesco II d'Este, Vitali makes it clear that the infinity of his canons mirrors the infinity of the prince's virtues: "il tributo [cf. "Opfer"!] di questi canoni musicali, la forma de quali nel proprio giro non havendo termine, ne nota finale, saranno in questo almeno proportionati al concerto di tante virtù, che nel petto di V.A.S. concordano così aggiustatamente con l'eternità" ["the tribute of these musical canons, the form of which in their own course does not have an end or final note, will at least be proportionate to the so many virtues which in the breast of Your Serene Highness concord so well with eternity"]. Bach may well have known this work, which, like his, comprised a great variety of contrapuntal pieces and could have been known in Germany through the printed edition. With his first and last canon he thus could have paid his particular respects to the king, just as in courtly productions the operatic *licenza* – the homage to the patron – normally occurred at the beginning or end.

---

[121] *Das 'Musikalische Opfer'*, p. 60. Further parallels are observed by Schenk in *Das Problem der Invention bei Bach und Beethoven*, Österreichische Akademie der Wissenschaften, phil.-hist. Klasse, *Anzeiger*, CXIV, 1977, pp. 91f.

* * *

We have seen that Bach indicated specific instruments – violins and flute – for only three components of the *Musical Offering*: the 'masquerade' canon, with three gods and a king, and the two peroration pieces, for King Frederick himself. I believe that he reserved these instruments for special effect here, and that they should therefore not be applied to the other canons.[122] None of these contains the brilliant idiomatic writing for violin which we have in the large leaps at the end of the 'Agamemnon' canon. In this piece the prescribed instruments serve also to differentiate the 'duet' from the accompanying bass. The canon *per tonos*, on the other hand, should be performed on tempered keyboard instruments, so that it can return to its key of departure (b♯ = c). Bach's music for keyboard instruments does not normally specify the instrument in the score (as opposed to the title). Thus he probably intended those canons of the *Musical Offering* without designation of instruments to be played on the keyboard, like those of the *Goldberg Variations*, the *Canonic Variations* BWV 769, or the *Art of Fugue*. With two instruments it would be possible not only to perform those passages which do not lie under two hands, but also to play easily from the original abbreviated notation.[123] The secular character of the work of course excludes the organ. Carl Philipp Emanuel Bach and Johann Friedrich Agricola report in their necrology that Bach improvised the three-part ricercar on a "Pianoforte".[124] Since Bach was invited by Frederick "to try out his Silbermann fortepianos, which stood in several rooms of the palace",[125] it would seem likely that he conceived the *Musical Offering* with these instruments in mind.

Now for the title "*Musicalisches Opfer*". It belongs to a large family of baroque titles which consist of the adjective 'musical' plus a noun, and often form a rhetorical figure, a metaphor. We are reminded of Schein's *Banchetto musicale* (1617), Frescobaldi's *Fiori musicali* (1635), Schütz's *Musicalische Exequien* (1636), Krieger's *Musicalische Ergetzlichkeit* (1684), Reinken's *Hortus Musicus* (1688), Vitali's *Artificii musicali* (1689), and particularly Muffat's synonymous *Armonico tributo* (1682). Bach certainly knew these collections of

---

[122] Contrary to NBA, pp. 71-79, and KB, p. 119.

[123] Only for the four-part enigmatic canon would each player have to write out his two parts in score.

[124] [Lorenz MIZLER], *Musikalische Bibliothek*, IV, Leipzig, Verfasser, 1754, p. 166. Cf. also Jacob ADLUNG, *Anleitung zur musikalischen Gelahrtheit*, Erfurt, Jungnicol, 1758, p. 961 ("Fortepiano"), Ernst Ludwig GERBER, *Historisch-biographisches Lexikon der Tonkünstler*, Leipzig, J. G. I. Breitkopf, 1790, I, 88 ("Forte Piano").

[125] FORKEL, p. 10. The king esteemed these instruments so highly that he eventually collected fifteen of them – MIZLER, *loc. cit.*, footnote.

Frescobaldi (see below, pp. 462f) and Reinken,[126] probably also Vitali's. Less obvious is the ancestry of his particular noun, but an additional clue is provided by the verb that accompanies it in the very first sentence of the dedication: "Ew. Majestät weyhe hiermit ... ein Musicalisches Opfer" ["To Your Majesty I hereby consecrate a Musical Offering"]. It is unlikely that a man of Bach's culture "in humanioribus" would, on such an occasion, have chosen his words without careful consideration of the literary and rhetorical traditions. It is equally unlikely that he would have taken as his model an author who published in German. For his subheadings and inscriptions he preferred Latin. The expression "to consecrate an offering" to a patron was not uncommon during the age of humanism, when even the Church was not disturbed by such 'pagan' formulations.[127] Thus Joachim du Bellay dedicated his *Defence et illustration de la langue francoyse* (Paris, 1549) as an 'offering' to his uncle, the cardinal Jean du Bellay. Our humanists' sources flowed, of course, from classical antiquity. Though Curtius devotes only a few pages to "Exordialtopik", he provides valuable insight into the *topoi* of dedications: "Statius sends his friend Gallicus a poem for his convalescence and compares his action to an offering to the gods (*Silvae*, I. iv.31ff). Roman poets are accustomed to refer to the dedication as a 'consecration' ['Weihung'] (*dicare, dedicare, consecrare, vovere*). Christian authors like to consecrate their work to God".[128] Bach had himself composed a group of cantatas on texts from Georg Christian Lehms's *Gottgefälliges Kirchen-Opffer* (Darmstadt, 1711).[129]

To what ancient authority may Bach have turned for counsel other than to his proven friend Quintilian? The Latin concept of 'offering' in an exordium is employed by our rhetor only once: in the proem (exordium) to the fourth book of his *Institutio oratoria*, precisely the one which we have most frequently quoted. It occurs, in fact, immediately before he states his program for the following part of his work: to explain the *ordo*, the five parts of the forensic speech (IV.Pr.6). His offering at this point is no mere formality, but rooted in a significant biographical event, as Bach's was to be: he was re-

---

[126] Cf. the arrangements BWV 965f.

[127] See Wolfgang LEINER, *Der Widmungsbrief in der französischen Literatur (1580-1715)*, Heidelberg, Winter, 1965, pp. 7ff, 56ff.

[128] CURTIUS, p. 96. Such offerings were also classified as a species of insinuation – C. WEISE, p. 169: "Endlich ist ein sonderlichs Stücke der Insinuation, welche Votum, und Servitiorum oblationem begreifft, darinnen man durch gute Wündsche und durch Darbietung aller willigen Dienste sich selbst angenehm machen wil" ["Finally, there are particular insinuation pieces which comprise *votum* and *servitiorum obligationem*, in which one wants to make oneself pleasing by offering all willing services"].

[129] Elisabeth NOACK, *Georg Christian Lehms, ein Textdichter Johann Sebastian Bachs*, «Bach Jahrbuch», LVI, 1970, pp. 7-18.

cently honored by an appointment from Domitian as tutor to the emperor's nephews. Now feeling particularly conscious of the need to fulfill great expectations, he hastens to do what he had overlooked at the beginning of his work, namely to invoke the help of the muses. This tardiness he excuses with the example of the greatest poets, who "invoked the muses not only at the beginning of their works, but even further on, when they had come to some important passage, they repeated their offerings (*repeterent vota*) and employed a new prayer", and he beseeches the muses and the emperor for help (IV.Pr.4). Such invocations were, of course, a normal component of internal exordia. Again there is an analogy to the *Musical Offering*, for Bach too had actually begun his work (with the three-part ricercar improvised in Potsdam) before he made his *votum* to the king: "Ich fassete demnach den Entschluß", "Dieser Vorsatz ist nunmehr ... bewerkstelliget worden" ["I thereafter resolved", and then "This intention is now ... fulfilled"]. Quintilian then undertakes

to explain the order (*ordo*) of the forensic cases, which are extremely varied and manifold; [to set forth] what the function of the *exordium* is, the plan of the *narratio*, the credibility of the *argumentatio* – whether we prove what [we have] related or refute what has been said against [us] – [and] how much force is in the *peroratio* – whether the memory of the judge must be refreshed by a brief repetition of the facts or (what is far more effective) whether his emotions must be stirred (IV.Pr.6).[130]

How could Bach's intention in the *Musical Offering* be more succinctly summarized than in these words? Surely we need no longer assume that "this time Bach relinquished a[ny] higher idea to join together all these ingenious single pictures to an artistic unity"[131] or that "no model existed for [the] disposition".[132]

Bach had also musical precedents: a theoretical one in the passage from Mattheson cited above (p. 423), and a practical one in the organ Masses of Frescobaldi's *Fiori musicali*, particularly the first of the three.[133] It is well

---

[130] This is about as close as Quintilian comes to summarizing the components of the speech. Since all classical rhetoricians wrote continuous prose without headings and enumerations, one should not expect to find a neatly numbered system (e.g. for the five forensic qualities or the five epideictic virtues). Their works were, however, easily and frequently reduced by humanist authors to such systems in the form of entire books of tables or 'alberi', with all concepts arranged in categories by headings, subheadings, and sub-subheadings.

[131] SPITTA, II, 676.

[132] KB, p. 123. Harry L. Levy has demonstrated in an unpublished lecture that Rubens modelled his cycle of paintings on the life of Maria Medici after the sections of the classical epideictic oration – cf. «Proceedings of the American Philological Association», CV, 1975, p. 46. A similar influence could be traced to a greater or lesser extent in much triumphal and panegyric art of antiquity and the early modern period.

[133] Venice, Vincenti, 1635; Kassel, Bärenreiter, 1954.

known that he studied Frescobaldi's music,[134] possessed a copy of this work,[135] and followed the Italian composer's practice when he notated the six-part ricercar in score. But no further relationship has been observed between the organ Masses and the *Musical Offering*. Nor has it been recognized until recently that, under the influence of Italian humanism, even the music of the Mass had become infiltrated with Ciceronian rhetoric.[136] Frescobaldi's "Toccata avanti la missa" and "Ricercar dopo il Credo" at the beginning of the two main divisions of the Mass (Mass of the Word and Mass of the Eucharist, respectively)[137] correspond to the Ciceronian *principium* and *insinuatio* which introduced the *narratio* and *argumentatio*, respectively, and thus to Bach's dual ricercars.[138] On the other hand, the two canzonas "dopo l'epistola" and "post il Comunio" serve as the last organ pieces of the two main Mass sections and thus have the functions of the *egressus* or small internal peroration (IV.iii.11f) and of the peroration proper, at the end of the *argumentatio*. Frescobaldi uses canzonas here because, as the most modern (with tempo designations!), subjective, and lively type of piece in the organ Mass,[139] they are best suited to release the affects which were characteristic of the classical peroration. By Bach's time, of course, the canzona had developed into the sonata.[140] Frescobaldi's "toccata cromatica per la levatione", framed by the second ricercar and second canzona (*insinuatio* and *peroratio*) may be seen not only as

---

[134] See C. P. E. Bach's letter of 13 January 1775 to Forkel, *Dok.*, III, p. 288.

[135] SPITTA, I, 418.

[136] W. KIRKENDALE, *L'Aria di Fiorenza*, Florence, Olschki, 1972, pp. 35-40. John O'MALLEY, S. J., *Praise and Blame in Renaissance Rome*, Durham NC, Duke UP, 1979, deals with classical rhetoric in the sermons at the papal court.

[137] The first Mass consists of the following items:

[*Liturgy of the Word*]:	[*Liturgy of the Eucharist*]:
Toccata avanti la Messa	Recercar dopo il Credo
	Alio modo, si placet
Kyrie pieces	Toccata cromatica per la levatione
Canzon dopo la Pistola	Canzon post il Comune
	Alio modo, si placet

The second and third Masses deviate only slightly from this arrangement by adding a "Toccata avanti il recercar" and, in the third Mass, by giving specific song titles (*Bergamasca, Girolmeta*) for the final pair of canzonas.

[138] See above, p. 80, note 229, with reference to the German ecclesiastical rhetorician J. C. Böhmer, 1713.

[139] Cf. PRAETORIUS, pp. 16 and 24 [*recte:* 22]: "recht weltlich", "frisch, frölich unnd geschwind" ["quite worldly", "fresh, joyous, and fast"].

[140] A few years after Bach's death, Christophe Moyreau published five lengthy suites beginning with an overture and concluding with a concerto (nos. 1, 3), sonata (nos. 2, 4), or both (no. 5), preceded by a second overture – cf. Pierre GUILLOT, *Les livres de clavecin de Christophe Moyreau*, «Recherches sur la musique française classique», XI, 1971, pp. 189-193.

an *argumentatio* but perhaps also as an inspiration for Bach's use of chromaticism in the theme of his first *argumentatio* canon. In any case, chromaticism and dissonance are hallmarks of both Elevation pieces and the *argumentatio in musica*. And, finally, Bach's decision to provide musical equivalents to Quintilian's alternative *narrationes* and *perorationes* could have been influenced by Frescobaldi's Kyries and canzonas "alio modo, si placet". With the Italian organ Mass the cantor of St. Thomas's thus found a precedent for the realization of a large-scale, functional, rhetorico-musical cycle, including dual exordia, chromatic argumentatio, and modern, 'affective' peroration. That this model for his work has hitherto been overlooked may be attributed to the Lutheran orientation of most research on Bach. But, as Erich Schenk has rightly stressed,[141] his genius was not limited by narrow confessional horizons; his debt to the Italians (and, we should now add, to the ancient Romans) is far greater than generally realized.

From the historical and rhetorical perspective the central problem of the *Musical Offering* now appears in a different light. A thematically unified musical work of moderate length has no obstacle to cyclic performance[142] once the sequence of its components has been understood. When these components are functionally analogous to the parts of an oration, such performance is as desirable as is the uninterrupted delivery of a speech. According to my interpretation, one of the two *narrationes* or two *perorationes*, respectively, might be omitted ad libitum, in the manner of the optional components of the oration or of Frescobaldi's Mass cycles.

Music of renaissance and baroque composers, who had been immersed in the study of Latin rhetoric while in school, cannot be adequately understood on the basis of our twentieth-century curricula, where rhetoric hardly exists any longer as an academic discipline and instruction in music theory is too often limited to mere descriptive analysis of sounds in a vacuum.[143] Because of this, Bach's instrumental music has come to be regarded (and performed) as 'abstract', its rhetorical basis and function no longer understood.[144] To

---

[141] P. 66.

[142] DAVID, pp. 40ff, quoted a relevant passage from FORKEL (p. 22), describing Bach's manner of improvising cycles of independent, contrasting pieces on a single theme.

[143] E.g. DAVID's chapter "Analyses" (pp. 103-152).

[144] An exception is KLOPPERS' rhetorical study of Bach's organ music (pp. 56-196). Cf. also Isolde AHLGRIMM and Erich FIALA, *Bach und Rhetorik*, «Österreichische Musikzeitschrift», IX, 1954, pp. 342-346, on the Inventions. SPITTA, who began his career as a classical philologist, had already observed (I, 666) that Bach compared these contrapuntal keyboard pieces to speech [thus anticipating the *Musical Offering*]. Anton Webern's highest praise for the *Art of Fugue* as "ein Werk, das völlig ins Abstrakte führt" ["a work which leads completely to the abstract"] has been characterized

comprehend earlier composers we must try to reconstruct their educational and intellectual environment, restore the priority of humanistic methods and systematically exclude narrow and anachronistic modern attitudes, unknown to them.

* * *

Finally, let us turn to the biographical facts, where further evidence, of circumstantial nature, can easily be found. Bach had studied rhetoric, of course, not only for the *Musical Offering*, but since his earliest years. At the excellent lyceum in Ohrdruf he had learned more Latin and rhetoric than any other subjects, and at the school of St. Michael in Lüneburg he progressed to more advanced readings in Latin authors, including Cicero's letters, orations, and philosophical works.[145] At the beginning of his tenure at the school of St. Thomas in Leipzig he taught Latin himself, and throughout his life he seems to have explained the rules of composition from the theory of rhetoric.[146] In letters of recommendation for a student he emphasized the training "in humanioribus" imparted at St. Thomas's.[147] Another cantor, Heinrich Bokemeyer at the ducal school in Wolfenbüttel, alludes in fact to the *stilus latinus* of the Ciceronians precisely when he defends canonic writing against Mattheson's attack.[148] But how did Bach come upon the idea of imi-

---

by Hans Gunther HOKE as "nicht nur seine eigene, sondern auch die Auffassung breiter Kreise musikhistorisch halbgebildeter Intellektueller" ["not only his own view, but also that of a large class of intellectuals with a very modest knowledge of music history"] – *Neue Studien zur 'Kunst der Fuge' BWV 1080*, «Beiträge zur Musikwissenschaft», XVII, 1975, p. 101. Also R. GERBER, pp. 65f, regarded Bach's late works as merely abstract and quadrivial. The writings of those authors who have recognized the importance of rhetoric for music deserve more attention from students of the Renaissance and Baroque. But it is necessary also to begin reading and quoting the ancient rhetoricians themselves, not merely the later music theorists, who are dependent upon them.

[145] SPITTA, I, 184ff, 214.

[146] SPITTA, II, 6f, 13; see also II, 64, and FORKEL, pp. 17 and 24: "... jedes Stück unter seiner Hand gleichsam wie eine Rede sprach"; "Er sah die Musik völlig als eine Sprache, und den Componisten als einen Dichter an" ["Under his hand every piece spoke like an oration", "He regarded music as a language, the composer as a poet"].

[147] *Dok.*, I, 48ff. Very high linguistic standards were set by Bach's direct predecessor as cantor at St. Thomas's, Johann Kuhnau. He read not only Latin and Greek, but also Hebrew, and applied this knowledge systematically to his musical compositions. See Othmar WESSELY, *Zur ars inveniendi im Zeitalter des Barock*, «Orbis musicae», I, 1972, pp. 113-140.

[148] "Wendet man aber ein: Es sey mit den *Canonibus* gezwungen Werk, und sie contentirten ein galant-gewehntes Ohr nicht; so dienet zur Antwort: Ein *Stilus latinus*, so pur nach den gemeinen *regulis Syntacticis* eingerichtet ist, kämmt gleichfals gezwungen und läppisch heraus. Gleichwohl kann ein galanter Ciceronianer der Syntactischen Regeln nicht entbehren. Wer also das *Artis est, occultare artem* recht zu practisiren weiss und ein zur Music aufgelegtes Naturell dabey *adhibirt*, der wird schon ein *delicates* Gehör zu vergnügen *capable* seyn" ["But if one objects: canons are forced pieces and do not satisfy an ear accustomed to the gallant [style], then a servicable answer is: also a Latin style arranged merely according to the rules of syntax will likewise turn out forced and foolish.

tating Quintilian in music? Undoubtedly from contacts with his philologist colleagues, particularly Johann Matthias Gesner (1691-1761, Plate XII.1), who had been appointed co-rector of the gymnasium in Weimar in 1715, two years before our composer left that city, and was to serve as Bach's rector at the Thomasschule in Leipzig from 1730 until he became professor at the University of Göttingen in 1734.[149] In 1738 the distinguished philologist published a monumental edition of Quintilian, including in it a lengthy footnote which was soon to become famous in Bach literature (Plates XII.2-3).[150] It is a commentary on a passage in which Quintilian illustrates the capacity of the human mind to perform more than one function simultaneously, referring to the cithara player who sings, plays, and beats time all at once (I.xii.2f). Here Gesner informs Quintilian's shade that this is nothing compared to Bach's playing the organ with hands and feet while directing and correcting his musicians, singing their cues, and so on. That Gesner praised his former colleague so lavishly may have been motivated in part by the censure of Bach published by Johann Scheibe on 14 May 1737.[151] However, Quintilian gave Gesner no pretext to counter Scheibe's strictures of Bach's "turgid" style, but only to praise him as a performing musician, as Scheibe himself had already done.[152] Much more adequate was the defense of Bach by the Leipzig university rhetorician Johann Abraham Birnbaum in 1738, surely in consultation with the composer. It immediately addresses the most insulting part of Scheibe's diatribe: the designation of Bach as a mere "Musikant".[153] As Birnbaum's second installment (1739) reveals, Bach was not flattered by Scheibe's

---

Nevertheless, a gallant Ciceronian cannot do without the rules of syntax. Thus whoever knows how to practice correctly the art of concealing the art and applies thereby a natural talent for music, he will be capable of pleasing a delicate ear"] – in Johann MATTHESON, *Critica Musica* cit., IV, 249.

[149] On Gesner see *Allgemeine deutsche Biographie*, IX, Leipzig, Duncker & Humblot, 1879, pp. 97-103; Luigi ANSBACHER, *Sulla cantata profana No. 209* [perhaps not by Bach], in *Bach-Gedenkschrift 1950* cit., pp. 163-177; Friedrich SMEND, *Johann Sebastian Bach und Johann Matthias Gesner*, «Gymnasium», LVII, 1950, pp. 295-298; Werner BÜRGER and Johannes SCHWINN, *Johann Matthias Gesner (1691-1761): Seine Beziehungen zu Ansbach und J.S.Bach*, in *Bachwoche Ansbach … 1991*, Ansbach, Bachwoche, 1991, pp. 122-130.

[150] *M. Fabii Quinctiliani De institutione oratoria libri duodecim … perpetuo commentario illustrati a Io. Matthia Gesnero*, Göttingen, Vandenhoeck, 1738, p. 61. The references to it by Schmutzer 1772, Kirnberger-Schulz 1773, Hiller 1784 ("ein grosser Gelehrter, … der berühmte Hofrath Gesner"; "a great scholar, … the famous *Hofrat* Gesner"), and Gerber 1790 are quoted in *Dok.*, III, pp. 238, 260, 403, 468. The Latin footnote itself is reproduced with a German translation in *Dok.* II, pp. 33ff, and in English translation in *The Bach Reader*, ed. Hans T. David, New York, Norton, 1945, p. 231.

[151] *Critischer Musikus*, Leipzig, B. C. Breitkopf, 1745², p. 62.

[152] Contrary to SMEND, p. 298, Gesner's note did not reveal "inner comprehension for the spirit of Bach's art as an oration, as a language in sounds".

[153] BIRNBAUM, reprinted in SCHEIBE, p. 841.

[or even Gesner's?] praise of his manual dexterity, but wished to appear as a master of musical rhetoric:[154]

Die Theile und Vortheile, welche die Ausarbeitung eines musikalischen Stücks mit der Rednerkunst gemein hat, kennet er so vollkommen, dass man ihn nicht nur mit einem ersättigenden Vergnügen höret, wenn er seine gründlichen Unterredungen auf die Aehnlichkeit und Uebereinstimmung beyder lenket; sondern man bewundert auch die geschickte Anwendung derselben, in seinen Arbeiten. Seine Einsicht in die Dichtkunst ist so gut, als man sie nur von einem großen Componisten verlangen kann.

He has such perfect knowledge of the parts [i.e. *dispositio*] and merits [rhetorical *virtutes*] which the working out [i.e. *elaboratio*] of a musical piece has in common with rhetoric, that one not only listens to him with satiating pleasure when he focuses his conversations [*inter al.* with the rhetoricians Gesner and Birnbaum] on the similarity and correspondences of both [music and rhetoric]; but one also admires *their clever application in his works* [!]. His insight into poetry [including Homer – regarded by Quintialian, X.i.46f, as the model and inspiration of all eloquence] is as good as one can expect from a great composer.

What better evidence could we wish for Bach's rhetorical concept of the *Musical Offering* than this first-hand testimony to his perfect understanding of the *partes orationis* in music as well as in speech and to his custom of conversing with rhetoricians on the relationships between rhetoric and music? Is it not time that we look for "their clever application in his works"? Significantly, the defense was written not by a musician, but by a rhetorician of the old school, a competent philologist for whom the musician Scheibe was no match. The issue of the Scheibe/Bach polemics was not merely a personal one, but possibly reflected an antagonism of two larger factions in Leipzig: on the one hand, the conservatives, Bach, Gesner, and Birnbaum;[155] on the other, the progressive group of Gottsched and his disciples, none of whom was more fanatic than Scheibe. Gottsched's brand of Ciceronianism was modern, vernacular, and Scheibe postulated the fashionable gallant style. Bach may well have known that Gottsched had dedicated his *Ausführliche Redekunst* to the Prussian crown prince Frederick in 1736, and he certainly knew that in the 1740s the gallant style flourished

---

[154] BIRNBAUM, in SCHEIBE, p. 997, my italics. Cf. FORKEL, p. 69, who calls Bach "den größten musikalischen Dichter und den größten musikalischen Declamator, den es je gegeben hat" ["the greatest musical poet and the greatest musical orator who ever existed"].

[155] Birnbaum's style was characterized as "ciceronisch" in the *Neue Zeitungen von gelehrten Sachen*, Leipzig, Grossen, 1735, p. 603.

at the Prussian court,[156] where the sovereign and his musicians, including C. P. E. Bach, were a generation younger than he. When he came to present a work to the king, he chose, notwithstanding the one concession with the gallant sonata, to state his position clearly as master of the old, rhetorical music, not as a mere "Musikant", and thus to dissociate himself from the new trend represented by Scheibe. He may well have regarded the *Musical Offering* partly as his own answer to the assailant, and it is very likely that he again consulted with Birnbaum (d. 1748) while planning the work.[157] Its completion and publication, however, he delayed for nine years (1738-47), surely heeding the famous admonition of Horace for a literary work: "nonumque prematur in annum" ["let it age for nine years" – *Ars poetica*, 388],[158] quoted by Quintilian on the very first page of his *Institutio*, i.e. in the introductory epistle! It would seem safe to assume that Bach had been planning at least the rhetorical *dispositio* of his complex musical oration long before his visit to Potsdam, and that the contact with Friedrich provided the stimulus for its completion. Once he made the plan, he could execute it with any suitable theme.

Yet Bach must have sought also to satisfy his patron personally. Frederick the Great was one of the few elite who still prided themselves on being disciples of Cicero and hence of Quintilian.[159] Already in his youth, as he wrote to Voltaire, he chose Cicero as his "friend and consoler" while he was under strict arrest. During the Seven Years' War the king took Cicero's works with him to the battlefield: the *Tusculanae disputationes*, *De natura deorum*, *De finibus*. And still in his old age (1779) he ordered his bureaucrats to have more ancient authors, including Cicero, translated into the vernacular.[160] There were few cities in Germany with a Cicero cult comparable to that of Potsdam. One of these was Leipzig, with its university and book publishers. Here, in

---

156 Quantz's chapters on musical performance are much indebted to Gottsched's treatment of *elocutio*.

157 From MIZLER, I/4, 1738, p. 62, we know that Birnbaum had "eine gute Einsicht in die Musik" and played "ein artiges Clavier" ["had a good insight into music" and played "the clavier nicely"].

158 The entire work of Horace was applied to music by MIZLER, III/2, pp. 605-635, who used, on p. 607, the formulation "musikalisches Opfer" in the sense of "serenade").

159 Eduard ZELLER, *Friedrich der Große als Philosoph*, Berlin, Weidmann, 1886, *passim* and especially note 117, reluctantly quotes many remarks in which Frederick expressed his great love of Cicero, e.g. to Voltaire, 6 July, 1737: "J'aime infiniment Cicéron" ["I love Cicero infinitely"]. See also T. ZIELINSKI, *Cicero im Wandel der Jahrhunderte*, Leipzig/Berlin, Teubner, 1908², p. 307.

160 As a child, Frederick learned Latin only until his eleventh year, secretly under the tutorship of his mother, against his father's will. Throughout his life he read the ancient authors in French translations.

the stronghold of Ciceronian rhetoric, Bach must have learned, at least from hearsay, of Frederick's partiality.

We need not be surprised that Bach did not reveal openly his grandiose rhetorico-musical plan, which now comes to light after so many years. Like the enigmatic canons, the Latin acrostic and *sententiae*, the entire work was a high play of wit, destined, perhaps as a reciprocating challenge, for an elevated personage who not only was a Ciceronian, but also had a more than ordinary understanding of music. If Bach had explained his secret to the king, he would have destroyed his compliment, or at least its subtlety; to have alluded to it in the newspaper announcement, directed at the 'profanum vulgus', would have been no less than an insult. Artists, writers, composers in the humanistic tradition guarded jealously the secrets of their work from the unenlightened public, as we have known for some time.[161] Bach's intention could not have been different. *Musica reservata* is only one manifestation of the humanistic concept of a high art, intelligible only to the elite, since its effect is based on understanding, not mere sensual pleasure. This tradition too was part of the revival of ancient rhetoric. Quintilian's words "docti rationem componendi intelligunt, etiam indocti voluptatem" ["the learned understand the principle of artistic composition, yet the ignorant receive [only] pleasure" – IX.iv.116] echo a passage from Cicero [?] quoted by Johann Joseph Fux in his *Gradus ad Parnassum*:[162]

Audi in hanc rem loquentem Ciceronem: Caeteri, inquit, cum legunt orationes bonas aut poëmata, probant oratores & poëtas, necque intelligunt, qua re commoti probent, quod scire non possunt, ubi sit, nec quid sit, nec quomodo factum sit, id quod eos maxime delectat.	Listen to Cicero speaking on this matter: 'Others', he says, 'when they read good orations or poems, commend the orators and poets, but do not understand what moves them to commendation, because they cannot know where, what, or how that is made which delights them most'.

Bach's friend and pupil Lorenz Mizler, who published a German translation of Fux's *Gradus* in 1742, epitomized the *eruditio musica* with his Correspondirende Societät der musikalischen Wissenschaften in Deutschland, founded in 1738

---

[161] E.g. from Edward WIND in his fascinating book *Pagan Mysteries in the Renaissance*, New York, Norton, 1968[2]. He cites – with irony – also Conrad Celtes, who could not hold his tongue and divulged his newly acquired erudition – p. 252f. Or William S. HECKSCHER, *Melancholia (1541): An Essay in the Rhetoric of Description by Joachim Camerarius*, in *Joachim Camerarius*, ed. Frank Baron, Munich, Fink, 1978, pp. 79f, on Dürer, who maintained silence on occult matters in order to add to his humanistic credentials. Cf. also Edward E. LOWINSKY, *Secret Chromatic Art in the Netherlands Motet*, New York, Columbia UP, 1946, *passim*.

[162] Vienna, Ghelen, 1725, p. 240. The passage is not contained in Cicero's rhetorical works.

... [um] so wohl was die Historie anbe-
langt, als auch aus der Weltweisheit, Ma-
thematik, Redekunst [!] und Poesie dazu
gehöret, in vollkommenen Stand zu setzen.

... to bring to perfection the musical
sciences, not merely what concerns history,
but also what pertains to them in philosophy, mathematics, *rhetoric*, and poetry.[163]

Members were admitted only by election; their number was limited to, but
never quite reached, twenty, and included Christoph Gottlieb Schröter, Heinrich Bokemeyer (see above, p. 449), Telemann, Stölzel, Spiess, and Handel
(honorary member).[164] "Mere practical musicians" could not be admitted,
"because they are incapable of contributing anything to the reception and improvement of music".[165] Members agreed to defend any one of their number
who was attacked in print,[166] as Bach was supported by Mizler and Schröter
against Scheibe even before he joined the society[167] in June 1747, as the fourteenth member (B-a-c-h = $2 + 1 + 3 + 8 = 14$).[168] For this occasion he composed the *Canonic Variations* BWV 769 and the six-part enigmatic canon
BWV 1076, and had the required portrait[169] painted by E. G. Haussmann.
Like the other members, he was now obliged to submit at least one work each
year to the society.[170] Such works were circulated regularly by the secretary
Mizler to the membership in the society's "Paket".[171] H. G. Hoke identified
the *Musical Offering* as Bach's contribution for 1748 and argued plausibly that
Bach intended the *Art of Fugue* as his final magnificent fulfillment of this requirement in 1749, before he was dispensed by virtue of becoming sixty-five
years of age.[172] These conclusions are based on a letter of 1 September 1747

---

[163] MIZLER, I/4, 1738, p. 74 (my italics). The society's statutes and other relevant information
are given here, pp. 73-76, and, revised and expanded, in III/2, 1746, pp. 346-362.

[164] III/2, p. 357.

[165] "Blose practische Musikverständige können deswegen in dieser Societet keinen Platz finden, weil sie nicht im Stande sind, etwas zur Aufnahme und Ausbesserung der Musik beyzutragen"
– I/4, p. 74; III, p. 349.

[166] III/2, p. 354.

[167] I/4, pp. 62-73 (reprint of Birnbaum's first defence of Bach); II/1, 1740, pp. 146ff (condem-
nation of Scheibe and mention of Birnbaum's second defence); III/1, 1746, pp. 203ff, 235.

[168] *Dok.*, III, 78, and F. SMEND, *Johann Sebastian Bach bei seinem Namen gerufen*, Kassel, Bärenreiter, 1950, p. 27. Bach's entry, like his compositions for the society (see below), was prepared well
in advance – see HOKE, p. 98.

[169] MIZLER, III/2, p. 353.

[170] III/2, p. 350: "jährlich wenigstens eine Abhandlung" ["at least one treatise each year"].
Though for most members this was a literary work, the wording "in der Ausübung nützlich" and
"die practische Musik immer höher bringen[d]" ["useful in the practice" and "raising practical music still higher"] left Bach free to write his "Abhandlung" in music.

[171] 1/4, p. 74; III/2, p. 350; *Dok.* II, 437.

[172] HOKE, pp. 100f; cf. MIZLER, III/2, p. 355, on the dispensation. The title "Art of Fugue"
connects with the classical tradition (*Ars rhetorica, Ars poetica, Ars amatoria*, etc.).

to Spiess, in which Mizler mentions visiting Bach and being told of "his trip to Berlin and the story of the fugue that he played for the king, which very soon will be engraved in copper and a copy included in the *Paket* of the Society".[173] With the *Musical Offering* Bach thus did his duty both to the king and to the society. Such an eventuality was already foreseen in the statutes: "When great amateurs and noble patrons of the musical sciences help to advance the intentions of the Society through their generosity ... the Society will show its gratitude by preparing musical compositions dedicated to such persons".[174] We do not know, however, whether Frederick ever patronized this first 'German Musicological Society', just as we do not know to what extent he appreciated the rhetoric of Bach's musical homage. But with the help of Quintilian, we now begin to understand it. Should not the *Neue Bach-Ausgabe* reissue the work with its *disiecta membra* arranged in the manner that properly conveys the composer's brilliant ideas?[175]

[*Continued in ch. 3*]

---

[173] *Dok.*, II, p. 437: "seine Berlinische Reise u. Geschicht von der Fuge, die er vor dem König gespielt, ... welche nächstens in Kupfer wird gestochen werden, u. in dem Packet der Soc. ein Exemplar zum Vorschein kommen". Since the *Musical Offering* and the *Art of Fugue* are among the very few works of Bach printed during his lifetime, it is quite possible that these editions, like BWV 769 and 1076, have some connection with the plans of the society to publish works from the "Paket" (MIZLER, III/2, p. 350), even though the editions seem to have been initiated by the composer.

[174] "Wenn große Liebhaber und vornehme Gönner der musikalischen Wissenschaften die Absichten der Societät durch ihre Freygiebigkeit befördern helfen, soll solche ... ihre Dankbarkeit durch verfertigte musikalische Stücke auf dergleichen Personen bezeugen" (I/4, pp. 75f; III/2, p. 354).

[175] The only satisfactory edition is still Ludwig Landshof's 'Urtext', Leipzig, Peters, 1937. This article does not, of course, exhaust all the parallels between Quintilian's treatise and the *Musical Offering*; scholars will surely discover additional ones.

APPENDIX I

Canon 4, a 2 per augmentationem, contrario moto (solution of Friedrich Smend)

Double hyperbole "insuper addita"

APPENDIX II

TABLE OF CONCORDANCES

QUINTILIAN

Proem to Book IV
Vota [to the Muses and the Emperor]

BACH [176]

Title / Dedication
"Ex. Mayestät weyhe ... ein Musicalisches Opfer"

Exordium I (Principium)

Ductus officio reipublicae aut non mediocis exempli
Extemporalis oratio
Neque diu moraturos
Docere
Simplex, ex proximo sermo
Delectare
Agitare
Miseratio
E contrario ductis, superbum
Breviter

Ricercar a 3

Theme from the head of State; audience in Potsdam
Improvisatory, free episodes prominent
Short episodes, frequent changes of style
Fugal elements, 'learned' style
Simple rhythms
Triplet episodes
Alla zoppa, Pyrrhic rhythm
Sighs, chromatic melody
Inversion of chromatic melody
Summary of various devices to be used later

Narratio brevis

Percursio

Brevis
Gravius ac sanctius
Varietas, mutationes
Ne pares tractus
Oratio perpetua

Canon Perpetuus super Thema Regium

Summary of motives to be elaborated in the five *Canones diversi*
Only five measures long
'Royal' style
Variety of rhythmic motives
Mixed meters [177]
Perpetual canon

Narratio ornata [178]

Transitus efficiat sententiam
Res diversissimas colligentem
Partitio

1. *f*: Ne quid naturae adversum
    Redditio contraria
  e: Robur
    Homer: Achilles idle, then rises, "swift-footed"

[5] *Canones diversi*

Acrostic
Five *canones diversi[ssimi]*
Division into five canons

1. Crab canon, one staff, *genus subtile*
    Retrograde motion
    Simple rhythm
    Slow and fast (running) rhythms, respectively; *anabasis* ("rises")

---

[176] The five printer's units are separated by horizontal lines. The left column consists of key words, not complete quotations, from Quintilian; ellipses are therefore not indicated.

[177] Cf. p. 430.

[178] "*f*" stands once more for the five forensic, "*e*" for the five epideictic virtues.

2. *f*: Qualis in comoediis etiam in mimis

    Translationibus crebrior, figuris iucundior
    Sententiis dulcis
    Mite ac placidum, blandum et humanum
e: Pulchritudo
    Homer: Three gods and a king
        Jupiter's thunderbolt
        Mars marshalling scattered troops
        Neptune
        Agamemnon pre-eminent
        "Such did Jupiter make Agamemnon"

2. *Genus medium, stilus theatralis, ethos, mimesis*
Subjectio [see also below, 2e: *katabasis, circulus, mimesis*]
Ingratiating music

Richer instrumentation (violins)
Richer instrumentation (violins)
Katabasis
Motives separated in pitch, Pyrrhic rhythm

Circulus (waves), 'rocking', Pyrrhic rhythm
Large leaps, Pyrrhic rhythm
Mimesis (canon at the unison, imitating the gods)

3. *f*: Simplicitatis imitatio

    Acumen
e: Infirmitas
    Homer: Tydeus, bellator parvus
    Apheleia

3. Canon by contrary motion, *genus subtile*, diminution, narrow range
High range
[As above, *simplicitas*]
[Small stature of Frederick]
Diminution; high, narrow range

4. *f*: Magnificentia
    Amplitudo paeanis
    Incrementum [augmentatio]
    Double hyperbole
e: Fortuna, dignitas
    Pindar: double hyperbole for Hercules

4. *Genus grande*, 'royal' style
Paean rhythm
Augmentation
Twice rise above ambitus [double hyperbole]
[As above, *magnificentia*]
Double hyperbole

5. *f*: Evidentia
    Ex accidentibus
    Magna virtus
e: Gloria
    Homer: six-step gradatio (klimax) for seven heroes

5. Rising modulation *per tonos*, leading to:
Profusion of accidentals
Genus grande: paean and dactylic rhythm
[As above, *evidentia*]
Six-step *gradatio*

4-5. Sententia. Fortuna dignitatem et gloriam parit

4-5. Sententia: fortuna, gloria

Egressus

Finis narrationis
In aliquam laetum locum
Iactatio
Maxime ornare
Cohaeret et sequitur

Fuga canonica

After five *canones diversi*
'Pleasant' music
Contrapuntal artistry
Extended length
Thematically related

Exordium II (Insinuatio)

Insinuatio surrepat animas

Ricercar a 6

Unobtrusive, disguised entries, no differentiation of tone color (keyboard)

[Argumentatio]

Quaestiones
Hortor ad quaeredum et inveniri posse fateor

Probatio (accusatio)
Simplicior [quam refutatio]
E contrario ductis
Clamosa

Refutatio
Necque ex aliis locis quam in probatione

Mille artes

Neget, molliat, minuat
Avertat; flexus

Peroratio in adfectibus
Liberior
Plenior
Totus eloquentiae aperire fontes
Quae pathos concitavit, ethos mitigat

Eloquentia regnat
Maxime debet crescere oratio
Fictam orationem induere personis, defunctos excitare
Concitare adfectos

Sicut amantes

Cum ad summam perduxerimus, relinquamus
Miserationem discutere urbane dictis
Velocior

Peroratio in rebus

Rerum repetitio, enumeratio, figuris varianda

Cum pondere
Sine recta repetitione

[Two enigmatic canons]

Riddle canons
"Quaerendo invenietis"

Canon a 2
Only two voices, half as long as *Canon a 4*
Contrary motion
(𝄾 ♩♩♩ -motives, etc.

Canon a 4
Theme related to *Canon a 2* (*thema regium* with upbeat, conjunct motion)
Four voices, twice as long as previous canon (and:)
Descending subdominant sequence
Winding figures

Sonata
No longer strict style of canon or fugue
Fuller instrumentation, four movements
Affective style, pathos, tempo indications
Pathos dispersed by *ethos* of fourth movement
Royal performer
Highest pitch
Largo: declamatory sighs in upper parts, lamento bass
Allegro: syncopated and Pyrrhic rhythm, concertizing
Andante: passionate sighs, echo effects, E♭-pathos
Abrupt ending
Allegro: ethos, triplets
Fast, breathless, few rests

Canon perpetuus

Some thematic material from *probatio*-canon, but varied
Alla breve time
Contrary motion (opposite of *imitatio recta*)

XIII.

A REVIEW OF THE FACSIMILE EDITION OF J. S. BACH'S
MUSICAL OFFERING

When the notation of a source is problematic or ambiguous for the modern reader, susceptible to varying interpretations by different editors, a facsimile is justified, indeed necessary. Thus editions of major medieval manuscripts have often included not only a transcription and commentary but also a facsimile, so that the reader can test the editor's interpretations against the original. On the other hand, facsimiles of relatively recent sources, with few notational problems, often provide little more information than a good critical edition, and in a less legible form. But the original edition and unique source of Bach's *Musical Offering* is a special case, for it was printed in a complex and unconventional format. A facsimile would enable the reader to visualize immediately the arrangement of its unbound horizontal and vertical folios and bifolios much more easily than a verbal description could allow. This would be no small convenience for the study of a work which, because of the problematic arrangement of its source, has been subject to more misunderstandings than any other major composition of a major composer.

The Peters edition[1] places the unbound facsimile pages (30 of them printed) loosely in a pocket, likewise the five-page preface in German and English. As far as the printing is concerned, this edition has only minor defects. If the facsimile were to show the original arrangement of folios and bifolios, it would not have tacitly transformed six of the folios into three bifolios, creating a discrepancy with the text of the preface, which mentions the "single leaves" (and, incidentally, refers to the bifolios as "folios"). Also, by an innocent ruse apparently intended to reduce costs, the same half-tone negative has been used on two different bifolios for five different pages, four of

---

[1] *Johann Sebastian Bach: Musikalisches Opfer, BWV 1079*, ed. Christoph Wolff, Peters, Leipzig, 1977.

them blank and one with a line-image superimposed from another negative. If, as stated in the preface, these two bifolios were reproduced from copies in Munich and Leipzig respectively, five pages would not show the identical pattern of spots and smears.

Professor Wolff begins his preface with a brief summary of the historical circumstances, from the memorable audience with Frederick the Great on 7 May 1747 and Bach's three-part improvisation on the king's theme to the newspaper advertisement of 30 September announcing the publication of the completed work. It is curious that he believes that the dedication, normally the last part of a literary or musical work to be written, refers only to the three-part ricercar and that Bach, when he wrote it on 7 July, "still had no clear conception of the whole extent of the work" – especially when we have read, in the paragraph immediately preceding, that "the expanded project in the sense of a multipartite monothematic instrumental work must, then, have achieved firm outlines soon after Bach's return [from Potsdam]". Why would a composer print the dedication of his work after completing only the first piece of the cycle? Bach's words, after all, are clear enough:

... wegen Mangels nöthiger Vorbereitung, die Ausführung nicht also gerathen wollte, als es ein so treffliches *Thema* erforderte. Ich fassete demnach den Entschluß, und machte mich sogleich anheischig, dieses recht Königliche *Thema* vollkommener auszuarbeiten, und sodann der Welt bekannt zu machen. Dieser Vorsatz ist nunmehro nach Vermögen bewerkstelliget worden ...	... for lack of necessary preparation the execution [of the task] did not succeed as well as such an excellent theme demanded. I then resolved and promptly undertook to *work out* this very royal theme *more perfectly* and then make it known to the world. This resolve *has now been carried out as well as possible* ... [my italics].

Did not Bach write the entire cycle in order to "work out" the royal theme? For the introductory ricercar alone he would never have used the high-sounding words "musical offering", "consecrate", and "make known to the world". (In comparison with these words, Mizler's remark that Bach showed him only the first ricercar at the beginning of July carries no weight). And Wolff again continues with a disclaimer: "Nevertheless the compositional work must have been completed soon after". Everyone who publishes knows how much time is needed for mailing, engraving, mailing again, printing music, and finally publishing an advertisement: 7 July to 30 September is little enough for this work. We must, then, leave the dedication as it stands, brief but magnificent, a testimony eloquent in every word, not referring immodestly to only one of the thirteen pieces but presenting the whole.

As Wolff correctly states, "the layout ... of the original print ... led to numerous speculations and controversial conclusions". But he believes that in conjunction with his edition of the work in the *Neue Bach-Ausgabe*, "which commendably permitted a comparative autopsy of the collated extant copies of this print to appear, decisive new understandings could be achieved for the first time". Unfortunately, the reviewer, after testing this substantial claim, has been forced to conclude that the "autopsy" has only produced yet more indecisive misunderstandings. The root of the problem, leading to unsolvable difficulties, is that Wolff (not Bach, as stated) "arranged the print ... in three fascicles, within which the loose leaves or folios respectively were held together by the title wrappers". Correct is Wolff's distinction of five printer's units,[2] but not their sequence (indicated by the letters A to E, retained here for simplicity's sake) or their combination into three "fascicles". According to his arrangement, units A (title page and dedication; one horizontal bifolio) and B (ricercar *a 3* and first *canon perpetuus*; three horizontal folios) would form the first "fascicle", unit C (trio sonata and second *canon perpetuus*; bifolio cover and three bifolios for the three separate parts) the second, and units D (the five short, numbered canons and the *fuga canonica*; one vertical bifolio) and E (ricercar *a 6* and two enigmatic canons; four horizontal folios) the third. But can that be? None of the extant copies is bound in this manner. Only unit C was provided with a bifolio cover, and for good reason: only here are there three separate instrumental parts that need to be held together. By an imperfect analogy with this cover, Wolff imagined that the bifolios A and D must also have served as "covers", for the loose folios of B and E respectively, thus forming two "fascicles". In this "handelsübliches Exemplar" ["customary trade copy"] the dedication would be separated from the title-page by the first two pieces of the cycle (insertion of B in A), the fuga canonica interrupted by the six-part ricercar and the two enigmatic canons (insertion of E in D), and a vertical bifolio (D) would serve as a "cover" for horizontal folios (E). Such a confusion of signatures, lacerating the content and diverging 90°, could hardly be regarded as "customary". In only one copy does unit A still exist as a bifolio, with the fold along the top as it left the printing press; in all the others the fold is cut open, so that title and dedication can be bound as successive pages. In the book trade, such opening of uncut signatures is customary, not a "mutilation", as Wolff would believe. Speculations such as this "fascicle" theory are not only flawed, but also misleading – a far cry from objective *Grundlagenforschung*.

---

[2] Cf. above, p. 418, Table 1.

The unsuspecting reader might be delighted with this "customary trade copy" if he did not know that since the 1920s nearly 30 different cyclic arrangements have been advocated, over half of them by Wolff alone.[3] His preface does not reveal this, unless the "numerous speculations and controversial conclusions" are understood to include his own. In the face of this confusion, compounded by the "fascicle" theory, he eventually finds it "very clear that the idea of a sophisticated cyclic structure to be realized in a cyclical performance has to he rejected".[4] Why, then, does he subsequently continue to construct new "solutions"?[5] Did Bach publish his work and then, like Wolff, repeatedly change his mind about the order of its pieces? The preface now returns to the verdict that "the *Musical Offering* does not represent a cyclical work which relies on a compulsory order of movements, and it is not to be played as such", yet concedes that "its conception operates as a closed unity".

With one exception (Peters, 1867), the printer's units of the *Musical Offering* were left intact until the 1920s. The Bach-Gesellschaft had published the work in the sequence suggested by Spitta: A B D E C. But H. T. David (1937), like many others, preferred to rearrange the canons even within the single printer's units, assuming that the engraver had not followed the sequence intended by the composer. Wolff propagates David's implausible notion by asserting that some canons were placed according to "considerations of printing technology":[6] not wanting to "waste" paper, "Bach composed those canons in order to fill up the space which would [otherwise] remain empty" after the larger pieces. This uniquely unartistic motive, attributed by David to an insensitive engraver, is now ascribed to the composer himself.

David believed that unit E marked the end, for it concluded with the signature of the engraver Johann Georg Schübler. Wolff therefore designates this unit with the last letter, E. Schübler's signature appears here, however, not because E marks the end of the entire cycle, but because it is the last unit in score. Unit C was not suitable for this, because it consisted of separate parts and because half of it was engraved not by J. G. Schübler but by an apprentice, probably his younger brother[7] – a fact that escaped Wolff's "autopsy". If

---

[3] *Der Terminus 'Ricercar' in Bachs Musikalischem Opfer*, «Bach-Jahrbuch», LIII, 1967, p. 72; *Ordnungsprinzipien in den Originaldrucken Bachscher Werke*, in *Bach-Interpretationen*, ed. M. Geck, Göttingen, Vandenhoeck, 1969, pp. 13f; *New Research on Bach's Musical Offering*, «Musical Quarterly», LVII, 1971, p. 407; *Neue Bach-Ausgabe*, VIII/1, Kassel, Bärenreiter, 1974, and *Kritischer Bericht* (henceforth *KB*), 1976, p. 125. Cf. above, p. 419, note 11.

[4] *New Research*, pp. 403f.

[5] *KB*, p. 125.

[6] *KB*, pp. 106, 122.

[7] Wolfgang WIEMER, *Die wiederhergestellte Ordnung in Johann Sebastian Bachs Kunst der Fuge*,

E were indeed the last unit, it would conclude the work with the one canon which is not in the key of the cycle. Instead of taking this as an indication that E does not belong at the end, Wolff interprets it as "an infallible [!] sign that Bach cherished no cyclic intention".[8]

The numerous rearrangements of the cycle – all of them arbitrary, since based on subjective aesthetic criteria – favor 'symmetrical' patterns (David, Gerber, Wolff), e.g.: ricercar *a 3*, five canons, sonata, five canons, ricercar *a 6*. There are several things wrong with this sequence, in addition to the violence it does to the source. First, Bach did not write ten canons, but nine canons and a lengthy (canonic) fugue. Because of its unique length (78 mm), this fugue cannot be regarded as a counterpart to canons of four and five measures in a 'symmetrical' pattern. Second, the above arrangement would conclude the cycle with a ricercar, i.e. a prelude (the six-part ricercar was in fact written as an internal prelude, to introduce the second half of the cycle).[9] Third, 'symmetry', in the visual sense, does not exist in acoustical categories: music, like oratory, unfolds in time, not in space, its form is linear. Fourth, 'symmetry' would place the climax of the work, the fully instrumented, multi-movement, strongly affective sonata, in the middle – contrary to all principles of rhetorical *dispositio*, not to mention court protocol. Quintilian, the most relevant authority for Bach's work, admonished (IX.iv.23) "cavendum ne descrescat oratio" ["take care that the eloquence does not diminish"], and to this day, even in American political conventions, the most important orator speaks at the end. Bach's unit C, finally presenting the royal flautist and his entourage, could not be followed by anticlimactic music. But after abandoning any cyclic concept Wolff still adheres to the notion of symmetry by designating the sonata as the central unit (C) and fascicle (II): "It is irrefutable [!] that Bach, by framing the sonata with the two ricercars, intended a certain symmetry in the sequence of fascicles in the original print; likewise, that the sum of the canon movements (ten) possesses symbolic qualities".[10] But even if the number of canons did correspond to the number of the Ten Commandments, what relevance would that have in this secular work? Here again, Wolff becomes inextricably tangled in his circular thought: on the one hand, unit C is to be in the "center", but on the other hand it is

---

Wiesbaden, Breitkopf & Härtel, 1977, pp. 40-46, quoted in an addendum sheet to Wolff's facsimile edition. For further informaion on the engravers, see the article of Gregory BUTLER, quoted above, p. 418, note 7.

  [8] *KB*, p. 122.

  [9] On the preludial function of ricercars, from the earliest to the latest, see chapters 2 and 3.

  [10] *KB*, p. 124; cf. *New Research*, p. 404.

not, for it is preceded in the facsimile edition by only two pieces and followed by nine. "The form of publication of the original print is congenial to the structure of the work as a whole", yet (in the next paragraph) "every sequential arrangement of the movements is necessarily an interference with the plan of the original printing".[11]

When the editor, in half a dozen publications on the *Musical Offering* within a decade, continually brings such fundamental contradictions (matched only by categorical, "infallible", "irrefutable", pronouncements): can the editions in the *Neue Bach-Ausgabe* and in facsimile be regarded as authoritative? Their effect is to make the *Musical Offering* unperformable (and thus, incidentally, to help bring musicology into disrepute with performers). Conscientious musicians, having been told so emphatically that the work has no particular order of movements, will obviously be reluctant to attempt still another subjective rearrangement.

What are we to make of these endless problems? What sequence of movements can one suggest, after so many different 'solutions'? We must, of course, return to the original edition, as Bach intended it, and throw the accumulated ballast overboard. Spitta and the editor of the Bach-Gesellschaft indeed went to this source and presented the correct sequence, though without knowing why it was correct. An article by this reviewer has demonstrated how Bach, like other composers in the humanist tradition, learned from the wisdom of Classical antiquity.[12] He made the thirteen pieces of the *Musical Offering* correspond precisely to the parts of the forensic oration, as described by Quintilian. (In 1738 Johann Matthias Gesner, Bach's friend and rector of the Thomas-Schule, published a commentary on this important classic, with a long footnote in praise of Bach). These correspondences are not few and vague, but numerous and concrete, often witty, and can be traced not only in every detail of the music but also in the literary inscriptions. The Leipzig rhetorician, Johann Abraham Birnbaum had good reason to say, when defending Bach against Johann Adolph Scheibe in 1739:[13]

Die Theile und Vorteile, welche die Ausarbeitung eines musikalischen Stücks mit der Rednerkunst gemein hat, kennet er so vollkommen, dass man ihn nicht nur mit einem ersättigenden Vergnügung hö-	He has such perfect knowledge of the parts and merits which the working out of a musical piece has in common with rhetoric, that one not only listens to him with satiating pleasure when he fo-

---

[11] *KB*, p. 125.

[12] See above, ch. 12, and the continuation, ch. 3.

[13] Reprinted in Scheibe's *Critischer Musikus*, Leipzig, B. C. Breitkopf, 1743, p. 997, and quoted here with my italics.

ret, wenn er seine Gründliche Unterredungen auf die Aehnlichkeit und Uebereinstimmung beyder lenket; sondern man bewundert auch die geschickte Anwendung derselben in seinen Arbeiten.

cuses his conversations on the similarity and correspondences of both [music and rhetoric]; but one also admires *their clever application in his works*. His insight into poetry is as good as one can expect from a great composer.

For those who no longer know what to do with this edition some good news remains: since the pages are loose, it is easy to salvage the expensive investment by rejecting the "three-fascicle" arrangement and putting the folios and bifolios in the order already accepted by Spitta and the Bach-Gesellschaft. But the preface will have to be rewritten.

XIV.

THE BAROQUE MOZART*

In his well known letter of 10 April 1782, Mozart wrote to his father: "Ich gehe alle Sonntage um 12 uhr zum Baron von Suiten – und da wird nichts gespiellt als Händl und Bach. – Ich mache mir eben eine Collection von den Bachischen Fugen – so wohl Sebastian als Emanuel und Friedemann Bach. – Dann auch von den händelschen" ["I go every Sunday at 12 o'clock to Baron van Swieten's – and nothing is played there but Handel and Bach. – At the moment I am making a collection of the fugues of Bach – those of Sebastian as well as Emanuel and Friedemann. Then also of Handel"]. Although these encounters with north German repertoire, which Baron Gottfried van Swieten had brought with him from Berlin to Vienna after his diplomatic mission in Prussia, were undoubtedly important for Mozart, they should be seen in a broader context. Some works of Bach and Handel were already known in Vienna, and interest in them was not an isolated phenomenon in the imperial city. Rather, it was sustained by a current of historicism existing at least since the beginning of the century, from the time of Johann Bernhard Fischer von Erlach, architect of Charles VI, and Johann Joseph Fux, imperial chapel master. Fischer built the court library, which Van Swieten later was to direct, and wrote a famous treatise entitled *Historische Architektur* with reproductions of buildings from all historical periods known to him – not only of classical antiquity, but even of ancient Egypt and the Near East. Fux's *Gradus*

---

* Since this lecture is a largely a synthesis of earlier reseach, it is published here without documentation, referring the reader to the following: Alfred HEUSS, *Mozart als Meister des Archaisierens*, ZfMw, IX, 1927, pp. 566f; Erich SCHENK, *Zur Tonsymbolik in Mozarts 'Figaro'*, «Neues Mozart-Jahrbuch», I, 1941, pp. 114-134; Reinhold HAMMERSTEIN, *Der Gesang der geharnischten Männer: Eine Studie zu Mozarts Bachbild*, AfMw, XIII, 1956, pp. 1-24; Leopold M. KANTNER, *Der Symbolwert von Archaismen untersucht in Opern der Klassik und Romantik*, in *De Ratione in Musica: Festschrift Erich Schenk zum 5. Mai 1972*, Kassel, Bärenreiter, 1975, pp. 156-186, and especially W. KIRKENDALE, *Fugue and Fugato in Rococo and Classical Chamber Music*, Durham NC, Duke UP, 1979, ch. 7, *Wolfgang Amadeus Mozart*, containing further arguments and literature.

ad Parnassum, printed at the emperor's expense, is comparable to Fischer's work insofar as it intends to teach the *stile antico*, then identified with Palestrina. Both publications represent not merely the personal taste of their authors, but also the interest of the court and of Charles VI in particular. As head of the Holy Roman Empire, this "Sacred Imperial and Catholic Royal Majesty" preferred the ecclesiastic style, counterpoint, for representation of the court, as a means to consolidate his rights to power. This predilection of the Hapsburgs remained up to the time of Beethoven. From it issued a strong tradition of composition in fugal style which terminated only with the arrival of Napoleon and the end of the empire. Many instrumental fugues were written in Vienna particularly for Mozart's emperor, Joseph II – a repertoire to which I dedicated a monograph. Immediately after his arrival in Vienna, Mozart relied upon this 'weakness' of the emperor, as one reads in a letter of 24 March 1781 to his father: "Ich möchte ihm mit Lust meine opera durchpeitschen, und dann brav Fugen spillen, denn das ist seine Sache" ["I should love to whip through my opera for him and then politely play fugues, for that is what he likes"]. Two years later he reports on one of his concerts: "spielte ich alleine eine kleine Fuge (weil der Kayser da war)" ["I played alone a short fugue (because the emperor was present")]. Mozart obviously knew fugues of the Josephinian era, and he had improvised fugues since his early youth. And it is possible that already in 1770 Padre Martini showed him in Bologna his copies of Bach's *Musical Offering* and *Art of Fugue*. In any case, Mozart already had considerable familiarity with fugal style, not only of Bach, before ever meeting Van Swieten.

During the years of the Sunday visits in Van Swieten's house (1782-83), Mozart composed no less than 22 fugues and fugal fragments, not in the modern Italian style of his Viennese contemporaries, but intentionally imitating the archaic north German counterpoint. These compositions can be designated 'style-imitations'. Mozart's extraordinary capacity for assimilating the styles of other composers is, of course, well known (cf. his letter of 7 Feb. 1778). But, obviously, he could not content himself with mere imitation, and this, I believe, is the reason why 19 of the 22 fugues remained fragmentary.

Van Swieten and Emperor Joseph II were not the only persons who incited Mozart to compose fugues. On 20 April 1782 he sent to his sister the fugue in C-major K. 394, explaining that his fiancée Konstanze was in love with the fugues of Bach and insisted that he compose similar pieces himself. The subject of this fugue (Ex. 1) is characterized by two sequential motives such as are found in innumerable fugue subjects of the Baroque. Mozart may have thought of the fugue in the same key from the beginning of Bach's *Well Tempered Clavier* (Ex. 2).

Ex. 1. Mozart: Fugue in C-major, K. 394.

Ex. 2. J. S. Bach: Fugue in C-major, *Das wohltemperierte Klavier*, I, 1.

These progressions are so characteristic for baroque fugues that later composers used them to obtain an archaic effect. When Beethoven in 1822 wrote his overture *The Consecration of the House* on the occasion of the reopening of the Theater in der Josephstadt, he chose the baroque French overture as the most suitable form for the solemn occasion. The transition to the fugal allegro (Ex. 3) consists of the same ascending motive which Mozart had used in the second measure of his fugue. Beethoven's fugue subject (Ex. 4) is no other than a rhythmic variant of the descending sequence at the beginning of Mozart's subject, as is clearly recognizable when it is reduced to its basic notes (Ex. 5). With his typical obstinacy, Beethoven repeats excessively his sequential motive, thus creating an exaggerated mannerism. He entitled the piece "Overture in the Style of Handel". In 1839, Louis Spohr published his Historical Symphony, with each of its four movements in the style of a different epoch. The first, entitled "Period of Bach-Händel, ca. 1720", consists of a fugue with a subject using our descending sequence (Ex. 6). Thus we see

Ex. 3. Beethoven: Overture *Die Weihe des Hauses* Op. 124, mm. 83f, transition to the fugue, mm. 83f.

Ex. 4. *Ibid.*: mm. 88-92, fugue subject.

Ex. 5. *Ibid.*: simplification of the subject.

Ex. 6. Louis Spohr: *Historische Sinfonie* Op. 116, first movement, mm. 8-11, fugue subject.

that Mozart, Beethoven, and Spohr associated this baroque theme-type directly with Bach and Handel.

Mozart returned again to a fugue subject with the descending sequential motive in his overture to *The Magic Flute*. This piece, like Beethoven's, uses ingredients typical of the French overture: a slow introduction with dotted rhythms, followed by a fugal allegro. In the third measure of the fugato theme (Ex. 7) we find the descending sequence, employed, however, in a new manner. Instead of continuing the sequence, Mozart repeats the motive at the same pitch – something which a baroque composer would never have done. Such repetitions of short motives are characteristic of the rococo/preclassical period. Now, eight years after meeting Van Swieten, Mozart no longer speaks the baroque language, but that of the Italian *opera buffa*. We know, in fact, that he 'borrowed' the theme from a piano sonata of Muzio Clementi.

Ex. 7. Mozart: *Die Zauberflöte* K. 620, overture, mm. 16-21f.

The subject with the sequential motives is only one example of a baroque theme-type. Thematic invention in the baroque era is based largely on a quantity of well known theme-types which were infinitely varied from one composition to another. Sequential themes, fragments of an ascending scale or a descending chromatic line were utilized continuously in a great variety of rhythmic configurations or melodic variants. It would be mistaken to regard such types as the result of poverty of invention, since they were employed also by the greatest composers, imaginatively and in new ways. This is true also of baroque poetry, which had at its disposal a complete vocabulary of *topoi* which were described and classified in manuals, as were the musical-rhetorical figures. These could be learned rationally by any musician, but the success of their employment depended upon the talent of the individual.

The third and last of the fugues completed by Mozart under the influence of Bach and Handel, K. 426, utilizes two of the most characteristic baroque theme-types. Its subject, in c-minor (Ex. 8), is based on the tonic and the fifth above (*c* and *g*), framed by the two adjacent notes, i.e. the minor sixth and the leading note. This universal theme-type is almost always characterized by the descending leap of the diminished seventh. It is heavily loaded with affective content and used frequently in baroque music for texts expressing sorrow and pain. To give it a name, I have designated it 'pathotype'. A few examples: the a-minor fugue from the second book of *The Well Tempered Clavier* (Ex. 9), the fugue "And with His stripes" in Handel's *Messiah* (for 'wounds', Ex. 10), the subject of the fugue in Haydn's quartet Op. 20, no. 5 (Ex. 11), the fugue in the Kyrie of Mozart's Requiem (Ex. 12). These similarities, in the vast majority of cases, are not to be seen as direct influence of one composer on another. The baroque theme-types were so diffused that they must be under-

Ex. 8. Mozart: Fugue in c-minor, K. 426.

Ex. 9. J. S. Bach: Fugue in a-minor, *Das Wohltemperierte Klavier*, II, 20.

Ex. 10. Handel: *Messiah*, no. 22, fugue "And with His stripes".

Ex. 11. J. Haydn: Quartet Op. 20, no. 5, fugue.

Ex. 12. Mozart: *Requiem* K. 626, Kyrie fugue.

stood as standard components of the universal language of the epoch. But in the case of K. 426, Mozart seems to have been motivated by a composition known to him, by Joseph Starzer (Ex. 13), his predecessor as director of the performances of Handel's oratorios promoted by Van Swieten.

Ex. 13. J. Starzer: Ballet *Gli Orazi e i Curiazi*.

The pathotype is often combined with another standard symbol of lament, the chromatic descent. The best known example of this combination is the *thema regium* of J. S. Bach's *Musical Offering* (Ex. 14). Mozart utilizes the same combination in his fugue K. 426. Upon a first hearing, one might attribute this piece to a late baroque composer and be surprised to learn that it is by Mozart. But a closer examination reveals that it comes from the classical period, not the Baroque. In the baroque themes, the chromatic descent is almost always harmonized with sequences of dominant sevenths, so that all notes form part of these chords (cf. the reduction, Ex. 15). Mozart, however, amply transforms them into non-harmonic notes, thus using them not as components of a chord, but as chromatic auxiliary notes. Thus he produces a gallant, slightly sentimental effect, typical for the rococo and late eighteenth century (Ex. 16), certainly not of the Baroque. It is such modifications which keep the old theme-types alive. Nevertheless, no other composition of Mozart

Ex. 14. J. S. Bach: *Musikalisches Opfer*, thema regium.

Ex. 15. Chromatic melody with sequential harmony.

Ex. 16. Chromatic melody without sequential harmony.

is so strongly tied to the Baroque: this fugue is the strictest and most elaborate from the second half of the eighteenth century. It presents the subject in inversion (Ex. 17) and in no less than six different strettos. That Mozart esteemed the piece highly is evident from his arrangement of it for string orchestra five years later (K. 546).

Ex. 17. Mozart: Fugue in c-minor, K. 426, mm. 35-38, inversion of the subject.

The keyboard pieces discussed thus far, the 'style copies', are an eloquent testimony of the influence of Bach on the music of Mozart. But most of his attempts at composing fugues remained fragmentary, often no more than an exposition. Mozart certainly realized that the style of the baroque fugue would remain foreign to him, but also that it offered something valuable which he could utilize in his own compositions. This he did by proceeding to introduce fugal sections into his multi-movement works. The future of contrapuntal writing did not consist in fugues, but in fugatos, combined with the classical forms such as sonata, rondo, variations, or scherzo. Mozart was the first composer to create such a combination, which I have labelled "terza pratica". He arrived there through his fugue fragments, since a fugato is nothing else but a fragmentary fugue. His best known essays in this genre are the finales of the Quartet in G-major K. 387 and of the Jupiter Symphony K. 551, and the overture to the *Magic Flute*. The quartet is the first case of a fugato integrated with sonata form (1782, the year after his move to Vienna).

The rondo finale of Mozart's last string quintet, K. 614, contains one of the most masterly combinations of old and new style. Its baroque-like thematic unity is radically different from the rondo of his time. Instead of the usual classical form (ABACABA) with contrasting B- and C-sections, Mozart develops the entire movement from a single A-theme: A A' A A" A A' A (A' in place of B, A" in place of C). The rondo theme is first presented in absolute homophony and is clearly articulated in antecedent and consequent phrases – the usual classical balance of 4 + 4 measures (Ex. 18). But behold what Mozart makes of this melody in the central section of the movement, A″: he no longer presents the two phrases in succession, but simultaneously as the two subjects of a double fugato (Ex. 19). Translating his thoughts into the language of the baroque, he transposes the theme into the minor mode and converts its first half into a sequence, no longer of four, but of five measures. (The sequence, particularly with this motif, was one of the preferred means of baroque composers to spin out the subject of an instrumental fugue). The second half, through the transposition to minor tonality, becomes a variant of the pathotype, with the downward leap of the diminished seventh, so often found in baroque fugues. These baroque elements – sequence and pathotype – were already latently present in the homophonic presentation of the theme. We sense a satisfaction when they receive their intrinsic baroque expression in the fugato. The section with the highly contrapuntal elaboration creates an enormous intensity. It forms the central culmination of the movement.

Ex. 18. Mozart: Quintet K 614, fourth movement, mm. 1-8.

Ex. 19. *Ibid.*: mm. 111-116, fugato.

Mozart employs a fugato in a very different manner in his sextet *Ein musikalischer Spaß* K. 522. This exquisite "musical joke" is a caricature not so much of the incompetent village musicians as of the composer without talent. In the rondo finale we find a pedestrian fugato on a feeble subject which has no relationship with the rest of the movement. The countersubject without the slightest interest consists of the simple cadential suspension of the sixteenth and seventeenth centuries (Ex. 20). During the mid-eighteenth century unimaginative composers frequently ended their fugue subjects with this worn-out formula which Mozart, in his witty parody, elevates to the rank of a countersubject. He understood that, in the hands of untalented composers, a fugato could easily degenerate into a mere mechanical procedure, as verified in the nineteenth century.

Ex. 20. Mozart: *Musikalischer Spaß* K. 522, fourth movement, mm. 250ff.

Expressive baroque devices are found, of course, also in Mozart's vocal music. The chromatic descent or *passus duriusculus* had been for generations a symbol of sorrow and pain, especially in the "Crucifixus" of the Mass and the laments of *opera seria*. Mozart utilizes this rhetorical-musical figure not only in the conventional manner, but also, as Erich Schenk observed, in an equivocal sense, in a subtle parody. In the second act of *The Marriage of Figaro* the gardener complains to the count that someone jumped out of a window and broke his flower pots. To protect the culprit Cherubino, who had been surprised in the chamber of the countess, the shrewd Figaro asserts that he himself had fled in that manner, and in order to be more convincing he pretends to have injured himself: "Stravolto m'ho un nervo del piè" ["I sprained my foot"], sung to a painful chromatic descent (Ex. 21). The contemporary audience still recognized the ambiguous situation and understood that Figaro was lying. This use of the language of *opera seria* in a comic context illustrates in an exemplary manner how *opera buffa* parodied *opera seria*.

Ex. 21. Mozart: *Le nozze di Figaro* K. 492, act II, finale, mm. 602-606.

Mozart intentionally used *stile antico* to represent also the age of persons, as Alfred Heuss and Leopold Kantner have observed. In the song *Die Alte* K. 517, an old woman as *laudator temporis acti* recalls with nostalgia the good old days and deplores the dissolute *mores* of the present. Here Mozart consciously avails himself of the style of the preceding half century and writes a baroque *Generalbasslied*, unique for his time, such as one might find in a collection like the *Augsburger Tafel-Confect* (1733-37) of Valentin Rathgeber, surely known to Mozart's father, who came from Augsburg. Similarly in *Don Giovanni* Mozart has Donna Elvira sing in the dotted rhythm of the French late Baroque, to indicate that this woman abandoned by Don Giovanni is no longer the youngest (Act I, no. 8). And at the end of this opera there is a fugato on a school-masterly subject to teach the morale: "Questo è il fin di chi fa mal", "l'antichissima canzon" ["This is the end of him who does wrong", "the very ancient song"].

Also in *The Marriage of Figaro* Mozart utilizes unmodern style to express old ideas. When he wishes to characterize the tyrannical old aristocrat Count Almaviva he resorts to the idioms of the *ancient régime*, the ceremonial style of the court of Louis XIV (cf. above, ch. 7). When the count commands "silence", the accompaniment introduces the pompous scalar ascent familiar from the slow introductions to the French overtures of Lully (Ex. 22). In another scene he orders his wife: "Va' lontan dagli occhi miei" ["Get out of my sight"] with the imperious dotted rhythm of the French overture and the rising scale which since the time of Lully expressed power and sovereignty (Ex. 23). In his Requiem, Mozart composed a French *grave* for the King of Heaven, the "Rex tremendae majestatis" (see ch. 7).

The relationship of Mozart with the *ancien régime*, with the society of the eighteenth century represented by these old styles, becomes problematic. In

Ex. 22. *Ibid.*: mm. 737ff.

Ex. 23. *Ibid.*: mm. 64-70.

Vienna he was kicked out by the majordomo of the archbishop of Salzburg. *Figaro* was his revenge, but also his downfall, for the Viennese *noblesse* did not forgive him for showing on the stage how a roguish servant outwits an aristocrat. With the exception of Van Swieten, the aristocracy then boycotted his subscription concerts and hired other piano teachers for their daughters.

Two years before his death, Mozart was again attracted to Bach, this time by his vocal music. Accompanying Prince Carl Lichnowsky to Leipzig, he remained much impressed by the performance of some motets of Bach in the church of St. Thomas. A contemporary witness reported that after a few measures Mozart exclaimed joyfully: "Was ist das? ... Das ist doch einmal etwas, woraus sich was lernen lässt" ["What is that? ... That is indeed something to learn from"]. He requested a manuscript copy and took it home with him. It is still in Vienna: the motet "Singet dem Herrn ein neues Lied" BWV 225, which contains, like most of Bach's sacred music, a chorale.

Thus we arrive at the finale of *The Magic Flute*, where we hear something unimaginable: a protestant chorale on the operatic stage. Again Mozart's imagination was stimulated by the music of Bach, as Reinhold Hammerstein demonstrated in an excellent article. Tamino must overcome the final test, passing through fire and water, before being reunited with Pamina. Two men in armour lead him before a pyramid and read to him an inscription on the stone: "Der, welcher wandert diese Straße voll Beschwerden, / wird rein durch Feuer, Wasser, Luft und Erden; / wenn er des Todes Schrecken überwinden kann, / schwingt er sich aus der Erde himmelan" ["He who walks this path full of obstacles purifies himself with fire, water, air, and earth. If he is able to conquer the terror of death, he will rise from earth towards heaven"]. This text is sung to the melody of the Lutheran chorale "Gott vom Himmel sieh' darein". Why did Mozart choose this melody? Hammerstein maintains that it is because of Luther's text, which speaks of "Silber, geprüft und geläutert von Feuer" ["silver, purified and ennobled by fire"], that is the same trial by fire which Tamino must undergo.

The chorale melody is introduced and accompanied by two counterpoints. The first, a rising motive (Ex. 24), is the musical-rhetorical figure of the *anabasis*, employed here to illustrate the words "he will *rise* from earth towards heaven". At the same time the motion in steady eighth notes, also

Ex. 24. Mozart: *Die Zauberflöte* K. 620, act II, finale, mm. 196f.

in the bass, describes the steps of him "who *walks* this path". Also this is a normal baroque idiom. The second counterpoint appears as a chromatic descent (Ex. 25). This *passus duriusculus* modifies like an adverb the verb 'to walk', showing that the path is "full of obstacles" or "Beschwerden". At the same time the rhythm of this motive interrupted by rests forms the rhetorical figure of the *suspiratio* ['sigh'] and underlines the hardness of Tamino's route. We see how much content is condensed by Mozart into these few measures: with the intentional employment of four different figures he expresses simultaneously a multitude of contents. The procedure is the same as that employed by Bach for the chorale settings of his cantatas and organ preludes, that is to illustrate and underline the sense of the chorale text by adding musical-rhetorical figures as counterpoints.

Ex. 25. *Ibid.*: mm. 199ff.

Why is the archaic style used here by Mozart? Hammerstein observed that the text, unlike the normal dialogues and monologues of opera, is not direct speech, but an inscription visible only to the initiated and declaimed by the two men in armour. Mozart therefore had to make the text stand out, distinguishing it from its context. To obtain this result, no traditional operatic style – recitative, aria, ensemble – would have been suitable. For him the Bachian counterpoint, like the Masonic ritual of this opera, represented a strict rule, an esoteric discipline. He utilizes the contrapuntal chorale setting as a ceremonial symbol, secularizing it and freeing it from the protestant liturgy, placing it at the service of the humanitarian ideals of his own time.

One of the first persons to understand the multiple historical strata of *The Magic Flute* was Beethoven. Schindler reports that the younger master greatly esteemed this Singspiel of Mozart: "Stellte Beethoven unter andern Mozarts *Zauberflöte* aus dem Grunde am höchsten, weil darin fast jede Gattung, vom Lied bis zum Choral und der Fuge, zum Ausdruck kommt" ["Beethoven rated Mozart's *Magic Flute* highest because almost every genre, from the song to the chorale and fugue, finds expression there"]. Also Goethe was fascinated by *The Magic Flute* and planned to write a sequel to the libretto. He surely appreciated the vast historical dimensions of Mozart's opera, comparable to *Faust*, ranging from ancient Egyptian occultism to Hellenistic mysticism, psalms of the Old Testament, Lutheran Reformation, and eighteenth-century Masonry.

The past, that which has become history, has always belonged to our Western artistic expression. Not by chance was the mother of the muses called Mnemosyne, 'Memory'. Again and again, ancient knowledge, images, and formulations have lent their wisdom to the present. If we understand the age and the diffusion of constant elements such as *topoi*, theme-types, musical-rhetorical figures, we acquire criteria for their variants, the individual historical manifestations.

I hope to have demonstrated with my few examples that Mozart not merely imitated baroque styles, but used them in a new manner, often with wit and always with great intelligence.

XV.

ANCIENT RHETORICAL TRADITIONS IN BEETHOVEN'S
MISSA SOLEMNIS

"Frau von Weissenthurn wishes to hear something about the ideas upon which you based your composition of the Mass".[1] This request was addressed to Beethoven in a conversation book of December 1819, that is, at a time when his *Missa solemnis* was not yet completed, but already much discussed. We do not know the reply. Later, writers have sought those "ideas" in the secularized religiosity of German Idealism, or simply in the realm of feeling. But did Beethoven himself conceive his ideas so indistinctly? Some of his older contemporaries had still known musical ideas as rational exposition of thought, musical formulations as carriers of meaning. Since the dawn of Humanism, music had appropriated, in both theory and practice, the entire sophisticated apparatus of rhetoric. As *ars bene dicendi* it had fulfilled with great refinement the tasks of *docere* as well as *movere* and *delectare*; it was to be not only enjoyed but also understood. However, by the time Beethoven arrived in Vienna this musical intelligibility had few advocates left among the musical public. Kant was no longer aware of it when he wrote that music speaks "through nothing but feelings without concepts" and is "more pleasure than culture".[2] The storm of Romanticism swept away musical rhetoric, just as it broke up the iconographical traditions of the visual arts and the stock of literary *topoi*. But language, whether verbal, pictorial, or musical, owes its effectiveness, indeed its very function as a vehicle for the expression of ideas, to the conventional association of certain modes of expression with certain mean-

---

[1] "Frau v. Weissenthurm wünscht, etwas von den Ideen zu hören, welche Sie Ihrer Composition der Messe zum Grund gelegt haben", *Ludwig van Beethovens Konversationshefte*, Berlin, Hesse, 1941-43, and Leipzig, Deutscher Verlag für Musik, 1968-99, I, 167. The writer is Joseph Karl Bernard. Johanna Franul von Weissenthurn (1773-1847) is the actress, singer, and playwright to whom Beethoven dedicated the song WoO 120.

[2] "durch lauter Empfindungen ohne Begriffe", "mehr Genuß als Cultur" – *Kritik der Urtheilskraft* (1790), § 53. *Kant's gesammelte Schriften*, Berlin, Reimer, 1913, V, 328.

ings. But the romantic 'original genius' and those who built his cult despised what they regarded as the 'dry rationalism' of such traditions, rejected that which may be learned as 'artificial' and 'unnatural', and no longer understood the depth and wit of an art that had matured with the Enlightenment.

Beethoven – was he the storm, or the tree in the storm? Many years ago Erich Schenk pointed to "Barock bei Beethoven",[3] and since then it has become clear that in that great farewell to the "European memory" (Curtius) the master was not merely the impetuous innovator who is celebrated in popular literature. Today we see that he not only retained traditional thought to an unexpected degree,[4] but even uncovered much older, buried traditions, and formed musical "ideas" in the plain and concrete sense of the century in which he was born – naturally with an incomparably freer, personal vocabulary. And this nowhere so profoundly as in his *Missa solemnis*, the work which belongs to the oldest musical tradition, the one which he believed to be his greatest.[5] Frau von Weissenthurn may now, somewhat belatedly, be provided with a partial answer.

The orchestra opens the Kyrie "assai sostenuto", with repeated tonic chords and complete absence of melodic motion. The first Kyrie-invocation of the chorus follows with the same music (Ex. 1a). This motif had opened countless orchestral Masses of the generation before Beethoven, typically in the form shown in Ex. 1b.[6] It is a *topos*, a traditional formulation for this text, traceable in festive Masses via Biber's *Missa Sancti Henrici* (1701)[7] and the

---

[3] *Beethoven und die Gegenwart: Festschrift Ludwig Schiedermair zum 60.Geburtstag*, Berlin/Bonn, Dümmler, 1937, pp. 177-219.

[4] Warren KIRKENDALE, *Fugue and Fugato in Rococo and Classical Chamber Music*, Durham NC, Duke UP, 1979, pp. 203-271.

[5] Ludwig van BEETHOVEN, *Briefwechsel*, Munich, Henle, 1996-98, nos. 1293, 1468, 1479, 1550.

[6] Leopold Hofmann, for example, begins nearly two-thirds of his 32 Masses in this manner – cf. Hermine PROHÁSZKA, *Leopold Hofmann und seine Messen*, «Studien zur Musikwissenschaft», XXVI, 1964, thematic catalogue; and Beethoven's teacher Albrechtsberger employs it frequently in his orchestral Masses – cf. Andreas WEISSENBACK, *Thematisches Verzeichnis der Kirchenkompositionen von Johann Georg Albrechtsberger*, «Jahrbuch des Stiftes Klosterneuburg», VI, 1914, nos. 3, 52, 66, 128, 145, 156. Karl PFANNHAUSER, *Zu Mozarts Kirchenwerken von 1768*, «Mozart-Jahrbuch», 1954, p. 162, gives examples by Georg Reutter, Ferdinand Schmidt, and Johann Georg Zechner. Cf. also the Masses of Fux, K. 14, 15, 28, Mozart, K. 139, 258, and the Mass by Johann Georg Lickl misattributed to Mozart (H. C. Robbins LANDON, *Mozart fälschlich zugeschriebene Messen*, «Mozart-Jahrbuch», 1957, p. 93). The formula is used satirically in the notorious "Schulmeistermesse", US-Wc ms. M2010 A9 etc., attributed in various sources to F. Aumann, F. X. Brixi, F. L. Gassmann, J. Haydn, M. Haydn, L. Mozart, and W. A. Mozart; the most widely accepted attribution, to Franz Aumann, is based on a comment of Giuseppe CARPANI, *Le Haydine*, Milan, Buccinelli, 1812, p. 112, which does not identify the Mass. Cherubini's *Deuxième Messe solennelle*, Paris, chez l'auteur, n.d. [composed 1811] presents a characteristically French version with double dotting.

[7] DTÖ, XLIX: *Messen von Heinrich Biber, Heinrich Schmeltzer, Johann Caspar Kerll*, Vienna, 1918, p. 1.

Ex. 1a. Beethoven: *Missa solemnis.*

Ex. 1b. Kyrie-*topos.*

polychoral *Missa salisburgensis* (Ex. 1c)[8] at least as far back as Cavalli's *Missa concertata* (1656, Ex. 1d).[9] In nearly every case it announces a *Missa solemnis*, with trumpets and drums. It has been demonstrated that slow tempo and

Ex. 1c. Pseudo-Benevoli [Biber? 1682?]: *Missa salisburgensis.*

Ex. 1d. Cavalli: *Missa concertata* (1656).

---

[8] DTÖ, XX: *Orazio Benevoli: Festmesse und Hymnus,* Vienna, 1903. Cf. Ernst HINTERMAIER, *'Missa salisburgensis': Neue Erkenntnisse über Entstehung, Autor und Zweckbestimmung,* «Musicologia Austriaca», I, 1977, pp. 154-196.

[9] London, Faber, 1966. Also Cavalli's setting of "Christe" to a falling third in long notes and repeated after a rest, is very similar to Beethoven's.

avoidance of melodic and harmonic movement belonged since the middle baroque era to the musical decorum of the King of Heaven.[10] The topos reflects the ancient conception of God as the one who possesses *apatheia*, is free from all passions and, as the first cause of being, is himself immovable – the concept taken over from the Stoics by the Greek Fathers into Western theology. Beethoven's formulation, unlike those of his predecessors, begins on a weak beat, thus removed still further from the dynamics of human passions. It is a borderline case of gesture in music: movement which is almost at a standstill. The invocation of Christ in the middle section shifts to the traditional triple time, andante, i.e. more human movement for Him who was also human.

In the Gloria, the prescribed gestures of the liturgy find their counterparts in the rhetorical figures of the music. The celebrant, when intoning "Gloria in excelsis Deo", raises his arms to express joy,[11] and Beethoven, like so many of his predecessors, begins the movement with a rapidly rising melody, the rhetorical figure of the *anabasis* (Ex. 2a-c). At the words "adoramus te", where

Ex. 2a. Beethoven: *Missa solemnis.*

Ex. 2b. Albrechtsberger: *Missa desponsationis B.M.V.*, 1785 (Weißenbeck no. 88).

---

[10] See above, ch. 7.

[11] Cf. *Caeremoniale episcoporum iussu Clemntis VIII*, Rome, Typ. linguarum externarum, 1600, f. 192: "Gloria in excelsis Deo: disiunctis, elevatisque manibus" ["with hands separated and raised"]; Pierre LE BRUN, *Explication litérale, historique et dogmatique des cérémonies de la Messe*, I, Paris, Delaune, 1716, pp. 175f, *Touchant la manière de dire le Gloria in excelsis*: "C'est un geste que l'amour des choses célestes a toujours fait faire, pour montrer qu'on voudroit les embrasser & les posséder" ["It is a gesture which the love of divine things has always made to show that one wished to embrace and possess them"]. Cf. also *Lamentations*, 3:41: "Let us lift up our heart with our hands unto God in the heavens". Beethoven's motif is rhythmically interesting in that it is actually duple meter in a context of 3/4 time; cf. the undesignated shift to 3/2 for the "Gratias", m. 45. It was probably in connection with one of these passages that Beethoven noted in a sketch: "den Rithmus von 3 Täkte im Gloria anzeigen" ["indicate the rhythm of 3 measures in the Gloria"] – Gustav NOTTEBOHM, *Zweite Beethoveniana*, Leipzig, Rieter-Biedermann, 1887, p. 474 – intending a designation such as he made in the string quartet Op. 131.

Ex. 2c. Id., *Missa S. M. Magdalenae*, 1802 (Weißenbeck no. 141).

the priest bows his head,[12] composers suddenly lower the pitch and dynamics.[13] With a plunge from fortissimo to pianissimo Beethoven intensifies this gesture to a musical *proskynesis* (measures 80ff, 100ff).

At the invocation of the "Pater omnipotens" God is again depicted in music. We are not surprised that Beethoven realizes the omnipotence much more vehemently than his predecessors do. The familiar downward leap of an octave on "omnipotens"[14] is stretched here to a twelfth – a huge, powerful gesture akin to the style of the heroic opera of the time. Beethoven also reserved the first entry of the trombones for the one word "omnipotens", *fff* (mm. 185ff). Only after the Mass was completed did he add these instruments,[15] having carefully calculated their effect and noted in his sketches "omnipotens ganze Orgel posaun im Pedal".[16] A reviewer writing in 1828 finds that "a better indication of the correct use of trombones could not easily be found".[17]

---

[12] Cf. Le Brun, p. 185, note 4.

[13] E.g. Leopold Hofmann (Prohászka, p. 94), Haydn's *Heiligesse* (1796), Paisiello's first Mass (1803, "per la cappella del Primo Console", US-Wc ms. ML96 P212), Beethoven's first Mass (1807), Schubert's first Mass (1814), Seyfried's third Mass (Leipzig, Hofmeister, pl. no. 1044 = ca. 1824-25), Preindl's sixth Mass (Op. 12, US-Wc ms. M2010 P92). Ignaz Schnabel's *Grande Messe* in F differentiated these two words by setting them *a cappella* in whole notes (US-Wc ms. M2010 A2 S34).

[14] It usually occurs in dotted rhythm ♩·♪♩, e.g. in Haydn's *Missa Sancti Nicolai* (1772) and *Missa in tempore belli* (1796), Cherubini's second Mass, Schubert's second Mass (1815), etc. The emphasis of "omnipotens" by a long, sustained note on the first syllable is likewise traditional; cf. Haydn's *Heiligmesse* (1796) and Tomaschek's *Missa solemnis* Op. 46 (US-Wc ms. M2010 T64).

[15] Nottebohm, p. 153; *Konversationshefte*, III, 342, 365 (June-July 1823); *Briefwechsel*, V, 131, no. 1655 (letter to Schindler, July 1823). It was common practice at this time to notate the brass instruments and timpani on a separate score; cf. the autograph of Mozart's *Don Giovanni*, Peter Winter's *Sanctus* in D major (US-Wc ms. M2010 A2 W82), Danzi's Mass in E-flat (US-Wc ms. M2010 A2 D2), Schnabel's Mass in F, etc.

[16] D-BNba 110, p. 1; cf. the indication in the score, "Pieno Org. con Ped.", and Beethoven's entry in a conversation book of March 1820, referring to the Credo: "ganzes orchester erst bei patrem omni potentem d.h. Pauke u. Trompete trombonen" ["full orchestra only at 'patrem omnipotentem', i.e. timpani, trumpets, and trombones"] – *Konversationshefte*, I, 371. Christoph Straus, in his *Missa Veni sponsa Christi*, introduced "Patrem omnipotentem" with a clarino fanfare – Guido Adler, ed., *Handbuch der Musikgeschichte*, Berlin, Keller, 1930², I, 513. Cf. also Beethoven's first Mass.

[17] "ein besseres Hindeuten auf den richtigen Gebrauch der Posaunen möchte es nicht leicht geben" – [Georg Christoph] Grossheim, «Caecilia», IX, 23.

Also the setting of "judicare" in the Credo (mm. 221ff) uses the trombones 'correctly' to symbolize divine power.[18] The Old Testament associated them with the voice of God (*Exod.* 19:16, *Zach.* 9:14),[19] and the New Testament could easily transfer them to His heralds, the angels. This instrumental language had become the musical equivalent of *Matthew* 24:31: "And He shall send His angels with a great sound of a trumpet, and they shall gather together His elect from the four winds".[20] The Last Judgement from the Pericope Book of Emperor Henry II may serve as an example for the iconographical tradition (Plate XV.1). The chord on which Beethoven's trombones enter was selected only after long deliberation:[21] a-flat minor, with seven flats, transcends normal tonal experience – an extreme harmonic setting for the *extremum judicium*.[22]

The "judicare" passage combines simultaneously two different rhythms: long notes and eighth-note tremolos (mm. 223ff). The declamation of "judicare" on long notes was standard practice, in both orchestral and *a cappella* Masses.[23] Also this simplest of rhythms reflects the ancient ethical concept which we recognized in the Kyrie-*topos*. Not only the Stoics, but also the Old Testament knew that, as the prototype of the just judge, God is immovable: "You, however, the lord of virtue, judge with tranquility".[24] The Chris-

---

[18] Anglo-Saxons may wonder why Beethoven employs trombones rather than trumpets to announce the Last Judgement. This usage is understandable when we realize that the angels' instrument of the Vulgate, the *tuba* (St. Jerome's uniform Latin translation for the variety of Hebrew and Greek words designating horn-like instruments), translated throughout the English Bible as "trumpet", is always rendered in German as 'Posaune', i.e. trombone. The scriptural instrument, of course, is not to be identified with either modern type. For centuries artists depicted it as a horn-shaped instrument (cf. Plate XV.1) or as a straight buisine, even after the introduction of the coiled trumpet and the slide trombone in the fifteenth century; cf. Reinhold HAMMERSTEIN, *Die Musik der Engel: Untersuchungen zur Musikanschauung des Mittelalters*, Bern, Franke, 1962, p. 213.

[19] Cf. ORIGEN, *In Jeremiam Homilia*, V, in P.G. XIII, 319C, and Beethoven's "Pater omnipotens". Further instances of trumpets and trombones to symbolize divine presence in literature and music are given by Wilhelm EHMANN, *Tibilustrium: Das geistliche Blasen*, Kassel, Bärenreiter, 1950, pp. 51-57.

[20] Gounod, in attempting to achieve a similar effect in his St. Caecilia Mass (1855) found that he needed no less than twenty-five trombones!

[21] NOTTEBOHM, p. 155.

[22] Cf. GROSSHEIM, p. 25: "eine höchst originelle Akkordefolge" ["a highly original sequence of chords"].

[23] E.g. Reutter's *Missa S. Caroli* (1734, DTÖ, LXXXVIII, 41), Jommelli's *Missa a 4 voci* (US-Wc ms. M2010 A2 J64), Michael Haydn's *Missa in Dominica Palmarum* (1794, DTÖ, XLV, 118) and *Missa sub titulo St. Francisci* (1803, DTÖ, XLV, 71), Tomaschek's *Missa solemnis*, etc. M. Haydn's *Missa Sanctae Crucis* (1762; Vienna, Doblinger, 1949, p. 18), without orchestral accompaniment, simulates a trumpet effect with a fanfare melody.

[24] "Tu autem, dominator virtutis, cum tranquillitate judicas" – *Book of Wisdom*, 12:18.

tian treatises on virtues have transmitted this image to modern times without alteration.[25]

The other rhythmic component, the tremolo, likewise has its traditional role here, where it represents the trembling of those awaiting their judgment. Here we recall the lines of the "Dies irae", "Quantus tremor est futurus, Quando judex est venturus" ["How much trembling there will be when the judge is about to arrive"], set to tremolos by composers such as Straus, Kerll, and Mozart.[26]

In the preceding Gloria Beethoven employed the tremolo in a nearly identical situation, namely, for the invocation of Christ enthroned in heaven, "qui sedes ad dexteram Patris"[27] (m. 271). The association of the throne with the judge's chair is clear from the same text in the Credo ("sedet ad dexteram Patris. Et iterum venturus est cum gloria, judicare vivos et mortuos"), and it was visible to Christians since the early Middle Ages through the iconographical grouping of *majestas* and Last Judgement. Beethoven accompanies the tremolo with the majestic dotted rhythm,[28] the musical emblem of the Sun King, which during the eighteenth century had become the *topos* for majesty *par excellence*.[29]

Tremolos also appear, a few pages earlier, for the word "peccata" (m. 256). And in the Sanctus there is an extraordinary array of them (mm. 30-33). It surely has a theological basis. Caesarius, sixth-century bishop of Arles, wrote: "with simultaneous trembling and rejoicing they will exclaim: 'Sanctus, sanctus, sanctus'".[30] Indeed, the "tremor" of the tremolos[31] on the minor ninth chord is followed directly by the "gaudium" of the festive vio-

---

[25] Cf. above, pp. 227ff, 231f.

[26] DTÖ, LIX: *Drei Requiem ... aus dem 17. Jahrhundert*, Vienna, 1923, pp. 13, 78f. Abbé Vogler, like Beethoven, combines tremolos for "tremor" with long notes for "judex" (Requiem, Mainz, Schott, 1822). On Johann Erasmus Kindermann's association of the tremulant register of the organ with the trembling at the Last Judgement in 1655 cf. Hans Heinrich EGGEBRECHT, *Zwei Nürnberger Orgel-Allegorien des 17. Jahrhunderts*, «Musik und Kirche», XXVII, 1957, p. 172.

[27] Biber's *Missa Alleluia* employs six trumpets for this text; see Guido ADLER, *Zur Geschichte der Wiener Messenkomposition in der zweiten Hälfte des XVII. Jahrhunderts*, «Studien zur Musikwissenschaft», IV, 1916, p. 26.

[28] Also in Cherubini's *Deuxième Messe solennelle*.

[29] Cf. above, ch. 7.

[30] "Cum tremore simul et gaudio clamabunt: 'Sanctus, sanctus, sanctus'" – no. CCLXXXI of the sermons falsely attributed to Augustine; see P.L. XXXIX, 2277.

[31] A much less marked use of tremolo in the Sanctus is found in Beethoven's first Mass, Cherubini's *Messe à trois voix* in F (1808; Paris, Conservatoire, pl. no. 657 [= 1810]), Schubert's first Mass (1814), Cherubini's *Quatrième Messe solennelle* (1816; Paris, chez l'auteur, n.d.), Seyfried's fourth Mass (Vienna, Haslinger, pl. no. 5084 [= 1827/28]), and Hummel's third Mass, Op. 111 (*Ibid.*, pl. no. 5495 [= 1830]).

lin figures for "pleni sunt coeli". The rhetoric of the Sanctus is further illuminated through the pianissimo tremolos on the identical minor ninth chord for a passage of similar religious content in the finale of the Ninth Symphony: "Über Sternen muss er wohnen" ["He must dwell above the stars", mm. 650-654].[32]

But the musical discourse on God is not exhausted with these more or less traditional images. With the mention of the Trinity[33] in the Credo, it is intensified to dogmatics, in a way which has few antecedents. The text of the Credo, as formulated by the Councils of Nicaea and Constantinople, had aimed particularly at affirming the divinity of Christ and of the Holy Ghost, denied by the Arians and Macedonians, respectively. Beethoven clearly underlines the ancient dogma when he not only heralds each of the three divine persons with an orchestral introduction, the prerogative of gods and kings in opera, but even uses the same orchestral ritornello and Credo-motif to introduce the "unum Deum" (mm. 1-4), the "unum Dominum Jesum Christum" (mm. 34-36), and the "Spiritum Sanctum" (mm. 265-67, with a slight distinction, mentioned below). With this thematic unity he applies the century-old technique of the "Credo Mass", which repeats the word "credo" before various articles of the Creed.[34] But he reduces the usual number of repetitions, reserving the second and third appearances of the motif for the second and third holy person. This usage might well be compared with the long-lived iconographical type which portrayed Father, Son, and Holy Ghost as three similar figures.[35] Perhaps the best-known representative of this type, which was cultivated from the tenth until at least the sixteenth century, is the elder Hol-

---

[32] Another clue to the meaning of Beethoven's trombones is the note in the sketches for this movement: "auf Welt Sternenzelt [i.e., "Ahnest du den Schöpfer, Welt? Such' ihn über'm Sternenzelt"] forte Posaunenstösse" ["For 'world, starry tent' strong trombone blasts"] – NOTTEBOHM, p. 186.

[33] Rudolf GERBER, *Aufbaugesetze in Beethovens 'Missa solemnis'*, «Das Musikleben», V, 1952, pp. 317-321, hypothesized that the quasi-ternary proportions between the various sections of the Gloria and Credo may have been intended to symbolize the Trinity. I regard such an intention as unlikely with composers later than J.S. Bach.

[34] Cf. Georg REICHERT, *Zur Geschichte der Wiener Messenkomposition in der ersten Hälfte des 18. Jahrhunderts*, ms. diss., Vienna, 1935, pp. 27-57; id., *Mozarts 'Credo-Messen' und ihre Vorläufer*, «Mozart-Jahrbuch», 1955, pp. 117-144.

[35] Others united three heads on one body or three faces on one head; cf. Karl KÜNSTLE, *Ikonographie der christlichen Kunst*, Freiburg, Herder, 1926-28, I, 221-233; Alfred HACKEL, *Die Trinität in der Kunst: Eine ikonographische Untersuchung*, Berlin, Reuther & Rechard, 1931, ch. 3; Adelheid HEIMANN, *Trinitas Creator Mundi*, «Journal of the Warburg Institute», II, 1938-39, p. 46; J. J. M. TIMMERS, *Symboliek en Iconographie der Christelijke Kunst*, Roermond, Maaseik, 1947, pp. 64f; Ernst H. KANTOROWICZ, *The Quinity of Winchester*, «Art Bulletin», XXIX, 1947, pp. 73-85, especially fig. 8 and note 69; Wolfgang BRAUNFELS, *Die Heilige Dreifaltigkeit*, Düsseldorf, Schwann, 1954, pp. IX, LI.

bein's *Coronation of the Virgin*, in Augsburg (Plate XV.2). One which Beethoven may very well have known is the famous Töpfer altar of ca. 1515 in the church of St. Helen in Baden near Vienna (Plate XV.3), a town frequently visited by him in his later years.[36] The altar had originally stood in Vienna's cathedral. It was sold to Baden after Benedict XIV, in 1745, forbade such portrayals because of their implication of tritheism.[37] Particularly objectionable from the theological point of view was the representation of the Holy Ghost in human form. Beethoven, however, makes a fine distinction. He makes only the first two orchestral ritornellos perfectly identical (mm. 1-4, 34ff); the third is abbreviated and in a different key (mm. 265ff). In setting the texts which immediately follow the ritornellos, he then uses identical music only for "in unum Deum" (mm. 5ff) and "in unum Dominum" (mm. 37ff), different music for "in Spiritum Sanctum" (mm. 267ff). This use of the same music for Father and Son is rare in Credo settings,[38] and therefore was probably calculated consciously by the composer, to express the concept "I and my Father are one" (*John* 10:30).[39] By deriving the ritornello of the Holy Ghost thematically from that of the Father and Son, Beethoven achieves a perfect musical equivalent of the words that follow: "in Spiritum Sanctum qui ex Patre Filioque procedit" ["the Holy Ghost which *issues from* the Father and Son"].

"Et incarnatus est", the words which proclaim the greatest mystery of the Christian doctrine and commemorate, as it were, the beginning of the Christian era, had, for centuries, been set off from their context in the Mass by a marked change of style. In the Renaissance they were often highlighted with a *noema* (homophonic interpolation). But in the mid-eighteenth century, composers such as Wagenseil, Richter, and the so-called Neapolitan school tended to employ here the modern *concertante* style, with solo voices and often elaborate virtuosity.[40] The *non plus ultra* of this Incarnatus type is in Mozart's c-minor Mass, K. 427. In the early romantic era the trend was reversed: the

---

[36] Documented for 1817, 1821, 1822, 1824, and 1825.

[37] Brief of 1 October to the Bishop of Augsburg, in BENEDICT XIV, *Opera omnia*, XV, Prato, Tip. Aldina, 1845, pp. 570-580. The Töpfer altar probably originated, like Holbein's painting, in Augsburg. On a differentiated treatment in the Masses of Mozart, cf. Manfred Hermann SCHMID, *Padre e Figlio: il Gloria nel segno del 'Domine Deus' in Mozart*, paper for the conference *Mozart e il sentire italiano*, Rome, 26 Jan. 2007.

[38] But it occurs in Cherubini's second Mass, in Hummel's first Mass, Op. 77 (Vienna, Haslinger, pl. no. 2751 [= 1818]) and, for "Domine Deus" and "Domine Fili", in the Gloria of Cavalli's Mass. In Masses of the Renaissance and Baroque the identity of divine persons was often represented by figural canons.

[39] The Scriptures always differentiate between the Father-Son on the one hand, and the Holy Ghost, on the other; cf. LE BRUN, p. 266.

[40] Cf. Karl Gustav FELLERER, *Der Palestrinastil und seine Bedeutung in der vokalen Kirchenmusik des achtzehnten Jahrhunderts*, Augsburg, Filser, 1929, p. 315; Ernst TITTEL, *Österreichische Kirchenmusik*, Vienna, Herder, 1961, p. 145.

stile antico now gives the text a nimbus of awe and solemnity. This solution is only natural for the generation of Wackenroder, Tieck, E.T.A. Hoffmann, and Thibaut, which extolled the 'Palestrina style' as the true ideal of sacred music. Thus composers such as Salieri,[41] Danzi,[42] and Witt[43] set the "Incarnatus" of their orchestral Masses as an *a cappella* insert, a musical correspondence to the prescribed genuflection of the priest at this point.[44] Beethoven composed here a quasi-'Gregorian' melody; it was recognized already by the reviewer of the first performance as a kind of plainchant: "The pathetic, monotonous plainchant for the words 'Et incarnatus est' in the Credo has an awesome effect".[45] Chant melodies, of course, continued to be used in the Mass throughout the eighteenth century; but by Beethoven's time they were relatively rare, especially in orchestral Masses. The one composer who still used them extensively is Michael Haydn, in his *a cappella* Masses for Advent and Lent. It is significant that in some of these he limits the borrowed melody to the "Incarnatus" and expressly labels it "Corale".[46] In the *Missa dolorum B.M.V.* (1762)[47] it is set in the style of a harmonized chorale, in the *Missa tempore Quadragesima* of 1794[48] note against note, with the plainchant melody (Credo IV of the *Liber Usualis*) appearing in the soprano.[49] I have little doubt that Beethoven knew such works of Michael Haydn, at that time the most popular composer of sacred music in Austria.

In sketches from the beginning and end of his career we find harmonizations of plainchant melodies: the *Lamentations* and the "Pange lingua".[50]

---

[41] Cf. Rudolf NÜTZLADER, *Salieri als Kirchenmusiker*, «Studien zur Musikwissenschaft», XIV, 1927, p. 161.

[42] Mass in E-flat (note 15, above).

[43] "Missa par Vitt organiste a Wurstburg" [*sic*], US-Wc ms. M2010 W83.

[44] Cf. *Caeremoniale episcoporum*, p. 199: "Et incarnatus est &c.: Episcopus genuflectit, & pariter omnes de choro genuflectunt" ["... the bishop and likewise all in the choir genuflect"].

[45] "Von schauervoller Wirkung ist der pathetische, eintönige Choral auf die Glaubensworte: et incarnatus est", ANON., AmZ, XXVI, 1824, col. 439.

[46] It will be remembered that in Italian this means 'plainsong', and that in German both 'Gregorian' chant and Protestant hymn are designated as 'Choral'.

[47] Düsseldorf, Schwann, 1962, p. 13.

[48] DTÖ, XLV, 130.

[49] Other instances of plainchant melodies in Masses of the late eighteenth and early nineteenth centuries include the *tonus peregrinus* in Mozart's Requiem (for "Te decet") and the eighth psalm tone for "Et in Spiritum Sanctum ..." in Diabelli's Pastoral Mass, Op. 147 (1830; Augsburg, Böhm, n.d.). Some composers used archaic headings when they, like Beethoven, wrote in a neo-Gregorian or neo-Palestrina style. Thus, Anton André, in his (orchestral) Mass Op. 43 (Offenbach, André, pl. no. 3894 [= 1819]) introduces the second "Osanna" with four measures note-against-note, *a cappella*, in "Tempo di canto Gregoriano"; and Seyfried labels the recurring whole-note cantus-firmus motif in the Credo of his fourth Mass as "Chorale".

[50] Joseph SCHMIDT-GÖRG, *Ein neuer Fund in den Skizzenbüchern Beethovens: Die Lamentatio-*

When he began work on the *Missa solemnis*, he noted his intention: "In order to write true church music – look for all the plainchants of the monks".[51] From such studies, not to mention his exercises in modal counterpoint for Haydn and Albrechtsberger, he learned to write the Dorian melody for "Et incarnatus est". From his notes and sketches it is evident that he regarded the 'Gregorian' modes primarily as a means of religious expression. In 1809 he wrote: "In the old church modes the devotion is divine, I exclaimed, and God let me express it someday".[52] And in 1818, when he first thought of writing a choral symphony: "A pious song in a symphony, in the old modes – Lord God we praise Thee – alleluja".[53] The mode used here in the "Incarnatus" appears in sketches of 1816, where he notes the authentic and plagal forms of the Dorian scale; and the also designation "dor" among the earliest sketches for the Kyrie may refer to this mode.[54] However, these jottings hardly influenced his choice of mode for the "Incarnatus". Did he have a particular reason for using the Dorian? No one has ever asked. We can now show that he arrived at his decision by a circuitous, speculative route, with the help of Gioseffo Zarlino's *Istitutioni harmoniche* of 1558. Conversation books from December 1819 and January 1820 document his search for this work. In December Joseph Czerny wrote, "We have some old Italians – Zarlino", and the following month Karl Peters, Lobkowitz's administrator, communicated: "We have Zarlino", i.e. in the prince's library.[55] In Zarlino's chapter *"Della natura o prop[r]ietà delli modi"* we learn about the Dorian mode: "Cassiodorus says, that it is the donor of modesty and the preserver of chastity".[56]

---

nen des Propheten Jeremias, «Beethoven-Jahrbuch», III, 1957-58, pp. 107-110; id., Das gregorianische Pangue-lingua bei Beethoven, in Johner-Festschrift: Der kultische Gesang der abendländischen Kirche, Cologne, Bachem, 1950, pp. 109-111.

[51] "Um wahre Kirchenmusik zu schreiben – alle Kirchenchoräle der Mönche ... zu suchen" – Beethoven's journal of 1818, quoted in Alexander Wheelock THAYER, Ludwig van Beethovens Leben, IV, Leipzig, Breitkopf & Härtel, 1907, p. 130.

[52] "In den alten Kirchentonarten ist die Andacht göttlich rief ich dabey aus, u. Gott laße mich es einmal darstellen" – Georg KINSKY, Briefe, Dokumente von Scarlatti bis Stravinsky: Katalog der Musikautographen-Sammlung Louis Koch, Stuttgart, Krais, 1953, p. 57.

[53] "Frommer Gesang in einer Sinfonie in den alten Tonarten – Herr Gott dich loben wir – alleluia" – NOTTEBOHM, p. 163.

[54] GB-Lbm ms. add. 29997, f. 13. Konversationshefte, I, 27 (February-March, 1818).

[55] "Wir haben einige alte Italiener – Zarlino" and "Wir haben den Zarlino" – Konversationshefte, I, 100, 193.

[56] "Caßiodoro dice, che è donatore della pudicitia & conservatore della castità" – Gioseffo ZARLINO, Istitutioni harmoniche, Venice, s.n., 1558, pp. 301f. Similarly Marin MERSENNE, Quaestiones celeberrimae, Paris, Cramoisy, 1623, 1675: "castitatis, majestatis, & constantiae custos" ["custodian of chastity, majesty, and constancy"]; and Giovanni Battista DONI, Compendio del trattato de' generi e de' modi della musica, Rome, Fei, 1635, p. 87: "donatore della pudicitia" ["giver of modesty", after Cassiodorus].

Zarlino is citing a letter of Cassiodorus to Boethius ca. 508 A.D.: "Dorius pudicitiae largitor et castitatis effector est".[57] And he can further lean on the authority of Agamemnon, who, "before departing from his homeland to go to the Trojan War, put his wife Clytemnestra in custody of a Dorian musician".[58] Is further proof needed for Beethoven's intelligent choice of the Dorian, the 'chaste' mode, when he wanted to allude to the mystery of the virginal conception?[59] We need only add that in his only other modal composition, the slow movement of the string quartet Op. 132, he again followed these authors in matching the mode with the idea to be expressed.[60] This "Heiliger Dankgesang eines Genesenen an die Gottheit in der lidischen Tonart" ["Sacred song of thanksgiving of a convalescent to the Divinity in the Lydian mode"] surely owes its mode to Zarlino's communication: "Cassiodorus believes ... that the Lydian mode is a remedy for fatigue of the soul, and similarly for that of the body".[61] Finally, we may adduce that the first sketches of the "Incarnatus" have been accurately dated as December-January 1819-20,[62] i.e. the same two months in which the notes on Zarlino were made in the conversation books!

One of the most prominent features of the "Incarnatus" is the long, slow trill in the high register of the flute. Also the very few eighteenth-century Masses which include this instrument[63] tend to employ it for the "Incarna-

---

[57] P.L. LXIX, 571B. As part of his autodidactic program Beethoven had abstracts from Boethius made for him by his friend Karl Pinterics – cf. Anton SCHINDLER, *Biographie von Ludwig van Beethoven*, Münster, Aeschendorff, 1860, II, 163. The fact that Cassiodorus refers to the ancient Greek modes, rather than the medieval ones does not affect our argument. In *Monumenta Germaniae Historica, Auctorum Antiquissimorum tomus XII: Cassiodori senatoris variae*, ed. Theodor Mommsen, Berlin, Weidmann, 1894, p. 70, "pudicitiae" is misread as "prudentiae".

[58] "avanti che si partisse della patria, per andare alla guerra troiana, diede la moglie Clitennestra in guardia ad un musico dorico" – ZARLINO, p. 302. Likewise Pierre de RONSARD, *Meslanges*, Paris, 1560, preface.

[59] It has not yet been determined whether Beethoven took a particular chant as his model. Two Dorian melodies with Marian texts begin with the same three or four notes, respectively, as his melody: the hymn "Ave maris stella" (LU 1259) and Perotin's monophonic conductus "Beata viscera Mariae Virginis" (I-Fl ms. Plut. 29.1, f. 422; D-W ms. 1206, f. 156*v*, etc.). The ascending intervals *d-a-c* used by Beethoven were even considered as a theoretical model for a Dorian incipit; cf. the melody-type for the first mode, "Primum quaerite" in JOHANNES AFFLIGEMENSIS, *De musica cum tonario* (ca. 1100), Rome, American Institute of Musicology, 1950, p. 86, and Bernhard MEIER, *Die Tonarten der klassischen Vokalpolyphonie*, Utrecht, Oosthoek, Scheltema & Holkema, 1974, p. 191.

[60] W. KIRKENDALE, *Fugue and Fugato*, pp. 250f, and below, p. 541.

[61] "Vuole Caßiodoro, ... ch' lidio sia remedio contra le fatiche dell'animo & similmente contra quelle del corpo", p. 303. Cf. CASSIODORUS in P.L. LXIX, 571C.

[62] *Ludwig van Beethoven, Skizzen und Entwürfe: Drei Skizzenbücher zur Missa Solemnis*, I: *Ein Skizzenbuch aus den Jahren 1819/20*, Bonn, Beethoven-Haus, 1952, pp. 11-17 of the preface, and the Dorian theme on p. 17 of the sketchbook.

[63] E.g. only fifteen of the 243 orchestral Masses in D-MÜs – Heinrich STUTE, *Studien über den*

tus", just as Diabelli's Pastoral Mass does later. Haydn's *Schöpfungsmesse* achieves a similar effect with the flute register of the obbligato organ.[64] There can be little doubt that the flute was chosen because of its pastoral associations. But in some cases, including Beethoven's *Missa solemnis*, the rhetoric goes still further. Ignaz Seyfried, in his review of the first edition, already suspected that the 'fluttering' figures of the flute depict the Holy Ghost in the traditional form of a dove, hovering above the Virgin: "seems to allude to the fluttering heavenly messenger in the form of a dove".[65] This interpretation could appear bold at first sight. It has often been repeated, but never justified. But a credible witness may be summoned. Fluttering thirty-second-note figures appear also in the first of Biber's 'Rosary' Sonatas, together with the dove in the miniature Annunciation which adorns the music.[66] Beethoven makes his intention very clear by having the flute enter exactly on the words "de Spiritu Sancto" (m. 134). Like the trombones for "omnipotens", the flute trill was a calculated afterthought, added to the finished score.[67]

In portraying the Holy Ghost in the form of a dove, artists since the second century followed the evangelists' description of the baptism of Christ.[68] In Annunciation scenes they often painted rays emanating from the dove and reaching the Virgin's ear, in accord with the idea of early Christian and medieval mystics that Mary conceived through the ear – thus the illustration of the Incarnatus in a sixteenth-century Credo cycle by Marten de Vos or the frontispiece of a book on the *Annunziata* of 1619 (Plates XV.4f).[69] Of the many literary formulations, I cite only pseudo-Augustine, "the Virgin was impregnated by means of the ears";[70] the widely diffused song "Gaude, Virgo, Mater Christi / Quae per aurem concepisti" ["Rejoice, Virgin, mother of Christ, who conceived through the ear"];[71] and Walther von der Vogelweide,

---

Gebrauch der Instrumente in dem italienischen Kirchenorchester des 18. Jahrhunderts, Quakenbrück, Keinert, 1929, p. 16.

[64] Also Preindl's first Mass.

[65] "scheint ... auf den in Tauben-Gestalt flatternden Himmelsboten anzuspielen" – «Caecilia», IX, 1828, p. 226.

[66] DTÖ, XXV: *Heinrich Franz Biber: Sechzehn Violinsonaten*, Vienna, 1905, p. 3.

[67] NOTTEBOHM, p. 153. The autograph of Beethoven's correction was at one time in the possession of Johannes Brahms.

[68] Matthew 3:16, Mark 1:10, Luke 3:22, John 1:32. Cf. above, the representation of the Holy Ghost with human form. The dove symbol was the only type approved by Benedict XIV, *loc. cit.*

[69] Another example, from ca. 1530 (Museum Langenargen), is reproduced in the Italian version of this article, p. 231.

[70] "virgo auribus impregnabatur" – P.L. XXXIX, 1988: *Sermo CXXI, in Natali Domini*, attributed to Ambrosius Autpertus.

[71] Ulysse CHEVALIER, *Repertorium hymnologicum*, Louvain, s.n., 1892-1921, I, 420, III, 251f, IV, 147, locates this incipit in thirteen sources from the fourteenth to sixteenth centuries.

"Durch ir ôre enpfienc si den vil süezen" ["Through her ear she conceived the very sweet one"].[72] So literally did the medieval mind understand the pre-incarnate Christ as *logos* – the word enters the body through the ear. (Also the closely related notion of fertilization by breath or sound, widely diffused in both Christian and Oriental cultures, may be remembered in this connection).[73] Although we cannot know whether Beethoven was aware of these long-lived theological and iconographical traditions, and although we must admit that all music is heard through the ear, I am tempted to point out that the prominent sound of the flute not only corresponds to the light colors of the dove in paintings, but also, issuing as it does from a reedless wind instrument, renders the fertilizing breath of the Holy Ghost much more directly than the painted rays could do. It will be remembered that the Latin word '*spiritus*' means 'breath', and especially this significance determined composers' choice of the instrument. At the end of the "Incarnatus" the flute becomes silent, and with the words "Et homo factus est" we leave the mystic sphere of the medieval modes and return with an emphatic gesture to major-minor tonality, the realm of man. The intention is clear from a note on this passage in the sketches: "here human".[74]

The "Crucifixus" is a paradigm of rhetorical figures traditional for this text: *tmesis*, tremolo, syncopation, diminished seventh chords, *cross*ed melodic intervals (tenor, m. 158), etc. Rather than list the parallels which can be found in almost any eighteenth-century Mass, I refer again to a passage from Biber's 'Rosary' Sonatas, this time one depicting the crucifixion.[75] Here is the same combination of *tmesis* and tremolo as used by Beethoven. Three notations in the sketchbooks further illuminate the rhetoric of the "Crucifixus". First, for the slow movement of the string quartet Op. 18, no. 1, allegedly inspired by the grave scene from *Romeo and Juliet*,[76] we find sketches combining tremolos and the *tmesis* rhythm, with the heading "les derniers soupirs"

---

[72] *Die Gedichte Walthers von der Vogelweide*, Berlin, De Gruyter, 1950[11], p. 49. Further literary and pictorial examples are given by Rudolph Hugo HOFMANN, *Das Leben Jesu nach den Apokryphen im Zusammenhange aus den Quellen erzählt und wissenschaftlich untersucht*, Leipzig, Voigt, 1851, pp. 77f; Yrjö HIRN, *The Sacred Shrine: A Study of the Poetry and Art of the Catholic Church*, London, Macmillan, 1912, pp. 296-300; and Ernest JONES, *Die Empfängnis der Jungfrau Maria durch das Ohr: Ein Beitrag zu der Beziehung zwischen Kunst und Religion*, «Jahrbuch der Psychoanalyse», VI, 1914, pp. 137ff. In 1662 Molière parodied the concept drastically with one of the most famous lines in French comedy: he has the innocent young Angès ask her stern guardian "si les enfants ... se faisoient par l'oreille?" – *L'école des femmes*, I.i.

[73] As illustrated by JONES, *loc. cit.*

[74] "hier menschlich" – D-BNbh BSk 1/49, p. 59.

[75] DTÖ, XXV, 48.

[76] THAYER, II, 1910[2], p. 186.

["the last sighs"].[77] Second, in a sketch-book for the *Missa solemnis* the note "Crucifixus in ♯ Ton" ["Crucifix in sharp/cross key" – the German "Kreuz" means both 'sharp' and 'cross'][78] shows Beethoven's interest in notational symbolism, even though this was not employed in the finished work. Third, among sketches for the death of Clärchen in *Egmont* there is the remark "Death could be expressed by a rest".[79] The passage "passus et sepultus est" ["He suffered and was buried"] is closely related to Mozart's music for the death of the Commendatore in *Don Giovanni*, I.ii. In the Mass, death comes with the long rests in the orchestra, on "sepultus est", and with the *morendo* of the few remaining voices.[80] But the section ends with a fermata on a bare fourth, i.e. a chord which lacks finality and requires a resolution (m. 187). Could there be a more subtle indication that Beethoven understood Christ's entombment not as an end, but as a transition?

The message of the resurrection is then proclaimed by the tenor. Throughout the Mass it is this voice which introduces new events[81] – a usage which can be related to the traditional role of the tenor voice as *testo*, as well as to the more recent operatic function of the heroic tenor as leader (cf. the "Held" in the Ninth Symphony). The words "secundum scripturas" in the sentence on the resurrection reflect the concern of the early Christian apologists to reconcile the doctrines of the New Testament with those of the Old.[82] Musically, the 'old' scriptures are rendered by one of the few *a cappella* passages in the Mass, and by archaic harmonies, in sixteenth-century style.

Some more details in the Credo are worth noting. The word "mortuos" is set not only to the usual *piano subito* and long, low notes, but also to 'dead' chords, without a third. Lasso employed such a chord for the word "mortem" in his motet "Tristis est anima mea".[83] Beethoven translates the idea of expectation literally into music with the prominent anticipations in the violins si-

---

[77] NOTTEBOHM, p. 485.

[78] D-Bds ms. Artaria 180.

[79] "Der Tod könnte ausgedruckt werden durch eine Pause" – NOTTEBOHM, pp. 277, 527. Cf. Hans-Heinrich UNGER, *Die Beziehugen zwischen Musik und Rhetorik im 16.-18. Jahrhundert*, Würzburg, Triltsch, 1941, pp. 70f, for similar ideas in theory (Calvisius 1592: "In interitu ... onmes voces silent"; "in death ... all voices are silent") and practice (Hans Leo Haßler, "Ich scheid' und stirbe", "I depart and die"; Heinrich Schütz, "und gab seinen Geist auf", "and gave up the ghost").

[80] Cf. also Cherubini's second Mass.

[81] Cf. also Beethoven's first Mass, Gloria, mm. 75-135.

[82] Cf. 1 *Cor.* 15:4: "resurrexit tertia die, secundum Scripturas" ["He was resurrected the third day, according to the scriptures"].

[83] *Modulorum ... secundum volumen*, Paris, Le Roy & Ballard, 1565; *Sämtliche Werke*, V, Leipzig, Breitkopf & Härtel, 1895, p. 48.

multaneous with "et exspecto" (mm. 289-292). The repetition of "exspecto" is a less ingenious, more conventional procedure of musical rhetoric.[84] Another conventional repetition is that of the word "non" in the phrase "cujus regni non erit finis" (mm. 262ff). However, other composers invariably complete the phrase by following the repetitions of "non" with "erit finis". Beethoven's terminal repetition of "non", in the form "non erit finis, non, non, non", has a precedent only in the satirical "Schulmeister-Messe" which parodies the "Non mi lasciare, no, no, no!" of the Italian secular cantata, with an intention which we would not want to attribute to Beethoven (Ex. 3). That we must ascribe this passage to his Promethean will to overcome mortality goes without saying,[85] but it is also apparent that at this point he has come dangerously close to the ridiculous.

Ex. 3. "Schulmeister-Messe".

non e - rit fi - nis, non non non non

The fact that Beethoven sets the articles of faith beginning with "Credo in Spiritum Sanctum..." rapidly in monotone declamation (Ex. 4a) has frequently been interpreted as proof of indifference towards Catholic dogma.[86] However, this section of the text is not one which lends itself to extensive musical exegesis. Its length, its short, uniform phrases, and its abstract content demand a declamatory setting. Indeed, such settings were usual in Masses at least from the seventeenth to the early nineteenth century.[87] Diabelli even employed here the recitation formula of a psalm tone (see note 49, above). We may relate Beethoven's treatment of dogma to his well-known statement that

---

[84] 'Expectation' was usually heightened by rests between the repetitions – e.g. Jommelli's *Messa a 4* (US-Wc ms. M2010 A2 J65), Naumann's *Missa solenne* (Vienna, Bureau des Arts et d'Industrie, pl. no. 167 [= 1803]), Beethoven's first Mass, Jean Martini's *Messe solennelle* (Paris, 1808), etc.

[85] Otto WEINREICH, *Trigemination als sakrale Stilform*, «Studie e materiali», IV, 1928, pp. 198-206, demonstrates the wealth of emphatic ternary repetitions in cult, rite, and magic. On the conventional repetition of "non" cf. Johann KUHNAU, *Texte zur Leipziger Kirchen-Music*, «Monatshefte für Musikgeschichte», Leipzig, 1710, XXXIV, 1902, p. 152.

[86] E.g. by Otto SCHILLING TRYGOPHORUS, *Beethovens Missa solemnis*, Darmstadt, Bergsträßer, 1923, p. 68, who attempts to make Beethoven a Lutheran.

[87] E.g. Cavalli's *Missa concertata*, Lotti's Mass for three voices (from the library of Archduke Rudolph, published as "Studentenmesse", Vienna, Universal Edition, 1913), Jommelli's *Missa a 4 voci*, Haydn's *Missa Cellensis*, *Missa in tempore belli*, *Heiligmesse*, Tomaschek's, *Missa solemnis*, Weber's 2.*ème* *Messe solennelle* (1818; Paris, Richault, n.d.), Cherubini's fourth Mass, etc.

Ex. 4a. Beethoven: *Missa solemnis*, Credo, mm. 268-275.

religion and figured bass are "closed subjects, on which there should be no
further dispute".[88] Declamation on a quasi monotone often serves for affirma-

---

[88] "in sich abgeschlossene Dinge, über die man nicht weiter disputieren soll" – SCHINDLER, II,
162.

tive statements which reject contradiction. Similarly in the Gellert song "Bitten", Op. 48, no. 1, Beethoven had employed six measures of repeated notes for the words "Herr! meine Burg, mein Fels, mein Hort" ["Lord! My fortress, my rock, my refuge", Ex. 4b].[89] The relation of this idea to the Credo is confirmed through his later use of the Credo-motif for a canon with the text "Gott ist eine feste Burg" WoO 188 ["God is a solid fortress", Ex. 4c]. Here in the *Missa solemnis* the monotone declamation of dogma combines simultaneously with the determined Credo-motif to form a most forceful expression of faith.[90] Earlier in the Credo, at "Deum de Deo" (mm. 61-64) and "Deo

Ex. 4b. Beethoven: "Bitten", Op. 48, no. 1, mm. 27-32.

Ex. 4c. Beethoven: "Gott ist eine feste Burg", WoO 188.

---

[89] Also Philipp Emanuel Bach presented repeated notes in his setting of this text – cf. Ernst BÜCKEN, *Die Lieder Beethovens: Eine stilkritische Studie*, «Neues Beethoven-Jahrbuch», II, 1925, p. 36.

[90] Not only the employment, but also the shape of Beethoven's Credo motif grew out of the eighteenth-century tradition of the Credo-Mass. Such Masses form their four-note Credo motives by using the word twice in succession, frequently beginning with a falling minor third, as in the *Missa*

vero" (m. 67), Beethoven used the notes of the 'solid' major triad, the alpha and omega of music, for unshakable dogma, as composers long before him had done and baroque theorists had expounded.[91] With "Deo vero" this expression is intensified by unison; with "lumen de lumine" it is in C major, which had a tradition as key of "light".

Also in the subject of the final fugue "Et vitam venturi saeculi" (mm. 309ff) the major triad retains its old symbolism of perfection and fulfillment,[92] now for the life after death. The leisurely tempo – incomprehensible to the first reviewers[93] – the subdued dynamics and the mild turn to the subdominant are not common in fugues.[94] (Beethoven employed them for similar effect in the fugue of the string quartet Op. 131). Thus life everlasting is envisioned not in the traditional manner as a vigorous physical existence, but as peace, removed from the bustle and noise of life on earth. It is perhaps the longest of all vocal fugues,[95] on the solitary height of the *Hammerklavier* sonata and the *Große Fuge*. The sovereign mastery of compositional technique exhibited here may justify the suggestion that Beethoven was contemplating his own "vitam venturi saeculi", his immortality as an artist. Such an idea was not foreign to him in these years. In March and April 1823 we find the following entries about the Mass in *Konversationshefte*: "It is a work of eternity", "You will be glorified, because your music [is] religion. ... You will rise with me from the dead, because you must".[96] The connection between the "Et vitam

---

solemnis; cf. REICHERT, *Mozarts 'Credo-Messen'*, p. 125. In sketches Beethoven noted: "es kann durchaus überall 2 mal Credo Credo" ["it can absolutely be everywhere twice Credo Credo" – D-BNbh 110, p. 3].

[91] Cf. Rolf DAMMANN, *Das Musikbegriff im deutschen Barock*, Cologne, Volk, 1967, pp. 40ff, 439-444.

[92] *Ibidem.*

[93] SEYFRIED, «Caecilia», IX, 1828, 230: "matt und schleppend" ["feeble and draging"]. ANON., AmZ, XXVI, 1824, col. 439: "so könnte auch nicht geleugnet werden, dass gerade dieser zögernde, ängstlich erwartete Schluss die früheren Eindrucke schwächt, weil sich eben gar kein denkbarer Grund dazu auffinden lässt, als der Wille, einen eigenen Weg zu wandeln. In manchen Fällen ist es doch angemessener, den hergebrachten Formen treu zu bleiben. Wer fühlt sich bey einer feurigen Prachtfuge von Naumann, Haydn, Mozart nicht hoch begeistert ...?" ["thus it could not be denied that precisely this hesitating, timidly expected conclusion weakens the earlier impressions, because no conceivable reason at all can be found for it, other than the intention of going one's own way. But in many cases it is more suitable to remain true to the traditional forms. Who does not feel highly inspired by a splendid fiery fugue of Naumann, Haydn, Mozart?"]. However, Beethoven's particular departure from tradition is meaningful for the *pax aeternitatis* (cf. note 164).

[94] W. KIRKENDALE, *Fugue and Fugato*, pp. 270f.

[95] The only rival for this title may be the "Et vitam" fugue in Cherubini's *Credo* of 1806. In the fugues of both composers, the length matches the idea of eternity, as does, on a smaller scale, Beethoven's sixfold [!] sequence on "saeculi", mm. 351-356.

[96] "Es ist ein Werk der Ewigkeit", "Sie werden verherrlicht, weil Ihre Musik Religion. Sie werden mit mir von Todten auferstehen, weil Sie müssen", III, 112, 160.

venturi saeculi" and Beethoven's own life and afterlife may be confirmed by a note on the sketches for this fugue:[97] "Applaudite amici", an anticipation of his famous last words, "Plaudite amici, comoedia est finita" ["Applaud, friends, the comedy is finished"].

At the beginning of the Sanctus a short but significant passage attracts our attention: four measures for brass ensemble (mm. 9-12). If we recall that the Sanctus from the very beginning, in *Isaiah* (6:3), was the hymn of the seraphim above the temple of Jerusalem, and that trumpets/trombones were the instruments of both the angels and the temple priests, then we can recognize the appropriateness of the instrumentation. However, we have here also a more recent musical tradition, namely that of the German 'Turmmusik' ['tower music'] of the Renaissance and Baroque. This too was associated with the music of the angels. Thus the Stadtpfeifer Hornbock in Kuhnau's *Musicalischer Quack-Salber* testified: "We know from experience that when our city pipers in the festive season play a religious song with nothing but trombones from the tower, then we are exceedingly moved, and imagine that we hear the angels singing".[98] And in the depiction of tower music on the title page of Pezel's *Hora Decima* (Leipzig, 1670; Plate XV.6) we see players in angelic form. Beethoven's miniature tower sonata is therefore a very fitting introduction for the Sanctus, the ancient song of the heavenly host.

The repertoires of the tower and the liturgy were not unrelated. Since the sixteenth century at least, the tower musicians joined the church choirs when polyphonic music was performed.[99] Much of the music played from the towers consisted of harmonizations of the same popular religious songs which were sung in the services – in Catholic countries especially – after the Josephinian reforms promoted the use of the vernacular. Among the most widely sung texts were the various "Heilig-Lieder", paraphrases of our Sanctus text.[100] One of their melodies found its way into Masses of Joseph and Michael Haydn and into Joseph Preindl's collection of *Melodien aller deutschen Kirchenlieder, welche im St. Stephansdom in Wien gesungen werden*.[101] Catho-

---

[97] D-BNbh BSk 1/49, p. 78.

[98] "Die Erfahrenheit giebet es, wenn unsere Stadt-Pfeiffer etwa zur Fest-Zeit ein geistliches Lied mit lauter Trombonen vom Thurme blasen, so werden wir über alle massen darüber beweget, und bilden uns ein, als hören wir Engel singen" – Dresden, Miehen & Zimmermann, 1700, p. 435.

[99] Walter SERAUKY, *Musikgeschichte der Stadt Halle*, I, Halle/Berlin, Waisenhaus, 1935, p. 289; EHMANN, p. 41.

[100] Cf. those published from 1808 on, listed in Wilhelm BÄUMKER, *Das katholische deutsche Kirchenlied in seinen Singweisen*, Freiburg, Herder, 1883-1911, IV, 740-743.

[101] Carl Maria BRAND, *Die Messen von Joseph Haydn*, Würzburg, Triltsch, 1941, pp. 298f.

lic communities, such as Vienna[102] and Salzburg,[103] cultivated tower music hardly less than the Lutheran,[104] some still in Beethoven's time. His connection with the long and honorable tradition is certain: in 1812 he made a late contribution to the vanishing repertoire, composing three trombone *equales* WoO 30 for the towermaster Franz Xaver Glöggl in Linz.[105]

The independent orchestral movement inserted between the Sanctus and Benedictus, entitled "Praeludium", seems to be unique among orchestral Masses, yet it makes perfect sense in the light of earlier liturgical practice. When polyphonic composition extended the length of the Sanctus, it became necessary to have the Consecration precede, rather than follow the Benedictus, in order not to delay the celebrant unduly. In pontifical Masses since the sixteenth century the Consecration and Elevation of the Host were accompanied by improvised or composed organ music. Such Elevation music, marking the climax of the entire liturgy, is described in the *Caeremoniale episcoporum* of 1600: "In the Solemn Mass [the organ] is played ... with a rather grave and sweet sound while the most sacred Sacrament is raised".[106] Similarly Adriano Banchieri, in his *Organo suonarino*, says: "at the Elevation played, but softly, and something grave which moves to devotion".[107] It is quite possible that this frequently reprinted and widely diffused book was among the "old Italians" mentioned in the conversation book of December 1819. In composing music which fits these descriptions so precisely, Beethoven was evidently cognizant of the practice and took care to conceive his work in every detail as a *missa solemnis*. This explains the musical style of the movement, that of a polyphonic organ improvisation: sostenuto, with sonorous harmonies, suspensions, and pedal point. It is played with "sweet sound", not rising above the "piano" dynamic indicated by Banchieri. Here and in the *Caeremoniale* the

---

[102] A German Stadtpfeifer wrote: "hab Ich der Stadt Wien damals 1 Jahr auf S. Stephans Thurm für einen gesellen gedient" ["At that time [ca. 1570] I served the city of Vienna for one year as a journeyman in the tower of St. Stephen"] – Hans ENGEL, *Spielleute und Hofmusiker im alten Stettin zu Anfang des 17. Jahrhunderts*, «Musik in Pommern», I, 1932, offprint, p. 4.

[103] Well into the eighteenth century, at least – cf. Hermann SPIES, *Die Tonkunst in Salzburg in der Regierungszeit des Fürsten und Erzbischofs Wolf Dietrich von Raitenau (1587-1612)*, «Mitteilungen der Gesellschaft für Salzburger Landeskunde», LXXII, 1932, pp. 78-81.

[104] In Leipzig until 1806 – EHMANN, p. 35.

[105] Cf. Othmar WESSELY, *Zur Geschichte des Equals*, in: *Beethoven-Studien: Festgabe der österreichischen Akademie der Wissenschaften zum 200. Geburtstag von Ludwig van Beethoven*, Vienna, Böhlau, 1970, pp. 341-360.

[106] "In Missa solemni pulsatur ... dum elevatur Sanctissimum Sacramentum graviori, & dulciori sono" – f. 52.

[107] "si suona alla Levatione, ma piano & cosa grave che muovi alla devotione" – Venice, Amadino, 1605, p. 38. On the *grave* see also above, pp. 72ff.

word "grave" implies both the slow tempo and the low register – Beethoven omits the violins and subdivides the violas and 'cellos. A parallel passage in the Ninth Symphony further illuminates his intention: the shorter but very similar orchestral interlude for low woodwinds and divided violas and 'cellos, marked "divoto" (cf. Banchieri's "devotion"), introducing the words "Ihr stürzt nieder, Millionen" ["You prostrate yourselves, millions", mm. 627ff]; this text completes the analogy, for the congregation kneels during the Consecration.

By the late eighteenth century the orchestra frequently replaced the organ for instrumental interludes of the Mass,[108] so that the Elevation and various items of the Proper were represented by movements of symphonies,[109] by virtuoso concertos,[110] and even by military fanfares.[111] Although Beethoven too employs the orchestra for the Elevation, his quasi-organ style is close to the legitimate tradition of organ music. He was familiar with this tradition from his youth, when he himself supplied the improvised organ interludes for the Rhenish service: a manuscript from Siegburg contains the rubric "Moderato, played before the Alleluia by L. von Beethoven".[112] In composing his own Elevation music for the *Missa solemnis*, he prevents the arbitrary insertion of a foreign orchestral movement and likewise binds the unreliable hands of an improvising organist – just as he and later nineteenth-century composers wrote out the cadenzas for their concertos.[113] The title "Praeludium" of this movement has often been construed as designating a 'prelude' to the Benedictus. However, in Beethoven's time the verb *präludieren* was the normal ex-

---

[108] W. KIRKENDALE, *Fugue and Fugato*, p. 36; Stephan BONTA, *The Uses of the Sonata da Chiesa*, JAMS, XXII, 1969, pp. 72f. The function of Beethoven's movement was easily recognized by SEYFRIED in his review of 1828, p. 227: "Anstatt des während der Consecration vorgeschriebenen Orgelspiels, hat unser Componist eigens ein Präludium ... gesetzt" ["Instead of the prescribed organ playing during the Consecration our composer set expressly a prelude"].

[109] E.g. in a Mass celebrated in Bonn on the occasion of the entry of Beethoven's patron Count Waldstein into the *Deutschrittersorden* – Joseph HEER, *Zur Kirchenmusik und ihrer Praxis während der Beethovenzeit in Bonn*, «Kirchenmusikalisches Jahrbuch», XXVIII, 1933, pp. 138f.

[110] E.g. by Dittersdorf in Bologna, 1763: "Bei dem Graduale spielte ich mein Konzert mit aller möglichen Anstrengung" ["During the Gradual I played my concerto with all possible exertion"] – Karl Ditters von DITTERSDORF, *Lebensbeschreibung*, Leipzig, Breitkopf & Härtel, 1801, p. 117.

[111] Cf. Charles BURNEY, *The Present State of Music in Germany, the Netherlands, and United Provinces*, London, Becket, 1773, pp. 115f: [in Augsburg] "there was a rude and barbarous flourish of drums and trumpets at the elevation of the Host, which was what I had never heard before, except at Antwerp". At a Mass for the installation of a bishop in Paris 1802, a military band played such pieces as "Ah! le bel oiseau, maman" during the Elevation; Michel BRENET, *La musique militaire*, Paris, Piccard, n.d., pp. 87f.

[112] "Moderato, wird vor dem Alleluja gespielt von L. von Pethoven", HEER, p. 132.

[113] Apparently he thought of supplying such pieces also for his first Mass; among sketches for the *Hammerklaviersonate* we find the note "Preludien zu meiner Messe" – NOTTEBOHM, p. 353.

pression for improvising organ music during the church service.[114] There can, then, be no doubt that with the word "Praeludium" Beethoven intended an allusion to the tradition and style of organ improvisation, a comcept which we have traced back to Aristotle.[115]

A striking and significant effect is achieved in the last measure of the Prae-ludium (m. 110), where a link with the Benedictus is established by the entry of the solo violin. At this moment the Consecration of the Host is completed and Christ becomes present on the altar. The effect of the sudden entry of the very high, bright solo violin (g''') into the dark, low orchestral background can not only be characterized by, but even identified with, the words "lux in tenebris", for it is thus that St. John referred to the coming of the Savior (1:5), the "lux vera" (1:9), the "lumen de lumine" which dispels the darkness of sin. Again the interpretation is strengthened by liturgical parallels: the 'Wandlungskerze', the candle lighted at the altar at the moment of Transubstantiation – the candle too is a symbol of Christ, since it consumes itself in giving light – and the 'Elevation bell', with its bright sound.[116]

The Benedictus then brings to perfection the late-eighteenth-century type of mild, ecstatic movement heard while the Host is exhibited on the altar. Such movements very often achieve their effect with subdominant tonality, predominantly solo voices, and obbligato solo instruments,[117] most commonly the organ, as the traditional instrument of Elevation music.[118] Beethoven originally considered a concertino of four obbligato instruments[119] – violin, horn, bassoon, and 'cello – as in André's Mass Op. 43 of 1819. He finally chose the solo violin to accompany Him "qui venit in nomine Domini" ["who comes in the name of the Lord"], as J. S. Bach did in the Advent cantata BWV 132. The extended orchestral introduction continues to serve as Elevation music, as it does in the Masses of Haydn and his contemporaries.

---

[114] Cf. Beethoven's note in a conversation book of March-May 1819: "preludiren des Kyrie vom organisten stark u. abnehmend bis vor dem Kyrie piano" ["improvisation for the Kyrie by the organist, strong and decreasing to piano before the Kyrie"] – *Konversationshefte*, I, 33.

[115] Cf. above, p. 72.

[116] Cf. LE BRUN, pp. 480, 400; Peter BROWE, *Die Elevation in der Messe*, «Jahrbuch für Liturgiewissenschaft», IX, 1929, pp. 37-43; Ludwig EISENHOFER, *Handbuch der katholischen Liturgik*, Freiburg, Herder, 1933, II, 163.

[117] E.g. the flute in Leopold Mozart's Mass in C (New York, Fox, 1963) and in Albrechtsberger's *Missa in C pro coronatione Francisci II Budae peragenda* (1792, Weissenbäck no. 97); the viola in Michael Haydn's *Missa solemnis* in G (Klafsky no. I, 38, DTÖ, LXII, p. vi); and the violin and 'cello in Salieri's Mass in D (NÜTZLADER, p. 161).

[118] E.g. the "Orgelmessen" of J. Haydn (1766 and ca. 1775), Mozart K. 259 (1776), M. Haydn (1805, Klafsky no. I, 24), and Albrechtsberger (1796 and 1801,Weissenbäck nos. 111 and 134).

[119] Alexander Wheelock THAYER, *Chronologisches Verzeichniss der Werke Ludwig van Beethovens*, Berlin, F. Schneider, 1865, p. 142; NOTTEBOHM, p. 149.

With verbal expression temporarily exhausted by the presence of Christ, Beethoven comes into his purely symphonic element. However, in order to make the meaning of this long orchestral section absolutely clear, he prefixes it with a single presentation of the text "Benedictus, qui venit in nomine Domini" (mm. 114-117), in the manner of the old *Devisenarie* ['motto aria']. It is declaimed on a monotone, since it is to serve merely as a heading for the movement.

Whoever has followed the rhetoric thus far will recognize the initial long, slow *katabasis* in the flutes and solo violin as the descent of Christ upon the altar. Is it the analogy to the Nativity that leads so naturally to the style of the pastoral Mass, with its gently rocking trochaic melodies in 12/8 meter?[120] Beethoven was doubtless familiar with at least some of the more recent representatives of this large musical progeny of St. Luke.[121] Yet his direct model was not a pastoral Mass, but another Christmas composition: Handel's *Messiah*. We know from the sketches that Beethoven studied this while working on the Mass.[122] Here he is clearly indebted to the aria "He shall feed His flock",[123] and thus we may see very concretely in his *katabasis* the coming of the Good Shepherd.

The Benedictus has a close relative: the slow movement of the string quartet Op. 59, no. 2. In both works there is a single violin soaring high above its accompaniment in long, smooth triplets (Exx. 5a-b) with occasional steep descents to the lowest register (Exx. 6a-b). I do not regard this similarity as entirely accidental. According to Czerny, the slow movement of the quartet was conceived by Beethoven while looking at the starry heavens and thinking of the music of the spheres.[124] Its ethereal, seraphic style must have appeared to be the most suitable one to express the presence of the heavenly visitor in the Mass.

---

[120] On this style, see above, pp. 27ff.

[121] The earliest *Missa pastoritia* is probably that by Francesco Sale in Tyrol, 1589 (*Missarum solemniorum ... Primus tomus*). In the eighteenth and early nineteenth centuries the genre was widely cultivated in Italy, Austria, and southern Germany – cf. Alois Augustin DIMPFL, *Die Pastoralmesse*, ms. diss. Erlangen, 1945. The extensive repertoire of Bohemian pastoral music made little use of the familiar quasi-siciliano idiom preferred in the Austro-Italian settings of the "Incarnatus" and "Benedictus" – cf. Camillo SCHOENBAUM, *Harmonia pastoralis Bohemica*, in *Festschrift für Walter Wiora zum 30. Dezember 1966*, Kassel, Bärenreiter, 1967, pp. 348-356. Composers of pastoral Masses are listed in W. KIRKENDALE, *Beethovens Missa solemnis*, 1971, note 109.

[122] W. KIRKENDALE, *Fugue and Fugato*, p. 216 (e).

[123] This seems to have been recognized already in 1828 by GROSSHEIM, pp. 25f. Part of the aria was copied by Beethoven in the sketchbook GB-Lbl ms. add. 29997, f. 26v, which contains also sketches for the *Missa solemnis*.

[124] THAYER, *Beethovens Leben*, II, 1910², p. 532. Cf. *Konversationshefte*, I, 230, III, 128, V, 164, and above, p. 19, on Beethoven's interest in astronomy.

Ex. 5a. Beethoven: String Quartet Op. 59, no. 2, second movement, mm. 37-40, 42-45.

Ex. 5b. Beethoven: *Missa solemnis*, Benedictus, mm. 200ff.

The setting of the Agnus Dei is unusual in that it has three rather than two complete presentations of the sentence "Agnus Dei, qui tollis peccata mundi, miserere nobis" before the "Dona nobis pacem".[125] However, the harmonic

---

[125] A departure which I have seen again only in Hummel's second Mass, Op. 80, Vienna, Has-

Ex. 6a. Beethoven: String Quartet Op. 59, no. 2, second movement, mm. 69-72.

Ex. 6b. Beethoven: *Missa solemnis*, Benedictus, mm. 155ff.

plan adheres to the normal eighteenth-century practice of beginning in the relative or tonic minor and returning to the tonic only with the "Dona nobis pacem", conceived as an independent movement. From the "Miserere" section it may suffice to mention a single rhetorical moment. The minor key is the one which Beethoven once designated in his sketches as "b-minor black

linger, pl. no. 3019 [= ca. 1820]. Beethoven could hardly have known that this threefold literal repetition was the earlier form of the Agnus Dei, as it was sung in the ninth and tenth centuries (and to this day in the Lateran church – cf. Guillaume DURAND [d. 1296], *Rationale divinorum officiorum* [Mainz], Fust & Schoeffer, 1459, f. [64]: "in ecclesia lateranensi non dicitur 'Dona nobis pacem'"), and that only in the eleventh and twelfth centuries, during times of stress, did the "Dona nobis pacem" replace the "miserere nobis" of the third sentence.

key".[126] Operas and oratorios of the eighteenth century had reserved it for the expression of distress. Here it is intensified by bassoon and bass solo, which add 'depth' to 'blackness', characterizing the plea for mercy as a humble call 'de profundis' – for centuries melodies creeping in the depths had been a *topos* for humility – and anticipating later events in the "Dona nobis pacem". For intellectual density this final movement has hardly a rival in the history of the Mass and therefore deserves detailed scrutiny. The pastoral idiom of the Italian Baroque returns – peace is again Arcadian happiness. However, not content merely to depict peace, Beethoven contrasts it with its opposite, war – just as he introduces violent discord and the words "nicht diese Töne" ["not these sounds"] into the "Ode to Joy". Though such a dramatic procedure is most unusual in a Mass,[127] it was intelligible and, alas, justified then as now.

More than any other passage in the *Missa solemnis*, it is the military episodes which have puzzled commentators: "It may be difficult to decipher what the composer really intended with this phrase";[128] or: "Moreover, what the strange trumpet fanfare, the interpolated recitative, the fugal instrumental section [i.e. the fugato] which only distrurbs the flow of the ideas ... really mean to say, – what the dull, unrhythmical, bizarre timpani strokes basically signify, heaven only knows".[129] Schindler even recommended that the military passages be omitted in performance.[130] One other work, and only one, is invariably mentioned in this connection: Haydn's *Missa in tempore belli*, which also includes trumpet fanfares and drum rolls in the "Dona". While there can be little doubt that the *Missa solemnis* was influenced directly by this Mass and others by Haydn, I should like to point out its place in a much more ancient tradition. The oldest collection of prayers for the Mass, the so-called

---

[126] "h moll schwarze Tonart", among b-minor sketches for Op. 102, no. 2 – NOTTEBOHM, p. 326. This characteristic was not assigned to the b-minor key by authors which Beethoven might have known, such as Schubart. Johann MATTHESON, *Das neu-eröffnete Orchester*, Hamburg, author, 1713, pp. 249ff, believed only that b-minor was "bizarre, unlustig und melancholisch" ["bizarre, apathetic, and melancholy"], but f-minor "drücket eine schwartze, hülfslose Melancholie schön aus" ["expresses beautifully a black, helpless melancholy"].

[127] Also Beethoven's first Mass and Cherubini's *Messe à trois voix* in F interrupt the peaceful mood of the "Dona" with troubled episodes on the words "Agnus Dei".

[128] "Was der Tonsetzer mit dieser Phrase eigentlich beabsichtigt habe, möge schwer zu entziffern seyn", ANON., AmZ, XXVI, 1824, col. 440.

[129] "Was übrigens die wunderliche Trompeten-Fanfarre, das eingemengte Recitativ, der fugirte, den Ideenfluss nur störende Instrumental-Satz ... eigentlich sagen will, – was die dumpfen, unrhythmischen, bizarren Pauken-Schläge im Grund bedeuten sollen, mag der liebe Himmel wissen" – SEYFRIED, p. 230; SCHINDLER, II, 79. Cf. also THAYER, *Beethovens Leben*, IV, 1907, p. 352.

[130] II, 79.

Leonine Sacramentary,[131] already contained *Missae tempore hostili*, motivated by the siege of Rome by the barbarians in the fifth and sixth centuries. From occasional prayers in time of war (cf. LU 1867) a fixed votive liturgy eventually developed (*Missa pro pace*, LU 1285-87).[132] Also musical military idioms had invaded the Mass long before Haydn and Beethoven. Dufay already wrote an *Et in terra ad modum tubae*.[133] When Renaissance composers based their parody Masses on French chansons, they did not exclude the ever popular battle chanson from their models. Thus Jannequin used his famous chanson *La Guerre* (ca. 1528), the prototype of battle pieces, for his Mass *La Bataille*, published in 1532.[134] This was followed by a long series of battle Masses, such as Tomás Luis de Victoria's *Missa pro victoria*,[135] Giovanni Anerio's immensely popular *Missa de la battaglia*,[136] Pietro Lappi's *Missa sopra la battaglia*,[137] Adriano Banchieri's *Missa in sono tubae*,[138] Christoph Straus's Masses *ad modum tubarum* and *cum tympanis ac 5 tubis campestribus*,[139] Carlo Grossi's Mass *Capriccio guerriero*,[140] and Francesco Foggia's *Missa detta la battaglia*.[141] Such compositions, however, did not remain without negative reactions, e.g. from Nicola Vicentino in 1555[142] and from the Council of Trent on 8 August 1562.[143]

Battaglia music had an uninterrupted existence until far into the nineteenth century, and Beethoven himself contributed his "Battle Symphony" for Wellington's victory, a work frequently underestimated when considered apart from its genre. And as early as 1809, when the French troops invaded

---

[131] P.L. LV, 21-156.

[132] Cf. Anton BAUMSTARK, *Friede und Krieg in altkirchlicher Liturgie*, «Hochland», XIII/1, 1915-16, pp. 257-270.

[133] DTÖ, XIV/XV: *Sechs Trienter Codices*, Vienna, 1900, pp. 145ff.

[134] *Liber decem missarum*, a collection published by Jacques Moderne, Lyon, 1532 and 1540.

[135] *Missae*, Madrid, Ioannes Flandrus, 1600; *Opera omnia*, Leipzig, Breitkopf & Härtel, 1909, VI, 26-58.

[136] 1605, with many manuscript copies and nine new editions to 1689; Regensburg, Pustet, 1955 («Musica Divina», 11).

[137] *Missarum ... liber secundus*, Venice, 1608.

[138] In Johann Donfrid's *Corolla Musica*, Trier, Zetzner, 1628.

[139] *Missae 8, 10, 11, 12, 12 et 20 voc.*, Vienna, Formica, 1631.

[140] *Armonici accenti ... op. 2*, Venice, Magni, 1657.

[141] *Octo Missae*, Rome, Fei, 1663; *Messe a tre, quattro e cinque voci*, Rome, Mutii, 1675. Not all such Masses were parodies. Rudolf GLÄSL, *Zur Geschichte der Battaglia*, Leipzig, Thomas & Hubert, 1931, pp. 44, 86, mentions three of the above.

[142] *L'antica musica ridotta alla moderna prattica*, Rome, Barré, 1555, f. 79bis*v*.

[143] *Concilium Tridentinum Diariorum, Actorum ... Nova Collectio*, tomus VIII, Freiburg, Herder, 1919, p. 918.

Austria, he had made sketches for a battle piece.[144] Considering the great impact of the march music of post-revolutionary France upon Beethoven's *œuvre*, we are not surprised to find notations for a march as part of the earliest sketches for the Agnus Dei.[145]

Fanfare melodies for *clarini* or trumpets are not uncommon in orchestral Masses of the eighteenth century,[146] not to mention the field Masses of the military camps, which used trumpets in place of bells (for Introit, Elevation, etc.). However, in the orchestral Masses these instruments merely reinforce the tuttis, and the character of their fanfares is usually joyous and festive.[147] Beethoven's Mass is unique in its extended solo passage for trumpets and timpani in the unmistakable and menacing form of a battle fanfare (mm. 170ff). For full understanding of this passage, it would be of interest to know whether Beethoven used an actual military signal of his time and, if so, what it signified. Unfortunately there is little hope of making such a discovery, for the signals had long been not only a strict secret of the trumpeters' guild, but also a military secret and therefore seldom committed to writing. Thus Johann Ernst Altenburg, in his *Versuch einer Anleitung zur heroisch-musikalischen Trompeter- und Pauker Kunst* of 1795, did not print a single military signal.[148]

---

[144] NOTTEBOHM, p. 162: "auf die Schlacht Jubelgesang". Cherubini, whose first Requiem was highly admired by Beethoven, ended his Coronation Mass of 1825 (Paris, chez l'auteur) with a "Marche religieuse, executée, après la messe, le jour du sacre de Charles X pendant la Communion du Roi".

[145] NOTTEBOHM, p. 150; Johannes WOLF, *Beethoven Kirchenmusiker?*, in *Beethoven-Zentenarfeier*, Vienna, Universal-Edition, 1927, p. 125.

[146] Cf. STUTE, pp. 21f. A characteristic example is Fux's *Missa corporis Christi* of 1713, *Sämtliche Werke*, Ser. I, Bd. 1, Graz, Akad. Druck- u. Verlagsanstalt, 1959. According to Stute, a Mass of Antonio Buroni (formerly in D-MÜs?), contains an indication for an unwritten vocal "cadenza col clarino" on the word "miserere".

[147] Also in Haydn's *Missa in tempore belli*.

[148] Cf. p. 94: "Da die Kunstverwandten diese Feldstücke blos nach dem Gehöre von einander zu erlernen pflegen, so hat mich dieses sowol, als der zu befürchtende Vorwurf einer Entdeckung ihrer Geheimnisse billig davon abgehalten, dieselben durch Noten bekannt zu machen" ["Since the professionals learned these field pieces only from each other by ear, not only this, but also the fear of the reproach for revealing their secrets rightly deterred me from making these known through notation"]. The only extant examples before the nineteenth century are those written in two manuscripts ca. 1600 and published in *Das Erbe Deutscher Musik, Reichsdenkmale*, Bd. 7: *Trompetenfanfaren, Sonaten, und Feldstucke*, Kassel, Bärenreiter, 1936. These pieces have little in common with Beethoven's fanfares. Only the signals "Aufs Pferd (Montacawalla)" and especially "Wache (Auged = Guet)" bear some resemblance to the trumpet parts in the second episode (m. 326). They are published also in Georg SCHÜNEMANN, *Sonaten und Feldstücke der Hoftrompeter*, ZfMw, XVII, 1935, p. 161. Leopold NOWAK, *Beethovens 'Fidelio' und die österreichischen Militärsignale*, «Österreichische Musikzeitschrift», X, 1955, p. 373, argued a close relationship between the fanfare of Beethoven's opera and those of the Austrian army. However, the only source quoted for the latter, Archduke Karl's *Dienst-Reglement für die kaiserlich-königliche Infanterie*, Vienna, 1807-1808, contains, in the copies which I consulted, only drum rolls, no trumpet signals. The Austrian trumpet

Trumpets and drums formed, of course, an essential part of the *Missae solemnes* for the most festive occasions.[149] But Beethoven's prominent use of a military fanfare may be regarded as particularly appropriate for a Mass dedicated to a member of the imperial family, Archduke Rudolph. Altenburg emphasized that Emperor Joseph II, Rudolph's grandfather, had introduced trumpets and drums to his dragoons in 1774; that the highest paid trumpeters in Europe were those in imperial service; and that the patron of the trumpeters' guild, the archangel Gabriel, was at the same time the protector of the imperial residence.[150] Rudolph had been much in need of such protection in 1809 when Napoleon's troops had forced him to leave Vienna and Beethoven wrote the sonata *Les Adieux* for him. Indeed, the passage in the Mass may be regarded as a product of Beethoven's personal experience in that year. Ferdinand Ries relates how the composer spent the night of 11 May with great fear in his brother's cellar, as the city was bombarded by French artillery.[151] Beethoven must have known what Altenburg knew: "But frightful and terrible is the sound of the trumpet when it announces the near advance of the enemy".[152] Only if we imagine ourselves in such a situation will we feel the full impact of the first military episode, ominous in its initial piano dynamic,

signals have been attributed, without the slightest evidence, to Michael Haydn. More relevant would be the French military signals of the early nineteenth century, but an examination of such material has thus far yielded no results.

[149] Such as listed in the *Diarium cantus figuralis aliarumque functionum musicae totius anni* from Herzogenburg, 1751, quoted by REICHERT, *Zur Geschichte der Wiener Messenkomposition*, p. 2. Cf. Fr[anz Xaver] GLÖGGL, *Kirchenmusik-Ordnung: Erklärendes Handbuch des musikalischen Gottesdienst*, Vienna, Wallishauser, 1828, §16, p. 36: "Vom Gebrauch der Trompeten und Pauken in der Kirche": "nur an doppelten Festen erster und zweiter Klasse" ["On the use of trumpets and timpani in the church": "only for duplex feasts of the first and second class"].

[150] "Endlich ist hier noch anzuführen, daß Kayser Joseph II. 1774 die Trompeten und Pauken auch bei den Dragoner Regimentern, durchgängig einzuführen geruhet hat" ["Finally is to be mentioned here that in 1774 Emperor Joseph II deigned to introduce trumpets and drums throughout the dragoon regiments"] – pp. 25, 52. "In Römischen Kayserlichen Diensten steht sich ein Feldtrompeter am besten" ["In the Roman Imperial service a field trumpeter has the best situation"] – p. 40. "So ist es auch als ein Vorzug anzusehen, daß vor allen andern Musikern, den Trompetern der Erzengel Gabriel, als ein besonderer Patron, und zwar als ein solcher, der zugleich die R. Kayserliche Residenz beschützt, vorgesetzt ist, diesem aber die Trompete vorzüglich gewidmet sey" ["Thus it is to be seen as an advantage, that archangel Gabriel is assigned to the trumpeters, before all other musicians, as a particular patron, as one who at the same time protects the imperial residence, and that the trumpet is preferentially dedicated to him"] – p. 32. Also when they were most threatened by the Turks, the Hapsburgs sought help from Gabriel – cf. Anna CORETH, *Pietas Austriaca*, «Mitteilungen des Österreichischen Staatsarchivs», VII, 1954, p. 116.

[151] Franz WEGELER and Ferdinand RIES, *Biographische Notizen über Ludwig van Beethoven*, Coblenz, Baedeker, 1845, p. 121.

[152] "Fürchterlich und schrecklich aber ist der Schall der Trompete, wenn er den nahen Anmarsch des Feindes verkündet", p. 24.

terrifying in its slow crescendo (mm. 164-188), the "near advance".[153] Such extraordinary, paralyzing tension demands drastic expression in the next vocal entry. And this appears: *recitativo accompagnato* (m. 174). This style is not entirely unknown to the Ordinary of the Mass, as Adler believed,[154] but it is, nevertheless, extremely rare. The opera composer Cavalli used it, likewise for an emphatic invocation, on "Domine Deus",[155] and Haydn, in his only cantata-Mass – which honors the patron saint of music – employs it before the "Incarnatus" aria. In his songs, Beethoven had already turned to recitative in exceptional moments of great psychological tension. The plea for mercy in the Mass, marked "ängstlich" ["frightened"], reveals the same intention as another non-operatic vocal work, the song "Der Wachtelschlag" WoO 129 (1803), which breaks momentarily into recitative at the words "Schreckt dich im Wetter der Herr der Natur, bitte Gott, bitte Gott!" ["If the lord of nature frightens you in the storm, pray to God"].[156]

Peace is eventually restored and the pastoral music returns. It leads into a fugato (mm. 216ff) on a subject from Handel's Hallelujah chorus. I have no doubt that Beethoven borrowed it consciously. We have seen that he studied *Messiah* while composing the Mass (above, p. 524). Why does he quote Handel at this point? It is clear that this triumphant theme, which everyone could associate with the "hallelujah" text, is very appropriate after the danger of war has been averted. There is, however, a deeper reason. Just as Napoleon and the French were for Beethoven representatives of war, Wellington and the English were the restorers of peace. And Handel's oratorios, then as now, were regarded as English music, their enthusiastic performances in Germany and Austria during the Wars of Liberation had been tantamount to political propaganda. As in the "Battle Symphony" the patriotic song of the French succumbs to that of the English, so in the Mass the military fanfares cede to the most popular piece in the repertoire of English sacred music.

A clue for the understanding of the second troubled episode in this rondo-like movement (ABACA) is provided by Beethoven's subtitle "Bitte um innern und äussern Frieden" ["Plea for inner and outer peace"]. That the first episode, with its *battaglia* language, represents the disturbance of "outer"

---

[153] Cf. in the sketches: "piano ... pauken in h und fis nur von weitem, agnus dei hiermit gleich anfang" ["piano ... timpani in b and f-sharp only from a distance, begin the Agnus immediately with this"] – NOTTEBOHM, pp. 464, 151.

[154] P. 33.

[155] *Missa concertata*.

[156] In sketches for the "Dona" Beethoven noted: "durchaus simple Bitte Bitte Bitte" – NOTTEBOHM, p. 465.

peace is not to be contested. May we then, following an indication of the composer, interpret the second, with its extended and restless orchestral fugato (presto, mm. 266ff), as the disturbance of "inner peace"?[157] The 'inner' struggle is distinguished from the external strife by the intellectual device of the fugato, and by an 'inner' thematic relationship between one of the fugato subjects and the 'peace' motif of the principal section (mm. 107f). The first episode had no such connection with the rest of the movement; it remained an 'external' interpolation.

The episodes can be best understood in relation to a much older practice. They are tropes, inserted into the liturgical text and expanding its ideas. Until well into the sixteenth century, the Agnus Dei was a favored text for the troping process,[158] and its tropes occasionally reflect, as Beethoven's do, the strife of the times, e.g.: "fer opem tribulatis, dona nobis pacem" ["bear strength/aid to the troubled, give us peace"] from the thirteenth century or "Agnus Dei, defensor nostri, adveni" ["Agnus Dei, our defender, come"] from the sixteenth.[159] Edmund Martène's *De antiquis ecclesiae ritibus* of 1702, reprinted in 1736, still states that the Agnus Dei was recited "not continuously, but interpolated and mixed with private prayer",[160] a formulation which can be traced back at least to the twelfth century.[161] The outburst of recitative in Beethoven's first episode, with its strongly subjective style of dramatic monody, comes indeed close to a "private prayer".

It has not yet been recognized that the reference to inner and outer peace in Beethoven's heading is not a subjective invention of the composer,[162] but is deeply rooted in ancient theological concepts. Prayers for inner and outer peace had formed an essential part of the liturgy from the earliest centuries

---

[157] Only this sequence, not that of the heading, could be artistically justified. In a sketch, Beethoven first wrote "darstellend äusseren Frieden" ["representing the external peace"], then added the words "u. inneren" ["and inner"] – cf. Harry GOLDSCHMIDT, *Zwei Skizzenblätter: ein Beitrag zur Programmatik Beethovens*, «Musik und Gesellschaft», III, 1953, pp. 55ff.

[158] Cf. the "Tropi ad Agnus Dei" in *Analecta Hymnica Medii Aevi*, ed. Clemens BLUME and Guido M. DREVES, XLVII: *Tropi Graduales*, Leipzig, Reisland, 1905, pp. 371-405; Charles ATKINSON, *The Earliest Settings of the* Agnus Dei *and its Tropes*, ms. diss., University of North Carolina, 1975.

[159] *Ibid.*, pp. 383, 387.

[160] "non continue, sed interpolate et mixtim cum private oratione" – Antwerp, De La Bay, 1736², I, 419.

[161] Joannes BELETH († 1182), *Rationale Divinorum Officiorum*: "non continue, sed interpolate ac sejunctim cum oratione interposita" ["not continuously, but interpolated and joined with interposed prayer"] – P.L. CCII, 55A.

[162] E.g. Paul NETTL, *Beethoven-Handbook*, New York, 1956, p. 145: "These words show the subjectiveness of Beethoven's work".

XV.1. Last Judgement, pericope book of Emperor Henry II. D-Mbs Cod. Lat. 4452, ca. 1022, f. 201v. Cf. p. 506.

XV.2. Coronation of the Virgin. By Hans Holbein sr. (1460/70-1524), Bayerische Staatsgemälde-Sammlungen. Cf. p. 509.

of the Christian era.[163] Beethoven's dual concept is fully developed in twelfth- and thirteenth-century commentaries on the "Dona nobis pacem". Alanus de Insulis, in his *Summa de arte praedicatoria*, distinguishes "three kinds of peace: peace of the time, peace of mind, and peace of eternity".[164] This threefold distinction embraces the dualistic interpretation of the Agnus Dei, for the third kind of peace, "pax aeternitatis", is accessible only to the dead,[165] and it therefore has its place in the Requiem Mass, where the "Dona nobis pacem" is altered to "Dona eis requiem sempiternam". Alain's great contemporary, Pope Innocent III, assigns inner and outer peace to the first and second "miserere", respectively, of the Agnus Dei; then both species combined, to the "Dona": "We therefore say 'miserere nobis' for the soul; likewise 'miserere nobis' for the body; 'dona nobis pacem' for both: so that we have spiritual peace of mind and temporal peace of body".[166] The dichotomy of "pax interna – pax externa" still belongs to the *topos* fund of baroque treatises on virtues, such as Wilhelm Friedrich von Efferen's *Manuale politicum de ratione status* of 1630.[167] That Beethoven attached particular importance to the peace of mind is revealed by the note in his sketches for the Agnus Dei: "Strength of the sentiments of inner peace above all ... Victory!".[168] Does the word "victory" in this context allude to the familiar image of the Lamb of God carrying the flag of victory?

We have arrived at the end of our path through the score. Since I have been speaking of a heading, I may look back on the other singular inscription in this Mass, the famous "Von Herzen – Möge es wieder – zu Herzen gehen!" ["From the heart – may it go again to the heart"]. This too is hardly, as hitherto believed, a romantic effusion of the composer's overflowing heart. Again we hear an echo of older theological parlance. The motto stands not at the head of the entire Mass, but at the beginning of the Kyrie only. And did

---

[163] Cf. BAUMSTARK.

[164] "tres species pacis: pax temporis, pax pectoris, et pax aeternitatis" – P.L. CCX, 156A – continuing: "Prima pax in temporalium prosperitate consistit, secunda ex mentis tranquillitate provenit, tertia in jucunditate vitae coelestis existit" ["The first peace consists in the prosperity of the times, the second issues from the tranquillity of the mind, the third exists in the delight of heavenly life"].

[165] Cf. above, the discussion of the "Et vitam" fugue.

[166] "Dicamus ergo 'miserere nobis' quantum ad animam; item 'miserere nobis' quantum ad carnem; 'dona nobis pacem' propter utramque: ut habeamus pacem pectoris spiritualem, et pacem corporis temporalem" – *De Sacro Altaris Mysterio*, P.L. CCXVII, 908D. These words are also found, almost literally, in Guillaume DURAND (d. 1296), *Rationale Divinorum Officiorum*, [Mainz], Fust & Schoeffer, 1459, f. [64].

[167] Frankfurt, Schönwetter, pp. 871ff.

[168] "Stärke der Gesinnungen des inneren Friedens über alles ... Sieg!" – NOTTEBOHM, p. 151.

not Jacques Bossuet, the great theologian of Louis XIV, call the Kyrie text "the language of the heart"?[169]

"I believe that I have treated the text as it has seldom been treated". When Beethoven wrote these words about his first Mass to Breitkopf & Härtel,[170] he was surely aware that he had taken unusual care of musical exegesis. But how much more does his statement apply to the *Missa solemnis*, where every textual concept, indeed almost every word is musically interpreted![171] (Nowhere did Richard Wagner exhibit his insensitivity towards older music so blatantly as when he said of this work: "The text is not comprehended by us ... according to its conceptual significance, but it serves ... merely as material for the voices").[172] But ever since the times of Galilei and Doni theorists had warned against undue concentration on single words.[173] And indeed, in the long chain of images in the Gloria and Credo, Beethoven indulges in such an endless, reckless, monumental wealth of conceptual mosaics, that his contemporaries were dismayed. The accepted balance between form and content was distorted; an avalanche buried moderation and convention. The complete freedom, the maturity of a late style could not easily be comprehended. Timidly the first reviewers voiced their discomfort at the fragmentation, the too rapid changes of key, tempo, and dynamics, the transitions too abrupt to be followed by the listener.[174] And Goethe, who

---

[169] Undocumented reference by Wilhelm WEBER, *Beethovens Missa solemnis*, Leipzig, Schlosser, 1908[2], p. 49, who, strangely enough, does not connect it with Beethoven's motto. I have not located the passage in Bossuet's voluminous writings. Cf. the similar formulations in Goethe's *Faust*, I.544 and II.9685f.

[170] "Von meiner Messe ..., glaube ich, daß ich den Text behandelt habe, wie er noch wenig behandelt worden" – 8 June 1808; *Briefwechsel*, II, 15.

[171] Cf. [Joseph] FRÖHLICH's perceptive review in «Caecilia», IX, 1828, p. 42f: "Jedes Instrument, jede Figur, jedes *p., pp., for., cresc.*, jedes Schleifen und Stossen ist berechnet, und muss nach dem Character der Stelle wie dieser durch die Worte und die in denselben enthaltenen Bilder bestimmt ist, immer anders gegeben werden. Auf diese Weise bekömmt manche Figur, die dem ersten Anblicke nach nichtssagend, gemein, ja dem Texte widersprechend erscheint, eine grosse, herrliche Bedeutung" ["Every instrument, every figure, every *p, pp, for., cresc.*, every slur and stroke is calculated and must always be interpreted differently, according to the character of the passage, determined by the words and the images contained therein. In this way many a figure, which at first appears insignificant, ordinary, indeed contradicting the text, receives a great, splendid meaning"].

[172] "Der Text wird von uns ... nicht seiner begrifflichen Bedeutung nach aufgefasst, sondern er dient ... lediglich als Material für den Stimmgesang", *Gesammelte Schriften und Dichtungen*, Leipzig, Fritzsch, 1871-83, IX, 103.

[173] *Dialogo di Vincentio Galilei nobile fiorentino della musica antica et della moderna*, Florence, Marescotti, 1581, p. 88f; Giovanni Battista DONI, *Lyra Barberina*, Florence, Typis Caesareis, 1763, II, 73: "L'errore consiste in questo, che in vece di esprimere o imitare tutto il concetto ... si mettono ad esprimere le parole separate" ["The error consists of this: instead of expressing or imitating the concept as a whole, ... one goes about expressing the single words"].

[174] ANON., AmZ, XXVI, 1824, col. 439: "Die Behandlung des Credo ist in der That ungewöhn-

in these years expressed his dislike of "überfüllte Musik",[175] would probably have felt no differently. However, we must recognize that Beethoven does achieve unity in the Gloria and Credo by linking contrasting episodes with short orchestral ritornellos and by using recurring motives for identical or different texts.[176] This structural coherence is not, as has been suggested, an innovation of the great symphonist, but is found in the Gloria and Credo movements of orchestral Masses since the mid-seventeenth century.

Frau von Weissenthurn's question could not have been more apposite. What distinguishes the *Missa solemnis* from the vast contemporary production is above all the intense concern with ideas. This led the composer to undertake extensive preparatory studies, from the translation, declension, or conjugation of single Latin words of the text with the help of a dictionary,[177] to the collection of plainchants, the examination of sacred music in Archduke Rudolph's library,[178] and the occupation with musical *ethos* in ancient treatises. And it is clear that, much more than has been hitherto suspected, the master occupied himself with theology and liturgics, isolated as he was in his deafness and withdrawing more and more into a world of images and speculation. He obviously wished to say the last word on the subject.[179] We begin to understand the unusually long gestation period of four and a half years.

Beethoven's acquaintance with the various musical, literary, iconographical, theological, and liturgical traditions is sometimes more, sometimes less de-

---

lich und höchst originell; sowohl die Grundtonart, B dur, als das Zeitmaass wird oft, vielleicht etwas gar zu oft gewechselt, und das Ohr ist beynahe kaum vermögend, den raschen Wechsel aufzufassen" ["The treatment of the Credo is indeed unusual and highly original; not only the basic tonality, B-flat major, but also the tempo are often changed, perhaps even somewhat too frequently, and the ear is hardly able to perceive the quick change"]. SEYFRIED, p. 229 (on the Gloria and Credo): "Der oftmalige, doch wohl gar zu häufige, unmotivierte Wechsel des Zeitmaasses, der Ton- und Tactarten, gibt ein zerstücktes Bild ... und erzeugt gewissermasen jenes beengende Gefühl, so aus Mangel an Einheit, aus der gleichsam blos rhapsodischen Behandlungs-Weise zu entspringen pflegt" ["The repeated, indeed presumably too frequent, unmotivated change of the tempo, of the keys and measures creates a fragmented picture ... and, to a certain degree, that oppressive feeling, which arises from lack of unity and the merely rhapsodic treatment"]. Cf. also *Briefe von Moritz Hauptmann, Kantor und Musikdirektor an der Thomasschule zu Leipzig, an Franz Hauser*, Leipzig, Breitkopf & Härtel, 1871, II, 269f.

[175] *Briefe*, Hamburg, Wegner, 1967, IV, 146, letter to Zelter, 6 June 1825. The present writer confesses that he does not appreciate the noisier sections of the *Missa solemnis*.

[176] In sketches Beethoven designated his Gloria-motif as "ritornell" – BNbh BSk 1/49, pp. 29, 32.

[177] Even to the extent of deriving "Pilatus" from "pilo": "pilato – pilo berauben, plündern, mit Wurfspiess versehen pilatus"; manuscript in D-Bds, quoted by J. WOLF, p. 124.

[178] Cf. p. 511 and Beethoven's letter of 29 July 1819 – *Briefwechsel*, IV, 298.

[179] He pursued a similar intention in other late works, especially in the *Große Fuge*; cf. pp. 553ff.

monstrable. The evidences of it are incontestable for the trombone chords and flute trills to symbolize the power of God and the dove of the Holy Ghost, for the authority of Zarlino on the character of the Dorian mode, for the traditions of the pastoral Mass, tower and Elevation music, and for the quotation from Messiah. That he knew the Töpfer altar or Michael Haydn's use of plainchant melodies for the "Incarnatus" is very probable. Still within the realm of possibility is his acquaintance with Biber's 'Rosary' Sonatas, with *battaglia* Masses, with the passages on Elevation music in the *Caeremoniale episcoporum* and in Banchieri's treatise, and with the account of military music in Altenburg's book. It is less likely that he knew first hand the works of the Church Fathers or Bossuet.[180] However, the patristic writings were so consistently copied by later authors, and famous theological formulations were so well preserved in popular pious literature, that a knowledge of them could be derived from any number of sources. A few links in the chain are sufficient to demonstrate the continuity in the European history of ideas and to show the appropriateness of Beethoven's formulations.

The century in which Beethoven was born had already brought not only the antiliturgical reforms of Joseph II, but also such thorough studies of historical sources as Lodovico Muratori's *Liturgia Romana Vetus* (1748) and Martin Gerbert's *De cantu et musica sacra* (1774).[181] In theological and liturgical matters Beethoven must have enlisted the advice of learned specialists for his *opus magnum*, just as painters used to do in working out an iconographical program. We find a clue to the identity of a helper in a conversation book early in 1820: "Kanne has just produced a history of the Mass. It is still in the censorship office".[182] August Friedrich Kanne was the most talented, original, and alcoholic of Beethoven's intimate companions, a human encyclo-

---

[180] However, the manuscript quoted by WOLF, *loc. cit.*, contains a general reference in Beethoven's own hand: he translates the Latin words as they were used "bey Kirchenvätern" ["in the church fathers"]! Cf. also THAYER, *Beethovens Leben*, IV, 1907, p. 334.

[181] Cf. also Anton L. MAYER, *Liturgie, Aufklärung und Klassizismus*, «Jahrbuch für Liturgiewissenschaft», IX, 1929, pp. 67-127.

[182] "Kanne hat soeben eine Geschichte der Messe geliefert. Liegt noch bey der Censur" – *Konversationshefte*, I, 242. The writer is Janitschek. On Kanne cf. SCHINDLER, *Biographie*, I, 72, 227f; II, 165-168; Constantin von WURZBACH, *Biographisches Lexikon des Kaiserthums Österreich*, X, Vienna, Hof- u. Staatsdruckerei, 1863, pp. 438-443; THAYER, *Beethovens Leben*, V, 1908, pp. 4f; Theodor FRIMMEL, *Beethoven-Handbuch*, Leipzig, Breitkopf & Hartel, 1926, I, 247f; Wilhelm HITZIG, *Ein Brief Friedrich August Kannes*, «Der Bär», IV, 1927, pp. 42-52; Imogen FELLINGER, *Friedrich August Kanne als Kritiker Beethovens*, Gesellschaft für Musikforschung, *Bericht über den internationalen musikwissenschaftlichen Kongress Bonn 1970*, Kassel, Bärenreiter, 1971, pp. 383-386; Heinrich ULLRICH, *Beethovens Freund Friedrich August Kanne*, «Österreichische Musikzeitschrift», XXIX, 1974, pp. 75-80; *id.*, *Friedrich August Kanne (1779-1833): Das Schaffen*, «Studien zur Musikwissenschaft», XXX, 1979, pp. 155-262.

pedia,[183] a former student of theology, and composer of a Mass himself.[184] He had become Vienna's most perceptive music critic and protagonist of Beethoven's music, and finally was to serve him as torchbearer at his funeral and as necrologist. Beethoven esteemed him highly and consulted him repeatedly on artistic questions. Unfortunately, the history of the Mass does not seem to have survived the censorship. At least it was never published.[185] (Kanne is known to have destroyed some of his manuscripts). If it could someday be found, I venture to predict that it would throw further light on Beethoven's composition. But even if Beethoven did not read it, he very probably benefited from it through Kanne's advice, and he surely read his friend's *Beytrag zur Musik-Geschichte des Mittelalters*[186] and his essays *Über die musikalische Malerey*[187] and *Über die Harmonie in der Tonkunst in Beziehung auf ihre Verwandtschaft mit der Malerey, Plastik und Dichtkunst.*[188]

---

[183] Heinrich LAUBE's "Reisenovelle" *Beethoven und Kanne* (1833): "ein Atlas von Gelehrsamkeit" ["an Atlas/atlas of erudition"] – *Gesammelte Werke*, Leipzig, Hesse, 1908, VI, 76. SCHINDLER, II, 165: "ein Mann von universeller Bildung" ["a man of universal culture"].

[184] Reviewed in AmZ, XIII, 1811, col. 505ff.

[185] Theophil Antonicek kindly searched for Kanne's manuscript for me in the major Viennese libraries and the remains of the Zensurarchiv.

[186] AmZ, I, Vienna, 1817, cols. 209ff, 213ff, 221ff, dealing, however, only with secular music.

[187] *Ibid.*, II, 1818, cols. 373-380, 385-391, 393ff, pp. 401-405. Beethoven's copy of «Cecilia», VIII, 1826 (D-BNba 757) contains his marginal glosses to Gottrfied WEBER's article *Über Tonmalerei*, pp. 125-171. Kanne's remark on the "adoramus" accords with Beethoven: a composer "wird einen desto schöneren Contrast zu bilden im Stande seyn, wenn er die Stelle 'adoramus te' mit dem Schauder heiliger Andacht ausdrückt" ["a composer will be able to create all the more beautiful contrast if he expresses the passage 'adoramus te' with the shudder of holy devotion"]. However, his subsequent words on the setting of the Mass recall the attitude of Galilei and Doni (above, note 173): "Wir meinen, man soll den Sinn des aus Worten bestehenden ganzen Satzes zu einer Richtschnur nehmen, & danach seine Musik componiren, also nicht einzelne Worte" ["We believe one should take as a guide the meaning of the entire sentence consisting of words, and compose one's music according to that, i.e. not single words". He looks with disfavor on composers "die ... alles ausdrücken ... und jedes einzelne auszudrücken suchen" ["Who ... express everything ... and try to express every single thing"] – col. 402.

[188] «Conversationsblatt: Zeitschrift für wissenschaftliche Unterhaltung», III, Vienna, 1821, pp. 69ff, 787-790, 801ff, 811ff, 821ff, 833-837. The sentence "Ja selbst der von einer Krankheit Genesende fängt an zu singen, sobald er sich wieder seiner Kraft bewusst wird" ["Indeed, even one who is recovering from an illness begins to sing, as soon as he again becomes conscious of his strength"], p. 836, may have influenced Beethoven's formulations "Heiliger Dankgesang eines Genesenen" ["Holy song of thanksgiving of one recovered"], and "Neue Kraft fühlend" ["Feeling new strength"] in Op. 132 (1825).

XVI.

GREGORIAN STYLE
IN BEETHOVEN'S STRING QUARTET OP. 132

The theme of the slow movement of Beethoven's string quartet Op. 132 has long been compared to plainchant (German: "Choral"), but not yet identified with a specific liturgical melody. Beethoven's title for the movement, "Heiliger Dankgesang eines Genesenen an die Gottheit in der lidischen Tonart" ["Sacred Song of Thanksgiving to the Divinity by one recovered from an illness, in the Lydian mode"] already in the year 1825 was a clear reference to consciously archaic writing – at the time when German romantic poets were rediscovering the Middle Ages and converting to Roman Catholicism. We must first ask whether Beethoven used 'Gregorian' melodies and then, if the answer seems to be positive, whether he continued the venerable tradition of selecting *cantus firmi* on the basis of their textual content.

The theme consists of five sections, each consisting of eight half notes. The fifth begins like the fourth and deviates from it only with the last three notes. All four (five) melodies correspond to liturgical chants:[1]

1. Alleluia verse "Salvum me fac, Deus" from the *Missa votiva pro vitanda mortalitate* (GR [139]).

Beethoven: phrase 1

℣ Sal - vum__ me_____ fac

---

[1] Various chants with incipits (5-7 notes) which correspond to Beethoven's melodies – both in the sketches and in the definitive version – are contained in J. R. BRYDEN and David G. HUGHES, *Index of Gregorian Chant*, Cambridge MA, Harvard UP, 1969. In evaluating them as possible models for Beethoven we must consider their accessibility, the potential relevance of their texts, and also the repeated notes (not indicated in the *Index*). The four melodies quoted here were selected by these criteria. Both the *Index* and the various liturgical books contain, of course, only a selection of the melodies actually used in the liturgies.

2. Hymn "Christe redemptor omnium, con-
serva tuos famulos" (Stäblein,[2] pp. 80f,
98, also with two other texts).

Chri- ste_____ re - dem - ptor

Beethoven: phrase 2

3. Hymn "Mediae noctis tempore" (Stäblein,
p. 448; transposed a fifth upwards).

Me - di - ae no - ctis___

Beethoven: phrase 3

4. Introitus "Venite adoremus Deum" for Saturday of the Ember week in September
(GR 371).

Ve - ni - te_____ , ad - o -
[remus]

Beethoven: phrase 5 (and 4)

An employment of plainchant melodies is indicated not only by the correspondences notated above, but also by Beethoven's catholic environment in
Bonn and Vienna; his resolve, at the time of his work on the *Missa solemnis*,
"in order to write true church music – look for all the liturgical chants of the
monks";[3] by his formulation of the theme as a *cantus firmus* in uniform long
notes; and – in the last adagio section – by the use of a 'Choralfuge', i.e. in catholic countries a fugue on a subject taken from a Latin or German liturgical melody.[4] A symbolic intention is suggested by Beethoven's preoccupation with concrete ideas, especially with religious concepts, in the *Missa solemnis*; by his
recourse to older stylistic features in order to express these ideas;[5] by the allusion

---

[2] Bruno STÄBLEIN, *Monumenta Monodica Medii Aevi*, I, *Hymnen* (1), Kassel, Bärenreiter, 1956.

[3] "Um wahre Kirchenmusik zu schreiben – alle Kirchenchoräle der Mönche ... zu suchen";
Alexander Wheelock THAYER, *Ludwig van Beethovens Leben*, IV, Leipzig, Breitkopf & Härtel,
1907, p. 130.

[4] Johann Georg ALBRECHTSBERGER, *Gründliche Anweisung zur Composition*, Leipzig, J. G. I.
Breitkopf, 1790, ch. XXVII: "Von der Fuge mit einem Choral". Beethoven composed three such
fugues during his lessons with Albrechtsberger.

[5] For many examples, see above, ch. 15.

to his own illness in the title, for which no liturgical text could be more relevant than "Salvum me fac, Deus"; by the possible influence on the rubrics "Dankgesang eines Genesenen" and "Neue Kraft fühlend" from an article of his close friend August Friedrich Kanne, who had once studied theology and probably served as a consultant to Beethoven on the composition of the *Missa solemnis*;[6] and by the choice of a 'Gregorian' mode.[7] Since we could demonstrate that Beethoven, with his Dorian "Incarnatus" in the *Missa solemnis*, selected the 'chaste' mode according to the specification of Zarlino,[8] it is not surprising to see that he followed the same authority when he decided to use the Lydian mode for his "Song of Thanksgiving" after an illness. According to Zarlino, "Cassiodorus contends ... that the Lydian is a remedy for fatigue of the mind and likewise for that of the body".[9] Zarlino's allusion is again to the letter of Cassiodorus to Boethius ca. 508 A.D.: "The Lydian was devised against excessive troubles and weariness of the spirit, it refreshes with relaxation and strengthens with delight".[10] John Milton, very knowledgeable in music, Latin, and Italian, was surely influenced by Cassiodorus or Zarlino when he wrote in *L'Allegro* (ca. 1632-34), lines 135f, "And ever against eating cares / Lap me in soft Lydian airs". And similarly Dryden-Handel in *Alexander's Feast* (1736), no. 16: "Softly sweet in Lydian measures / Soon he sooth'd the soul to pleasures".

Two arguments, however, speak more strongly against Beethoven's adoption of the melodies quoted above: accessibility and sketches. As far as I know, the two hymns had not appeared in print by Beethoven's time,[11] though the one with the three 'Redemptor'-texts might possibly have been known to him through the Redemptorists in Vienna, often mentioned in his conversation books.[12] His second and third *cantus firmi* do not correspond to the hymns from their first notation in the sketches, but were the result of a melodic me-

---

[6] *Ibid.*, pp. 536f and note 188.

[7] A more extended discussion of the *Heiliger Dankgesang* in my *Fugue and Fugato in Rococo and Classical Chamber Music*, Durham NC, Duke UP, 1979, pp. 249-255, includes further information on Beethoven's preoccupation with plainchant, church modes, and the *Choralfuge*.

[8] See above, pp. 511f, where it is shown that Beethoven consulted Zarlino's work and selected the "chaste" Dorian mode to symbolize the virginal conception.

[9] "Vuole Caßiodoro, ... che 'l Lidio sia remedio contra le fatiche dell'animo, & similmente contra quelle del corpo" – *Istitutioni harmoniche*, Venice, s.n., 1558, p. 303.

[10] "Lydias contra nimias curas animaeque taedia repertus, remissione reparat, et oblectatione corroborat" – P.L. LXIX, 571C.

[11] The sources listed by Stäblein are limited to a selection of the most important older manuscripts. For Beethoven, only Austrian manuscripts could come into question.

[12] *Ludwig van Beethovens Konversationshefte*, ed. Georg Schünemann, Berlin, Hesse, 1941-43, I, 323, 347f, 351; III, 141, 159f, 255.

tamorphosis[13] – which of course contraindicates the adoption of older melodies.[14] The two other phrases, on the other hand, correspond melodically in
their first appearance in the sketches to the definitive version. Their plainchant
versions, as Mass propers, could have been more widely diffused than the two
hymns. The introitus "Venite adoremus" indeed belongs to the oldest chants;
its text and melody are found together in many manuscripts since the ninth
century,[15] though hardly printed before 1908. The melody quoted for "Salvum
me fac, Deus", however, is not present among the alleluias in manuscripts,[16]
and a preliminary examination of printed Graduals (ten, 1501-1791, exclusively from Romance countries) likewise does not produce it. The votive Mass
"pro vitanda mortalitate" was introduced already in 1348 by Clement VI on
the occasion of the black plague,[17] but the manuscripts generally include only
the spoken text, almost never with melodies.[18] I find the text "Salvum me fac,
Deus" (Ps. 69) as an Alleluia verse for the first time in the "Missa votiva contra
pestem" in a *Graduale Cartusiense* of Seville, 1630, then in the "Missa votiva
pro vitanda mortalitate" of the Graduals of Mecheln 1859, Marseille 1872,
and Regensburg 1872/73 (*Editio Ratisbonensis*), with four different melodies,
none of which corresponds to the *Graduale Romanum*.[19] The version which coincides with Beethoven's melody appears for the first time in Graduals of Tournai 1883 and Solesmes 1895, and one must suspect that it is a recent adaptation, to be attributed to the French Benedictines. I have not been able to
determine from where the melody was taken and whether it was set to the "Salvum" text already before 1825.[20]

---

[13] The earliest sketches are contained in the Roda-sketchbook D-BNbh NE 47, where the definitive version of the five phrases appears on f. 8. All preceding versions are quoted in the musical
examples of Cecilio de RODA, *Un quaderno di autografi di Beethoven del 1825*, «Rivista musicale italiana», XII, 1905, pp. 69-81, where the following corrections may be made: 1) the order of the first
two musical examples should be reversed; 2) the fourth note in Beethoven's third phrase in example
14 is not b', but a', and 3) the words transcribed by Roda, p. 71, as "Doch Du gabst mir wieder
Kräfte, mich des Abends zu finden", should read "... mich des Lebens zu freuen".

[14] Beethoven could have rejected an earlier version or, when it resembled the final version, have
first quoted it inexactly from memory and later corrected it.

[15] Information from Dom Jean Claire, Solesmes.

[16] According to the alleluia file of Karl-Heinz Schlager, which is fairly complete for the period
up to ca. 1400.

[17] Victor LEROQUAIS, *Les sacramentaires et les missels manuscrits des bibliothèques publiques de
France*, Paris, s.n., 1924, II, 296 et passim.

[18] Reference from Michel Huglo.

[19] Karl-Heinz SCHLAGER, *Thematischer Katalog der ältesten Alleluia-Melodien aus Handschriften
des 10. und 11. Jahrhunderts*, Munich, Ricke, 1965, p. 62, believed that the Alleluia "Salvum me fac
servum" in the ms. I-Bu 2679, without musical notation, could be identical to "Salvum me fac,
Deus". But the text is different – cf. GR 93.

[20] No documentation for the provenance exists in Solesmes.

Beethoven's four phrases are very similar also to the style of German protestant chorales. However, a comparison with the many thousand melodies
published by Bäumker and Zahn revealed few correspondences,[21] and no text
as relevant as "Salvum me fac, Deus".

Though we can say nothing conclusive about the genesis of Beethoven's
melodies, as positive result remains the demonstration that they are in any
case in 'Gregorian style'. Perhaps he wished to produce his own imitation
of liturgical plainchant (as in the "Incarnatus" of his *Missa solemnis*)[22] and
succeeded better than he realized.

---

[21] For Beethoven's first phrase cf. Johannes ZAHN, *Die Melodien der deutschen evangelischen
Kirchenlieder*, Gütersloh, Bertelsmann, 1889-93, nos. 1294 and 1296; for the second phrase, no.
499 (without Beethoven's first note, *g'*, which, however, was added only to the definitive version)
and no. 622 (corresponds almost exactly to the penultimate version, RODA, ex. 15); for the third
phrase cf. no. 1259 (almost identical with the first sketches related to the final version, RODA, ex.
8, pp. 72f.

[22] See above, pp. 510f and note 59.

XVII.

THE *GREAT FUGUE* OP. 133: BEETHOVEN'S *ART OF FUGUE*

More than any other work of Beethoven, the *Great Fugue* Op. 133 has aroused only extreme opinions, favorable and unfavorable. The first criticism, in 1826, was rather drastic:[1]

Aber den Sinn des fugirten Finale wagt Ref. nicht zu deuten: für ihn war es unverständlich, wie Chinesisch. Wenn die Instrumente in den Regionen des Süd- und Nordpols mit ungeheuern Schwierigkeiten zu kämpfen haben, wenn jedes derselben anders figuriert und sie sich *per transitum irregularem* unter einer Unzahl von Dissonanzen durchkreuzen, wenn die Spieler, gegen sich selbst mißtrauisch, wohl auch nicht ganz rein greifen, freylich, dann ist die babylonische Verwirrung fertig; dann gibt es ein Concert, woran sich allenfalls die Marokkaner ergötzen können.

But the reviewer does not dare to explain the meaning of the fugal finale [Op. 133 as the original finale of the quartet Op. 130]: for him it was incomprehensible, like Chinese. When the instruments have to struggle with tremendous difficulties in the regions of the south and north poles; when each of them has a different figuration and they cross each other with accented passing notes[2] and an immense number of dissonances; when the players, distrustful of each other, do not play quite in tune; then indeed, the Babylonian confusion [*Genesis* 11:7-9] is complete; then there is a concert in which, at most, the Moroccans can take delight.

Schindler agreed:[3]

Diese Composition scheint ein Anachronismus zu seyn. Sie sollte jener grauen Vorzeit angehören, in welcher die Ton-

This composition seems to be an anachronism. It should belong to those grey olden times when the relationships of

---

[1] Anonymous, in AmZ, XXVIII, 1826, col. 310. D. F. Tovey (1911) and E. Walker (1920) still maintained that the work had been definitely abandoned as unperformable.

[2] On the *transitus irregularis*, cf. *Ludwig van Beethoven's Studien im Generalbasse, Contrapuncte und in der Composistions-Lehre*, ed. Ignaz Ritter von Seyfried, Vienna, T. Haslinger [1832], p. 19.

[3] Anton SCHINDLER, *Ludwig van Beethoven*, Münster, Aeschendorff, 1860³, II, 115.

verhältnisse noch vermittelst mathematischer Berechnung bestimmt wurden. Unbedenklich darf solche Combination als die höchste Verwirrung des speculativen Verstandes betrachtet werden, deren Eindruck wohl in alle Zeiten einer babylonischen Verwirrung gleichen wird. Hierbei kann nicht mehr von Dunkel im Gegensatz zur Klarheit die Rede seyn.

sound were still determined by means of mathematical calculation. Such a combination can be regarded unhesitatingly as the greatest aberration of the speculative intellect, and at all times its impression will resemble Babylonian confusion. Here one can no longer speak of darkness in contrast to clarity.

T. Helm and J. de Marliave, in their books on Beethoven's string quartets, avoid the *Great Fugue*, W. Altmann and D. G. Mason pass negative judgements. The work was praised enthusiastically as early as 1826 by Anton Halm,[4] in 1859 by Zellner,[5] and thereafter by Lenz,[6] H. Scherchen,[7] S. Grew,[8] and E. Ratz.[9] A more recent evaluation is from no less a pen than Igor Stravinsky's:[10]

Now, at 80, I have found new joy in Beethoven. The *Great Fugue*, for example, now seems to me the most perfect miracle in music. ... It is also the most absolutely contemporary piece of music I know, and contemporary forever. ... Hardly birthmarked by its age, the *Great Fugue* is, in rhythm alone, more subtle than any music of my own century. ... I love it beyond everything.

The unprecedented difficulty and recklessness of the work made it a challenge for commentators. Arnold Schering gave a poetic explanation as a Walpurgis Night,[11] highly imaginative, but without convincing evidence. Those

---

[4] Cf. the letter printed in Alexander Wheelock THAYER, *Ludwig van Beethovens Leben*, V, Leipzig, Breitkopf & Härtel, 1908, pp. 298f: "Ihr höchstes Meisterwerk" ["Your highest masterpiece"].

[5] «Blätter für Musik», V, 10, quoted in Wilhelm von LENZ, *Beethoven: Eine Kunst-Studie*, Hamburg, Hoffmann & Campe, 1855-1860, V, 290-293.

[6] *Ibid.*, p. 253: "der über jede Beschreibung erhabene, namenlos geniale Riesen-Satz" ["giant movement ... sublime beyond description ..."].

[7] Hermann SCHERCHEN, *Beethovens Große Fuge*, «Die Musik», XX, 1928, pp. 401-420.

[8] Sydney GREW, *The Grosse Fuge*, «Music and Letters», XII, 1931, pp. 140-147, 253-261.

[9] Erwin RATZ, *Die Originalfassung des Streichquartettes Op. 130 von Beethoven*, «Österreichische Musikzeitschrift», VII, 1952, pp. 81-87.

[10] *My Reflections on Being Eighty*, «The Observer», London, 17 June 1962. Stravinsky acknowledged receipt of the ms. and offprint of the present article (the author's first musicological publication) with two notes: "Greetings to Dr. Kirkendale and *so much thanks* for sending me your so important 'The *Great Fugue* Op. 133' ..." (13 Dec. 1962) and "Greetings to J. Warren Kirkendale and thanks for his remarkable article on Beethoven's '*Great Fugue*' ..." (19 Sept. 1963) – quoted here as a minuscle addendum to the composer's published correspondence, illustrating again his tolerance for musicology; photocopies filed with the original offprint in I-Rvat.

[11] *Beethoven und die Dichtung*, Berlin, Junker & Dünnhaupt, 1930, pp. 351ff.

fond of metaphysical interpretations, so frequent in the literature on Beethoven, have inevitably regarded it as a 'transcendental struggle'.[12] Even more writers limit themselves to formalistic and aesthetic analysis, 'explaining' the work merely out of itself.[13] A favorite solution has been to press it into the Procrustean bed of the sonata-cycle or sonata-movement. But the composer's point of departure and intention, the two most vital aspects of any investigation, are to be found neither in vague philosophical speculation nor in abstract formal schemes, but, as we shall demonstrate, in the very nature of counterpoint; the explanation is based on biographical and philological facts. The present study attempts to show, for the first time, to what extent the *Great Fugue* is rooted in historical tradition.

The discussion may be preceded by a brief outline of the formal structure:[14]

OVERTURA (mm. 1-30). A sort of thematic catalogue quoting the four main versions of the first theme (x) in the reverse order of their appearance in the fugue (x^4, x^3, x^2, x^1) and in a circle of fifths (G-C-F-B♭).

A-SECTION. Allegro (mm. 31-158). B♭ major, **C**-time. A 'regular' *double fugue* on x^1 and the dotted second theme (y). Exposition, counter-exposition (with a free counterpoint in triplets), 'middle entries', x^1 syncopated (m. 111), a

Ex. 1. Beethoven: Op. 133, mm. 30-35, y- and x^1-themes (A-section).

[12] E.g. RATZ, pp. 85f: "And that is the meaning of the 'Great Fugue': in it the temporary antithesis between the *ego* and the world is overcome; the *ego* now experiences in itself the governance of those divine spiritual powers which are operative in the entire visible and invisible world. But this unity must always be won anew through struggle. And Beethoven's life is a perpetual struggle ...""!

[13] SCHERCHEN and GREW have written the most extensive studies of this kind (*opp. cit.*).

[14] Cf. also the versions of Scherchen and Grew. The analysis of V. D'INDY, followed by all French writers and D. G. MASON, is misleading, for it does not recognize the D-section (see below) as a fugue. D'INDY, RATZ and other modern musicians have attempted to restore the *Great Fugue* as finale of the quartet Op. 130. I dealt with this question and came to the conclusion that the 'restoration' is not justified – *Fugue and Fugato in Rococo and Classical Chamber Music*, Durham NC, Duke UP, 1979², pp. 255ff.

group of entries with both themes in diminution (m. 139, y transformed into triplets), coda (m. 147).

B-SECTION. Meno mosso (mm. 159-232), G♭ major,[15] 2/4. *Double fugato* on x^2 and a new countersubject (z), framed and interrupted by homophonic entries of the z-theme. Stretto on x (m. 193). The accompaniment in repeated sixteenth-notes, which, like the homophonic passages in general, does not occur in the sketch of this fugato, is not new for a fugue.[16]

Ex. 2. Beethoven: Op. 133, mm. 167-170, z- and x^2-themes (B-section).

C-SECTION. Allegro molto (mm. 233-272), B♭ major, 6/8. Episode on x^3 (a diminution of x^2) with a trill-figure as countersubject and an answer at the fifth at the beginning, but otherwise not fugal.

Ex. 3. Beethoven: Op. 133, mm. 238f, x^3-theme (C-section).

D-SECTION. (1) A♭ major (mm. 273-413), 6/8. *Fugue* on x^4 (augmentation of x^2) with two countersubjects using the first three notes of x^3 (in inversion) and x^2; the trill-figure from C is transformed to become the cadence of x^4. Exposition, entries of the first half of x^4 in a circle of fifths (m. 308), episode (m. 325), entries of the second half of x^4 in a circle of fifths (m. 350, entries on the same notes as in mm. 308ff), canonic, sequential episode (6 × 4 mm.) on the head motive of x^4 (mm. 380-402). Almost all of D (1) is derived from x.
(2) Episode (mm. 414-492), E♭ major etc., 6/8. Free fantasy on variants of x and y, hardly fugal, after a brief *double fugato* on variants of x and y (mm. 416-432). Pedal point at the end (E♭, mm. 477-492).

15 The fugato was originally intended to begin in D♭ – sketch, D-BNbh Mh 101, pp. 4f.
16 Cf. W. KIRKENDALE, *Fugue and Fugato*, pp. 69f.

Johann Georg Albrechtsbergers,
K. K. Hoforganistens zu Wien

gründliche

Anweisung

zur

Composition;

mit

deutlichen und ausführlichen Exempeln,

zum Selbstunterrichte,

erläutert;

und mit

einem Anhange:

Von der Beschaffenheit und Anwendung aller jetzt üblichen
musikalischen Instrumente.

Leipzig,
bey Johann Gottlob Immanuel Breitkopf, 1790.

XVII.1. Johann Georg Albrechtsberger: *Gründliche Anweisung zur Composition*, Leipzig, J. G. I.
Breitkopf, 1790. Cf. p. 551.

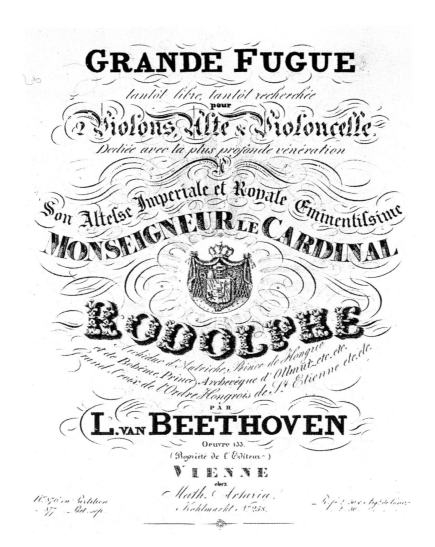

XVII.2. Ludwig van Beethoven: first edition of the *Große Fuge* Op. 133, Vienna, Artaria [1827], dedicated to Archduke Rudolph. Cf. p. 553.

Ex. 4. Beethoven: Op. 133, m. 288-297, x^4-theme (D-section).

B' -SECTION. Reprise of the Meno mosso (mm. 493-510), A♭ major, 2/4. Forte, x^2 combined with its own inversion, z, and a trace of y. Measures 493-500 repeated in mm. 501-508 with parts exchanged (double counterpoint). Transition (mm. 511-532).

C' -SECTION. Reprise of the Allegro molto (mm. 533-564), B♭ major, 6/8 (x^3). CODA (mm. 565-741). (1) New, free homophonic section (mm. 565-656) on the semitone step from x^3. Includes a hocket characteristic of Beethoven's late quartets (m. 581; the latent two-part writing of x becomes real).
(2) The coda proper (mm. 657-741). Reminiscences of what preceded. Finally (m. 716), a new, syncopated variant of y combined with x^4.

The arrangement Overtura-A-B-C-D-B'-C'-Coda may not, of course, be regarded as a succession of closed sections, for all components are developed from the same thematic material (x) and the seams are concealed. For example, x^3 from the C-section is further employed in D, and the reprise of B (B') still belongs tonally to D (A-flat).

When Beethoven began work on the gigantic fugue of the *Hammerklavier* sonata Op. 106 and the *Great Fugue*, he had already written many short fugatos;[17] but his published works offered him no point of departure for an independent, large-scale fugal movement. Somehow he had to orient himself. Is it not likely that he referred to his contrapuntal studies[18] with Haydn and Al-

---

[17] KIRKENDALE, *op. cit.*, pp. 225ff (chart) lists 55 fugatos, fugues and projected fugues in Beethoven's instrumental works.

[18] A corrupted selection of Beethoven's exercises and studies was published by Ignaz von SEYFRIED (as above, note 2); a critical selection by Gustav NOTTEBOHM, *Beethovens Studien*, I: *Beetho-*

brechtsberger (1792-95) and to those prepared for his pupil Archduke Rudolph (ca. 1809), to whom he dedicated Opp. 106 and 133? He had already
returned to them for the chorale fugue in Op. 132.[19] But he had not yet fully
exploited their potential. We shall now show that they served him well in his
largest fugal work.

Beethoven had worked numerous exercises in Fuxian species counterpoint for Haydn, and he was still recommending the practice of species to the
Archduke in 1823.[20] In search of a countersubject for the main theme (x) of
Op. 133 he tried out every conceivable species, with 2, 3, 4, and 6 notes respectively against each note of the theme.[21] The style of the fugal sections in
the finished composition is still determined by the species principle: *the jux-
taposition of various uniform ostinato rhythms*, for example with one (m. 194,
493), three (m. 86, 139), four (m. 31, 167, 493), and six (m. 58) notes against
one, as well as the fourth species (syncopation, mm. 111, 139). The various
voices maintain their own rhythm for many measures at a time: quarter,
eighth, sixteenth notes, dotted rhythm, etc. This is what prompted the contemporary critic to complain that each part "has a different figuration".
The y-theme too, which was first sketched in uniform eighth notes,[22] belongs
in its final form to a particular species, "*contrappunto puntato*".[23] The rhyth-

---

vens Unterricht bei J. Haydn, Albrechtsberger und Salieri, Leipzig, Rieter-Biedermann, 1873.
Although Seyfried's inaccuracies and supposititious comments have long been exposed by NOTTE-
BOHM (*Beethoveniana*, Leipzig, Rieter-Biedermann, 1872, pp. 154-203), they are still sometimes
quoted as authentic. The source used by Seyfried and Nottebohm is the Beethoven-Autograph 75
in A-Wgm. On the basis of many newly identified autographs, references in the letters and conversation books, the inventory of books and music in Beethoven's estate, contemporary reports etc., I provided listings of the theoretical works and of the baroque music and fugues which Beethoven definitely knew (*op. cit.*, pp. 206-224). Among other autographs consulted, the following contain
sketches for Op. 133. References to them are provided also from NOTTEBOHM, *Zweite Beethoveniana*
(henceforth "II"), Leipzig, Rieter-Biedermann, 1887, and Hans SCHMIDT, *Verzeichnis der Skizzen
Beethovens* [= SV], «Beethoven-Jahrbuch», VI, 1965/68, pp. 7-128.

   1) D-B Mus. ms. autogr. Beethoven 9, fasc. I, Ia, II, V. Nottebohm, II, 1f, 5f. SV 26.
   2) D-B Mus. ms. autogr. Beethoven 11, fasc. 2, fol. 26v-27, 30. Nottebohm, II, 250. SV 28.
   3) D-B Mus. ms. autogr. Beethoven 24 (Kullak sketchbook, 1825-26), ff. 1-5, 7v-10, 12. SV 30.
   4) D-B Mus. ms. Artaria 214, 6 f. (now in PL-Kj). SV 23.
   5) D-BNbh NE 47 (Bh 680), ff. 35, 36-37, 39, 40r-v. Described by the former owner, Cecilio
      DE RODA, *Un quaderno di autografi di Beethoven del 1825*, «Rivista musicale italiana»,
      XII, 1905, pp. 734-738. SV 104.
   6) D-BNbh, Mh 101 (Bh 687), 7 fol. SV 150.

   [19] Cf. *Fugue and Fugato*, pp. 254f.

   [20] Letter of 1 July 1823 to Rudolph – Ludwig van BEETHOVEN, *Briefwechsel*, Munich, Henle,
1996-98, V, no. 1686.

   [21] D-BNbh NE 47, ff. 35, 36v, 37; RODA, pp. 735f. Beethoven tried out also the 'joy' theme of
the Ninth Symphony in its 6/8-form as a countersubject to the x-theme – f. 35, Roda's Ex. 99.

   [22] NOTTEBOHM, II, 6.

   [23] Franz Xaver RICHTER, *Harmonische Belehrungen*, ms. B-Br II.6292, pp. 189f; Johann Anton

mic combinations change with each section (A, B, C, etc.) and even with each entry of the subject.

For the whole conception of the work the following passage from Albrechtsberger's treatise on musical composition (Plate XVII.1) is of greatest significance:[24]

Die Vergrößerung (*augmentatio*), die Verkleinerung (*diminutio*), die Abkürzung (*abbreviatio*), die Zerschneidung (*syncope*), die Engführung (*restrictio*) des Fugenthema sind die Hauptfiguren (Zierlichkeiten) und Künste in einer Fuge. Doch kann man selten alle zugleich in einer einzigen Fuge anbringen.

Augmentation, diminution, abbreviation, syncopation, and stretto of the fugue subject are the principal figures (adornments) and artifices in a fugue. Yet one can rarely employ all of them at once in a single fugue.

Beethoven was especially interested in this passage, for he twice copied in his sketches almost all of the musical examples which Albrechtsberger gives for the "main figures". These sketches, unknown to Nottebohm, were identified for the first time by the present author,[25] who has related the contrapuntal "figures" to the theory and practice of rhetoric.[26] Beethoven obviously found a challenge in the last sentence of the quotation: to "employ all of them at once in a single fugue". He made this his principle of composition, his means of building up a large-scale fugue, and this, more than anything else, accounts for the unusual length of the work. All of the contrapuntal artifices listed by Albrechtsberger are employed here: augmentation (x^4 or D), diminution (m. 139; x^3 or C),[27] abbreviation (mm. 308, 378, etc.), syncopation (mm. 111, 139, 716) and stretto (m. 193 and many free or fragmentary strettos, including those with one part augmented or diminished). Of these devices, syncopation is very rare. Albrechtsberger himself is one of the few composers who followed Fux's recommendation to present the subject in syncopation towards the end of a

---

ANDRÉ, *Lehrbuch der Tonsetzkunst*, Offenbach, André, 1832-1843, II, 10, but without Beethoven's repetition of notes at the same pitch.

[24] Johann Georg ALBRECHTSBERGER, *Gründliche Anweisung zur Composition*, Leipzig, J. G. I. Breitkopf, 1790, p. 189.

[25] KIRKENDALE, *Fugue and Fugato*, pp. 209f (c, d, e), 213 (k), 215 (c). The sketches are in D-BNbh Mh 46, and a photocopy of unknown provenance in D-BNba, An 251/2. They belong surely to the other extracts from theoretical works which Beethoven made for Archduke Rudolph.

[26] Above, pp. 76f.

[27] In the sketches Beethoven designated the x^3-theme as "abbreviatur" – D-B Beethoven-Autograph 9, fasc. 2, f. 4.

fugue[28] (e.g. in his quartets Op. 1, nos. 3 and 5, Op. 2, no. 4, Op. 3, no. 6).[29] Beethoven employs it both in the normal values (m. 111; since x^1 is itself already syncopated, this is actually double syncopation) and in diminution (m. 139).

The final proof that Albrechtsberger's treatise was the point of departure for the *Great Fugue* is given by the continuation of the passage quoted above:[30]

Es giebt noch eine Zierlichkeit, wo man nämlich die Noten des Satzes mit einem Suspir theilt, welche aber nicht so schön und männlich ist, als die fünf vorhergehenden. Sie könnte Interruptio, zu teutsch: Unterbrechung genannt werden. Man sehe ein Beyspiel:

There is still another adornment, viz., in which the notes of the subject are separated by a rest, but this is not as handsome and manly as the preceding five. It could be called 'interruption', in German 'Unterbrechung'. See an example:

Ex. 5. Albrechtsberger: *Grundliche Anweisung*, p. 195.

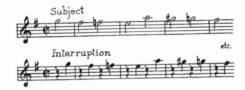

Here we discover the source of the peculiar rhythmisation of Beethoven's x^1-theme,[31] one of the most puzzling aspects of the *Great Fugue* (cf. Ex. 1). This "adornment" is mentioned in very few treatises on counterpoint.[32] It is significant that Albrechtsberger suggests the name himself ("could be

---

[28] Johann Joseph Fux, *Gradus ad Parnassum*, Vienna, van Ghelen, 1725, p. 149. Cf. also Mozart's fugato K. 387/1V (coda).

[29] A comprehensive catalogue of the sources for Albrechtberger's fugal chamber music is provided in Kirkendale, *Fugue and Fugato*, pp. 290-296.

[30] Albrechtsberger, p. 194.

[31] The x^1-form of the theme is relatively infrequent in the sketches. It appears for the first time in the sketch-book D-B Beethoven-Autograph 9, fasc. 2, f. 6, and D-BNbh NE 47, f. 40. On the notation of two tied eighth notes in place of a quarter note and for recent literature on Op. 133 cf. an article of David B. Levy to be published in the «Beethoven Forum».

[32] I examined 90 printed and manuscript theoretical treatises from the seventeenth to early nineteenth centuries, listed *op. cit.*, pp. 335-339. Albrechtsberger was probably influenced, directly or indirectly, by Quintilian's illustrations of *interruptio* (*Institutio oratoria*, IX.ii.54). This ancient rhetorical figure is defined by Lodovico Carbone, *De elocutione oratoria*, Venice, G. B. Ciotti, 1592, p. 287, as "figuram qua inchoatae sententiae cursus ita revocatur, ut inde eius pars alia non dicta, intelligatur" ["a figure in which the movement of a thought [already] begun is revoked, so that the other part of it, not spoken, is thence understood"].

called").[33] Johann Gottfried Walther, in his manuscript *Praecepta* of 1708, illustrates its employment in canons, but does not name it.[34] Marpurg defines it briefly: "The imitation can be interrupted by some rests, and the progress of the melody thus delayed. This is called an interrupted imitation, *imitatio interrupta*".[35] He includes the "fuga per imitationem interruptam" as the fifth of six categories of fugues classified by the type of imitation employed. But his only musical example (tab. III, fig. 3) is that given by Walther. The device is very rare in fugal repertoire.[36] Apart from a free application in Contrapunctus XI of J. S. Bach's *Art of Fugue*, I find it only in Albrechtsberger's quartet fugue Op. 1, no. 1. Albrechtsberger was no longer able to take his musical examples for syncopation and interruption from fugues of Bach and Handel, as he did for the other "principal figures", but had to draw upon his own works. His example of syncopation is taken from his quintet-fugue Op. 3, no. 6, that of interruption from Op. 1, no. 1. Beethoven was determined to leave none of the musical-rhetorical figures listed by Albrechtsberger unused, not even the most exceptional ones.

The word *recherchée* on the title page of the first edition (*Grande Fugue, tantôt libre, tantôt recherchée*, Plate XVII.2)[37] has always been interpreted merely as 'strict' as opposed to *libre*, at best with reference to the obvious derivation from the Italian *ricercar*. Ever since the *Musica nova* of 1540, 'ricercar' had come to designate more often a learned, highly contrapuntal piece than the free, improvisatory type of prelude for lute to which the name was first ap-

---

[33] The term is related to the *tmesis* of the *Figurenlehre* (Vogt, Spiess), which, however, designates only the general procedure of incision and not this special case.

[34] *Praecepta der musikalischen Composition*, Leipzig, Breitkopf & Härtel, 1955, pp. 198ff.

[35] "so kann diesebe [= die Nachahmung] vermittelst einiger Pausen unterbrochen und der Fortgang des Gesangs dadurch aufgehalten werden. Dieses heißt eine unterbrochene Nachahmung, *imitatio interrupta*" – Friedrich Wilhelm Marpurg, *Abhandlung von der Fuge*, Berlin, Haude & Spener, 1753-54, I, 8, also 22, paraphrased by J. G. Siegmeyer, *Theorie der Tonsetzkunst*, Berlin, Schuppel, 1822, p. 225. Marpurg says later (I, 25) that *interruptio* is normally used only as a means of varying middle entries of the fugue subject. Beethoven copied from his treatise examples of the contrapuntal artifices, and he possessed a copy of the French edition of 1801 – cf. Kirkendale, pp. 208 and 210. Johann Anton André, *Lehrbuch der Tonsetzkunst*, Offenbach, André, 1832-43, II, 10, gives an example of *interruptio* which is rhythmically similar to Marpurg's (but not as a means of thematic metamorphosis), calling it "contrapunto alla zoppa" (*contrapunctus claudicans*) or "limping counterpoint". But Richter understands by 'alla zoppa' the rhythm quarter-half-quarter note – *Anmerkungen*, pp. 189f, and symphony F[8], DTB III/1, p. xli.

[36] The examples in Richard William Harpster, *The String Quartets of Johann Georg Albrechtsberger*, ms. diss., University of Southern California, 1976, p. 15, are merely rests on the downbeat, not interrupted imitation, i.e. modification of a fugue subject.

[37] Vienna, Artaria, 1827. The English translation as "*Great Fugue*" is inadequate, for, unlike the German *Große Fuge*, it conveys an idea of "greatness", very welcome to the admirers of the work, but not in keeping with the composer's meaning of 'large'.

plied.[38] In theoretical writings of the eighteenth century, when the ricercar was superseded by the fugue, the term signified especially a fugue which made lavish use of contrapuntal artifices. Beethoven may very well have read in Marpurg[39] that

wenn eine solche strenge Fuge weitläufig ausgearbeitet wird, noch allerhand andere Kunststücke, wozu die vielerley übrigen Gattugen der Nachahmung, des doppelten Contrapuncts, des Canons und der Tonwechselung Gelegenheit geben, damit vergesellschaft werden: so nennet man ein solches Stück alsdann mit einem italienischen Nahmen ein *Ricercare* oder eine *Ricercata*, eine Kunstfuge, eine Meisterfuge.	when a strict fugue is worked out at length and combined with all sorts of other artifices occasioned by the many other species of imitation, of double counterpoint, of canon, and of modulation, then such a piece is called by an Italian name a *ricercare* or a *ricercata*, an art-fugue (*Kunstfuge*), a master-fugue.

André recommends that, before a fugue is composed, its subject should be tested for its capacity to be used in contrapuntal artifices (augmentation, diminution, stretto etc.),[40]

deren mehr oder weniger jede Fuge enthalten soll, und *wenn sie alle enthält*, [sie] eine Ricercata (Kunstfuge) genannt wird.	of which any fugue should contain some, and *when it contains all of them*, [it] is called a ricercata (*Kunstfuge*).

Heinrich Christoph Koch writes in 1802:[41]

Wenn die strenge Fuge noch mit verschiedenen ungewöhnlichern und künst-	If strict fugue is combined with various unusual and ingeious imitations, it is

---

[38] Cf. above, pp. 48f.

[39] I, 19f. Cf. also Johann Gottfried WALTHER, *Musicalisches Lexicon*, Leipzig, Deer, 1732, s.v. 'Ricercare': "künstliche Fuge" ["fugue with many artifices"].

[40] *Vierstimmige Fuge nebst deren Entwurf und den allgemeinen Regeln über die Fuge*, Offenbach, André, 1827², p. 9, my italics. The work was first published in 1799 as an answer to Karl Spazier's criticism of the fugato in André's symphony Op. 4 – cf. KIRKENDALE, pp. 187-190.

[41] *Musikalisches Lexikon*, Frankfurt, Hermann, 1802, col. 609. The *Great Fugue* corresponds also to Langlé's definition of the "ricercatto": "Le ricercatto se compose de plusieurs sujets et contre-sujets. ... Toutes les parties qui composent une fugue y sont employées, comme sujet, contre-sujet, réponse, renversement, imitation, stretto et pédale ...; quant aux modulations elles sont arbitraires, on peut, si l'on veut, faire tous les tours d'harmonie, majeurs, mineurs, soit avec des diésis, soit avec des bémols ...; mais un ricercatto bien fait a toujours un motif principal" ["The ricercato is made up of several subjects and countersubjects. ... All the elements which go to make up a fugue are used in it. ... As for the modulations, they are arbitrary; you can, if you wish, run the whole gammut of harmonies, major and minor keys, with sharps or flats. And finally, it is a sort of caprice or fugal prelude; but a well-written ricercatto always has a principal motive" – cf. Beethoven's *x*-theme] – Honoré Francois Marie LANGLÉ, *Traité de la Fugue*, Paris, l'auteur, 1805, p. 54.

lichen Nachahmungen vermischt wird, so pflegt man sie alsdann eine Ricercata oder eine Kunstfuge zu nennen.	customarily called a *ricercata* or *Kunstfuge*.

As is well known, J. S. Bach hid the word 'ricercar' in an acrostic[42] used as a heading for his *Musical Offering*, a work overloaded with contrapuntal devices. The historical term had become a theoretical one. With the word *recherchée* Beethoven underlined his intention to "employ all [of the artifices] at once in a single fugue".[43]

This plan resulted, as is evident from the analysis given above, in a compound movement. Although it is to be regarded as a single fugue, it actually consists of two fugues (A and D^1), two fugatos (B and part of D^2) and several more or less homophonic sections. Altogether not more than 45 percent is fugal. The freer sections, which we do not need to examine further here, serve to relax tension and constitute perhaps part of the "poetic element" which Beethoven required of the fugue:[44]

Eine Fuge zu machen ist keine Kunst, ich habe deren zu Dutzenden in meiner Studienzeit gemacht. Aber die Phantasie will auch ihr Recht behaupten, und heut' zu Tage muss in die althergebrachte Form ein anderes, ein wirklich poetisches Element kommen.	It takes no great skill to write a fugue; I wrote dozens of them in my student days. But the imagination also claims its due, and in this day and age another, a really poetic element must enter into the old traditional form.

The division of the work into several sections, each with its own tempo, time and key signature, was interpreted by Lenz as a particular innovation (when he quotes Zellner's analysis of 1859, adding his own commentary in parentheses):[45]

'In schulgerechtem Sinn keine Fuge, dem widerspricht die formelle Dehnung, die Gliederung in mehrere rhythmisch selbständige Abschnitte' (das ist eben die Beethovensche Neufuge).	'Not a fugue in the academic sense; this is contradicted by the formal extension, the division into several rhythmically independent sections'. [Lenz:] (That is precisely the Beethovenian new-fugue).

---

[42] "**R**egis **I**ussu **C**antio **E**t **R**eliqua **C**anonica **A**rte **R**esoluta".

[43] André had followed a similar procedure, but wth a very different intention – cf. KIRKENDALE, *Fugue and Fugato*, p. 190, quotation from his *Vierstimmige Fuge*.

[44] LENZ, V, 219.

[45] *Ibid.*, p. 290.

But this division is by no means new, for the early history of the fugue consists largely of the development from many-sectioned, polythematic ricercars, fantasias, canzonas, and capriccios of the seventeenth century to the single-sectioned, monothematic fugue. If, in the history of music, a distant parallel to the *Great Fugue* is to be found, it is in these pieces. One may compare, for example, the easily accessible fantasia of Sweelinck printed in the *Anthology of Music*,[46] with its gigantic length, the diminution, single and double augmentation of the subject, the continual succession of new counterpoints; or Frescobaldi's canzona and Froberger's capriccio in the same volume,[47] with their sections comprising variations of the theme with different time signatures. If it were not improbable that Beethoven knew this repertory,[48] one would be inclined to believe that he was indebted to the ancient variation-ricercar[49] and that the word *recherchée* in the heading had not only a theoretical, but also a historical meaning.

The extensive employment of variation and fugue has long been recognized as characteristic of Beethoven's late works. Common to both are the exploitation of a single theme or thematic complex, and the general lack of repetitions of sections. The thematic economy and formal freedom of these two procedures explain Beethoven's preference for them in his most mature works. Of these, the *Great Fugue* is especially characteristic, for it combines both principles. Not only the variation of the themes themselves, but also the differentiation of the sections by means of new contrapuntal figures corresponds to the practice of variation.[50]

The contrapuntal and homophonic sections are differentiated consistently from each other also in their dynamics. Here Beethoven adheres to a traditional fugal practice which we have observed in the rococo period.[51] At that time dynamic indications were still generally limited to homophonic movements and, in fugues, to occasional homophonic episodes. Fugues seldom

---

[46] Adam ADRIO, *Fugue*, vol. 1, Cologne, A. Volk, 1960, no. 4.

[47] Nos. 6 and 7.

[48] But not impossible. Beethoven himself possessed a fugue of his friend Anton Reicha on a theme of Frescobaldi, divided by double bars into four sections – KIRKENDALE, *Fugue and Fugato*, pp. 193, 195, 219.

[49] The term applied by Wihelm FISCHER in *Handbuch der Musikgeschichte*, ed. Guido Adler, Frankfurter Verlagsanstalt, 1924, p. 483. This variation technique is, of course, by no means restricted to pieces entitled "ricercar", as the above-mentioned works of Frescobaldi and Froberger show.

[50] Yet one may not go so far as to divide the whole work into numbered variations, as D'Indy did. Beethoven himself declared that the fugato in his Eroica-Variations Op. 35 "keine Variation genannt werden kann" ["may not be called a variation"] – letter of 8 April 1803, to Breitkopf & Härtel, *Briefwechsel*, I, 159. In Op. 133 he varies his theme in the manner of the thematic transformations of the symphonic poem, which he thus anticipates.

[51] *Fugue and Fugato*, pp. 75f.

had more than a *"f"* at the beginning, for they required "strength and emphasis",[52] "a firm, powerful stroke of the bow".[53] Gentler dynamics were considered 'gallant' and associated with homophonic episodes:[54]

Wenn man aber die Zwischensätze mit zärtlichen und schmeichelhaften Gedanken, *welche auch ein Piano leiden* oder mit Läufern und Triolen, oder mit Gedanken des Theater- und Kammerstyls, welche in vielen Terzen oder Sexten einhergehen, verfertigt: so wird die Fuge eine Galanterie-Fuge genannt.	If, however, the episodes are composed of tender and blandishing ideas *which tolerate a piano*, or with runs and triplets, or with ideas from the theater and chamber style, going around in many thirds or sixths: under these circumsances, the fugue is called a gallantry fugue.

Beethoven accordingly provides the contrapuntal parts of his work, the two fugues (sections A and D), with an unrelenting *fortissimo* throughout their entirety (128 and 141 measures respectively!). After all, *forte* performance of fugues was the norm in Albrechtsberger's time.[55] The homophonic sections, on the other hand, are predominately *piano*, like those of the rococo composers. The 'gallantry-fugato' in the first B-section (*meno mosso*), with its accompaniment of repeated sixteenth notes and "tender and blandishing ideas which tolerate a *piano*", is played *pianissimo*; but its reprise (B') is *forte*, for here the homophonic accompaniment is omitted and the texture is radically thickened by the combination, in double counterpoint, of the x^2-theme with its own inversion. In a sketch of this section (B') Beethoven noted: "in ... [here he quoted the beginning of x^2 and z] forte kleiner contrepoint".[56]

---

[52] "Kraft und Nachdruck" – Christian Friedrich Daniel SCHUBART, *Ideen zu einer Ästhetik der Tonkunst*, Vienna, Degen, 1806 (written 1784-85), p. 59.

[53] "einen festen, kraftigen Bogenstrich" – anonymous review of Monn's and Gassmann's fugal quartets in AmZ, X, 1808, col. 439. Even at the beginning of the 19th century, dynamic variety was not expected in a fugue. In 1811 Abbé. Vogler claimed that the alteration of *p* and *f*, "was in den Fugen nicht gewöhnlich ist" ["which is unusual for fugues"], as his innovation – Georg Joseph VOGLER, *System für den Fugenbau*, Offenbach, André, ca. 1817, preface dated 1811. During the composition of the fugue in the 'cello sonata Op. 102, no. 2 (1815) Beethoven still found it necessary to note an explicit reminder in the sketches: "Bei allen Fugen piano u. forte" ["in all fugues piano and forte"] – NOTTEBOHM, II, 319. Reicha, advocating the employment of dynamic nuances in fugues, deplored the traditional manner of performance: "La manière dont on exécute vulgairement les fugues ... est une espèce de barbarie: c'est à qui criera ou jouera plus fort!" ["The common manner of performing fugues ... is a kind of barbarism: it is a question of who can shout or play the loudest!"] – Anton REICHA, *Traité de haute composition musicale*, Paris, 1824-26; p. 1097 in the edition of Carl Czerny, Vienna, Diabelli, 1832.

[54] ALBRECHSTBERGER, p. 172 (my italics).

[55] The dynamic gradations added in Felix Weingartner's edition for orchestra (New York, Kalmus, n.d.) contradict both Beethoven's intention and the traditional performance practice.

[56] D-B Beethoven-Autograph 9, fasc. 2, f. 4.

It is well known that Beethoven wrote the main theme of Op. 133 for the first time among sketches for the opening measures of the quartet Op. 132,[57] before he had arrived at the final version of the latter.[58] The obvious thematic relationship between Op. 132 (first movement, mm. 1, 75), Op. 133 (*x*-theme), and Op. 131 (first movement; seventh movement, mm. 1, 22) has been unduly stressed by commentators. After all, thematic community *per se* does not make a work better, for it can be mere technical manipulation. More important is to recognize, as Erich Schenk has done, that Beethoven returns here to the baroque art of varying theme-types. It has long been generally acknowledged that in the baroque period thematic conception is largely a metamorphosis of universal theme-types.[59] One of the most widespread of these universal types is that which I have designated as "pathotype".[60] This motive-type or theme-type consists of the first and fifth scale degrees in minor, framed by the diminished seventh of the sixth and seventh degree, in any melodic succession (the most common are 5\1/6\7 and 5/6\7/1) or rhythmic variation. In vocal music it is inseparable from words expressing sorrow, affliction, grief. A vast number of examples could be given. It is especially common as a fugue theme. But in the *Great Fugue* Beethoven uses the venerable formula in an entirely new manner. For the first time in its long history, the type is employed in a major key (Bb), transferred to the supertonic. The diminished seventh which frames the fifth (c'-g'; see Ex. 2) is in turn framed by the octave (bb-bb).[61] A singular feature of this subject is that, from the third note onward, it contains its own inversion. (For this reason its variant form at mm. 416ff can be considered either as the normal form or as the inversion). The form in which the theme first appears (in dotted half notes) has been well characterized as the "supreme monumentalization ... of the traditional idiom".[62]

The fact that Beethoven allows both of his themes (*x* and *y*) to appear simultaneously in the first entry (m. 31) is not to be interpreted as an "intensification" in relationship to the fugues of the piano sonatas Opp. 106 and

[57] D-B Beethoven-Autograph 11, fasc. 2, ff. 26v-27; NOTTEBOHM, II, 250.

[58] Not until *ibid.*, f. 29.

[59] Erich SCHENK, *Über Begriff und Wesen des musikalischen Barock*, ZfMw, XVII, 1935, p. 391: "vielfach nichts anderes als variative Ausgestaltung der Universal-Thementypen".

[60] *Fugue and Fugato*, pp. 91f and 112, identifying three dozen examples from the second half of the eighteenth century in fugues for instrumental ensemble. Cf. also above, pp. 491f.

[61] Riemann's 'correction' (THAYER, V, 296, footnote) of the variant readings of the theme in mm. 28 and 33 is not justified; the notation of the autograph is unambiguous.

[62] Erich SCHENK, *Barock bei Beethoven*, in *Beethoven und die Gegenwart: Festschrift Ludwig Schiedermair zum 60. Geburtstag*, Berlin, Dümmler, 1937, p. 215.

110.[63] It is simply determined by the instrumentation. Unlike keyboard fugues, which nearly always begin with a single theme, it had been customary in the Austrian quartet-fugues to begin with two subjects. This was the norm for most of Albrechtberger's fugues for string ensemble, and Haydn too adheres to this tradition of the multiple fugue in his quartet fugues Op. 20 "con due", "tre" and "quattro soggetti".

In its indebtedness to Austrian fugal tradition and particularly to Albrechtsberger's theory and practice the *Great Fugue* is, of course, not an isolated phenomenon among Beethoven's late works. To show it in this context we may indicate here other direct and indirect influences of the teacher.[64] (By far the greater part of Albrechtsberger's instrumental music consisted of fugues: 99 for keyboard[65] and 159 for string instruments). In the sketches for the fugue of the 'cello sonata Op. 102, no. 2 Beethoven tried out strettos (*Engführungen*) with entries of the thema at intervals of three, two and one measures respectively,[66] for he had been taught by Albrechtsberger to write strettos with entries at increasingly shorter time intervals.[67] In the last section of the *Heiliger Dankgesang* in the Lydian mode in the quartet Op. 132 he returned to a particular type of fugue which he had practised with him: the chorale fugue.[68] For the use of an ecclesiastical mode and a chorale theme in a fugue for string quartet he could have found precedents in the works of Albrechtsberger, who composed a fugal quartet "modi phryggi"; his keyboard fugue Op. 1, no. 6 on the chorale "Christus ist erstanden" was arranged for string quartet; the string trio Op. 8, no. 4 has a fugue on "Herr, ich glaube".[69] The dovetailing of entries in Opp. 132 and Op. 133 (sections A and D) corresponds to Albrechtberger's theory and practice.[70] In writing

---

[63] RATZ, p. 84.

[64] Correspondences with Albrechtsberger's theory and pratice are pointed out where they exist. It goes without saying that I do not claim to account for Beethoven's style solely in this way.

[65] Alexander SCHRAMECK-KIRCHNER, *J. G. Albrechtsbergers Fugen für Tasteninstrumente*, ms. diss., Vienna, 1954.

[66] Designated "erste Enge", "2te Enge", and "3te Enge" – Miller-Koch-Scheide sketch-book, US-PR, SV 364, p. 47.

[67] ALBRECHTSBERGER, pp. 193f, copied by Beethoven – cf. SEYFRIED, pp. 204ff (the passage is authentic). The procedure was recommended also by MARPURG, I, 120, and others. Cf. *Fugue and Fugato*, pp. 72, 210, 233.

[68] *Fugue and Fugato*, pp. 205, 254. Cf. ALBRECHTSBERGER, chapter 27: "Von der Fuge mit einem Chorale". Beethoven had written three such fugues on themes given to him by Albrechtsberger.

[69] *Fugue and Fugato*, pp. 296, 292; also 249, 252f.

[70] Cf. *Fugue and Fugato*, pp. 62f. The second voice "fängt also gleich über oder unter der letzten Note der vollendeten ersten Stimme an" ["thus begins immediately above or below the last note of the first voice" – ALBRECHTSBERGER, p. 183] in almost all of Albrechtsberger's fugues. This pro-

the fugue theme of the piano sonata Op. 110 Beethoven may have recalled Albrechtsberger's quartet-fugue Op. 1, no. 4:

Ex. 6. Albrechtsberger: Quartet fugue Op. 1, no. 4.

Ex. 7. Beethoven: Piano sonata Op. 110, third movement, mm. 27-31.

The quartet-fugue in C-major,[71] written by Beethoven for Albrechtsberger in 1795, had already used the theme of another fugue from the same collection:

Ex. 8. Albrechtsberger: Quartet fugue Op. 1, no. 3.

Ex. 9. Beethoven: Quartet fugue in C-major.

Further thematic relationships to fugues of Albrechtsberger are found in the fugues of Beethoven's Op. 102, no. 2 (Albrechtsberger Op. 19, no. 5), Op. 124 (Albrechtsberger Op. 1, no. 2 [keyboard], Op. 8, no. 1, Op. 24, no. 5) and Op. 125 (Albrechtsberger Op. 8, no. 6). In these cases there is no question of direct quotation or imitation, but merely similarity of theme-type. The heading *"con alcune licenze"* of the fugue in the *Hammerklavier* sonata Op. 106, similar to the *"tantôt libre"* in Op. 133, is a reminiscence of Albrechtsberger's custom of writing the word *"Licenz"* (or *"Lic."*) over the

cedure already characterized the early ricercars and was often replaced by intervening codettas in baroque fugues – see above, p. 63.

71 «Nagels Musik-Archiv», no. 186, Kassel, Nagel, 1955.

permissible exceptions to the rules of strict counterpoint in the fugues of his pupils.[72]

In many respects, the fugue in Op. 106 is to be interpreted in the same way as Op. 133. Peculiar to both is the unprecedented, almost exaggerated employment of contrapuntal artifices, which in turn leads to great length. (The fugue Op. 106 even makes use of the extremely rare device of retrograde motion; Beethoven took this directly from Marpurg's treatise on fugue,[73] as is proven by his transcript of Marpurg's examples of retrograde motion among the sketches for Op. 106).[74] In this respect, both fugues have no connection with those of the Austrian chamber music from the second half of the eighteenth century, which make almost no employment of contrapuntal artifices.[75]

Without the suggestion of a great theoretical compendium the *Great Fugue*, that "giant movement", would never have been written. As a practical composition it has roots in the tradition of the baroque *Kunstbuch* (skillbook).[76] Here its direct prototype is J. S. Bach's *Art of Fugue*. We know that Beethoven was familiar with this work.[77] The *Great Fugue* was his *Art of Fugue*, his *summary of the various fugal techniques* – hence the subsequent dedication to his pupil in counterpoint Archduke Rudolph, for whom he had originally copied the passage from Albrechtsberger, the clue to our interpretation.

The differences between the two compositions separated by momentous changes in the world of thought are obvious: Bach's work relatively static and didactic, Beethoven's dynamic and emotional, etc. Beethoven wrote *his* version, the freest and most subjective of all *Kunstbücher*; "imagination" and the "really poetic element" have asserted their rights.[78] That he, unlike Bach, was obliged to take his point of departure (and no more) from theory in no way prevented him, at the height of his powers, from writing an extraordinary and highly original work. Only before the background of tradition can its uniqueness and the personal accomplishment of the composer be determined.

---

[72] Cf. NOTTEBOHM, *Beethoven's Studien*. Albrechtsberger often uses the word in his *Anweisung*. Francescoantonio VALLOTTI (1697-1780), consistently strict, does not admit such freedoms: "le leggi del contrappunto debbono, per mio parere, osservarsi sempre da principio sino al fine, e il fare altrimenti è una licenza ardita e senza scusa" ["The laws of counterpoint must ... always be observed, from the beginning to the end; to do otherwise is a bold and inexcusable licence"] – *Trattato della moderna musica*, Padua, Basilica del Santo, 1950, p. 351.

[73] MARPURG, II, tab. 16, fig. 1-2.

[74] Boldrini sketch-book, p. 8 – NOTTEBOHM, II, 351f. The fugue of the sonata Op. 110 employs even double diminution.

[75] *Fugue and Fugato*, pp. 73ff.

[76] On the 'Kunstbuch' cf. Erich SCHENK, *"Das Musikalische Opfer" von Johann Sebastian Bach*, «Anzeiger der Österreichischen Akademie der Wissenschaften», phil.-hist. Klasse, XC, 1953, p. 55, and «Die Musikforschung», XXIV, 1971, pp. 486f.

[77] *Fugue and Fugato*, p. 214.

[78] Beethoven's words, quoted above, p. 555.

XVIII.

"SEGRETO COMUNICATO DA PAGANINI":
A HISTORY OF HARMONICS ON THE VIOLIN

The literature on Paganini's 'secret'[1] is as extensive as it is futile and sensational, and the first word in the title of the present paper is surely enough to frighten away any respectable scholar. Previous discussions, from the romantic rumors of a pact with Satan to the rational explanation of violinistic techniques now public domain, have been implicitly unanimous in one point: that Paganini himself never committed his "secret" to writing. The discovery of an autograph document expressly labelled "segreto" may justify a return to the popular subject.

The location of the original manuscript of this document could not be ascertained. I found a photograph of it in the Maia Bang Hohn collection of Paganiniana in the Library of Congress.[2] Those items of this collection which are listed in Maia Bang's own manuscript catalogue have been used repeatedly by biographers of Paganini. Hitherto inaccessible was a quantity of uncatalogued material, apparently added to the collection sometime between the writing of the catalogue and the death of Maia Bang in 1940. While working as a librarian in the Music Division of the Library of Congress I catalogued this material in a supplement to Maia Bang's catalogue. There our photograph

---

[1] E.g. Godefroi Engelbert ANDERS, *Niccolo Paganini, sa vie, sa personne, et quelques mots sur son secret*, Paris, Delaunay, 1830; Spartaco COPERTINI, *Il segreto di Paganini*, «Il Piccolo di Parma», 14 April 1920; Roberto MANTOVANI, *Le Secret de Paganini*, Paris, 1922; Albert JAROSY, *Nouvelle théorie du doigté (Paganini et son secret)*, Paris, M. Eschig, 1924; Edgar ISTEL, *The Secret of Paganini's Technique*, «Musical Quarterly», XVI, 1930, pp. 101-116; Carl FLESCH, *Apropos of Paganini's Secret*, «The Strad», L, 1939, pp. 205-207; S. L. SALZEDO, *Paganini's Secret at last*, London, Nicholson & Watson, 1946; A. GIORDANO, *Il segreto di Paganini visto da un liutaio*, paper delivered at the conference *Paganini: divo e comunicatore*, Genoa, 3-5 December 2004. See also Gian Carlo CONESTABILE, *Vita di Niccolo Paganini* [1851], nuova edizione con aggiunte e note di Federico Mompellio, Milan etc., Soc. Ed. Dante Alighieri, 1936, pp. 389-426.

[2] On this collection cf. Harold SPIVACKE, *Paganiniana*, «The Library of Congress Quarterly Journal of Current Acquisitions», II, 1945, pp. 49-67.

bears the number 998. A comparison with known Paganini autographs leaves no doubt as to the authenticity.

The document consists of two leaves of music manuscript paper, probably forming a single bifolio. One leaf bears a double certification of authenticity and tells about the past history of the document:[3]

[Fol. 1, right column:]

I hereby certify that this / manuscript is in the hand / writing of my grandfather / Nicolo Paganini, the / celebrated violinist. / Parma, March 27th, 1900. / [Signed] Andrea Paganini.

[Another hand:]

Visto, si dichiara vera / ed autografa la firma / del Sig. Andrea Paganini / sopra apposta e chi / rilascia su carta libera / per semplice norma / amministrativa / Vigiotto di Parma, / 27 Marzo 1900 / [stamp] Il Sindaco / F. Mozzeti.

[Seen, it is declared the true and autograph signature of Sig. Andrea Paganini above (and) who renders it on unstamped paper for simple administrative measure, Vigiotto di Parma, 27 March 1900, the Mayor F. Mozzeti].

[Fol. 1, left column, another hand:]

This document was purchased by / me from Signora Massima [?] Fedora Germi, / the wife of L. G. Germi in 1883 who was / the advocate for Nicolò Paganini, for whom / it was written, & I have now / presented it to Miss Valentina Crespi / as a token of my esteem. / G. C. Duncan Aug. 5, 1921.[4]

The second leaf (see Plate XVIII.1) turns out to be a demonstration of the method of performing continuous scales of artificial harmonics with double stops in parallel thirds. The text and the music are in Paganini's handwriting, the staves enclosed in square brackets are my own:

[Fol. 2:]

Segreto comunicato e raccomandato da Paganini al suo caro amico L. G. Germi. / Armonici a doppie corde di terza.

[Secret communicated and recommended by Paganini to his dear friend L. G. Germi. Harmonics in double stops at the interval of a third].

---

[3] This certification was made for Mr. Duncan (see below – hence the use of English) while the document was in his possession.

[4] On Crespi and Duncan see Postscriptum, below, pp. 579f.

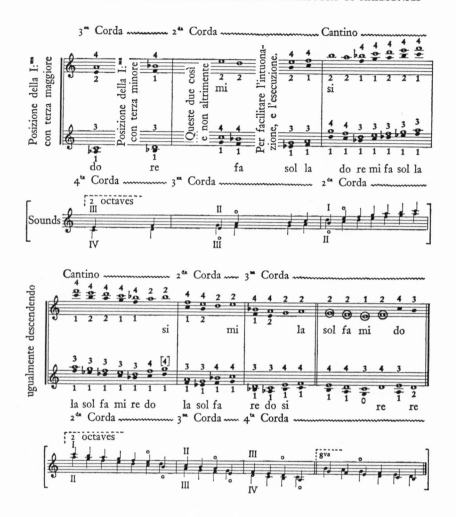

Mio caro Germi, ti prego per l'Amicizia / che mi professi, di lacerare la presente tosto / che l'avrai letta, e di non farti ve- / dere ad ese- / guirgli, perché ti rappiran- / no il segreto, e se / potessi ti comuniche- / rei un poco della mia magia / per abbili- / tarti ad eseguirli sul muso di chiunque / senza timore di propagarli. Addio.
Li poco ubbidienti quattro Armonici / qui sopra fatti ⊙ deesi appoggiare il dito

My dear Germi, I beg you, for the friendship which you profess to me, to tear up the present [paper] as soon as you have read it, and not to let yourself be seen performing it, because they will steal the secret from you; and if I could I would communicate a little of my magic to you, to enable you to perform it in the face of anyone without fear of propagating it. Addio.

con qualche grado di soppressione / ma non sono necessari.[5]

The not very obedient four harmonics made here above ⊙ one must place the finger with some degree of pressure but they are not necessary.[5]

The recipient of the document, Luigi Guglielmo Germi (1786-1870) in Genoa, was not only Paganini's advocate, the administrator of his vast fortune, but also his closest friend, most faithful correspondent, and an amateur violinist. We can hardly reproach him for not following his friend's exhortation to destroy the paper as soon as he read it. The words "secret" and "magic", used here and frequently by Paganini in writings and conversations, can be considered typical of his mode of expression. For example:[6]

Sehr oft kam Paganini in seinen Gesprächen mit mir darauf zurück, daß er der Welt einst, nachdem er seine Reisen vollendet und sich gleichsam in die Ruhe zurückgezogen haben werde, ein musikalisches Geheimnis mittheilen wolle, was in keinem Conservatorium der Musik zu erlernen sey.

Paganini very often repeated in his conversations with me that he intended some day, after he had finished his travels and as it were retired, to communicate to the world a musical secret which is to be acquired in no conservatory of music.

As proof of the efficacy of this "secret" Paganini cited the miraculous transformation of Gaetano Ciandelli from a mediocre 'cellist to a virtuoso within three days, and certified it on paper for his biographer: "Giacomo Ciandelli of Naples became the first violoncellist of the Royal Theaters there through the magic communicated to him by Paganini, and he could be the first in Europe".[7] Here again we find the words "magic" and "communicated by Paganini". Similarly in letters to Germi: "But to tell you the truth, a certain magic issued from my performance which I could not describe to you", 1 July 1818; "I shall not tell you of the magic which came out of my instrument in the con-

---

[5] The four encircled notes are not harmonics, but make use of a trick not employed in legitimate violin playing: the string is pressed lightly at a non-nodal point and 'squeaks' to produce a note an octave higher than written. The vertcal lines of text: 1) "First position with major third"; 2) "Second position with minor third"; 3-4) "These two thus and not otherwise, to facilitate the intonation and the performance"; 5) "Descending in the same manner".

[6] Julius Max SCHOTTKY, *Paganini's Leben und Treiben als Künstler und als Mensch*, Prague, Calve, 1830, pp. 276-278.

[7] "Gaetano Ciandelli di Napoli per la magia comunicatagli da Paganini divenne primo Violoncello dei R. R. Teatri cola, e potrebbe essere il primo d'Europa", *ibid.*, p. 279. The story is repeated by François Joseph FÉTIS, *Notice biographique sur Nicolo Paganini*, Paris, Schonenberger, 1851, p. 79, and refuted by S. L. SALZEDO, *Paganini and Ciandelli*, «The Strad», L, 1934, pp. 109-111.

cert given here", i.e. in Karlsruhe, February 1831.[8] The word "secret" as employed by Paganini is not to be taken too seriously. He uses it frequently and indiscriminately in his notebooks for culinary recipes and prescriptions of quack doctors, for anything from ravioli to a laxative.

When did Paganini send the document to Germi? If we look at his famous 24 Capricci Opus 1, we find that they make no use whatsoever of harmonics, although they do exploit every other conceivable violinistic effect. However, this cannot necessarily be construed as evidence that our document postdates the composition of the caprices (presumably first decade of the nineteenth century), for we know that Paganini already employed harmonics in his playing at Lucca, i.e. between the fall of 1805 and the summer of 1808.[9] Probably he did not wish to make his "secret" known even in 1818, when he had the caprices published by Ricordi, and for this reason did not include passages in harmonics.[10] On the other hand, by 1830 every ramification of his artificial double harmonics had been revealed in a publication by Carl Guhr (see below), so he would not have sent his "secret" to Germi after that year. Guhr observed that Paganini employed especially thin strings to facilitate the production of harmonics: "Paganini's playing requires thin strings for the following reasons: ... Second, the harmonics, especially the artificial ones, respond better in the higher positions".[11] Through letters written to Germi from Naples we learn that Paganini procured strings for him in 1820: "Tomorrow I shall order the [violin] strings for you in order to forward them to you when they are made", 2 August; "With the first ship which departs I shall send you the strings", 27 October; "I have bought the strings for you and shall send them to you by sea", 12 December.[12] The connection of the "segreto comunicato" with these letters suggests that the document might have been sent to Germi in this year 1820, if not earlier.[13]

---

[8] "ma a dirti il vero scaturì dalla mia esecuzione una certa magia che non saprei descriverti"; "non ti parlerò della magia che scaturì dal mio strumento nel concerto dato qui" – *Epistolario*, I, Milan/Geneva, 2006, pp. 122, 653.

[9] See the quotation at the end of this article.

[10] Occasional indications of harmonics in posthumous editions of these and other works of Paganini have been added by editors. Paganini may, of course, have played passages in harmonics which he did not notate as such.

[11] "Paganinis Spiel erfordert aus folgenden Gründen schwache Saiten: ... 2.[tens] Sprechen die Flageolet Töne, besonders die künstlichen, auf schwachen Saiten in den höheren Lagen besser an" – p. 3.

[12] "Domani ti comanderò le corde armoniche per inoltrartele quando saranno fatte"; "Col primo bastimento che partirà ti spedirò le corde armoniche"; "Ti ho comperate le corde, e te le spedirò per mare" – *Epistolario*, I, 188, 192f.

[13] The words "corde armoniche", however, do not mean strings "suitable for harmonics", but simply "for musical instruments", as opposed to ordinary strings or cords.

Paganini's harmonics impressed the contemporary audiences more than any other single feature of his playing. Johann Heinrich Küster praised them as early as 1819, nine years before Paganini first left Italy: "This is proven above all by Paganini, who knows how to apply them with unbelievable dexterity, good taste, and in an ingenious manner, single as well as double, without ever missing a single one".[14] A report of a concert in the Redoutensaal in Vienna mentions "his wonderfully sweet flageolet notes, for which, in virtue of their frequent employment, he seems to cherish almost too great a partiality".[15] The Prague correspondent of the *Osservatore Triestino* admires "his double stops in harmonics, as things of ultimate perfection".[16] In bad virtuoso tradition, Paganini did not feel obliged to adhere strictly to the original notation of a composition; Wilhelm Speyer reported to Ludwig Spohr in a letter of 17 September 1829:[17]

Höchst interessant war der Vortrag der Beethovenschen Sonate [Op. 24]. Um Ihnen das Wunderlichste davon zu erzählen, so vernehmen Sie, dass er nach der Wiederholung des ersten Teils des Rondos das Thema in Flageolett-Oktav-Doppelgriffen hören liess!	The performance of Beethoven's sonata [Op. 24] was extremely interesting. To tell you the most bizarre part of it, learn that after the repetition of the first section of the rondo he let the theme be heard in harmonic double stops of the octave!

On 18 December 1829, Paganini played a concert for the Frankfurt Museum: "There he most brilliantly developed ... his eminent skill in the alternation of normal playing with passages in harmonics".[18] Gottfried Weber, although quasi-illiterate, is more specific:[19]

Sein Flageolettspiel ist in der That etwas ganz Anderes, als das, was man bisher	His playing in harmonics is indeed something quite different from that which was

---

[14] "Diess beweiset vor andern Paganini, der sie mit unglaublicher Fertigkeit, gutem Geschmacke und auf sinnreiche Weise, einfach wie doppelt . . . anzubringen weiss, ohne dass ihm ein einziger versagt" – AmZ, XXI, 1819, col. 701 (see below).

[15] "seine wundersüßen Flageolettöne, für welche er, vermöge derselben öfteren Anwendung, eine fast allzugroße Vorliebe zu hegen scheint" – unsigned review, AmZ, XXX, 1828, col. 310.

[16] "le sue corde doppie a flageolet, come cose dell'ultima perfezione" – quoted in Arturo CODIGNOLA, *Paganini intimo*, Bergamo, Nave, 1935, pp. 64f.

[17] Edward SPEYER, *Wilhelm Speyer der Liederkomponist 1790-1878*, Munich, Drei Masken, 1925, p. 103.

[18] "Aufs Glänzendste entwickelte er darin ... seine eminente Fertigkeit in Abwechslung der gewöhnlichen Spielart mit den Flageolet-Passagen" – «La Flora», Munich, 25 December 1829, quoted by SCHOTTKY, p. 218.

[19] Carl GUHR and Gottfried WEBER, *Paganinis Kunst, die Violine zu spielen*, «Caecilia», XI, 1829, pp. 76-86; the passage quoted is from a footnote on p. 83, signed "GW".

auf dem Instrumente kannte; es ist nicht das, auf die wenigen, grade als Aliquottöne der leeren Saiten sich darbietenden Töne beschränkte, und aus der lückenhaften Reihe dieser wenigen sogenannten natürlichen oder leeren Flageolettöne, ängstlich eine zusammenhängende Tonfigur zusammenlesende, und nur einzelne dabei entstehenden Lücken durch Greifen mit dem ersten und Anlehnen eines höheren Fingers (durch sogenannte künstliche oder gegriffene Flageolettöne) ausfüllende, sondern ein durch keine Schwierigkeit beschränktes Gebrauchen jedes zu jeder beliebigen Melodie erforderlichen, künstlichen Flageolet-Tones, sogar zu ganzen zweistimmigen Melodieen, – was freilich ans Unbegreifliche grenzt.

hitherto known on the instrument; it is not limited to just the few partial tones rendered by the open strings; it does not timidly gather together a connected phrase from the incomplete series of these few so-called natural or open harmonics and fill out only single, thus created gaps by stopping with the first finger and touching with a higher one (through so-called artificial or stopped harmonics); but [it is] the employment, limited by no difficulty, of every artificial harmonic necessary for any given melody, even for whole two-part melodies, – which truly borders on the incomprehensible.

Carl Seidel found that Paganini's double harmonics "spoke intensely to the heart and ... truly enchant".[20] Eugene Sauzay reported, after Paganini's debut in Paris (1831): "all of us practiced for months nothing else but pizzicati with the left hand and double harmonics".[21] Few writers were critical of the virtuoso's acrobatics. In the «Allgemeine Musikalische Zeitung» of 21 October 1829 we read: "too many harmonics";[22] and Ludwig Spohr's words – notwithstanding the dedication from Carl Guhr – recall the sound judgment of Leopold Mozart (see below, no. 15 and p. 574):[23]

Besonders die sogenannten künstlichen Flageolet-Töne müssen, weil sie von dem natürlichen Tone des Instruments ganz abweichen, als untauglich verworfen werden. ... So grosses Aufsehen der berühmte Paganini in neuester Zeit durch das Wiedererwecken des veralteten und schon ganz vergessenen Flage-

Especially the so-called artificial harmonics must be rejected as useless, because they deviate completely from the natural sounds of the instrument. ... However much attention the famous Paganini has attracted in most recent times through the revival of the antiquated and already completely forgotten harmo-

---

[20] "mächtig zum Herzen redeten, und ... wahrhaft bezaubern" – SCHOTTKY, p. 132, footnote.
[21] Carl FLESCH, p. 205.
[22] "zu viele Flageoletgriffe" – unsigned review, AmZ, XXXI, 1829, col. 695.
[23] Louis SPOHR, Violinschule, Vienna, Haslinger, 1832, p. 108.

oletspiels und durch seine eminente Fertigkeit darin auch gemacht hat und so verführerisch ein solches Beyspiel seyn mag, so muss ich doch allen jungen Geigern ernstlich rathen, ihre Zeit nicht bey dem Studium desselben zu verlieren und darüber Nützlicheres zu versäumen. Als Autorität für diese Ansicht kann ich die grössesten Geiger aller Zeiten anführen, z.B. Pugnani, Tartini, Corelli, Viotti, Eck, Rode, Kreutzer, Baillot, Lafont u. a., von denen auch nicht einer in Paganinis Weise flageolet gespielt hat.

nics and through his eminent skill therein, and however seductive such an example may be, yet I must seriously advise all young violinists not to waste their time with the study of the same and thereby neglect more useful things. As authority for this view I can cite the greatest violinists of all time, e.g. Pugnani, Tartini, Corelli, Viotti, Eck, Rode, Kreutzer, Baillot, Lafont, etc., not one of whom played harmonics in Paganini's manner [but cf. below, p. 571, no. 15].

How much of Paganini's "secret" was really new? The sources for a history of harmonics include the following:

A. PRE-PAGANINI: PREDOMINANTLY MUSICAL COMPOSITIONS, FRENCH AND ITALIAN, ca. 1738-1801.

1. Jean-Joseph Cassanea de MONDONVILLE (1711-72): *Les sons harmoniques: sonates a violon seul avec la basse continue par M.ʳ Mondonville œuvre 4.° ... à Paris et à Lille ... avec privilège du Roy*, author, and Boivin, Le Clerc [ca. 1738]. Six sonatas, in B minor, C, G, A, F, and G, preceded by a four-page "Avertissement utile pour jouer les sonates dans le goût de l'auteur".

2. Charles de LUSSE (born ca. 1720): *Six sonates pour la flute traversière avec une tablature des sons harmoniques par M. de Lusse Iᵉʳ œuvre ... à Paris chez l'auteur* [1751].

3. L'ABBÉ LE FILS [Joseph-Barnabé Saint-Sévin, 1727-1803]: *Duo italien de Bertolde* from the *Deuxième recueil d'airs français et italiens, avec des variations pour deux violons ... chez l'auteur* [Paris, ca. 1754].

4. Domenico FERRARI (ca. 1722-80): *VI sonate a violino solo e basso dedicate a sua eccellenza il signor principe Don Lorenzo Corsini di Domenico Ferrari ... opera 1ᵃ, ... chez M.ʳ Huberty, Paris* [between 1756 and 1760].

5. L'ABBÉ LE FILS: *Principes du violon pour apprendre le doigté de cet instrument et les différends agréments dont il est susceptible, dédiés a Monsieur le Marquis de Rodouan de Damartin par M.ʳ L'Abbé le Fils, ordinaire de l'Académie Royale de Musique ... à Paris chez Des Lauriers ... A. P. D. R.* [1761]. Pages 72-73: "Des sons harmoniques".

6. Charles CHABRAN [Carlo Chiabrano, born ca. 1723]: *Six Solos for a Violin, with a thorough-bass for the harpsichord* [Op. 1], London, Peter Welcker [1763]. Sonatas nos. 2 (second and third movements) and 5 (first movement), with passages in "sons armoniques", the latter reprinted in Jean-Baptiste CARTIER, *L'art du violon*, Paris, Decombe, 1798, pp. 94-101.

7. Jean-Jacques ROUSSEAU (1712-78): *Dictionnaire de musique*, Paris, Duchesne, 1768. Pages 449f: article *Sons harmoniques ou sons flutés*. Plate G, fig. 3: *Table des sons harmoniques sensibles et appréciables sur le violoncelle* (eight natural harmonics, without musical notation).

8. Pierre Nicholas HOUSSET dit LA HOUSSAYE (1735-1818): *Sei sonate a violino solo e basso dedicate all'illustrissimo signor di Montribloud di Pietro La Houssaye opera prima*, Paris, Sieber [ca. 1773].

9. Francesco GALEAZZI, *Elementi teorico-pratici di musica con un saggio sopra l'arte di suonare il violino*, Rome, Pilucchi Cracas, 1791-96, I, 172-177: "Delle voci armonici".

10. Francesco CAMPAGNOLI (1751-1827): *Metodo della meccanica progressiva per suonare il violino*, Turin, n.d., pp. 185-188: "L'arte di suonare a monocordo e d'eseguire i suoni armonici", with five short pieces for two violins, in which the upper part uses artificial harmonics (Allemanda, Andante, Allegro, Andantino, Minuetto).

B. POST-PAGANINI: PREDOMINANTLY GERMAN DIDACTIC WORKS, 1815-1840

11. J. G. E. MAASS: *Ueber die Flaschinettöne, besonders der Saiten*, AmZ, Leipzig, XVII, no. 29, 19 July 1815, col. 477-487, and *Beilage: Tafel der Flageolet-Töne*.

12. Johann Heinrich KÜSTER: *Einiges über die Ausübung der Flageolettöne auf der Violine, Ibid.*, XXI, no. 42, Leipzig, 20 October 1819, col. 701-707, and four pages of music as *Beilage*.

13. Joseph BREYMANN: *Abhandlung über die Flageolet-Töne*, AmZ, Vienna, IV, 1820, col. 505-508, 561-564, 569-572, 577ff, 593ff, 603f.

14. Niccolò DE GIOVANNI: *Metodo teorico pratico per ben fare sul violino gli armonici semplici, trillati e doppi*. Manuscript, quoted by CONESTABILE/MOMPELLIO with the following comment: [24]

> Explains the technique of harmonics according to the method of Paganini. This manuscript belongs to Prof. Franzoni, who, questioned by me about the year in which it was written, replied: 'I infer from what my teacher Domenico De Giovanni told me, that the little book was written in the 1820s about 1827 or 28, the period in which De Giovanni had several encounters with Paganini in Genoa'.

15. Carl GUHR (1787-1848): *Ueber Paganini's Kunst, die Violine zu spielen: ein Anhang zu jeder bis jetzt erschienenen Violinschule nebst einer Abhandlung über das Flageoletspiel in einfachen und Doppeltönen. Den Heroen der Violine Rode, Kreutzer, Baillot, Spohr zugeeignet von Carl Guhr Director und Kapellmeister des Theaters zu Frankfurt a/M.*, Mainz, B. Schott's Söhne, plate no. 3194. Preface dated November 1829. A French edition, *L'art de jouer le violon de Paganini ...*, was published by Schott in Paris, and an English edition by Novello in London.

---

[24] "Spiega la tecnica dei suoni armonici secondo il metodo di Paganini. Questo manoscritto è posseduto dal prof. Franzoni, il quale, da me interrogato circa l'anno in cui venne scritto, mi rispose: 'Deduco, da quanto mi disse il mio maestro Domenico De Giovanni, che quel libretto fu scritto negli anni dal 1820 circa 1827 o 28, epoca in cui il De Giovanni ebbe parecchi incontri col Paganini in Genova'" – p. 641.

Nos. 4-13 of the thirteen *Übungsstücke für das Flageolet einfach und doppelt* (pp. 34-38 of the German edition) were composed by Johann Heinrich Küster. Guhr's report originally appeared in «Caecilia», XI, 1829 – see above, note 19 – whence it was immediately translated into French by Fétis for his «Revue Musicale», December 1829.

16. Joseph von BLUMENTHAL: *Abhandlung über die Eigenthümlichkeit des Flageolet (sons harmoniques oder sons flutés) als Anleitung zur practischen Ausübung desselben auf der Violine, verfasst, und dem Herrn Ig. Fr. Edl. v. Mosel s. k. k. apostoli. Majestät wirklicher Hofrat achtungsvoll gewidmet von Jos. v. Blumenthal. 43tes Werk ... Wien, bei Ant. Diabelli und Comp.* (plate no. 3032 [= 1829]).

17. Karl WLCŽEK. Schottky, in 1830, mentions "that Herr von Blumenthal in Vienna published a harmonics method of his own; [and] that Herr Karl Wlcžek in Prague is occupied with a similar work".[25] Apparently it was never published.

18. Justus Johann Friedrich DOTZAUER (1783-1860): *Violoncell-Flageolett-Schule: ein Hülfsmittel zum Studium reiner Intonation nebst einem Anhang über das Pizzicato mit den Fingern der linken Hand, Op. 147*, Leipzig, Hofmeister, plate no. 2239 [= 1837].

19. ANONYMOUS: *Paganini's Method of Producing the Harmonic Double Stops*, London, 1840.

Natural harmonics had, of course, been used ever since the later Middle Ages on the *trompette marine*. This instrument was still played in France during the early decades of the eighteenth century by its last and greatest virtuoso, Jean-Baptiste Prin, who, like Johann Gletle and Lorenzo de Castro, also composed music for it.[26] The earliest application of harmonics to the violin is credited by Marpurg and subsequent authors to Mondonville.[27] In the *Avertissement* preceding the sonatas *Les sons harmoniques* (ca. 1738) Mondonville briefly describes the production of single, natural harmonics. He uses them sporadically throughout the six sonatas both in the violin and the continuo violoncello to facilitate changes of position, designating them by the sign "∿" and, for all harmonics except the first, by two notes resembling double stops, one for the position of the finger and one for the actual pitch. The *Tablature des sons harmoniques* in the six sonatas Op. 1 of the French flautist

---

[25] "dass Hr. von Blumenthal in Wien eine eigene Flageoletschule nach Paganini herausgab; [und] daß sich Herr Karl Wlcžek zu Prag mit einem ähnlichen Werke beschäftigt" – pp. 132f.

[26] Prin called himself "enseignant à montrer à jouer de la trompette marine" ["teacher of showing how to play the marine trumpet"] and wrote a manuscript *Mémoire sur la trompette marine avec l'art d'apprendre a jouer de cet instrument sans maître, par le St. Jean-Baptiste Prin, maître a dancer de Paris et musicien de la Ville de Strasbourg* – F. W. GALPIN, *Monsieur Prin and his Trumpet Marine*, «Music and Letters», XIV, 1933, pp. 19f.

[27] «Historisch-kritische Beyträge zur Aufnahme der Musik», I, 1754, p. 469; cf. also Lionel de LA LAURENCIE, *L'École française de violon de Lully a Viotti*, Paris, De La Grave, 1922-24, I, 428.

Charles de Lusse (Paris, author [1751]) appears to have been inspired by Mondonville's publication. The earliest reference to harmonics on the violoncello associates them with Martin Berteau (Bertaud, Bertolde, d. 1756), the founder of the French school of 'cello playing. Rousseau states in his article on harmonics: "To judge them [harmonics] well, it is necessary to have heard M. Mondonville on his violin, or M. Bertaud on his violoncello, bring forth successions of these beautiful sounds".[28] The *Duo italien de Bertolde* in the *Deuxième recueil* of L'Abbé le Fils (ca. 1754)[29] is probably the next publication after Mondonville's to employ harmonics. Here we still find only natural harmonics, indicated for the first time with a zero, as they are today. About this time two Italian violinists were attracting attention at the Concert Spirituel: Carlo Chiabrano[30] and Domenico Ferrari. Their success may have been due partly to the novel use of harmonics featured in their later publications. Ferrari's sonata Op. 1, no. 5 (ca. 1756-60) ends with a menuet composed entirely of harmonics.[31]

By this time Paganini's "secret" had already been discovered: artificial harmonics are written and described for the first time in 1761 by L'Abbe le Fils in his *Principes du violon*. He calls them "sons harmoniques qui se font par le moyen de deux doigts" ["harmonics which are made by means of two fingers"], as opposed to natural harmonics "par le moyen d'un seul doigt" ["by means of a single finger" – pp. 72f], and uses a square white note to indicate the position of the stopping finger:

His examples consist of diatonic and chromatic scales and a menuet which uses exclusively natural and artificial harmonics and is written as played rather than as sounded.[32] The earliest sonata to employ artificial harmonics, no. 1 in Chiabrano's collection of 1763, was followed a decade later by La Houssaye's Op. 1, no. 1 (ca. 1773), where the harmonics are designated by the word "armonico".[33]

---

[28] "Il faut, pour en bien juger, avoir entendu M. Mondonville tirer sur son Violon, ou M. Bertaud sur son Violoncelle, des suites de ces beaux *Sons*", p. 449.

[29] De LA LAURENCIE, II, 236.

[30] Fétis confused Carlo with Francesco, a guitarist and less important composer; hence La Laurencie and *Riemann-Lexikon* (twelfth edition) still attribute the sonatas of Carlo to Francesco.

[31] DE LA LAURENCIE, II, 237.

[32] The recording which accompanies David BOYDEN, *History of Violin Playing from its Origins to 1761*, London, Oxford UP, 1965, includes a performance of this menuet.

[33] De LA LAURENCIE, I, 430 and II, 506.

The following genealogies of teachers and pupils reveals that four of our artists of harmonics can be traced back to the two great Italian violin schools of the eighteenth century:

PIEDMONTESE SCHOOL

Somis

Chiabrano   Leclair

L'Abbé

PADUAN SCHOOL

Tartini

Ferrari   La Houssaye

(The nature of harmonics must have been well known to Tartini, who had discovered combination tones on the violin and delighted in theoretical speculations). But the real arena for the display of harmonics was the Concert Spirituel in Paris. All of the artists mentioned above were closely associated with this organization. Mondonville played there from 1737 and directed the concerts from 1755 to 1762. Berteau made his debut in 1739, L'Abbé followed in 1741, La Houssaye in 1745, Chiabrano in 1751, and Ferrari in 1754.

In Germany harmonics enjoyed no such popularity. Indeed, musicians of taste disapproved of them:[34]

Wenn nun auch das beständige Einmischen des sogenannten Flascholets noch dazu kömmt; so entstehet eine recht lächerliche, und, wegen der Ungleichheit des Tones, eine wider die Natur selbst streitende Musik, bey der es oft so still wird, daß man die Ohren spitzen muß, bald aber möchte man wegen dem gähen und unangenehmen Gerassel die Ohren verstopfen. [Footnote:] Wer das Flascholet auf der Violin will hören lassen, der thut sehr gut, wenn er sich eigens Concerte oder Solo darauf setzen läßt, und keine natürliche Violinklänge darunter mischet.

When, in addition, the so-called flageolet notes are continually mixed in, then begins quite ridiculous music, contending against nature with its inequality of tone, often so faint that one must prick up one's ears, but soon one would want to plug them up because of the sudden and unpleasant clatter. [Footnote:] He who wishes to perform flageolet notes on the violin does well to have special concertos or solos [= sonatas] composed for it and not to mix in any natural violin sounds.

---

[34] Leopold MOZART, *Versuch einer gründlichen Violinschule*, Augsburg, Lotter, 1756, p. 107. Cf. also above, pp. 569f, Louis Spohr.

This comment of Leopold Mozart's is further evidence that the art of playing in harmonics was already highly developed in 1756. In German countries the technique continued to be associated with the less reputable type of musician. The vagabond fiddler Jakob Scheller (1759-1803) made a specialty of it. Ernst Ludwig Gerber heard him perform "one of the most splendid concertos of Hoffmeister" in 1794: "He played the whole first theme of the rondo in harmonics on his instrument with such trueness, lightness, and purity, that it was in no way distinguishable from organ pipes".[35]

The list of sources given above falls clearly into two groups of 9-10 works each. The first group is exclusively Italo-French and extends from about 1738 to ca. 1791. The second group is separated from the first by a gap and is predominantly German. This gap explains Spohr's statement that Paganini "revived" the "antiquated" and "completely forgotten" technique of harmonics. There can be no doubt that this technique was unfamiliar in Austria, Bohemia, and Germany at the time of Paganini's appearance – the contemporary reviews are full of astonishment at the novelty, and our theoretical sources from the early nineteenth century emphasize that the subject of harmonics had never been adequately expounded (see below). Paganini's harmonic virtuosity went far beyond that of his predecessors and was surely quite new. He could justly claim as his "secret" the artificial harmonics in double stops, employing all four fingers simultaneously; there is no earlier record of this. Also the pseudo-harmonics (see above, note 5) appear to be his invention. The strongest testimony to the impact of Paganini's harmonics is the fact that they directly gave birth to a new type of treatise, the *Flageoletschulen* or special harmonic methods which I have listed (nos. 12, 14-19).

J. G. E. Maass observes in his purely theoretical essay of 1815 that "so few players achieve significant skill in the production of harmonics. ... To this end, however, the knowledge of the nature and origin of these sounds would have to be more widely disseminated among the artists".[36] He mentions only one type of artificial harmonic, that in which the string is touched a fourth above the stopped note, sounding two octaves

---

[35] "eines der herrlichsten Concerte von Hoffmeister"; "Den ganzen ersten Satz [= Thema] des Rondo spielte er in Flageolettönen auf seinem Instrumente so wahr, leicht und rein, daß es auf keine Weise von Pfeifwerken zu unterscheiden war" – *Neues historisch-biographisches Lexikon der Tonkünstler*, Leipzig, A. Kühnel, 1812-14, IV, 47.

[36] "so wenig Spieler in Hervorbringung der Flaschinettöne eine bedeutende Fertigkeit erlangen. ... Zu diesem Ende müsste freylich auch die Kenntnis von der Natur und Entstehungsart dieser Töne unter den Künstlern allgemeiner verbreitet werden" – col. 478ff.

higher.[37] He does not mention Paganini, and there was probably no influence exerted in either direction. Four years later J. H. Küster opens the series of treatises inspired by Paganini. After praising the latter's harmonic artistry (see above, p. 568) he asserts: "The path which leads to these advantages is known to only a few, is trodden by even fewer, and, if I am not mistaken, has never been adequately unveiled to the performing artist in writings".[38] The contents of Küster's essay can be indicated by its rubrics: "Eine kleine Anleitung zum Flageolet-Spiele auf der Violine, sowohl in einfachen als doppelten Tönen (Doppelgriffen)", "Von den Griffen mit einem festen und einem losen Finger", "Von der Art, die Flageolettöne zu schreiben". Küster is the first to publish artificial harmonics in double stops. He employs two systems of notation: a) for the purpose of demonstration he writes the touched notes and indicates the interval above the stopped notes by a Roman numeral, e.g.:

---

[37] The various types of artificial harmonics and their inclusion by L'Abbé, Campagnoli, Paganini, Maass, Küster, Guhr, Blumenthal, and Dotzauer (= A, C, P, M, K, G, B, D) can be tabulated as follows:

No. of harmonic	Division of stopped string by the touching finger	Interval of touching finger above stopped note	Interval of sound above stopped note	Mentioned by					
1.	1/2	Octave	Octave			K	G		D
2.	1/3	Fifth	Twelfth	C	P	K	G	B²	D
3.	1/4	Fourth	Double octave	A C	P M	K	G	B¹	D
4.	1/5	Major third	Double octave plus major third	A C	P	K	G	B³	D
5.	1/6	Minor third	Double octave plus fifth			(K)	(G)	(B⁴)	D
6.	1/7	Flat minor third	Double octave plus flat minor seventh					(B⁵)	

KÜSTER admits that the very high harmonics are not pleasant (col. 704). BLUMENTHAL lists five "forks" ("Gabeln") and declares the fourth and fifth to be impracticable (p. 7).

[38] "Der Weg, der zu diesen Vortheilen führt, ist nur Wenigen bekannt, wird von noch Wenigeren betreten, und, wenn ich nicht irre, ist er nie in Schriften dem ausübenden Künstler hinlänglich enthüllt worden" – col. 703.

for the first chord in Paganini's document; b) to this rather awkward notation he prefers writing the notes at their actual pitch, indicating the first, second, third *armonico* by "A^1", "A^2", "A^3", etc. Neither of these systems survived. As long as there was no generally accepted notation, harmonic playing was propagated mainly by verbal tradition and composers rarely prescribed it in their scores. Yet it was not Baillot and Ernst who first devised the modern system of notation, as Andreas Moser assumed.[39] It had already been developed by L'Abbé, Paganini, and Maass. Breymann's thorough and learned article, on the other hand, apparently inspired by work of the physicist Ernst Cladni,[40] is of mathematical/acoustical nature, hardly addressing musical practice and not mentioning harmonics in double stops.

The most significant of the *Flageoletschulen* is that of the Frankfurt conductor and violinist Carl Guhr,[41] known also as the composer of a violin concerto "in Paganini's style".[42] Guhr had the opportunity to hear Paganini in August and September 1829 (if not earlier), when the virtuoso gave six concerts in the city on the Main. At the beginning of his treatise he writes:[43]

Da ich längere Zeit so glücklich war, diesen großen Meister öfter zu hören und mich mit ihm über die Art seines Spiels zu unterhalten, so bemühte ich mich, weil er sehr bedächtig Allem auszuweichen suchte, was das Geheimnis seiner Kunst (wenn ich es so nennen darf) betraf, ihn genau zu beachten und das, worin er sich von allen übrigen Meistern der Violine absondert, selbst zu erforschen. ... [Ich] fasste nun den Entschluß, ... besonders das so selten in Lehrbüchern vollständig besprochene Flageolet-Spiel in eine Art von System zu bringen. ... Ganz mit Unrecht hat die neuere Violinschule das Flageoletspiel gänzlich vernachlässigt, da es, auf sinnreiche Weise, mit Beurtheilung und Geschmack an-

Since I was for a long period of time so fortunate to hear this great master often and to converse with him on the manner of his playing, and since he very cautiously sought to evade everything which concerned the secret of his art (if I may call it this), I endeavoured to observe him exactly and to investigate myself that which separates him from all other masters of the violin. ... [I] decided ... to formulate in a sort of system especially the playing of harmonics, which is rarely discussed completely in instruction books. ... The modern violin school has totally neglected the playing of harmonics; [this is] quite unjustifiable, since, when it is employed ingeniously, with judgement and taste, it is not only of the greatest ef-

[39] *Geschichte des Violinspiels*, Berlin, Hesse, 1923, p. 435.

[40] *Die Akustik*, Leipzig, Breitkopf & Härtel, 1802.

[41] Cf. W. H. RIEHL, *Karl Guhr*, in Riehl's *Musikalische Charakterköpfe*, Stuttgart, Cotta, 1899[7], II, 257-277.

[42] *Le Souvenir de Paganini, 1ᵉʳ Concerto* in E, Op. 85, Mainz, Schott.

[43] P. 1.

gebracht, nicht nur von der größten Wirkung ist, sondern auch vorzüglich die
zarte Führung des Bogens ... befördert.

fect, but also excellently promotes the
delicate conduct of the bow.

In his attempt to distinguish rationally between Paganini's technique and that
of other violinists Guhr isolates six features (p. 4): 1) *scordatura*; 2) an individual style of bowing; 3) pizzicato with the left hand; 4) single and double harmonics; 5) performance on the G-string; and 6) [other] *tours de force*. The
fact that Guhr devotes his treatise almost exclusively to the fourth of these
confirms the impression given by the contemporary reviews: Paganini's harmonics attracted more attention than any other feature of his playing. Like
L'Abbé and Paganini, Guhr uses scales for most of his examples – diatonic
and chromatic, in single and various double stops. Paganini's diatonic scale
in thirds is found on page 30, the essential difference being that Guhr does
not cross the parts for the third and seventh double stop as Paganini had done
"per facilitare l'intuonazione" by interpolating a natural harmonic. Guhr
takes over Küster's two systems of notation literally, together with their rubric, the statement on the "delicate conduct of the bow", and ten "Übungsstücke". Only the latter are acknowledged.

Blumenthal declares apologetically at the end of his *Abhandlung* (p. 18)
that he has written it "blos auf ausdrückliches Begehren der Verlags-Hand-
lung" ["only at the explicit desire of the publisher"], Diabelli. He gives, like
Guhr, a fully developed system of natural and artificial harmonics, including
scales and double stops at all intervals and bowed trills (cf. above, De Giovanni). Like the other treatises, Blumenthal's uses two staves to explain the production of artificial harmonics. The twelve "Übungsstücke" on well-known
operatic melodies at the end of the work (pp. 19-24)[44] are then written on
only one staff as played, the stopped notes being indicated in double harmonics by half notes. The first chord of Paganini's document appears thus:

The anonymous English publication, *Paganini's Method of Producing the
Harmonic Double Stops* of 1840, is a tiny booklet containing nothing new –
the exercises at the end (pp. 15-20) are taken from Guhr. In spite of its late

---

[44] The limited repertoire of the *trompette marine* likewise consisted largely of arrangements of
operatic airs – cf. GALPIN, p. 19.

date and indebtedness to Guhr it still claims to "divulge the secret". No part of Paganini's performance, says the author,[45]

has appeared so unaccountable, as his method of producing the harmonics. We, of course, allude to those movements which are executed by him, in which the double stops are introduced.

The method by which he accomplishes this apparent miracle, has hitherto remained a secret; or, only known to the few (for it is not impossible that others may have made the same discovery as ourselves). It is our object then to divulge the secret, so that the public at large may have the benefit of it.

Through the *Flageoletschulen* Paganini's 'secret harmonic art' became the resource of the destitute, finding application in the countless encore trifles which bolster the vanity of the virtuosos and cause discerning listeners to follow Princess Elisa: in Lucca, said Paganini,[46]

veranstaltete [ich] alle vierzehn Tage bei den feierlichen Zirkeln ebenfalls ein grosses Concert, wobei aber die regierende Fürstin Elisa Baciocchi, Prinzeß von Lucca und Piombino, Napoleon's geliebteste Schwester, nicht jedesmal erschien oder bis an den Schluß ausharrte, weil die Flageolet-Töne meiner Violine ihre Nerven zu sehr erschütterten.

Every two weeks I organized a large concert likewise at the solemn gatherings; but here the ruling sovereign Elisa Baciocchi, Princess of Lucca and Piombino, Napoleon's most beloved sister, did not appear each time or endure to the end, because the harmonics of my violin shook her nerves too vehemently.

POSTSCRIPTUM

In a letter of 19 January 2006 Professor William Ramp of the University of Lethbridge, a great grandnephew of George Duncan, very kindly sent me the following communication on two of the persons mentioned in Paganini's document:

George Cuthbertson Duncan, M.D., was born near Port Dover, in what is now Ontario, Canada, 21 Aug. 1852 and died in London, England, on 27 Nov. 1935. He studied medicine at McGill University in Montreal, but then moved overseas, setting up a 'society' practice in London and on the Continent which was said to have included, for a time, Elizabeth, empress of Austria. Some time in the 1890s he ceased

---

[45] P. 1.

[46] SCHOTTKY, p. 365. I agree with Elisa, and apologize to my readers for having written an article on this superficial composer and circus artist.

the active practice of medicine and took up the life of an amateur collector and re-
storer of paintings and stringed instruments. His specialty in the former seems to
have been 16th- and 17th-century works of the Spanish and various Italian schools,
and, in the latter, violins and 'cellos by the 17th- and 18th-century Cremonese lu-
thiers. He appears also to have served as an informal agent and consultant to various
monied collectors, and may have had a hand in the collection of art for Elizabeth's
palace, Achilleion on Corfu. He lived a peripatetic existence between two residences:
the Hotel Cavour in Milan and the Charing Cross Hotel in London. His circle in Italy
included ... the Duchess of San Teodoro (married ... to the Roman archaeologist Rodolfo Lanciani). Few records of his collecting and restoring activities survive, though
they were enough to attract the intese interest of Arthur F. Hill, the London violin
dealer and biographer of Stradivari. He testified that in London Duncan collaborated
with the Voller brothers in the production and sale of faked "old master" violins:
"Dr. Duncan practically keeps the Vollers going". "We know Dr. Duncan to be a
rogue".[47]

Duncan appears ... as a patron and friend of ... young women pursuing musical
careers, one being ... Valentina Crespi. The 1921 date of Dr. Duncan's gift to Crespi
may perhaps be significant: in the early 1920s he was involved in a lawsuit against the
Italian government pertaining to legislation banning or restricting the export of Italian works of art and other cultural treasures. It is perhaps possible that he gave the
ms. to Crespi because he feared that he might no longer be able to take it out of the
country.

Valentina Crespi was a talented concert violinist, of mixed Italian and Romanian
parentage. She trained at the Royal Conservatory in Milan, at Paris under Armand
Parent, and in Budapest under Jenō Hubay. She was at one time a protégée (according to her New York agent) of the queen of Romania. She performed in England,
America, and on the Continent before the First World War, and was still touring
in America after the war. She also performed for some early radio broadcasts in
the U.S. in the 1920s, and composed incidental music for silent films. In the mid-
1930s she was living in Lausanne and apparently was till there in the 1940s. ... She
was ... owner of a 1699 Stradivari violin, which is still called the "Crespi" Stradivari;
it is at present in the collection of the Royal Academy of Music in London.

---

[47] John DILWORTH et al., *The Voller Brothers*, London, British Violin Makers' Association,
2006, pp. 17ff.

Three things we owe especially to Schenk. One was the awareness of the great impact of Italy on music of the 16-18th centuries. Schenk had profound knowledge of Baroque and Viennese Classical music and he realized how important Italy's influence on Austria was in the 17-18th centuries. Another thing which Schenk emphasized is that it is not enough to *describe* music, to make formal analyses, but we must try to *explain the content*, the meaning of the music. The third thing was the importance of *concrete* (e.g. biographical) information. We developed a severe allergy to abstract writing such as aesthetics and the 'critical theories' fashionable today, so easily constructed and communicating so little, lacking contact with specific historical reality.[6]

– *The subject of your dissertation, – i.e.* Fugue and Fugato in Rococo and Classical Chamber Music – *was that your own choice?*

– I chose this topic myself before going to Vienna (Rudolf Gerber had advised me against it, and wanted me to work on Grell, Herzogenberg, or Kiel!), but Schenk was very interested in it because he liked to show the influence of the Baroque on Viennese Classical music. My book was first written and published in German, but there is a later English translation which contains many more sources and composers.

– *What did you do after finishing your dissertation?*

– I wanted to do something quite different, so I began to work on Italian music and went back to the sixteenth century. After my first year in Italy I went in 1963 to the U.S., where I had never lived before. After a short time on the staff of the Music Division of the Library of Congress I received the position of an assistant professor at the University of Southern California in Los Angeles. As you may know, America often puts the conservatory into the university and has hardly any independent conservatories. This university had an excellent music school. They had faculty there with worldwide reputation, such as Jascha Heifetz and Gregor Piatigorsky; graduate students staged fully professional operas twice a year. But musicology was only a small minority, which is not a good situation for academic work. So after four years I went to North Carolina, to Duke University, which did not have a music school. There musicology was part of the faculty of arts, where it belongs. I

---

[6] Ernst Robert CURTIUS "particularly mistrusted the tendency ... to replace the empirical account of phenomena with abstract categories and theoretical explanations" – *Essays on European Literature*, Princeton UP, 1973, p. XII. Unfortunately for serious scholarship, readership is in direct proportion to the broad and abstract nature of the topic, and too many writers have allowed themselves to be seduced by this situation. Fewer readers are interested in the specialized and concrete studies which constitute the real contributions to knowledge – cf. below, note 13.

was responsible for setting up the graduate program (not in its current form, which provides for a Ph.D. also in composition).[7]

– *When did you leave the U.S.?*

– My 16-year sojourn in the U.S. was interrupted by several years' research in Italy. After being offered a chair by the University of Pavia in 1982 I was appointed to the chair of musicology at the University of Regensburg. It was like moving into a professor's paradise: an autonomous institute exclusively for music history, no bloated administration,[8] department meetings, etc. And there is no other part of Germany where I would love to live except Bavaria. Regensburg had the best library of the eight Bavarian universities. It is one of the oldest cities north of the Alps, and as a historian I like to live in places with such a long history. The city was not damaged by the war; it is full of medieval churches. It is close to the mountains, which was good for me, since I am a passionate alpinist. And it is close to Italy. Some of my best students there were Italian. The university was not yet affected by the budget cuts which came after my retirement.

I should mention another important event in my life: the year after I left the U.S. and before I went to Bavaria I spent as visiting professor at the Harvard University Center for Italian Renaissance Studies [1982/83]. The Center is located in the villa of Bernard Berenson in Florence. It has a splendid library, which is continually extended. We lived on the grounds of the villa. There were about a dozen fellows from different countries (including Hungary) and different disciplines. I had very good possibilities to make contacts with representatives of history, art history, literature, etc. We had lunch together every day, and former fellows and other scholars passing through Florence also came to give lectures. In one year I could meet much of the world of Renaissance scholars, which was very stimulating.

– *After your retirement in 1992, how do you live and work now?*

– When I was teaching in Bavaria we were travelling back and forth between Regensburg and Rome. Since my 'retirement' I live all the time in Rome, except for the summer, which I spend on our island in Ontario [Birch Island, Kahshe Lake, Muskoka]. In the music section of the German Historical Institute in Rome we have one of the very best musicological libraries in Europe.

---

[7] Cf. Edward LOWINSKY, *On the Matter of a Doctor's Degree for Composers*, «College Music Society Symposium», III, 1963, pp. 43-52.

[8] The university did have a chancellor, but he was paid less than the professors, and instead of telling them what to do, asked what he could do for them. Bavarian universities are run entirely by the professors, not by professional administrators, students or alumni, as in the American academic buyers' markets.

The Italian libraries and archives, on the other hand, are very rich in primary sources. I had been working for many years in Florentine archives when preparing my book on the musicians of the Medici. My favorite place to work is the Vatican Library. There I can meet the best humanistic scholars of the world. Since I do not have room in my apartment in Rome for all the books that I had in my house in Germany, I left the musicological literature in the Vatican Library,[9] and I walk only fifteen minutes to consult it there.

– *After having lived and taught on both sides of the Atlantic, how would you compare the predominant tendencies of musicology in America and Europe?*[10]

– I was privileged to work in the U.S. in the 1960s and '70s, which were a great period of American musicology.[11] It may have been the best in the world at that time. That was not because American musicologists are necessarily better. It was simply because there were so many of them, still including European immigrants and their pupils. With over two thousand members in the American Musicological Society and only a couple of journals, one could select the very best manuscripts for publication. However, I have become disappointed with some of the developments in recent years, especially the sometimes arrogant 'new musicology', which largely abandoned – to its own detriment – historical method and source-based research, often in favor of abstract 'theories' and the ahistorical social sciences.[12] The A.M.S., which was so strong before, has allowed itself not only to embrace ephemeral fads (successions of '-isms' – the American 'band-wagon' phenomenon), but also to become a kind of political lobby for special-interest groups. Once this happens, you have no longer objective historiography, but ideology and thought control, dangerously close to that of totalitarian regimes of the extreme left

---

[9] A preliminary catalogue is listed below, p. 604, which does not include the acquisitions after 2000.

[10] For a comparison of the German and American university systems, cf. Erwin PANOFSKY, *Meaning in the Visual Arts*, Garden City, Doubleday, 1955, pp. 321-346.

[11] In spite of its frequent location as a minority in departments indifferent, even hostile to scholarship. On the unique, still unsolved problems of American music departments, see the editorial by Paul Henry LANG, «Musical Quarterly», L, 1964, pp. 215-226. On the crisis afflicting all of the humanities in recent decades, see Alan BLOOM, *The Closing of the American Mind: How Higher Education has Failed Democracy and Improverished the Souls of Today's Students*, New York, Simon & Shu7ster, 1987, Parts One and Three; Lynne V. CHENEY, *Telling the Truth: Why Our Culture and Our Country have Stopped Making Sense – and What we can do about it*, ibid., 1995; and Roger KIMBALL, *Tenured Radicals: How Politics has Corrupted our Higher Education*, New York, Harper & Row, 1990.

[12] Cf. my remarks in *La storia, le scienze sociali e le nozze medicee del 1589*, «Rivista italiana di musicologia», XXXIV, 1999, pp. 389-394.

and right ('political correctness', laudable in everyday life, but disastrous when imposed upon curricula, appointments, and historical scholarship).[13] The colleagues in Eastern Europe know very well what that means. Ideology has nothing to do with truth; it operates with distortion and becomes mere propaganda.

---

[13] It has become almost impossible for a gifted young scholar who has occupied himself exclusively with works of art produced by white, heterosexual, European males more than a couple of centuries ago to receive an academic appointment. But alternative topics of research have proved rather disappointing. A disproportionate obsession with feminism, 'sexuality', and 'gender' *ad nauseam* has been become obligatory also for those who simply fear being stigmatized as 'nonconformists'. (In 2007 the executive director of the A.M.S., presumably in deference to 'big brother', actually sent a questionnaire to all members, requesting them to report, albeit anonymously, their "sexual orientation"!). Already in 1979 an eminent scholar of the humanities, Paul Oskar KRISTELLER, recognized an approaching catastrophe: "I was educated in a *humanistisches Gymnasium* in Berlin in which I learned a great deal of Greek, Latin, French and German literature as well as history". "The steady decline of our educational system makes it increasingly difficult for future scholars to acquire the linguistic and other skills essential for the serious pursuit of historical studies, and the exclusive emphasis on the contemporary world which has reached the proportions of a 'cultural revolution' undermines any interest which the lay public may have in the past. The scholar is under constant pressure, not to attain new knowledge through fresh research, but to communicate to the general public all that is known [e.g. *Handbücher der Musikwissenschaft* or the undocumented compilations of music dictionaries] ... in a diluted and sometimes distorted fashion. ... Thus he may be led, as a result of popular pressure and weak training, to cultivate a kind of fake scholarship instead of the real thing, relying on translations rather than on the original texts, on secondary rather than on primary sources, on vague clichés instead of precise concepts, on abstract formulas instead of concrete nuances, [on recent trendy, ephemeral literature in English, ignoring much more relevant, still useful older publications in ancient and modern foreign languages], and concerning himself with fashionable theories and ideologies rather than with the historical facts and documents [since this requires a long preparation, travel, and hard, time-consuming work!], and with artificial problems that are in vogue but unrelated to the historical events and hence incapable of any satisfactory solution. ... There is a widespread quest for broad synthesis and a contempt for details and nuances". "The validity of all scholarly contributions will not be decided by the preconceptions of academic cliques or claques, or by the shifting basis of intellectual fashion designers and opinion makers". "The world of scholarship, ... if it yields to political or social pressures, it does so at its own risk, and must consider whether that price is worth paying". – *Renaissance Thought and its Sources*, New York, Columbia UP, 1979, pp. 1, 11ff. In the *AMS Newsletter* of Feb. 2005, pp. 2f, the president of the American Musicological Society observed, apparently with satisfaction, an enormous increase in the *quantity* [!] of papers and 19th-20th-century topics at the Society's annual meetings during the past thirty years. The espousal of 'diversity' at all costs in academic circles is part of a wider trend, affecting Christianity as a whole. On the eve of his election to the papacy as Benedict XVI, my musically competent, brilliant former colleague at the University of Regensburg Cardinal Joseph Ratzinger warned courageously and effectively of the tyranny of relativism, "i.e. drifting here and there with every wind of teaching. ... A dictatorship of relativism is developed, which recognizes nothing as definite and allows as final measure only one's own ego and wishes" – a welcome antidote to the "diversity" pusillanimously touted by administrators of American universities and "learned" societies, who, wishing as good politicians to be all things to all people, have presided over the destruction of the priority of mankind's greatest treasure – our precious heritage of older European culture – in curricula and appointments, and allowed venerable, well-founded canons to disappear which provided shared worthwhile knowledge as the basis of intelligible communication among educated persons. (My 'Eurocentrism' does not necessarily deny the value of other cultures, but recognizes that exotic ones are less relevant to ours and can never be well understood by many Western observers, not fluent in the respective languages etc.).

German musicology is no longer at as high a level as it was until the middle of our century. It too now tends to neglect primary sources, no longer to search in archives for unknown documents (partly because there are fewer left to be found easily), but to sit at home and make formal-aesthetic analyses. There is less interest now in the earlier periods of music history, which I find most worthwhile and fascinating, with more opportunities to engage in 'problem-solving'. The Italians have the advantage of having so much source material right in their own country.[14] But by 'sources' I of course understand not merely music manuscripts, but also archival documents, a wide variety of old manuscript and printed literary texts, and in some cases products of the visual arts.

Two years ago [in 1994] I was visiting professor at Moscow State University. I was asked to go there as a consultant to advise how a chair of musicology might be established. It is a very important university, but it does not have music history there. This is located only at the conservatory, where it does not belong. Before arriving I prepared a report summarizing the advantages and disadvantages of the academic systems I know.[15] The whole thing proved to be an exercise in futility, because the university simply does not have the resources to establish a musicological program. They cannot buy many Western publications, and they could not do so during the last eighty years of economic mismanagement. The country has great human and natural resources, but it has yet to develop a system of providing adequate funds for higher education and humanistic research. I found this rather sad, because I met there some very intelligent and diligent students.

I must say that I am favorably impressed by the situation in Budapest. I always found it respectable that a small country like Hungary could produce such a serious journal as *Studia Musicologica*. You have a very nice building, good facilities for working, and plenty of equipment. I was pleased to meet colleagues here. Many of them I knew by reputation, but the only one I had met personally is Professor Somfai, with whom I had correspondence already in the early sixties. In 1956 I tried to come to Hungary to examine sources in the National Library, but it was impossible in that troubled year.[16]

– Your research goes in different directions. You worked in archives collecting biographical data, you worked extensively on the connections of music with

---

[14] This has led to much useful but merely descriptive, mechanical work – inventories, catalogues, bibliographies – and a certain reluctance to use these sources for interpretive historiography or interdisciplinary *Geiste*swissenschaft, attributable also to the location of a majority of Italian musicologists in conservatories rather than universities.

[15] See below, p. 604, *Comments*.

[16] Revolt against Soviet domination and flood of Hungarian refugees to Vienna.

sister arts, and you published different articles on a sort of hermeneutics of mu-sic. How could you summarize the common ground of these studies?

– The music that we study is a phenomenon of the past. In my view it can therefore be understood only by historical methods. I am perhaps rather ex-treme in the position I take, because I believe that to understand any work of art from the past we must go back and try to go through the same kind of educational process that people in those times had. This can mean, for exam-ple, studying Latin rhetoric, which was a major part of the curriculum in ear-lier times and which now has completely disappeared. We have found that some important musical phenomena could be explained only with reference to Cicero and Quintilian [cf. their listings in our Index of Names]. People today think of rhetoric only as the demagogic speech of politicians, often without con-tent. But this negative use of the word became prevalent only in the nineteenth century. I especially like the Renaissance because of the great interest the peo-ple then held in the culture of the past, particularly of Classical antiquity.

I would not only say that to understand works of the past we somehow have to immerse ourselves in the whole culture of that period. I would go further and say that we should systematically exclude ideas and notions that came only later.[17] Karl Marx and Sigmund Freud (not to mention Heinrich Schenker or fashionable modern philosophers) are hardly relevant for the Re-naissance, or even for Mozart and Beethoven, because people then had never heard of them. If we use these modern methods we are going to arrive at ana-chronistic results which are, of course, dubious.

– How is it possible to get a close contact with a period which lies many centuries behind us?

– I like an idea of Descartes (notwithstanding the damage done by his dis-respect for memory/tradition and his influence on sterile positivism): that you should not accept statements made by other people until you go back to first principles and prove them yourself. In music-historical research this means going back to the primary sources. If you think about what we know about the past: we know something only because someone – a participant or a wit-ness of the event – wrote it down, and this written documentation has come down to us. We know hardly anything else. If someone wants to find informa-tion which is new and reliable – and this is crucial in historical research – he finds it by examining and interpreting new sources. I ascribe great importance to this, and it explains, e.g., my efforts to combine all information on the Flor-entine court musicians.

---

17 Cf. CURTIUS, p. 501: "to liberate ourselves from the mental attitudes of the present and to read ancient texts without modern preconceptions".

I find it very important to do biographical research. In recent decades (e.g. Carl Dahlhaus), the great relevance of biography has not been fully recognized. One reason for this was that many popular biographical works were rather novelistic. But in speaking of biography I mean a scholarly reconstruction of the composer's life, based on sources. We have some eminent classical works in this field, dealing mostly with great masters.[18] But we certainly need to deal also with the lives of lesser known composers, because without them we do not have an adequate picture of earlier times. I believe that the more we know about the composer's life, the less superficial our understanding of his music will be. We must know about his education, about the society in which he moved, the patronage he received. Music was composed by individuals, and I like becoming acquainted with them. That is why I enjoyed the research in archives that I did for nearly forty years on the lives of Florentine musicians and Emilio de' Cavalieri.

– *Even if biographical work is so fascinating for you, it is often said that documents found in archives are dead things. How are you able to fill them with life?*

– Documents are anything but dry. I find them far more interesting than modern paraphrases. They connect us directly with the past. Especially letters are fascinating. Their writers speak to us directly and thus come back to life. I have always felt that writing about music should have human interest. It should also go beyond the readership consisting of musicologists and should say something for other educated people who might be interested in the subject. There are a couple of ways of bringing in human interest. One which I have already hinted at is to try to deal with the content of the music; another is biographical work.

Music was written by human beings for human beings, and this is sometimes forgotten when people write about music as a kind of abstract pattern of sounds (or practice exclusively descriptive formal analysis or textual criticism). Hanslick's unfortunate concept of music as "tönend bewegte Form", for example, caused much damage, especially for twentieth-century composers.

– *Do you regard music as a special kind of language?*

---

[18] A conscientious scholar will want to communicate only *new* information and insights and not be content with writing a general monograph on the life and works of a well-researched "great master" (the easy road to ephemeral fame), where there can be few new findings. What we need are not broad surveys (commercial compilations), but specialized source-based studies, presenting new information – not merely articles (not to mention the surfeit, especially in Italy, of quickly produced papers for conferences), but also unfragmented research in comprehensive monographs. For this we have no shortage of good, but unduly neglected composers and repertoires (e.g. baroque vocal music, extant almost entirely in mss., as yet with little bibliographical control).

– Yes, indeed. Music should express something, and we have to try to find out how it expresses human emotions, experiences, and ideas. This is certainly not a new idea. We can go back to the ancient Greek 'doctrine of *ethos*' or the so-called *Affektenlehre* of the German Baroque. Of course not every kind of music lends itself to an interpretation of its content. I found many meaningful features in a madrigal of Marenzio and Vecchi, and in Beethoven's *Missa solemnis*, but I would not have succeeded very well with Palestrina or with Haydn's instrumental music.

– *Do see any changes in these concepts over the centuries?*

– In the Middle Ages the system of the seven liberal arts classified music together with astronomy and mathematics, not with the language arts of grammar and rhetoric. Music was regarded as a kind of earthly counterpart to the music of the spheres, to the divine harmony of the universe. In those centuries the composers were less concerned with the expression of meaning in music.[19]

The great change came with the Renaissance, with Humanism. Humanists were very much interested in language, in the word, in literary studies. This change focused the attention on the meaning of the text to be set to music. It happened in the time of Josquin, ca. 1500, and was an equivalent of the humanist respect for the word. This change, which I regard as the most important one in the history of music, can be illustrated with contemporary writings. They frequently speak about music as a kind of "oration". But this concept became lost in the nineteenth century, with the reaction against rational aspects of musical composition. There emerged the cult of the 'original' genius who 'creates' everything out of his own feeling.[20] This 'confessional' art, I think, was not an improvement, but led to some excessively sentimental and bombastic music.

– *If we accept that much earlier music was a vehicle of meaning, what kind of methods can help us to decipher it?*

– A full answer to this complex question is provided only in our publications. I think one way to learn how to deal with the content of music is to read

---

[19] This well-worn simplification still has validity in general, though recent research has demonstrated that a preoccupation with musical expression of text and affect was not entirely absent during the Middle Ages – cf. Klaus Wolfgang NIEMÖLLER, *Tradition und Innovation des Affekt-Denkens im Musikschrifttum des 16. Jahrhunderts*, in *Tugenden und Affekte in der Philosophie, Literatur und Kunst der Renaissance*, ed. Joachim Poeschke *et al.*, Münster, Rhema, 2002, pp. 77-93. Our readers will recognize that our source-based historical method differs fundamentally from that of books by aestheticians on "musical meaning".

[20] Cf. KRISTELLER, p. 256: "Modern writers find it difficult to believe that God created the world out of nothing, but they see no difficulty in assuming that a human artist, even a minor artist, creates his art out of nothing. They should know that ... our productive imagination does not produce anything out of nothing, but works by freely recombining past impressions and experiences".

not only musicological journals, but also some of the best work of art historians and literary historians, who have more direct access to 'meaning'. But the work of a music historian is not much different from that of the scholars of these sister disciplines. In both cases we are concerned with finding contemporary documents relating to these earlier productions, with trying to explain these productions in the sense of their own time.

For this reason I am rather skeptical about the *Rezeptionsforschung* which became very popular in Germany in the last decades. This may have its value, but all it tells us is about the tastes of people who lived after the composer. This has no relevance to the production of the work itself. That is why we have to move backward, not forward. Once the work is composed, it is finished, and nothing more is going to influence the statement which the composer made with it. What follows tends to be the topic of a kind of sociological research. I think Theodor Adorno had an unfortunate influence on German musicology, making it the handmaid of sociology. In sociology everything becomes abstract, dealing with masses of anonymous consumers who listen to the music without understanding it, because they do not think historically. The taste of the average concertgoer is not such an important subject for musicology. *Rezeptionsforschung* can be really useful only in one case: namely, if you can prove the influence of earlier music on a later composer. Exactly this was the topic of my dissertation, in which I sought to demonstrate the traces of baroque influences on Viennese Classical music.

– *Have you received some direct inspiration from art historians?*

– Definitely. Perhaps the best work that ever has been done in humanistic disciplines is that of iconologists. Iconology is a method developed especially by Aby Warburg and later by Fritz Saxl, Edgar Wind, Erwin Panofsky, William Heckscher, *et al.* It aims at interpreting the *meaning* of the work, and it has been especially successful in dealing with Renaissance paintings, because these works were generally based on literary sources, either from the Scripture or from Classical literature.[21] It often happens that every detail of a picture is determined by some ancient literary source(s). Humanist scholars helped the painters to develop iconological programs, and we cannot understand the paintings if we regard them merely from the so superficial aesthetic point of view. We must identify the literary sources, and that is why a classical education is indispensable.[22] I tried to apply this method to music itself first in the

---

[21] Cf. note 25 and p. 605, Giorgione.

[22] The greatest threat to the humanities today is the loss of familiarity with the great Graeco-Roman and Judeo-Christian cultures. My esteemed colleague Martin Staehelin was once told by a student: "I don't need to know anything about the Mass; I'm studying *musicology*"!

case of Beethoven's *Missa solemnis*,[23] pointing out many details where the composer interpreted older ideas in the Mass text with musical means. I developed it further in the article on the symbolism of the circle.[24]

The other important aim of iconologists is to identify and describe motives that had a continuity over a longer period of time. This also gave a strong impulse to my own work. If we examine a composer in isolation we easily imagine that much of what he did was new. This may be only a misinterpretation if we do not know enough about his predecessors. If we come to know them better, we realize that much of that which seemed to be new had already been done before. As Goethe once said: "We are original only because we do not know anything".

A similar method in literary history is *topos* research. The *topoi* are literary equivalents of iconological motives: they are certain modes of expression and formulation which have a very long history. An eminent scholar in this field was Ernst Robert Curtius with his *Europäische Literatur und das lateinische Mittelalter*. He showed that one cannot begin to understand a literary work unless one knows what the author himself had known, what he had read. The traces go back very often to ancient Greek and Latin literature. His method can be applied with great benefit also to music.[25]

---

[23] Above, ch. 15.

[24] Above, ch. 1.

[25] The introduction of the method and terminology of *topos*-research to musicology occurred first with U. Kirkendale's monograph, *Antonio Caldara: Sein Leben und seine venezianisch-römischen Oratorien*, 1966 (where the word "*topos*" occurs frequently throughout the volume), and her paper *The King of Heaven and the King of France: History of a Musical Topos* (cf. *Abstracts of Papers Read at the ... Annual Meeting of the American Musicological Society*, 1969, pp. 27f), finally published in 2006 and in this volume, ch. 7. And the cited articles on Beethoven and on the *circulatio* (here ch. 1 and 15; also ch. 2 and 12) might be regarded as the first attempts at a systematic application of the iconological method – the tracing of motive-traditions and of the connections with ancient authors as a means to explain content – *to music itself*. (When the paper on Beethoven's *Missa solemnis* was presented at the Bibliotheca Hertziana in Rome, Wolfgang Lotz, director of that splendid institution concluded: "That is iconology"). Nevertheless, this method is still unfamiliar to musicologists. Their approximation to art history has been almost exclusively in the area of iconography, describing visual art which depicts notated music or musical subjects, rather than explaining the meaning of musical compositions. An example is the good contribution of James Haar to the volume *Meaning in the Visual Arts: Views from the Outside. A Centennial Commemoration of Erwin Panofsky (1892-1968)*, ed. Irving Lavin, Princeton, Institute for Advanced Study, 1995, where the author honestly admits that he will discuss "the use of notation in painting and decorative art". However, the two musicological articles in this volume claiming to deal with "iconology" and "meaning" (a fourth one, on ventriloquism in the cinema, is irrelevant) miss completely the point of Panofsky's research. Yet they undertake to instruct us on "what obstacles must be overcome", creating – very much "from the outside" – such obstacles, instead of producing concrete examples of solutions. Ellen Rosand confuses the issue by consistently speaking of musical "iconography" in an article entitled *Music and Iconology*, denying that the method "can be concerned with the meaning of works of music as opposed to their form" and advocating an isolation from the neighbouring visual and literary disciplines which is diametrically opposed to Panofsky's broad approach. Leo Treitler's article indulges precisely in the kind of writing decisively refuted by iconologists: vague, abstract aesthetics, focused

– The topoi *and the iconological commonplaces appear in the works of great artists, but they are also present with their less eminent contemporaries. Can you define what makes an artifact into a great work?*

– No, I do not indulge in abstract definitions or aesthetics. This is something which cannot be explained in a few words. The *topoi* and the iconological motives are rather constant during a long period of time. But great artists always add something to them, they vary them,[26] sometimes using an old style to express intelligently a specific meaning (e.g. above, pp. 495f for Figaro, "die Alte", and Donna Elvira). These changes can distinguish a real genius from his predecessors and imitators. But we cannot know what he added unless we know what had been there before. In different periods we have completely different ways of expressing ourselves in music. But there are still some constant elements which continually appear in modified forms and in new contexts.[27]

I like to think of the work of a music historian as consisting largely of contextualization, i.e. of re-establishing lost connections. We first hear a work in isolation and then we try to re-integrate it into the net of connections it had with the past and the time of its composition. These connections became lost during the time that separates us from the composition, they are no longer obvious to us. We cannot understand a ricercar, including those of J. S. Bach's *Musical Offering*, unless we know something about ancient rhetoric and the liturgical practice of the 16th-18th centuries in Italy. Our most important task is to reconstruct such lost contexts. The more such connections we are able to reconstruct, the more credible and interesting our interpretation will be.

– Behind your intensive interest in the music of the past I feel a certain concept about the place of music in human life. How would you summarize this?

---

on composers from the romantic and postromantic periods, where the old rhetorical *topoi* and iconological motifs were no longer well understood, but largely abandoned. The work of iconologists is, fortunately, very concrete (as meaning must be), and the best of it has been done, of course, on the Renaissance, where most great painting was based on ancient literary sources ('Nachleben der Antike') which need to be identified by scholars who read widely in ancient literature. (Hopefully, U. Kirkendale's discovery of the ancient literary source explaining all details of Giorgione's so-called "Tempesta" will still be published). But neither Rosand nor Treitler seems aware of the fundamental lesson of such 'source-based' research. Only one contribution to the volume, by Marc Fumaroli, rightly emphasizes the affinity of iconology to *topos*-reseach. Another, by Willibald Sauerländer, describes the damage done by deconstructionism (see above, p. 123, note 150). – The remarks made in my interview, and the title of our present volume, both formulated before publication of the one in Princeton, necessitate this footnote.

[26] Cf. KRISTELLER, p. 249: "I sometimes wonder whether the greater finesse of literature and art before the nineteenth century may be due to the very fact that the writers and artists had to find new variations on given themes that were well-known to themselves and to their audiences".

[27] Cf. Reinhold HAMMERSTEIN, *Über Kontinuität in der Musikgeschichte*, in *Musicologia Humana* cit., pp. 13-41.

– I believe that music was at its best when it was serving something that was higher than the individual. Until the end of the eighteenth century these were two institutions: the Church and the courts (not to mention genuine folk music, not yet commercialized, which I also enjoy). The composers were not pouring out their own private sentiments or 'intellectual' constructions, that may not be of interest to anyone else, but they were serving the higher purpose of the Church, the glory of God, or the state. These purposes kept music somewhat more objective and not overly sentimental. Then in the nineteenth century we have *Trivialmusik*, a degeneration. And in the twentieth century we get – still worse – incoherent cacophony (the emperor's new clothes, according to Hans Christian Andersen's wisdom) and commercial rock/pop music, the latter being both a cause and effect of the end of civilization as we knew it. Earlier music had its task in edifying the audience, but rock music is the ultimate depravity and banality, the brutal, often antisocial expression of the immature and uneducated urban proletariat, acoustical environmental pollution produced by musically untrained vocalists and 'heavy metal'.

– *All the things you are concerned with belong to the past. Do you feel no gap between your research on earlier times and your life in the late twentieth century?*

– The past gives me a very wide selection from which I can chose those problems I find most challenging to solve, those things I regard as most interesting and worthwhile. Of course I feel an enormous 'gap'. As a historian I live with the past. Anyone who received his formal education in the 1940s and '50s has experienced many changes. We have had an immense technological revolution with the advent of computers, which are extremely useful in many ways, especially for word processing and for the marvelous union catalogues of libraries, which facilitate our work greatly. But Internet's 'fast information' (most of it of a quality comparable to 'fast food') is endangering the culture of the book; many students no longer have the patience to engage in extensive searches in libraries or to read books there, but prefer to sit at home in front of a computer screen. And technology is pushing out the historical disciplines from education.[28] From the media one has the impression that almost the entire population is interested only in the short-lived present. This is impoverishing our lives. A world that has no awareness of the great achievements of the past destroys the value of present life.

---

[28] Cf. CURTIUS, pp. 408f: "Education is no longer valued as an end in itself, but only for its practical utility". "Those countries in which the details of democratic education have been realized are continually in danger of failing into intellectual enslavement, ... a planetary despotism in which technology would continue to develop and the higher activities of the spirit would perish".

We are very fortunate in having an enormous heritage of artistic production from nearly three millennia (the best of it not from the more recent past), and I think it is unfortunate to spend one's life without becoming acquainted with it, and not merely music. I believe it would be a good investment for the state to support education in the historical disciplines. There would be fewer problems with drugs and crime if young people learned about things which are really worthwhile, of lasting value. It is obviously short-sighted to marginalize the humanities, not providing sufficient support for them, but favoring merely utilitarian, financially profitable activity. If this thinking continues to predominate, we are threatened with the demolition of our civilization and with a new barbarism.

– *Thank you, Professor Kirkendale.*

XX.

ON "SOURCES" FOR MUSIC HISTORY

LETTER TO THE EDITOR
OF THE «JOURNAL OF THE AMERICAN MUSICOLOGICAL SOCIETY»,
18 MARCH 2006

Ever since 1999, when this Journal began listing bibliographies at the end of articles, a consistent system of headings has not been imposed by the editors. While this may not always be necessary, it has lead to some terminological confusion which in some cases may be seen as both a cause and an effect of a serious methodological error. The heading "Works Cited", employed 46 times during the seven years 1999-2005, is correct enough. Problematic is the nomenclature "secondary sources" for lists consisting exclusively or almost exclusively of secondary literature.[1] It is used 14 times unqualified and another eight times with a different but similar adjective such as "printed", "published" "modern", "other", etc. Apparently it is not always understood that in historical research a "source" is by definition and by hydrographic analogy always "primary" (the first and usually most reliable communication of certain information), that "primary source" is thus a pleonasm (forced on us by the incorrect use of the word 'source') and "secondary source" or "reference source", an oxymoron.

Since the music we study is a phenomenon of the past, it could be argued that a historical approach is the most valid one for its understanding. Historiography – as opposed to prehistory, anthropology, and to a certain degree ethnology – begins with written records of civilized peoples. The concrete information which we have about individuals, preferably identifiable, and their works is available to us only insofar as it was written down either by themselves or by contemporary witnesses before being forgotten. Thus the publication of sources and source-based research has enjoyed a certain priority in serious historical writing, notwithstanding valiant attempts to deal with non-written traditions. Venerable monuments of erudition such as Migne's *Patro-*

---

[1] Cf. the critique in W. KIRKENDALE, *La storia, le scienze sociali*, p. 392.

logiae, the *Rerum Italicarum Scriptores*, the *Fontes Rerum Austriacarum*, the *Monumenta Germaniae Historica*, or the *Rerum Britannicarum Medii Aevi Scriptores* have a very long shelf-life. They could almost claim immortality, were it not for the occasional discovery of new sources for the same or related documents and the refinement of philological/editorial techniques.

Of the two principal activities of a historian – a) the discovery/presentation of hitherto unknown sources and b) their interpretation as a means of explaining historical phenomena – the former is an indispensable prerequisite for the latter, since no interpretation will be valid which is not based on solid facts. The former possesses a high degree of objectivity, while the latter, the more it departs from the sources, the more it becomes vulnerable to subjective judgements or trendy attitudes ("-isms"), which can be superseded, e.g. by the presentation of new sources or even by closer attention to the old ones. Although sources can need to be evaluated critically, to deny literary texts meaning other than from the irrelevant, anachronistic, and inconsistent interpretations by the historically unprepared modern reader, as occurred with the fad of deconstructionism, is no less than a retreat from the philologist-historian's major responsibility: to rediscover and reveal authors' intentions at the time of writing – a capitulation motivated, one might suspect, by lack of preparation and a disinclination to undertake the hard work necessary for such research. If literature has no meaning, what reason would we have for studying it? The discipline could be declared bankrupt.

If someone were to ask my opinion regarding the choice of a topic for research, my first question might be: "What hitherto unknown or inadequately studied sources are available for this topic"? In the absence of such, I would have little confidence that much new and reliable information would be forthcoming, and I would suggest looking for a more promising topic, of which enough still exist. Though America's geographical distance from the major depositories of sources and a certain lack of ease with ancient and modern languages – not to mention history – have largely discouraged such work as the above-mentioned *monumenta*, some American musicologists, with the help of independent study, microfilms, travel, etc. succeeded very well in overcoming such obstacles. One need only mention the splendid publications of the American Institute of Musicology, the *Census-Catalogue of Manuscript Sources of Polyphonic Music 1400-1550*, or the *Monuments of Renaissance Music*. Much activity, on the other hand, is of a commercial rather than scholarly nature (great-master monographs, undocumented compilations for music dictionaries, even broad surveys of entire epochs or genres, i.e. textbooks for college students, that lucrative American invention), where the communication of new information cannot be a priority and readers are not made aware of the importance of source-based research. As a result, some writers actually refer to the *New Grove Dictionary of Music* or *Die Musik in Geschichte und Gegenwart* as their "source" [!], thus destroying their own credibility.

Many of the articles in the Journal which used the word 'source' incorrectly in the headings of the bibliographies are well researched and have not suffered the negative consequences of such terminology (unlike some less serious publications). Thus I do not wish my remarks to be understood as a criticism of their content. But it is disconcerting to see a reputable journal listing secondary literature (even *A History of Western Music*, encyclopedias, and the abstract writings of philosophers who never laid eyes on a source or, *ergo*, made a concrete contribution to the history of music) as the "sources" of an author's information – taken from what others have already published, often not even for the first time and without adequate documentation. The misleading captions are unfortunately found even at the end of good articles of authors who have not participated in the widespread abandonment of historical method and concrete source-based research in the name of a 'New Musicology' more interested the ahistorical social sciences and in abstract critical theories.

During fifteen years of teaching at American universities, one of the few books which I could recommend to monolingual students was Oliver Strunk's *Source Readings in Music History*, which certainly had a salutary influence in the U.S. Yet sometimes this influence also backfired. While I was a student at the University of Vienna, I once encountered a young man who had come from America for a semester of graduate study and was already having difficulty using a library catalogue. He justified that he read no foreign language by saying: "That is not necessary for musicologists today because Strunk has translated everything". Strunk himself confessed to me that he regretted having omitted certain caveats from his anthology. I would have preferred that instead of writing in his preface about "sparing the reader from constant reference to the original texts" he had *prescribed* this necessity, as did Paul Oskar Kristeller.[2] If a third edition were ever to be published, it would be helpful if an editor, more experienced in work with sources than vulnerable to the thought control of 'political correctness', made it clear that a translation is no longer a source (notwithstanding the high quality of Strunk's translations; in Italy one says "tradutore – traditore"), and at least pointed out the existence of huge and extremely important biographical and institutional categories most worthy of the designation 'sources' yet excluded from the anthology: old manuscripts

---

[2] Above, p. 586, note 13.

in libraries (not merely music manuscripts!) and documents in archives (letters, diaries, expense accounts, payrolls, etc.). The first edition of the reader already limited itself to texts which were previously published and thus known, in some cases even in English translation. This policy was unaltered in the second edition. The *Bach Reader* is a similar case.

The mere usage of a term, no matter how widely diffused,[3] does not justify the propagation of an error in scholarly writing.[4] A long list of secondary literature under a rubric "... Sources", appended to an article however good, will not teach or encourage students of historical musicology to make the necessary distinction and to undertake source-based research. Such encouragement has recently been provided in a tangible manner by endowments for the funding of travel. This is a good beginning, though much more needs to be done, also in the classroom and in publications. An easy and significant improvement would be made if the Journal's bibliographies were to use only the heading "Works Cited" or, even better, to distinguish strictly between "Sources" and their opposite [!], "Secondary Literature". It is clear to me that not all of the Journal's current readership will agree with my comments, which, moreover, violate my own principle of practicing, rather than talking about, musicology.[5]

---

[3] Dictionary definitions reflecting indiscriminate usage are, of course, inadequate for historical scholarship. While one need not yet object to the *Oxford English Dictionary*, 1964 ("Source: ... original documents serving as material for the historical study of a subject", compromised in 1971 by an adverb: "especially of an original or primary character"), the later editions no longer intend to be a guide for good English usage, but include atrocious colloquialisms such as "gonna", "wanna", and "sort of" (adverb), not to mention obscenities, all of which might better have been reserved for a dictionary of slang.

[4] A distinguished historian provided a succinct confirmation: "I agree most wholeheartedly with your criticism of the phrase 'secondary sources'. These are 'secondary literature', they are not sources. The term is being used incorrectly" (letter of Ronald Witt, 1 May 2006).

[5] The editor of the Journal did not dare publish this letter, fearing it would be "divisive". But he paid me a compliment by recognizing that my view of musicology differs from that "now current in the [American] profession". The Journal has already provided precedents for publishing some articles and reviews which could be regarded as divisive and offensive by all previous generations of serious historical musicologists (see, for only one example of many, vol. LIX, p. 476).

BIBLIOGRAPHICAL REFERENCES

Under "the *neighboring* disciplines" in the subtitle of this volume are understood only the humanities – Mnemosyne, her daughter Clio, and their legitimate offspring: history, classical philology and rhetoric, literature, art history (especially iconology), patristics, liturgics, political theology, etc., not the ahistorical and abstract social sciences, aesthetics, or linguistics. Of the publications which appeared in more than one version ("a", "b", etc.), the later versions – including those in this volume – contain revisions of the earlier ones, sometimes slight, sometimes substantial (especially in ch. 4, 9, and in the discussion of the five numbered canons in ch. 12, now rewritten). A bibliography of works cited has not been included, since these can be traced easily through the authors' names and the titles of anonymous works in the index. Translations of quotations in foreign languages have been added reluctantly; a few quotations from easily accessible secondary literature have been given only in translation. Future addenda and corrigenda will be filed in I-Rvat Fondo Kirkendale 2236.

1. **a)** *Circulatio-Tradition, Maria lactans, and Josquin as Musical Orator*, AMl LVI, 1984, pp. 69-92. **b)** *La tradizione della circulatio, Maria lactans e Josquin come musico oratore*, «Quadrivium», n.s. VIII, 1997, pp. 117-164, with seven plates added; separately as «Studi e materiali per la storia dell'Accademia Filarmonica», XIII, Bologna, A.M.I.S., 1997. **c)** *Zur Circulatio-Tradition und Josquins Maria lactans*, in *Chormusik und Analyse II*, ed. Heinrich Poss, Mainz, Schott, 1997, I, 11-41, with seven plates. The article was prepared as a lecture for the competition for the chair of musicology, U. Regensburg, 1982. **Papers**: Duke U., U. Marburg, U. Regensburg, U. Toronto, U. Göttingen, Fifteenth-Century Conference 1982 (U. Regensburg), IMS congress 1982 (U. Strasbourg), Harvard U. Center for Italian Renaissance Studies (Villa I Tatti, Florence), U. Turin, Congress of the International Society for the History of Rhetoric 1983 (Johns Hopkins U., Florence), U. Tübingen, U. Milan, Slovenian Academy of Sciences (U. Ljubljana), U. Pavia, Accademia Filarmonica (Bologna, on the occasion of the author's admittance as honorary member), Istituto Banfi (Reggio Emilia), U. Rome (Sapienza), Moscow State U., U. Toruń, Collège de France (awarded with the College's medal), U. and Conservatory Bari, Hungarian Academy of Sciences (Budapest).

2. **a)** *Ciceronians versus Aristotelians on the Ricercar as Exordium, from Bembo to Bach*, JAMS XXXII, 1979, pp. 1-44. Reviewed in «Wolfenbütteler Renaissance-Mitteilungen», IV/1, 1980, pp. 8f, by Ludwig Finscher. **b)** *Ciceroniani contro Aristotelici sul ricercar come exordium, da Bembo a Bach*, SM XXVI, 1997, pp. 3-54. **c)** Abridged (lecture): *Antike Rhetorik und italienische Instrumentalmusik der Renaissance*, in *Das antike Rom in Europa*, ed. Hans Bungert («Schriftenreihe der Universität Regensburg», XII), Regensburg, Mittelbayerische Druckerei, 1986, pp. 123-139. The article resulted from an invitation to contribute to *De ratione in musica*, a Festschrift for Erich Schenk dealing with the relationships of music and language, a subject which Schenk had continually illuminated in his brilliant lectures and seminars at the University of Vienna. **Papers**: SUNY Buffalo, annual meeting AMS 1978 (Minneapolis), Duke U. Humanism Conference, U. Utrecht, F. U. Berlin, Warburg Institute (U. London), U. Hamburg, U. Cologne, U. Heidelberg, U. Freiburg, Hochschule für Musik (Vienna), U. Bologna, U. Padua, U. Pisa, U. Regensburg, Slovenian Academy of

Sciences (U. Ljubljana), Istituto Banfi (Reggio Emilia), U. Pavia, Istituto Storico Germanico (Rome), Moscow State U., Hungarian Academy of Sciences (Budapest).

3. *On the Rhetorical Interpretation of the Ricercar and J. S. Bach's Musical Offering*, SM XXVI, 1997, pp. 331-376.

4. **a)** *Franceschina, Girometta, and their Companions in a Madrigal "a diversi linguaggi" by Luca Marenzio and Orazio Vecchi*, AMl XLV, 1972, pp. 185-235. **b)** *La Franceschina, la Girometta e soci in un madrigale «a diversi linguaggi» di Luca Marenzio e Orazio Vecchi*, in *Il madrigale tra Cinque e Seicento*, ed. Paolo Fabbri, Bologna, Il Mulino, 1988, pp. 249-331. **c)** Abridged in: *Madrigali a diversi linguaggi von Luca Marenzio – Orazio Vecchi, Johann Eccard und Michele Varotto*, Wolfenbüttel, Möseler, 1975 («Das Chorwerk», CXXV), pp. III-XII, with edition of the music, pp. 1-19. **Papers**: congress of the Gesellschaft für Musikforschung 1970 (U. Bonn), annual meeting AMS 1972 (Dallas), Duke U., Harvard U. Center for Italian Renaissance Studies (Villa I Tatti, Florence), Renaissance conference at Villa Serbelloni (Bellagio), U. and Musikhochschule Frankfurt, Bibliotheca Hertziana (Rome), Holland Festival Oude Muziek (Utrecht), Moscow State U., Hungarian Academy of Sciences (Budapest).

5. **a)** *La favola della 'nascita dell'opera' nella Camerata fiorentina demitizzata da Emilio de' Cavalieri*, «Rivista italiana di musicologia», XXXVII, 2002, pp. 131-141. **b)** *The Myth of the 'Birth of Opera' in the Florentine Camerata Debunked by Emilio de' Cavalieri: A Commemorative Lecture*, «Opera Quarterly», XIX, 2003, pp. 631-643, with five illustrations added. **Papers**: Rome, Santa Maria in Aracoeli, 11 March 2002 (Soprintendenza per il Patrimonio Storico di Roma-Lazio, inauguration of the author's commemorative inscription in the Cavalieri chapel on the 400th anniversary of the composer's death), annual meeting Società Italiana di Musicologia 2002 (Padua).

6. *Il primo Orfeo di Monteverdi, Francesco Rasi: compositore, poeta, cantante, omicida*. Lecture, Cremona, Scuola di paleografia musicale (U. Pavia), 2 June 1986, on the occasion of the conferral of an honorary doctorate. First published in this volume. Complete versions of Rasi's biography: **a)** *Zur Biographie des ersten Orfeo, Francesco Rasi*, in *Claudio Monteverdi: Festschrift Reinhold Hammerstein zum 70. Geburtstag*, ed. Ludwig Finscher, Laaber, Laaber-Verlag, 1986, pp. 297-335. **b)** revised in W. KIRKENDALE, *The Court Musicians in Florence*, 1993, pp. 556-603.

7. *Il Re dei Cieli e il Re di Francia: su un* topos *musicale nella maniera di Lully*, RIdM XXXIX, 2004, pp. 53-106. **Papers**: annual meeting AMS 1969 (St. Louis, with abstract), congress of the Gesellschaft für Musikforschung 1970 (U. Bonn), Duke U., Columbia U. faculty seminar, annual meeting Società Italiana di Musicologia 2004 (U. Lecce, revised and expanded).

8. *The War of the Spanish Succession Reflected in Works of Antonio Caldara*, AMl XXXVI, 1964, pp. 221-233. **Paper**: Annual meeting AMS 1963 (U. Washington, Seattle).

9. **a)** *The Ruspoli Documents on Handel*, JAMS XX, 1967, pp. 222-273, 518f. Alfred Einstein Award, 1968. **b)** Reprinted in *Baroque Music II: Eighteenth Century*, ed. Ellen Rosand, New York, Garland, 1985 («Garland Library of the History of Western Music», VI), pp. 96-148. **Paper**: California chapter AMS 1965 (U. C. Riverside).

10. *Orgelspiel im Lateran und andere Erinnerungen an Händel: Ein unbeachteter Bericht in* «Voiage historique» *von 1737*, «Die Musikforschung», XLI, 1988, pp. 1-9.

11. **a)** *Handel with Ruspoli: New Documents from the Archivio Segreto Vaticano, December 1706 to December 1708*, SM XXXII, 2003, pp. 301-348; addenda and corrigenda *ibid.*, XXXIII, 2004, pp. 249f. **b)** *Händel bei Ruspoli: Neue Dokumente aus dem Archivio Segreto Vaticano, Dezember 1706 bis Dezember 1708*, «Händel-Jahrbuch», L, 2004, pp. 309-374. **Papers**: Archivio di Stato Rome 1992, Handel Institute (King's College, U. London, 2002), annual meeting Società Italiana di Musicologia 2003 (Rome).

12. **a)** *The Source of Bach's 'Musical Offering': the 'Institutio oratoria' of Quintilian*, JAMS XXXII, 1980, pp. 88-141. Deems Taylor Award 1981. **b)** Reprinted in *Eighteenth- and Nineteenth-Century Source Studies*, New York, Garland, 1985, ed. Ellen Rosand («Garland Library of the History of Western Music», VIII), pp. 96-149 . **c)** Abridged: *Die 'Institutio oratoria' als Modell des 'Musikalischen Opfers'*, in *Neue Zürcher Zeitung*, 25/26 Oct. 1980,

pp. 67f. **d**) Abridged: *Die 'Institutio oratoria' als Modell des 'Musikalischen Opfers'*, in *Bach-Tage Berlin: Vorträge 1970 bis 1981*, ed. Günther Wagner, Neuhausen-Stuttgart, Hännsler-Verlag, 1985, pp. 249-262. **e**) *La fonte dell'«Offerta musicale» di Bach: Quintiliano, «Institutio oratoria»*, in *Musica poëtica: Johann Sebastian Bach e la tradizione europea*, ed. Maria Teresa Giannelli, Genoa, Edizioni culturali internazionali, 1986, 133-190; published without the author's knowledge, and with numerous errors. **f**) Abridged: *Bach und Quintilian: Die 'Institutio oratoria' als Model des 'Musikalischen Opfers'*, in *Musik in Antike und Neuzeit*, ed. Michael von Albrecht, Frankfurt etc., Peter Lang, 1987, pp. 85-58. Contains new information on the five numbered canons. **g**) Reprint of (f) in *Bach-Woche Ansbach ... 1991: Offizieller Almanach*, Ansbach, 1991, pp. 39-58. **Papers** (presented by W.K. for U.K.): U. and Musikhochschule Frankfurt, King's College (U. London), F. U. Berlin, U. Kiel, Österreichische Gesellschaft für Musik (Vienna), Duke U., annual meeting AMS 1979 (New York), U. Cologne, U. Bonn, Schweizerische Musikforschende Gesellschaft (U. Basle), U. and E.T.H. Zürich, U. Bologna, Berliner Bach-Tage 1980, Bryn Mawr College, SUNY (Stony Brook), U. Heidelberg, Harvard U. Center for Italian Renaissance Studies (Villa I Tatti, Florence), U. Regensburg, Stadtbibliothek Munich, Slovenian Academy of Sciences (U. Ljubljana), U. Pavia, Bach-Woche Ansbach, Moscow State U., Hungarian Academy of Sciences (Budapest), Council of Europe (Como), Cosarara (Cremona).

13. *Bach, Johann Sebastian: Musikalisches Opfer, BMW 1079, Facsimile of the original edition, Leipzig 1737, ed. Christoph Wolff (Peters, Leipzig, 1971)*, review, «Music and Letters», LXII, 1981, pp. 91-95.

14. *Mozart barocco*, lecture, in *Album Amicorum Albert Dunning in occasione del suo LXV compleanno*, ed. Giacomo Funari, Turnhout, Brepols, 2002, pp. 403-414. **Papers**: U. Chicago, U. of Southern California, California chapters of AMS (U. C. Berkeley), Duke U.; conference *Bach, Mozart e la tradizione barocca*, Internationale Stiftung Mozarteum and Associazione Mozart Italia, Rovereto 2000.

15. **a**) *Beethovens Missa solemnis und die rhetorische Tradition*, «Sitzungsberichte der Österreichischen Akademie der Wissenschaften», phil.-hist. Klasse, CCLXXI, 1971, pp. 121-158. Reviewed in «Studia Musicologica», XIV, 1972, pp. 441f, by Vera Lampert. **b**) Slightly abridged: *New Roads to Old Ideas in Beethoven's Missa solemnis*, «Musical Quarterly», LVI, 1970, pp. 665-701. **c**) Repint of (b) in *The Creative World of Beethoven*, ed. Paul Henry Lang, New York, Norton, 1971, pp. 163-199. **d**) Revised version of (a) in *Ludwig van Beethoven*, ed. Ludwig Finscher, Darmstadt, Wissenschaftliche Buchgesellschaft, 1982 («Wege der Forschung», CDXXVIII), pp. 52-97. **e**) *La 'Missa solemnis' di Beethoven e la tradizione retorica*, in *Beethoven*, ed. Giorgio Pestelli, Bologna, Il Mulino, 1988, pp. 215-258; cf. also p. 293. The Italian version contains typographical errors, due to insufficient availability of proofs while mountain climbing. **Papers**: Österreichische Akademie der Wissenschaften (Vienna, invitation to commemorate the bicentenary of Beethoven's birth, 1970), Greater New York Chapter of AMS 1970 (CUNY), Bibliotheca Hertziana (Rome), Duke U., U. Regensburg, U. Pavia, U. Karlsruhe, Gnesin Institute (Moscow), U. Warsaw, U. Kraków, Hungarian Academy of Sciences (Budapest).

16. *Gregorianischer Stil in Beethovens Streichquartett Op. 132*, in Gesellschaft für Musikforschung, *Bericht über den internationalen musikwissenschaftlichen Kongress Berlin 1974*, Kassel, Bärenreiter, 1980, pp. 373-376. **Papers** (augmented): annual meeting AMS 1973 (Chicago), T. U. Berlin, Duke U., congress of the Gesellschaft für Musikforschung 1974 (Berlin), U. Oxford, King's College (U. London), U. Cambridge, U. Mainz, U. Munich, U. Zürich.

17. **a**) *The 'Great Fugue' Op. 133: Beethoven's 'Art of Fugue'*, AMl XXXV, 1963, pp. 14-24. **b**) W. KIRKENDALE, *Fuge und Fugato in der Kammermusik des Rokoko und der Klassik*, diss., U. Vienna, 1961. **c**) *Op. cit.*, Tutzing, Schneider, 1966, pp. 292-303. **d**) *Fugue and Fugato in Rococo and Classical Chamber Music*, Durham NC, Duke UP, 1979, pp. 255-269. **Papers**: U. Bonn, U. Vienna, Congress of the Gesellschaft für Musikforschung 1962 (Kassel), annual meeting AMS 1962 (Ohio State U.), Hungarian Academy of Sciences (Budapest).

18. *"Segreto comunicato da Paganini"*, JAMS XVIII, 1965, pp. 394-407. **Papers**: California chapters of the AMS 1965 (Stanford U.), U. of Southern California, Duke U.
19. *Történészként a multtal élek együtt: Beszélgetés Warren Kirkendale-lel*, «Muzsika», XIV/1, Jan. 1997, pp. 21-25, with two photos (to be filed in I-Rvat). Another version was broadcast by the Hungarian radio.

ADDENDA TO THE BIBLIOGRAPHY OF PUBLICATIONS
IN *MUSICOLOGIA HUMANA: STUDIES IN HONOR OF WARREN
AND URSULA KIRKENDALE*, FLORENCE, LEO S. OLSCHKI, 1994, pp. 575-579

Nos. 1 b-c, 3, 5 a-b, 6, 7, 11 a-b, 14, 19, above.

Warren Kirkendale:

Comments on the Study of Musicology at the University ... on the occasion of a visiting professorship at Moscow State University, Rome, 1994, ms., 30 pp., to be filed in I-Rvat.
[Letter to the Editor], JAMS XLVIII, 1995, pp. 533-539.
Prolusione, in *La scuola polifonica romana del Sei-Settecento: Atti del convegno internazionale di studi in memoria di Laurence Feininger, Trento ... 1996*, Trent, Provincia autonoma di Trento, 1997, pp. 41f.
Caldara e Metastasio fra Roma e Vienna, Accademia Nazionale di Santa Cecilia, *Festival di Pasqua 1998: Celebrazioni per il terzo centenario della nascita di Pietro Metastasio*, Rome, Accademia Nazionale di Santa Cecilia, 1998, pp. 11-18.
Un antidoto contro le «impertinenze» di un saggista politico, «Il saggiatore musicale», V, 1998, pp. 141-150.
La storia, le scienze sociali e le nozze Medicee del 1589, RIdM XXXIV, 1999, pp. 389-394.
Emilio de' Cavalieri e le sue Lamentazioni [notes for the program of a performance in Rome, Palazzo Rospigliosi, Holy Week, Apr. 2000, to be filed in I-Rvat].
Cavalieri, Emilio, in *Die Musik in Geschichte und Gegenwart*, Personenteil, IV, Kassel, Bärenreiter, 2000, col. 463-471.
Music of Louis Lemaire Painted by Jean-Baptiste Oudry, 1725, «Imago Musicae», XVI/XVII, 1999/2000, pp. 254f.
Catalogo sistematico del primo nucleo musicologico nel Fondo Kirkendale della Biblioteca Apostolica Vaticana [desk-top edition], Rome, 2000, 361 pp. Copies in I-Rvat, Pontificio Istituto di Musica Sacra, and Istituto Storico Germanico, Rome. Addenda to be catalogued in I-Rvat.
Emilio de' Cavalieri, 'Gentiluomo Romano': His Life and Letters, His Role as Superintendent of all the Arts at the Medici Court, and His Musical Compositions. With addenda to *L'Aria di Fiorenza* and *The Court Musicians in Florence*, Florence, Olschki, 2001, 551 pp., 64 plates. Reviewed in «Early Music Review», no. 72, July 2001, pp. 7f, by Barbara Sachs; «Giornale della musica», Feb. 2002, p. 21, by Fiorenza Rossetto; «Musicologia Austriaca», XX, 2001, pp. 227ff, by Herbert Seiffert; «Piano Time», XX, no. 186, 2002, by Franco Onorati; «L'Indice», XIX, no. 6, 2002, p. 27, by Dinko Fabris; «Ricerche di storia sociale e religiosa», no. 61, 2002, no. 6, by Vittorio Bracco; «L'osservatore romano», 12/13 Aug. 2002, p. 3, by Antonio Braga; «Oggi e domaini», XXX/9, Sept. 2002, p. 39, by Marco Della Sciucca; «Die Musikforschung», LV, 2002, pp. 429f, by Bernhard Schrammek; «Renaissance Studies», XVI, 2002, pp. 594-597, by Noel O'Regan; «Renaissance Quarterly», LVI, 2003, pp. 179f, by Ann E. Moyer; «Notes», LXI, 2004, pp. 428-430, by Murray Bradshaw. RIdM XL, 2005 [*sic*?], in preparation.
To the reviews of *The Court Musicians in Florence* listed in *Emilio de' Cavalieri*, p. 434, may be added «Early Music Review», LXXVII, Feb. 2002, pp. 4f, by Barbara Sachs; «Ars Lyrica», XIV, 2004, pp. 97-102, by Edward Rutschman.

[Commemorative inscription for the 400th anniversary of the death of Emilio de' Cavalieri, S. Maria in Aracoeli, Rome, 2002; transcribed in *La favola* and *The Myth*].

Review of Don Harrán, *Salamone Rossi: Jewish Musician in Late Renaissance Mantua*, Oxford UP, 1999, in «Renaissance Studies», XVI, 2002, pp. 266-270.

Kirkendale, in *Die Musik in Geschichte und Gegenwart*, Personenteil, X, Kassel, Bärenreiter, 2003², col. 164ff.

Ursula Kirkendale:

Antonio Caldara: Life and Venetian-Roman Oratorios, translated and revised by W. Kirkendale, Florence, Leo S. Olschki, 2007.

In preparation: An extensive iconological study identifying the subject matter of Giorgione's so-called *Tempesta* through an ancient author (bibliographical data hopefully to be listed eventually in the *Bibliography of the History of Art*).

INDEX OF PERSONS AND TITLES

Numbers followed by "n" refer only to notes on the respective pages. Christian names of authors of modern secondary literature, indicated here with initials, can be found in the notes. Titles of anonymous and collective publications and of songs are included in this index.

"À Paris sur petit pont": 196
Aaron, Pietro: 26n, 51n
Abbé le Fils (Joseph-Barnabé Saint-Sévin): 570, 573f, 576n, 577
Abele, Matthias: 248
Abert, H.: 225
Acciaiolo, Nicolò: 232n
Achilles: 433, 435, 437n, 439, 443, 446, 448, 475
Adams, John Quincy: 73, 90n
Ademollo, A.: 287, 288n, 318n
Andersen, Hans Christian: 594
Adler, G.: 14, 505n, 507n, 531
Adlung, Jacob: 460n
Adorno, T.: 222, 591
Adrio, A.: 556n
Aeschylos: 237
Agamemnon: 433, 436f, 439, 443, 445f, 448, 460, 476, 512
Agricola, Johann Friedrich: 182, 185, 460
– Martin: 182
Ahlgrimm, I.: 464n
Aim, Gio. Antonio: 332
Alanus de Insulis: 13, 25n, 230, 533
Alberti, Leon Battista: 14
Albertonio, Francesco: 187ff
Albertus Magnus: 16
Albrecht, M. von: 89n, 101n
Albrechtsberger, Johann Georg: 77, 271, 502n, 504f, 523n, 540, 549-553, 557, 559ff; pl. XVII.1
Alciati, Andrea: 10n; pl. I.1
Aldobrandini, Gio. Francesco: 190
– Pietro, card.: 208
Aldus: s. Manuzio:

Alessandro VIII, pope: 404n
Alexander the Great: 242
Alexander VIII Ottoboni, pope: 367
Alexandre, I.: 402n
Alföldi, A.: 241n, 243n, 252n
Alfonso el Sabio: 26
Allacci, L.: 177n
Allori, Alessandro: 208
Allorto, R.: 151n
Allsop, P.: 390n
Alouette: 157
Altenburg, Johann Ernst: 529f, 536
Altmann, W.: 546
Alvito, duke of: 310
Amadei, Federigo: 274n, 275, 326
– Filippo (Pippo): 307
Ambrose, St.: 55
– Z. P.: 124n
Amerbach, Bonifacius: 39
American Institute of Musicology: 596
Amico, Bernardino: 247
Ammirato, Scipione: 170
Amorevole, Battista: 138
Analecta Hymnica: 532n
Anders, G. E.: 563n
Andraschke, P.: 223n
André, Johann Anton: 510n, 523, 550fn, 553ffn
d'André, Lucrezia: 318f, 363, 390, 401n, 402; pl. XI.12
Andrea, trombonist: 332
– violinist: 331
Andreini, Giovanni Battista: 160n, 176n, 178n
Andrews, R.: 194n

Handschin, J.: 39n, 186n
Hanley, E.: 273n, 319n
Hansell, S. H.: 294n, 307n
Hanslick, E.: 97, 589
Hapsburg: 488
– Archduke Rudolph von: 530, 535, 551n, 561; pl. XVII.2
Hardouin-Mansart, Jules: 247
Harpster, R. W.: 553n
Harrán, D.: 89n, 203n
Harries, K.: 14n
Harris, E.: 351n, 363n, 365n, 366fn, 374fn, 378fn, 383n, 385n, 386f, 389, 390n, 392n, 393, 395n, 401n, 412
Harrison, D.: 100n
Hartmann, K.-G.: 182n
Harvey, William: 13n
Harwood, E.: 117n
Haskell, F.: 326n
Haßler, Hans Leo: 515n
Hauptmann, M.: 535n
Haussmann, Elias Gottlieb: 470
Hautecœur, L.: 14n, 238n, 246n, 247
Hawkins, John: 287
Haydn, Joseph: 5, 191, 491, 502n, 505n, 513, 516, 519n, 520, 523, 527ffn, 531, 549f, 559, 590
– Michael: 251n, 502n, 506n, 510, 520, 523n, 530n, 536
Hayneccius, Martin: 181, 184n, 185
H.D.: 135f
Heartz, D.: 41n
Heawood, E.: 386n, 391n, 392
Heckscher, W. S.: 25n, 469n, 591
Heer, J.: 522n
Heider, G.: 21n
Heifetz, Jascha: 583
Heimann, A.: 508n
Heine, Heinrich: 250
Heinichen, Johann: 289n
Helen of Troy: 276

TIBERGRAPH
CITTÀ DI CASTELLO • PG
FINITO DI STAMPARE NEL MESE DI LUGLIO 2007

«HISTORIAE MUSICAE CULTORES»

Diretta da LORENZO BIANCONI